# Organizational Behavior
## The State of the Science

### Second Edition

**Gregory Bedny and David Meister**
*The Russian Theory of Activity: Current Applications to Design and Learning*

**Michael T. Brannick, Eduardo Salas, and Carolyn Prince**
*TeamPerformance Assessment and Measurement: Theory, Research, and Applications*

**Jeanette N. Cleveland, Margaret Stockdale, and Kevin R. Murphy**
*Women and Men in Organizations: Sex and Gender Issues at Work*

**Aaron Cohen**
*Multiple Commitments in the Workplace: An Integrative Approach*

**Russell Cropanzano**
*Justice in the Workplace: Approaching Fairness in Human Resource Management, Volume 1*

**Russell Cropanzano**
*Justice in the Workplace: From Theory to Practice, Volume 2*

**James E. Driskell and Eduardo Salas**
*Stress and Human Performance*

**Sidney A. Fine and Steven F. Cronshaw**
*Functional Job Analysis: A Foundation for Human Resources Management*

**Sidney A. Fine and Maury Getkate**
*Benchmark Tasks for Job Analysis: A Guide for Functional Job Analysis (FJA) Scales*

**J. Kevin Ford, Steve W. J. Kozlowski, Kurt Kraiger, Eduardo Salas, and Mark S. Teachout**
*Improving Training Effectiveness in Work Organizations*

**Jerald Greenberg**
*Organizational Behavior: The State of the Science, Second Edition*

**Uwe E. Kleinbeck, Hans-Henning Quast, Henk Thierry, and Hartmut Häcker**
*Work Motivation*

**Martin I. Kurke and Ellen M. Scrivner**
*Police Psychology Into the 21st Century*

**Joel Lefkowitz**
*Ethics and Values in Industrial and Organizational Psychology*

**Manuel London**
*Job Feedback: Giving, Seeking, and Using Feedback for Performance Improvement, Second Edition*

# Organizational Behavior
## The State of the Science
### Second Edition

Edited by

## Jerald Greenberg
*The Ohio State University*

LAWRENCE ERLBAUM ASSOCIATES, PUBLISHERS
2003    Mahwah, New Jersey                    London

*50495409

Lawrence Erlbaum Associates, Inc., Publishers
10 Industrial Avenue
Mahwah, NJ  07430

Cover design by Kathryn Houghtaling Lacey

**Library of Congress Cataloging-in-Publication Data**

Organizational behavior : the state of the science / [edited by]
Jerald Greenberg

    p.   cm.

Includes bibliographical references and index.
ISBN 0-8058-4031-1 (c : alk. paper)
ISBN 0-8058-4541-0 (pbk : alk. paper)
1. Organizational behavior   I. Greenberg, Jerald.
  HD58.7 .O717 2003
  302.3'5 —dc21                                  2002033869
                                    CIP

Printed in the United States of America
10   9   8   7   6   5   4   3   2   1

*To my dad, Ben, for teaching me the value of hard work,
and for demonstrating it with his actions*

# Contents

## Part III: Cross-Level Themes

## Part IV: Commentary

# Series Foreword

Edwin A. Fleishman
Jeanette M. Cleveland
*Series Editors*

There is a compelling need for innovative approaches to the solution of many pressing problems involving human relationships in today's society. Such approaches are more likely to be successful when they are based on sound research and applications. This *Series in Applied Psychology* offers publications, which emphasize state-of-the-art research and its application to important issues of human behavior in a variety of societal settings. The objective is to bridge both academic and applied interests.

Recent years have seen the rapid growth and development of the field of organizational behavior (OB). The empirical bases, theoretical development, and methodological foundation of the field continue to evolve. The first edition of the book *Organizational Behavior: The State of the Science* recognized these dramatic changes as well as the need to assess these developments. That book, conceived and edited by Jerald Greenberg, brought together a set of prominent scholars in the field of OB to write original chapters to examine the historical roots of the field, to evaluate its present status, and to offer needs for future research and directions. Special focus was on the field's value and worth as a scientific and practical endeavor.

This second edition recognizes that the pace of development in this field, since 1994, has resulted in additional topics and issues that need to be reviewed and assessed. The need for critical reflection about the science of OB, which inspired the first volume, is still appropriate. Encouraged by the success of the first edition, and by his colleagues in the field, Dr. Greenberg has again undertaken this challenging task.

Jerald Greenberg, is in a particularly appropriate position to observe developments in the field of OB. He has been a leading contributor to its development over the years. Currently Abramowitz Professor of Business Ethics at Ohio State University, he is a former Chair of the Organizational Behavior Division of the Academy of Management and has been honored by the Society of Industrial and Organizational Psychology for his research publications in this area. He is the senior author of the widely adopted textbook *Behavior in Organizations*, now in its 8th edition.

In this second edition of *Organizational Behavior: The State of the Science*, Professor Greenberg has, again, brought together leading scholars in the field who identify additional issues and topics that have emerged and need to be reviewed and assessed. The original chapters in this second edition are all on new topics that reflect the growth in the field in the past decade. The need for critical reflection about the science of OB, which inspired the first volume, is paramount throughout. All authors in this second edition, are new to this edition, providing some fresh viewpoints. The book concludes with an integrative chapter, including a critical evaluation of the earlier presentations.

To provide further cohesion to the presentations, chapters are organized around "what was, what is, and what will be" as seen through the eyes of acknowledged leaders in the field. The book's goal is clearly to set an agenda for future research in the field of organizational behavior.

The book can be used as a companion to the first edition, for a comprehensive coverage of the field of OB. Since it includes mainly new material and coverage of different topics, it can be used alone as an especially updated view of the field. As with the first volume, the book is appropriate for researchers and teachers in organizational behavior as well as for consultants and managers who want to keep up to date with issues in this field. The book should be of particular value for use in doctoral seminars on organizational behavior, human resource management, and organizational psychology. Because it chronicles what is now happening in the field of organizational behavior, the book should also be a useful reference book for years to come.

# Preface

I always found it fascinating, even inspiring, to learn what experts in the field of organizational behavior (OB) had to say about their specialized areas of expertise. How did they feel about what is going on, and where did they think their subfields should be going? Published articles that gave the field's leaders opportunities to express these opinions were few and far between. This was unfortunate, I believed, because these expert opinions always helped stimulate my own thinking about the topics under consideration. Whether I agreed or disagreed with the experts, I always learned from their observations.

Fortunately, in exchange for a beverage or two at a SIOP or Academy of Management meeting, I found it was possible to get some of the field's most influential scholars to share their observations in person. In fact, when groups of us would convene, it was impossible to keep some of them from doing otherwise, whether or not they were so prompted. This, I always thought to myself, was where "the real learning" occurred at these meetings. It was less from listening to the carefully crafted presentations of individual research studies than from the sharing of opinions about what's going on in the field. It was in these conversations that opinions were formed, ideas were developed, and plans were put into place that ended up shaping the field for years to come.

"What if we could assemble that wisdom in one place, a volume that could be accessed by all?" I wondered about a decade ago. The answer took the form of the first edition of this book—a collection of chapters by leaders in the field of OB who were asked to report on "the state of the science" in their respective subfields—or, as I put it when describing their mission, "what was, what is, and what should be." The resulting book was very well received, but given the fast-paced nature of our field, it's not surprising that the various contributions became dated in just a few years. As this became apparent to many of my colleagues, requests trickled in to update that book. Indeed, they were correct; it was necessary to do so. Many of the "hot topics" on which we reported back in 1994 have cooled today, and more than a few of the "cutting-edge ideas" have since become dull with the passage of time.

Although the substance of that first edition may be less useful than it was originally, I do not believe that the underlying mission—to report on the state of the science of OB—has become any less important. In fact, given how dramatically the field has grown over the past decade (as witnessed by gains in the number of people attending our conferences and in the number of journal pages on which our work appears), it appears that the need for critical reflection about the science of OB that inspired that first volume has become greater than ever. It was with the goal of meeting this need that I have prepared the latest edition of this book.

As with the first edition, I have assembled a group of OB's most prolific and highly regarded scholars, individuals representing the wide variety of subfields that are represented in the our journals. I then asked them to share their thoughts about their specific specialty area—its past, its present, and its prospects for the future. My intent, as it was earlier, was to encourage those of us who toil in the trenches of OB to step back and engage in serious self-reflection. So, instead of plowing ahead with our work—too often, myopically—the time has come once again to assess critically our efforts to date. In essence, that's what this book is designed to do: Its intent is to encourage us to pause and reflect, to think about our field's course more carefully before moving ahead with it. Because we often lose sight of the big picture while engaging in our everyday pursuits, I thought it would be useful to have some of the field's leaders encourage us to engage in a bit of scientific self-reflection. Although this exercise might cause us to feel awkward or uneasy—or even be professionally painful at times (as is typical of any consciousness-arousing experiences)—there can be no doubt that any adjustments that result will pay off handsomely for the future of our field.

In contrast to the first edition of this book, which examined OB from a very broad perspective (including micro-issues, macro-issues, research methods, teaching OB, and OB practice), I have devoted this edition exclusively to the individual-level and group-level processes as well as the key methodological issues that interest most of today's OB scholars. In so doing, of course, these chapters also address a broad array of important practical issues with which we also are concerned. This is in keeping with "where the action is" in mainstream OB. As such, most readers will find the coverage in this edition to be more reflective of the field of OB as they encounter it.

Specifically, the chapters in this book cover a wide range of OB topics. I have divided these into three sections that roughly distinguish between *in-*

*dividual processes* (e.g., affect, stress, and self-fulfilling prophecies), *interpersonal processes* (e.g., diversity, justice, reputations, dysfunctional behavior, and conflict), and *cross-level themes* (e.g., construct validity, and cross-cultural issues). I realize, of course, that this particular categorization is somewhat arbitrary and that its wisdom can be challenged. Indeed, all of the topics presented here focus on individual, interpersonal, and cross-level processes to some extent. To readers who take exception to this admittedly arbitrary categorization I apologize, but to those who find the organizing heuristic useful, I am pleased to be of service. Regardless, what matters most here is not how I have organized the various contributions, but what the authors have to say about their fields. It is on this that readers should focus most carefully. After all, it is this opportunity to "have an audience with the experts" that represents the value added by this book.

I would be remiss in writing these remarks if I failed to acknowledge a special feature of this book—the commentary chapter by one of our field's most important scholars, Edwin A. Locke. I asked Professor Locke to comment on the state of the field of OB as a whole as reflected by the contributions to this book. His essay, which concludes this volume, connects the various individual contributions by acknowledging a common limitation of our work—vagueness in the definitions we use. With characteristic candor and insight, Locke provides a service to the field of OB by challenging us all to be more precise in our conceptualizations. His remarks represent the ultimate exercise in elevating our self-consciousness about our work, which is exactly what this book is all about.

In case it is not clear by now, this book is aimed at a professional audience. Professors and graduate students in OB and allied fields (e.g., industrial/organizational psychology, human resource management, sports management, public policy management, social psychology, and others) stand to benefit by reading it closely. Each chapter offers a detailed analysis of the state of the science with respect to a highly topical aspect of OB. But, these contributions are more than mere reviews of the literature to guide those seeking a conceptual map of a particular area. By encouraging us to engage in critical self-assessment of our empirical and conceptual work, the contributors to this book force us to be highly introspective. Whether or not you agree with their observations, ignoring them is a luxury we cannot afford. If, after reading any given chapter, you find yourself reassessing your thinking about the topic, then its author has been successful. In that case, as a field, we all cannot help but benefit.

*Jerald Greenberg*
Columbus, Ohio

# About the Contributors

**Jerald Greenberg**, PhD, is the Abramowitz Professor of Business Ethics and Professor of Management and Organizational Behavior at the Ohio State University's Fisher College of Business. Professor Greenberg is widely recognized as one of the founding fathers of the field of organizational justice. Acknowledging his pioneering contributions in this area, Professor Greenberg has received numerous professional honors from the Organizational Behavior Division of the Academy of Management, including the *William A. Owens Award*, the *New Concept Award*, and on two occasions, the *Best Paper Award*. He is a highly sought-after speaker throughout the world and has published extensively, with over 130 professional chapters and journal articles to his credit. He also has co-authored or co-edited 18 books, including *Behavior in Organizations, Advances in Organizational Justice,* and the *Handbook of Organizational Justice.* In recognition of his lifelong contributions to organizational behavior, Dr. Greenberg has been inducted as a Fellow of both the American Psychological Association and the American Psychological Society. Professor Greenberg also is past chair of the Organizational Behavior Division of the Academy of Management.

**Herman Aguinis** (www.cudenver.edu/~haguinis) is an associate professor of management at the University of Colorado at Denver. He received his PhD in industrial/organizational psychology from the University at Albany, State University of New York. He has published over 40 journal articles in *Academy of Management Journal, Academy of Management Review, Journal of Applied Psychology, Personnel Psychology,* and elsewhere. He is the recipient of several awards including the *Journal of Organizational Behavior* Best Paper Award (1996) and the Academy of Management Research Methods Division *Advancement of Organizational Research Methodology Award* (2001). He is past Program Chair for the Iberoamerican Academy of

Management and currently serves as an elected Executive Committee Member of the Human Resources Division of the Academy of Management, as Associate Editor for *Organizational Research Methods*, and on the editorial board of the *Journal of Applied Psychology* and other journals. He has been a visiting scholar at universities in the People's Republic of China (Beijing and Hong Kong), Malaysia, Singapore, Argentina, and Spain.

**Sigal G. Barsade** received her PhD from the Haas School of Business, University of California, Berkeley, and is an associate professor of organizational behavior at the Yale School of Management, Yale University. Her research primarily focuses on how work behavior is influenced by employee emotion and affective processes, such as group emotional contagion, affective diversity in teams, trait affect, moods, affective organizational culture, emotional norms, emotional attributions, and emotional intelligence. She has recently published articles about emotional contagion and its influence on group behavior, affective diversity in senior management teams, and a model of group affect in *Administrative Science Quarterly* and *Organizational Behavior and Human Decision Processes*.

**Rebecca J. Bennett**, PhD (Northwestern, 1991), is Professor of Management and the Associate Director of the Family Business Center at the University of Toledo. She is a member of the Academy of Management, Society for Industrial and Organizational Psychology, Society for Human Resource Management. Her research interests include employees' responses to fair and unfair punishment, employee deviance, conflict and conflict resolution, forgiveness, and empowerment. Her research has been presented at many national and international conferences and has been published in journals such as *Academy of Management Journal, Journal of Applied Psychology, Human Performance, Journal of International Conflict Management*, and *Organization Behavior and Human Decision Processes*, as well as in several edited volumes. Dr. Bennett serves as an ad hoc reviewer for many management journals.

**Fred R. Blass** is a PhD student currently studying Organizational Behavior and Human Resources Management in the Department of Management at Florida State University. He earned a master's degree in Administrative Science from George Washington University. His research interests include personal reputation, and aspects of social influence such as mentoring and organizational politics.

**Arthur P. Brief** received his PhD from the University of Wisconsin–Madison in 1974 and currently is the Lawrence Martin Chair of Business at Tulane's A. B. Freeman School of Business, with a courtesy appointment in the Department of Psychology. He also is Director of the William B. and Evelyn Burkenroad Institute for the Study of Ethics and Leadership in Management. Professor Brief is a recipient of the Academic Leadership Award from the Aspen Institute's Initiative for Social Innovation Through Business and the World Resources Institute for integrating social and environmental concerns into business education. His latest book is *Attitudes in and Around Organizations*. Professor Brief was co-editor of Lexington Books' series "Issues in Organization and Management" and currently is co-editor of Lawrence Erlbaum Associates's "Organization and Management Series." In January 2003, he will become Editor of the *Academy of Management Review*. Professor Brief is a Fellow of the Academy of Management, the American Psychological Association, and the American Psychological Society as well as a member of the Society of Organizational Behavior.

**Jason A. Colquitt** is an Assistant Professor of Management at the University of Florida's Warrington College of Business. He earned his PhD in Business Administration at Michigan State University's Eli Broad Graduate School of Management. He earned his BS in Psychology at Indiana University. Dr. Colquitt's research interests include organizational justice, team effectiveness, and personality influences on learning and task performance. He has published several articles on these and other topics in the *Academy of Management Journal, Journal of Applied Psychology, Personnel Psychology,* and *Organizational Behavior and Human Decision Processes.* Professor. Colquitt also is co-author of *Organizational Justice: A Primer,* and co-editor of the *Handbook of Organizational Justice.*

**Cary L. Cooper** is BUPA Professor of Organizational Psychology and Health, and Deputy Vice Chancellor of the University of Manchester Institute of Science and Technology (UMIST). He is the author of over 80 books and over 300 academic journal articles. He is Founding Editor, *Journal of Organizational Behavior;* co-editor of the medical journal *Stress & Health;* and former co-editor, *International Journal of Management Review.* He is a Fellow of the British Psychological Society, the Royal Society of Arts, the Royal Society of Medicine, the Royal Society of Health, and an Academician of the Academy for the Social Sciences. He is President of the British Academy of Management and a Companion of the (British) Institute of Management. He is a Fellow of the (American) Academy of Management and recipient of its 1998 Distinguished Service Award. Professor Cooper was awarded a CBE in the Queen's Birthday Honours List for his contribution to health.

**Kurt T. Dirks** is currently an associate professor at the John M. Olin School of Business at Washington University in St. Louis. He received his PhD in organizational behavior from the University of Minnesota. His research is focused on trust in the workplace, including its antecedents, consequences, and processes. He also conducts research on feelings of ownership. The research has been published in the *Academy of Management Review,* the *Journal of Applied Psychology,* and *Organization Science.*

**Ceasar Douglas** is Assistant Professor of Management at Florida State University. He received a PhD in Management from the University of Mississippi, a master's degree in business Administration from Grand Valley State University in Michigan, and a bachelor's degree in Biology from Illinois Wesleyan University. Dr. Douglas teaches courses in Organizational Behavior and Strategic Management, and he has research interests in the areas of work team development, leadership, leader political skill, and temporary workforce issues. He has published articles in *Sam Advanced Management Journal, Supervision,* and the *Employee Responsibilities and Rights Journal.* Prior to his academic career, Dr. Douglas worked 15 years as a manufacturing manager for Clorox Company, Sun Chemical, Hexcel Chemical, and Herman Miller. Before his business experience, he had a career as a professional football player in the National Football League, with the San Francisco 49ers and the Chicago Bears, and in the Canadian Football League, with the Edmonton Eskimos.

**Dov Eden** is the Lilly and Alejandro Saltiel Professor of Corporate Leadership and Social Responsibility at Tel Aviv University's Faculty of Management. Since completing his PhD in organizational psychology at the University of Michigan in 1970, he has been at Tel Aviv University, where he chaired the Organizational Behavior Program, directed the Israel Institute of Business Research, and served as academic director of executive training. He is a Fellow of APA and of SIOP and a member of the Academy of Management, the Israel Psychological Association, and the Society for Research on Organizational Behavior. He is presently associate editor of *Academy of Management Journal* and has served on the editorial boards of *Journal of Applied Psychology, Organizational Behavior and Human Decision Processes, Leadership Quarterly,* and *Megamot Israel Behavioral Sciences Quarterly.* His research interests include leadership, motivation, expectation effects and self-fulfilling prophecy, management training, and job stress and vacation relief.

**Jeffrey R. Edwards** is the Belk Distinguished Professor of Management at the Kenan-Flagler Business School, University of North Carolina. He research examines person–environment fit, stress and coping, cognitive models of attitudes, work–family issues, and research methods, including topics such as difference scores, polynomial regression, and measurement and construct validation using structural equation modeling. He is editor of *Organizational Behavior and Human Decision Processes,* associate editor of *Organizational Research Methods,* and has served on the editorial boards of the *Journal of Applied Psychology, Personnel Psychology,* the *Academy of Management Review,* the *Journal of Management,* and the *Journal of Organizational Be-*

*havior*. He has been elected to the Society of Organizational Behavior, is past division and program chair of the Research Methods Division of the Academy of Management, and is founder and coordinator of RMNET, the electronic question-and-answer network of the Research Methods Division.

**Gerald R. Ferris** is the Francis Eppes Professor of Management and Professor of Psychology at Florida State University. Formerly, he held the Robert M. Hearin Chair of Business Administration, and was Professor of Management and Acting Associate Dean for Faculty and Research in the School of Business Administration at the University of Mississippi from 1999 to 2000. Before that, he served as Professor of Labor and Industrial Relations, of Business Administration, and of Psychology at the University of Illinois at Urbana–Champaign from 1989 to 1999, and as the Director of the Center for Human Resource Management at the University of Illinois from 1991 to 1996. Ferris received a PhD in Business Administration from the University of Illinois at Urbana–Champaign. He has research interests in the areas of social influence processes in human resources systems, and the role of reputation in organizations. Ferris is the author of articles published in such journals as the *Journal of Applied Psychology, Organizational Behavior and Human Decision Processes, Personnel Psychology, Academy of Management Journal,* and *Academy of Management Review.* Ferris serves as editor of the annual series *Research in Personnel and Human Resources Management.*

**Joanne H. Gavin** is the recipient of the Otto Alois Faust Doctoral Fellowship in Character and Health (2000–2002) and she is currently working on her PhD in organizational behavior at the University of Texas at Arlington. Ms. Gavin earned her MBA and BS in Business Administration at the University of New Orleans. Her research interest is in the area of personal character, decision making, and executive health. She is co-author of articles appearing in the *Academy of Management Executive, Applied Psychology: International Review,* and the *Academy of Management Journal.* Ms. Gavin is also co-author of several chapters in books such as *International Review of Industrial and Organizational Psychology* and *Psychology Builds a Healthy World.* In 2001, she presented a paper entitled "Transcendent Decision-Making: Defining the Role of Virtue-Based Character in the Decision-Making Process" at the Society for Business Ethics. This paper served as the foundation work for her dissertation.

**Jorge A. Gonzalez** is an Assistant Professor of Management at the University of Wisconsin–Milwaukee and received his PhD in Management from Texas A&M University. He does research in the areas of diversity in organizations, organizational commitment, organizational identification, and cross-cultural management. His research has been published in *Personnel*

*Psychology* and the *Journal of International Business Studies*. His area of teaching is international business.

**Christine A. Henle** is an Assistant Professor of Management at the University of North Carolina at Charlotte. She received her PhD in industrial/organizational psychology from Colorado State University. Her research interests include workplace deviance, organizational justice, employment law, and human resources management. She has published her work in psychology and management journals as well as edited books. She has also done consulting work in various human resource management areas including job analysis, selection, training, and performance management.

**Robert W. Kolodinsky** is Assistant Professor of Management at James Madison University in Harrisonburg, Virginia. He did his doctoral studies in Organizational Behavior and Human Resources Management at Florida State University. His research interests include social influence processes in organizations, social and political skill, human resource systems, performance appraisal issues, perceptions of politics, leadership, leader–member exchange theory, and spiritual issues in the workplace. He has published several journal articles and book chapters, and papers on which he was the primary author have won Best Paper awards at two conferences. Kolodinsky is a three-time small business owner and a small business founder.

**Edwin A. Locke** is Dean's Professor of Leadership and Motivation (Emeritus) at the R. H. Smith School of Business at the University of Maryland, College Park. He received his BA from Harvard in 1960 and his PhD in Industrial Psychology from Cornell University in 1964. He has published over 220 chapters, notes, and articles in professional journals, on such subjects as work motivation, job satisfaction, incentives, and the philosophy of science. He also is the author or editor of nine books, including *A Theory of Goal Setting and Task Performance* (Prentice-Hall, 1990, with G. Latham), *Handbook of Principles of Organizational Behavior* (Blackwell, 2000), and *The Prime Movers: Traits of the Great Wealth Creators* (AMACOM, 2000). Dr. Locke is a Fellow of the American Psychological Association, the American Psychological Society, and the Academy of Management. He was a winner of the Outstanding Teacher–Scholar Award at the University of Maryland, the Distinguished Scientific Contribution Award of the Society for Industrial and Organizational Psychology, and the Career Contribution Award from the Academy of Management (Human Resource Division).

**Judi McLean Parks** is the Reuben C. & Anne Carpenter Taylor Professor of Organizational Behavior at the John M. Olin School of Business at Washington University in St. Louis. She received her PhD in organizational behavior from the University of Iowa. Her research focuses on conflict and conflict resolution, the "psychological contract" between employers and employees, the impact of perceived injustice, as well as the effect of gender and ethnicity on perceived justice. Recently, she has begun to explore organizational identity and its relationship to conflict in organizations. An author of numerous articles and chapters, her research has been published in a variety of journals, including *Academy of Management Journal, Journal of Applied Psychology,* and *Organizational Behavior and Human Decision Processes.*

**Debra L. Nelson**, PhD, is the CBA Associates Professor of Business Administration and Professor of Management, Oklahoma State University. She is the author of over 70 journal articles and book chapters, and six books. Dr. Nelson's research has been published in the *Academy of Management Executive, Academy of Management Journal, Academy of Management Review, MIS Quarterly, Journal of Organizational Behavior,* and other journals. Her books include *Stress and Challenge at the Top: The Paradox of the Successful Executive; Organizational Leadership; Preventive Stress Management in Organizations; Gender, Work Stress and Health;* and *Organizational Behavior: Foundations, Realities, and Challenges, 4e.* Dr. Nelson is recognized with numerous teaching and research awards, including the Regents Distinguished Teaching Award, the Burlington Northern Faculty Achievement Award, and the Greiner Graduate Teaching Award. She has served on the editorial review boards of the *Journal of Occupational Health Psychology, Academy of Management Executive,* and the *Journal of Organizational Behavior.*

**James Campbell (Jim) Quick** is Professor of Organizational Behavior and Director of the Doctoral Program in Business Administration, the University of Texas at Arlington. Internationally recognized with his brother for their influential and groundbreaking theory of preventive stress management, he has over 100 book, journal, encyclopedia, and clinical publications. He was Founding Editor of APA's *Journal of Occupational Health Psychology.* He is a Fellow of the Society for Industrial and Organizational Psychology, the American Psychological Association, the American Institute of Stress, and was awarded an APA Presidential Citation. He has received over $235,000 in research support. He was APA's stress expert to the National Academy of Sciences (1990). He is listed in *Who's Who in the World* (7th edition). He was awarded the Maroon Citation by the Colgate University Alumni Corporation, and the Legion of Merit by the U.S. Air Force. He is married to the former Sheri Grimes Schember.

**Jonathan D. Quick** is Director, Essential Drugs and Medicines Policy (EDM), for the World Health Organization, Geneva. EDM works to ensure for people everywhere access to safe, effective, good quality essential drugs that are prescribed and used rationally. He joined WHO in 1995 after 20 years in international health, serving in Pakistan, Kenya, and over 18 other countries in Africa, Asia, and Latin America. He has authored or edited 10 books, including as Senior Editor of *Managing Drug Supply* (1997–1978), and over 40 articles and chapters on essential drugs, public health, and stress management. He is a Diplomate of the American Board of Family Practice, and a Fellow of both the Royal Society of Medicine (UK) and the American College of Preventive Medicine. He earned an AB degree *magna cum laude* from Harvard University, and an MD degree with distinction in research and an MPH from the University of Rochester.

**Belle Rose Ragins** is a Professor of Management at the University of Wisconsin–Milwaukee. Her research interests focus on diversity and mentoring in organizations. Her work has been published in such journals as *Academy of Management Journal, Academy of Management Review, Academy of Management Executive, Journal of Applied Psychology,* and *Psychological Bulletin*. She recently authored (with David Clutterbuck) *Mentoring and Diversity: An International Perspective* (2002). Dr. Ragins has received eight national awards for her research, including the Sage Award for scholarly contributions to management, the American Society for Training and Development Research Award for best published paper in 1999, the American Psychological Association Placek Award, and five Best Paper Awards from the National Academy of Management. She served on the editorial board of the *Academy of Management Journal,* and is currently on the editorial boards of the *Journal of Applied Psychology* and the *Journal of Vocational Behavior*.

**Sandra L. Robinson** (PhD, Northwestern University) is Associate Professor of Organizational Behavior as well as an Associate Member of the Psychology Department at the University of British Columbia. Dr. Robinson's research interests include trust, managing employment relationships, psychological contracts, betrayal, workplace deviance, and workplace aggression. Her publications have appeared in various journals, including *Harvard Business Review, Administrative Science Quarterly, Academy of Management Review, Journal of Applied Psychology, Journal of Organizational Behavior,* and *Academy of Management Journal*. Dr. Robinson serves on the editorial boards of *Academy of Management Journal* and *Journal of Applied Psychology* and is an Associate Editor of the *Journal of Management Inquiry*. She also is a past board member of the Organizational Behavior Division of the Academy of Management and a current board member of the Western Academy of Management.

**Sandra E. Spataro** is an Assistant Professor of organizational behavior at the Yale School of Management. Her research examines the influences of organizational social structures on individuals' work experiences, including how demographic diversity among co-workers affects the performance of work tasks and other work experiences, how demographic differences between co-workers influence cooperation and peer evaluations, and the formation and implications of informal status and power hierarchies in organizations. Recent publications include "Getting to Know You: The Influence of Personality on the Alignment of Self-Other Evaluations of Demographically Different People" (with F. J. Flynn & J. A. Chatman, *Administrative Science Quarterly*, 46 (3):414–442) and "When Differences Do (and Do Not) Make a Difference: How Individual Identities Influence Reactions to Diversity" (in M. Neale, E. Mannix, & J. Polzer [Eds.], *Research on Managing Groups and Teams*, Volume 4). She received her PhD from the Haas School of Business at the University of California, Berkeley.

**Darren C. Treadway** is a PhD candidate at Florida State University in Organizational Behavior and Human Resource Management. He received a master's degree in Business Administration from Virginia Tech and a bachelor's degree from Concord College in West Virginia. Darren's research interests include the role of age in the workplace, reactions of diverse groups to organizational politics, multilevel processes in organizations, and work–family conflict. Before his doctoral studies, Darren worked for 8 years as an operations and human resource manager.

# I

## Individual Processes

# 1

# The Affective Revolution in Organizational Behavior: The Emergence of a Paradigm

Sigal G. Barsade
*Yale University*

Arthur P. Brief
*Tulane University*

Sandra E. Spataro
*Yale University*

"Our task, you might say, is to discover the reason that underlies unreason."

—Herbert A. Simon (1989, p. 23)

A new research paradigm is emerging within organizational behavior (OB), in both theory and empiricism, based on the increasing recognition of the importance of affect to organizational life. In his classic book, *The Structure of Scientific Revolutions*, Kuhn (1970) described a paradigm as a scientific achievement that involves the creation of a constellation of research values, techniques, and beliefs, which offer a model for the type of investigation people within the scientific community should be following. A paradigm must be sufficiently compelling to draw scientists from other, competing types of research activity and open-ended enough to leave many new problems for these researchers, and those following them, to solve in the scientific enterprise. As we show, the study of affect in organizations is developing into such a paradigm.

When examining the emergence of the affective paradigm among organizational scholars in this chapter, we argue that this evolution of research *within* OB affective scholarship can be best described as following the steps of a Kuhnian scientific revolution.[1] We want to be clear, however, that we follow the Kuhnian steps heuristically, rather than literally, to help our understanding of the process of change in this field. As many scholars including Kuhn (1970) himself have pointed out (e.g., Brief, 1998; Jones, 1998; Pfeffer, 1993), the social sciences as a whole, including organizational behavior, do not yet have one dominant paradigm.[2] However, Kuhn's model is a powerful lens through which to examine the marked changes over the past half-century in affective research in organizational behavior. As questions and pursuits that historically have occupied organizational scholars studying affect are being swiftly supplanted by new questions and new methods, we observe a new cross-disciplinary paradigm emerging and argue in favor of its occurrence.

We begin by describing *"Where we were,"* in a preparadigmatic stage of diverse and richly construed perspectives and models of early affect researchers, such as that of Hersey (1932), who conducted an in-depth longitudinal study of the daily emotions and performance of a group of skilled railroad workers, or that of Fisher and Hanna (1931) in whose work on worker psychopathology we see the first hints of dispositional affect theory to return over half a century later. Based on a historical review by Weiss and Brief (2002), we discuss how this work narrowed into the accepted

---

[1]Kuhn's model posits that scientific knowledge advances through a combination of incremental evolutionary steps and then, dramatically, via marked, path-changing revolutions. The first stage in Kuhn's model is collection of a "pool of facts" (p. 15), when researchers confront "… the same range of phenomena, but not usually all the same particular phenomena, describe and interpret them in different ways" (p. 17), forming preparadigmatic schools. In this preparadigmatic stage, each school approaches part of the collection of facts in a particular way, identifies a theoretical emphasis, and presents a specific understanding of the phenomenon at hand. Eventually, Kuhn argued, a dominant paradigm gains preeminence. At this point the scientific field moves to the next stage of "normal" science. Normal science is the iterative, puzzle-solving, "mopping up operations" (p. 24) in which scientists largely spend their time trying to solve a puzzle "… that no one before has solved or solved so well" (p. 38). However, when some puzzles cannot be solved or anomalies emerge, a crisis occurs, and from this crisis arises the next stage—the emergence of a scientific revolution. The scientific revolution involves the blurring of the old paradigm, and a struggle for preeminence between the old paradigm and a new paradigm. The field is then reconstructed through the change of basic theoretical generalizations and assumptions, altering its methods with the identification of new questions and goals.

[2]The lack of a dominant paradigm in organizational behavior technically precludes the present occurrence of scientific revolution. This is because, as described earlier in Kuhn's model, a scientific field must go through a preparadigmatic stage (where the social sciences currently stand from a Kuhnian perspective), and then a normal science stage in which everyone follows the same paradigm, to subsequently have a "revolution."

dominant paradigm of affect defined as job satisfaction. We detail how the field then entered a period of "normal" iterative science revolving around this central concept, solving puzzles about the antecedents and consequences of job satisfaction. We then describe how a crisis of confidence ensued, sparked particularly by the conspicuous and persistent absence of empirical support for the intuitive notion that job satisfaction is a predictor of job performance.

We discuss how this crisis of confidence, coinciding with a profound methodological and theoretical revolution in the study of affect in psychology (Fiske, 2001), coupled with an integration of long-held sociological perspectives, then led away from the "normal science" of job satisfaction research to the beginnings of an affective scientific revolution, which we discuss in the *"Where we are now"* section.

In this section we show that the early job satisfaction paradigm is being replaced by richer theory, stronger measures, more sophisticated methods, and most importantly, a broader understanding of affective constructs and how they influence organizational life. Research has shifted away from focusing on self-reported worker satisfaction to a dramatically more broad understanding of affective experience. The current broader conceptualization of affect incorporates a myriad of constructs such as mood, trait affect, specific emotions, and emotional labor—all now directly linked to cognitive, behavioral, and emotional organizational outcomes. These offer a base for robust investigation of affect as cause and consequence of organizational behavior using both sociological and psychological perspectives. There is a continuing move away from studying emotions as only an intrapsychic experience and toward examining the social aspects of affect with an understanding of how people influence each other affectively, both consciously and subconsciously, with group emotion becoming an increasingly rich field of inquiry. We also point out the foreshadowing of the type of multimodel hybrid paradigm we hope for the field. Weiss and Cropanzano's (1996) "Affective Events Theory" leads the way in this as does the construct of emotional intelligence (Mayer, Caruso, & Salovey, 1999; Salovey & Mayer, 1990).

We posit in our section describing *"Where we are going"* that there will be continuing growth of this affective revolution, with more questions asked and puzzles solved. We discuss how emerging research is demonstrating that specific, discrete emotions, such as anger, joy, and envy, manifest differently in both how they arise in an individual and how they affect the focal individual and those around him or her. This will lead to an increasing value being placed on differentiating specific emotions from one another and investigating the distinct antecedents and consequences of each (Ekman & Davidson, 1994; but also see Ortony & Turner, 1990). We expect to see an expansion of the study of affect to broader levels of analysis than has been done to date. We suggest that we should be examining affect at the organizational level—through constructs such as affective culture, as well as examining affect more deeply at the intrapsychic level—through more subconscious and developmentally based affective processes. Furthermore, we expect that inquiries into the role of neuropsychology will gain momentum within the field (e.g., LeDoux, 1996; Panksepp, 1998). Critical to these deepening perspectives are the ability of methodological tools to recognize and analyze the role of affect in individuals and in social settings, and to keep up with more sophisticated conceptual models of affect (e.g., Cartwright, 2000). Thus, we expect new techniques of measuring and detecting emotions to be advanced. These methods will help scaffold the validity and reliability of the new paradigm, as well as offer a fertile field to increase the investigative breadth of research.

Ultimately, because of the tremendous complexities of understanding human behavior, which is more difficult to decipher than the physical sciences on which Kuhn mainly focused, we predict the future of study of affect in organizations will emerge into a paradigmatic multimodel hybrid that Kuhn may not have foreseen. We expect that a divergence of views and lenses with which to view organizational phenomena, rather than competition between them, will inspire the hybrid paradigm that will mark knowledge of affect in organizational behavior. That is, rather than having one paradigm "win" the field of affect in organizational behavior through the triumph or victory of some miniparadigms over others for being "more correct," we suggest that an embracing of multiple theoretical, methodological, and disciplinary perspectives, with which to view and understand affect in organizations, will occur. Given the nature of the human phenomenon, this type of multimodel paradigmatic hybrid could lead to the strongest revolution yet in our understanding of organizations and the people who live within them.

## WHERE WE WERE:
## THE "BLOOMING OF A THOUSAND THEORIES"
## NARROWED TO THE
## "JOB SATISFACTION" PARADIGM

### The Blooming of a Thousand Theories

Affective states were not always perceived as irrational, annoying, statistical "noise" that interfered with the true understanding of rational organizing. Their beginning in organizational study was much more robust, dramatic, and complete. Very early on, classical sociologists exploring the psychic experiences of workers in capitalistic institutions studied the concept of "worker alienation," characterized by the boredom and mental numbness that could arise in highly specialized factories and with the emotional isolation of workers from each other (Marx, 1842–1844/1971; see Seeman, 1959, for a discussion of these early conceptualizations of "worker alienation"). As early as the 1930s, inquiry into affect at work was characterized by broad conceptualizations of the potential causes (e.g., both individual and situational considerations) and implications (at work, with family, in society, etc.) of affect. For example, the Hawthorne studies, which began in 1927, focused on the "adjustment" and "maladjustment" of a worker to his situation. These researchers studied level of adjustment as a function of both the social conditioning the worker brought to the workplace and the physical circumstances of the workplace itself (Roethlisberger & Dickson, 1939)—an early explication of a person–situation interaction. Work by Fisher and Hanna (1931) gave early attention to "temperamental" or personality influences on the experience and expression of emotion. Further, Robert Hoppock's 1935 book *Job Satisfaction* actually focused more on societal than on business implications of job satisfaction and used many differing methodologies to examine these implications. Some very mainstream correlational studies of organizational conditions, as opposed to individual differences, as antecedents of job satisfaction were developing in this decade as well (see Kornhauser & Sharp, 1932, for an early and prototypical example of this type of research). Lastly, a richness of methods, including experience sampling of affect through daily emotion checklists (four times per day, for 10–13 weeks; Hersey, 1932), diaries, case studies, and interviews (Hoppock, 1935), characterized the research into affect at work during this time.

## The Affect-as-Job Satisfaction Paradigm

Despite the early proliferation of ideas and methodologies to explore affect at work, by the end of the 1930s, both the focus of affect research and the methods used to approach it converged around the organizational causes and implications of job satisfaction.[3] This convergence continued through the 1940s, with scientists focused on World War II efforts, and therefore on a major advantage of survey methodology: the ability to quickly and efficiently test and classify many people. This rather narrow domain of research could be characterized, until the late 1950s and 1960s, by an emphasis on positive description rather than theory development or deductive theory testing (Weiss & Brief, 2002). Even some potentially rich ideas for theory development, like March and Simon's (1958) suggestion that satisfaction could be understood in terms of predictability of instru-

---

[3]A rich and thorough history of job satisfaction research is examined by Weiss and Brief (2002), and is the basis for the historical summary we offer here.

mental relationships on the job, were largely ignored and never investigated empirically (Brief, 1998).

Research on job satisfaction in the 1950s lacked immediate potency. However, some notable developments during this time sowed the seeds for future advancements. These included: Herzberg and colleagues' introduction of the notion that satisfaction and dissatisfaction were not simply opposites (Herzberg, Mausner, & Snyderman, 1959); the beginnings of a focus on equity as a cause of satisfaction (e.g., Homans, 1961; Patchen, 1961), which took hold in the 1960s; and, from the Human Relations school, born out of the lessons of the Hawthorne studies, the groundwork for Hackman and Oldham's (1975) job characteristics model and other task design approaches (e.g., Campion & Thayer, 1985) helping to predict job satisfaction.

As Weiss and Brief (2002) noted, the 1950s contained examples of a phenomenon often repeated in the scientific process—the "discovery" of something that had actually garnered attention in past cycles of research development. For example, Weitz's (1952) discoveries of intrapersonal consistencies with respect to the experience and expression of emotion ignored research from the 1930s that suggested the same (e.g., Fisher & Hanna, 1931). Similarly, some claim Weitz's advancements were forsaken in the new "dispositional approach" sparked in the 1980s (e.g., Judge, 1992).

Following the unfulfilled promise of theory advancement and stagnant methodological progress in the 1950s, the 1960s were a time of reawakening in job satisfaction research. Theory development and the use of theory-driven measures regained prominence. Theoretical development was exemplified in Vroom's (1964) *Work and Motivation*, which characterized prior job satisfaction research as plainly intuitive about how rewards and punishments might affect job attitudes and lacking in fundamental theory. Vroom's own theories, including expectancy theory, were firmly rooted in social psychological principles and set the stage for further theory development, including the systematic examination of a potential association between satisfaction and performance.

Other discrepancy theories also emerged in the 1960s. Adams's (1963, 1965) equity theory linking satisfaction to a person's comparison of his or her own perceived ratio of inputs to outcomes to another's ratio of inputs to outcomes implied a link between evaluation of an experience and resulting satisfaction. In 1969, Locke was the first job satisfaction theorist to consider satisfaction explicitly as emotion—or at least to label it as such. Consistent with Adams's equity theory, Locke (1969) argued that emotions, such as satisfaction, result from evaluations (similar to the current concept of "cognitive appraisal").

Also important in the 1960s was work at the University of Minnesota on the theory of work adjustment (see Dawis & Lofquist, 1984, for a summary), centered primarily around the concept of "mutual correspondence," or the extent to which individuals and work environments met one another's needs. This work not only outlined the fit model that underlay much existing theory, it also put forth the Minnesota Satisfaction Questionnaire (MSQ), a facet-based measure of job satisfaction still used today. Similarly important advancements in theory-driven methodology came from the Job Descriptive Index (JDI; Smith, Kendall, & Hulin, 1969), a highly influential and still popular measure of job satisfaction.

The proliferation of both theoretical and methodological idea generation that occurred during the 1960s was followed by a period of consolidation and relative quiet in the 1970s. Salancik and Pfeffer's (1978) introduction of social information processing theory was one of the few significant theoretical developments in organizational research on job satisfaction during this time period. Social information processing asserted that jobs are ambiguous stimuli and expressions of affect and attitudes from co-workers influence individuals' interpretations of these ambiguities. This was the first explicit advancement of the notion that attitudes could be directly influenced by the expressed attitudes of one's co-workers. Further, Pfeffer and Salancik's ideas suggested that, because satisfaction was socially influenced it could not be reliably predicted only by job characteristics, but was rather transient and based, in part, on the opinions of others. Landy's (1978) opponent process theory of job satisfaction also offered an intriguing hypothesis that every time a deviation in feelings from one's equilibrium level of job satisfaction occurred, an opponent process would bring back satisfaction into balance. Although theoretically provocative, this theory never progressed to empirical testing and support.

Nonetheless, the 1970s brought useful activity in the form of reviews of the satisfaction and motivation literature, which helped organize and consolidate thinking around existing streams of research (e.g., Lawler, 1973; Locke, 1976; Mitchell, 1974). Otherwise, there was little new job satisfaction theory development occurring, with the marked exception of work examining specific elements of the work environment and how they affected motivation and other attitudes at work. These include Lawler's (1971) work on pay and Hackman and Oldham's (1975) models of job design. As in the 1950s, the relative quiet of the 1970s set the stage for more radical advances in the following decade. Up until that time, however, job satisfaction was the affective variable of choice. It was an often attempted, if unsuccessful, predictor variable of job performance,[4] and made a standard dependent measure to be predicted by a number of variables ranging from workplace ergonomics to organizational culture.

---

[4]See Judge, Thoresen, Bono, and Patton's (2001) measurement error focused article.

The use of job satisfaction as the primary representation of workplace affect was limited, given the construct of job satisfaction certainly does not encompass the totality of richness of affective experience and, in fact, has some directly cognitive components—in measurement, if not in definition (Brief & Roberson, 1989; Organ & Near, 1985). Weiss (2002) offered a compelling argument that although job satisfaction is certainly affective, in that it consists of a valenced evaluation, it lacks many other defining features of moods and emotions (e.g., it is not a state, does not have a subjective experiential character, and has no typical physiological correlates; but, see Brief, 1998). Also, even if one ignores research clearly defining job satisfaction from both a cognitive and affective perspective (e.g., Brief, 1998; Motowidlo, 1996) and if one takes the most affectively theoretical definition of job satisfaction given by Locke (1976),"a pleasurable or positive emotional state resulting from the appraisal of one's job or job experiences"(p. 1300), the construct of job satisfaction does not begin to sound the depth of the affective construct. Thus, from theoretical, methodological, and predictive perspectives, it was not a very satisfactory operationalization of affect at work.

## WHERE WE ARE NOW:
## THE BEGINNINGS OF A REVOLUTION

The crisis that sparked the shift in affective paradigm and the beginnings of the affective revolution was not a lack of ability to understand the construct of job satisfaction. This part of the "mopping up operation" of normal science (Kuhn, 1970, p. 24) had been thoroughly addressed—with, to date, more than 12,000 studies on job satisfaction published (Spector, 1996). Rather, it was mainly the disenchantment with the construct's inability to relate to important organizational outcomes, mainly job performance, that served as the "crisis" that opened organizational behavior scholars to the possibility of other ways to characterize affect at work. This rationale was explicitly stated in Staw and colleagues' work, particularly in the seminal Staw, Bell, and Clausen (1986) study. They built a strong theoretical case, based on recent psychological evidence, and offered empirical support that trait affect measured as early as adolescence could predict study participants' job satisfaction up to almost 50 years later, even across different careers and jobs. Staw's work coincided with and took advantage of the rising tide of methodological sophistication and interest in affective personality within psychology at the time (e.g., Watson & Clark, 1984).[5] By

---

[5]Not directly related to affect, Staw and colleagues' articles regarding dispositional affect and consistency in job attitudes (see also Staw & Ross, 1985) were also a precursor to a more general trait versus state argument that occurred within the field of organizational behavior. Mirroring the critical view against personality and dispositional constructs in the psychological literature (e.g., Mischel, 1968)                                    *(continued on next page)*

confirming the relative stability of job attitudes resulting from trait measures of affect, the Staw et al. (1986) article gave impetus to view affect at work more broadly. The very act of showing the importance of another type of affect at work, a type of affect other than job satisfaction, was a turning point in the affective revolution as researchers began to broaden their affective constructs, both as cause and consequence.

## Affect Elaborated: The Fueling of the Affective Revolution From Models in Psychology and Sociology

To understand the progression of the affective revolution as it spread through organizational behavior is to understand how the construct of affect became increasingly differentiated and nuanced. Questions asked and areas explored by organizational scholars within the affective domain were also profoundly influenced by cutting-edge work in psychology (which was and is undergoing its own "affective revolution," see Kihlstrom, 1999) and the integration of work done by sociological scholars—many of whom were testing their theories in explicitly organizational domains.

*The Basic Nature of Affect.*    An overarching view of affect divides it into two basic categories: trait affect and state affect. Trait affect, the affect examined by Staw and colleagues, is a long-term, stable predisposition in individuals to perceive the world around them as either primarily positive or negative (e.g., Watson, 2000). One's trait affect characterizes the way affect tends to be experienced and expressed (Goldsmith & Campos, 1986). It does not need a specific target but rather is a generalized tendency toward having a particular level of positivity and negativity, which then permeates all of an individual's experiences (Lazarus, 1991). Extensive work by psychologists studying

---

[5] *(continued)*      traits were greatly out of favor in organizational research as compared to situational approaches (e.g., Salancik & Pfeffer, 1978). Part of this seemed to be for political reasons within the field of organizational behavior—both liberal and conservative. From a liberal perspective, it was thought discriminatory to study variables that people couldn't develop or change (e.g., Davis-Blake & Pfeffer, 1989). On the conservative side, why study variables that management could not change? Staw's work successfully challenged this resistance to traits. In fact, Staw's first article examining the longitudinal consistency in men's job satisfaction across employer and occupation (Staw & Ross, 1985) showed more about the importance of dispositional factors in organizational behavior in general than about affect per se. Thus, the argument about the existence and usefulness of affective traits was a focus of an implicit state–trait debate that would rage in organizational behavior (e.g., Davis-Blake & Pfeffer, 1989; House, Shane, & Herold, 1996; Staw, in press), but seems ultimately solved by a perspective taking into account the main effects of both states and dispositions, as well as the interaction between them. This has occurred specifically within the field of emotions (e.g., Lazarus & Cohen-Charash, 2001) as well as in organizational behavior in general (e.g., Brief, 1998; Chatman, 1989; Spataro, in press).

affect has focused on the trait of positive affect, the degree to which a person is high in enthusiasm, energy, mental alertness, and determination (Watson, Clark, & Tellegen, 1988; Watson & Tellegen, 1985), and on the trait of negative affect, the degree to which one feels subjective distress, such as irritability, anxiety, or nervousness (e.g., Brief, Burke, George, Robinson, & Webster, 1988; Watson & Pennebaker, 1989).

State affect can be divided into two general categories, moods and specific emotions, and these two categories are primarily differentiated by intensity, duration, and specificity. Emotions are intense, relatively short-term affective reactions to a specific environmental stimulus. As opposed to moods, which are longer lasting but more diffuse, emotions have a clear cause or object and are more focused and intense (Frijda & Mesquita, 1994). Emotions are more likely to change beliefs than moods (Schwarz, Bless, Bohner, Harlacher, & Kellerbenz, 1991) and are more likely to disrupt or influence activity (Lazarus, 1991). The antecedents of moods are not as distinct as those of emotions, and are so diffuse, individuals may not realize they are experiencing them, nor that moods are influencing their behavior (Forgas, 1992).

State and trait affect are related so closely that they have been described as the "former [state affect] being provoked in a specific context, the latter (background) influencing this provocation" (Lazarus, 1991, p. 47). Although state affect is a shorter term reaction with greater fluctuation than trait affect (Tellegen, 1985), trait affect at the personality level helps to determine state affect (Lazarus, 1991). Thus, the moods an individual typically experiences will reflect his or her overall trait affect; and, other individuals with whom a given individual interacts regularly will perceive and characterize the person by his or her underlying trait affect, as a function of the person's typically expressed moods.

## Increased Sophistication of Affective Constructs and Methods

A variety of continued advances, conceptual and methodological, in basic psychological and sociological research have bolstered the momentum of the affective revolution in organizational behavior. Examples of these include advances in research focusing on (a) the dimensionality of affect, (b) basic/discrete affect, and (c) the social construction of affect. Difficult as it may be, organizational behavior scholars must stay abreast of these advances, including the debates that surround them, as their substance is at the very heart of how we conceive of and measure affective states and traits. We now briefly examine each of the perspectives and discuss how each has influenced organizational behavior research to date.

*The Dimensional Approach.*   One model for understanding the nature of moods and emotions is the dimensional approach, which seeks to ascertain those broad factors that best describe affective experience.[6] The exact nature of this dimensionality is hotly debated in social psychology (e.g., Cacioppo, Gardner, & Bernston, 1997, 1999; Feldman Barrett & Russell, 1998; Green, Salovey, & Truax, 1999; Russell & Carroll, 1999; Russell & Feldman Barrett, 1999; Watson & Tellegen, 1999; Watson, Wiese, Vaidya, & Tellegen, 1999; for an example of the very limited research on the structure of affect in the workplace, see Burke, Brief, George, Roberson, & Webster, 1989). The debate centers on the affective circumplex, advanced by Russell (1980). He argued that affective experience can be represented by a circle, with two main axes being degree of pleasantness and activation. Alternatively Watson and Tellegen (1985) proposed a different orientation of the primary axes, focusing on constructs combining pleasantness and energy, which they labeled positive and negative affectivity. The issues involved are complex and very much caught up in recent advances in neuroscience (e.g., Davidson, 1998; Gray, 1994; Harmon-Jones & Allen, 1998; Isen, 2002; LeDoux, 1996). We do not attempt to resolve the debates here; but rather, give a taste of their flavor. For example, many affect researchers conceptualize happiness and sadness as diametric opposites (e.g., Larsen & Diener, 1992; Russell, 1980). When people are happy they tend to smile, laugh, and seek out others; but when sad, they frown, cry, and may withdraw from others (e.g., Shaver, Schwartz, Kirson, & O'Connor, 1987). Alternatively, the evaluation space model (ESM) of Cacioppo and Berntson (1994) posits that positive affect (e.g., happiness) and negative affect (e.g., sadness) can co-occur but over time tend not to. Recent evidence indicates this is so (Larsen, McGraw, & Cacioppo, 2001).

Organizational researchers have incorporated most aspects of the dimensionality approach. For example, some organizational researchers rely on Russell's (e.g., 1980) affective circumplex model as the correct way of viewing the dimensionality of state affect and, therefore, study pleasantness (e.g. see Isen, in press, and Isen & Baron, 1991, for a review) or pleasantness and energy as independent constructs (e.g., Barsade, in press; Bartel & Saavedra, 2000). However, other organizational researchers follow Watson's work (e.g., Watson et al., 1988) and treat state affect as comprised of two dimensions of combined activation (or energy) and pleasantness (e.g., Brief et al., 1988; Brief, Butcher, & Roberson, 1995). Although to our knowledge, no one in the organizational literature has embraced Cacioppo and Berntson's (1994) highly attractive evaluation space

---

[6]The concept of a dimensionality approach to affect was proposed as far back as Wundt (1905/1991), who, based on evidence from introspection, suggested three dimensions to account for differences between affect: pleasure–displeasure, excitement–calm, and strain–relaxation. These dimensions are very similar to those being discussed today.

model, it is, as we describe more fully later in this chapter, the type of hybrid model we expect to see emerging in the future study of affect in organizations. This integrative, hybrid perspective is also implicit in Larsen and Diener's (1992) approach toward the overarching question of the dimensionality of affect. They suggest focusing not on one "most appropriate" dimensionality but rather on the importance of matching the most relevant affective dimension to the particular construct researchers are interested in examining.

*The Categorical Approach: Basic and Discrete Affect.* There are researchers who oppose the dimensionality approach just stated, as they believe that it overly simplifies affective experience. For example, as Lazarus (1991) stated:

> Much of value is lost by putting these [emotional] reactions into dimensions, because the simplifying or reductive generalizations wipe out important meanings about person–environment relationships, which the hundreds of emotion words were created to express. If we want to know what makes people or any given person angry, for example, the task is not facilitated—in fact it is actually undermined—by a pre-occupation with the so-called underlying response dimensions, which supposedly transcend emotion categories. Anger, then, becomes only a kind of unpleasant activation, when in reality it is a complex, varied, and rich relational pattern between persons. (pp. 63–64)

When determining how to divide emotions categorically, there is a school of research that has asserted there exists a core set of universal emotions—anger, fear, sadness, disgust, surprise, and happiness—and that these basic emotions are preprogrammed responses humans and other animals have evolved to cope with their environments (e.g., Izard, 1992; Weisfeld, 1997). This basic affect approach, advanced mainly by evolutionary psychologists (based on the work of Darwin, 1872/1970), focuses on nonverbal behavior, particularly facial expressions. In fact, the universal recognition of facial expression has been used as evidence for the evolutionary nature of emotional responses and for the basic affect approach (e.g., Ekman & Friesen, 1971; Keltner & Ekman, 2000).[7] This area of work has spurred some very interesting cross-cultural studies of emotion, including inter- and intranational differences in emotion expression and norms (e.g., Eid & Diener, 2001), and in the understanding of emotional expressions (Elfenbein & Ambady, 2002). This type of research has been

---

[7]There has traditionally been a debate about whether recognition of facial expression and affective norms are universal or culturally specific. More recent research combines both the universal and culturally specific approaches (e.g. Eid & Diener, 2001; Fiske, Kitayama, Markus, & Nisbett, 1998).

shown to have direct relevance in the organizational context (see Elfenbein, Marsh, & Ambady, 2002, for a review).

Directly related to the basic affect approach is the discrete category approach to emotions. This approach divides the affective experience into discrete categories, with a similar evolutionary and functionalist rationale as used in the basic approach to emotion described previously. However, it is significantly more inclusive, and contains many more types of emotions than the six mentioned. This discrete approach to emotions is one of the most promising areas in affective organizational research (see Lazarus & Cohen-Charash, 2001 for a thorough review); and, we discuss it in depth in the "Where We Are Going" section later.[8]

*The Social Constructionist Approach.* Psychological approaches to categorizing and characterizing affect stand in contrast to sociological perspectives that focus much less on distinguishing and recognizing specific affect, per se. This is because, in their extreme, sociological perspectives maintain that, as emotions are contextually defined, there are potentially as many emotions as there are situations (Kemper, 1978). That is, rather than conceiving of affect as coming from within people, sociologists construe affect as a product of socially created systems of meaning, negotiated among actors (e.g., Griffiths, 1995; Parrott & Harre, 1996). As Fineman (2000) explained, "… physical sensation, such as a churning stomach, is undoubtedly a real feeling, but it is only 'revulsion' when labeled and/or performed in a manner consistent with repulsive circumstances and behaviour" (p. 9). Sociologists, and specifically social constructionists, attempt to understand the aspects of situations that assign meaning and offer interpretations of emotional experiences in social settings—a cognitive appraisal theory approach.

Despite agreement among sociologists that emotions are contextually defined, there is variation in the lenses used to view and interpret situations. Some social constructionists (Gordon, 1989; Harre, 1986) and symbolic interactionists (Hochschild, 1983; Shott, 1979) focus on how specific social structures and local norms shape individual behavior, and, particularly, the

---

[8]There is an approach that combines the dimensional and categorical approaches discussed previously; this is the prototypical approach (Shaver et al., 1987). It does so by showing that there are varying levels of hierarchies of affect that people use in their mental representations. At the top of the hierarchy is an overarching, superordinate differentiation: positive and negative affect. This is similar to the positive and negative affect talked about in the dimensional approach. These two categories then branch out into six "basic category" branches: love, joy, anger, sadness, fear, and surprise—quite similar to the emotions studied by basic affect researchers. These six categories then further divide into 25 subordinate level categories. These lower levels of categories encompass the more specific emotions found in the "basic affect" approach. This approach has been very helpful to affect researchers to define the relevant emotions within the constructs they are studying.

experience and expression of affect (e.g., Hochschild, 1983; Scheff, 1990). Roles such as salesperson, mother, and accountant, as well as contexts such as library, McDonald's, and board meeting, are all governed by rules of conduct that proscribe acceptable behaviors and also shape the experience and expression of emotion. These constructionists examine the situation in terms of these "rules" and the structure that supports them to understand how meaning is conferred on emotional experiences. The rules can also be internally constructed by the employees based on their perception of the appropriate professional rules of conduct. For example, Yanay and Shahar (1998), in a study of the socialization of psychologists in training, examined how the psychologists' approach to their emotional labor can be seen as a negotiation of their own professional identity, roles, and values.

Other constructionists attend less to structure and norms and more to relationships and, specifically, interrelationships between social groups, with affect understood as feelings about shifts in the balance of power and status between interdependent social groups (e.g., Barbalet, 1995; Kemper, 1991). For example, in situations where a shift in power or status among groups poses a threat to one's vested interests, that person's experience of fear or anxiety is an expression of this specific threat. The meaning of the emotion still comes from the situation; but in this case, the situation is construed in terms of power and status relationships rather than norms and social structure.

Perhaps the greatest impact of social constructionist approaches to studying affect on organizational behavior research has come from work in emotional labor (for a review, see Thoits, 1989). In general, the sociological paradigm is based on the idea that social structure and, particularly, aspects of stratification, are the primary drivers of human behavior. Numerous sociological studies from the 1960s through the 1980s related these variables to affective experiences within organizations as well (e.g., Collins, 1975; Goffman, 1967; Kemper, 1981; Smith-Lovin, 1988). In fact, by explicitly examining the secondary effects of workplace affect on the lives and health of those whose jobs demand they manage their display of affect at work, Hochschild's (1983) studies of service providers were, in their own right, as significant a spark on the affective revolution in organizational behavior as was Staw's work on dispositional affect. Her 1983 book, *The Managed Heart: Commercialization of Human Feeling,* introduced the concept of "emotional labor," work performed by service workers required to project expected and organizationally desirable emotions in their interactions with clients, regardless of actual emotions felt.

Whereas Hochschild's original thesis asserted the negative effects of emotional labor on the private lives of the workers she studied, research in this area has been extended to explore both antecedents and consequences of emotional labor, inside and outside the workplace. Adjustment to contextual factors that regulate expression of affect has served as the basis for extensive work in sociology and organizational behavior on the functions and dysfunctions of managing the expression of emotions. Rafaeli and Sutton's emotional labor research in organizations (Rafaeli & Sutton, 1987, 1989, 1990, 1991; Sutton & Rafaeli, 1988) continued in this tradition and was an important spark in the affective revolution, putting the concept of emotional labor squarely on the affect-in-organizations map. This work served as a significant catalyst for much of the work in emotional labor that followed.

However, there have been some difficulties with how this line of research has progressed. Despite high levels of interest and substantive work, efforts to clarify the antecedents and consequences of emotional labor in organizations have suffered from disagreements as to the definition of "emotional labor" and from failure to agree on empirical methods for assessing it (Haertel & Zerbe, 2000). This may explain the mixed set of outcomes regarding the functionality of emotional labor in organizations. Among the positive outcomes, emotional labor has been related to both self-esteem and self-efficacy (Seeman, 1991), self-expression (Clark & LaBeff, 1982), emotional adaptability (Schaubroeck & Jones, 2000), enhanced task accomplishment (Rafaeli & Sutton, 1989), improved vendor–client interaction (Gross & Stone, 1964), and increased customer compliance with service providers (Rafaeli & Sutton, 1991). Emotional labor also has been shown to lead to negative consequences, including emotional exhaustion, cynical job attitudes, and decreased psychological attachment to jobs (Kruml & Geddes, 2000), as well as decreases in both job identification and job involvement among employees (Schaubroeck & Jones, 2000). These mixed findings may serve as their own crisis call for sociological scholars. In the meantime, there is still work to be done among organizational researchers to reconcile these findings and ultimately to determine the best methods and theories to understand the influence of emotional labor in organizations.

## The Beginning of the Affective Revolution in Organizational Behavior: Empirical Evidence

*Trait Affect.* The importance of this expanded, richer view of affect to the field of organizational behavior is supported by the blaze of new research in the field (for a review see Brief & Weiss, 2002; Staw, in press). For example, with regard to trait positive affect, a plethora of work has been conducted examining the influence of trait affect on organizational processes. A small sampling of this work shows trait positive and negative affect predicting work group mood (George, 1989), perceptions of job stress and strain (e.g., Brief et al., 1988; George, 1990; Mak & Mueller, 2000), perceptions of job characteristics and job satisfaction (e.g., Brief et al., 1995; Fortunato & Stone-Romero, 2001; Kraiger, Billings, & Isen, 1989; Levin & Stokes, 1989;

Watson & Slack, 1993), accuracy in perceiving informal patterns of social interaction (Casciaro, Carley, & Krackhardt, 1999), work achievement and social support (e.g., Spector, Fox, & Van Katwyk, 1999; Staw, Sutton, & Pelled, 1994), perceptions of fairness (Skarlicki, Folger, & Tesluk, 1999), tardiness, early departure, absenteeism and other counterproductive employee behavior (e.g., Aquino, Lewis, & Bradfield, 1999; Beugre, 1998; Douglas & Martinko, 2001; Duffy, Ganster, & Shaw, 1998; George, 1989; Iverson & Deery, 2001), organizational commitment (Cropanzano, James, & Konovsky, 1993), managerial decision making and potential (Staw & Barsade, 1993), supervisor ratings (e.g., Wright & Staw, 1999), and prosocial and helping behaviors (George, 1991). Many of these relationships also have been found to hold true in a variety of urban and rural international work settings as varied as China, Australia, and the United Arab Emirates (e.g., Chiu & Kosinski, 1999; Hui, Law, & Chen, 1999; Iverson & Maguire, 2000; Shaw, Duffy, Ali Abdulla, & Singh, 2000).

*State Affect.* Based on a similar eruption of research within psychology, state affect, and particularly mood, has been shown to be predictive of the quality of people's cognition, social interactions, helping and prosocial behavior, and persistence and task success (see Fiedler & Forgas, 1988; Forgas, 2001; Mayne & Bonanno, 2001; Moore & Isen, 1990, for reviews of this literature). Organizational researchers also have greatly expanded their work in the influence of state affect on organizational life (see Isen & Baron, 1991, for a review). For example, positive mood has been shown to relate positively to prosocial and helping behaviors at work (George, 1990, 1991; George & Bettenhausen, 1990; George & Brief, 1992), negotiation outcomes (e.g., Barry & Oliver, 1996; Thompson, Nadler, & Kim, 1999), and creative problem solving (see Isen, 1999, for a review of the induced affect–creativity link literature), including very recent findings of positive (Amabile, Barsade, Mueller, & Staw, 2002; Madjer, Oldham, & Pratt, in press) and negative (Zhou & George, 2001) relationships between positive affect and creativity in work settings. Positive mood also has been related negatively to absenteeism (George, 1989; Pelled & Xin, 1999) and turnover (Cropanzano et al., 1993; George & Jones, 1996). For a more complete review of research on the consequences of mood in the workplace see Staw et al. (1994).

*Emotional Labor.* As indicated earlier, emotional labor has been studied from the perspective of individuals attempting to manage their own displayed affect, including, for instance, positive affect displayed by stewardesses (Hochschild, 1983), the negative and positive emotional mix displayed by bill collectors and police interrogators (Rafaeli & Sutton, 1991), and the controlled emotions of paralegals (Pierce, 1995). Nonetheless, research on affect management is not restricted to individuals' attempts to manage their own affect. Included in this body of research are investigations about interpersonal affect management, or attempts by individuals to manage the emotions of others (e.g., Francis, 1994; Thoits, 1996; Van Maanen & Kunda, 1989; Yanay & Shahar, 1998). Most of the work in this area has looked at interactions across status levels (e.g., stewardesses to passengers, store clerks to customers, service providers to clients), where the lower status individual is chartered with managing his or her own affect, as well as the affect experienced by the higher status other, perpetuating the organization's social stratification (e.g. Hochschild, 1983). Recent work by Lively (2000) extends hierarchical emotional management investigations to the peer level. In her study of law firms, she introduced the notion of "reciprocal affect management," whereby co-workers of similar status—paralegals—voluntarily rely on each other to help manage their emotion in the workplace, thus enabling the perpetuation of status hierarchies as partially carried out through emotional inequalities between paralegals and attorneys.[9]

*The Social Sharing of Affect.* The study of the social nature of affect has been a natural complement to the primarily intrapsychic approach to affect in organizations. The workplace is comprised of many people working together, and it is very helpful to understand how the social aspects of affect influence work life in general, and groups in specific. There is a long history of study in the social sharing of affect (see Levy & Nail, 1993, for a review). For example, the sharing, or contagion, of emotions has been examined as far back as 400 B.C., when Hippocrates coined the term "hysteria" to refer to the passing of an agitated state from unmarried women to other unmarried women (Veith, 1965). More recently, Le Bon's (1895) classic examination of contagion in the context of crowd behavior and McDougall's (1923) examination of the "group mind" typified the interest of behavioral theorists in the general phenomenon of contagion. Inducing emotional contagion can be either a subconscious process or an intentional attempt at affective influence, as seen in the following definition of emotional contagion: "… a process in which a person or group influences the emotions, or behavior of another person or group

---

[9]As work on the management of emotions, and specifically emotional labor, becomes more social in nature, that is, looking at interpersonal and reciprocal emotion management, it is important to note its distinction from the "social sharing of emotions" literature to be discussed later in the chapter. The focus in emotion management research is on the contextually determined guidelines of appropriateness and desirability of emotions in that particular context, and the constraints such expectations place on emotion expression in the workplace. Emotion management is a process of adaptation to these "display rules," and inquiries into its effects and determinants are rooted in modes of conformity to externally imposed guidelines for emotional expression. The social sharing of emotion, on the other hand, focuses on the processes by which emotions are transmitted and shared among co-workers, with less emphasis on the role of the context in directing and constraining which emotions are displayed and to what extent.

through the conscious or unconscious induction of affect states and behavioral attitudes" (Schoenewolf, 1990, p. 50).

Historically, much research of the social sharing of emotions was linked to the study of hysteria (often called hysterical contagion, e.g., Phoon, 1982) and the fairly infrequent cases of mass psychogenic illness (such as the well known "June Bug" study, where Kerchoff and Back [1968] found that stress spread through friendship networks in an organization and led to hysterical contagion among employees). Current research examines less dramatic yet more prevalent day-to-day contagion effects (e.g., Hatfield, Cacioppo, & Rapson, 1992, 1993, 1994; Hsee, Hatfield, Carlson, & Chemtob, 1990; Hsee, Hatfield, & Chemtob, 1992; Sullins, 1991), and this lower key, day-to-day contagion is particularly relevant to work settings. This is because workplace emotional contagion is generally expected to be the result of a constant, subtle, continuous transfer of moods among individuals and groups and, perhaps, through entire organizations. A direct workplace application of this can be seen in a service encounter study by Pugh (2001) who found that the display of positive affect by bank tellers was positively correlated with customers' positive affect following the interaction, as well as with customers' positive evaluations of service quality.

Although almost all psychological research has focused on dyadic contagion, researchers studying contagion among members of larger groups, both in the laboratory (e.g., Barsade, in press) and field (e.g., Bartel & Saavedra, 2000; Totterdell, 2000; Totterdell, Kellett, Teuchmann, & Briner, 1998), have found that the phenomenon not only exists but can influence group and individual level processes. Kelly and Barsade (2001) reviewed research into these mostly implicit, subconscious ways of sharing group affect (including behavioral entrainment and vicarious learning) and also proposed more explicit, conscious mechanisms such as "affective impression management." Such a concept is particularly salient to our emerging understanding of emotions in the leadership process. Preliminary work by George (1995, 2000) and others (Lewis, 2000) has shown that leader mood can influence followers' moods. And, as Hsee, Hatfield, and Chemtob (1990) showed, this influence can occur in the other direction as well. Recent work in the political science realm is a good source of information for organizational theorists in this area, as researchers have begun to explicitly examine the affective demeanor of political candidates and their influence on attitudes (Kinder, 1994; Ottati, Steenbergen, & Riggle, 1992) or voting outcomes (Glaser & Salovey, 1998). As the role of leaders is such a critical one within groups and organizations, we expect to see substantially more affect-infused leadership research.

Recent research supporting the social aspects of affect parallels and helps explain another growing area of inquiry—the processes and effects of shared emotions of group members. Research in this area highlights the fact that a "shared affective bond" is not a new concept, but rather, one that was discussed implicitly in the group cohesiveness (Ashforth & Humphrey, 1995), morale (Muchinsky, 1983), and organizational climate literatures (see Schneider & Reichers, 1983, for a review). However, shared affect bonds did not begin to be defined clearly and explicitly studied until the work of George (1990). She explicitly focused on "affective work-group tone," defining it as "consistent or homogenous affective reactions within a group" (p. 108). George found that this group affective tone was significantly negatively related to absenteeism, positively related to better customer service in a study of retail sales groups (George, 1995), and positively related to organizational spontaneity (George & Brief, 1992).[10] Barsade, Ward, Turner, and Sonnenfeld (2000), in their theory of group affective diversity, expanded on George's homogeneous conceptualization of group affect. They did this by emphasizing not only the importance of looking at mean level group affect and similarities in group members' affect, but also by specifically theorizing about and examining how affective differences among group members influence group behavior. The authors built a detailed theory of affective similarity-attraction that parallels the more cognitively based similarity-attraction theory. In doing so, they found, in a sample of top management teams, that the affective diversity of the team could serve as an important predictor of group processes, such as cooperation, conflict, level of CEO participativeness versus authoritarianism with the team, as well as firm financial performance. Kelly and Barsade (2001) and Barsade and Gibson (1998) provided a thorough review of the group affect literature, offering a model of group affect, which includes multiple levels of analysis—looking at group affect from a "bottom up" and "top down" perspective.

There is a fascinating and important research spark in the social sharing of affect carried out by Rime and colleagues looking at the precursors, processes, and consequences of the social sharing of affect. Rime, Mesquita, Philippot, and Boca (1991) tracked how often and through what processes people socially share their emotions as well as how this sharing of emotions influences the sharer's subsequent affect and health (Finkenauer & Rime, 1998; Pennebaker, Zech, & Rime, 2001). Rime and his colleagues showed that this sharing, in and of itself, is affect-inducing to the parties involved in the sharing (Christophe & Rime, 2001). Rime's work implies a collective emotional knowledge that forms among people as a result of social sharing of their affect (e.g. Rime, 1995). Given the emotional knowl-

---

[10]Similar to the state–trait debate that the groundbreaking work of Staw et al. (1986) brought up, George's work prompted and coincided with a large methodological debate about best aggregation practices in studying work groups (George, 1990; George & James, 1993; Yammarino & Markham, 1992). These two streams of research show that the study of affect in organizations has reverberated and rippled out to even broader advances in organizational behavior.

edge base that this can create in a group, as well as the individual level effects on the people with whom the emotions are being shared, this is a construct organizational researchers should be aggressively pursuing.

## The Case of Emotional Intelligence

An understanding of how the roles of affect and cognition may be entwined comes together nicely in a recent stream of research examining emotional intelligence. The construct of emotional intelligence systematically takes into account the role of affect in life functioning and, by integrating cognitive processes, explicitly recognizes the relationship between affect and cognition.[11] Salovey and Mayer (1990) described "emotional intelligence" as "... the ability to monitor one's own and others' feelings and emotions, to discriminate among them and to use this information to guide one's thinking and actions" (p. 189). Their view has evolved over time into a four-factor model described by Mayer, Salovey, and Caruso (2000) and Salovey, Woolery, and Mayer (2001) as consisting of (a) *perception, appraisal, and expression of emotion* (being able to identify your own and others' emotions, to discriminate between feelings and their honest and dishonest expression, and to accurately express your own emotions); (b) *emotional facilitation of cognitive activities* (using emotions to facilitate judgment, problem solving, and creativity—and redirecting and prioritizing thinking based on feelings); (c) *understanding and analyzing emotional information and employing emotional knowledge* (understanding how different emotions are related, the causes and consequences of emotions, transitions between emotions, and understanding complex feelings and contradictory emotional states); and (d) *emotional regulation* (managing your own emotions—being open to unpleasant and pleasant feelings, monitoring and reflecting on emotions, being able to engage or detach from emotional states, and being able to manage emotions in other people).

There is much more methodological and theoretical work to be done with the emotional intelligence construct, particularly regarding its role in organizations.[12] Some early findings show that emotional intelligence

---

[11]This is not to evoke the affect–cognition debate that raged in psychology starting with Zajonc's (1980) seminal article positing that "preferences need no inferences"; that is, affect and cognition are separate processes, and that affect needs no cognitive input and can occur before cognition. This led to opposition by cognitive appraisal theorists such as Lazarus (1981, 1982). There is now ample neurophysiological as well as behavioral evidence helping to resolve the debate, showing that these two processes can operate independently and can also influence each other (e.g., Murphy, 2001). Although this debate may seem to be an unnecessary tempest in a teapot, in retrospect it was a necessary step to force the field to move from a complacent prerevolutionary state and into a mindset that forced a consideration of the more expanded role of affect.

[12]It is particularly important to do vigorous methodological work on this construct to avoid it turning into an all-encompassing panacea for managerial ills as has been done in some of the popular management literature.

(construed of as an ability [e.g., Mayer, Salovey, & Caruso, 2000]) is positively related to social skills (Schutte et al., 2001), empathy (e.g., Ciarrochi, Chan, Caputi, & Roberts, 2001), and, within an organizational context, hiring decisions in simulated and actual settings (Barsade, Doucet, & O'Hara, 2002; Fox & Spector, 2000). The construct of emotional intelligence offers much promise of expanding our understanding of organizational life, not only at the individual level but also at the group level of analysis (Druskat, 2001; see also Bass, 2002).

## WHERE WE ARE GOING: A REVOLUTION TO A MATURE, HYBRID AFFECTIVE PARADIGM

The affective revolution within the organizations field has just begun and a full paradigm development is years away. We are certain there are unexplored areas of affect at work that will emerge as important as, or more important than those we have discussed so far. First, we posit that some of these areas likely will be natural outgrowths of what has been occurring so far in the revolution, such as the study of discrete emotions at work or more research on the organizational level of analysis as compared to the current emphasis on individual and group levels of analysis. Other approaches we suggest are less immediately obvious, or currently methodologically possible, such as an organizational neuroscience approach to affect. We also argue that some ways of understanding affect, such as the role of subconscious affective processes, have largely been ignored or, as in the case of psychoanalytic theory, have largely been shunned in our field. These schools of thought can offer rich insights into conventional areas of organizational behavior as well as those areas not often explored within our field. We also discuss other developmental approaches, such as attachment theory, that have not been so much shunned as relatively ignored, and how they also can be productively integrated into organizational research. We describe how methodological approaches such as experience sampling methodologies, using, for example, beepers, e-mail, or other daily tracking mechanisms, promise large influence on our ability to track and predict affective processes over time and thereby give us a much needed understanding of "everyday" moods and emotions. Last, we discuss our vision of a mature hybrid paradigm in which knowledge of affect in organizations across disciplines, across levels of analysis, and across methods, can be used to more completely understand the domain of affect in organizations.

## Discrete Affect in Organizations

Most organizational research has focused on general mood or on trait affect, referring to positive and negative affectivity. This emphasis on the more overarching aspects of affect, however, can hinder our study of specific affect, as it can mask the causes and consequences of the discrete emotions (Lazarus & Cohen-Charash, 2001). For example, anger and fear are both negative, high-energy emotions but what causes each, how each might influence perceptions, and how different kinds of people might deal with each are matters generally not attended to in the organizational literature, as they have been in the psychological literature (e.g., Bodenhausen, Sheppard, & Kramer, 1994; Izard, 1993; Izard, Ackerman, Schoff, & Fine, 2000; Keltner, Ellsworth, & Edwards, 1993; Lerner & Keltner, 2001; Roseman, 1991; Roseman, Spindel, & Jose, 1990; Timmers, Fischer, & Manstead, 1998; Zummuner & Fischer, 1995). In fact, the study of discrete emotions in organizational behavior is in its infancy.

Discrete affect researchers in organizational behavior have generally focused on organizational antecedents of certain workplace emotions, such as unfairness (e.g., Bennett, 1998; Weiss, Suckow, & Cropanzano, 1999) or status (e.g., Tiedens, 2001; Tiedens, Ellsworth, & Mesquita, 2000). Gibson (1995) conducted one of the few studies that systematically explored the antecedents, expression, and consequences of a variety of discrete emotions. Gibson examined accounts of emotional episodes, recording the differing antecedents and consequences of the specific emotions of anger, fear, sadness, joy, acceptance, disgust, and anticipation at work. He found that depending on the emotion, there were different antecedents, expression of the emotion, and consequences. For example, feeling anger at work tended to be caused by factors reflecting injustices (e.g., criticism of the person, having suggestions ignored, or a response to corporate layoffs); perpetrated mainly by superiors or the company as a whole; and was expressed to the people causing the anger a little over half the time. This is in contrast to fear, an emotion caused by factors related to uncertainty (e.g., failure by self, threats external to the organization, and lack of corporate support for the person); associated with superiors, self, and to a lesser extent, external agents; and was almost never expressed to the agent causing the fear.

Research on the consequences of discrete affect in organizational life, although preliminary in nature, has focused mainly on negative emotions such as anger (e.g., Davis, LaRosa, & Foshee, 1992; Fitness, 2000; Glomb, 1999), including negative emotions specifically found in negotiation situations (e.g., Allred, 1999; Davidson & Greenhalgh, 1999; Glomb & Hulin, 1997; Pillutla & Murnighan, 1996), envy at work (e.g., Cohen-Charash, 2000; Duffy, Shaw, & Stark, 1997), jealousy (Miner, 1990; Vecchio, 1995), anxiety—particularly in response to organizational change such as layoffs and mergers (e.g., Astrachan, 1991, 1995), depression (Rosenthal, 1985), guilt (e.g., Millar & Tesser, 1988), and shame (e.g., Poulson, 2000). There has been very little work on the role of positive discrete affect in organizations, such as hope, happiness, compassion, and love (with few exceptions, e.g., Allred, Mallozzi, Matsui, & Raia, 1997; Gibson, 1995; Weiss, Suckow, & Cropanzano, 1999). However, the case for studying more positive emotions at work has begun to be made more explicitly, for example, through Fredrickson's (2000) broaden-and-build model of positive emotions and the advent of "positive psychology" (e.g., Seligman & Csikszentmihalyi, 2000; Snyder & Lopez, 2002).

Further revealing the early state of research about specific emotions at work, almost all of the studies have taken place in a laboratory or simulated setting, or used scenario or recall designs. Very few researchers have ventured into the field to examine the role of specific emotions, with the exception of a few mainly qualitative studies (e.g., Bonifacio, 1991). Thus, there is much theoretical and methodological work to be done on the predictive role of discrete affect in organizations, especially with regard to positive emotions.

Leary's (2000) model of social emotions addresses an interesting aspect of discrete affect, which may be particularly relevant to the social settings of organizational life. Leary defined social emotions as those "… emotions that are aroused by real, imagined, anticipated, or remembered encounters with other people" (p. 331) and that are uniquely relevant to the person's social involvements (Frijda & Mesquita, 1994). The emotions he discussed—shame/embarrassment, hurt feelings, jealousy, social anxiety, social sadness, loneliness, pride, and love—are based on the concept of relational devaluation, or "… indications that others do not regard their relationship with the individual to be as important, close or valuable as the individual desires" (Leary, 2000, p. 336). Relational devaluation is a phenomenon likely to be important in organizational settings because of the continual social comparisons and interaction between employees and managers—a specific context rife with opportunities for this type of devaluation. Overall, the shift to the study of the causes, nature, and function of discrete affect is one of the most promising and underdeveloped areas in the affective revolution; we expect to see many more questions asked and puzzles solved in this field.

## A Question of Levels: Organizational Level Affect

Much of the new work we anticipate seeing in the affective revolution will involve the expansion of levels of study, both upward and downward. Most organizational affective research to date has focused on individual or group level affect. Moving upward in level from there, we predict a progression toward examining organizational level affect, particularly in the areas of organizational culture and socialization. This has already begun with regard to socialization. There has been some preliminary work in the emotional socialization of medical students (Hafferty, 1988), and Pratt and Barnett (1997) offered a promising foray into this realm with their study of how Amway distributors explicitly use emotions, including ambivalent emotions, to teach recruits to "unlearn" prior responses and then relearn new cognitions and behaviors. Work in affective organizational socialization is also intimated in Gibson's (1995) work through his argument that organizations shape emotional "scripts" by differentially encouraging and suppressing emotional expression. This type of work is related to emotional labor in that the rules and rewards for this labor can become affective cultural norms translated through implicit and explicit socialization practices.

On an explicitly organizational level, we propose the as yet untested idea of affective organizational culture as an important concept to be integrated into conventional organizational culture research. The idea is based on the notion that organizations hold affective tones and normative rules that are part of the organizational landscape in the same way that value-based norms and rules have been held and studied in organizations (e.g., O'Reilly, 1989; Schein, 1991). Organizational affective culture research may have direct applicability and particularly important ramifications for the cross-cultural aspects of managing within and across organizations. As we discussed earlier, research in psychology already has begun to focus on cross-cultural aspects of emotional display and norms (e.g., Eid & Diener, 2001). This area will become increasingly critical within the organizational realm, particularly given the prevalence of multinational companies and projects where people from different affective cultures need to productively interact. Researchers have begun to explore these areas (Cooper, Doucet, & Pratt, 2002), and we predict tremendous growth in research on this topic.

## A Question of Levels: The Subconscious World of Affect in Organizational Behavior

Further, we predict an entirely new world awaits organizational researchers in expanding the levels of analysis to the even more downward "intrapsychic" level. Specifically, we foresee questions and answers that pursue the less conscious, or subconscious, influences of affect in the workplace. For example, research shows that people have a tendency to mimic others' nonverbal actions and facial expressions, which can happen unintentionally, uncontrollably, and subconsciously (Hatfield, Cacioppo, & Rapson, 1994). There is then an affective influence on the person's own feelings as a result of this mimicking (e.g., facial efference theory; Zajonc, 1985; Zajonc, Murphy, & Inglehart, 1989). These findings have served as the theoretical base for the contagion processes discussed in the organizational studies cited earlier in this chapter (e.g., Barsade, in press; Bartel &

Saavedra, 2000; Totterdell, 2000; Totterdell et al., 1998).[13] We expect interest in this topic to grow.

Another perspective on subconscious processes specifically involves peoples' emotional unconscious and how it plays out in our conscious lives on learning, influence, and thought (Kihlstrom, 1999). The emotional unconscious is described as the conscious awareness of one's emotional state, but a lack of awareness of the source of that state (which can come from a current or past experience; Kihlstrom, Mulvaney, Tobias, & Tobis, 2000). Because of this, the emotions people feel can serve as an expression of implicit memories that reflect the influence of a past event on ongoing experience, whether or not that event is consciously remembered. Support for the importance of this emotional unconscious on our judgment, decision making, and memory can be seen through mood-congruence findings showing that moods can operate without our awareness (e.g., Singer & Salovey, 1988), as well as the effects of "mere exposure" (Zajonc, 1968, 2001), affective priming (Monahan, 1998; Murphy, Monahan, & Zajonc, 1995), and implicit perception, memory, and emotion (see Kihlstrom, 1999, for a review).[14]

Last, a rich source for hypothesizing about the role of subconscious emotions on conscious actions, thoughts, and feelings in organizations comes from the psychodynamic school within psychology (e.g., Freud, 1900/1999; Klein, 1987; Winnicott, 1986). The psychodynamic perspective not only

---

[13]There is direct research supporting the automatic, continuous, nonverbal mimicking and feedback among individuals (Hatfield, Cacioppo, & Rapson, 1994). A two-step process has been found in which people first engage in an innate tendency (Doherty, 1998; Levenson, 1996), seen already in newborns (Field, Woodson, Greenberg, & Cohen, 1982; Haviland & Lelwica, 1987), to mimic others' nonverbal behavior, including facial expressions (Lundqvist & Dimberg, 1995), body language (Chartrand & Bargh, 1999), speech patterns (Ekman, Friesen, & Scherer, 1976), and verbal tones (Hietanen, Surakka, & Linnankoski, 1998; Neumann & Strack, 2000). The second step of the contagion process involves "feedback": experiencing the affect being mimicked, through a reaction to visceral, glandular, and muscular responses (see Hatfield et al., 1994, for a review). This facial feedback hypothesis has found much support (Hatfield, Cacioppo, & Rapson, 1992), although there have also been critiques of it (Cacioppo, Berntson, Larsen, Poehlmann, & Ito, 2000).

[14]The movement to study subconscious affective processes has distanced itself theoretically and empirically from the psychodynamic Freudian perspective to the point that some psychologists, such as Singer (1997) have gone so far as to ask "... whether it is useful any longer to case discussion of conscious processes in the terminology of psychoanalytic metapsychology. In view of the great advances in modern cognitive psychology, might it not be better to attempt the integration of psychoanalytically derived observations in the more general operationalized and empirically data-rich sphere of modern cognitive and social-personality psychology?" (p. 758). Other leading psychologists studying the emotional unconscious support this view by focusing explicitly on the rejection of Freud's work as the basis of psychoanalysis, rather than on other theoretical advances in psychodynamic theory, including object–relations theory as explicated by Klein and colleagues (e.g. Kihlstrom, 1999). However, other researchers such as Westen (1998a, 1998b, 2000) and Panksepp (2000) take a more explicitly integrative and broad approach to the combination of the social-cognition view of the subconscious with the psychoanalytic view—explicitly taking into account progression in psychoanalytic theory.

takes into account more immediate influences, both conscious and unconscious, of people's surroundings, but also takes a longer term developmental approach to what people bring into their life situations, including their work. From an organizational perspective, psychoanalytic research asks "What do employees bring with them into the organization as a result of their past, their development, and their subconscious strivings that then influences how they behave, even if they do not realize it?"

Although research based on a psychoanalytic perspective seems intuitively useful, within organizational behavior it has influenced hypothesis generation more than hypothesis testing (e.g., Diamond, 1993; Fineman, 1993; Gabriel, 1999; Kets de Vries, 1990, 1991, 1997; Kets de Vries & Miller, 1984, 1985, 1986; Kilberg, 1995). These theories need to be tested to provide evidence regarding their validity and utility in organizational behavior research. Given that psychoanalytic theory and methods have continued to develop—both methodologically and theoretically—along with other fields in psychology, a promising foundation for psychodynamic research in organizational behavior comes from increasingly rigorous empirically psychoanalytically based research in psychology. Take, for example, the classic psychodynamic construct of "transference," where "representations of significant others, stored in memory, are activated and used in new social encounters on the basis of a new person's resemblance to a given significant other" (Berk & Andersen, 2000, p. 546; otherwise known as the "You vaguely remind me of that kid in elementary school who I hated, and I don't like you much either" phenomenon; Kelly & Barsade, 2001, p. 109). Rigorous laboratory work by Andersen and colleagues (Andersen & Glassman, 1996; Andersen, Glassman, Chen, & Cole, 1995; Glassman & Andersen, 1999a) has shown how transference is activated and how people's past emotional histories are brought in, transferred onto new people, and influence perceptions and behavior (see Glassman & Andersen, 1999b, for a review). It is very likely that transference occurs in organizations as employees meet new co-workers, customers, and clients, and may well be fertile ground for understanding previously inexplicable organizational dynamics.

An explicitly organizational example of the influence of psychodynamic processes on organizational behavior tested using an experimental design can be seen in Astrachan's (1995) study of anxiety and layoffs. He studied ego defenses stemming from feelings of anxiety that were stimulated in study participants due to pending layoffs in a merger and acquisition simulation. His study showed how affective and attitudinal responses to an impending layoff could be predicted by the underlying psychoanalytic theory of ego defenses, specifically *denial* (when people disregard or discredit the sources of anxiety), *splitting* (when people polarize good feelings and bad feelings—such as attachment and rejection or love and hate—feelings that are actually not mutually exclusive or dichotomous), and *projection* (when people attribute good qualities to one individual or group, whereas bad qualities are attributed to another individual or group that is then scapegoated).

Along similar lines as psychodynamic perspectives, another useful source for future research is attachment theory (e.g., Ainsworth, Blehar, Waters, & Wall, 1978; Bowlby, 1973, 1980, 1982). This theory inherently is based on the emotional subconscious and is an affective developmental theory that sheds light on how less conscious processes influence more conscious behaviors, thoughts, and emotions. Attachment theory is concerned with how early attachments to primary caregivers influence individuals' internal working emotional models of themselves and others, manifesting themselves in their current feelings and behaviors. Bowlby (1973, 1980, 1982) first studied attachment relationships between babies and their primary caregivers and hypothesized that early attachment experiences influence one's perception of one's own worthiness (high or low) and the dependability of other people (high or low). Ainsworth et al., (1978) extended this work and found three types of attachment styles that corresponded to how babies responded to brief separation from these caregivers: secure attachment (self: comfortable with relationships without fearing rejection; others: viewed as available, trustworthy, and helpful); anxious–ambivalent attachment (self: wanting closeness but being concerned about possible rejection due to intermittent reinforcement from the primary caregiver; others: inconsistently available over whom no control is felt); and avoidant attachment (self: attempting to avoid dependency or closeness, coming from being consistently rejected when trying to develop this closeness; others: viewed as untrustworthy or unavailable, and the self not worthy or needing of attachment).

Hazan and Shaver (1987) first paralleled this research in adult interpersonal and affective behavior, finding three similar attachment styles to those of Ainsworth et al. (1978), which they then explicitly extended into the work domain (Hazan & Shaver, 1990). Since then, other researchers have begun to study the influence of adult affective attachment styles on variables important to organizational researchers, such as having difficulties at work (Hardy & Barkham, 1994), mental categorization and creative problem solving (Mikulincer & Sheffi, 2000), differential satisfaction with employment contracts (Krausz, Bizman, & Braslavsky, 2001), delegation and organizational structure (Johnston, 2000), group behavior (Smith, Murphy, & Coats, 1999), spillover in work–family balance attempts (Sumer & Knight, 2001), and work stress intensity and job satisfaction (Schirmer & Lopez, 2001).

However, there is still much work to be done using attachment theory within an organizational context. For example, researchers could examine the results of interactions among co-workers depending on their shared, or not shared, attachment styles. Attachment theory could be particularly relevant to the question of dealing with layoffs or how people differentially respond to organizational recruitment and socialization efforts. Also, whereas attachment styles seem to stay steady, there is some indication in a 20-year longitudinal study that they can be changeable for some people across life experiences (Iwaniec & Sneddon, 2001). This offers potential for organizations to help create more secure attachment styles, or at minimum, lead managers to consider what type of styles they may be recreating by their behavior toward their employees.

## Tracking Affective Patterns: "Everyday Emotion"

Methodological advances through everyday experience methods (Reis & Gable, 2000), such as experience sampling methodology (ESM) have allowed a much more precise view of how affect develops and affective processes occur in daily experience (e.g., Alliger & Williams, 1993). Everyday experience sampling involves taking multiple samples of affective daily experience, which provides the ability to more closely track the antecedents and consequences of daily feelings and actions. For example, using this type of methodology, recent work by Nezlek and colleagues has found relationships between affective constructs such as anxiety, depression, and general mood with daily events, self-awareness, and psychological adjustment (Nezlek, 2001; Nezlek & Gable, 2001; Nezlek & Plesko, in press). This method can also be used to address long-held debates in the affective literature. For example, Zelenski and Larsen (1999) used ESM to track research participants three times a day for a month, asking about what affect they were experiencing. In doing so, they actually helped not only to see the cyclicity of affect in daily life but also to answer basic questions about the dimensional versus discrete affect model on states and traits discussed earlier in the chapter. There have been a few studies applying types of ESM techniques explicitly to organizations (e.g., Amabile, Barsade, Mueller, & Staw, 2002), but as of yet, not many. We predict that the ESM method will grow enormously in popularity and will open up a completely new understanding of the more microprocesses of affect and its causes and consequences.

## Neuroscience and Affect

Thus far, in our elaboration of "where we are going" with affect research, we have focused on affective processes that are invisible to the conscious eye but highly influential through subconscious processes. Another opportunity to increase understanding by turning inward comes from examination of the physiological and neurophysiological underpinnings of affect (see Damasio, 1994; Isen, 2002; Lane & Nadel, 2000; LeDoux, 1995, 1996; Panksepp, 1998). Although physiological evidence from psychology laboratory experiments has been used as the theoretical underpinning of some affective studies in work settings, such as emotional contagion, discussed earlier, these processes have not been tested directly within the field context or in support of other forces in organizational life.

Basic research on the brain and affect has strong theoretical relevance, if not yet practical applicability, to the organizational domain. Along these lines, Brief and Weiss (2002) noted that understanding of these physiological underpinnings of affect should be applied more directly in organizational behavior, though, as of now, methodological complications render this line of research exceedingly difficult. Initial studies in this area have focused on the consequences of removing, either intentionally through surgery or via life's accidents, specific areas of the brain (Fox & Davidson, 1984). This research, as well as laboratory research studying brain asymmetry in responses to stimuli (e.g., Tomarken, Davidson, & Henriques, 1990), has helped psychologists determine the relevance of the cortical and limbic systems in understanding how affect functions in the brain (e.g., Damasio, 1994; LeDoux, 1995, 1996; LeDoux & Phelps, 2000). These methods can be limited in their degree of accuracy. However, neuroimaging, using magnetic resonance imaging (e.g., Pine et al., 2001) and positron emission tomography (e.g., Kishimoto, 1993; Pietrini et al., 2000) offer more exact visualization of the activity of the brain responding to emotional stimuli (see Grossenbacher, 2001, for a review). It now seems impractical to use this tool in organizational settings, but one day some organizational scholars, as trained neuroscientists, may employ new technologies that allow them to understand the physiological activity of people's brains as their workdays unfold, an additional, but by no means exclusive tool for enhancing our understanding of affect in organizations.[15]

## CONCLUSIONS: THE REVOLUTIONARY ZENITH— A MATURE HYBRID PARADIGM

Ultimately, the affective revolution should culminate in using all the relevant knowledge we can cull from all paradigms, levels of analysis, and scientific disciplines. A successful hybrid paradigm will allow seemingly disparate data from multiple fields to join together to describe, understand, and predict affective processes in organizations. A particular para-

---

[15]We are definitely not suggesting a future move to a completely reductionist approach to studying affect in organizations. This would be antithetical to the mature hybrid paradigm we have been promoting throughout the chapter, and now discuss more specifically in our conclusion. This is because the concept of a mature hybrid paradigm explicitly promotes the necessity of knowledge from many paradigms, on many levels of analysis, to fully understand human emotions, cognitions, and behavior. See Lazarus (1991, pp. 186–187) for an excellent discussion of the specific intellectual problems with a completely reductionistic psychophysiological paradigm.

digm would not "win out" because each is contributing a piece to a larger puzzle. As researchers of the influence of affect on people's emotions, cognitions, and behavior in organizations, we are pursuing a sophisticated composite of life in organizations, which should reflect and incorporate all the various sources and explanations that drive these processes.

In some ways, the very nature of our suggestion of a hybrid paradigm does not suit the purely Kuhnian perspective, which describes progression in science as the "winning" of one paradigm over another, rather than the coexistence of paradigms into a hybrid. However, although we appreciate and use Kuhn's perspective as a heuristic with which to understand the advances in our field, we do not feel constrained by its ultimate predictions. It seems quite plausible that understanding sciences based on people rather than on laws of physics may take a different path. The complexity of understanding people versus things may require the power of every bit of interdisciplinary paradigm sharing we can get. Other organizational and psychological scholars seem to have suggested the same. For example, Porter (1996), in his reflection on 40 years of organization studies, stated the following:

> Some will argue that while organization studies may be a multidisciplinary field, it definitely is not an integrated interdisciplinary one. I agree. But that is probably not an attainable, or perhaps, even desirable objective. In fact, if it becomes a single new discipline itself, I would probably begin to worry about the possible dangers of too much convergence. I think a worthy and more reachable goal, at least for the present time, is to strive for increased cross-disciplinary attacks on common intellectual problems as they relate to organizations. This, I predict, is what we probably will see with expanding frequency during the next 40 years. At least, I hope so, because this is where I think we will find valuable lodes of intellectual and scholarly ore. (p. 263)

Similarly, Jones 1998, in his *Handbook of Social Psychology* chapter reviewing major developments in five decades of social psychology, explicitly discussed the "vigorous hybrid" (p. 34), of knowledge that has come from the interdisciplinary work between social psychologists and cognitive psychologists.[16] It may be that the mechanisms of the human mind, and heart, cannot be explained by one paradigm, or one approach, in the same way that the laws of physical sciences can be.

---

[16]Some scholars, such as Jones (1998), reject the idea that the crises in social psychology are paradigmatic crises in a Kuhnian sense. For example, Brief suggested that the crisis concept does not apply to the organizational sciences (Brief, 1998, p. 85) in the same way as Kuhn laid out, because it relates to the understanding of human behavior within organizations. However, as Pfeffer (1993) argued, Kuhn may still be correct with regard to the political and resource allocation benefits that come with following a clear, stringent, and coherent paradigm development process. This can be seen particularly when comparing the benefits the coherent paradigms give fields such as economics as compared to the multiparadigmatic field of organizational behavior. However, as we argue in this chapter, we strongly question the intellectual benefits that would come from this type of coherent paradigm within the organizational behavior field.

The study of affect in organizational behavior is in the midst of a revolution. Revolutions, like the one underway, follow from crises of inadequacy or malfunction of existing paradigms. In affect research, such crises were early failures to discover a job satisfaction/job performance link, and insufficiently differentiated perspectives on the nature of affect and how it operates in organizations. Recent advances in this field may seem like natural, evolutionary results, building incrementally on each previous forward step, as is often the perspective of observers looking at a revolution from the outside (Kuhn, 1970). But if, when looking at the current state of the field, we keep an eye to the farthest horizons of these early stirrings, the dramatic shift in momentum in affect research—with support galvanized by important and robust methodological, empirical, and theoretical work across disciplinary clearly revolutionary. ¡*Viva la affect!*

## ACKNOWLEDGMENTS

We would like to thank Yochi Cohen-Charash and Andreas Xenachis for their helpful comments.

## REFERENCES

Adams, J. S. (1963). Toward an understanding of inequity. *Journal of Abnormal Psychology, 67*, 422–436.

Adams, J. S. (1965). Inequity in social exchange. In L. Berkowitz (Ed.), *Advances in experimental social psychology* (Vol. 2, pp. 267–299). New York: Academic.

Ainsworth, M. D. S., Blehar, M., Waters, E., & Wall, S. (1978). *Patterns of attachment.* Hillsdale, NJ: Lawrence Erlbaum Associates.

Alliger, G. M., & Williams, K. J. (1993). Using signal-contingent experience sampling methodology to study work in the field: A discussion and illustration examining task perceptions and mood. *Personnel Psychology, 46*, 525–549.

Allred, K. G. (1999). Anger and retaliation: Toward an understanding of impassioned conflict in organizations. In R. J. Bies, R. J. Lewicki, & B. H. Sheppard (Eds.), *Research in negotiation in organizations* (Vol. 7, pp. 27–58). Stamford, CT: JAI.

Allred, K. G., Mallozzi, J. S., Matsui, F., & Raia, C. P. (1997). The influence of anger and compassion on negotiation performance. *Organizational Behavior and Human Decision Processes, 70*, 175–187.

Amabile, T., Barsade, S. G., Mueller, J., & Staw, B. (2002). *Emotions and creativity in teams: A longitudinal field study.* Unpublished manuscript.

Andersen, S. M., & Glassman, N. S. (1996). Responding to significant others when they are not there: Effects on interpersonal inference, motivation, and affect. In R. M. Sorrentino & E. T. Higgins (Eds.), *Handbook of motivation and cognition: Vol. 3. The interpersonal context* (pp. 262–321). New York: Guilford.

Andersen, S. M., Glassman, N. S., Chen, S., & Cole, S. W. (1995). Transference in social perception: The role of chronic accessibility in significant-other representations. *Journal of Personality and Social Psychology, 69,* 41–57.

Aquino, K. L., Lewis, M. U., & Bradfield, M. (1999). Justice constructs, negative affectivity, and employee deviance: A proposed model and empirical test. *Journal of Organizational Behavior, 20,* 1073–1091.

Ashforth, B. E., & Humphrey, R. H. (1995). Emotion in the workplace: A reappraisal. *Human Relations, 48,* 97–125.

Astrachan, J. H. (1991). *Mergers, acquisitions, and employee anxiety: A study of separation anxiety in a corporate context.* New York: Praeger.

Astrachan, J. H. (1995). Organizational departures: The impact of separation anxiety as studied in a merger and acquisitions simulation. *Journal of Applied Behavioral Science, 31,* 31–50.

Barbalet, J. M. (1995). Climates of fear and sociopolitical change. *Journal for the Theory of Social Behaviour, 25,* 15–33.

Barry, B., & Oliver, R. L. (1996). Affect in dyadic negotiation: A model and propositions. *Organizational Behavior and Human Decision Processes, 67,* 127–143.

Barsade, S. G. (in press). The ripple effect: Emotional contagion in groups. *Administrative Science Quarterly.*

Barsade, S. G., Doucet, L., & O'Hara, L. (2002). *Emotions in the hiring process: Emotional intelligence, emotional contagion and empathy.* Unpublished manuscript.

Barsade, S. G., & Gibson, D. E. (1998). Group emotion: A view from top and bottom. In D. Gruenfeld, E. Mannix, & M. Neale (Eds.), *Research on managing groups and teams* (pp. 81–102). Stamford, CT: JAI.

Barsade, S. G., Ward, A. J., Turner, J. D. F., & Sonnenfeld, J. A. (2000). To your heart's content: The influence of affective diversity in top management teams. *Administrative Science Quarterly, 45,* 802–836.

Bartel, C., & Saavedra, R. (2000). The collective construction of work group moods. *Administrative Science Quarterly, 45,* 197–231.

Bass, B. M. (2002). Cognitive, social, and emotional intelligence of transformational leaders. In R. E. Riggio & S. E. Murphy (Eds.), *Multiple intelligences and leadership* (pp. 105–118). Mahwah, NJ: Lawrence Erlbaum Associates.

Bennett, R. J. (1998). Taking the sting out of the whip: Reactions to consistent punishment for unethical behavior. *Journal of Experimental Psychology: Applied, 4,* 248–262.

Berk, M. S., & Andersen, S. M. (2000). The impact of past relationships on interpersonal behavior: Behavioral confirmation in the social–cognitive process of transference. *Journal of Personality and Social Psychology, 79,* 546–562.

Beugre, C. D. (1998). Understanding organizational insider-perpetrated workplace aggression: An integrative model. In P. A. Bamberger & W. J. Sonnenstuhl (Eds.), *Research in the sociology of organizations: Vol. 15. Deviance in and out of organizations* (pp. 163–196). Stamford, CT: JAI.

Bodenhausen, G. V., Sheppard, L. A., & Kramer, G. P. (1994). Negative affect and social judgment: The differential impact of anger and sadness. *European Journal of Social Psychology, 24,* 45–62.

Bonifacio, P. (1991). *The psychological effects of police work: A psychodynamic approach.* New York: Plenum.

Bowlby, J. (1973). *Attachment and loss: Separation* (Vol. 2). New York: Basic Books.

Bowlby, J. (1980). *Attachment and loss: Loss* (Vol. 3). New York: Basic Books.

Bowlby, J. (1982). *Attachment and loss* (2nd ed.). New York: Basic Books.

Brief, A. P. (1998). *Attitudes in and around organizations.* Thousand Oaks, CA: Sage.

Brief, A. P., Burke, M. J., George, J. M., Robinson, B. S., & Webster, J. (1988). Should negative affectivity remain an unmeasured variable in the study of job stress? *Journal of Applied Psychology, 73,* 193–198.

Brief, A. P., Butcher, A. H., & Roberson, L. (1995). Cookies, disposition, and job attitudes: The effects of positive mood-inducing events and negative affectivity on job satisfaction in a field experiment. *Organizational Behavior and Human Decision Processes, 62,* 55–62.

Brief, A. P., & Roberson, L. (1989). Job attitude organization: An exploratory study. *Journal of Applied Social Psychology, 19,* 717–727.

Brief, A. P., & Weiss, H. M. (2002). Organizational behavior: Affect in the workplace. *Annual Review of Psychology, 53,* 279–307.

Burke, M. J., Brief, A. P., George, J. M., Roberson, L., & Webster, J. (1989). Measuring affect at work: Confirmatory analyses of competing mood structures with conceptual linkage to cortical regulatory systems. *Journal of Personality and Social Psychology, 57,* 1091–1102.

Cacioppo, J. T., & Berntson, G. G. (1994). Relationship between attitudes and evaluative space: A critical review, with emphasis on the separability of positive and negative substrates. *Psychological Bulletin, 115,* 401–423.

Cacioppo, J. T., Berntson, G. G., Larsen, J. T., Poehlmann, K. M., & Ito, T. A. (2000). The psychophysiology of emotion. In M. Lewis & J. M. Haviland-Jones (Eds.), *Handbook of emotions* (2nd ed., pp. 173–191). New York: Guilford.

Cacioppo, J. T., Gardner, W. L., & Berntson, G. G. (1997). Beyond bipolar conceptualizations and measures: The case of attitudes and evaluative space. *Personality and Social Psychology Review, 1,* 3–25.

Cacioppo, J. T., Gardner, W. L., & Berntson, G. G. (1999). The affect system has parallel and integrative processing components: Form follows function. *Journal of Personality and Social Psychology, 67,* 839–855.

Campion, M. A., & Thayer, P. W. (1985). Development and field evaluation of an interdisciplinary measure of job design. *Journal of Applied Psychology, 70,* 29–43.

Cartwright, J. (2000). *Evolution and human behavior: Darwinian perspectives on human nature.* Cambridge, MA: MIT Press.

Casciaro, T., Carley, K. M., & Krackhardt, D. (1999). Positive affectivity and accuracy in social network perception. *Motivation and Emotion, 23,* 285–306.

Chartrand, T. L., & Bargh, J. A. (1999). The chameleon effect: The perception–behavior link and social interaction. *Journal of Personality and Social Psychology, 76,* 893–910.

Chatman, J. A. (1989). Improving interactional organizational research: A model of person–organization fit. *Academy of Management Review, 14,* 333–349.

Chiu, R. K., & Kosinski, F. A. (1999). The role of affective dispositions in job satisfaction and work strain: Comparing collectivist and individual societies. *International Journal of Psychology, 34*, 19–28.

Christophe, V., & Rime, B. (2001). Exposure to the social sharing of emotion: Emotional impact, listener responses and secondary social sharing. In W. G. Parrott (Ed.), *Emotions in social psychology: Essential readings* (pp. 239–250). Philadelphia: Psychology Press/Taylor & Francis.

Ciarrochi, J., Chan, A., Caputi, P., & Roberts, R. (2001). Measuring emotional intelligence. In J. Ciarrochi & J. P. Forgas (Eds), *Emotional intelligence in everyday life: A scientific inquiry* (pp. 25–45). Philadelphia: Psychology Press/Taylor & Francis.

Clark, R. E., & LaBeff, E. E. (1982). Death telling: Managing the delivery of bad news. *Journal of Health and Social Behavior, 23*, 366–380.

Cohen-Charash, Y. (2000). *Envy at work: A preliminary examination of antecedents and outcomes.* Unpublished doctoral dissertation, University of California, Berkeley.

Collins, R. (1975). *Conflict sociology.* New York: Academic.

Cooper, D., Doucet, L., & Pratt, M. (2002). *I'm not smiling because I like you: Cultural differences in emotion displays at work.* Manuscript in preparation.

Cropanzano, R., James, K., & Konovsky, M. A. (1993). Dispositional affectivity as a predictor of work attitudes and job performance. *Journal of Organizational Behavior, 14*, 595–606.

Damasio, A. R. (1994). *Descartes' error: Emotion, reason and the human brain.* New York: Putnam.

Darwin, C. (1970). *The expression of the emotions in man and animals.* Chicago: University of Chicago Press. (Original work published 1872)

Davidson, M. N., & Greenhalgh, L. (1999). The role of emotion in negotiation: The impact of anger and race. In R. J. Bies, R. J. Lewicki, & B. H. Sheppard (Eds.), *Research in negotiation in organizations:* (Vol. 7, pp. 3–26). Stamford, CT: JAI.

Davidson, R. J. (1998). Affective styles and affective disorders: Perspectives from affective neuroscience. *Cognition and Emotion, 12*, 307–330.

Davis, M. A., LaRosa, P. A., & Foshee, D. P. (1992). Emotion work in supervisor–subordinate relations: Gender differences in the perception of angry displays. *Sex Roles, 26*, 513–531.

Davis-Blake, A., & Pfeffer, J. (1989). Just a mirage: The search for dispositional effects in organizational research. *Academy of Management Review, 14*, 382–400.

Dawis, R. V., & Lofquist, L. H. (1984). *A psychological theory of work adjustment.* Minneapolis: University of Minnesota Press.

Diamond, M. A. (1993). *The unconscious life of organizations: Interpreting organizational identity.* Westport, CT: Quorum Books/Greenwood.

Doherty, R. W. (1998). Emotional contagion and social judgment. *Motivation and Emotion, 22*, 187–209.

Douglas, S. C., & Martinko, M. J. (2001). Exploring the role of individual differences in the prediction of workplace aggression. *Journal of Applied Psychology, 86*, 547–559.

Druskat, V. U. (2001). Building the emotional intelligence of groups. *Harvard Business Review, 79*, 80–91.

Duffy, M. K., Ganster, D. C., & Shaw, J. D. (1998). Positive affectivity and negative outcomes: The role of tenure and job satisfaction. *Journal of Applied Psychology, 83*, 950–959.

Duffy, M. K., Shaw, J. D., & Stark, E. M. (1997, April). *The Saleri syndrome: Consequences of envy in groups.* Paper presented at the meeting of the Society for Industrial and Organizational Psychology, St. Louis, MO.

Eid, M., & Diener, E. (2001). Norms for experiencing emotions in different cultures: Inter- and intranational differences. *Journal of Personality and Social Psychology, 81*, 869–885.

Ekman, P., & Davidson, R. J. (Eds.). (1994). *The nature of emotion: Fundamental questions.* New York: Oxford University Press.

Ekman, P., & Friesen, W. V. (1971). Constants across cultures in the face and emotions. *Journal of Personality and Social Psychology, 17*, 124–129.

Ekman, P., Friesen, W. V., & Scherer, K. (1976). Body movement and voice pitch in deceptive interaction. *Semiotica, 16*, 23–27.

Elfenbein, H. A., & Ambady, N. (2002). On the universality and cultural specificity of emotion recognition: A meta-analysis. *Psychological Bulletin, 128,* 203–235.

Elfenbein, H. A., Marsh, A., & Ambady, N. (2002). Emotional intelligence and the recognition of emotion from the face. In L. F. Barrett & P. Salovey (Eds.), *The wisdom of feelings: Processes underlying emotional intelligence* (pp. 37–59). New York: Guilford.

Feldman Barrett, L., & Russell, J. A. (1998). Independence and bipolarity in the structure of current affect. *Journal of Personality and Social Psychology, 74*, 967–984.

Fiedler, K., & Forgas, J. (Eds.). (1988). *Affect, cognition, and social behavior: New evidence and integrative attempts.* Toronto, Canada: Hogrefe.

Field, T. M., Woodson, R., Greenberg, R., & Cohen, D. (1982). Discrimination and imitation of facial expressions by neonates. *Science, 218*, 179–181.

Fineman, S. (1993). Organizations as emotional arenas. In S. Fineman (Ed.), *Emotion in organizations* (pp. 9–35). Thousand Oaks, CA: Sage.

Fineman, S. (Ed.). (2000). *Emotions in organizations* (2nd ed.). London: Sage.

Finkenauer, C., & Rime, B. (1998). Keeping emotional memories secret: Health and subjective well-being when emotions are not shared. *Journal of Health Psychology, 3*, 47–58.

Fisher, V. E., & Hanna, J. V. (1931). *The dissatisfied worker.* New York: Macmillan.

Fiske, A. P., Kitayama, S., Markus, H. R., & Nisbett, R. E. (1998). The cultural matrix of social psychology. In D. T. Gilbert, S. T. Fiske, & G. Lindzey (Eds.), *Handbook of social psychology* (4th ed., Vol. II, pp. 915–981). New York: Oxford University Press.

Fiske, S. T. (2001). Seek out the magician: Contrarian tricks of mere simplicity make affect appear and disappear from social psychology. In J. A. Bargh & D. K. Apsley (Eds.), *Unraveling the complexities of social life: A festschrift in honor of Robert B. Zajonc* (pp. 11–21). Washington, DC: American Psychological Association.

Fitness, J. (2000). Anger in the workplace: An emotion script approach to anger episodes between workers and their superiors, co-workers and subordinates. *Journal of Organizational Behavior, 21*, 147–162.

Forgas, J. P. (1992). Affect in social judgments and decisions: A multiprocess model. *Advances in Experimental Social Psychology, 25*, 227–275.

Forgas, J. P. (2001). Introduction: Affect and social cognition. In J. P. Forgas (Ed.), *Handbook of affect and social cognition* (pp. 1–24). Mahwah, NJ: Lawrence Erlbaum Associates.

Fortunato, V. J., & Stone-Romero, E. F. (2001). Positive affectivity as a moderator of the objective-task characteristics/perceived-task characteristics relationship. *Journal of Applied Social Psychology, 31,* 1248–1278.

Fox, N. A., & Davidson, R. J. (1984). Hemispheric substance of affect: A developmental model. In N. A. Fox & R. J. Davidson (Eds.), *The psychology of affective development* (pp. 353–382). Hillsdale, NJ: Lawrence Erlbaum Associates.

Fox, S., & Spector, P. E. (2000). Relations of emotional intelligence, practical intelligence, general intelligence, and trait affectivity with interview outcomes: It's not all just 'G.' *Journal of Organizational Behavior, 21,* 203–220.

Francis, L. (1994). Laughter, the best mediation: Humor as emotion management in interaction. *Symbolic Interaction, 17,* 147–163.

Fredrickson, B. L. (2000). Why positive emotions matter in organizations: Lessons from the broaden-and-build model. *Psychologist-Manager Journal, 4,* 131–142.

Freud, S. (1999). In J. Crick (Trans.) & R. Robertson (Ed.), *The interpretation of dreams.* New York: Oxford University Press. (Original work published 1900).

Frijda, N. H., & Mesquita, B. (1994). The social roles and functions of emotions. In S. Kitayama & H. R. Markus (Eds.), *Emotion and culture: Empirical studies of mutual influence* (pp. 51–87). Washington, DC: American Psychological Association.

Gabriel, Y. (1999). *Organizations in depth.* London: Sage.

George, J. M. (1989). Mood and absence. *Journal of Applied Psychology, 74,* 317–324.

George, J. M. (1990). Personality, affect, and behavior in groups. *Journal of Applied Psychology, 75,* 107–116.

George, J. M. (1991). State or trait: Effects of positive mood on prosocial behaviors at work. *Journal of Applied Psychology, 76,* 299–307.

George, J. M. (1995). Leader positive mood and group performance: The case of customer service. *Journal of Applied Social Psychology, 25,* 778–794.

George, J. M. (2000). Emotions and leadership: The role of emotional intelligence. *Human Relations, 53.*

George, J. M., & Bettenhausen, K. (1990). Understanding prosocial behavior, sales performance, and turnover: A group-level analysis in a service context. *Journal of Applied Psychology, 75,* 698–709.

George, J. M., & Brief, A. P. (1992). Feeling good—doing good: A conceptual analysis of the mood at work-organizational spontaneity relationship. *Psychological Bulletin, 112,* 310–329.

George, J. M., & James, L. R. (1993). Personality, affect, and behavior in groups revisited: Comment on aggregation, levels of analysis, and a recent application of within and between analysis. *Journal of Applied Psychology, 78,* 798–804.

George, J. M., & Jones, G. R. (1996). The experience of work and turnover intentions: Interactive effects of value attainment, job satisfaction, and positive mood. *Journal of Applied Psychology, 81,* 318–325.

Gibson, D. E. (1995). Emotional scripts and organization change. In F. Massarik (Ed.), *Advances in organization development* (Vol. 3, pp. 32–62). *Norwood, NJ: Ablex.*

Glaser, J., & Salovey, P. (1998). Affect in electoral politics. *Personality and Social Psychology Review, 2*, 156–172.

Glassman, N. S., & Andersen, S. M. (1999a). Activating transference without consciousness: Using significant-other representations to go beyond what is subliminally given. *Journal of Personality and Social Psychology, 77*, 1146–1162.

Glassman, N. S., & Andersen, S. M. (1999b). Streams of thought about the self and significant others: Transference as the construction of interpersonal meaning. In J. A. Singer & P. Salovey (Eds.), *At play in the fields of consciousness: Essays in honor of Jerome L. Singer* (pp. 103–140). Mahwah, NJ: Lawrence Erlbaum Associates.

Glomb, T. M. (1999). Anger and aggression in organizations: Antecedents, behavioral, components, and consequences. *Dissertation Abstracts International, 59*, 6,101.

Glomb, T. M., & Hulin, C. L. (1997). Anger and gender effects in observed supervisor–subordinate dyadic interactions. *Organizational Behavior and Human Decision Processes, 72*, 281–307.

Goffman, E. (1967). *Interaction ritual.* Garden City, NY: Doubleday.

Goldsmith, H. H., & Campos, J. J. (1986). Fundamental issues in the study of early temperament: The Denver twin temperament study. In M. E. Lamb, A. L. Brown, & B. Rogoff (Eds.), *Advances in developmental psychology* (Vol. 4, pp. 231–283). Hillsdale, NJ: Lawrence Erlbaum Associates.

Gordon, S. L. (1989). The socialization of children's emotions: Emotional culture, competence, and exposure. In C. I. Saarni & P. Harris (Eds.), *Children's understanding of emotion* (pp. 319–349). New York: Cambridge University Press.

Gray, J. A. (1994). Three fundamental emotion systems. In P. Ekman & R. J. Davidson (Eds.), *The nature of emotions: Fundamental questions* (pp. 243–247). New York: Oxford University Press.

Green, D. P., Salovey, P., & Truax, K. M. (1999). Static, dynamic, and causative bipolarity of affect. *Journal of Personality and Social Psychology, 76*, 856–867.

Griffiths, M. (1995). *Feminism and the self: The web of identity.* London: Bloomsbury.

Gross, E., & Stone, G. P. (1964). Embarrassment and the analysis of role requirements. *American Journal of Sociology, 70*, 1–15.

Grossenbacher, P. G. (Ed.). (2001). *Finding consciousness in the brain: A neurocognitive approach.* Amsterdam: John Benjamins.

Hackman, J. R., & Oldham, G. R. (1975). Development of the job diagnostic survey. *Journal of Applied Psychology, 60*, 159–170.

Haertel, C. E. J., & Zerbe, W. J. (2000). Commentary: Reconciling research findings. In N. M. Ashkanasy, C. E. Haertel, & W. J. Zerbe (Eds.), *Emotions in the workplace: Research, theory, and practice* (pp. 215–217). Westport, CT: Quorum Books/Greenwood.

Hafferty, F. W. (1988). Cadaver stories and the emotional socialization of medical students. *Journal of Health & Social Behavior, 29*, 344–356.

Hardy, G. E., & Barkham, M. (1994). The relationship between interpersonal attachment styles and work difficulties. *Human Relations, 47*, 263–281.

Harmon-Jones, E., & Allen, J. B. (1998). Anger and frontal brain activity: EEG asymmetry consistent with approach motivation despite negative affective valence. *Journal of Personality and Social Psychology, 74,* 1310–1316.

Harre, R. (Ed.). (1986). *The social construction of emotions.* Oxford, England: Basil Blackwell.

Hatfield, E., Cacioppo, J., & Rapson, R. L. (1992). Primitive emotional contagion. In M. S. Clark (Ed.), *Emotion and social behavior. Review of personality and social psychology* (Vol. 14, pp. 151–177). Newbury Park, CA: Sage.

Hatfield, E., Cacioppo, J., & Rapson, R. L. (1993). Emotional contagion. *Current Directions in Psychological Science, 2,* 96–99.

Hatfield, E., Cacioppo, J., & Rapson, R. L. (1994). *Emotional contagion.* New York: Cambridge University Press.

Haviland, J. M., & Lelwica, M. (1987). The induced affect response: 10-week-old infants' responses to three emotion expressions. *Developmental Psychology, 23,* 97–104.

Hazan, C., & Shaver, P. R. (1987). Romantic love conceptualized as an attachment process. *Journal of Personality and Social Psychology, 52,* 511–524.

Hazan, C., & Shaver, P. R. (1990). Love and work: An attachment–theoretical perspective. *Journal of Personality and Social Psychology, 59,* 270–280.

Hersey, R. B. (1932). *Workers' emotions in shop and home: A study of individual workers from the psychological and physiological standpoint.* Philadelphia: University of Pennsylvania Press.

Herzberg, F., Mausner, B., & Snyderman, B. (1959). *The motivation to work.* New York: Wiley.

Hietanen, J. K., Surakka, V., & Linnankoski, I. (1998). Facial electromyographic responses to vocal affect expressions. *Psychophysiology, 35,* 530–536.

Hochschild, A. R. (1983). *The managed heart: Commercialization of human feeling.* Berkeley: University of California Press.

Homans, G. C. (1961). *Social behavior: Its elementary forms.* New York: Harcourt, Brace, & World.

Hoppock, R. (1935). *Job satisfaction.* New York: Harper.

House, R. J., Shane, S. A., & Herold, D. M. (1996). Rumors of the death of dispositional research are vastly exaggerated. *Academy of Management Review, 21,* 203–224.

Hsee, C., Hatfield, E., Carlson, J. E., & Chemtob, C. (1990). The effect of power on susceptibility to emotional contagion. *Cognition and Emotion, 4,* 327–340.

Hsee, C. K., Hatfield, E., & Chemtob, C. (1992). Assessments of the emotional states of others: Conscious judgments versus emotional contagion. *Journal of Social and Clinical Psychology, 11,* 119–128.

Hui, C., Law, K. S., & Chen, Z. X. (1999). A structural equation model of the effects of negative affectivity, leader–member exchange, and perceived job mobility on in-role and extra-role performance: A Chinese case. *Organizational Behavior and Human Decision Processes, 77,* 3–21.

Isen, A. M. (1999). Positive affect. In T. Dalgleish & M. J. Power (Eds.), *Handbook of cognition and emotion* (pp. 521–539). Chichester, England: Wiley.

Isen, A. M. (in press). Positive affect and decision making. In M. Lewis & J. Haciland (Eds.), *Handbook of emotions* (3rd ed.). New York: Guilford.

Isen, A. M. (2002). A role for neuropsychology in understanding the facilitating influence of positive affect on social behavior and cognitive processes. In C. R. Snyder & S. J. Lopez (Eds.), *Handbook of positive psychology* (pp. 528–540). London: Oxford University Press.

Isen, A. M., & Baron, R. A. (1991). Positive affect as a factor in organizational behavior. In B. M. Staw & L. L. Cummings (Eds.), *Research in organizational behavior* (pp. 1–53). Greenwich, CT: JAI.

Iverson, R. D., & Deery, S. J. (2001). Understanding the "personological" basis of employee withdrawal: The influence of affective disposition on employee tardiness, early departure, and absenteeism. *Journal of Applied Psychology, 86*, 856–866.

Iverson, R. D., & Maguire, C. (2000). The relationship between job and life satisfaction: Evidence from a remote mining community. *Human Relations, 53*, 807–839.

Iwaniec, D., & Sneddon, H. (2001). Attachment style in adults who failed to thrive as children: Outcomes of a 20-year follow-up study of factors influencing maintenance or change in attachment style. *British Journal of Social Work, 31*, 179–195.

Izard, C. E. (1992). Basic emotions, relations among emotions, and emotion cognition relations. *Psychological Review, 99*, 561–565.

Izard, C. E. (1993). Organizational and motivational functions of discrete emotions. In M. Lewis & J. M. Haviland (Eds.), *Handbook of emotions* (pp. 631–641). New York: Guilford.

Izard, C. E., Ackerman, B. P., Schoff, K. M., & Fine, S. E. (2000). Self-organization of discrete emotions, emotion patterns, and emotion-cognition relations. In M. D. Lewis & I. Granic (Eds.), *Emotion, development, and self-organization: Dynamic systems approaches to emotional development* (pp. 15–36). New York: Cambridge University Press.

Johnston, M. A. (2000). Delegation and organizational structure in small businesses: Influences on manager's attachment patterns. *Group and Organization Management, 25*, 4–21.

Jones, E. E. (1998). Major developments in five decades of social psychology. In D. T. Gilbert, S. T. Fiske, & G. Lindzey (Eds.), *Handbook of social psychology* (4th ed., pp. 3–57). New York: Oxford University Press.

Judge, T. A. (1992). The dispositional perspective in human resource research. In G. Ferris & K. Rowland (Eds.), *Research in personnel and human resource management* (pp. 31–72). Greenwich, CT: JAI.

Judge, T. A., Thoresen, C. J., Bono, J. E., & Patton, G. K. (2001). The job satisfaction–job performance relationship: A qualitative and quantitative review. *Psychological Bulletin, 127*, 376–407.

Kelly, J. R., & Barsade, S. G. (2001). Mood and emotions in small groups and work teams. *Organizational Behavior and Human Decision Processes, 86*, 99–130.

Keltner, D., & Ekman, P. (2000). Facial expressions of emotion. In M. Lewis & J. M. Haviland-Jones (Eds.), *Handbook of emotions* (2nd ed., pp. 236–249). New York: Guilford.

Keltner, D., Ellsworth, P. C., & Edwards, K. (1993). Beyond simple pessimism: Effects of sadness and anger on social perception. *Journal of Personality and Social Psychology, 64*, 740–752.

Kemper, T. D. (1978). *A social interactional theory of emotions.* New York: Wiley.

Kemper, T. D. (1981). Social constructionist and positivist approaches to the sociology of emotions. *American Journal of Sociology, 87*, 336–362.

Kemper, T. D. (1991). An introduction to the sociology of emotions. In K. T. Strongman (Ed.), *International review of studies on emotion* (pp. 301–349). New York: Wiley.

Kerchoff, A. C., & Back, K. W. (1968). *The June-bug: A study of the hysterical contagion.* New York: Appleton-Century-Crofts.

Kets de Vries, M. (1990). Leaders on the couch. *Journal of Applied Behavioral Science, 26*, 423–431.

Kets de Vries, M. (1991). *Organizations on the couch: Clinical perspectives on organizational behavior and change.* San Francisco: Jossey-Bass.

Kets de Vries, M. (1997). Leaders who self-destruct: The causes and cures. In R. P. Vecchio (Ed.), *Leadership: Understanding the dynamics of power and influence in organizations* (pp. 233–245). Notre Dame, IN: University of Notre Dame Press.

Kets de Vries, M., & Miller, D. (1984). Group fantasies and organizational functioning. *Human Relations, 37*, 111–134.

Kets de Vries, M., & Miller, D. (1985). Narcissism and leadership: An object relations perspective. *Human Relations, 38*, 583–601.

Kets de Vries, M., & Miller, D. (1986). Personality, culture, and organization. *Academy of Management Review, 11*, 266–279.

Kihlstrom, J. F. (1999). The psychological unconscious. In L. A. Pervin & O. P. John (Eds), *Handbook of personality: Theory and research* (2nd ed., pp. 424–442). New York: Guilford.

Kihlstrom, J. F., Mulvaney, S., Tobias, B. A., & Tobis, I. P. (2000). The emotional unconscious. In E. Eich, J. F. Kihlstrom, G. H. Bower, J. P. Forgas, & P. M. Niedenthal (Eds.), *Cognition and emotion* (pp. 30–86). New York: Oxford University Press.

Kilberg, R. R. (1995). Integrating psychodynamic and systems theories in organization development practice. *Consulting Psychology Journal: Practice and Research, 47*, 28–55.

Kinder, D. R. (1994). Reason and emotion in American political life. In R. Schank & E. Langer (Eds.), *Beliefs, reasoning, and decision making: Psycho-logic in honor of Bob Abelson* (pp. 277–314). Hillsdale, NJ: Lawrence Erlbaum Associates.

Kishimoto, H. (1993). Positron emission tomography and affective disorders. In T. Kariya & M. Nakagawara (Eds.), *Affective disorders: Perspectives on basic research and clinical practice* (pp. 99–112). Philadelphia: Brunner/Mazel.

Klein, M. (1987). In J. Mitchell (Ed.), *The selected Melanie Klein.* New York: The Free Press.

Kornhauser, A. W., & Sharp, A. A. (1932). Employee attitudes: Suggestions from a study in a factory. *Personnel Journal, 10*, 393–404.

Kraiger, K., Billings, R. S., & Isen, A. M. (1989). The influence of positive affective states on task perceptions and satisfaction. *Organizational Behavior and Human Decision Processes, 44*, 12–25.

Krausz, M., Bizman, A., & Braslavsky, D. (2001). Effects of attachment style on preferences for and satisfaction with different employment contracts: An exploratory study. *Journal of Business and Psychology, 16*, 299–316.

Kruml, S. M., & Geddes, D. (2000). Catching fire without burning out: Is there an ideal way to perform emotion labor? In N. M. Ashkanasy & C. E. Haertel (Eds.), *Emotion in the workplace: Research, theory, and practice* (pp. 177–188). Westport, CT: Quorum Books/Greenwood.

Kuhn, T. S. (1970). *The structure of scientific revolutions* (2nd ed). Chicago: University of Chicago Press.

Landy, F. J. (1978). An opponent process theory of job satisfaction. *Journal of Applied Psychology, 63*, 533–547.

Lane, R. D., & Nadel, L. (2000). *Cognitive neuroscience of emotion.* New York: Oxford University Press.

Larsen, J. T., McGraw, A. P., & Cacioppo, J. T. (2001). Can people feel happy and sad at the same time? *Journal of Personality and Social Psychology, 81*, 684–696.

Larsen, R. J., & Diener, E. (1992). Promises and problems with the circumplex model of emotion. In M. S. Clark (Ed.), *Emotion. Review of personality and social psychology, No. 13* (pp. 25–59). Thousand Oaks, CA: Sage.

Lawler, E. E. (1971). *Pay and organizational effectiveness: A psychological view.* New York: McGraw-Hill.

Lawler, E. E. (1973). *Motivation in work organizations.* Monterey, CA: Brooks/Cole.

Lazarus, R. S. (1981). A cognitivist's reply to Zajonc on emotion and cognition. *American Psychologist, 36*, 222–223.

Lazarus, R. S. (1982). Thoughts on the relations between emotion and cognition. *American Psychologist, 37*, 1019–1024.

Lazarus, R. S. (1991). *Emotion and adaptation.* New York: Oxford University Press.

Lazarus, R. S., & Cohen-Charash, Y. (2001). Discrete emotions in organizational life. In R. Payne & C. L. Cooper (Eds.), *Emotions in organizations* (pp. 45–81). Chichester, England: Wiley.

Leary, M. R. (2000). Affect, cognition, and the social emotions. In J. P. Forgas (Ed.), *Feeling and thinking: The role of affect in social cognition* (pp. 351–356). New York: Cambridge University Press.

Le Bon, G. (1895). *The crowd: A study of the popular mind.* London: Ernest Benn.

LeDoux, J. E. (1995). Emotion: Clues from the brain. *Annual Review of Psychology, 46*, 209–235.

LeDoux, J. E. (1996). *The emotional brain: The mysterious underpinnings of emotional life.* New York: Simon & Schuster.

LeDoux, J. E., & Phelps, E. A. (2000). Emotional networks in the brain. In M. Lewis & J. M. Haviland-Jones (Eds), *Handbook of emotions* (2nd ed., pp. 157–172). New York: Guilford.

Lerner, J. S., & Keltner, D. (2001). Fear, anger, and risk. *Journal of Personality and Social Psychology, 81*, 146–159.

Levenson, R. W. (1996). Biological substrates of empathy and facial modulation of emotion: Two facets of the scientific legacy of John Lanzetta. *Motivation and Emotion, 20*, 185–204.

Levin, I., & Stokes, J. P. (1989). Dispositional approach to job satisfaction: Role of negative affectivity. *Journal of Applied Psychology, 74*, 752–758.

Levy, D. A., & Nail, P. R. (1993). Contagion: A theoretical and empirical review and reconceptualization. *Genetic, Social, and General Psychology Monographs, 119*, 233–284.

Lewis, M. (2000). Self-conscious emotions: Embarrassment, pride, shame and guilt. In M. Lewis & J. M. Haviland-Jones (Eds.), *Handbook of emotions* (2nd ed., pp. 623–636). New York: Guilford.

Lively, K. J. (2000). Reciprocal emotion management. *Work and Occupations, 27*, 32–63.

Locke, E. A. (1969). What is job satisfaction? *Organizational Behavior and Human Decision Processes, 4*, 309–336.

Locke, E. A. (1976). The nature and causes of job satisfaction. In M. D. Dunnette (Ed.), *The handbook of industrial and organizational psychology* (pp. 1297–1349). Chicago: Rand McNally.

Lundqvist, L. O., & Dimberg, U. (1995). Facial expressions are contagious. *Journal of Psychophysiology, 9*, 203–211.

Madjer, N., Oldham, G. R., & Pratt, M. G. (in press). There's no place like home: The contributions of work and non-work creativity support to employees' creative performance. *Academic Management Journal.*

Mak, A. S., & Mueller, J. (2000). Job insecurity, coping resources and personality dispositions in occupational strain. *Work and Strain, 14*, 312–328.

March, J. G., & Simon, H. A. (1958). *Organizations.* New York: Wiley.

Marx, K. (1971). *The early texts.* (D. McLellan, Ed.). Oxford, England: Blackwell. (Original work published 1842–1844)

Mayer, J. D., Caruso, D., & Salovey, P. (1999). Emotional intelligence meets traditional standards for an intelligence. *Intelligence, 27*, 267–298.

Mayer, J. D., Caruso, D., & Salovey, P. (2000). Selecting a measure of emotional intelligence: The case for ability scales. In R. Bar-On & J. D. A. Parker (Eds.), *Handbook of emotional intelligence* (pp. 320–342). San Francisco: Jossey-Bass.

Mayer, J. D., Salovey, P., & Caruso, D. (2000). Models of emotional intelligence. In R. J. Sternberg (Ed.), *Handbook of intelligence* (pp. 396–420). New York: Cambridge University Press.

Mayne, T. J., & Bonanno, G. A. (Eds.). (2001). *Emotions: Current issues and future directions.* New York: Guilford.

McDougall, W. (1923). *Outline of psychology.* New York: Scribner.

Mikulincer, M., & Sheffi, E. (2000). Adult attachment style and cognitive reactions to positive affect: A test of mental categorization and creative problem solving. *Motivation & Emotion, 24*, 149–174.

Millar, K. U., & Tesser, A. (1988). Deceptive behavior in social relationships: A consequence of violated expectations. *Journal of Psychology, 122*, 263–273.

Miner, F. C., Jr. (1990). Jealousy on the job. *Personnel Journal, 69*, 88–95.

Mischel, W. (1968). *Personality and assessment.* New York: Wiley.

Mitchell, T. R. (1974). Expectancy models of job satisfaction, occupational preference and effort: A theoretical, methodological, and empirical appraisal. *Psychological Bulletin, 81*, 1053–1077.

Monahan, J. L. (1998). I don't know it but I like you: The influence of nonconscious affect on person perception. *Human Communication Research, 24*, 480–500.

Moore, B. S., & Isen, A. M. (Eds.). (1990). *Affect and social behavior.* Cambridge, England: Cambridge University Press.

Motowidlo, S. J. (1996). Orientation toward the job and organization. In K. R. Murphy (Ed.), *Individual differences and behavior in organizations* (pp. 175–208). San Francisco: Jossey-Bass.

Muchinsky, P. M. (1983). *Psychology applied to work.* Homewood, IL: Dorsey.

Murphy, S. T. (2001). Feeling without thinking: Affective primacy and the nonconscious processing of emotion. In J. A. Bargh & D. K. Apsley (Eds.), *Unraveling the complexities of social life: A festschrift in honor of Robert B. Zajonc* (pp. 39–53). Washington, DC: American Psychological Association.

Murphy, S. T., Monahan, J. L., & Zajonc, R. B. (1995). Additivity of nonconscious affect: Combined effects of priming and exposure. *Journal of Personality and Social Psychology, 69*, 589–602.

Neumann, R., & Strack, F. (2000). Mood contagion: The automatic transfer of mood between persons. *Journal of Personality and Social Psychology, 79*, 211–223.

Nezlek, J. B. (2001). Day-to-day relationships between self-awareness, daily events, and anxiety. *Journal of Personality, 70*, 249–275.

Nezlek, J. B., & Gable, S. L. (2001). Depression as a moderator of relationships between positive daily events and day-to-day psychological adjustment. *Personality and Social Psychology Bulletin, 27*, 1692–1704.

Nezlek, J. B., & Plesko, R. M. (in press). Trait adjustment as a moderator of the interactive effects of positive and negative daily events on daily psychological adjustment. *Personality and Social Psychology Bulletin.*

O'Reilly, C. (1989). Corporations, culture and commitment: Motivation and social control in organizations. *California Management Review, 31*, 9–25.

Organ, D. W., & Near, J. P. (1985). Cognition vs. affect measures of job satisfaction. *International Journal of Psychology, 20*, 241–254.

Ortony, A., & Turner, T. J. (1990). What's basic about basic emotions? *Psychological Review, 97*, 315–331.

Ottati, V. C., Steenbergen, M. R., & Riggle, E. (1992). The cognitive and affective components of political attitudes: Measuring the determinants of candidate evaluations. *Political Behavior, 14*, 423–442.

Panksepp, J. (1998). *Affective neuroscience: The foundations of human and animal emotions.* New York: Oxford University Press.

Panksepp, J. (2000). On preventing another century of misunderstanding: Toward a psychoethology of human experience and a psychoneurology of affect [Comment on "Experimental psychology and psychoanalysis: What we can learn from a century of misunderstanding"]. *Neuro-Psychoanalysis, 2*, 240–255.

Parrott, W. G., & Harre, R. (1996). Some complexities in the study of emotions. In R. Harre & G. Parrott (Eds.), *The emotions* (pp. 1–38). London: Sage.

Patchen, M. (1961). *The choice of wage comparisons.* Englewood Cliffs, NJ: Prentice-Hall.

Pelled, L. H., & Xin, K. R. (1999). Down and out: An investigation of the relationship between mood and employee withdrawal behavior. *Journal of Management, 25,* 875–895.

Pennebaker, J. W., Zech, E., & Rime, B. (2001). Disclosing and sharing emotion: Psychological, social, and health consequences. In M. S. Stroebe & R. O. Hansson (Eds.), *Handbook of bereavement research: Consequences, coping, and care* (pp. 517–543). Washington, DC: American Psychological Association.

Pfeffer, J. (1993). Barriers to the advance of organizational science: Paradigm development as a dependent variable. *Academy of Management Review, 18,* 599–620.

Phoon, W. H. (1982). Outbreaks of mass hysteria at workplaces in Singapore: Some patterns and modes of presentation. In J. W. Pennebaker & L. R. Murphy (Eds.), *Mass psychogenic illness: A social psychological analysis* (pp. 21–31). Hillsdale, NJ: Lawrence Erlbaum Associates.

Pierce, J. (1995). *Gender trials: Emotional lives in contemporary law firms.* Berkeley, CA: University of California Press.

Pietrini, P., Guazzelli, M., Basso, G., Jaffe, K., & Grafman, J. (2000). Neural correlates of imaginal aggressive behavior assessed by positron emission tomography in healthy subjects. *American Journal of Psychiatry, 157,* pp. 1722–1781.

Pillutla, M. M., & Murnighan, J. K. (1996). Unfairness, anger, and spite: Emotional rejections of ultimatum offers. *Organizational Behavior and Human Decision Processes, 68,* 208–224.

Pine, D. S., Grun, J., Zarahn, E., Fyer, A., Koda, V., Li, W., Szeszko, P. R., Ardekani, B., & Bilder, R. M. (2001). Cortical brain regions engaged by masked emotional faces in adolescents and adults: An fMRI study. *Emotion, 2,* 137–147.

Porter, L. W. (1996). Forty years of organization studies: Reflections from a micro perspective. *Administrative Science Quarterly, 41,* 262–269.

Poulson, C. F., II. (2000). Shame and work. In N. M. Ashkanasy & C. E. Haertel (Eds.), *Emotion in the workplace: Research, theory, and practice* (pp. 250–271). Westport, CT: Quorum Books/Greenwood.

Pratt, M. G., & Barnett, C. K. (1997). Emotions and unlearning in Amway recruiting techniques: Promoting change through "safe" ambivalence. *Management Learning, 28,* 65–88.

Pugh, S. D. (2001). Service with a smile: Emotional contagion in the service encounter. *Academy of Management Journal, 44,* 1018–1027.

Rafaeli, A., & Sutton, R. I. (1987). Expression of emotion as part of the work role. *Academy of Management Review, 12,* 23–37.

Rafaeli, A., & Sutton, R. I. (1989). The expression of emotion in organizational life. In L. L. Cummings & B. M. Staw (Eds.), *Research in organizational behavior* (Vol. 11, pp. 1–42). Greenwich, CT: JAI.

Rafaeli, A., & Sutton, R. I. (1990). Busy stores and demanding customers: How do they affect the display of positive emotion? *Academy of Management Journal, 33,* 623–637.

Rafaeli, A., & Sutton, R. I. (1991). Emotional contrast strategies as means of social influence: Lessons from criminal interrogators and bill collectors. *Academy of Management Journal, 34,* 749–775.

Reis, H. T., & Gable, S. L. (2000). Event-sampling and other methods for studying everyday experience. In H. T. Reis & C. M. Judd (Eds.), *Handbook of research methods in social and personality psychology* (pp. 190–222). New York: Cambridge University Press.

Rime, B. (1995). The social sharing of emotion as a source for the social knowledge of emotion. In J. Russell, Fernandex-Dols, A. S. R. Manstead, & J. C. Wellenkamp (Eds.), *Everyday conceptions of emotion: An introduction to the psychology, anthropology, and linguistics of emotion* (Vol. 81, pp. 475–489). Norwell, MA: Kluwer.

Rime, B., Mesquita, B., Philippot, P., & Boca, S. (1991). Beyond the emotional event: Six studies on the social sharing of emotion. *Cognition and Emotion, 5,* 435–465.

Roethlisberger, F. J., & Dickson, W. J. (1939). *Management and the worker.* Cambridge, MA: Harvard University Press.

Roseman, I. J. (1991). Appraisal determinants of discrete emotions. *Cognition and Emotion, 5,* 161–200.

Roseman, I. J., Spindel, M. S., & Jose, P. E. (1990). Appraisals of emotion-eliciting events: Testing a theory of discrete emotions. *Journal of Personality and Social Psychology, 59,* 899–915.

Rosenthal, S. (1985). Mourning and depression in organizations. In V. Colkan (Ed.), *Depressive states and their treatment* (pp. 201–219). New York: Aronson.

Russell, J. A. (1980). A circumplex model of affect. *Journal of Personality and Social Psychology, 39,* 1161–1178.

Russell, J. A., & Carroll, J. M. (1999). On the bipolarity of positive and negative affect. *Psychological Bulletin, 125,* 3–30.

Russell, J. A., & Feldman Barrett, L. (1999). Core affect, prototypical emotional episodes, and other things called emotion: Dissecting the elephant. *Journal of Personality and Social Psychology, 76,* 805–819.

Salancik, G. R., & Pfeffer, J. (1978). A social information processing approach to job attitudes and task design. *Administrative Science Quarterly, 23,* 224–253.

Salovey, P., & Mayer, J. D. (1990). Emotional intelligence. *Imagination, Cognition, and Personality, 9,* 185–211.

Salovey, P., Woolery, A., & Mayer, J. D. (2001). Emotional intelligence: Conceptualizations and measurement. In G. J. O. Fletcher & M. S. Clark (Eds.), *Blackwell handbook of social psychology: Interpersonal processes* (pp. 279–307). Malden, MA: Blackwell.

Schaubroeck, J., & Jones, J. R. (2000). Antecedents of workplace emotional labor dimensions and moderators of their effects on physical symptoms. *Journal of Organizational Behavior, 21,* 163–183.

Scheff, T. J. (1990). *Microsociology: Discourse, emotion, and social structure.* Chicago: University of Chicago Press.

Schein, E. H. (1991). *Organizational culture and leadership.* San Francisco: Jossey-Bass.

Schirmer, L. L., & Lopez, F. G. (2001). Probing the social support and work strain relationship among adult workers: Contributions of adult attachment orientations. *Journal of Vocational Behavior, 59*, 17–33.

Schneider, B., & Reichers, A. E. (1983). On the etiology of climates. *Personnel Psychology, 36*, 19–39.

Schoenewolf, G. (1990). Emotional contagion: Behavioral induction in individuals and groups. *Modern Psychoanalysis, 15*, 49–61.

Schutte, N. S., Malouff, J. M., Bobik, C., Coston, T. D., Greeson, C., Jedlicka, C., Rhodes, E., & Wendorf, G. (2001). Emotional intelligence and interpersonal relations. *Journal of Social Psychology, 141*, 523–536.

Schwarz, N., Bless, H., Bohner, G., Harlacher, U., & Kellerbenz, M. (1991). Response scales as frames of reference: The impact of frequency range on diagnostic judgements. *Applied Cognitive Psychology, 5*, 37–49.

Seeman, M. (1959). On the meaning of alienation. *American Sociological Review, 24*, 783–791.

Seeman, M. (1991). Alienation and anomie. In J. Robinson, P. Shaver, & L. Wrightsman (Eds.), *Measures of personality and social psychological attitudes* (pp. 291–371). San Diego, CA: Academic.

Seligman, M. E. P., & Csikszentmihalyi, M. (2000). Postive psychology: An introduction. *American Psychologist, 55*, 5–14.

Shaver, P., Schwartz, J., Kirson, D., & O'Connor, C. (1987). Emotion knowledge—further exploration of a prototype approach. *Journal of Personality and Social Psychology, 52*, 1061–1086.

Shaw, J. D., Duffy, M. K., Ali Abdulla, M. H., & Singh, R. (2000). The moderating role of positive affectivity: Empirical evidence from bank employees in the United Arab Emirates. *Journal of Management, 26*, 139–154.

Shott, S. (1979). Emotion and social life: A symbolic interactionist analysis. *American Journal of Sociology, 84*, 1317–1334.

Simon, H. A. (1989). Making management decisions: The role of intuition and emotion. In W. H. Agor (Ed.), *Intuition in organizations: Leading and managing productively* (pp. 23–39). Thousand Oaks, CA: Sage.

Singer, J. L. (1997). "What is consciousness?" Commentary. *Journal of the American Psychoanalytic Association, 45*, 753–759.

Singer, J. A., & Salovey, P. (1988). Mood and memory: Evaluating the network theory of affect. *Clinical Psychology Review, 8*, 211–251.

Skarlicki, D. P., Folger, R., & Tesluk, P. (1999). Personality as a moderator in the relationship between fairness and retaliation. *Academy of Management Journal, 42*, 100–108.

Smith, E. R., Murphy, J., & Coats, S. (1999). Attachment to groups: Theory and management. *Journal of Personality and Social Psychology, 77*, 94–110.

Smith, P. C., Kendall, L. M., & Hulin, C. L. (1969). *The measurement of satisfaction in work and retirement: A strategy for the study of attitudes.* Chicago: Rand McNally.

Smith-Lovin, L. (1988). Impressions from events. In L. Smith-Lovin & D. R. Heise (Eds.), *Analyzing social interaction: Advances in affect control theory* (pp. 35–70). New York: Gordon & Breach.

Snyder, C. R., & Lopez, S. J. (Eds.). (2002). *Handbook of positive psychology* (pp. 731–744). London: Oxford University Press.

Spataro, S. (in press). When differences do (and do not) make a difference: How individual identities influence reactions to diversity. In M. Neale, E. Mannix, & J. Polzer (Eds.), *Research on managing groups and teams, Vol. 4.* Stamford, CT: JAI.

Spector, P. (1996). *Industrial and organizational psychology: Research and practice.* New York: Wiley.

Spector, P. E., Fox, S., & Van Katwyk, P. T. (1999). The role of negative affectivity in employee reactions to job characteristics: Bias effect or substantive effect? *Journal of Occupational and Organizational Psychology, 72,* 205–218.

Staw, B. M. (in press). The dispositional approach to job attitudes: An empirical and conceptual review. In B. Schneider & B. Smith (Eds.), *Personality and organization.* Mahwah, NJ: Lawrence Erlbaum Associates.

Staw, B. M., & Barsade, S. G. (1993). Affect and managerial performance: A test of the sadder-but-wiser vs. happier-and-smarter hypotheses. *Administrative Science Quarterly, 38,* 304–331.

Staw, B. M., Bell, N. E., & Clausen, J. A. (1986). The dispositional approach to job attitudes: A lifetime longitudinal test. *Administrative Science Quarterly, 31,* 56–77.

Staw, B. M., & Ross, J. (1985). Stability in the midst of change: A dispositional approach to job attitudes. *Journal of Applied Psychology, 70,* 469–480.

Staw, B. M., Sutton, R. I., & Pelled, L. H. (1994). Employee positive emotion and favorable outcomes at the workplace. *Organization Science, 5,* 51–71.

Sullins, E. S. (1991). Emotional contagion revisited: Effects of social comparison and expressive style on mood convergence. *Personality and Social Psychology Bulletin, 17,* 166–174.

Sumer, H. C., & Knight, P. A. (2001). How do people with different attachment styles balance work and family? A personality perspective on work–family linkage. *Journal of Applied Psychology, 86,* 653–663.

Sutton, R. I., & Rafaeli, A. (1988). Untangling the relationship between displayed emotions and organizational sales: The case of convenience stores. *Academy of Management Journal, 31,* 461–487.

Tellegen, A. (1985). Structures of mood and personality and their relevance to assessing anxiety, with an emphasis on self-report. In A. H. Tuma & J. D. Maser (Eds.), *Anxiety and the anxiety disorders* (pp. 681–706). Hillsdale, NJ: Lawrence Erlbaum Associates.

Thoits, P. A. (1989). The sociology of emotions. *Annual Review of Sociology, 15,* 317–342.

Thoits, P. A. (1996). Managing the emotions of others. *Symbolic Interaction, 19,* 85–109.

Thompson, L. L., Nadler, J., & Kim, P. H. (1999). Some like it hot: The case for the emotional negotiator. In L. L. Thompson, J. M. Levin, & D. M. Messick (Eds.), *Shared cognition in organizations: The management of knowledge* (pp. 139–161). Mahwah, NJ: Lawrence Erlbaum Associates.

Tiedens, L. Z. (2001). Anger and advancement versus status and subjugation: The effect of negative emotion expressions on social status conferral. *Motivation & Emotion, 25*, 233–251.

Tiedens, L. Z., Ellsworth, P. C., & Mesquita, B. (2000). Stereotypes of status and sentiments: Emotional expectations for high and low status group members. *Personality and Social Psychology Bulletin, 26*, 560–574.

Timmers, M., Fischer, A. H., & Manstead, A. S. R. (1998). Gender differences in motives for regulating emotions. *Personality and Social Psychology Bulletin, 24*, 974–985.

Tomarken, A. J., Davidson, R. J., & Henriques, J. B. (1990). Resting frontal brain asymmetry predicts affective responses to films. *Journal of Personality and Social Psychology, 59*, 791–801.

Totterdell, P. (2000). Catching moods and hitting runs: Mood linkage and subjective performance in professional sport teams. *Journal of Applied Psychology, 85*, 848–859.

Totterdell, P., Kellett, S., Teuchmann, K., & Briner, R. B. (1998). Evidence of mood linkage in work groups. *Journal of Personality and Social Psychology, 74*, 1504–1515.

Van Maanen, J. V., & Kunda, G. (1989). Real feelings: Emotional expression and organizational culture. In L. L. Cummings & B. M. Staw (Eds.), *Research in organizational behavior* (Vol. 11, pp. 43–104). Greenwich, CT: JAI.

Vecchio, R. P. (1995). The impact of referral sources on employee attitudes: Evidence from a national sample. *Journal of Management, 21*, 953–965.

Veith, I. (1965). *Hysteria: The history of a disease*. Chicago: University of Chicago Press.

Vroom, V. H. (1964). *Work and motivation*. New York: Wiley.

Watson D. (2000). *Mood and temperament*. New York: Guilford.

Watson, D., & Clark, L. A. (1984). Negative affectivity: The disposition to experience aversive emotional states. *Psychological Bulletin, 96*, 465–490.

Watson, D., Clark, L. A., & Tellegen, A. (1988). Development and validation of brief measures of positive and negative affect: The PANAS scales. *Journal of Personality and Social Psychology, 54*, 1063–1070.

Watson, D., & Pennebaker, J. W. (1989). Health complaints, stress, and distress: Exploring the central role of negative affectivity. *Psychological Review, 96*, 234–254.

Watson, D., & Slack, A. K. (1993). General factors of affective temperament and their relation to job satisfaction over time. *Organizational Behavior and Human Decision Processes, 54*, 181–202.

Watson, D., & Tellegen, A. (1985). Toward a consensual structure of mood. *Psychological Bulletin, 98*, 219–235.

Watson, D., & Tellegen, A. (1999). Issues in the dimensional structure of affect—Effects of descriptors, measurement error, and response formats: Comment on Russell and Carroll. *Psychological Bulletin, 125*, 601–610.

Watson, D., Wiese, D., Vaidya, J., & Tellegen, A. (1999). The two general activation systems of affect: Structural findings, evolutionary considerations, and psychobiological evidence. *Journal of Personality and Social Psychology, 76*, 820–838.

Weisfeld, G. E. (1997). Discrete emotions theory with specific reference to pride and shame. In N. L. Segal, G. E. Weisfeld, & C. C. Weisfeld (Eds.), *Uniting psychology* and biology: Integrative perspectives on human development (pp. 419–443). Washington, DC: American Psychological Association.

Weiss, H. M. (2002). Deconstructing job satisfaction: Separating evaluations, beliefs and affective experiences. Human Resource Management Review, 12, 173–194.

Weiss, H. M., & Brief, A. P. (2002). Affect at work: A historical perspective. In R. L. Payne & C. L. Cooper (Eds.), Emotions at work: Theory, research, and application in management (pp. 133–171). Chichester, England: Wiley.

Weiss, H. M., & Cropanzano, R. (1996). Affective events theory: A theoretical discussion of the structure, causes and consequences of affective experiences at work. Research in Organizational Behavior, 18, 1–74.

Weiss, H. M., Suckow, K., & Cropanzano, R. (1999). Effects of justice conditions on discrete emotions. Journal of Applied Psychology, 84, 786–794.

Weitz, J. (1952). A neglected concept in the study of job satisfaction. Personnel Psychology, 5, 201–205.

Westen, D. (1998a). The scientific legacy of Sigmund Freud: Toward a psychodynamically informed psychological science. Psychological Bulletin, 124, 333–371.

Westen, D. (1998b). Unconscious thought, feeling, and motivation: The end of a century–long debate. In R. F. Bornstein & J. M. Masling (Eds.), Empirical perspectives on the psychoanalytic unconscious: Empirical studies of psychoanalytic theories (Vol. 7, pp. 1–43). Washington, DC: American Psychological Association.

Westen, D. (2000). Integrative psychotherapy: Integrating psychodynamic and cognitive–behavioral theory and technique. In C. R. Snyder & R. E. Ingram (Eds.), Handbook of psychological change: Psychotherapy processes & practices for the 21st century (pp. 217–242). New York: Wiley.

Winnicott, D. W. (1986). Transitional objects and transitional phenomena: A study of the first not-me possession. In P. Buckley (Ed.), Essential papers on object relations: Essential papers in psychoanalysis (pp. 254–271). New York: New York University Press.

Wright, T. A., & Staw, B. M. (1999). Affect and favorable work outcomes: Two longitudinal tests of the happy-productive worker thesis. Journal of Organizational Behavior, 20, 1–23.

Wundt, W. (1905). Grundriss der Psychologie (7th rev. ed.). Leipzig: Engelman. [Cited in R. L. Lazarus (1991). Emotion and adaptation. Oxford, England: Oxford University Press.]

Yammarino, F. J., & Markham, S. E. (1992). On the application of within and between analysis: Are absence and affect really group-based phenomena? Journal of Applied Psychology, 77, 168–176.

Yanay, N., & Shahar, G. (1998). Professional feelings as emotional labor. Journal of Contemporary Ethnography, 27, 346–373.

Zajonc, R. B. (1968). Attitudinal effects of mere exposure. Journal of Personality and Social Psychology Monograph Supplement, 9, 1–27.

Zajonc, R. B. (1980). Feeling and thinking: Preferences need no inferences. American Psychologist, 39, 151–175.

Zajonc, R. B. (1985). Emotion and facial efference: A theory reclaimed. *Science, 228,* 5–21.

Zajonc, R. B. (2001). Mere exposure: A gateway to the subliminal. *Current Directions in Psychological Science, 10,* 224–228.

Zajonc, R. S., Murphy, S. T., & Inglehart, M. (1989). Feeling and facial efference: Implications of the vascular theory of emotion. *Psychological Review, 96,* 395–416.

Zelenski, J. M., & Larsen, R. J. (1999). Susceptibility to affect: A comparison of three personality taxonomies. *Journal of Personality, 67,* 761–791.

Zhou, J., & George, J. M. (2001). When job dissatisfaction leads to creativity: Encouraging the expression of voice. *Academy of Management Journal, 44,* 682–696.

Zummuner, V. L., & Fischer, A. H. (1995). The social regulation of emotions in jealousy situations: A comparison between Italy and the Netherlands. *Journal of Cross-Cultural Psychology, 26,* 189–208.

# 2

---

# Stress, Health,
# and Well-Being at Work

---

James Campbell Quick
*The University of Texas at Arlington*

Cary L. Cooper
*University of Manchester Institute of Science and Technology*

Debra L. Nelson
*Oklahoma State University*

Jonathan D. Quick
*World Health Organization*

Joanne H. Gavin
*Marist College*

Stress and health at work are important for two reasons, one economic and one humanitarian. The economic rationale for the concern for workplace stress is based on the direct and indirect organizational costs of workplace stress. Absenteeism, strikes, turnover, grievances, accidents, health care costs, and compensation awards are multicause organizational problems with direct economic costs to which stress may be a contributing causal factor (Macy & Mirvis, 1976; Quick, Quick, Nelson, & Hurrell, 1997). In addition, communication breakdowns, faulty decision making, and poor quality of working relations are also multicause problems at work with indirect economic costs to which stress can be a contributing causal factor (Kahn, Wolfe, Quinn, Snoek, & Rosenthal, 1964). The emotional suffering endemic to organizational life has both economic costs, even if hard to calculate, as well as a human burden (Frost & Robinson, 1999). Further, the humanitarian rationale for the concern for workplace stress is based on the moral and ethical grounds that employees should be treated as ends in themselves, with dignity and respect (Aristotle, 310/1998; Solomon, 1992). Right and fair treatment at work is important in and of itself, and contributes to good physical, psychological, emotional, and spiritual health.

Workplace stress is a health risk rooted in the early days of the Industrial Revolution, the heart of which was the factories and mills of Manchester, England in the mid-1800s. Over the next 100 years these factories and mills gave way to large, modern corporations, and more recently to the appearance and disappearance of dot.com companies in the technology sector of the New Economy, over 200 of which went out of business in 2000 (Rosch, 2001). Kahn et al., (1964) studies in role conflict and ambiguity brought attention to the organizational and psychological stress associated with work in large corporations that dominated the industrial landscape of the mid-20th century. During their rise, psychiatry had an early concern with industrial mental hygiene and "preventive management." Elkind (1931) applied a national mental hygiene agenda to workplace issues of industrial relations, human nature in organizations, management, and leadership. Later, the American Psychological Association (APA) formed a cooperative agreement with the National Institute for Occupational Safety and Health (NIOSH) for job stress and psychological disorders in the workplace (Sauter, Murphy, & Hurrell, 1990).

## STRESS—THE TEST AMERICANS ARE FAILING?

Contrary to the *Business Week* headline "Stress: The Test Americans Are Failing," Americans are passing the stress test when life expectancy is the operational measure. American men and women extended their average life expectancy at birth by over 50% in less than a century, from less than 50 years in 1900 to over 75 years for before the mid-1980s (*Vital Statistics of the United States*, 1988). Further, some stress is good, and not all stress is bad. The stress response is a normal psychophysiological response to stressful or traumatic events, environmental demands, and interpersonal conflicts (Quick, Quick, & Gavin, 2000). In spite of this normalcy of the stress response, stress poses a risk to health when it is experienced too frequently, too intensely, for too prolonged a period of time, or when the stress-induced energy is mismanaged. Further, despite the success as measured by life expectancy at birth, stress is still a direct contributing cause or indirectly implicated in over 50% of all human morbidity and mortality (Cooper & Quick, 1999, 2003). In the United

States and all developed countries, the 10 leading causes of death account for about 80% of all deaths. Stress is directly implicated in four causes (heart disease, strokes, injuries, and suicide and homicide) and indirectly implicated in a further three (cancer, chronic liver disease, and emphysema and chronic bronchitis). These broader health statistics help to frame the context for workplace stress.

## Job Stress—An Epidemic?

Although we are living longer, we may be suffering more. This has been called the Age of Anxiety based in part on a 1 SD increase in anxiety levels within the U.S. population over the period from 1952 to 1993 (Twenge, 2000). Anxiety disorders, one of the two most common presenting complaints for stress, affect one in every six people in the United States and one in every five employed people in the United Kingdom (Cooper & Quick, 1999). The 2001 Labor Day survey by The Marlin Company in collaboration with the American Institute of Stress found 35% reporting that their jobs are harming their physical and emotional health. In addition, 50% of employees reported a more demanding workload than a year earlier and 42% said job pressures are interfering with their personal relationships. As early as 1980, NIOSH identified stress and psychological disorders in the workplace as one of the top 10 occupational health hazards in America (Millar, 1984; Sauter et al, 1990). Layoffs and downsizing continued through the 1990s, with their adverse effects on employee, managerial, and executive stress (Morris, Cascio, & Young, 1999). The American Institute of Stress calls job stress a health epidemic based on a set of indicators, including self-report surveys, unscheduled absence data, violent incidents at work, and job loss numbers (Rosch, 2001b).

Translated literally from the Greek, epidemic means "upon the people" (Tyler & Last, 1998). Epidemiology is the basic science and most fundamental practice of public health and preventive medicine. Epidemics of infection are often assessed on three indicators, which are (a) the percentage of the population affected by the disease, (b) the rate of spread of the disease, and (c) the intensity of the adverse impact of the disease. Whereas the ancients often lacked adequate knowledge to do little more than observe victims and record mortality, the evolution of preventive medicine from the mid-1800s affords greater power to stop epidemics (Wallace & Doebbeling, 1998). Treatment alone is rarely effective in the management of epidemics.

## MAJOR HISTORICAL THEMES

The stress concept has its origins in medicine and physiology. Walter B. Cannon hypothesized the existence of the stress response circa 1915 based on his physiological research. He first called it "the emergency response" (Benison, Barger, & Wolfe, 1987) and then the stress response, distinguishing stress from strain (Cannon, 1935). Cannon's primary interest was in the sympathetic nervous system components of the stress response as well as the central role of emotions, especially "the fighting emotions" as he called them, in triggering the stress response (Cannon, 1915/1929). Selye (1976) was the physician scientist most closely associated with the stress concept based on his extensive endocrine (hormone) system research and his explication of stress's role in the diseases of maladaption and adverse health effects. The combined research of these two physician scientists, both rooted in the earlier research of Claude Bernard, framed our basic understanding of the psychophysiology of stress (Rosch, 2001a).

The second half of the 20th century saw the proliferation of theories of organizational stress by a wide range of social psychologists, industrial engineers, sociologists, and organizational behaviorists. Cooper (1998b) presented 10 leading theories, which range from narrowly defined theories of specialized aspects of stress or strain such as burnout, the sojourner, and control, to more robust theories with broader applicability in the workplace. We focus on the latter theories and review the person–environment fit model, the managerial stress and psychosocial model, the demand–control model, the effort–reward model, and the preventive stress management model. In addition, we consider measures of workplace stress and finally, the issue of healthy and productive work.

## Organizational Stress and Person–Environment Fit

Kahn et al. (1964) were the first to bring the stress concept into an organizational and work context with their seminal studies in role conflict and ambiguity. The original studies were concerned with the nature, causes, and consequences of these two kinds of organizational stress and, more broadly, with the impact of organization on individual. This social psychological adaptation of the stress concept in organizations focused attention on the stressful aspects of role taking in organizations and was extended into a person–environment fit approach to stress (Edwards & Cooper, 1990). In a more recent review of two competing versions of the person–environment fit approach, Edwards (1996) drew complimentary conclusions from impact of the two versions on strain. In both versions, person–environment fit was related to two forms of strain, which were tension and dissatisfaction. Further, the fit between environmental supplies and employee values (S–V fit) was primarily linked to dissatisfaction, whereas the fit between environmental demands and employee abilities (D–A fit) was primarily linked to tension. Quick, Nelson, Quick, and Orman (2001) extended the person–environment fit approach with an isomorphic theory of stress that examines dynamic effect spirals for improving fit and reducing strain.

## Managerial Stress, Psychosocial Factors, and Preventive Medicine

Cooper and Marshall (1978) went beyond the problems of role conflict and ambiguity to focus attention on the additional sources of stress for managers in complex industrial organizations. Their expanded model of sources of managerial stress shown in Fig. 2.1 includes factors intrinsic to the job, career development, organizational structure and climate, interpersonal relations at work, and factors outside the organization, such as family demands, which have spillover effects into the workplace. This approach to organizational stress goes well beyond physical sources of stress and iden-

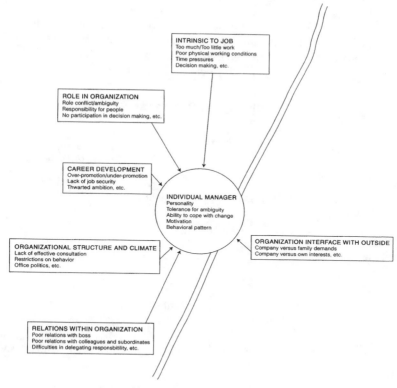

FIG. 2.1   Sources of Managerial Stress. Note: From "Sources of Managerial and White Collar Stress," by C. L. Cooper and J. Marshall, in *Stress at Work* (p. 83), by C. L. Cooper and R. Payne (Eds.), Copyright © 1978 by John Wiley & Sons Limited: Chichester, England. Reprinted with permission.

tifies a wide range of psychosocial demands of the workplace, which are contributing sources of stress for managerial and white collar employees.

From a complimentary framework, Levi (1979) examined stress and stress reactions in the context of an ecological model of psychosocial factors and health for the U.S. Surgeon General. Levi gave important consideration to high-risk situations, high-risk groups, and high-risk reactions, showing how psychosocial factors can lead to disease. He brought special attention to life change events and to psychosocial factors in hypertension and cardiovascular diseases. Levi proposed that preventive medicine offers an intervention approach for ameliorating the adverse effects of these psychosocial factors. Thus, medical, psychological, and organizational research had established by the 1970s that workplace stress factors were potential health risks for people in organizations.

## The Demands–Control Model

A major theory of job stress that developed during this same time period came to be known most commonly as the demands–control model shown in Fig. 2.2. Jobs in the high-strain cell in the model are characterized by high job demands combined with low job decision latitude (low control) and pose

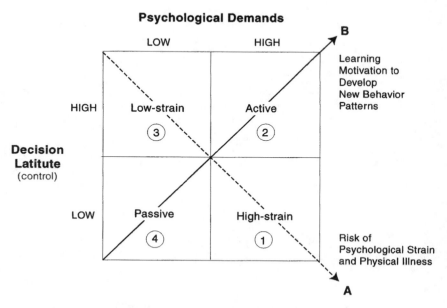

FIG. 2.2   Demands–control model of work stress. From "Current Issues Relating to Psychosocial Job Strain and Cardiovascular Disease Research," by T. Theorell and R. A. Karasek, 1996, *Journal of Occupational Health Psychology, 1,* p. 11. Reprinted with permission.

the greatest health risk for job incumbents. The original health risks identified were exhaustion, depression, job and life dissatisfaction, illness days, and elevated consumption of tranquilizers and sleeping pills (Karasek, 1979). Subsequent research on the demand–control model has focused on the cardiovascular risks associated with high strain job (Karasek et al., 1988; Theorell & Karasek, 1996). A third dimension that is sometimes added to this model is social support. House (1981) was the first to extensively explore the issue of social support in the context of work stress. More recently, Lynch (2000) examined the extensive medical and psychological evidence concerning the health risks associated with social isolation.

## The Effort–Reward Model

From a medical sociological perspective, Siegrist (1996) argued that the exchanges in work life between the individual and the organization should be balanced and reciprocal in nature. Specifically, he suggested that occupational groups who experience lower levels of status control are more likely to have high incidence of high effort–low reward (or, high-cost/low-gain) imbalance, leading to higher stress and strain as indicated in Fig. 2.3. Other research suggests that worker compensation stress claims are the result of an imbalance between the needs of employees and the demands of the organization (Woodburn & Simpson, 1994). Finally, this sociological view is consistent with well-established research on the effects of socioeconomic status. Specifically, Adler, Boyce, Chesney, Folkman, and Syme (1993) found that those at the bottom of the socioeconomic status ladder have the highest incidence of morbidity and mortality.

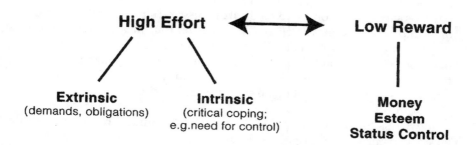

FIG. 2.3 Effort–reward model of work stress. From "Adverse Health Effects of High-Effort/Low-Reward Conditions," by J. Siegrist, 1996, *Journal of Occupational Health Psychology, 1,* p. 30. Reprinted with permission.

## Preventive Stress Management

Prevention is always the best public health strategy for any disease epidemic. If job stress is in fact a health epidemic, then prevention holds the best hope for addressing this epidemic (Elkin & Rosch, 1990; Quick, Quick, Nelson, & Hurrell, 1997; Quick & Tetrick, 2003). The theory of preventive stress management is based on translating the public health notions of prevention into an organizational context and overlaying them on a stress process model as shown in Fig. 2.4 (Quick, Nelson, & Quick, 1998). The prevention strategies in the figure are classified into primary, secondary, and tertiary. Primary prevention aims to modify and manage the demands of the work environment. Secondary prevention aims to modify and manage the individual's response to these demands. Tertiary prevention aims to help and provide aid to those in frank distress. From a public health perspective, primary prevention is always the preferred point of intervention. This implies for workplace stress and health that job redesign efforts and other interventions that alter, modify, or eliminate stressful work conditions are the preferred category of stress management program (Quick, Nelson, & Simmons, 2000; Quick & Quick, 1997).

## Stress Measures in the Workplace

Assessment and surveillance activities are a second distinguishing feature of the public health notions of prevention. That is, preventive intervention is based on diagnostic information developed by the measurement of stress in the workplace. Valid, reliable stress measurement requires multiple psychological, environmental, and medical measurements (Quick, Quick, & Gavin, 2000). Stress instruments fall into four construct categories. These are measures of (a) environmental demands and sources of stress; (b) healthy, normal stress response; (c) modifiers of the stress response; and (d) psychological, behavioral, and medical distress and strain. For the purposes of workplace stress measurement, we focus on four measures that offer a range of construct assessment. For a more clinical assessment of organizational stress, Levinson's (in press) classic approach to organizational diagnosis is an excellent resource. Hurrell, Nelson, and Simmons (1998) critically reviewed the measurement of job stressors and strain.

*Job Stress Survey (JSS).*    Spielberger (1994) found job pressure and lack of organizational support as the two primary sources of job stress of a wide range of employees in diverse occupations. The JSS measures the severity and the frequency of 30 different job demands. Examples from the JSS scale items are "excessive paperwork" and "poorly motivated co-workers." Severity and frequency scores are also computed for 10-item

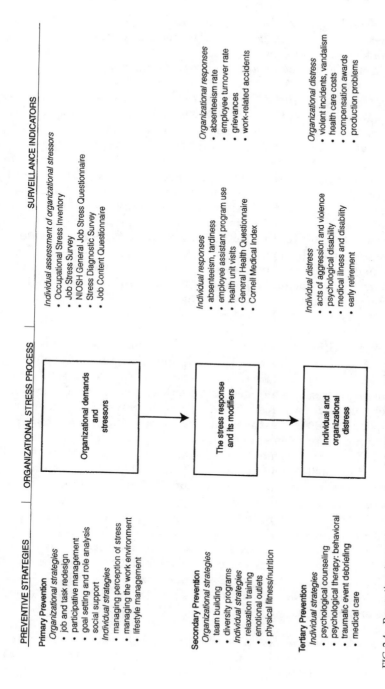

FIG. 2.4   Preventive stress management model. Adapted from "The Theory of Preventive Stress Management in Organizations," by J. D. Quick, J. C. Quick, and D. L. Nelson, in *Theories of Organizational Stress* (p. 259), by C. L. Cooper (Ed.), 1998, Oxford, England: Oxford University Press. Reprinted with permission.

Job Pressure and Organizational Support subscales that were factor analytically derived from the 30 JSS items. The subscales show considerable internal consistency and subsequent testing of the JSS consistently finds these two factors across work contexts (Vagg & Spielberger, 1998).

*NIOSH Generic Job Stress Questionnaire.* The Generic Job Stress Questionnaire (Hurrell & McLaney, 1988) was developed by the NIOSH and contains measures of 13 different job stressors as well as a host of measures of individual distress and modifiers of the stress response. The questionnaire assesses constructs within domains contained in the NIOSH job stress model (Hurrell & Murphy, 1992). Specific stressor, distress, and modifier variable constructs were selected for conclusion in the instrument on the basis of a content analysis of the job stress literature and the scales selected to measure these constructs were adapted from scales with known reliability and validity. The instrument was designed to be modular in form so that the diagnostician or stress researcher can select individual scales, or the entire instrument can be used. Various investigators into a variety of languages (including Japanese and Finnish) have translated the questionnaire and normative data on the questionnaire are currently being gathered.

*Occupational Stress Inventory (OSI).* The OSI measures three domains of adjustment: occupational stress, personal strain, and coping resources (Osipow & Davis, 1988; Osipow & Spokane, 1992). Six occupational stress scales measure role overload, role insufficiency, role ambiguity, role boundary, responsibility, and the physical environment. Four personal strain scales measure vocational strain, psychological and/or emotional problems, interpersonal problems, and physical illnesses. Four coping scales measure recreational activities, self-care, social support, and rational/cognitive coping. Plotting standardized scores on each of the 14 scales procedures a "stress profile" for an individual manager or executive, or can be used to develop organizational profiles as shown in Fig. 2.5. The figure shows stress, strain, and coping profiles in five U.S. Air Force organizations, two of which are large industrial maintenance depots (AFMC—Air Force Materiel Command), two of which are pilot training units (AETC—Air Education and Training Command), and one of which is a combat unit (ACC—Air Combat Command). The most notable differences are in occupational stress and individual strain among these five organizations.

*Pressure Management Indicator (PMI).* The PMI is a measure developed from the earlier Occupational Stress Indicator (OSI) and based on the Cooper and Marshall (1978) stress model. The PMI is used increasingly as a

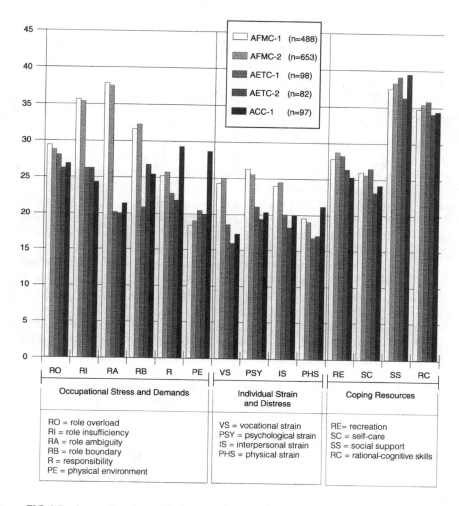

FIG. 2.5   Occupational stress in five U.S. Air Force organizations. From J. A. Adkins, Lieutenant Colonel, USAF, BSC, courtesy of the United States Air Force.

diagnostic instrument in Europe, and is more reliable, more comprehensive, and shorter than the OSI (Cooper, Sloan, & Williams, 1988; Williams & Cooper, 1998). The PMI measures sources of pressure, such as workload, relationships, work–home balance, and daily hassles; individual differences, such as Type A behavior/drive, locus of control, and social support; and job stress effects, such as job satisfaction, security, mental health, and physical symptoms.

## Healthy and Productive Work

A less historically well-known theme in workplace stress, health, and well-being is that of healthy organizations. Maslow called for healthy work environments as early as the 1960s, whereas Murphy and Cooper (2000) presented the most recent definition and evidence concerning healthy and productive work. Much happened in the intervening 40 years. An international tradition aimed at defining and encouraging the healthy workplace design through the identification of physical and psychosocial health risk factors coupled with redesign interventions to enhance mental health and psychological well-being grew up in that time (Hurrell & Murphy, 1992; Quick, Murphy, & Hurrell, 1992; Sauter, Murphy, & Hurrell, 1990). The APA and NIOSH, through a cooperative agreement, stimulated these initiatives with a three-pronged strategy for healthy workplace design, health promotion at work, and surveillance of health risks (Landy, Quick, & Kasl, 1994).

Whereas this perspective focuses attention on attributes of the organization, individual characteristics cannot be ignored because some are inherently unhealthy. For example, Von Dusch (1868) was the first to call attention to excessive involvement in work as a health risk factor for cardiovascular problems. Rosenman and Friedman (1977) labeled this Type A behavior pattern 100 years later and Rosenman (1996) explored in detail the role of personality and behavior in cardiovascular disease. This view is broadly consistent with Lazarus's (1995) psychological theory of work stress and with Levinson's (1985) psychoanalytic theory of executive stress. These theories of stress look to the individual and the individual's responses to explain the experience of stress, at work and beyond.

## CURRENT STATE OF AFFAIRS

There is good news and bad news in the current state of affairs. The good news is that our knowledge of stress management strategies, both what organizations can do and what individuals can do, has expanded steadily over the past 50 years. The tools and techniques available for managing workplace stress in healthy and productive ways have expanded and are more broadly understood by managers and employees alike. The bad news is that workplace stress has shifted and increased, as previously noted. Global competition has increased the pressures on organizations and individuals, resulting in a variety of changes in the workplace, both in the United States and Europe. This has important implications for people's health and for the management of risks. However, positive structures, roles, and processes are emerging to help.

## Global Competition: A New Reality

Global competition is creating a new organizational reality on the industrial landscape that is, in many cases, driving up work stress and creating health risks for people at work (Gowing, Kraft, & Quick, 1998). Organizations and businesses are facing increasingly competitive environments that place employees at risk of obsolescence, job loss, and adverse health systems, processes, and structures to support employees in meeting the ever-increasing challenges that both individuals and organizations face in the present economic climate. Pressure and change are watchwords resulting from the global competition. Thus, work life is changing in the United States and Europe (Lawler, 1996). Change is often experienced as a threat to well-being or survival (Staw, Sandelands, & Dutton, 1981). As a result of this predisposition to experience change as a threat, individuals, groups, and organizations often respond with well-learned responses that may not be appropriate to the changed reality. The tension and rigidity occasioned by these stressful times sap competence, capability, and productivity as energy and resources are committed to defense, not achievement or accomplishment. Hence, "threat-rigidity effects" emerge.

Seen as a threat, change carries with it the fear of impending loss and of costs for individuals and organizations. Hobfoll's (2001) conservation of resources theory of stress clearly suggests that the experience of loss contributes most to a person's experience of stress. Organizational strategies to guard against loss often include mergers and acquisitions, or employment or asset downsizing. Both strategies enhance a sense of managerial and executive control coupled, with placing many employees on the defensive. Thus, employees become less open to new information and management controls behavior more strictly. This cycle of defensiveness and rigidity may well be counterproductive in the face of the new organizational reality.

*Mergers & Acquisitions.* Marks (1994) coined the phrase "organizational MADness," referring to the impact of mergers, acquisitions, and downsizing that result in a fearful, suspicious, and cynical workforce. In addition to global competition, several other forces lead to MADness: government deregulation, technological change, total quality management (TQM) or other reengineering movements, delayering, broader economic conditions, and corporate rationalization.

Earlier, Marks and Mirvis (1985b) found the merger syndrome, a defensive, "fear-the-worst" response, to be a common response to the uncertainty and stress of a merger. Those at the top of the acquired organization report disbelief, uncertainty, fear, and stress. Lower level employees circulate rumors of mass layoffs and forced relocations, pay freezes, loss of benefits, and plant closings. Fear of job loss after a merger or acquisition was the top-ranked worry of 54% of the senior executives in the 1,000 largest U.S. companies; the second most common worry was burnout, reported by 26% of the executives (Robert Half International, 1991). These concerns are not limited to hostile takeovers. Crisis management should be the order of the day (Marks & Mirvis, 1985a). Instead of managing crises, senior managers too often seal themselves off, become less accessible, and limit their lines of communication, leaving their staff uninformed about the changes in the organization.

Merger syndrome is manifested by increased centralization and decreased communication that leaves employees in the dark about what is happening in the merger. Rumors are fueled by this communication breakdown. In addition, employees focus on worst-case scenarios and become preoccupied with the merger. The result is that employees are distracted, productivity decreases, and key people leave the company. One *Wall Street Journal* survey found that nearly 50% of executives in acquired firms seek other jobs within 1 year and another 25% plan to leave within 3 years.

*Downsizing.*    The early 1990s began a process of economic slowdown, plant closings and layoffs, and budget cutbacks. This mood of austerity affected private and public sector organizations alike. More organizations are working toward balanced budgets and fiscal responsibility; they are becoming "leaner and meaner" (Hirschhorn, 1983; Levine, 1980).

Leana and Feldman (1992) focused on layoffs. Several institutions play a role in how layoffs are implemented: companies, unions, and provincial and federal regulations. Other people are affected besides those laid off: spouses, children, parents, friends, and co-workers. Although about 2.5 million jobs were lost each year during the early 1980s in the United States, most of these blue collar, a different pattern has followed that period. Over one third of Fortune 1000 companies reduced their workforces 10% each year. They were reducing their workforces not because the company was losing money, but because they aimed to increase productivity and cut costs. Hourly workers in manufacturing still are the hardest hit, suffering about 50% of the job losses; the rest are spread fairly evenly over the other organizational levels. The downsizing that continued through the 1990s as a strategy to increase profitability and financial strength has not achieved that objective (Morris, Cascio, & Young, 1999). White collar workers were as vulnerable as blue collar workers. Job loss continues to be a problem and may even worsen.

Cascio (1993) drew two conclusions from his extensive work on downsizing. First, downsizing continues as long as overhead costs remain noncompetitive with domestic and international rivals. Second, there were risks for the employer, for former employees, and for employees who stayed on the job, which needed to be addressed.

## The Changing Workplace

While new technologies were transforming workplaces prior to the current era of global competition, the post-Berlin Wall period that ushered in this highly stressful period of international competition has led to a transformation of managerial roles, employee attitudes, working hours, work–life balance, and the psychological contract between the individual and the organization (Cooper, 1998a, 1999). John Chain, former Commander-in-Chief of the U.S. Air Force's Strategic Air Command, suggested that one had to reach back to the time of Martin Luther to find a time in Western history with the potential for such sweeping and dramatic change. Thus, the current period is characterized by a major restructuring of work such as has never been known since the Industrial Revolution. The result has been smaller organizations, with fewer people doing more and feeling much less secure.

*Managerial Roles.*   To examine the changes in the nature of managerial work and organizational life, Cooper (1998a) asked managers about the changes they had experienced in the last 2 years. Recent views see managerial work as becoming more "intensive" due to changes in organizational structures and increasing task fragmentation. When surveyed, managers indicated that the nature of the work they do and the demands placed on them had changed considerably and in a majority of cases they had little training to help them cope with these changes. The key findings were that:

- 82% of managers noted the proliferation in the amount of information that they now have to deal with.
- 76% identified that their reliance on interpersonal skills had become more important as management by the use of positional authority had become far more difficult.
- 60% said they were spending far more time dealing with organizational politics.
- 60% thought that their jobs had become more fragmented.

Observations from respondents about the way that change had been implemented referred to the naïve use of approaches such as delayering which "takes out" a layer of managers but rarely "takes out" the work they do. This creates role overload, increased task fragmentation, and reduced role clarity among the remaining managers. The impact of restructuring that is cost-driven change seems to have increased managerial overload and to have put managers under even more pressure. Not surprisingly, this usually results in them having to work very long hours.

*Employee Attitudes.*    A longitudinal study conducted in the United Kingdom from 1996 through 2000 found persistently high levels of change (Worrall & Cooper, 1997, 1998, 1999, 2001). Worrall and Cooper found that when organizational change is badly managed, the stressful and negative impact on managers is increased. In 47% of cases, managers who had been affected by restructuring did not think that the reasons for restructuring had been clearly communicated to them. In only 20% of cases did managers feel that they had been involved at all in the decision-making process about restructuring. Consequently, and particularly in privately held companies, restructuring is something that managers feel is done to them rather than something that is done with them. It is not surprising that these managers have often felt a heightened sense of powerlessness in their organizations as a direct result of badly managed organizational change. Restructuring has had a major negative impact on managers' sense of loyalty to their organization, their morale, their motivation, and their perceptions of just how secure their job really is.

The managers surveyed said that organizational change has "decreased" their loyalty, morale, motivation, and sense of job security since the mid-1990s. The negative impact of organizational change was greatest on managers' morale (64% said decreased), although this is followed closely by its impact on managers' sense of job security (60% said decreased). The impact of change on managers' motivation and loyalty (53% and 49% saying decreased respectively) is also marked. The changing workplace has both increased the level of stress for managers and had an adverse impact on their morale and attitudes.

*Working Hours.*    Another way in which the workplace has changed as a result of the global competition is in terms of working hours (Worrall & Cooper, 2000). In both the United States and the United Kingdom, working hours have been trending up through the late 1990s, and the British have very long working hours as compared to their European partners. However, productivity in the United Kingdom remains below that achieved in other European countries. In 2000, 40% of United Kingdom managers work in excess of 50 hours a week but that varies considerably by organizational level. Whereas 62% of senior executives work over 50 hours per week, only 24% of junior managers do the same.

In an average day, 91% of managers work longer than their contract hours with 28% working up to an hour over their contract and 28% working more than 2 hours over their contracted hours. There is a clear relationship between hours worked over contract and seniority, with 35% of directors and above working 2 hours a day over their contract hours, ranging down to 16% of junior managers. When analyzed by sector, managers in the public sector were less likely to work 2 hours or more over contract in an average day than managers in other sectors. In the public sector, 37% of managers claimed to be working over 2 hours per day over contract compared to 50% of managers in incorporated organizations.

*Work/Life Balance.* Work/life imbalance is a major source of stress for an important segment of the workforces in the United States and the United Kingdom. However, fewer managers are saying that work is more important than home, although this also varies by organizational level. In 1999 and 2000, 12% of managers thought that work was more important than home, down from 16% in 1997. Although 45% of junior managers see work as less important than home, this declines to around 24% for directors and above (Worrall & Cooper, 1997, 1999, 2000). Managers are still very conscious of the adverse effects that working long hours has on their relationships with their partners and children, their health, and their social lives. For all managers, 65% think that the amount of work they do has an adverse effect on their health and 72% think that it affects their relationship with their partner.

*The Psychological Contract.* As more organizations continue to experiment with outsource and market-test (in the case of the public sector), and utilize "interim management" and the like, more employees are selling their services to organizations on a freelance or short-term contract basis (Cooper, 1999). This creates a corporate culture of blue collar, white collar, managerial, and professional temps, or in other words, a "contingent workforce." In the United Kingdom, for example, more than one in eight workers are self-employed. Part-time work and the perception of people that they are on short-term contracts are growing faster than permanent full-time work. The number of men in part-time jobs has nearly doubled in the past decade, whereas the number of people employed by firms of more than 500 employees has slumped to just over one third of the employed population. These trends may foreshadow future organizations, organizations with only a small core of full-time, permanent employees working from a conventional office that buy most of the skills they need on a contract basis, either from individuals working at home or linked to the company by computers and modems (teleworking), or by hiring people on short-term contracts to do specific jobs or to carry out specific projects. Although companies can maintain the flexibility they need to cope with rapid market and economic changes (Cooper & Jackson, 1997; Handy, 1994; Makin, Cooper, & Cox, 1996), the health and well-being implications of this for individuals are not at all clear. However, managers and employees alike are experiencing increased job insecurity, lowered morale, and the erosion of motivation and loyalty.

## Health Implications

All of these changes in the workplace resulting from global competition and industrial restructuring have important and stressful effects on people at work, and place them at risk in terms of their health. The research on the stress and health effects of life change events has a very long history anchored in the early research of Adolph Meyer at Johns Hopkins Medical School on life charts (Winters, 1952). Holmes and Rahe took Meyer's core ideas of marking major life changes and major illnesses on life charts and formulated a scale for examining the health risks associated with life change events. This line of research found that individuals were at risk from 12 to 18 months following a major life change event. Rahe's (1994) subsequent research has found a pattern paralleling changes described in the changing workplace. Specifically, the number and severity of life change events has increased 40% over the past several decades. This systemic view of stress and health is consistent with Cannon's earlier formulations.

Cannon's (1935) concept of homeostasis states that people are designed for physiological balance and that when they experience stress, they are thrown out of balance. The imbalance from stressful events creates increased vulnerability, the potential for effortful compensation, and risk of functional problems. The immune system of the body also helps to safeguard the inner physiology. An organizational parallel to the immune system requires identifying vulnerabilities and available resources for fending off risks and threats, and then building behavioral inoculation programs around the resources and deficiencies. Three positive examples of helpful new tools for these stressful times include a structural innovation, a role innovation, and a process innovation. The structural innovation is the concept of an organizational health center, the role innovation is the concept of a chief psychological officer, and the process innovation is Schein's concept of organizational therapy.

*The Organizational Health Center.*   Adkins (1999) designed and implemented the concept of an organizational health center (OHC) in the U.S. Air Force as a structural mechanism for enhancing health and managing stress. The mission of the OHC was to maximize physical, psychological, behavioral, and organizational health by applying behavioral science technology to a workplace setting. Adkins's systemic organizational health program implemented the four strategies for reducing psychological disorders at work, as proposed by stress researchers at NIOSH (Sauter et al., 1990). This was possible because the OHC director worked directly for the chief executive officer (CEO). First, organizational change was managed using community resources, team building, and management coaching. Second, information, education, and communication for workers were enhanced through training and prevention programs, such as for workplace violence and suicide prevention. Third, enriched psychological services were provided through worksite-oriented support programs such as employee assistance, worksite wellness, and peer counseling. Fourth, surveillance and monitoring were done by collecting and reporting of indicator data.

The OHC director functioned as an internal consultant with the responsibility of looking after the health care of the organization as a whole rather than being identified with any single group—management or labor—within the organization. A 1-year evaluation found: (a) workers' compensation rates declined by 3.9%, following a 4.6% increase the previous year, exceeding the management-established goal of a 3% reduction and saving over $289,000 in workers' compensation costs; (b) health care utilization rates declined by 12%, yielding a saving of over $150,000 in recaptured productivity alone; and (c) deaths resulting from behavioral problems, including suicides, declined by 41%, resulting in cost savings of over $4 million.

*Chief Psychological Officer.* The OHC director worked directly for the CEO and therefore functioned much as a chief psychological officer (CPO) for the organization. The role of CPO is an innovative new role with important potential for the stress, health, and well-being of people at work. Organizations often have many chiefs: CEO, chief operational officer (COO), chief financial officer (CFO), and chief information officer (CIO). These officers are responsible for the critical resources and processes that influence the health of the organization. People may be the most important resource in any organization, especially in the information age. Yet responsibility for their support and development is often dispersed to functions such as personnel and human resources, the medical department, employee assistance programs (EAPs) for counseling and psychotherapy, and possibly an industrial chaplainry for their spiritual needs.

The role of CPO was crafted in the realignment and closure of the U.S. Air Force's largest industrial maintenance depot at Kelly Air Force Base, Texas (Quick 1997, Quick & Klunder, 2000). The process that led to this position began in July 1995 when the Base Realignment and Closure Commission recommended to U.S. President Bill Clinton the realignment and/or closure of a number of domestic military installations. The San Antonio Air Logistics Center was one of the military installations on the realignment and/or closure list. The industrial restructuring process affected the largest number of federal employees in U.S. history. The San Antonio Air Logistics Center at Kelly Air Force Base, Texas was the largest industrial employer in South Texas and one of the largest industrial facilities in the Department of Defense. An active duty U.S. Air Force psychologist was recruited to serve the commanding general/CEO as his organizational clinical psychologist; in essence, the CPO for the organization, responsible for the mental health and well-being of a workforce of 13,000 executives, managers, and employees. He initiated a Transition Life Advisor Program that deployed eight clinical social workers into major industrial areas that had been targeted for closure or realignment to deal with individuals identified as chronically most in need.

During the 6-year privatization and realignment process, which ended July 13, 2001, the San Antonio Air Logistics Center experienced some very positive results during very difficult times. There are three positive indicators in this regard. First, there has not been a single closure-related fatality in the organization during the closure, and only one psychiatrically related suicide. Although there was a significant decline in suicide rates throughout the Air Force, as reported by the Centers for Disease Control and Prevention for the period 1995 to 1999, the experience at Kelly is still noteworthy in this regard. Second, there were no incidences of workplace violence during the 6-year period. One FBI estimate indicates that 85% or more of workplace violence is preventable because stress often serves as the triggering event for the violence (Mack, Shannon, Quick, & Quick, 1998). Third, there was a cost avoidance of approximately $33 million during the 6-year period based on equal employment office estimates of complaints that did not happen. The Air Force estimates each employee complaint at a cost of about $80,000 to process, all costs considered. Using this case estimator and the number of cases expected during this period, civilian personnel found the number of cases to be approximately 25% below their estimate. Hence, a significant cost avoidance and savings resulted. The leadership's concern for people's health and well-being did not come at the expense of performance, where the Center continued to excel (Steely, 1999).

*Organizational Therapy.*   Schein is innovating a process of organizational therapy as a means for addressing the endemic stress and strain of work life (Quick & Gavin, 2000). Whereas prevention is always preferred from a public health perspective, tertiary prevention is essentially treatment intervention or therapy. During the process of managing the stress of an expanding business worldwide, ICI-Zeneca designed and implemented a six-level stress management strategy, the first level of which was to treat stress casualties (Teasdale & McKeown, 1994). The last level in the company's strategy was to improve the organizational culture. Schein suggested that an evolving practice of organizational therapy is needed to help organizations heal. Healthy organizations need to have natural homeopathic agents and immune systems that metabolize the stress, strain, and pain found in the workplace.

Organizational therapy is needed as one more approach to manage the stress and strain of organizational life. Frost and Robertson (1999) were concerned with the toxins and emotional pain, which are all too often endemic to organizational life. Their concern was for those who serve as therapeutic agents in organizations to metabolize and neutralize these toxins and emotional pain, often at the risk of their own health and well-being. They labeled those individuals who serve this therapeutic function as organizational heroes even though they have no formal organizational roles for engaging in their therapeutic and curative activities. Hence, organizational heroes are different from CPOs who have both formal roles and clinical training.

## Legal Liability and Risk Assessment

Ivancevich, Matteson, and Richards (1985) were among the first to express concern for the legal liability organizations were exposed to for workplace stress. Their approach was to formulate a preventive law strategy, develop a stress diagnostic system, involve top-level management, evaluate current programs, and document what was done. Litigation is costly on a number of dimensions, even for the "winners." For example, Frank S. Deux won a $1.5 million judgment against Allstate Insurance Company for job strain in a federal court (civil action no. 88–2099, U.S. District Court, Western District of Louisiana), only to have the judge vacate the judgment. The 2 years or more of litigation, trial, and appeals all carried emotional, material, and psychological costs for Deux and for Allstate Insurance Company. This is an increasingly important issue within the United Kingdom.

*Legal Issues.* The business costs of stress in the workplace are well established, as in the large-scale survey that found 19.5 million working days were lost in the United Kingdom during 1995 due to work-related illness, with by far the largest category of illness being "musculoskeletal, stress, anxiety, and depression" (Jones, Hodgson, Clegg, & Elliott, 1998). Organizations are experiencing an increase in personal injury claims against them, brought by employees who have suffered from the adverse effects of workplace stress (Earnshaw & Cooper, 1996). In the case of *Walker v. Northumberland County Council* (Industrial Relations Law Reports, 1995), an employee brought a claim against his employer because he had suffered a nervous breakdown as a result of the stress of an excessive workload. The case was settled out of court, but a more recent case was not. In the case of *Lancaster v. Birmingham City Council,* the employer admitted liability for the stress-related illness suffered by an employee and she was awarded damages by the court. In response to such developments, the U.K. Health and

Safety Executive (HSE) issued a discussion document prompting debate on the management of stress at work (HSE, 1999).

*Risk Assessment.* Recent years have seen a proliferation in legislation requiring employers to conduct risk assessments of their operations. In the United Kingdom, this includes the Control of Substances Hazardous to Health (COSHH) Regulations (1988/1994) and the Management of Health and Safety at Work Regulations (MHSWR, 1992). Whereas the current legislation focuses on physical hazards, such as chemicals, asbestos, use of display screen equipment, and so on, the emphasis has recently shifted to the risk associated with occupational stress (HSE, 1999). Employers are becoming increasingly aware that they must assess the risk posed by workplace stress and take adequate measures to control that risk—both to avoid business loss (including compensation claims) and to ensure a healthy workforce. There is good evidence linking the experience of occupational stress with serious psychiatric harm and physical disease, such as coronary heart disease (Cooper, 1996). There is growing evidence to support the effectiveness of organizational stress interventions, such as EAPs, in mitigating the experience of workplace stress (Berridge, Cooper, & Highley-Marchington, 1997). For example, Cooper and Sadri (1991) found that an in-house stress counseling program in a large organization reduced absenteeism by 60% in 1 year. This was later substantially confirmed in a study of a number of external EAPs (Highley-Marchington & Cooper, 1998).

*Risk Management.* A Royal Society Study Group (1992) that aimed to produce a multiscience approach to risk management highlighted instead the conflicting perspectives and the lack of a common understanding of risk. Many definitions of risk and alternative approaches to risk management exist (Rowe, 1990; Singleton & Hovden, 1987). Although there is no universally accepted definition of risk, Warner (1992), in the Introduction to the Royal Society report, argued that the term refers to "a combination of the probability, or frequency, of occurrence of a defined hazard and the magnitude of the consequences of the occurrence" (p. 4). A hazard might be understood as "the potential to cause harm," whereas a risk is "the likelihood of that potential being realized" in a given period of time (Health & Safety Commission, 1991, p. 41). Reflecting this understanding, a risk can be conceptualized as having two basic elements, one relating to the probability that an event, decision, or activity will have undesirable negative outcomes, and the other relating to the severity of those outcomes (Glendon & McKenna, 1995, p. 320).

In the United Kingdom, companies have a legal obligation to undertake risk assessments of their operations under MHSWR (1992) and other legislation. Risk assessment involves both hazard identification and risk evaluation and has been defined as a "process of estimating the probability and size of possible outcomes, and then evaluating the alternative courses of action" (Wharton, 1992, p. 7). The primary purpose of risk assessment is to determine the extent to which existing, or planned, control measures are satisfactory or need to be improved (Booth, 1993). Methods of risk assessment derive an estimate of the level of risk, or a risk rating, for a hazard. This is commonly achieved by estimating the probability of an event, the severity of the consequences, and the frequency of exposure; these figures (which may be based on subjective judgment) are multiplied together to give the risk level (see, e.g., Kazer, 1992; Steel, 1990; Waring, 1996). Events with severe consequences must be very rare, and very frequent events must have low consequences for the resultant level of risk to be acceptable. Frequent events with severe consequences represent an unacceptable risk. In an example cited by Waring (1996), a manufacturing plant identified the use of ethoxol as a hazard (this is a respiratory irritant and narcotic); the frequency of exposure was high as it is airborne, and levels varied between areas of the plant; the consequences were also high as the U.K. HSE has set maximum exposure limits that were exceeded in some areas. Using this simple formula, the risk would be assessed as unacceptably high and, if ethoxol could not be eliminated from the manufacturing process, risk control measures would have to be implemented to reduce exposure; for example, changes in handling procedures or a "no smoking/no eating" ban should be introduced in high-exposure areas.

## FUTURE RESEARCH AND THEORY

Researchers have made landmark contributions to our knowledge of work stress and health in the second half of the 20th century, and especially in the past decade. A shift is now called for from managing risks and vulnerabilities to emphasizing the positive and looking for sources of strength and resilience among individuals, which are important themes for the future. There remain many fruitful avenues for theory development and research along these lines. Three of these avenues are self-reliance, executive health, and eustress. Self-reliance is a positive pattern of relationship formation, and a source of strength both in personal and work life. Executives are role models for others in organizations, and the more we know about their health, the more we can lift them up as models for staying healthy under stress. The positive face of stress, eustress, can help us determine ways to make the workplace healthier and a source of greater fulfillment for individuals.

## Self-Reliance

We are in a new age of self-reliance in which people at work need fallback positions as alternatives to the work environment and the security of their workplace. This fundamental unpredictability and insecurity of future workplaces creates endemic stress, for which people must learn new and different coping and prevention strategies. Researchers have described self-reliance in various, but complementary, ways. All of these conceptualizations reveal self-reliance as a source of strength. Levinson (1996), for example, in a follow-up to his classic article "When Executives Burn Out," noted that his basic assumption that leaders take action to prevent stress seemed outdated. Because of increasing stress from increased competition among organizations and the related reengineering and downsizings, employees no longer looked to employers for support. Instead, Levinson suggested that they look to themselves in what he termed "a new age of self-reliance." Looking inside the self is the fallback position should the job fail the individual. Specific competencies and skills can become outdated, he argued, such that individuals must focus not on what they do but on who they are. By acting on who the individual truly is, he or she experiences less stress because the work and true selves are integrated. Individuals thus express self-reliance by understanding their most characteristic behaviors, and by enacting these behaviors in the workplace, and this in turn leads to less stress and more security.

Frese (1997) proposed that self-reliance is the ability to acquire knowledge and skills by oneself and to motivate oneself. He contended that self-reliance is dynamic, and requires a long-term orientation. It is an umbrella term for self-training and initiative, and the need for it stems from the changing nature of work. Increased competition and complexity, and trends toward working outside traditional organizational structures, increasingly require employees to take responsibility for their own learning and motivation. Hence, Frese's concept of self-reliance focuses on mastery and task performance skills. His is a concept of personal renewal through enhanced skill development and performance improvement.

Our own research on self-reliance is complementary to Frese's concept by focusing more attention to the interpersonal and interdependent aspects of self-reliance. Our ideas stem from the pioneering work of Ainsworth and Bowlby (1991), who examined infants' interactions with their primary caregivers to determine infants' characteristic patterns of early relationships. They proposed that the attachment process is a biological imperative, and that it leads to survival of the human species. Ainsworth and Bowlby saw three distinct patterns of attachment: secure (subsequently renamed self-reliant), avoidant, and anxious–ambivalent. Self-reliant patterns represent healthy and secure attachments, whereas avoidant and anxious–ambivalent patterns were insecure and unhealthy. Early childhood patterns of attachment become internal working models of relationships.

Attachment orientations persist in adulthood, and they are related to effectiveness and satisfaction at work (Hazan & Shaver, 1990). In the management literature, the attachment orientations are labeled self-reliant (secure), counterdependent (avoidant), and overdependent (anxious–ambivalent; Nelson, Quick, & Joplin, 1991). Adults who are self-reliant form close and supportive relationships with others both inside and outside the organization. Their secure internal working model leads to the formation of flexible, interdependent relationships with others. They are comfortable working alone, or asking for assistance from others, as each situation demands. Self-reliant individuals report fewer symptoms of distress, and are better able to develop the social supports needed for effective performance at work (Nelson, Quick, & Simmons, 2001).

The two insecure attachment patterns may lead to negative outcomes. Counterdependent individuals, for example, may overinvest in work, and are reluctant to ask for help when it is needed. They may reject offers of support, and find themselves isolated within the organization. Believing that others cannot be depended on, counterdependent people operate with the idea that it is best to depend only on oneself. Overdependent individuals often appear clingy and unable to provide support to others because of a preoccupation with their own needs. Like counterdependent individuals, overdependent people believe that others cannot be counted on. They often drain their social support providers by exhausting others' resources. Higher levels of distress symptoms and diminished well-being are reported by both counterdependent and overdependent individuals.

Self-reliance, in any of these three conceptualizations, appears to be a promising construct worthy of further exploration. It offers a way to examine a positive individual characteristic that may serve to guide individuals through distressful times in life. In particular, we need to determine ways that self-reliance can be encouraged and developed at work. How can individuals discover their own patterns of expressing who they truly are, as Levinson proposed? How can individuals take more responsibility for their own learning and motivation? How can interdependent behavior be developed in the workplace?

## Executive Health

Whereas many believe that the health of executives is something that we need not concern ourselves with given their ability to obtain the best medical care available, we recognize the central and critical role executives play in creating, enhancing, advancing, and maintaining the economic wealth of a nation. The loss of an executive, although not more morally tragic than the loss of any employee, can have a direct effect on the financial and emotional well-being of the entire company (Quick, Gavin , Cooper, & Quick, 2000). It is critical that executives and managers learn to build their strengths by maximizing their physical, psychological, spiritual, and ethical health while managing the risk that threatens their health.

The importance of executive health is becoming more apparent to everyone. This attention is demonstrated by the many centers of executive health that have begun opening around the country and the organizations that have begun sending their top managers to these centers. For example, General Motors has commissioned a major longitudinal study of 3,500 of its key executives in collaboration with four medical centers of excellence: Duke, Mass General (Harvard), Mayo Clinic, and Johns Hopkins.

*The Duke Executive Health Program.*   The Duke program has three distinguishing features, which are (a) its integration of the four major components of the comprehensive health assessment at one site, the Center for Living, within the Duke University Medical Center in Durham; North Carolina; (b) its strong practice foundation in preventive medicine, and (c) Executive Escapes. Duke's Executive Escapes are an innovative and attractive delivery mechanism for their comprehensive health assessment and intervention program. The core of Duke's preventive medicine orientation is a four-component health assessment, which is a comprehensive mind–body evaluation by physicians, clinical health psychologists, registered dieticians, and exercise physiologists. This comprehensive approach recognizes the multidimensionality of managerial and executive health while offering medical, behavioral, and psychological intervention for lifestyle change.

*What Can Organizations Do?*   Our review of the literature and evidence suggests three recommendations for organizations concerning the health of the managers and executives. These are to (a) proactively identify and manage known health risks, (b) emphasize prevention and health risk screening, and (c) encourage and endorse individual health enhancement and disorder prevention programs.

Known health risks arise in two forms, the first environmental and the second personal. There are an increasingly well-known set of health risk factors that are based in either the physical environment or the psychosocial environment. Identifying and managing known health risks is not necessarily highly complicated. Management may include simple actions such as avoidance of physical danger. For example, the CEO of a small company in the scrap metal industry who was decapitated by putting his head in a shredding machine and then telling the operator to turn it on was simply being foolhardy. However, Paul Chapparone's elaborate personal security systems are born of his experience of being held hostage as an executive in Tehran, Iran in the 1970s (Mack & Quick, in press). At a more personal level, organizations should manage the health risks of key executives, just as the federal government is systematically monitoring the health of Vice President Richard Cheney because of his known cardiovascular health risks.

Organizations can also benefit from the use of preventive medicine and public health with their managers and executives by emphasizing prevention and health risk screening. Health risk screening, which is a key basis for early intervention, is central to eliminating, correcting, and managing health problems before they cause serious or irreversible problems for a manager, executive, or the organization. Annual medical and psychological examinations or health checks make economic sense for organizations to fund on behalf of their managers and executives.

Finally, organizations can encourage a norm of health enhancement and disorder prevention plans on the part of their managers and executives. The executive culture is well attuned to the management of a portfolio of financial assets for the health and success of the enterprise. Managers and executives are accustomed to having a plan or plans for "managing the business." In a similar fashion, managers and executives should be encouraged to have a plan or plans for managing their health. The physical and psychological health are key assets for the business and, as we have previously seen, there are substantive costs and losses for the business especially when a key executive or manager is disabled or dies unexpectedly.

## Eustress: Positive Stress

The lion's share of existing stress research has focused on the prevention and resolution of the negative; that is, its focus has been on the prevention and management of distress. The emphasis has been on the negative in terms of identifying causes of distress, ways of coping with stressors, and healing the wounds of distress. Selye (1976) wrote about the importance of distinguishing between eustress (from the Greek *eu*, meaning good) and distress (from the Latin *dis* or bad). Many researchers, including Quick and Quick (1984), have acknowledged the presence of a positive form of stress, associating it with good health and high performance. Edwards and Cooper (1990) emphasized that eustress is not simply the absence of distress, and that one way to study eustress is to assess positive psychological states.

This positive stress has been described in various ways, and recognized in athletes and performing artists (e.g., opera singers) as being in the "zone" or in the "flow." Time is suspended, and there is pure joy and pleasure from immersion in productive activity. Yet in the research literature on work stress and health, eustress appears very infrequently. There is a regrettable lack of attention to defining eustress, identifying causes of eustress, identifying a process (similar to coping) of managing eustress, and finding ways of generating eustress at work.

Simmons (2000) defined eustress as the positive psychological response to a stressor that is indicated by the presence of positive psychological states. Eustress reflects the extent to which individuals appraise a situation or event as beneficial or as a potential enhancement of their well-being. Work situations elicit a mixture of both positive and negative responses in individuals. When assessing eustress as we have defined it here, the indicators of eustress should be positive psychological states, such as attitudes or emotions. Positive affect, meaningfulness, manageability, and hope may be good indicators of eustress (Simmons, 2000; Simmons & Nelson, 2001; Simmons, Nelson, & Neal, 2001). These indicators all represent an aspect of *active engagement*, which may be an important component of the eustress response at work.

Eustressed workers are actively engaged, meaning that they are immersed in and pleasurably occupied by the demands of the work at hand. Workers can be engaged and perceive positive benefits even when confronted with extremely demanding stressors. Some, in fact, may wish to proactively call up this response, and to prolong the experience of eustress. Nelson and Simmons (2003) referred to this process as *savoring*, and offered it as a complement to what is called coping in response to distress. They further suggested that individuals who likely engage in savoring are those who are optimistic, hardy, and self-reliant, and who possess an internal locus of control and a sense of coherence. As a complement to distress prevention, we need to study eustress generation, which consists of ways that managers can help employees engender and savor the eustress response at work.

As a beginning, researchers could identify the conditions at work that are most closely associated with feelings of active engagement and eustress. This line of research must then go beyond the identification to examine why employees respond in a eustressful way to these conditions. Finally, the linkage must be made between eustress at work and health.

Research on eustress can best be accomplished through interdisciplinary teams. There may be, as indicated by the work of Frankenhauser (1983, 1991), some physiological differences between the eustress response and the distress response, and these differences need elaboration and clarification.

## CONCLUSION

Work is a stressful and effortful activity, and that is not necessarily bad. Stress can be both a positive and a negative, the latter posing serious health risks for individuals and organizations. Positive stress (eustress) is essential to growth, development, and mastery as well as to achieving high levels of performance in a wide range of tasks and activities. Stress can neither be avoided by individuals nor eliminated from organizations and places of work. Stress can be managed and the stress-induced energy that is characteristic of work can be channeled in constructive and productive ways. Stress well managed enhances strength and contributes to competence. Whereas it is a universal human experience, there is also great variance across individuals in terms of what causes stress, what its immediate and health effects are on a specific individual, and how it is best managed in a healthy way.

The negative side of stress, often known as distress or strain, is accompanied by a variety of health problems and risks. Selye (1976) called the health problems associated with distress and strain the diseases of maladaption. Individuals and organizations pay a price for mismanaged stress, stress that is too intense, too frequent, or too prolonged. The price may be physical, psychological, behavioral, or emotional, and these costs have been well established over the nearly 90 years since the stress concept was first identified within the medical and physiological community. Within the last 50 years, organizational researchers have come to understand the effects of stress in the workplace, along with the human and economic costs associated with distress and strain at work.

Therefore, in one way there is nothing new in the ideas of stress, health, and well-being at work. In another way, there is everything new and that is attributable to the dramatically changing workplace in most industrialized nations. We have described the systemic changes that have taken place, especially during the past decade following the collapse of the Berlin Wall and the opening of markets and national borders. The increase in global competition has created increased and shifting pressures on people in workplaces. Managing change has become a key stress management skill for executives, managers, and employees alike. However, competition without cooperation becomes extremely destructive (Quick, Gavin, Cooper, & Quick, in press). Safeguarding the health of executives, managers, and employees is a first line of defense for organizations to ensure strength while guarding against distress and strain. We suggest that self-reliance is an essential skill for the new age of anxiety. The paradox of self-reliance is that individuals who are so have the capacities to both work autonomously and independently in the appropriate circumstances while also connecting in cooperative, secure, and supportive relationships when that is appropriate. Organizational cultures that place value on cooperation, collegiality, and mutual support create workplaces that are stronger and more resilient in ensuring the health and vitality of their employees while being productive at the same time.

# ACKNOWLEDGMENTS

We express our appreciation for two sources of support for their stress and health research over the past several years. First, BUPA, the largest medical insurance company and private hospital group in the United Kingdom, has substantially funded Cary L. Cooper's research group at the University of Manchester Institute of Science and Technology. Second, James Campbell Quick at The University of Texas at Arlington and Jonathan D. Quick at the World Health Organization appreciate a trust gift given to support their research. Partial support for this chapter came during a Faculty Development Leave awarded to James Campbell Quick by The University of Texas at Arlington and from Professor Cary L. Cooper's preparation for the 43rd MacLaren Lecture at the University of Aston, November 7, 2000. We would like to thank Marilyn Saba and Paige Dawkins for their help in the preparation of this manuscript, Joyce Adkins, PhD Lt. Col. BSC USAF in the Department of Defense for providing data courtesy of the U.S. Air Force, and Joel Quintans for the artistic management of that data. We thank Paul Rosch, Marilyn Macik-Frey, and Shen Schember Quick for helpful comments on an earlier drafts of the manuscript.

# REFERENCES

Adkins, J. A. (1999). Promoting organizational health: The evolving practice of occupational health psychology. *Professional Psychology: Research and Practice, 30,* 129–137

Adler, N. E., Boyce, W. T., Chesney, M. A., Folkman, S., & Syme, S. L. (1993). Socioeconomic inequalities in health: No easy solution. *Journal of the American Medical Association, 269,* 3140–3145.

Ainsworth, M. D. S., & Bowlby, J. (1991). An ethological approach to personality. *American Psychologist, 46,* 333–341.

Aristotle (1998). *Nicomachean ethics* (D. Ross, Trans.). Revised by J. L. Ackrill & J. O. Urmson. Oxford, England: Oxford World Classics. (Orginal work published 310)

Benison, S., Barger, A. C., & Wolfe, E. L. (1987). *Walter B. Cannon: The life and times of a young scientist.* Cambridge, MA: Belknap.

Berridge, J., Cooper, C. L., & Highley-Marchington, C. (1997). *Employee assistance programmes and workplace counselling.* Chichester, England: Wiley.

Booth, R. T. (1993). *Where's the harm in it? Risk assessment workbook.* Henley-on-Thames, England: Monitor Training.

Cannon, W. B. (1929). *Alternative satisfactions for the fighting emotions. Bodily changes in pain, hunger, fear and rage: An account of recent researches into the function of emotional excitement.* New York: Appleton. (Original work published 1915)

Cannon, W. B. (1935). Stresses and strains of homeostasis. *The American Journal of the Medical Sciences, 189,* 1–14.

Cascio, W. F. (1993). Downsizing: What do we know? What have we learned? *Academy of Management Executives, 7,* 95–104.

Cooper, C. L. (1996). *The handbook of stress, medicine and health.* Boca Raton, FL: CRC Press.

Cooper, C. L. (1998a). The changing psychological contract at work. *Work & Stress, 12,* 97–100.

Cooper, C. L. (1998b). *Theories of organizational stress.* Oxford, England: Oxford University Press.

Cooper, C. L. (1999). The changing psychological contract at work. *European Business Journal, 1,* 115–118.

Cooper, C. L., & Jackson, S. (1997). *Creating tomorrow's organizations: A handbook for future research in organizational behaviour.* Chichester, England: Wiley.

Cooper, C. L., & Marshall, J. (1978). Sources of managerial and white collar stress. In C. L. Cooper & R. Payne (Eds.), *Stress at work* (pp. 81–105). Chichester, England: Wiley.

Cooper, C. L., & Quick, J. C. (1999). *Fast Facts: Stress and strain* [Clinical monograph]. Oxford, England: Health Press.

Cooper, C. L., & Sadri, G. (1991). The impact of stress counseling at work. *Journal of Social Behavior and Personality, 6,* 411–423.

Cooper, C. L., Sloan, S. J., & Williams, S. (1988). *Occupational stress indicator management guide.* Oxford, England: NFER-Nelson.

Earnshaw, J., & Cooper, C. L. (1996). *Stress and employer liability.* London: Institute of Personnel and Development.

Edwards, J. R. (1996). An examination of competing versions of the person–environment fit approach to stress. *Academy of Management Journal, 39,* 292–339.

Edwards, J. R., & Cooper, C. L. (1990). The person–environment fit approach to stress: Recurring problems and some suggested solutions. *Journal of Organizational Behavior, 10,* 293–307.

Elkin, A. J., & Rosch, P. J. (1990). Promoting mental health at the workplace: The prevention side of stress management. *Occupational Medicine, 5,* 734–754.

Elkind, H. B. (Ed.). (1931). *Preventive management: Mental hygiene in industry.* New York: B. C. Forbes.

Frankenhauser, M. (1983). The sympathetic-adrenal and pituitary-adrenal response to challenge: Comparison between the sexes. In T. M. Dembroski, T. H. Schmidt, & G. Blumchen (Eds.), *Biobehavioral bases of coronary heart disease* (pp. 91–105). New York: Karger.

Frankenhauser, M. (1991). The psychophysiology of workload, stress, and health: Comparison between the sexes. *Annals of Behavioral Medicine, 13,* 197–204.

Frese, M. (1997). Dynamic self-reliance: An important concept for work in the twenty-first century. In C. L. Cooper & S. E. Jackson (Eds.), *Creating tomorrow's organizations* (pp. 399–416). Chichester, England: Wiley.

Frost, P., & Robinson, S. (1999). The toxic handler: Organizational hero—and casualty. *Harvard Business Review, 77,* 97–106.

Glendon, A. I., & McKenna, E. F. (1995). *Human safety and risk management.* London: Chapman & Hall.

Gowing, M. K., Kraft, J. D., & Quick, J. C. (1998). *The new organizational reality*. Washington, DC: American Psychological Association.

Handy, C. (1994). *The empty raincoat*. London: Hutchinson.

Hazan, C., & Shaver, P. R. (1990). Love and work: An attachment theoretical perspective. *Journal of Personality and Social Psychology, 52*, 511–524.

Health and Safety Commission. (1991). *Second report of the advisory committee on the safety of nuclear installations: Human reliability analysis—a critical review*. London: HMSO.

Health and Safety Executive. (1999). *Managing stress at work*. Sudbury, England: HSE Books.

Highley-Marchington, C., & Cooper, C. L. (1998). *An assessment of EAP's and workplace counselling in British organisations*. Norwich, England: HMSO.

Hirschhorn, L. (1983). *Cutting back*. San Francisco: Jossey-Bass.

Hobfoll, S. E. (2001). The influence of culture, community, and the nested-self in the stress process: Advancing conservation of resources theory. *Applied Psychology: An International Review, 50*, 337–370.

House, J. S. (1981). *Work stress and social support*. Reading, MA: Addison-Wesley.

Hurrell, J. J., & McLaney, M. A. (1988). Exposure to the job stress: A new psychometric instrument. *Scandinavian Journal of Work, Environment, and Health, 14*, 27–28.

Hurrell, J. J., Jr., & Murphy, L. R. (1992). Psychological job stress. In W. N. Rom (Ed.), *Environmental and occupational medicine* (pp. 675–684). New York: Little Brown.

Hurrell, J. J., Jr., Nelson, D. L., & Simmons, B. L. (1998). Measuring job stressors and strains: Where we have been, where we are, and where we need to go. *Journal of Occupational Health Psychology, 3*, 368–389.

Ilgen, D. R. (1990). Health issues at work: Opportunities for industrial/organizational psychology. *American Psychologist, 45*, 273–283.

Ivancevich, J. M., Matteson, M. T., & Richards, E. P., III. (1985). Who's liable for stress on the job? *Harvard Business Review, 64*, 60–72.

Jones, J. R., Hodgson, J. T., Clegg, T. A., & Elliott, R. C. (1998). *Self-reported work-related illness in 1995: Results from a household survey*. Sudbury, England: HSE Books.

Joplin, J. R. W., Nelson, D. L., & Quick, J. C., (1999). Attachment behavior and health: Relationships at work and home. *Journal of Organizational Behavior. 20* (6), 783-796.

Kahn, R. L., Wolfe, R. P., Quinn, R. P., Snoek, J. D., & Rosenthal, R. A. (1964). *Organizational stress: Studies in role conflict and ambiguity*. New York: Wiley.

Karasek, R. A. (1979). Job demands, job decision latitude, and mental strain: Implications for job redesign. *Administrative Science Quarterly, 24*, 285–308.

Karasek, R. A., Theorell, T., Schwartz, J. E., Schnall, P. L., Pieper, C. F., & Michela, J. L. (1988). Job characteristics in relation to the prevalence of myocardial infarction in the U.S. health examination survey (HES) and the health and nutrition examination survey (HANES). *American Journal of Public Health, 78*, 910–918.

Kazer, B. (1992). Risk assessment: Scattergram or bullseye. *The Health and Safety Practitioner, 10*(5), 40–41.

Landy, F., Quick, J. C., & Kasl, S. (1994). Work, stress and well-being. *International Journal of Stress Management, 1*, 33–73.

Lawler, E. E. (1996). *From the ground up: Six principles for building the new logic corporation*. San Francisco: Jossey-Bass.

Lazarus, R. S. (1995). Psychological stress in the workplace. In R. Crandall & P. L. Perrewe (Eds.), *Occupational stress: A handbook* (pp. 39–38). Washington, DC: Taylor & Francis.

Leana, C. R., & Feldman, D. C. (1992). *Coping with job loss: How individuals, organizations and communities respond to layoffs*. New York: Macmillan/Lexington Books.

Levi, L. (1979). Psychosocial factors in preventive medicine. In D. A. Homburg (Ed.), *Healthy people: The Surgeon General's report on health promotion and disease prevention background papers* (pp. 207–252). Washington, DC: U.S. Department of Health, Education, and Welfare.

Levine, C. H. (1980). *Managing fiscal stress*. Chatham, NJ: Chatham House.

Levinson, H. (1985). *Executive stress*. New York: New American Library.

Levinson, H. (1996, July–August). When executives burn out: A new age of self-reliance. *Harvard Business Review, 162*–173. (HBR Classic; original 1981)

Levinson, H. (in press). *Organizational assessment: A manual*. Washington, DC: American Psychological Association.

Lynch, J. J. (2000). *A cry unheard: New insights into the medical consequences of loneliness*. Baltimore: Bancroft.

Mack, D. A., & Quick, J. C. (in press). EDS: An inside view of a corporate life cycle transition. *Organizational Dynamics*.

Mack, D. A., Shannon, C., Quick, J. D., & Quick, J. C. (1998). Stress and the preventive management of workplace violence. In R. W. Griffin, A. O'Leary-Kelly, & J. Collins (Eds.), *Dysfunctional behavior in organizations: Vol. 1. Violent behavior in organizations* (pp. 119–141). Greenwich, CT: JAI.

Macy, B. A., & Mirvis, P. H. (1976). A methodology for the assessment of quality of work life and organizational effectiveness in behavioral economic terms. *Administrative Science Quarterly, 21,* 212–226.

Makin, P., Cooper, C., & Cox C. (1996). *Organizations and the psychological contract*. London: BPS Books.

Management of Health and Safety at Work Regulations, (1992). London: United Kingdom Legislation.

Marks, M. L. (1994). *From turmoil to triumph*. New York: Lexington Books.

Marks, M. L., & Mirvis, P. H. (1985a). Merger syndrome: Management by crisis. *Mergers & Acquisitions, 20,* 70–76.

Marks, M. L., & Mirvis, P. H. (1985b). Merger syndrome: Stress and uncertainty. *Mergers & Acquisitions, 20,* 50–55.

Millar, J. D. (1984). The NIOSH-suggested list of the ten leading work-related diseases and injuries. *Journal of Occupational Medicine, 26,* 340–341.

Morris, J. R., Cascio, W. F., & Young, C. E. (1999, Winter). Downsizing after all these years. *Organizational Dynamics,* 78–87.

Murphy, L. R., & Cooper, C. L. (2000). *Health and productive work: An international perspective*. London: Taylor & Francis.

Nelson, D. L., Quick, J. C., & Joplin, J. (1991). Psychological contracting and new-comer socialization: An attachment theory foundation. *Journal of Social Behavior and Personality, 6,* 55–72.

Nelson, D. L., Quick, J. C., & Simmons, B. L. (2001). Preventive management of work stress: Current themes and future challenges. In A. Baum, T. Revenson, & J. Singer (Eds.), *Handbook of health psychology* (pp. 349–364). Mahwah, NJ: Lawrence Erlbaum Associates.

Nelson, D. L., & Simmons, B. L. (2003). Health psychology and work stress: A more positive approach. In J. C. Quick & L. Tetrick (Eds.), *Handbook of occupational health psychology pp. 97–120.* Washington, DC: American Psychological Association.

Osipow, S. H., & Davis, A. S. (1988). The relationship of coping resources to occupational stress and strain. *Journal of Vocational Behavior, 32,* 1–15.

Osipow, S. H., & Spokane, A. R. (1992). *Occupational stress inventory: Manual, research version.* Odessa, FL: Psychological Assessment Resources.

Quick, J. C., (1997). Occupational health and stress: The role of the chief psychological officer in 21st century organizations. *Proceedings of the Ninth International Montreux Congress on Stress.* Co-sponsored by The American Institue of Stress, Biotonus Clinique Bon Port.

Quick, J. C., & Cooper, C. L., (2003) *Fast Facts: Stress and Strain.* Oxford, England: Health Press.

Quick, J. C., & Gavin, J. H. (2000). The next frontier: Edgar Schein on organizational therapy. *Academy of Management Executive, 14,* 30–44.

Quick, J. C., Gavin, J. H., Cooper, C. L., & Quick, J. D. (2000). Executive health: Building strength, managing risks. *Academy of Management Executive, 14,* 34–44.

Quick, J. C., Gavin, J. H., Cooper, C. L., & Quick, J. D. (in press). Working together: Balancing head and heart. In N. G. Johnson, R. H. Rozensky, C. D. Goodheart, & R. Hammond (Eds.), *Psychology builds a healthy world.* Washington, DC: American Psychological Association.

Quick, J. C., Joplin, J. R., Nelson, D. L., Mangelsdorff, A.D., & Fiedler, E., (1996). Self-reliance and military service training outcomes. *Military Psychology, 8* (4), 279–293.

Quick, J. C., & Klunder, C. (2000). Preventive stress management at work: The case of the San Antonio Air Logistics Center (AFMC). *Proceedings of the Eleventh International Congress on Stress.* The American Institute of Stress, Hawaii.

Quick, J. C., Murphy, L. R., & Hurrell, J. J., Jr. (1992). *Stress and well-being at work: Assessments and interventions for occupational mental health.* Washington, DC: American Psychological Association.

Quick, J. C., Nelson, D. L., Quick, J. D., & Orman, D. K. (2001). An isomorphic theory of stress: The dynamics of person–environment fit. *Stress and Health, 17,* 147–157.

Quick, J. C., Nelson, D. L., & Simmons, B. (2000). Work conditions. In N. Schmitt (Ed.), Encyclopedia of psychology (pp. 269–274). Washington, DC: American Psychological Association and Oxford University Press.

Quick, J. C., & Quick, J. D. (1997). Stress management programs. In L. H. Peters, S. A. Youngblood, & C. R. Greer (Eds.), *The Blackwell encyclopedia of human resource management* (pp. 338–339). Oxford, England: Basil Blackwell.

Quick, J. C., & Quick, J. D. (1984). *Organizational stress and preventive management.* New York: McGraw-Hill.

Quick, J. C., Quick, J. D., & Gavin, J. H. (2000). Stress: Measurement. In N. Schneiderman (Ed.), *Encyclopedia of psychology* (pp. 484–487). Washington, DC: American Psychological Association and Oxford University Press.

Quick, J. C., Quick, J. D., Nelson, D. L., & Hurrell, J. J., Jr. (1997). *Preventive stress management in organizations.* Washington, DC: American Psychological Association.

Quick, J. C., & Tetrick, L. (2003). *Handbook of occupational health psychology.* Washington, DC: American Psychological Association.

Quick, J. D., Nelson, D. L., & Quick, J. C. (1998). The theory of preventive stress management in organizations. In C. L. Cooper (Ed.), *Theories of organizational stress* (pp. 246–268). Oxford, England: Oxford University Press.

Rahe, R. H. (1994). "The more things change ..." *Psychosomatic Medicine, 56,* 307–309.

Robert Half International. (1991, September 9). [Press release]. New York: Author.

Rosch, P. J. (2001a). On the origins and the evolution of "Stress." *Health and Stress, 9,* 1–7.

Rosch, P. J. (2001b). The quandary of job stress compensation. *Health and Stress, 3,* 1–4.

Rosenman, R. H. (1996). Personality, behavior patterns, and heart disease. In C. L. Cooper (Ed.), *Handbook of stress, medicine, and health* (pp. 217–231). Boca Raton, FL: CRC.

Rosenman, R. H., & Friedman, M. (1977). Modifying Type A behavior patterns. *Journal of Psychosomatic Research, 21,* 323–331.

Rowe, G. (1990). Setting safety priorities: A technical and social process. *Journal of Occupational Accidents, 12,* 31–40.

Royal Society Study Group. (1992). *Risk: Analysis, perception, management.* London: The Royal Society.

Sauter, S. L., & Hurrell, J. J. (1999). Occupational health psychology: Origins, content, and direction. *Professional Psychology: Research and Practice, 30,* 117–122.

Sauter, S. L., Murphy, L. R., & Hurrell, J. J. (1990). Prevention of work-related psychological distress: A national strategy proposed by the National Institute of Occupational Safety and Health. *American Psychologist, 45,* 1146–1158.

Selye, H. (1976). *Stress in health and disease.* Boston: Butterworth.

Siegrist, J. (1996). Adverse health effects of high-effort/low-strain reward conditions. *Journal of Occupational Health Psychology, 1,* 30.

Simmons, B. L. (2000). *Eustress at work: Accentuating the positive.* Unpublished doctoral dissertation, Oklahoma State University, Stillwater, OK.

Simmons, B. L., & Nelson, D. L. (2001). Eustress at work: The relationship between hope and health in hospital nurses. *Health Care Management Review, 26,* 7–18.

Simmons, B. L., Nelson, D. L., & Neal, L. J. (2001). A comparison of the positive and negative work attitudes of home healthcare and hospital nurses. *Health Care Management Review, 26,* 64–75.

Singleton, W. T., & Hovden, J. (1987). *Risk and decisions.* Chichester, England: Wiley.

Solomon, R. C. (1992). Corporate roles, personal virtues: An Aristotelian approach to business ethics. *Business Ethics Quarterly, 2,* 317–339.

Spielberger, C. D. (1994). *Professional manual for the job stress survey (JSSS).* Odessa, FL: Psychological Assessment Resources.

Staw, B. M., Sandelands, L. E., & Dutton, J. E. (1981). Threat-rigidity effects in organizational behavior: A multilevel analysis. *Administrative Science Quarterly, 26,* 501–524.

Steel, C. (1990). Risk estimation. *The Health and Safety Practitioner, 8,* 20–21.

Steely, P. W. (1999). Expect excellence. *Kelly Observer, 34,* 4.

Teasdale, E. L., & McKeown, S. (1994). Managing stress at work: The ICI-Zeneca pharmaceutical experience 1986–1993. In C. L. Cooper & S. Williams (Eds.), *Creating healthy work organizations* (pp. 133–165). Chichester, England: Wiley.

Theorell, T., & Karasek, R. A. (1996). Current issues relating to psychosocial job strain and cardiovascular disease research. *Journal of Occupational Health Psychology, 1,* 9–26

Twenge, J. M. (2000). The age of anxiety? Birth cohort change in anxiety and neuroticism, 1952–1993. *Journal of Personality and Social Psychology, 79,* 1007–1021.

Tyler, C. W., Jr., & Last, J. M. (1998). Epidemiology. In R. B. Wallace & B. N. Doebbeling (Eds.), *Maxcy-Rosenau-Last public health & preventive medicine* (14th ed., pp. 5–33). Stamford, CT: Appleton & Lange.

Vagg, P. R., & Spielberger, C. D. (1998). Occupational stress: Measuring job pressure and organizational support in the workplace. *Journal of Occupational Health Psychology, 3,* 294–305.

*Vital Statistics of the United States, 1985, Life Tables, Vol. II, Section 6.* (1985). (DHHS Publication No. PHS 88-1104, January 1988). Washington, DC: U.S. Department of Health and Human Services, Public Health Service, National Center for Health Statistics.

Von Dusch, T. (1868). *Lehrbuch der herzkrankheiten* [Textbook of heart disease]. Leipzig, Germany: Verlag von Wilhelm Engelman.

*Walker v. Northumberland County Council.* Industrial Relations Law Reports (1995). London: IRLR.

Wallace, R. B., & Doebbeling, B. N. (1998). *Maxcy-Rosenau-Last public health & preventive medicine* (14th ed.). Stamford, CT: Appleton & Lange.

Waring, A. (1996). *Safety management systems.* London: Chapman & Hall.

Warner, F. (1992). Introduction. In Royal Society Study Group, *Risk: Analysis, perception, management* (pp. 1–12). London: The Royal Society.

Wharton, F. (1992). Risk management: Basic concepts and general principles. In J. Anesll & F. Warton (Eds.), *Risk: Analysis, perception, & management.* Chichester, England: Wiley.

Williams, S., & Cooper, C. L. (1998). Measuring occupational stress: Development of the Pressure Management Indicator. *Journal of Occupational Health Psychology, 3,* 306–321.

Winters, E. E. (Ed.). (1952). *The collected papers of Adolf Meyer: Vol. IV. Mental hygiene.* Baltimore: Johns Hopkins University Press.

Woodburn, L. T., & Simpson, S. (1994). Employee types: Who will be the next stress claimant? *Risk Management, 41,* 38–44.

Worrall, L., & Cooper, C. L. (1997). *Quality of working life survey.* London: Institute of Management.

Worrall, L., & Cooper, C. L. (1998). *Quality of working life survey.* London: Institute of Management.

Worrall, L., & Cooper, C. L. (1999). *Quality of working life survey.* London: Institute of Management.

Worrall, L., & Cooper, C. L. (2000). *Quality of working life survey.* London: Institute of Management.

# 3

# Self-Fulfilling Prophecies in Organizations

Dov Eden
*Tel Aviv University*

The Pygmalion effect is a special case of self-fulfilling prophecy (SFP; Merton, 1948) in which raising leader expectations regarding subordinate achievement produces an improvement in performance. Inspired by earlier research on the experimenter effect (Rosenthal, 1966), Rosenthal and Jacobson (1968) were the first to demonstrate the Pygmalion effect experimentally in the classroom. There has been some argument that teachers' naturally occurring expectations are usually realistic and that the Pygmalion effect is often small and practically unimportant (Jussim, 1991; Jussim & Eccles, 1995; see also Madon, Jussim, & Eccles, 1997, and Smith et al., 1998). Nevertheless, the Pygmalion effect is well established in educational psychology as confirmatory meta-analytic results accrue (Babad, 1993; Dusek, Hall, & Meyer, 1985; Harris & Rosenthal, 1985; Rosenthal, 1985, 1991a, 1991b; Rosenthal & Rubin, 1978). Moreover, organizational researchers have been accumulating field experimental support for the Pygmalion approach among adults in nonschool organizations (for reviews, see Eden, 1990a, 1993a, 1993b; Kierein & Gold, 2000; McNatt, 2000; White & Locke, 2000).

## THE EARLY PYGMALION EXPERIMENTS

King (1971) launched adult Pygmalion research. He was the first to publish an experimental replication of the Pygmalion effect among adults in a nonschool organization. He created the Pygmalion effect among hard-core unemployed trainees in industry. Eden and Ravid (1982) and Eden and Shani (1982) increased external validity by creating Pygmalion effects among military personnel, and in a different national and cultural milieu. Eden and Ravid also created a Galatea effect. Named for the statue that the mythical Pygmalion sculpted, the Galatea effect is a self-produced expectation effect among individuals whose *own* self-expectations have been raised, as distinct from Pygmalion effects that are produced among subordinates by inducing *their supervisors* to expect a lot of them. Expanding beyond dyadic manager–subordinate relationships, King (1974) pioneered also in applying the SFP concept to organizational development (OD). He showed that raising manager expectations for the outcomes of an OD intervention increased productivity gains. Eden (1990d) replicated the whole-group version of Pygmalion, producing the effect by raising leader expectations toward whole groups of subordinates. Based on these early experiments, Eden (1984, 1988b) developed a theoretical model of the Pygmalion leadership approach. Eden (1986, 1988a, 1990a) furthermore proposed some preliminary, practical implications of the Pygmalion effect for OD and for managerial consulting.

## ELABORATION EXPERIMENTS

The next several experiments extended the Pygmalion paradigm to different levels of the independent variable, to additional dependent variables, and to different populations. Oz and Eden (1994) moved from the study of the effects of high leader expectations to a replication of the SFP effect at the low end of the expectancy scale. Babad, Inbar, and Rosenthal (1982) had coined the term *Golem effect* to refer to the negative impact of low teacher expectations on performance. However, for ethical reasons, Babad et al. rightly had refrained from creating low expectations to study their debilitating effects and instead had employed a cross-sectional design. Oz and Eden studied the Golem effect experimentally in an ethically acceptable way by *averting* it. By leading supervisors to reinterpret low scores in prior ability tests as not being indicative of poor achievement potential, they showed experimentally that uprooting naturally formed low expectations, or preventing their crystallization, averted or attenuated the Golem effect. This has come to be known as de-Golemization.

All of these experiments involved performance as the dependent variable. Eden and Kinnar (1991) showed that the SFP approach could be applied to raise the volunteer rate for service in elite combat units, and Eden and Aviram (1993) showed that it could help speed reemployment among persons who had suffered recent job loss. Next, Eden and Zuk (1995) extended the SFP approach to seasickness and performance at sea. They showed that naval cadets who had been led to believe, supposedly on the basis of psychological tests and evaluations, that they would be able to overcome seasickness and perform well despite rough seas, actually did report less seasickness and did perform better at sea than their randomly assigned control comrades. The authors concluded optimistically that Pygmalion applications were limited only by our finite imagination.

## Women as Pygmalions and Galateas

All of these replications involved men. Several subsequent studies were dedicated to extending generalizability to women. In two experiments, Dvir, Eden, and Banjo (1995) showed that the Pygmalion effect can be produced among women. The Pygmalion effect did not emerge in Dvir's all-women experiment among cadets in an Israel Defense Forces (IDF) officer training course; it did emerge in Banjo's IDF experiment among men led by a man and among women led by a man, but not among women led by a woman. In a subsequent pair of experiments involving women only, Davidson and Eden (2000) replicated the de-Golemization effect twice among disadvantaged IDF women led by women, demonstrating the remedial value of the SFP effect. Mediation analysis in these last two experiments revealed that leader support, self-efficacy, and motivation mediated the effect; leaders whose expectations were raised were rated as better and more supportive leaders than the control leaders, and their subordinates reported greater self-efficacy and motivation. None of these experiments permitted cross-gender comparisons.

Finally, in a university-based community outreach project, Natanovich and Eden (2001) replicated the Pygmalion effect among male and female supervisors of male and female tutors and found Pygmalion effects among all four supervisor–tutor gender combinations. Thus, we can now safely conclude that the Pygmalion effect is equally applicable to men and women. Natanovich and Eden also produced confirmatory effects among Jewish and Arab supervisors and tutors, further extending external validity.

Thus, Pygmalion effects have now been created experimentally in a wide variety of populations and settings, and the role of leadership and self-efficacy in mediating the effects of expectations on performance has been demonstrated. These experimental findings confirm the Pygmalion-at-work model, according to which High Leader Expectations → Improved Leadership → Augmented Self-Efficacy → Greater Motivation → Intensification of Effort → Better Performance (Eden, 1990c).

## Pygmalion in Nonwork Settings

Not all adult Pygmalion research has been conducted in work or military organizations. Learman, Avorn, Everitt, and Rosenthal (1990) studied SFP effects among caregivers and their patients in a nursing home. Furthermore, in a creative quasi-experimental design, Chapman and McCauley (1993) found SFP effects among National Science Foundation awardees in a comparison of 7-year follow-up PhD completion rates among awardees and nonawardees. They interpreted the higher completion rate among awardees as both a Pygmalion effect and a Galatea effect arising from high mentor expectations and high self-expectations aroused by being bestowed this coveted award. Chapman and McCauley thus added higher education as a setting in which SFP effects have been demonstrated. This study also shows the relevance of the Pygmalion concept to extraordinarily talented individuals.

## Pygmalion in the Experimental Laboratory

A unique aspect of the Pygmalion research is that it has been conducted exclusively in the field. Perhaps researchers have deemed it difficult or impossible to instill credible high expectations experimentally in contrived situations. Perhaps it is simply an instance of a powerful pattern set by Rosenthal and Jacobson's (1968) original classroom experiment that determined the Pygmalion research paradigm for decades to come. Nevertheless, Gold (1999, see also Gold, 2001) broke this pattern with the first laboratory experiment on the Pygmalion effect. Leadership researchers have begun studying e-leadership, which is assuming greater importance as the electronic communications revolution expands interpersonal interaction beyond the face-to-face format of bygone generations (for review see Avolio, Kahai, & Dodge, 2000). Noting that all previous demonstrations of the Pygmalion effect had been in field situations in which leaders and subordinates interacted face-to-face, Gold set out to produce the first Pygmalion effect in a laboratory setting. The experimental task involved performance on a computer simulation involving a city-planning task. Crossed with his expectancy treatment, Gold had some of his participants interacting face-to-face and compared them with other participants using computer-mediated communication in a 2 (Expectancy high/control) × 2 (Face-to-face/not face-to-face) × 2 (computer-mediated/not computer-mediated) design. The manipulation check showed that leaders who were induced to expect more from their subordinates did so for all conditions. Analysis of variance detected no significant main effects of face-to-face communications or of computer-mediated communication. However, a significant interaction showed that a Pygmalion effect was produced in the combined face-to-face and computer-mediated communication condition. Comparing cell means revealed that high expectations boosted performance only in the combined face-to-face and computer-mediated communication condition. Gold suggested that perhaps the subordinates needed both communication conditions to interpret whatever high-expectancy cues the leaders were sending. Because the subordinates were working on a computer task, perhaps computer-mediated interpersonal interaction had to be bolstered by the richness of face-to-face encounter for high leader expectations to boost performance.

## Meta-Analytic Summaries of Pygmalion-at-Work Research

Two recent meta-analyses of the Pygmalion-at-work research have confirmed the Pygmalion effect and estimated its size. McNatt (2000) calculated an overall corrected estimate of the average effect of $d = 1.13$ (58 effect sizes, $N = 2,874$) in 17 studies. Using somewhat different inclusion criteria, Kierein and Gold (2000) found an overall average effect of $d = 0.81$ (13 effect sizes, $N = 2,853$) in nine studies. Thus, there is solid and consistent evidence for the internal and external validity of the Pygmalion effect among adults in organizations. Moreover, this effect is large.

# PYGMALION AND DECEPTION

Nearly all of the early published Pygmalion research employed deceptive experimental treatments to raise expectations. The leaders were typically duped into expecting more, and consequently unwittingly provided better leadership to subordinates expected to achieve more. This means that it was nonconscious mental processes that led them to treat their subordinates in accordance with their expectations. Once having internalized high expectations, the managers produced the SFP "automatically." Bargh and Chartrand (1999) explained how the SFP can operate "entirely nonconsciously" (p. 467) and summarized experimental evidence for the automatic activation of stereotypes in which participants nonconsciously act in accordance with their expectations toward others and thereby get others to act as expected with no awareness of the process by either party. Such so-called "dual-process models" in social psychology (Chaiken & Trope, 1999) acknowledge both conscious and nonconscious determinants of behavior.

Thus, in principle, individuals can be aware or unaware of their role in an interpersonal SFP process. However, the deceptive induction of high expectations in all the early SFP experiments seemed to render it uncertain whether similar productive outcomes would be obtained if managers were conscious of the process. Perhaps automaticity is integral to the SFP process, and inviting leaders to collaborate in a fully informed, joint attempt to produce it would make them conscious of the process and prevent its occurrence.

Moreover, feeding random information to leaders in organizational settings seems not to be the ideal way to create lasting, positive effects and to build trust between academics and managers. To advance the Pygmalion concept beyond basic research to application in management as a productive approach to leadership, it seemed necessary to develop ways to implement it without deceiving the intended beneficiaries. Here practical and ethical considerations may converge, for basing high expectations on random information both introduces ethical ambiguities and risks long-term consultant credibility. The training approach used in the next series of experiments involved the participating leaders as partners in the research and obviated the need for deception, thus bypassing the ethical uncertainties.

## PREVIOUS PYGMALION TRAINING INTERVENTIONS

The only previous nonschool research on Pygmalion training was Crawford, Thomas, and Fink's (1980) "Pygmalion at Sea" project in the United States Navy. Performance ratings of chronically low-performing sailors were improved by raising expectations of both the sailors and their supervisors. This was done through three workshops designed to (a) teach the commanders Pygmalion concepts to persuade them to reverse their negative expectations toward the sailors, (b) provide counseling-and-guidance training to senior enlisted supervisors, and (c) promote personal growth in separate workshops conducted for the low performers themselves. Comparisons of the experimental low performers with their shipmates and with low performers on other ships revealed improvements in performance and discipline among the former.

There were several serious, uncontrolled threats to internal validity in this quasi-experimental study, rendering its results somewhat equivocal (see Eden, 1988b, 1990c). Nevertheless, Crawford et al. (1980) pioneered the practical application of the Pygmalion concept. Their intervention was designed to make the personnel involved—both the commanders and the enlisted men—fully informed collaborators in creating positive SFPs. However, replication to test the effectiveness of Pygmalion training with adequate internal validity was still needed.

Weinstein et al. (1991) used a quasi-experimental design to assess a Pygmalion-based, collaborative, community-oriented, preventative intervention for ninth graders at risk for school failure. Teachers and other school staff, who served as Weinstein's collaborators, communicated positive expectations to low achievers. They also changed such aspects of school functioning as student responsibility, curriculum, and evaluation in accord with the high-expectancy culture they were trying to create. The authors dubbed their results "promising but not uniform" (p. 333). Pupils who were "at risk" attained higher grades, fewer disciplinary referrals, and better retention at year's end. However, these improvements were not maintained the following year with teachers who had not been involved in the project. Weinstein et al. (see also Weinstein, 2002) suggested that their intervention may not have been strong enough to effect lasting change.

The U. S. Navy's Pygmalion at Sea study has not been replicated, and nothing approaching the organizationwide and community scope of Weinstein et al.'s (1991) school project has ever been attempted in work organizations. Nevertheless, these early application efforts inspired the next series of Pygmalion training experiments in organizations.

## SEVEN PYGMALION TRAINING EXPERIMENTS IN ORGANIZATIONS

Progress in Pygmalion research, as well as the pioneering attempts by Crawford et al. (1980) and Weinstein et al. (1991) to apply the Pygmalion concept, sparked literature reviews (Eden, 1990b, 1993a, 1993b) that were quite sanguine about the potential for Pygmalion applications to improve leadership and boost productivity appreciably with relatively little investment. Buoyed by the optimism born of the success of the previous, basic experiments, my students and I (Eden et al., 2000) undertook a new, programmatic effort to use training to apply the Pygmalion concept and to evaluate its effects. This entailed developing a Pygmalion training workshop, training samples of managers, and evaluating the effectiveness of the training using rigorous experimental design. This program ultimately involved seven field experiments in seven organizations. In all seven experiments questionnaires measured leader and follower perceptions; three experiments also included analysis of objective performance data. Six were true experiments in which participating organizational units were assigned to conditions at random; one was a quasi-experiment. The individuals who were trained from the participating organizations were commanders in an infantry unit, counselors in a summer camp, managers in an industrial manufacturing plant, elementary school principals in a school district, branch managers in two banks (two different experiments), and department managers in a hospital.

### Pygmalion Leadership Style: The Independent Variable

Pygmalion Leadership Style (PLS) is a set of behaviors that managers use when they expect high performance from their subordinates. Based on empirical findings and on several theoretical models (e.g., Eden, 1988b, 1990c; Rosenthal, 1991a; Rosenthal & Rubin, 1978; Sutton & Woodman, 1989), it was hypothesized that these leader behaviors convey high expectations to subordinates and arouse high motivation and intensification of effort. PLS includes leader behavior that creates a supportive interpersonal climate, attributes subordinate success to stable, internal causes and their failures to ephemeral and external causes, and motivates subordinates by enhancing their self-efficacy (see elaboration in Eden, 1993b). The series of seven field experiments was an attempt to demonstrate that PLS training could be used to improve participants' managerial effectiveness.

The key difference between these seven experiments and those that preceded them was that, whereas in the earlier experiments the leaders typically had been duped into expecting more of their subordinates, in these seven the managers were fully informed of the aims of the workshops at the outset and they knew the true nature of the research in which they were participating. Thus, the training experiments tested the *applicability* of the Pygmalion paradigm more than the preceding experiments had. The managers who had produced the Pygmalion effects in the earlier experiments did so unwittingly. However, for training to get participating managers to choose to adopt PLS, they must be convinced of its superiority; they must become eager collaborators.

## The Pygmalion Workshop: The Experimental Treatment

The Pygmalion workshop developed into a training program that had three primary aims. The first was to increase participating managers' *attributed efficacy*; that is, to get them to believe that their subordinates were indeed capable of achieving more. This replaced the 5-minute treatment that we had implemented in the previous experiments to raise participants' expectations unwittingly. The second aim was to increase participants' *managerial self-efficacy* by getting them to believe in their own capacity to lead their subordinates to greater achievement. Third, several sessions were devoted to *behavioral skill training* to raise the participants' proficiency in enacting PLS behaviors.

The workshop opened with a 20-minute experiential warm-up exercise to demonstrate the meaning and power of the Pygmalion phenomenon in management (see description in Eden, 1990c, p. 163). This was followed by an interactive lecture on SFP in economics, medicine, science, education, and management; Pygmalion, Galatea, and Golem effects; and leadership as the prime mediator of the effects of manager expectations on subordinate self-efficacy, motivation, and performance. The remaining 2.5 days were interspersed with brief lecturettes on positive and negative SFP; general and specific self-efficacy, attributed efficacy, managerial self-efficacy, collective efficacy, and means efficacy (Eden, 1996, 2001); the effective management of attributions in the wake of success and failure; and managing organizational culture to enhance organizationwide SFP. Analysis of famous Pygmalion-like leaders (e.g., Lee Iacocca) was supplemented by examples offered up by the participants.

Next, a session was devoted to identification of the myriad opportunities to create Pygmalion effects. This set the stage for role playing to rehearse self-efficacy-enhancing leader behaviors in a variety of manager–subordinate situations using VCR for instant replay, feedback, and analysis. No structured role plays were provided; rather, the participants were encouraged to bring forth relevant situations from their own personal managerial experience. The procedure used for conducting these sessions itself embodies Pygmalion principles: A participant describes a supervisor–subordinate situation, articulates a Pygmalion goal for the interaction, role-plays the situation, and gets feedback, usually quite negative, from fellow participants. After viewing the video replay and discussing how to do it better, the participant defines an improvement goal, plays the role again, and gets feedback again, almost always positive, based on improved performance of the Pygmalion role with practice.

At the end of the role-playing sessions, the facilitator emphasized to the participants how the role-playing exercise epitomized the Pygmalion leadership process by (a) encouraging them to try something difficult; (b) providing constructive feedback about their performance; (c) getting them to try again, leading to improved performance; and (d) providing feedback attributing the success to their ability to expand their mastery of PLS, thereby reinforcing their learning, enhancing their managerial self-efficacy, and augmenting their motivation to apply PLS.

The workshop concluded with implementation planning at the individual, departmental, and organizational levels using printed forms that led the participants through a process of defining Pygmalion goals at different levels (individual subordinates, groups of subordinates, and departments) and for different time spans (immediate, several months, and a year). They were asked to foresee obstacles to transfer and implementation (e.g., overload, crises that demand immediate attention, subordinate resistance) and to plan how to overcome them. The workshop closed optimistically with a strong note of high expectations.

In the first several training experiments, the workshop lasted only 1 or 2 days. The training model was developed over time and was delivered as described earlier in the last several experiments. In Experiment 7, the workshop ended with a session in which bank branch managers presented their Pygmalion application plans to regional management. For a more detailed description of the workshop, see Eden et al. (2000).

In each experiment, leadership was measured before and after training as a manipulation check to validate the workshop as a means for getting the managers to change their behavior. The general hypothesis tested in all seven experiments was that PLS augments subordinates' self-efficacy, motivates intensification of effort, and culminates in improved performance. The specific variables included varied somewhat from experiment to experiment.

## Results of the Seven Pygmalion Training Experiments

Although the results were mixed, most of the experiments detected little evidence that the workshops improved participant leadership or that they aroused any response at all among the followers. Meta-analysis of 61 effects in the seven experiments yielded a small mean effect size ($r = .13, p < .01$). The contrast between this small effect and the medium-to-large effect produced by previous Pygmalion experiments is stark. It appears evident that producing the Pygmalion effect using a deceptive, 5-minute experimental treatment and creating it among informed participants in a training intervention are quite different enterprises. This difference is discussed later in terms of the efficacy–effectiveness distinction and in terms of future directions for Pygmalion research and application.

## MEANS EFFICACY: A NEW MOTIVATIONAL CONSTRUCT

Two expansions of the efficacy construct that have gained the attention of work motivation scholars in recent years are the distinction between general and specific self-efficacy and the distinction between self-efficacy and collective efficacy. Eden (1996, 2001) reconceptualized these distinctions and integrated them into a more general theoretical framework dubbed the internal–external efficacy model. This model distinguishes between general and specific efficacy beliefs as well as between internal and external sources of efficacy beliefs. He then created a 2-by-2 cross-classification of the sources of subjective efficacy using the internal–external and the general–specific dimensions. He defined and instantiated each of the resulting four sources of subjective efficacy.

According to this internal–external efficacy model, internal efficacy is conceived as including both general and specific self-efficacy. External efficacy is defined and elaborated as *means efficacy*. Means efficacy is an individual's belief in the utility of the tools available for performing a task. Tools can include implements (e.g., machines, computers, and violins), other persons (e.g., co-workers and supervisors), or bureaucratic means for accomplishing work (e.g., procedures and forms). Collective efficacy is classified as one type of means efficacy: It is the individual's belief in the ability of his or her team or department to perform well. Total subjective efficacy is comprised of self-efficacy (i.e., belief in one's own ability) and means efficacy (i.e., belief in the ability of the tools and other resources available for performing the task). The central hypothesis of the model is that motivation is maximized when both self-efficacy and means efficacy are high. The Pygmalion implication is that managers who desire to produce productive expectancy effects should act to enhance their subordinates' beliefs both in their own capacity to excel (i.e., their self-efficacy) and in the utility of the tools available to them (i.e., means efficacy); when managers arouse maximal total efficacy, maximal performance will result. To date, there have been two tests of the internal–external efficacy model.

## Boosting Means Efficacy Among Computer Users in a Social Service Organization

In the first empirical test of the means-efficacy construct, Eden and Granat-Flomin (2000) set out to build a measure of means efficacy and validate it by testing the hypothesis that raising means efficacy boosts performance expectations and enhances performance.

*Sample and Design.*    We conducted a true field experiment in one department of the Institute for Social Services (ISS, a pseudonym), a government social service organization that processes claims and effects payment of benefits mandated by law to entitled recipients. The department operates nationwide, with units dispersed throughout Israel in 17 major regional branch offices. These units were about to get a new computer system that included decision-support software designed to do many operations automatically, to do them fast, and to eliminate processing errors. We randomly assigned the branches to experimental and control conditions. We told the employees in the experimental branches that they were about to get a new computer system proven to be the best of its kind anywhere. Control personnel got the same computer system with no means-efficacy treatment.

*Measures.*    We devised a measure of *means efficacy* for the computer system comprised of 20 5-point items asking how much the respondent agreed that the computer was an efficacious work tool, "as distinct from your own personal ability." The stem "My present computer" was completed with such items as "is an efficient tool," "can serve its purpose at work," "is reliable," "saves time," "can recover fast from breakdowns," "is worth the money invested in it," "enables faster service to the client," and "can prevent snafus at work," pretest and posttest $\alpha = .95$ and .99, respectively. *General self-efficacy* was assessed using the 14-item version of Chen, Gully, and Eden's (2001) New General Self-Efficacy Scale (NGSE), which taps the respondent's overall sense of being able to muster the internal resources needed to succeed in challenging circumstances, pretest and posttest $\alpha = .94$ and .95. *Computer self-efficacy* was measured using 13 5-point items that asked the respondent "how much you believe you can operate your computer successfully." Examples of the 13 items that followed the stem, "I believe I can:" are, "operate the computer quickly," "recover fast from glitches in the system," and "give accurate service using the computer," pretest and posttest $\alpha$ = .95 and .97. *Performance* was operationalized in terms of mean time to account, defined as the number of days it took to get claim money deposited into the claimant's bank account.

*Treatment.*   The employees in all the participating branches got two days of training on the new computer system. An Information Technology director introduced the new system and emphasized that it had been developed 6 years earlier in the United States, where it had proved highly successful. In reality, the new system had been developed locally. After some general instruction, the department head divided the employees into two groups and sent them to adjacent rooms equipped with computer terminals for training exercises. Each room had enough terminals to accommodate about half the participants, who were not informed that the room assignments had been randomized by branch.

Midday on the first day of training, the experimenter delivered the experimental treatment. The department head introduced her and informed the participants that she was conducting university research and would be collecting data on a few occasions. The experimenter spent 7 minutes in each room. In the control room she walked about observing what the participants were doing, smiled, nodded, and made other natural gestures. In the experimental room, she took the podium and made a 7-minute presentation in which she emphasized that the aim of the research was to study the reliability of the new system and the ease with which it is adopted; that as part of the course we wanted to familiarize you with some of the advantages of the new system; that this system has been used in the United States for the past 6 years; that research in departments similar to yours showed drastic improvements in average net file-processing time, employee and client satisfaction, and such organizational dimensions as complaints, absence and tardiness rates, and error rate. She then screened colorful, graphic transparencies showing the advantages of the new system and repeated that it was much more efficient and convenient to use than the old system and that it enables employees to improve their performance and achieve excellence. After the final data collection, participants received oral and written debriefing that described the experiment, its purpose, method, findings, and implications.

*Manipulation Checks.*   The impact of the means-efficacy treatment was tested using repeated-measures analysis of variance of pretest–posttest differences between experimental and control branches in means efficacy, the independent variable that the treatment was designed to influence. The manipulation check detected a significant main effect of occasion showing that means efficacy increased in both conditions. This was expected because all the branches got a much improved computer system. However, a significant Treatment × Occasion interaction indicated that the increase was significantly greater in the experimental condition, corroborating the positive effect of the means-efficacy treatment on means efficacy among the experimental participants. Neither general self-efficacy nor computer self-efficacy was targeted by the treatment and neither was expected to be influenced by it; as predicted, both remained virtually unchanged across occasions in both conditions. Thus, the treatment selectively affected the variable it was intended to affect (means efficacy) and did not affect what it was not intended to affect (self-efficacy), strengthening the validity of the treatment. Analysis of measures of participants' expectations for improvement in service similarly showed differences between experimental and control branches as predicted.

*Performance Effect.* We compared the experimental and control branches in the mean number of days it took to deliver the service to clients before and after the installation of the new computer system. The experimental branches significantly and appreciably surpassed the control branches in pretest–posttest service time improvement, as predicted. Whereas time to account was reduced negligibly from 26 to 25 days in the control branches, it was nearly halved from over 28 to under 16 days in the experimental branches. This is the performance improvement that resulted from augmenting the experimental employees' means efficacy. Believing more in the new computer system, they got better service out of it, and rendered better service to their clients.

*Implications.* Our ISS experiment demonstrated that means efficacy can be measured reliably, that an experimental intervention can enhance means efficacy, and that enhancing means efficacy—without altering self-efficacy—can improve performance. This was the first validation of the internal–external efficacy model. It established means efficacy as a meaningful and useful motivational construct in its own right, as distinct from self-efficacy. It set the stage for an experimental demonstration of the usefulness of means efficacy in a training situation.

## The Total Efficacy Experiment in the IDF Anti-Aircraft Gunnery School

Next, Eden and Sulimani (2001, 2002) conducted an after-only randomized field experiment at the IDF Anti-Aircraft Gunnery School. The 16 instructors were noncommissioned officers assigned to a course to prepare them for their instructor role. As part of this preliminary training, we randomly assigned the instructors to two groups and gave each group a different 1-day workshop. The experimental group received Pygmalion training that included an opening lecture emphasizing the instructors' role in enhancing their trainees' total subjective efficacy, both self-efficacy and means efficacy. The workshop continued with role-playing exercises in which the participants rehearsed how to effect this enhancement. The control group was trained in interpersonal communication. The control workshop was opened with a lecture on basic concepts and moved to role-playing exercises that provided practice for application of the concepts taught. Then the instructors were dispersed and assigned to 7- to 8-week-long anti-aircraft gunnery specialty courses that are routinely delivered to small groups, ranging between three and six trainees per instructor. The sample numbered 8 experimental instructors and their 27 trainees and 8 control instructors and their 40 trainees. The trainees completed questionnaires during their courses. After the courses were over and the grades were submitted, a debriefing presentation was made for all the school's staff. It included description of SFP and Pygmalion effects, self-efficacy and means efficacy, past research, and full disclosure of the design and aims of the experiment. The hypothesis was that raising self-efficacy and means efficacy motivates improved performance.

*Manipulation Check.* The experimental trainees reported significantly and appreciably more self-efficacy and more means efficacy than the control trainees, as predicted. These were the manipulation checks; they show that the treatment (i.e., the workshop training) influenced the independent variables as intended. Thus, training instructors in using Pygmalion and total efficacy concepts resulted in their raising their trainees' self-efficacy and means efficacy to levels that exceeded those of the trainees of the control instructors. The treatment affected means efficacy more than self-efficacy, as evidenced by the effect sizes ($r = .43$ vs $.27$, respectively). The binomial effect size display (BESD; see Rosenthal & Rubin, 1982) equivalent of the means-efficacy effect size, $r = .43$, is a success rate of 71.5% versus 28.5% in the experimental and control conditions, respectively. For self-efficacy, the comparable percentages were 63.5% and 36.5%. Thus, the likelihood of an experimental trainee compared to a control trainee scoring above median on means efficacy was more than 2.5:1, whereas for self-efficacy it is appreciably less than 2:1, though still not negligible. For both efficacy variables, BESD indicates a practically important effect.

*Results.* The treatment did not influence general motivation significantly; however, it did affect means motivation as predicted. The effect size for means motivation, $r = .42$, translates to a BESD of 71% versus 29% in favor of the experimental trainees; again, this is a large effect. Finally, the experimental trainees significantly outperformed the control trainees on both a written test ($r = .27$, 63.5% vs 36.5%) and a performance test ($r = .57$, 78.5% vs 21.5%). The latter effect was the largest produced in this experiment, and was exceptionally large. Cohen (1988) defined an $r$ of .50 as "about as high as they come" (p. 81).

We had predicted that the efficacy and motivation variables would mediate the effects of the treatment on performance. However, using Baron and Kenny's (1986) criteria, neither self-efficacy, means efficacy, nor either motivation measure mediated. Furthermore, the hypothesis that self-efficacy and means efficacy interact in influencing performance was not confirmed. Regressing performance on both self-efficacy and means efficacy simultaneously revealed that means efficacy was a significant predictor of performance, whereas self-efficacy was not. The interaction term added in the next step was not significant. Thus, contrary to the hypothesis, after accounting for the main effects of the two efficacy variables, they did not combine interactively to affect performance. These mediation and moderation tests should be regarded with great caution because the small sample did not provide sufficient statistical power for definitive third-variable tests.

## THE CURRENT STATE OF PYGMALION RESEARCH

Eden and Sulimani's (2001, 2002) results have substantive implications for both efficacy theory and for Pygmalion training, and they provide an occasion to summarize the current state of Pygmalion and other SFP research in organizations. First, these results constitute the second field-experimental confirmation of the productive effects of boosting means efficacy. Successful replication should reduce suspicion that Eden and Granat-Flomin's (2000) confirmatory findings were one-time, idiosyncratic results. Furthermore, whereas Eden and Granat-Flomin's treatment was contrived and based on deception, Eden and Sulimani's treatment involved fully informed participants being trained to apply the internal–external efficacy model. The convergence of the results of two such different samples, experimental designs, and treatment procedures renders each a constructive replication of the other (Lykken, 1968). Therefore, practitioners can now base application of the means efficacy concept on replicated experimental evidence.

Moreover, the Anti-Aircraft Gunnery School results cast Pygmalion training in a new light. Instructors trained to produce Pygmalion effects *did* produce them. After seven largely unsuccessful attempts to produce Pygmalion effects in training experiments, the Anti-Aircraft Gunnery

School application succeeded. This can be counted as Experiment 8, undertaken in the wake of repeated attempts (Eden et al., 2000) that resulted in, at best, a small effect. Thus, the second implication of Eden and Sulimani's results is that practitioners can move ahead with Pygmalion training applications without deceiving clients knowing that there is an empirical basis for expecting success.

## Why is This Experiment Different From All Other Experiments?

Several unique features of the Anti-Aircraft Gunnery School experiment may have facilitated its success. First, adding means efficacy as a concept may strengthen the arsenal in the hands of instructors and supervisors with a new tool that previous participants in Pygmalion training did not have. In the Anti-Aircraft Gunnery School study it is clear that means efficacy made a difference. However, it is impossible to determine definitively whether or not a Pygmalion effect would have been produced in that experiment *without* the means–efficacy concept. Eden and Granat-Flomin's (2000) test of means efficacy, the only previous one, was in the tradition of deceptive experimentation and did not involve informed participants. Therefore, further research is needed to determine whether Pygmalion training can be effective without the means–efficacy concept.

Second, McNatt's (2000) meta-analysis revealed stronger Pygmalion effects in military settings and among men. Consistent with this, the most confirmatory of Eden et al.'s (2000) seven experiments was the only one that was conducted in the military and among all-male units. Thus, the fact that the Anti-Aircraft Gunnery School study took place among men in a military setting might have been in its favor. Replication among both genders in civilian organizations is needed to extend generalizability.

Third, in six of the seven Pygmalion training experiments, the participants were managers or supervisors. In the Anti-Aircraft Gunnery School study they were instructors. Perhaps the Pygmalion approach to training fits instructors better than managers. The modern Pygmalion notion was born in the classroom (Rosenthal & Jacobson, 1968). Pygmalion's home court may be the classroom after all.

Fourth, in most of the previous Pygmalion training studies the participants were experienced managers. Prior experience may have made them impervious to new ideas. Conversely, the Anti-Aircraft Gunnery School instructors were young, inexperienced, and eager to learn whatever might help them in their new role. This may have maximized their receptiveness to the training. After the debriefing, several experimental instructors approached us informally and volunteered their enthusiastic views of the utility of the Pygmalion approach. Although we did not quantify them, such reactions corroborated our sense of their exceptional receptiveness. The practical implication is that Pygmalion trainees should be selected for their openness to new experience or should be beginners who approach their roles with the earnest passion that the cynicism born of experience so often extinguishes.

Fifth, in five of the seven experiments, after the training the managers returned to the subordinates they had managed in the past. This means that they entered and left the training with prior knowledge of their subordinates' performance potential based on their own personal experience. It is difficult for workshop training to overcome crystallized low expectations and replace them with high expectations commensurate with the Pygmalion approach. Judging by frequent remarks made by many workshop participants, managers often cling to their low assessment of some of their subordinates and resist the idea that most can improve appreciably. In contrast, for participants who have no prior acquaintance with the subordinates to whom they are to be assigned, there is no need to overcome prior expectations; the "only" task before the facilitator is to implant high expectations for future subordinates. A recent experimental attempt to overcome prior acquaintance among civilian production supervisors did not produce a Pygmalion effect (Eden & Aloni, 2000). Thus, the absence of prior acquaintance probably gave the replication in the Anti-Aircraft Gunnery School a crucial advantage over previous Pygmalion training experiments.

Summarizing, the differences between Eden and Sulimani's successful training experiment and most of its unsuccessful predecessors include (a) the focus on means efficacy, (b) the military setting, (c) training instructors rather than managers, (d) participant inexperience, and (e) the lack of prior acquaintance. These five variables are potential moderators of expectation effects. How they interact to block or facilitate the Pygmalion effect is for future research to discover. Meantime, practitioners should bear in mind that these moderators have been confounded in previous research. Many Pygmalion experiments in military settings have involved command personnel who were new to their roles and who had no prior acquaintance with the subordinates toward whom their expectations were raised.

## FUTURE PYGMALION THEORY, RESEARCH, AND APPLICATION IN ORGANIZATIONS

Despite McNatt's (2000) meta-analytic finding, there does not seem to be anything inherently military about Pygmalion. The inherently greater order and discipline in military organizations, compared to civilian settings, may give experimenters greater control and therefore greater chances of producing effects in military organizations. That is, the advantage of military settings may be more in *detecting* the effect than in *producing* it. A hypothesis that is testable using meta-analysis is that experimental treatments in general (i.e., not only Pygmalion treatments) are more effective and succeed more often in military organizations than in civilian settings.

Furthermore, civilian managers in training workshops appear to resonate to the Pygmalion approach no less than do military participants (Eden et al., 2000). It is more likely the experience and prior acquaintance of the personnel involved, in both civilian and military settings, that moderate the impact of Pygmalion interventions. Therefore, civilian and military practitioners alike should focus Pygmalion applications on inexperienced managers slated to supervise subordinates whom they do not know personally, and should include means-efficacy training.

The Anti-Aircraft Gunnery School experiment shares one more feature with the two most successful of Eden et al.'s (2000) experiments: the training lasted only 1 day. Eden et al. started out with a 1-day workshop and increased it to 2 days and then to 3 days. The first two of the seven experiments involved 1 day of training and produced the most confirmatory results. Eden et al. noted—with consternation—that the longer the training became, the less effective it was. Several short-term training interventions have been reported enviably successful. Smoll, Smith, Barnett, and Everett (1993) trained Little League coaches in building players' self-esteem for 2½ hours; Barling, Weber, and Kelloway (1996) trained bank managers in leadership for 1 day; and Frayne and Geringer (2000) trained sales personnel in self-management for 8 hours. All three of these studies reported significant training effects. The evidence appears to indicate that 1 day of training or less can be more effective than 3 days. Have we been overtraining? Would more of Eden et al.'s seven experiments have succeeded had the training been briefer? Meta-analysis of managerial training including length of training as a moderator is in order.

## Means Efficacy Does Motivate Better Performance

Eden and Sulimani's (2001, 2002) experiment produced the first replication of the means-efficacy effect. It was also the second experiment in which means-efficacy had sizable impact on performance and self-efficacy had none. Eden and Granat-Flomin (2000) did not try to raise self-efficacy, and its lack of effect in their study had been predicted. In contrast, the Anti-Aircraft Gunnery School instructors had been trained in raising both means efficacy and self-efficacy and actually did raise both, as the manipulation checks revealed. Therefore, self-efficacy could have played a role. Nevertheless, multiple regression showed that means efficacy *did* influence performance, whereas self-efficacy *did not*.

Perhaps in jobs that involve heavy use of tools, means efficacy overshadows self-efficacy in determining performance. The internal–external efficacy model stipulates that tasks differ in the extent to which they are tool-dependent (Eden, 2001). Some tasks, such as auto repair, nursing, and air traffic control, require heavy use of tools, whereas others, such as proofreading, playing chess, and most kinds of retail sales, require little or no use of tools. Both confirmatory means-efficacy experiments to date involved highly tool-dependent jobs. These are the types of jobs in which practitioners should seek to augment means efficacy as a motivation booster.

## Needed: New Ways of Fostering Self-Efficacy

Adding means efficacy to the arsenal of managers and consultants should not deflect our attention from the need to devise more innovative ways to enhance *self*-efficacy. The emerging consensus regarding the central role of self-efficacy in job motivation has not been accompanied by new proposals of how to enhance it. Many of the classical examples are from other arenas, such as helping relieve counselees of their snake phobias (Bandura, 1997). An exception is Rowe and Kahn's (1998) concept of "congratulatory feedback" (p. 138). Discussing the importance of self-efficacy among the elderly, they recommended lavishing congratulations on an individual who has succeeded in overcoming serious obstacles and has performed an activity well despite the odds that disfavor success. Congratulatory feedback is of course relevant to many other kinds of individuals who have achieved success. Successful performance is too often taken for granted by managers and mentors. We need more such innovative ideas for ways of fostering self-efficacy.

## Specificity Matching Facilitates Hypothesis Confirmation

In the Anti-Aircraft Gunnery School experiment, we predicted that instructors trained in total efficacy concepts would be able to increase trainee motivation. Means–specific motivation (i.e., "desire to use the system you are being trained on") was influenced by the treatment, whereas general motivation (e.g., "desire to serve in anti-aircraft units") was not. Because both the experimental treatment and the performance measures were specific to particular weapon systems, these results bear out Eden's (1996) call for matching the specificity of the motivational measure to the specificity of the treatment and of the task performance predicted. This replicates for motivation what Davidson and Eden (2000) showed for self-efficacy, namely, that a measure that matches the specificity of the domain being studied confirms more hypotheses than measures that are either too general or too specific. "Specificity matching" of measures of self-efficacy, motivation, and performance should increase hypothesis confirmation in empirical studies involving these variables.

## Improvements in the Pygmalion Training Design

In the wake of the overall disappointing results of their seven Pygmalion training experiments, Eden et al. (2000) proposed a number of ideas for enhancing the impact of future PLS training. The subsequent encouraging results of Eden and Sulimani's (2001, in press) "Experiment 8" do not render these suggested improvements irrelevant or unimportant. These suggestions include enlisting the participants as collaborators in the research, not only as trainees in the workshops; building in resistance to posttraining transfer problems; more follow-up sessions after the training phase, which should be viewed as a beginning rather than an end; more on-site follow-up consultations; more Pygmalion action planning; involving higher management throughout the process; developing a divisional or regional Pygmalion culture; involving participating managers in devising criterion measures; getting the subordinates of the participating managers actively involved in the Pygmalion project; combining Pygmalion with other approaches to leadership, such as the transformational, charismatic, visionary, and leader–member exchange approaches; and selecting participating managers and organizations for readiness for Pygmalion leadership. These suggestions appear to be appropriate for any behavioral intervention in organizations. Being mindful of them during future Pygmalion interventions should augment their effectiveness.

## Efficacy Versus Effectiveness

It is possible that, despite the internal and external validity demonstrated in the earlier dozen or so overwhelmingly confirmatory experiments, the Pygmalion approach lacks "application validity," that is, the practical applicability that would render it an effective tool in the hands of managers. This goes beyond Campbell and Stanley's (1966) "external validity." Seligman (1995, 1996, 1998; see also Holon, 1996) suggested the terms *efficacy* and *effectiveness* to distinguish between psychotherapy recovery rates produced in controlled studies and in clinical practice, respectively. Cumulative findings show that some treatments achieve better recovery rates in controlled studies than in clinical practice whereas others work better in actual practice than in the highly controlled studies. Applying Seligman's terms, although early Pygmalion experimentation confirmed that the Pygmalion approach has a large measure of efficacy, the training experiments show that it has yet to pass the effectiveness test.

Deficient effectiveness appears to plague not only the Pygmalion approach. The effectiveness record of leadership training in general seems deficient. For example, searching Yukl's (2002) most recent general survey of the leadership literature does not reveal a single field-experimental confirmation of the effectiveness of *any* leadership application. There appear to have been precious few field-experimental demonstrations of the effectiveness of *any* approach to leadership. An exception is the field-experimental confirmation of the effectiveness of transformational leadership training among IDF officer cadets (Dvir, Eden, Shamir, & Avolio, 2002). This came in the wake of numerous confirmations of transformational leadership theory in causally equivocal, cross-sectional research and in several laboratory experiments that have shown transformational leadership's efficacy, but not its effectiveness. Dvir et al. have taken the first stride toward establishing the effectiveness of transformational leadership training. Thus, like other theory-based approaches to leadership training, Pygmalion training still lacks strong, convincing, or consistent empirical support for its effectiveness. Beyond Pygmalion, research is needed on the entire spectrum of leadership theories to establish their effectiveness. Pending such research, their practical applicability should be regarded as tentative. It is hoped that organizational behavior researchers will accept the challenge of effectiveness research.

## The Role of Awareness in Self-Fulfilling Prophecy

It appears that awareness of SFP effects on the part of managers being trained to produce them intentionally impedes the SFP process and prevents the emergence of expectation effects or at least reduces their magnitude. For the practitioner, this is bad news. One implication of it is that we need to devise ways of creating productive SFP that bypass client awareness and yet meet ever more stringent ethical restrictions. The search for such approaches could open up a whole new avenue of Pygmalion research.

There is another implication of the relative weakness of the Pygmalion effects produced in the training experiments. The cognitive processes set into motion when participating managers think about their subordinates and choose how to relate to them are different when the managers are aware of the impact of their expectations on their subordinates from when they are not aware. Commenting on this point, Lord and Emrich (2000) wrote, "Awareness that social information can affect judgments often differentiates between assimilation and contrast effects in social judgments" (p. 556). This may be the embryonic stage in a new phase of Pygmalion research that could deepen our understanding of the intrapersonal cognitive processes involved in the Pygmalion effect. In Lord and Emrich's witty words in the title of their article, the name of this game is "Thinking Outside the Box by Looking Inside the Box." Thus, the different results of Pygmalion studies with and without awareness may key into basic, cognitive issues that are worthy of exploration in the wider context of cognitive social psychology and leadership theory.

## Pygmalion in the Laboratory and e-Pygmalion

The significance of Gold's laboratory Pygmalion experiment is doublefold. First, he broke new methodological ground by taking Pygmalion into the laboratory. Second, he tested the Pygmalion phenomenon in the emerging realm of electronic interpersonal relationships. Gold conducted the first e-Pygmalion experiment. Hopefully, others will follow him in scrutinizing in the laboratory fine-grained aspects of interpersonal expectancy effects that are not readily amenable to articulation in field experimentation. Particularly fascinating is the opportunity afforded by computer-mediated research to study SFP effects under conditions of impoverished interpersonal stimulation. Rosenthal (1979) invested considerable effort in the experimental laboratory to reveal the perceptual basis for the communication of expectations, developing specifically for this purpose the Profile of Nonverbal Sensitivity (PONS). Using the PONS, Rosenthal and his colleagues have shown that individuals are capable of perceiving and responding to incredibly brief, barely threshold-level visual interpersonal stimuli that evidently bypass conscious processing (Rosenthal, Hall, DiMatteo, Rogers, & Archer, 1979). Individuals are astoundingly sensitive, even in perceiving strangers with whom they have "zero acquaintance" (i.e., with minimal prior exposure to visual stimuli; Ambady, Hallahan, & Rosenthal, 1995).

The testable implication of e-Pygmalion is that electronically transmitted expectations may affect receiver motivation and performance, even when the individuals involved in the interaction have never even laid eyes on one another. This raises several researchable questions: Can Pygmalion effects be routinely created exclusively via electronic media, where the communication is verbal but not visual? Rosenthal's PONS research has been conducted among participants with "zero acquaintance" but who had viewed each other very briefly at the outset of the experiment. Would similar results be obtained if they had never laid eyes on each other, and had only e-communication as a source of knowledge about each other? Because emerging technologies enable transmission of voice and video as well as written information, what is the effect of various combinations of verbal–written *and* oral and visual distance communication of expectations? What makes these questions particularly provocative is that Rosenthal (1991b) confirmed meta-analytically that "socioemotional support" is the most powerful mediator of interpersonal expectation effects. Socioemotional support includes "warm," nonverbal behaviors such as smiling, drawing physically near, nodding the head affirmatively, mellowing voice intonation, and several other nonverbal behaviors that are enacted by the leader (teacher or supervisor) and perceived by the follower (pupil or subordinate). In all previous Pygmalion research, these behaviors have been studied when the participants were interacting face-to-face. Is physical presence necessary for socioemotional support to be expressed and felt, or can "cold," electronically mediated, interpersonal communication provide sufficient support to mediate expectancy effects?

Avolio, Kahai, and Dodge (2000) summarized advances in research on e-leadership. Some of the same issues relevant to e-leadership are relevant to e-Pygmalion. Research on e-Pygmalion should become part and parcel of e-leadership research.

## ETHICAL CONSIDERATIONS: FUNCTIONAL TRUTH OR LITERAL TRUTH?

"There is a formula that perfectly fits painting: Lots of little lies for the sake of one big truth."

—Pierre Bonnard, French Reductionist–Impressionist Painter, 1867–1947,
as quoted in a wall epigraph at the *Bonnard Retrospective* exhibited
at the Museum of Modern Art in New York City in 1998

White and Locke (2000) discussed several problems with the Pygmalion approach and proposed some solutions. One of the important issues they raised was the ethical compromise inherent in conveying contrived information to managers to arouse high expectations toward subordinates. White and Locke argued against "creating the false impression among managers that some of their subordinates have the potential to shine (with the further implication that the other subordinates will not) with no actual supporting data" (p. 402, parentheses in original). White and Locke extended their discussion of the potential negative ramifications to organizational trust and justice as well as legal opportunities that deception might provide for individuals eager to play the role of aggrieved victim. White and Locke stated their position very clearly: "Expectations should not be deceptively manipulated in the workplace" (p. 402).

### High Versus Accurate Expectations

It is appropriate to begin the discussion of any ethical dilemma with a question. If you know clients will be motivated to try harder and will increase their likelihood of succeeding at some endeavor that is important to them if you tell them they have the wherewithal to succeed even though you are not basing this encouraging statement on specific, validated information regarding those particular individuals, is it ethically permissible to do so? Under these same conditions, is it ethical *not* to do so? If you convey such information, is it lying, or, to use psychology's euphemism, is it dissimulating? Is it *mis*leading? Is it *mis*information? Is the information "biased" and is conveying it therefore unethical practice?

*Authentic Relationships: Academic Psychology's Truth Bias.*      There seems to be a preponderance of opinion among psychologists that interpersonal relationships, including formal, professional relationships, should be "authentic" and always based on truth. This may seem to contradict the deliberate creation of the unwitting version of the Pygmalion effect, in which the experimenter or consultant bypasses participants' or clients' awareness and instills high expectations without specific knowledge of the actual ability levels of the individuals involved. The untruth inherent in this action is analogous to Bonnard's "little lies" that create "one big truth."

Taylor and Brown (1988; see also Taylor, 1989) articulated a construct they dubbed "positive illusions." Bolstered by evidence that they reviewed from a wide range of psychological research, Taylor and Brown argued that, by and large, individuals entertain favorable biases in self-perception that lead them to exaggerate their self-worth in the optimistic direction, including their estimates of their ability to affect their environments and their own personal futures. Furthermore, Taylor and Brown contended that such biases may be highly adaptive, ultimately leading to positive illusions that augment their psychological well-being. Taylor and Brown concluded that positive illusions are "a valuable human resource to be nurtured and promoted, rather than an error-prone processing system to be corrected" (p. 205). Furthermore, research shows that positive illusions and "unrealistic" high expectations can contribute even to improved physical health (Leedham, Meyerowitz, Muirhead, & Frist, 1995; Scheier & Carver, 1985; Taylor, Kemeny, Reed, Bower, & Gruenewald, 2000). This occurs despite the potential clash between the "unrealistic" positive self-illusions and psychology's basic assumption that successful coping and adjustment require accurate self-perception. This is the paradox of functional, positive self-illusions.

To support their general position, Taylor and Brown (1994) quoted Bandura's (1989) marvelously clear and accurate words, which seem virtually to echo the advantages of moderate positive illusions:

> It is widely believed that misjudgment produces dysfunction. Certainly, gross miscalculation can create problems. However, optimistic self-appraisals of capability that are not unduly disparate from what is possible can be advantageous, whereas veridical judgments can be self-limiting. When people err in their self-appraisals, they tend to overestimate their capabilities. This is a benefit rather than a cognitive failing to be eradicated. If self-efficacy beliefs always reflected only what people could do routinely, they would rarely fail but they would not mount the extra effort needed to surpass their ordinary performances. (p. 1177)

Similarly, elaborating the advantages of self-efficacy that overestimates ability, Maddux (1995) actually cited Taylor and Brown and invoked positive illusions to support his position:

> In the face of difficulties, people with a weak sense of personal efficacy develop doubts about their ability to accomplish the task at hand and give up easily, whereas those with a strong sense of self-efficacy increase their efforts to master a challenge when obstacles arise. Perseverance usually produces the desired results, and this success then increases the individual's sense of efficacy. Motivation toward difficult goals is enhanced by *overestimates* of personal capabilities (i.e., positive illusions, Taylor & Brown, 1988), which then become self-fulfilling prophecies when people set their sights high, persevere, and then surpass their usual level of accomplishment. (pp. 12–13, parentheses in original, italics added)

Is it the psychologist's job to help people rid themselves of positive illusions and overestimates of their capabilities? Would mentors who help people develop overestimates of their capabilities be guilty of ethical wrongdoing? Hardly. Deception is not deceit and deceptiveness is not deceitfulness. An experimenter using deception is not being deceitful toward research participants. This generalizes to teachers and managers who encourage struggling pupils and employees who want to succeed by assuring them that they can do better, even while harboring doubts about their capability to do so. Furthermore, this can be done without implying that others lack the capability to succeed.

A major consideration for the utility of positive illusions is the size of the discrepancy between the level of the self-expectations they embody and actual, present ability level. There seems to be a consensus that the gap should be moderate, not huge. Expecting people to do better than their last proven level of performance, but not *much* better all at once, should produce the motivation needed to try. Trying to achieve a goal one notch above the previous level of accomplishment may succeed; demanding immediate sky-high improvement will demotivate effort and impair accomplishment. However, the size of the discrepancy is a practical matter, not an ethical one.

## Functional Truth Versus Literal Truth: An Ethical Choice

A Russian trainer realized that a weightlifter attempting to lift 200 kilos was capable of doing so. This fine athlete would lift 195 and then 197.5. However, every time he attempted 200, he failed. The trainer suspected that the "magic" round number 200 was acting as a psychological barrier, rather than as a motivating goal. Next day he arrived at the gym early and, unbeknownst to the athlete, doctored the labels on the weight bars such that 197.5 kg was labeled 195 and 200 was labeled 197.5. That day, the athlete lifted 200 when it was labeled 197.5 but failed, as previously, to lift it when it was labeled 200.

—Amiram Vinokur

Did this trainer engage in unethical behavior? To be sure, the issue remains controversial, as not all psychologists agree with Taylor and Brown's position (e.g., Colvin & Block, 1994; Colvin, Block, & Funder, 1995). Despite Taylor and Brown's (1994) reasoned response to their critics, some scholars still remain unconvinced (e.g., Judge, Locke, Durham, & Kluger, 1998).

Knowledge of the productive power of such "false" expectations must impose an ethical burden on each and every one of us. Answers to two opposing questions must be weighed. First, knowing that it is based on random assignment or general knowledge of productive outcomes in previous research, is it ethical to convey such "false" information to managers? Second, given the experimental evidence for improved performance that all persons involved are striving to attain, is it ethically permissible *not* to convey such "false" information to managers? Furthermore, in light of the consistent findings of powerful, positive, and productive effects, is such information really "false"? In conveying unsubstantiated, generalized, positive information about subordinates to managers, we are telling "little lies" that convey a "big truth" akin to that described by Pierre Bonnard in the aforementioned quote. Will that serve our clients—subordinates, managers, and organizations—well or poorly? Would it be better either to say nothing or to convey only "little truths" about the subordinates that will obscure the big truth, which is that they can probably do better than you have expected them to do until now? Must we convey true information about the subordinates, including those who have scored below the median on whatever measures we have? Must we tell the whole truth even when we have solid evidence that this is likely to produce counterproductive Golem effects that are injurious to the manager, the subordinates, and the organization?

Each of us must resolve these ethical dilemmas as a basis for choosing to act or to abstain with regard to Pygmalion research and application. My personal resolution is to choose the "big truth" that I see embedded in the Pygmalion effect and to convey high expectations at every turn and to encourage others to do the same. I choose not to sacrifice the universally desired potential gains produced by expectation effects by refraining from "little lies" in the name of ethical purity. Whoever decides to desist from such application on ethical grounds must live with the knowledge that he or she has deprived others of the potential benefits. It is the nature of ethical dilemmas that such personal decisions are to be respected. Nevertheless, it is incumbent on each of us to take a clear stand on the issue.

My own choice is clear: Based on knowledge of the meta-analyzed results of over 20 internally and externally valid field experiments showing that raising expectations without regard for the aptitude of the particular individuals involved produces sizable and consistent performance increments, I deem it ethical to do so and unethical not to. Thus, I find myself in agreement with the spirit of White and Locke's (2000) statement, "We believe that Pygmalion interventions should focus on the capacity that all employees have to upgrade their skills and improve their performance ..." (p. 402). Moreover, I agree that conveying positive information about employees should not be done in a way that implies disparagement of other employees.

This ethical issue has accompanied research and application of the Pygmalion phenomenon from the beginning. There may be additional ways to cast it and think about it. I would welcome such thinking and discussion. Meantime, the statement that "half the people around here are below average" is indisputable statistical and *literal truth*. However, it is also likely to be demotivating and dysfunctional to that half of the population who score below the median and to detract from their utilization and development of whatever potential they do have. Conversely, Garrison Keillor's characterization of Lake Wobegon in his weekly National Public Radio program *Prairie Home Companion* as a place where "all the children are above average" is statistically and *literally false*. However, it is wholesome, *functional truth* that can inspire individuals to strive for greater achievement; this is the truth that organizational behavior scholars and practitioners should promote and promulgate. Think about that next time you hear someone define the Pygmalion effect in terms of conveying "false" information to managers.

## ACKNOWLEDGMENT

Work on this chapter was partially supported by the Lilly and Alejandro Saltiel Chair in Corporate Leadership and Social Responsibility.

## REFERENCES

Ambady, N., Hallahan, M., & Rosenthal, R. (1995). On judging and being judged accurately in zero-acquaintance situations. *Journal of Personality and Social Psychology, 69*, 518–529.

Avolio, B. J., Kahai, S., & Dodge, G. (2000). E-leadership and its implications for theory, research and practice. *Leadership Quarterly, 11*, 615–670.

Babad, E. Y. (1993). Pygmalion—25 years after interpersonal expectations in the classroom. In P. D. Blanck (Ed.), *Interpersonal expectations: Theory, research, and applications* (pp. 125–153). Cambridge, England: Cambridge University Press.

Babad, E. Y., Inbar, J., & Rosenthal, R. (1982). Pygmalion, Galatea, and the Golem: Investigations of biased and unbiased teachers. *Journal of Educational Psychology, 74*, 459–474.

Bandura, A. (1989). Human agency in social cognitive theory. *American Psychologist, 44*, 1175–1184.

Bandura, A. (1997). *Self-efficacy: The exercise of control*. New York: Freeman.

Bargh, J. A., & Chartrand, T. L. (1999). The unbearable automaticity of being. *American Psychologist, 54,* 462–479.

Barling, J., Weber, T., & Kelloway, E. K. (1996). Effects of transformational leadership training on attitudinal and financial outcomes: A field experiment. *Journal of Applied Psychology, 81,* 827–832.

Baron, R. M., & Kenny, D. A. (1986). The moderator–mediator variable distinction in social psychological research: Conceptual, strategic, and statistical considerations. *Journal of Personality and Social Psychology, 51,* 1173–1182.

Bass, B. M. (1998). *Transformational leadership: Industrial, military, and educational impact.* Mahwah, NJ: Lawrence Erlbaum Associates.

Campbell, D., & Stanley, J. (1966). *Experimental and quasi-experimental designs for research.* Chicago: Rand McNally.

Chaiken, S., & Trope, Y. (Eds.). (1999). *Dual-process theories in social psychology.* New York: Guilford.

Chapman, G. B., & McCauley, C. (1993). Early career achievements of National Science Foundation (NSF) graduate applicants: Looking for Pygmalion and Galatea effects in NSF winners. *Journal of Applied Psychology, 78,* 815–820.

Chen, G., Gully, S. M., & Eden, D. (2001). Validation of a new general self-efficacy scale. *Organizational Research Methods, 4,* 62–83.

Cohen, J. (1988). *Statistical power analysis for the behavioral sciences* (2nd ed.). Hillsdale, NJ: Lawrence Erlbaum Associates.

Colvin, C. R., & Block, J. (1994). Do positive illusions foster mental health? An examination of the Taylor and Brown formulation. *Psychological Bulletin, 116,* 3–20.

Colvin, C. R., Block, J., & Funder, D. C. (1995). Overly positive self-evaluations and personality: Negative implications for mental health. *Journal of Personality and Social Psychology, 68,* 1152–1162.

Crawford, K. S., Thomas, E. D., & Fink, J. J. (1980). Pygmalion at sea: Improving the work effectiveness of low performers. *Journal of Applied Behavioral Science, 16,* 482–505.

Davidson, O. B., & Eden, D. (2000). Remedial self-fulfilling prophecy: Two field experiments to prevent Golem effects among disadvantaged women. *Journal of Applied Psychology, 85,* 386–398.

Dusek, J. B., Hall, V. C., & Meyer, W. J. (Eds.). (1985). *Teacher expectations.* Hillsdale, NJ: Lawrence Erlbaum Associates.

Dvir, T., Eden, D., Avolio, B., & Shamir, B. (2002). Impact of transformational leadership on follower development and performance: A field experiment. *Academy of Management Journal, 45,* 735–744.

Dvir, T., Eden, D., & Banjo, M. L. (1995). Self-fulfilling prophecy and gender: Can women be Pygmalion and Galatea? *Journal of Applied Psychology, 80,* 253–270.

Eden, D. (1986). OD and self-fulfilling prophecy: Boosting productivity by raising expectations. *Journal of Applied Behavioral Science, 22,* 1–13.

Eden, D. (1988a). Creating expectation effects in OD: Applying self-fulfilling prophecy. *Research in Organizational Change and Development, 2,* 235–267.

Eden, D. (1988b). Pygmalion, goal setting, and expectancy: Compatible ways to raise productivity. *Academy of Management Review, 13,* 639–652.

Eden, D. (1990a). Consultant as Messiah: Applying expectation effects in managerial consultation. *Consultation, 9,* 37–50.

Eden, D. (1990b). Industrialization as a self-fulfilling prophecy: The role of expectations in development. *International Journal of Psychology, 25,* 871–886.

Eden, D. (1990c). *Pygmalion in management: Productivity as a self-fulfilling prophecy.* Lexington, MA: Lexington.

Eden, D. (1990d). Pygmalion without interpersonal contrast effects: Whole groups gain from raising manager expectations. *Journal of Applied Psychology, 75,* 394–398.

Eden, D. (1993a). Interpersonal expectancy effects in organizations. In P. D. Blanck (Ed.), *Interpersonal expectations: Theory, research, and applications* (pp. 154–178). Cambridge, England: Cambridge University Press.

Eden, D. (1993b). Leadership and expectations: Pygmalion effects and other self-fulfilling prophecies in organizations. *Leadership Quarterly, 3,* 271–305.

Eden, D. (1996, August). *From self-efficacy to means efficacy: Internal and external sources of general and specific efficacy.* Paper presented at the 56th annual meeting of the Academy of Management (Organizational Behavior Division), Cincinnati, Ohio.

Eden, D. (2001). Means efficacy: External sources of general and specific subjective efficacy. In M. Erez, U. Kleinbeck, & H. Thierry (Eds.), *Work motivation in the context of a globalizing economy* (pp. 65–77). Mahwah, NJ: Lawrence Erlbaum Associates.

Eden, D., & Aloni, G. (2000). *Pygmalion effects among blue-collar supervisors and subordinates: Is prior acquaintance a barrier?* (Working Paper No. 18/2000). Tel Aviv, Israel: Tel Aviv University, Faculty of Management.

Eden, D., & Aviram, A. (1993). Self-efficacy training to speed reemployment: Helping people to help themselves. *Journal of Applied Psychology, 78,* 352–360.

Eden, D., Geller, D., Gewirtz, A., Gordon-Terner, R., Inbar, I., Liberman, M., Pass, Y., Salomon-Segev, I., & Shalit, M. (2000). Implanting Pygmalion Leadership Style through workshop training: Seven field experiments. *Leadership Quarterly, 11,* 171–210.

Eden, D., & Granat-Flomin, R. (2000, April). *Augmenting means efficacy to improve service performance among computer users: A field experiment in the public sector.* Paper presented at the 15th annual meeting of the Society for Industrial and Organizational Psychology, New Orleans, LA.

Eden, D., & Kinnar, J. (1991). Modeling Galatea: Boosting self-efficacy to increase volunteering. *Journal of Applied Psychology, 76,* 770–780.

Eden, D., & Ravid, G. (1982). Pygmalion versus self-expectancy: Effects of instructor- and self-expectancy on trainee performance. *Organizational Behavior and Human Performance, 30,* 351–364.

Eden, D., & Shani, A. B. (1982). Pygmalion goes to boot camp: Expectancy, leadership, and trainee performance. *Journal of Applied Psychology, 67,* 194–199.

Eden, D., & Sulimani, R. (2001, April). *Making Pygmalion training effective: Greater mastery through augmentation of means efficacy.* Paper presented at the 16th annual meeting of the Society for Industrial and Organizational Psychology, San Diego, CA.

Eden, D., & Sulimani, R. (2002). Pygmalion training made effective: Greater mastery through augmentation of self-efficacy and means efficacy. In B. J. Avolio & F. J. Yammarino (Eds.), *Transformational and charismatic leadership: The road ahead.* (pp. 287–308) New York: Elsevier.

Eden, D., & Zuk, Y. (1995). Seasickness as a self-fulfilling prophecy: Raising self-efficacy to boost performance at sea. *Journal of Applied Psychology, 80,* 628–635.

Frayne, C. A., & Geringer, J. M. (2000). Self-management training for improving job performance: A field experiment involving salespeople. *Journal of Applied Psychology, 85,* 361–372.

Gold, M. A. (1999). *Pygmalion in cyberspace: Leaders' high expectancies for subordinate performance conveyed electronically versus face-to-face.* Unpublished doctoral dissertation, The University at Albany, State University of New York.

Gold, M. A. (2001, April). *Pygmalion in cyberspace: Leaders' electronic and face-to-face communications.* Paper presented at the 16th annual meeting of the Society for Industrial and Organizational Psychology, San Diego, CA.

Harris, M. J., & Rosenthal, R. (1985). Mediation of interpersonal expectancy effects: 31 meta-analyses. *Psychological Bulletin, 97,* 363–386.

Holon, S. D. (1996). The efficacy and effectiveness of psychotherapy relative to medications. *American Psychologist, 51,* 1025–1030.

Judge, T. A., Locke, E. A., Durham, C. C., & Kluger, A. N. (1998). Dispositional effects on job and life satisfaction: The role of core evaluations. *Journal of Applied Psychology, 83,* 17–34.

Jussim, L. (1991). Social perception and social reality: A reflection–construction model. *Psychological Review, 98,* 54–73.

Jussim, L., & Eccles, J. (1995). Naturally occurring interpersonal expectancies. *Review of Personality and Social Psychology, 15,* 74–108.

Kierein, N., & Gold, M. A. (2000). Pygmalion in work organizations: A meta-analysis. *Journal of Organizational Behavior, 21,* 913–928.

King, A. S. (1971). Self-fulfilling prophecies in training the hard-core: Supervisors' expectations and the underprivileged workers' performance. *Social Science Quarterly, 52,* 369–378.

King, A. S. (1974). Expectation effects in organization change. *Administrative Science Quarterly, 19,* 221–230.

Learman, L. A., Avorn, J., Everitt, D. E., & Rosenthal, R. (1990). Pygmalion in the nursing home: The effects of caregiver expectations on patient outcomes. *Journal of the American Geriatrics Society, 38,* 797–803.

Leedham, B., Meyerowitz, B. E., Muirhead, J., & Frist, M. H. (1995). Positive expectations predict health after heart transplantation. *Health Psychology, 14,* 74–79.

Lord, R. G., & Emrich, C. G. (2000). Thinking outside the box by looking inside the box: Extending the cognitive revolution in leadership research. *Leadership Quarterly, 11,* 551–579.

Lykken, D. T. (1968). Statistical significance in psychological research. *Psychological Bulletin, 70,* 151–159.

Maddux, J. E. (1995). Self-efficacy theory: An introduction. In J. E. Maddux (Ed.), *Self-efficacy, adaptation, and adjustment: Theory, research, and application* (pp. 3–33). New York: Plenum.

Madon, S., Jussim, L., & Eccles, J. (1997). In search of the powerful self-fulfilling prophecy. *Journal of Personality and Social Psychology, 72,* 791–809.

McNatt, D. B. (2000). Ancient Pygmalion joins contemporary management: A meta-analysis of the result. *Journal of Applied Psychology, 85,* 314–322.

Merton, R. K. (1948). The self-fulfilling prophecy. *Antioch Review, 8,* 193–210.

Natanovich, G., & Eden, D. (2001, April). *Pygmalion effects among outreach supervisors and tutors: Extending gender and ethnic generalizability.* Presented at the 16th annual meeting of the Society for Industrial and Organizational Psychology, San Diego, CA.

Oz, S., & Eden, D. (1994). Restraining the Golem: Boosting performance by changing the interpretation of low scores. *Journal of Applied Psychology, 79,* 744–754.

Rosenthal, R. (1966). *Experimenter effects in behavioral research.* New York: Apple-Century-Crofts.

Rosenthal, R. (Ed.). (1979). *Skill in nonverbal communication: Individual differences.* Cambridge, MA: Oelgeschlager, Gunn, Hain.

Rosenthal, R. (1985). From unconscious experimenter bias to teacher expectancy effects. In J. B. Dusek, V. C. Hall, & W. J. Meyer (Eds.), *Teacher expectations* (pp. 37–65). Hillsdale, NJ: Lawrence Erlbaum Associates.

Rosenthal, R. (1991a). *Meta-analytic procedures for social science.* Newbury Park, CA: Sage.

Rosenthal, R. (1991b). Teacher expectancy effects: A brief update 25 years after the Pygmalion experiment. *Journal of Research in Education, 1,* 3–12.

Rosenthal, R., Hall, J. A., DiMatteo, M. R., Rogers, P. L., & Archer, D. (1979). *Sensitivity to nonverbal communication: The PONS test.* Baltimore: Johns Hopkins University Press.

Rosenthal, R., & Jacobson, L. (1968). *Pygmalion in the classroom: Teacher expectation and pupils' intellectual development.* New York: Holt, Rinehart & Winston.

Rosenthal, R., & Rubin, D. B. (1978). Interpersonal expectancy effects: The first 345 studies. *Behavioral and Brain Studies, 3,* 377–386.

Rosenthal, R., & Rubin, D. B. (1982). A simple general purpose display of magnitude of experimental effect. *Journal of Educational Psychology, 74,* 166–169.

Rowe, J. W., & Kahn, R. L. (1998). *Successful aging.* New York: Dell.

Scheier, M. F., & Carver, C. S. (1985). Optimism, coping, and health: Assessment and implications of generalized outcome expectancies. *Health Psychology, 4,* 219–247.

Seligman, M. E. P. (1995). The effectiveness of psychotherapy: The *Consumer Reports* study. *American Psychologist, 50,* 965–974.

Seligman, M. E. P. (1996). Science as an ally of practice. *American Psychologist, 51,* 1072–1079.

Seligman, M. E. P. (1998). *Learned optimism: How to change your mind and your life* (2nd ed.). New York: Pocket Books.

Smith, A. E., Jussim, L., Eccles, J., VanNoy, M., Madon, S., & Palumbo, P. (1998). Self-fulfilling prophecies, perceptual biases, and accuracy at the individual and group levels. *Journal of Experimental Social Psychology, 34,* 530–561.

Smoll, F. L., Smith, R. E., Barnett, N. P., & Everett, J. J. (1993). Enhancement of children's self-esteem through social support training for youth sport coaches. *Journal of Applied Psychology, 78*, 602–610.

Sutton, C. D., & Woodman, R. W. (1989). Pygmalion goes to work: The effects of supervisor expectations in a retail setting. *Journal of Applied Psychology, 74*, 943–950.

Taylor, S. E. (1989). *Positive illusions: Creative self-deception and the healthy mind*. New York: Basic Books.

Taylor, S. E., & Brown, J. D. (1988). Illusion and well-being: A social psychological perspective on mental health. *Psychological Bulletin, 103*, 193–210.

Taylor, S. E., & Brown, J. D. (1994). Positive illusions and well-being revisited: Separating fact from fiction. *Psychological Bulletin, 116*, 21–27.

Taylor, S. E., Kemeny, M. E., Reed, G. M., Bower, J. E., & Gruenewald, T. L. (2000). Psychological resources, positive illusions, and health. *American Psychologist, 55*, 99–109.

Weinstein, R. S. (2002). *Reaching higher: The power of expectations in schooling*. Cambridge, MA: Harvard University Press.

Weinstein, R. S., Soule, C. R., Collins, F., Cone, J., Mehlhorn, M., & Simontacchi, K. (1991). Expectations and high school change: Teacher–researcher collaboration to prevent school failure. *American Journal of Community Psychology, 19*, 333–363.

White, S. S., & Locke, E. A. (2000). Problems with the Pygmalion effect and some proposed solutions. *Leadership Quarterly, 11*, 389–415.

Yukl, G. (2002). *Leadership in organizations* (5th ed.). Upper Saddle River, NJ: Prentice-Hall.

# II

## Interpersonal Processes

# 4

# Understanding Diversity in Organizations: Getting a Grip on a Slippery Construct

Belle Rose Ragins
*University of Wisconsin–Milwaukee*

Jorge A. Gonzalez
*University of Wisconsin–Milwaukee*

It is startling that within the course of only 10 years the term *diversity* evolved from relative obscurity to one of the most commonly cited issues facing managers and organizations today (Digh, 1998a; Robinson & Dechant, 1997; Society for Human Resource Management, 1997). Although diversity has always been a part of organizations, the recognition of diversity as an organizational issue became salient when demographers forecasted that White males would, for the first time, become the numerical minority in the workforce. In 1987 the Hudson Institute released a report predicting that women, immigrants, and people of color would constitute 85% of the new entrants into the workforce by the year 2000 (Johnston & Packer, 1987), and that White men would account for less than 40% of the labor force by the year 2010 (Loden & Rosener, 1991). Nearly overnight, books and articles appeared that addressed the challenge of diversity and forecasts for the impending "Workforce 2000" (Cox & Blake,

1991; Fernandez, 1991; Jackson & Associates, 1992; Loden & Rosener, 1991; Morrison, 1992; Thomas, 1990, 1991). Thus, the field of "diversity in organizations" was born, even though social scientists have studied the effects of racial and gender diversity in related contexts for well over 40 years (cf. reviews by Alderfer & Thomas, 1988; Konrad & Gutek, 1987; Triandis, Kurowski, & Gelfand, 1993; Williams & O'Reilly, 1998).

The Hudson report's predictions of Workforce 2000 were accurate. People of color are currently 27% of the workforce (U.S. Census, 2000), and are expected to comprise 36% of the workforce by the year 2025 (Fullerton, 1999). Women currently constitute a full 47% of the workforce (U.S. Census, 2000), and we are witnessing unprecedented workforce diversity in other areas as well. For example, people with disabilities are nearly 12% of the workforce (U.S. Census, 2000), gay men and lesbians constitute between 4% and 17% of the workforce (Gonsiorek & Weinrich, 1991), and 42% of employees will be 45 years of age or older by the year 2015 (Fullerton, 1999). Immigration trends are contributing to increasing religious diversity in the American workplace, and it is projected that Islam will be the second largest religion in the United States by the year 2010 (Digh, 1998b).

Given these demographic changes, most organizations recognize that there is no turning back with respect to diversity, that diversity is a fact rather than a fad, and that companies that do a good job with diversity will gain a competitive edge over those that do not. In recognition of the increasing significance of diversity, more than 70% of Fortune 500 companies have diversity initiatives (Digh, 1998a; Society for Human Resource Management, 1997), and U.S. companies are estimated to spend between $200 and $300 million a year on diversity training (Flynn, 1998).

The purpose of this chapter is to provide an overview of the field of workplace diversity. We start with a general introduction to the field and examine the debate involved with establishing a case for diversity. We then present various definitions of diversity and explore the dilemmas faced in defining this somewhat slippery construct. Next, we trace these dilemmas to the evolution of diversity as an emerging field in organizational behavior. Following this, we provide an overview of the current state of research and theory on workplace diversity. Finally, we offer projections and recommendations for the future of the field.

## THE DIVERSITY DEBATE

Although managers and practitioners view diversity as beneficial to organizations (Robinson & Dechant, 1997), organizational scholars are more divided on the effects of diversity on work group performance (see reviews by Jackson, Stone, & Alvarez, 1992; Milliken & Martins, 1996; Triandis et al., 1993; Webber & Donahue, 2001; Williams & O'Reilly, 1998).

## More Than Two Sides to the "Diversity Sword"?

There are two perspectives on workplace diversity. One perspective holds that diversity represents a valued and competitive advantage for organizations. For example, some studies have found that over time culturally diverse work teams make better decisions than homogeneous teams (McLeod, Lobel, & Cox, 1996; Watson, Kumar, & Michaelsen, 1993; see also review by Triandis et al., 1993).

However, other scholars observe that diversity may be a "two-edged sword" (Milliken & Martins, 1996), and point to evidence suggesting that diversity may create conflict and limit work group cohesiveness (cf. review by Jackson et al., 1992). Williams and O'Reilly (1998) concluded from their review that diverse groups are less able to provide for members' needs and have less integration, less communication, and more conflict than homogeneous groups. However, they also observed that group outcomes vary by the type of diversity, that we know little about how group and individual processes affect group outcomes, and that these effects may also be moderated by other variables that have not been investigated, such as culture, technology, and task design.

In recognition of the fact that the effects of diversity may vary by the type of diversity studied, Webber and Donahue (2001) conducted a meta-analysis of 24 studies of diversity and team performance. They compared studies that assessed effects of job-related diversity (i.e., functional background, industry, and occupation) and demographic diversity (age, gender, race, and ethnicity) and found that neither type of diversity had a relationship with team cohesion or performance. Rather than having positive or negative effects, their meta-analysis suggests that diversity may have no effect on team outcomes. In essence, there may be more than two sides to the diversity sword.

## Unexamined Issues in the Diversity Debate

It is important to recognize that any relationship found between team diversity and group outcomes may be due to processes underlying demographic group memberships. For example, Konrad (in press) observed that status and power effects that are correlated with group membership may be responsible for the negative relationships between diversity and group cohesiveness reported by Williams and O'Reilly (1998). This argument is aligned with a structuralist perspective, which holds that many observed group differences are a function of group differences in power and status in organizations (Kanter, 1977; Martin, 1985; Ragins & Sundstrom, 1989).

A larger issue that has not received much attention in the diversity debate is the effect of diversity on the overall performance of the organization. In fact, organizational outcomes may be affected by how the organization leverages its diversity, rather than by actual diversity (cf. Schneider & Northcraft, 1999). For example, Richard (2000) found that whereas racial diversity in organizations did not affect firm performance, it interacted with business strategy to have a positive impact on organizational outcomes. Similarly, Wright, Ferris, Hiller, and Kroll (1995) found a positive relationship between stock returns and the presence of exemplary affirmative action programs, suggesting that progressive diversity programs may have a positive relationship with organizational outcomes. Other scholars are quick to note that although the benefits associated with diversity may be contested, the costs associated with mismanaging diversity are quite clear (Jackson et al., 1992; Robinson & Dechant, 1997). These costs may include increased turnover and absenteeism among disenfranchised groups, and the organization becoming a target of costly lawsuits. In addition, organizations that develop a poor reputation with respect to diversity lose their competitive edge in recruiting the best talent, and may face indirect costs associated with restricted marketing of products to an increasingly diverse consumer base (Cox & Blake, 1991; Robinson & Dechant, 1997). Finally, it has been suggested that organizations that are sensitive to domestic cultural differences may also do a better job in the international marketplace (Fernandez, 1991).

## The Diversity Debate: A Moot Point?

On a practical level, debating the costs and benefits associated with diversity becomes a moot point. Organizations cannot choose whether or not to be diverse or ignore the diversity in their workforce, customer base, and business environments. It may be more beneficial to explore how organizations can capitalize and effectively manage the diversity in their business environment than to debate the relative costs and benefits of diversity. Along similar lines, because diverse work teams are a fact of life, it may be more important to study the processes underlying effective and ineffective teams, thus giving insights into methods for improving team performance, than to simply examine whether various types of diversity are associated with various team outcomes. However, before we even face this challenge, diversity scholars must first undertake the daunting task of defining the very construct of diversity.

## DEFINING DIVERSITY: DIVERSE PERSPECTIVES AND DILEMMAS

A review of the literature reveals a wide variety of opinions as to what constitutes the very construct of diversity. In this section, we identify some of the facets of diversity, and the dilemmas and issues raised in defining this complex and evolving construct.

## Micro Approaches to Diversity: Individual and Group Perspectives

One common approach to diversity is to define it in a very individualistic and general way. Specifically, diversity has been defined as all the ways in which people are similar and different from one another (Thomas, 1991; Triandis et al., 1993) and all the situations in which the actors of interest are not alike with respect to some attribute (Jackson et al., 1992). This definition incorporates demographic and group differences, as well as individual differences in personality, values, knowledge, skill, and abilities. Although the inclusiveness of this approach is appealing, it has also been criticized as belittling group differences based on power (Linnehan & Konrad, 1999) and discounting histories of societal oppression (Cox, 1995; Nkomo, 1995). In essence, defining diversity as all of the ways in which people differ may dilute diversity by treating all differences as equal, thus ignoring group differences that result in discrimination and unequal treatment in organizations (Linnehan & Konrad, 1999).

*Individual Perspectives.* Diversity has also been defined as the factors that shape an individual's experiences, values, and world perceptions. Loden and Rosener (1991) proposed that diversity involves primary and secondary dimensions. Primary dimensions are immutable differences that are inborn or represent one's core identity, such as race, ethnicity, gender, age, physical abilities/qualities, and sexual orientation. These dimensions have a primary influence in shaping the individual's self and worldview. In addition, individuals have secondary dimensions of diversity that can be modified or discarded throughout one's life. Secondary dimensions include educational background, geographic location, income, marital status, military experience, parental status, religious beliefs, and work experience. According to Loden and Rosener, primary and secondary dimensions interact to shape the individual's experiences, values, and perceptions.

*Group Perspectives.* Along similar lines, diversity has been defined from a group identity perspective. Specifically, Nkomo and Cox (1996) viewed identity as the key factor underlying diversity, and defined diversity as "a mixture of people with different group identities within the same social system" (p. 339). They identified a number of complexities involved with the concept of identity as a source of diversity. For example, individuals hold multiple group memberships, but different situations may increase or decrease the salience of group identities to the individual. In addition, two individuals may hold the same group membership but may differ in the impact of that group membership on their individual identities. Finally, they observed that all group identities are not equivalent in cultural and political history.

Whereas some definitions of diversity focus on factors that shape the individual, other approaches view diversity in terms of demographic group memberships. Implicit in this approach is the perception of group membership. For example, distinctions have been made between group memberships that are observable (e.g., gender, race, age, appearance, and some forms of disability) and those that are not easily observable (e.g., religion, sexual orientation, class, some forms of disability; Jackson, May, & Whitney, 1995; Pelled, 1996; Shaw & Barrett-Power, 1998). McGrath, Berdahl, and Arrow (1995) pointed out that an individual's demographic diversity may not only reflect underlying traits and attributes, but also may be a stimulus for evoking others' expectations about the individual's performance, traits, and attributes. Along parallel lines, Harrison, Price, and Bell (1998) offered the distinction between visible or "surface-level" diversity, which includes visible, immutable, and biological characteristics, and nonvisible or "deep-level" diversity, which includes such nonvisible attributes as attitudes, values, and beliefs.

*Job Performance Perspectives.* Diversity has also been defined in terms of the individual and group differences that affect job performance. One example is Jackson and Ruderman's (1995) view that diversity involves three domains: demographic diversity (e.g., based on gender, ethnicity, and age), psychological diversity (e.g., based on values, beliefs, knowledge), and organizational diversity (e.g., based on tenure, occupation, hierarchical level). McGrath et. al. (1995) extended this approach and proposed five dimensions of diversity: (a) demographic attributes that are socially meaningful in the society in which the organization is embedded (e.g., age, race, ethnicity, gender, sexual orientation, physical status, religion, and education); (b) task-related knowledge, skills, and abilities; (c) values, beliefs, and attitudes; (d) personality and cognitive and behavioral styles; and (e) status in the work group's embedding organization (e.g., rank, occupation, department, and tenure). In line with this approach, Thomas and Ely (1996) observed that diversity involves not just identity group memberships, but also the underlying perspectives and approaches to work held by members of different identity groups. Similarly, Pelled (1996) offered the construct of job-related diversity, which involves the experiences, skills, or perspectives needed for the task at hand. She proposed that demographic diversity should be viewed within the context of its level of job-relatedness and visibility. Northcraft, Polzer, Neale, and Kramer (1995) observed that functional diversity (involving cognitive and physical resources) and demographic diversity are interrelated; demographic group membership may serve as a "cue" for triggering stereotypes and expectations about job-related forms of diversity.

*Slippage in Defining the Construct.* This discussion reveals another level of complexity and raises some questions about the slippery construct of diversity. In particular, who defines diversity and where does diversity reside? Is diversity objective or subjective? Does the target or the perceiver define diversity? An individual's "surface-level" diversity may be salient to others, but may not be relevant or important to the individual. Moreover, nonvisible demographic group memberships (i.e., sexual orientation, class, religion) may not be salient to others, but may be central to the individual's own self-perception of diversity. In short, the individual's objective group membership may be quite different from others' perception of that membership, the individual's self-perception of that membership, and the degree to which that membership is important to his or her self-concept.

## Macro Approaches to Diversity: Organizational and Power Perspectives

Diversity has not only been defined at the individual and group level, but it has also been approached from more macro levels involving the organization, cultural systems, and society.

*The Organizational and Social System Perspective.* One macro approach defines diversity in terms of group culture within a social or societal system. For example, Cox (1993) viewed diversity in terms of the organizational context and defines cultural diversity as "the representation, in one social system, of people with distinctly different group affiliations of cultural significance" (p. 6). According to Cox, cultural groups refer to groups who share norms, values, or traditions that differ from those shared by other groups in an organization. Triandis (1995) took a broader cultural approach in defining diversity, and observed that diversity is a socially constructed phenomenon determined by the cultural–historical context and situation. He noted that salient dimensions of diversity vary from culture to culture, and proposed that diversity becomes important in situations where the group is heterogeneous and when power relations among social categories are in flux. Ferdman (1995) observed that group-level accounts of diversity do not provide a means to consider the linkages between the group's culture and the social identity of its members. He attempted to bridge this gap by viewing diversity as the individual's cultural identity, which focuses on the individual's personal experiences of group-level differences. Finally, Alderfer observed that individuals are members of multiple embedded groups in organizations, and that perspectives on diversity should examine the interrelationships among organizational groups (Alderfer, 1997; Alderfer, Alderfer, Tucker, & Tucker, 1980; Alderfer & Smith, 1982; Alderfer & Thomas, 1988).

*The Power Perspective.*    Diversity has also been defined from a power perspective, which views diversity as a reflection of the power relationships among groups in organizations (Alderfer, 1997; Linnehan & Konrad, 1999; Ragins, 1997; Ragins & Sundstrom, 1989). The power perspective is grounded in the idea that groups receive differential treatment in organizations (Nkomo, 1995), and that some groups face restricted power and privilege (Ely, 1995b). In this view, it is not just the group membership that is significant, but the power, status, and resources associated with that membership (Ragins, 1997). The power perspective interacts with individual-level, social identity perspectives on diversity. Specifically, an individual may choose not to identify with a group that has low power or is immersed in power conflicts with other groups in an organization. In addition, the power or status associated with an individual's group may affect the perception of that individual's diversity by others in the organization. For example, an individual may be a member of multiple groups, but others in the organization may view that individual primarily in terms of a group membership that is made salient by power dynamics. Although the power perspective has been applied primarily to demographic groups (i.e., race, gender, sexual orientation), it can also be applied to other dimensions of diversity that reflect the "haves and have-nots" in organizations (e.g., job type, exempt/nonexempt status, function, occupation).

*Assumptions Underlying Approaches to Diversity.*    A power perspective on diversity illuminates some assumptions underlying the very construct of diversity. Specifically, discussions about diversity or "diverse groups" often implicitly assume that diversity only exists among those in oppressed groups (Ely, 1995b; Nkomo, 1992). Nkomo (1992) observed that the prefix of "white" is usually suppressed when talking about groups or managers in organizations; managers are assumed to be White, Whites are not viewed as having a race, and when the construct of race is raised, it is framed as an issue or a problem. Ely (1995b) elaborated that discussions of diversity assume that "only people of color have a race; only women have a gender; only gay, lesbian, and bisexual people have a sexual identity" (p. 162). She observed that: "Diversity as a condition of relationship is lost to a notion of diversity as a set of attributes that reside in some people and not others. This leaves dominant groups fundamentally unchanged and relations of domination intact" (p. 162). Ely observed that as diversity is grounded in the constructs of dominance, privilege, and power, we can only define and understand diversity by simultaneously examining these constructs.

## Summary: Defining the Slippery Construct

In summary, it is apparent that there is diversity even in the way diversity is defined. Jackson and Ruderman (1995) concluded that "there is no consensus yet on what diversity means, nor is there consensus about which types of phenomena define the domain of diversity research" (p. 3). This conclusion is even more true today; it appears that the slippery construct of diversity has become "an empirical onion" that reveals more complexity with time and analyses. Over the course of the past 10 years, diversity has been viewed from individual, group, organizational, and societal perspectives. It has been defined in terms of identity groups, demographic groups, political groups, cultural groups, and power relationships among groups in organizations. Definitions of diversity have drawn on such factors and processes as visibility, job-relatedness, degree of immutability, and group power. Diversity has been viewed as residing in the individual, in the group, and in the organization. It has been viewed as a state, as a process, and as a political act.

Perhaps as is the case in any new field of inquiry, the definition of a construct emerges with the study of its properties, effects, and outcomes. Like any field, the field of workplace diversity has evolved over time and has been influenced by a number of related fields and streams of research. We now turn to examining how the field of workplace diversity evolved. This examination provides a useful perspective for viewing the current issues and challenges faced by diversity scholars.

## THE EVOLUTION OF DIVERSITY RESEARCH: BAGGAGE AND BENEFITS

With the release of the Hudson Institute's report on Workforce 2000 (Johnston & Packer, 1987), organizational scholars faced a sudden demand for insights about the impact of Workforce 2000 on individuals, work relationships, and organizations. Because there was no field of "diversity in organizations," these scholars drew on three closely related streams of research: research on women in management, research on organizational demography, and social–psychological research on identity and intergroup relations. Although these areas provided an important foundation for the field of workplace diversity, they also came with assumptions that became infused into the study of diversity. In fact, many of the limitations in the field of diversity are "baggage" that was inadvertently inherited from these related streams of research. We now examine the contributions and limitations of these three historical traditions.

## The Women in Management Tradition

The field of women in management (WIM) first emerged in the 1970s (see, e.g., Hennig & Jardim, 1976; Kanter, 1977; Nieva & Gutek, 1981) and became solidified as an independent field of investigation in the 1980s (Larwood, Stromberg, & Gutek, 1985; Powell, 1988; Stead, 1985; Wallace, 1982).

*Early Influences.* The WIM field looked to psychological studies of gender differences in personality and behavior in its early research and paradigm development (see Nieva & Gutek, 1981; Riger & Galligan, 1980). Consequentially, much of the early WIM research used a "trait approach" in which researchers examined whether female and male managers differed in a given trait, attribute, or characteristic. The advantage of the trait approach was that gender differences could be isolated and easily studied in laboratory settings. The problem with this approach was that it examined a given trait in isolation without considering the group or organizational context. For example, researchers may find that women communicate less in work groups than men do. However, if the woman is the sole female in an all-male group, this effect may be due to the group's gender composition rather than the subject's gender. The trait approach also takes a person-centered rather than a situation-centered approach in explaining gender differences in organizations (Riger & Galligan, 1980). Person-centered explanations for behavior ignore the context and assume a deficiency model by blaming the individual for organizational outcomes associated with group membership (Nkomo, 1992).

*Baggage and Benefits Inherited From the WIM Tradition.* The WIM field eventually recognized the limitations of the trait approach, and moved from an examination of "sex differences in x, y, or z" to a more complex examination of gender in organizations. The very construct of gender was reconceptualized using a poststructuralist feminist approach, and gender became viewed as a social and political construction that occurs within a gendered and political organizational context (Calás & Smircich, 1992; Ely, 1995a, 1995b; Fondas, 1997; Mumby & Putnam, 1992; Wharton, 1992). However, in spite of this paradigm evolution, early research on diversity adopted the readily accessible trait approach, perhaps in part because of its ease of use.

Although the WIM field provided a needed paradigm for viewing diversity in organizations, it came with some "baggage" that was adopted by the field of workplace diversity. In addition to its reliance on the trait tradition, at least three other limitations were passed along to the study of workplace diversity. First, diversity scholars tried to apply WIM research findings to diversity, but may not have recognized that many of the WIM studies used White, able-bodied, white-collar women who were assumed to be heterosexual, upper-to-middle-class Christians. In addition to restricted generalizability, an underlying assumption in the WIM field was that female managers only differed from their male counterparts on biological sex; there was little if any discussion on the experiences of female managers of color or lesbian managers. This silo approach to gender may be seen today in diversity research that examines one dimension of diversity (i.e., race or gender) without exploring the cumulative or interactive effects of multiple group memberships on workplace experiences (cf., Ferdman, 1995; Ragins, Cornwell, & Miller, in press).

Second, the WIM field had a historical tradition of examining gender as it relates to the workplace experiences of women, but not men. In fact, only recently have gender scholars examined the experience of being male in organizations (Cheng, 1999; Maier, 1999). We can see that research on diversity adopted this limitation; gender and race have typically been examined from the perspective of those in the minority; the experiences of majority members are rarely discussed or compared to the experiences of minority members in organizations.

The third limitation of the WIM field was that, by definition, the field focused on women who managed or sought to manage others, usually within large, male-dominated corporate settings. There was limited discussion or research on gender effects in other occupations and organizations. In contrast, the field of workplace diversity is charged with examining diversity among employees in all ranks, functions, and types of organizations. These disparities may explain why the study of diversity often takes the form of examining how managers (implicitly White) "manage other people's diversity" in corporate settings.

## The Demography Tradition

In addition to the WIM tradition, the field of diversity in organizations has also been guided by a 40-year stream of research on demography in organizations (see review by Williams & O'Reilly, 1998).

*Defining Demography.* Demography and diversity are sometimes viewed as overlapping areas of research, but Tsui and Gutek (1999) made the distinction that "diversity research refers to the study of the effects of diversity on the employment experiences of individuals, usually individuals who are in the minority categories" (p. 25). In contrast, demographic research "refers to the study of both the causes and consequences of the composition or distribution of specific demographic attributes of employees in an organization or units within it. Organizational demography researchers are interested in the effect of demography "on everyone, not only the minority individuals" (p. 26). In essence, diversity research is focused more on understanding the experiences of individuals whereas demographic research is concerned more with the effects of demography on group and organizational outcomes.

Tsui and Gutek (1999) distinguished between two approaches to demography: compositional demography and relational demography. Compositional demography involves the study of the effects of demographic compositions of work groups, departments, or organizations on group or organizational outcomes (Pfeffer, 1983). One example of this approach is the examination of the impact of the gender composition of a group on group outcomes. Tsui and Gutek observed that this approach assumes that group demography has the same impact on all group members, irrespective of individual demographic characteristics. Relational demography was developed to address this shortcoming. Relational demography examines the similarity or dissimilarity between the individual's demographic characteristics and that of the group (Tsui, Egan, & O'Reilly, 1992; Tsui & O'Reilly, 1989). An example of this approach is studying the impact of being the sole female in a primarily male group (Tsui & Gutek, 1999).

*Baggage and Benefits Inherited From the Demography Tradition.*
Research on organizational demography provided a significant foundation for the emerging field of workplace diversity. Diversity scholars recognized the importance of incorporating the demographic composition of groups and organizations in their research. However, although the demography approach provided an important perspective on the role of context, it also came with some limitations. As pointed out by Lawrence (1997), a key limitation of demographic research is that researchers may find a relationship between demography and outcomes, but are unable to explain why this occurs. Although all areas have limitations, this limitation is particularly restrictive because the diversity field is charged with understanding how diversity affects individuals, relationships, groups, and organizations. Lawrence (1997) observed that demographic variables cannot replace the study of subjective or psychological processes, and recent approaches have taken this criticism to heart by examining the cognitive and psychological processes associated with demographic differences (Elsass & Graves, 1997; Pelled, 1996), and the impact of organizational culture and context on work group demography (Carroll & Harrison, 1998; Chatman, Polzer, Barsade, & Neale, 1998). However, a number of assumptions in demographic research were adopted by diversity scholars, which may have contributed to some of the limitations in the field.

As discussed earlier, one limitation of the demography tradition is that individuals are viewed in terms of their objective group membership, but there is little information as to the subjective meaning of that group membership to the individual. Nkomo and Cox (1996) observed that group memberships may hold different meanings for different individuals and that these memberships may be affected by situational cues that go beyond work demography.

A related limitation of the demography tradition is that demographic characteristics are often studied in isolation (Lau & Murnighan, 1998). Individuals are viewed as having a race or a gender, but not both (Ferdman, 1995). In addition to ignoring the effects of multiple demographic memberships, there has been little study on the potential for interaction among group memberships (cf. Ragins et al., in press). Following the demographic tradition, diversity research often examines the independent effects of race and gender, but provides limited insights into the workplace experiences of women of color, or guidance on how race and gender may interact to affect workplace experiences.

A third limitation is that demographic studies have typically examined a relatively narrow set of characteristics that have minimal political or social consequences. For example, Pfeffer's (1983) early research on organizational demography examined the effects of organizational tenure, and subsequent research has focused on such demographic characteristics as education, functional background, occupation, and age (see review by Williams & O'Reilly, 1998). Although some demographic research has examined race and gender, there has been a lack of research on other demographic characteristics that fall under the domain of diversity in organizations (e.g., disability, class, or sexual orientation).

Along similar lines, Tsui and Gutek (1999) observed that demographic research often assumes that all types of demography are equivalent. For example, the effects of being the oldest person in a group of young co-workers is often viewed as equivalent to the effects of being the only Black employee in a group of White employees. This assumption does not recognize the cultural and historical differences between groups (Nkomo, 1992; Nkomo & Cox, 1996) or the power relationships among groups in organizations (Linnehan & Konrad, 1999; Ragins & Sundstrom, 1989). Pelled, Ledford, and Mohrman (1999) tested this assumption and found that demographic effects were varied by group membership. Individuals who were dissimilar from their groups on race and gender reported less inclusion, but those who differed on tenure and education reported more organizational inclusion.

In summary, although demographic research helped the field of workplace diversity examine the impact of work group and organizational demography on diversity, it also came with specific limitations that were incongruous with the goals and focus of diversity research. The most striking limitation is the inability of demographic research to explain the processes behind observed effects. Social–psychological research addressed this very issue, and we now turn to examining the impact of this tradition on the field of workplace diversity.

## The Social Psychological Tradition

Diversity theorists have recently turned to the well-established field of social psychology for insights into how diversity affects individuals and groups in organizations. Social psychologists have examined the processes involved with social identity and intergroup relations for well over 30 years, and diversity scholars recognize that this research tradition can provide a solid background for emerging theories on workplace diversity.

*Social Identity Theory.*    Although there are many different psychological theories that can be applied to the workplace, social identity theory has been the predominant theory used by diversity scholars. According to social identity theory, an individual's self-concept is based both on a personal identity, which involves idiosyncratic characteristics (e.g., personality, individual traits, physical characteristics) as well as a social identity, which involves the individual's sense of belonging to various groups (Tajfel, 1981; Tajfel & Turner, 1986). Social identity theory involves both the individual's self-categorization into social groups and the meaning assigned to that self-categorization (Pettigrew, 1986; Tajfel, 1981; Turner, 1981). This theory has been used to explain the social psychology of intergroup relations and the process by which individuals categorize themselves and others into "in-groups" and "out-groups" (Hogg & Abrams, 1988; Tajfel & Turner, 1986; Turner, 1987). Social identity theory is grounded on the idea that intergroup social comparisons take on an evaluative component, and this perspective has been used to examine such processes as group identification and intergroup conflict in organizations (see review by Ashforth & Mael, 1989).

*Baggage and Benefits Inherited From the Social Identity Tradition.*
Although social identity theory has had a positive impact on the workplace diversity field and may offer continued promise for the future, there are some limitations involved with applying social identity research to workplace diversity. One issue is that laboratory studies of social identity were focused on explaining the general cognitive processes involved with group categorizations, but were not developed to explain how these processes emerge in organizations, or the team and organizational outcomes associated with these processes (Brewer, 1995). A more troubling concern identified by Brewer (1995) is that many of these laboratory studies did not examine race or

gender, but created "in-groups" and "out-groups" based on artificial group memberships that have little relevance to organizational settings.

Another limitation of the social identity approach is that it does not address the effects of structural characteristics of organizations on the development of social identity and intergroup relationships (Brewer, 1995). For example, organizations that are racially segregated and have cultures that do not support diversity may have a different impact on members' social identities than organizations that are structurally integrated and have supportive cultures. In fact, Wharton (1992) contended that social identity theory cannot be applied to the workplace without examining the effects of macro organizational variables on the development of workplace social identities. She observed that: "Treating race and gender only as structural categories obscures the fact that the meaning and significance of these distinctions are likely to be themselves conditioned by organizational arrangements and processes" (p. 57). She proposed that segregated organizations that are discriminatory should increase the salience of social identities for group members that are isolated and face discrimination. Although a few theoretical models include organizational context (Brickson, 2000), most applications of social identity theory to the workplace assume a very micro perspective and do not consider the influence of organizational context on the development of social identities and intergroup relations in organizations.

Finally, social identity theory may suffer from the same limitation faced by demography theory: assuming equivalent and symmetrical effects of various group memberships. Both approaches assume that the processes underlying social identity or demography are the same for minority and majority group members, ignoring the impact of discrimination, stereotypes, and group differences in power on diversity processes. Some diversity scholars are beginning to recognize nonsymmetrical effects for group membership (e.g., Mueller, Finley, Iverson, & Price, 1999; Sessa & Jackson, 1995; Simon, Hastedt, & Aufderheide, 1997), but we need to extend this line of thinking by viewing social identity within the context of discrimination, power, and privilege.

*Promising Social Psychological Influences.* A number of psychological and sociological theories on interpersonal discrimination and intergroup relations address these issues and offer great promise for future research and theory on workplace diversity. For example, stigma theory (Goffman, 1974; Heatherton, Kleck, Hebl, & Hull, 2000), aversive racism (Dovidio & Gaertner, 1986; Gaertner & Dovidio, 2000), modern sexism (Benokraitis, 1997), status characteristic theory (Berger, Cohen, & Zelditch, 1972), status generalization theory (Webster & Foschi, 1988), and other theories related to interpersonal discrimination (Lott & Maluso, 1995) and racism (Dovidio & Gaertner, 1986; Eberhardt & Fiske, 1998) could complement social identity and demography perspectives, and provide critical insights for understanding the effects of diversity within organizational settings. These theories have been incorporated in some studies of workplace diversity (e.g., Brief, Dietz, Cohen, Pugh, & Vaslow, 2000; Mor Barak, Cherin, & Berkman, 1998), but have not been systematically included into paradigms, models, and theories of workplace diversity.

## Summary: Minimizing the Baggage and Maximizing the Benefits

In summary, we can see that the field of workplace diversity has been influenced over time by research traditions in the areas of WIM, organizational demography, and social identity. Each of these areas provided important insights that helped shape the field of workplace diversity, but they also came with limitations and conceptual baggage that is evident in current research on workplace diversity. It is interesting to note that social identity and demographic approaches actually complement each other in providing micro and macro perspectives on diversity in organizations; the baggage of one is essentially the strength of the other. In spite of this, diversity scholars have tended to use either one approach or the other without considering the possibility of integrating these approaches in their models or research.

We now turn to examining some of the major current research findings on workplace diversity. This view is informed by our understanding of the evolution of the field and the limitations that have been inherited from various research traditions.

## THE CURRENT STATE OF DIVERSITY: WHERE WE ARE NOW

In this section we review some of the key theories and research on workplace diversity. We start with a review of the research findings on organizational and relational demography, and the processes that may be responsible for some of these research findings. We then explore current findings on how social identity operates within the organizational context.

## Research on Organizational and Relational Demography

There has been a fair amount of research on the area of demography in organizations (for a comprehensive review, see Tsui & Gutek, 1999; Williams & O'Reilly, 1998). Researchers have examined the effects of demographic diversity in top management teams, work groups, and entire organizations.

*Top Management Team Demography.* A number of studies have examined the effect of the demographic composition of top management teams on organizational outcomes. This research draws on the strategic management literature and proposes that the composition and diversity among those in upper echelons have an important role in the formulation and implementation of strategy and ultimate firm performance (Finkelstein & Hambrick, 1990; Hambrick & Mason, 1984; Smith et al., 1994). This perspective holds that cognitive variations among those in higher ranks affect their strategic decisions, and that these decisions in turn affect firm performance. It should be noted that although cognitive diversity is viewed as the key factor underlying this process, most research has relied on demographic diversity as a proxy for cognitive diversity (Pfeffer, 1983), which presents certain limitations in this research (see Priem, Lyon, & Dess, 1999).

The studies in this area are consistent in illustrating that the demographic composition of top management teams affects organizational outcomes. Hambrick, Cho, and Chen (1996) found that diversity in function, background, and company tenure of top management teams had a positive relationship with growth in market share and profit. Murray (1989) found a positive relationship between the age and tenure diversity of the team, and firm adaptability and stock ratios. However, although heterogeneous teams performed better on long-term performance, homogeneous teams performed better on short-term performance under conditions of intense competition. Wiersema and Bantel (1992) also found a significant relationship between top management team demography and corporate strategic change, which was measured as absolute change in diversification level.

*Relational Demography Research.* A number of other studies examined the effects of relational demography on group and individual outcomes. This research indicates outcomes vary by the type of demography studied (Pelled, Ledford, & Mohrman, 1999; Ragins et al., in press). Moreover, conflicting results have been found even within a specific demographic category. For example, some relational demogaphy studies found that tenure heterogeneity was associated with higher turnover rates, but age heterogeneity did not have a significant effect (McCain, OReilly, & Pfeffer, 1983; Wagner, Pfeffer, & O'Reilly; 1984). In contrast, other research found that age heterogeneity was a stronger predictor of turnover than tenure heterogeneity in work teams (Jackson et al., 1991).

A number of studies have examined race and gender relational demography effects in organizations. Riordan and Shore (1997) found that work group productivity, work group commitment, and perceptions of advancement opportunities were associated with group similarities in race, but not age or gender. Tsui, et al. (1992) found that increasing work-unit diversity was associated with lower levels of psychological attachment. Of particular interest was their finding of nonsymmetrical effects for race and gender. In contrast to their female counterparts, men who differed from the group on the basis of gender were less likely to report being attached to the group, had increased absence, and reported a lower intention to stay in the organization. Similarly, whereas being different from others in the work unit did not affect people of color, this difference had a negative effect on White team members. In another study, Tsui and O'Reilly (1989) examined the impact of relational demography in supervisor–subordinate dyads. Race had no effect, but gender had a unilateral effect across all of the outcomes studied. Subordinates in mixed-gender dyads reported greater role ambiguity and role conflict, and their supervisors liked them less and rated their performance lower than subordinates in same-gender dyads.

*Deep-Level Diversity.*    Although most demographic research has examined visible demographic differences, some studies have investigated invisible differences, or "deep-level diversity" (Harrison et al., 1998). For example, Barsade, Ward, Turner, and Sonnenfeld (2000) examined the impact of affective fit in top management teams. Affective fit was described as the extent to which a member is similar to others in the group in an affective personality trait that influences emotional reactions. Groups that were diverse in affect were more likely to report conflict, stressful relationships, and less cooperation than groups that were homogeneous in affective fit.

Some research has compared the effects of visible and deep-level diversity. Jehn, Chadwick, and Thatcher (1997), for example, compared the effects of value congruence, a deep-level characteristic, and visible demographic dissimilarity on task and relationship conflict, performance, and member satisfaction. Different effects were found for these two forms of diversity. Gender diversity was associated with greater relationship conflict, whereas educational diversity was associated with greater task-oriented conflict. They also found less task and relationship conflict in groups that shared the deep-level characteristic of value congruence. Harrison et al. (1998) found that although both visible and deep diversity affected group cohesiveness, group similarity in surface-level dimensions (e.g., age, ethnicity, and gender) became less important, and similarity in deep-level diversity (e.g., satisfaction with work and supervision, organizational commitment) became more important over time. This suggests that deep and surface diversity may differ in their processes and effects, and that opportunities for interactions may moderate the relationship between team diversity and outcomes.

Although researchers are examining both deep and surface-level diversity, Powell (1998) observed that these forms of diversity present a dilemma for organizations. Organizations that seek fit in deep-level characteristics are praised for reinforcing core values but condemned for maintaining demographic homogeneity, whereas organizations that seek demographic diversity are praised for broadening their perspective but condemned for harming organizational cohesiveness. Powell noted that an increased understanding of the differences between deep and surface diversity can help organizations pursue these seemingly incompatible goals.

Along similar lines, there is some evidence that the organizational culture interacts with demography to affect team outcomes. Chatman et al. (1998) found that an organization's emphasis on individualistic or collectivistic values interacted with the organization's demographic composition to influence social interaction, conflict, productivity, and perceptions of creativity in group settings. They concluded that the benefits of demographic diversity are most likely to be realized in organizations that focus on common interests rather than individualism.

As discussed earlier in this chapter, one of the key limitations with demographic research is that it does not provide us with information on the "black box," or processes underlying the effects of demography on organizational outcomes (Lawrence, 1997). We now turn to an examination of research that attempts to shed some light on these issues.

## The Impact of Process Variables on Diversity in Organizations

A number of studies have explored the processes that shape the relationship between demographic diversity and outcomes. These processes include social integration, team conflict, team norms, and other decision-making processes.

*Social Integration.* O'Reilly, Caldwell, and Barnett (1989) found that the social integration of the team mediated the relationship between the team's tenure diversity and turnover; greater diversity led to less social integration in work groups, which in turn was related to greater individual turnover. They observed that social integration affects group attraction, cohesion, and satisfaction, and that these processes may account for the relationship between diversity and team outcomes. Along similar lines, Smith et al. (1994) assessed the influence of top management team demography on organizational performance using three alternative models: a demography model where only demography influenced performance, a process model in which both demography and process variables (social integration and communication) influenced performance directly, and an intervening model where process variables acted as a mediator for demography. These researchers found partial support for the process and intervening models but little support for the demography model, thus supporting the idea that team diversity influences outcomes through interpersonal processes.

   *Team Conflict.*    Team conflict is another process variable that may affect outcomes of diverse teams (cf. Eisenhardt, Kahwajy, & Bougeois, 1997). Pelled (1996) discussed the relationship between different forms of conflict and diversity. She classified diversity in terms of visibility and job-relatedness, and viewed conflict as either substantive or affective. Substantive conflict is based on disagreements about tasks, goals, decisions, and procedures, whereas affective conflict is interpersonally based and leads to such negative emotions as anger, fear, and distrust. Pelled argued that visible diversity (e.g., age, gender, race) is more likely to trigger affective conflict, whereas diversity in job-related demographic variables (e.g., education, tenure) is more likely to lead to substantive conflict. Pelled also hypothesized different outcomes associated with different types of conflict. In particular, she proposed that substantive conflict should lead to the positive outcome of increased performance on cognitive tasks, but affective conflict could result in negative outcomes, such as turnover. Pelled and her colleagues tested this idea and found some support for their model (Pelled, Eisenhardt, & Xin, 1999). In support of their model, functional background diversity was related to task conflict and race diversity was related to emotional conflict. However, gender diversity was not related to any form of conflict, and tenure diversity was related to task but not emotional conflict. In contrast to expected effects, greater emotional conflict was found among groups that had more age similarity than dissimilarity. In short, although some forms of diversity increased the conflict experienced in teams, the relationship between conflict and performance was not straightforward and was affected by the type of diversity studied.
   In another effort to examine the relationship between conflict and diversity, Simons, Pelled, and Smith (1999) examined the influence of debate and decision comprehensiveness on the relationship between team diversity and performance in top management teams. Debate was defined as team interactions that involved opposing views about tasks and strategic decision-making processes. Decision comprehensiveness was the extent to which an organization is exhaustive or inclusive in making and integrating strategic decisions (Fredrickson, 1984). They found that debate increased the tendency for diversity to enhance top management team performance, and that decision comprehensiveness partially mediated the interactive effects of diversity and debate on company performance.

   *Group Norms and Faultlines.*    Team norms may be another process variable that underlies the effects of group diversity. Specifically, Chatman and Flynn (2001) found that cooperative group norms mediated the relationship between group composition and work outcomes. Teams that were demographically diverse were more likely to have norms that emphasized less cooperation among its members, but this effect was also found to fade over time. In addition, groups were more likely to display cooperative norms when members had greater frequency of contact, and this effect was particularly salient for diverse teams. This supports the view that time and intergroup contact are important variables to consider when assessing workgroup diversity (e.g., Harrison et al., 1998).

Group faultlines may reflect another process that affects outcomes in diverse teams. Lau and Murnighan (1998) developed the idea of faultlines to explain how the alignment of individual member characteristics in a group affects outcomes. Faultlines determine the existence and strength of subgroups, and depend on the composition and alignments of multiple demographic attributes in a group. A work group may display several faultlines if there are several subgroups that share more than one distinctive characteristic. For instance, a team may have a subgroup of middle-aged White females who share similar tenure. Earley and Mosakowski (2000) used the faultline perspective in their study of subgroups and hybrid team cultures in transnational teams. Their findings suggest that homogeneous and highly heterogeneous teams have better long-term performance than moderately heterogeneous teams due to the absence of faultlines and strong subgroups.

Studying the process by which demography influences outcomes is promising to our understanding of diversity (cf. Jackson et al., 1995; Sessa & Jackson, 1995). As can be seen from our review, diversity scholars have examined such process variables as social integration, communication, group norms, faultlines, and conflict. Although an examination of these process variables adds to our understanding of how and why diversity affects outcomes, scholars have also taken a more macro approach in examining the effects of organizational numerical proportions on diversity outcomes.

## The Influence of Numerical Proportions

Diversity outcomes may be influenced by the sheer number of different employee groups in organizations. Kanter's (1977) theory of numerical proportions was developed to explain gender effects, but has been applied to other groups that are in the numerical minority (i.e., "tokens"). She proposed that numerical rarity affects majority members' perceptions of minority members. These perceptions include an increased awareness of minorities due to their high visibility, an exaggeration of differences between minority and majority groups, and a distortion of minority members' individual attributes to fit pre-existing group stereotypes. Minorities face heightened performance pressures, greater stereotyping, and increased boundaries between minority and majority groups as a consequence of these perceptions.

Some researchers have examined the effects of numerical proportions on women's experiences in organizations. Ely (1994, 1995a) found that the number of women in the upper echelons of organizations affected women's work relationships, their social constructions of gender, and their gender identity at work. Women in male-dominated firms were less likely than those in gender-integrated firms to identify with senior women or to see their authority as legitimate (Ely, 1994). She found a greater perception of competition among women and less likelihood of same-gender support in male-dominated than in gender-integrated firms. Ely (1995a) also found that women perceived greater differences between men and women in firms with few women at the top, and that gender perceptions were aligned with gender role stereotypes. Women in gender-integrated firms were better able to integrate expressions of masculine and feminine roles, regarded feminine attributes as a source of strength, and expressed less negative attitudes toward expressing masculine traits at work. Other researchers have also found support for the tokenism effect. Lyness and Thompson (2000) found that skewed gender ratios at top ranks were associated with female executives' reports of barriers to advancement and exclusion from informal networks. Tharenou (2001) found that male hierarchies impeded women's advancement into lower and middle-level management positions, and concluded that gender dissimilarity may impede the development of women's power at early career stages.

A study of relational demography by Riordan and Shore (1997) supports the idea that numerical proportions also matter in group settings, but found that the effects of numerical proportions varied by the individual's race or ethnicity. White group members showed lower levels of group commitment and reported less productivity when they were in groups composed of primarily minorities than when in groups that were primarily White or racially balanced. Similarly, African Americans in mostly White groups exhibited lower work group commitment than African Americans in mostly minority groups. However, in contrast to White participants, there were no significant differences in the commitment displayed by African Americans in racially balanced work groups from those in mostly minority groups. The researchers also found significant differences between the African American and Hispanic participants in the study, which points to the need to separately study race and ethnicity effects for different groups.

Tolbert, Simons, Andrews, and Rhee (1995) identified two conflicting perspectives on the effects of group proportions on team outcomes. The social–psychological perspective, which is based on theories of intergroup contact, predicts that because contact with minority groups reduces social prejudice (Allport, 1954), increasing the size of a minority group should result in decreased discrimination because of increased contact. An alternative intergroup competition perspective (Blalock, 1967) predicts the exact opposite effect: that increasing the size of the minority group would be viewed as a threat to scarce resources, which in turn would increase the probability of discriminatory behaviors. Their study of female faculty representation in sociology departments yielded support for the competition perspective; departments with a high proportion of female faculty were significantly less likely to increase their number of female faculty in the future than departments with a low number of female faculty.

These studies suggest that we need to examine diversity not only from an organizational and group perspective, but also from an individual perspective. We now turn to examining how social identity and intergroup relations theories have been applied to diversity in the workplace.

## Social Identity Theory: Managing Multiple Identities in Organizations

Social identity theory (Tajfel, 1981; Tajfel & Turner, 1986; Turner, 1987) has provided an important theoretical foundation for the field of workplace diversity (Milliken & Martins, 1996; Nkomo & Cox, 1996; Williams & O'Reilly, 1998). Social identity theory is concerned with the existence of multiple identities, the variability of the degree to which people identify with a social group, and the role of the social context in social identification (Deaux, 1993). Social identity theory not only explains our self-concept, but it also addresses the way in which we view and categorize others (Tajfel, 1981). According to self-categorization theory, individuals categorize themselves and others to simplify their environment (Markus & Cross, 1990; Turner, 1987). Visible group differences may trigger categorization, as well as stereotypes and assumptions about personality and deep-level forms of diversity.

*Applications of Social Identity Theory.* There are a number of theoretical articles that apply social identity to workplace diversity. For example, Wharton (1992) observed that race and gender are not objective categories, but are social constructions grounded in perception. She asserted that an understanding of social identity and perceptual classification processes is central to understanding how race and gender become relevant social categories in organizations. Schneider and Northcraft (1999) used social identity theory to explain diversity conflicts in organizations and examined how categorization processes affect diversity initiatives and organizational outcomes. Hogg and Terry (2000) applied self-categorization theory, a variant of social identity theory, to diversity in organizations. They examined how prototype-based processes affect sociodemographic diversity and minority group relations in organizations. Brickson (2000) used Brewer and Gardner's (1996) social identity classification model to develop a model of identification processes in organizations. Brickson also incorporated a macro perspective by proposing that contextual features of the organization, such as organizational, task, and reward structures activate identity orientations, which in turn influence organizational and individual outcomes of diversity.

*Social Identity Varies by Group Membership.*    Social identity and categorization processes may vary for minority and majority members in organizations. Demographic minorities may be more likely to see themselves in terms of the social category that makes them a minority, instead of other categories or characteristics (Deaux, 1993; Tajfel, 1981). The numerical distinctiveness of minority group membership is one explanation for this phenomenon, as minority members are in the numerical minority and often possess characteristics that make them distinct (Deaux, 1993). However, other researchers argue that social identities involving minority group memberships are not guided by numerical proportions or distinctiveness, but instead are governed by the social environment (e.g., Oakes & Turner, 1986). In support of this idea, Simon, Hastedt, and Aufderheide (1997) found that minority members are more likely to define themselves through group social identities than are majority members, but also found that this occurred only when the meaningfulness of group distinctions was high. In other words, minorities may focus on their group identity not because there are fewer of them, but because the environment they face (e.g., co-workers' actions and organizational climate) constantly reminds them that they are the minority. For instance, cases of gender discrimination in an organization may increase the salience of gender as a social identity for female employees.

*Organizational Influences on Social Identity.*    Organizational factors may affect the emergence and salience of social identities in organizations. An important factor here is the organization's diversity climate, which involves the extent to which majority members value efforts to increase minority representation and whether the qualifications and abilities of minority members are questioned (Kossek & Zonia, 1993). Perceptions of climate may be affected not only by the organization actions toward diversity, but also by the extent to which diversity is salient to the individual (e.g., Mor Barak et al., 1998), thus suggesting an interactional process.

The relationship between the organizational context and social identity is also addressed in embedded intergroup relations theory (Alderfer & Smith, 1982). This theory holds that organizational role identities are embedded in a social system. Because powerful organizational groups (i.e., top management) are often comprised of people who are members of particular identity groups, power relations at the group identity level (e.g., Black and White, male and female) characterize power relations among groups at the organizational level (e.g., managers and subordinates, haves and have-nots). An organizational context where differences among demographic groups are evident provides meaningfulness for demographic identification. This context ascribes a status to an identity by associating it with access to resources or power (Nkomo & Cox, 1996; Ragins & Sundstrom, 1989).

In summary, workplace diversity has been studied from organizational, group, and individual perspectives using organizational demography, numerical proportions, social identity, intergroup relations, and embedded group relations theories. Now that we have examined the current state of the field, let us direct our attention to the future, and explore the gaps, challenges, and issues that need to be faced by diversity scholars.

## WHERE WE NEED TO GO: THE CHALLENGE OF FUTURE RESEARCH ON WORKPLACE DIVERSITY

In the course of this chapter we identified many problems, issues, and dilemmas facing the field of workplace diversity. In this section, we highlight additional conceptual and empirical issues that need to be addressed in future research and theory on diversity in the workplace.

### Expanding Our Perspectives on Diversity

As discussed earlier, diversity has been defined and approached from a variety of perspectives. Diversity is a slippery and complex construct. It may be viewed as an objective or subjective state that involves visible or invisible differences. It may reside in the target, the perceiver of the target, or in the perceptual space that exists between these two entities. It can be approached from individual, dyadic, group, organizational, or societal perspectives. It can range from being a member of an oppressed group to being in a group that shares a set of values, attributes, or personality characteristics. Reactions to diversity can range from attraction to hate crimes.

The problem is not that we apply multiple perspectives to understand diversity; in fact, the complexity of this construct requires complexity in our approach. Our concern is the narrowness with which we approach the construct and the myopic lens that we often use to view the results of our research. These limitations are understandable, as diversity is a relatively slippery construct. Consider, for example, the slippage between an individual's "objective" group membership, the perception of that membership by others, and the degree to which the individual uses that group membership to define his or her social identity. To make matters even more complex, an individual's social identity in a group may be affected by co-worker's reactions to his or her "objective" demographic group membership. In this case, not only may an individual's group membership be misperceived, but that very misperception may influence the individual's future behavior, self-categorizations, and group interactions. Researchers who examine individual or group outcomes associated with a specific "type of diversity" need to account for these complexities. Although it may not be feasible to study or control for all of these factors, they should at least be considered when viewing the results of a given study.

Our understanding of diversity may also be enriched by the incorporation of a poststructuralist perspective in our theory and research (e.g., Calás & Smircich, 1992; Ely, 1995b; Fondas, 1997; Nkomo, 1992; Wharton, 1992). This perspective holds that many "objective" demographic group memberships (i.e., race, ethnicity, gender, class, sexual orientation, disability) reflect a subjective social meaning that is embedded in organizational and societal contexts linked to oppression and power. Research that simply examines outcomes associated with various demographic group memberships views diversity in a vacuum, and does not recognize the political and social meanings attached to race, gender, and other historically oppressed groups. Diversity scholars need to recognize that the individual's experience in an organization is partly a function of intergroup power relationships within the organization and society (Ragins, 1997). Along similar lines, just as we are beginning to understand the ways in which organizations are "gendered" to reflect the dominant group's (i.e., male) values and beliefs (Calás & Smircich, 1992), so do we need to understand how other characteristics of the dominant group affect the organization. We need to understand how organizational processes, functions, and systems reflect implicit racism, heterosexism, classism, ableism, and other forms of societal oppression. This perspective suggests that organizations not only reflect societal values, but are also agents of social control that perpetuate power differences between groups in society.

We can apply this poststructuralist perspective to future research. For example, an examination of the effects of race or gender within a given work group could benefit from including such variables as the diversity climate in the organization, the presence of a glass ceiling, the degree and type of social interaction between groups, power differences between groups, and other reflections of how race and gender are viewed in the organization. This approach may give insight into the relationship between the individual's personal experience of diversity and the social, political, and organizational factors that influence that experience.

## Expanding Our Study of Diversity

In addition to expanding our perspectives on diversity, we need to expand the way in which we study the construct. There are at least four areas that reflect the narrowness of our approach to studying workplace diversity.

First, we have focused our attention on a limited subset of groups in organizations. Much of our research has focused on race, ethnicity, and gender; we know little about the effects of sexual orientation, disability, religion, age, class, and appearance on workplace experiences, interactions, and outcomes. In addition, our research has focused on visible group memberships and has ignored invisible identities that are associated with social stigmas, stereotypes, and discrimination. We need research that examines how employees deal with invisible and stigmatized social identities in the workplace. We also need to examine differences among those with invisible stigmatized identities. For example, gay employees may face a different set of challenges in the workplace than employees who are in religious minorities, come from lower socioeconomic classes, or have invisible disabilities.

Second, we do not distinguish between minority groups in organizations. We often talk about "people of color" as if the experiences of different racial and ethnic groups are interchangeable. Research comparing "minority" and "majority" members often combine individuals from different ethnicities and races together into one group that is labeled the "minority" group. Even studies that examine a specific racial group may lose sight of important differences. For example, East Indians, Japanese, Koreans, and Hmong may be classified as Asian, even though these groups represent very different cultures, languages, religions, and social identities. Although an increasing number of employees are multiracial, we know little about this population. It is clear that more research is needed that examines the experiences and issues faced by specific identity groups in organizations.

Third, there has been a lack of research, or even recognition, of the effects of multiple group memberships in organizations. For example, individuals may be viewed as having either a race or a gender, but not both (Ferdman, 1995). This silo approach is limiting and may be misleading. For example, diversity scholars may gain insights into the experiences of women or African Americans in organizations, but end up knowing little about the unique experiences of African American women. In addition, we often assume that multiple group memberships are additive, but they may be synergistic (cf. Ragins et al., in press). For example, African American women may face unique barriers that extend beyond the cumulative effects associated with their race and gender; the "double whammy" associated with race and gender may in practice be a "triple whammy." It is clear that we need more research and theory that explores the effects of multiple group memberships in organizations.

Finally, most of our research has focused on managerial populations in corporations. This "Fortune 500" approach to studying diversity leaves us with little information about how diversity affects individuals and groups in different ranks, positions, occupations, and organizations. For example, we know little about diversity processes among individuals in blue collar, pink collar, trades or service occupations. We need more research that examines diversity processes and outcomes in a wider variety of ranks, professions, and organizations.

## Understanding the Processes Underlying Diversity

Future research on workplace diversity should examine not just the objective and subjective states associated with diversity, but also the process underlying diversity effects in organizations (e.g., Lawrence, 1997; Pelled, 1996). In particular, we need to understand how diversity affects, and is affected by, dyadic, group, and intergroup relationships.

To start, we need a better understanding of the conditions under which various group memberships become salient to the individual and others in the workplace. A number of potential research questions come to mind. For example, what individual, group, and organizational factors predict the salience of one identity over others? How do these factors combine to affect the perception of an individual's identity by others in the organization? Do the processes involved with salience differ for group memberships that are visible and invisible? What are the effects and interactions of different group memberships on these processes?

We also need to understand the processes involved with asymmetrical diversity effects in organizations. Existing research suggests that gender and racial group composition effects are asymmetrical (Konrad & Gutek, 1987; Mueller et al., 1999; Riordan & Shore, 1997; Yoder, 1991). For example, the experience associated with being the sole woman in a primarily male group is quite different than the experience of being the sole male in a primarily female group. One reason for this may be that individuals take the power and privilege associated with their group memberships into their work relationships (Ragins, 1997). More research is needed that illuminates the factors responsible for these asymmetrical relationships and examines how perceptions of power and status affect diverse relationships in organizations.

We also need to extend our understanding of the processes associated with diversity and intergroup relationships in organizations. As discussed earlier, diversity scholars have identified conflict, communication, group norms, and social integration as key processes that may explain research findings on diversity. However, there has been little discussion of other processes that may be more pertinent to groups that are marginalized in organizations. In particular, we need more research that examines how racism and other forms of social prejudice affect work relationships. As discussed earlier, there is a substantial body of social–psychological research on processes involved with social prejudice, interpersonal discrimination, and racism, but this research has not been systematically applied to diversity in the workplace. In addition, most of this research has focused on race and gender; we know little about how or whether these processes apply to other marginalized groups in organizations. It is clear that the field of diversity could benefit from a broader inclusion of these theories to the workplace.

Finally, we need to examine the specific processes associated with relationships, groups, and organizations that do a good job with respect to diversity (cf. Williams & O'Reilly, 1998). What are the characteristics and processes common to organizations, groups, and dyads that promote equality, effectiveness, and satisfaction in diverse relationships?

## Applying Multilevel and Historical Approaches to Diversity

We need to apply multilevel approaches in future theory and research on workplace diversity. Multilevel approaches could incorporate individual, interpersonal, and organizational levels of analyses (e.g., Ragins & Sundstrom, 1989). A multilevel approach is useful for at least two reasons. First, diversity has been approached and defined from individual, interpersonal, and organizational perspectives. Second, these levels interact with one another, and the effects of diversity may be most apparent at the intersection between various levels of analyses. For example, the treatment and impact of a gay employee in a heterosexual work team may be affected not just by the social identity of the gay employee or the relational demography of the work team, but by the broader influence of the organization's culture, workplace practices, and policies regarding sexual orientation diversity (e.g., Ragins & Cornwell, 2001).

In addition to using multiple levels of analysis, we need to apply historical perspective in our study of diversity. It is not just the use of a "snap shot" cross-sectional approach that limits our research, but also the assumption that individuals, groups, and organizations have no history, and that prior experiences are not a factor in current interactions. In contrast to this view, prior experiences may play a key role in individual, interpersonal, and organizational processes and outcomes. For example, an individual's prior experience with workplace discrimination may affect his or her social identity, group interactions, and organizational and career choices. Similarly, work teams that encountered conflict due to diversity in the past may seek comfortable homogeneous relationships in the future. On the organizational level, organizations with a history of large publicized lawsuits may approach diversity in a very different manner than companies lacking this experience. It is clear that more research and theory is needed that examines the effects of prior experiences on current behaviors, group interactions, and organizational policies associated with diversity in organizations.

In summary, instead of using a magnifying glass to study diversity at a given level of analyses at a single point in time, we need to broaden our scope to examine the effects of diversity over time using multiple levels of analyses. We now turn to examining the magnifying glass used in these analyses.

## Examining Our Own Assumptions and Biases About Diversity

The study of diversity is unique from other areas of research on organizational behavior. Some research on diversity is controversial and may evoke emotional reactions, discomfort, and even unconscious biases among writers and readers. There is little reason to assume that we are immune from the pervasive effects of prejudice, stereotypes, and stigma. These effects may be subtle and subconscious (e.g., Eberhardt & Fiske, 1998). For example, theories of aversive racism (Dovidio & Gaertner, 1986) hold that individuals may truly believe that they are not racist, but harbor racist feelings that result in subtle, but potent, biases. These feelings are usually unconscious, and involve discomfort, uneasiness, and fear of the minority group. Similar aversive prejudice processes involving gender and sexual orientation have also been proposed (Benokraitis, 1997; Ragins et al., in press).

A key question that comes to mind is whether aversive prejudice affects our research. We witness some troubling trends. To start, it is disturbing that there has been little research on the antecedents and consequences associated with racism, heterosexism, classism, and ableism in organizations. We know little about the effects of privilege, power, and discrimination, yet we find an increasing emphasis on the study of diversity in cognition, interpersonal styles, and personality traits. We do not mean to devalue this research; it is important to understand deep diversity and its relationship to other forms of diversity. The key question that must be asked and answered is whether our level of comfort affects our topic of study.

There are other indexes that trigger concern. As reviewed earlier, many studies on demography and social identity assume that group differences have equivalent effects; organizational tenure, for example, becomes equated with race in discussions of workplace diversity. Diversity is often defined as all the ways in which we are different, and this dilutes diversity by ignoring social, historical, and political consequences of group memberships (see Linnehan & Konrad, 1999). The constructs of power, dominance, and privilege are central to diversity (Ely, 1995b; Ragins, 1997), but are rarely included in studies of workplace diversity.

An assimilation perspective is often present in our research. Nkomo (1992) observed that we may use a deficit perspective and question why marginalized groups cannot "fit in" with the dominant culture in the organization, but do not acknowledge the underlying values or assumptions in this question. She noted that instead of asking how organizations can manage diversity, we need to ask how organizational processes contribute to the maintenance of racial domination and stratification in organizations. The assimilationist perspective is also evident in our treatment of race. Ely (1995b) observed that discussions of race become discussions about people of color and rarely focus on the experience of being White in an organization; White people are not regarded as having a race, and White becomes the dominant norm against which other groups are assessed. In fact, we know little about the culture, meaning, and effects of being White in organizations.

Linnehan and Konrad (1999) contended that we have moved from a study of the effects of intergroup inequality in organizations to taking a approach that obscures issues relating to discrimination, power, and privilege. We agree with this perspective, and observe a certain paradox in the field of workplace diversity. The stimulus for the development of the field was demographic changes in race and gender. We have now come full circle from an incomplete analysis of gender and race effects in organizations, to research on workplace diversity that excludes race and gender, and instead focuses on accessible, and arguably more comfortable, forms of diversity.

## CONCLUSION

In conclusion, diversity scholars face some formidable but surmountable challenges. They must examine a complex and controversial topic that has political, social, and historical implications. While traveling this slippery path, they must always keep one eye turned inward to examine whether their own biases, stereotypes, and preconceptions affect their method or focus of research. Although this self-assessment is important for all researchers, it becomes essential for those studying workplace diversity.

There are other challenges along this path. Scholars who study stigmatized groups face the possibility of becoming stigmatized themselves. Those who study groups in which they are not a member face questions regarding credibility and sensitivity, but those who study their own group face questions regarding objectivity. Questions relating to the value and limitations of advocacy research are always an issue.

In spite of these hurdles, we believe that diversity scholars can gain an incredible sense of reward from their research. In addition to broadening our understanding of diversity in organizations, they can contribute to the broader goals of promoting social justice and group equality in organizations.

# REFERENCES

Alderfer, C. P. (1997). Embedded intergroup relations and racial identity development theory. In C. E. Thompson & R. T. Carter (Eds.), *Racial identity theory: Applications to individual, group and organizational interventions* (pp. 237–263). Mahwah, NJ: Lawrence Erlbaum Associates.

Alderfer, C. P., Alderfer, C. J., Tucker, L., & Tucker, R. C. (1980). Diagnosing race relations in management. *Journal of Applied Behavioral Science, 16*(2), 135–166.

Alderfer, C. P., & Smith, K. K. (1982). Studying intergroup relations embedded in organizations. *Administrative Science Quarterly, 27*(1), 35–65.

Alderfer, C. P., & Thomas, D. A. (1988). The significance of race and ethnicity for understanding organizational behavior. In C. L Cooper & I. Robertson (Eds.), *International review of industrial and organizational psychology* (pp. 1– 41). Chichester, England: Wiley.

Allport, G. (1954). *The nature of prejudice.* Cambridge, MA: Addison-Wesley.

Ashforth, B. E., & Mael, F. (1989). Social identity theory and the organization. *Academy of Management Review, 14*(1), 20–39.

Barsade, S. G., Ward, A. J., Turner, J. D. F., & Sonnenfeld, J. A. (2000). To your heart's content: A model of affective diversity in top management teams. *Administrative Science Quarterly, 45*(4), 802–836.

Benokraitis, N. V. (1997). *Subtle sexism: Current practice and prospects for change.* Thousand Oaks, CA: Sage.

Berger, J., Cohen, B. P., & Zelditch, M., Jr. (1972). Status characteristics and social interaction. *American Sociological Review, 37*(3), 241–255.

Blalock, H. (1967). *Toward a theory of minority group relations.* New York: Capricorn.

Brewer, M. B. (1995). Managing diversity: The role of social identities. In S. E. Jackson & M. N. Ruderman (Eds.), *Diversity in work teams: Research paradigms for a changing workplace* (pp. 47–68). Washington, DC: American Psychological Association.

Brewer, M. B., & Gardner, W. (1996). Who is this "we"? Levels of collective identity and self-representations. *Journal of Personality and Social Psychology, 71*(1), 83–93.

Brickson, S. (2000). The impact of identity orientation on individual and organizational outcomes in demographically diverse settings. *Academy of Management Review, 25*(1), 82–101.

Brief, A. P., Dietz, J., Cohen, R. R., Pugh, S. D., & Vaslow, J. B. (2000). Just doing business: Modern racism and obedience to authority as explanations for employment discrimination. *Organizational Behavior and Human Decision Making Processes, 81*(1), 72–97.

Calás, M. B., & Smircich, L. (1992). Using the "F" word: Feminist theories and the social consequences of organizational research. In A. J. Mills & P. Tancred (Eds.), *Gendering organizational analysis* (pp. 222–234). Newbury Park, CA: Sage.

Carroll, G. R., & Harrison, J. R. (1998). Organizational demography and culture: Insights from a formal model and simulation. *Administrative Science Quarterly, 43*(3), 637–667.

Chatman, J. A., & Flynn, F. J. (2001). The influence of demographic heterogeneity on the emergence and consequences of cooperative norms in work teams. *Academy of Management Journal, 44*(5), 956–974.

Chatman, J. A., Polzer, J. T., Barsade, S. G., & Neale, M. A. (1998). Being different yet feeling similar: The influence of demographic composition and organizational culture on work processes and outcomes. *Administrative Science Quarterly 43*(4), 749–780.

Cheng, C. (1999). Masculinities from margin to center: Studies on gender, status, and representation. *Journal of Men's Studies, 7*(3), 295–430.

Cox, T. H., Jr. (1993). *Cultural diversity in organizations: Theory, research and practice.* San Francisco: Berrett-Koehler.

Cox, T. H., Jr. (1995). The complexity of diversity: Challenges and directions for future research. In S. E. Jackson & M. N. Ruderman (Eds.), *Diversity in work teams: Research paradigms for a changing workplace* (pp. 235–246). Washington, DC: American Psychological Association.

Cox, T. H., Jr., & Blake, S. (1991). Managing cultural diversity: Implications for organizational competitiveness. *Academy of Management Executive, 5*(3), 45–67.

Deaux, K. (1993). Reconstructing social identity. *Personality and Social Psychology Bulletin, 19*(1), 1–12.

Digh, P. (1998a). Coming to terms with diversity. *HR Magazine, 43*(12), 117–120.

Digh, P. (1998b). Religion in the workplace: Make a good-faith effort to accommodate. *HR Magazine, 43*(13), 85–91.

Dovidio, J. F., & Gaertner, S. L. (Eds.). (1986). *Prejudice, discrimination and racism.* San Diego, CA: Academic Press.

Earley, P. C., & Mosakowski, E. (2000). Creating hybrid team cultures: An empirical test of transnational team functioning. *Academy of Management Journal, 43*(1), 26–49.

Eberhardt, J. L., & Fiske, S. T. (Eds.). (1998). *Confronting racism: The problem and the response.* Thousand Oaks, CA: Sage.

Eisenhardt, K. M., Kahwajy, J. L., & Bourgeois, L. J. (1997). How management teams can have a good fight. *Harvard Business Review, 75*(4), 77–86.

Elsass, P. M., & Graves, L. M. (1997). Demographic diversity in decision-making groups: The experiences of women and people of color. *Academy of Management Review, 22*(4), 946–973.

Ely, R. J. (1994). The effects of organizational demographics and social identity on relationships among professional women. *Administrative Science Quarterly, 39*(2), 203–238.

Ely, R. J. (1995a). The power in demography: Women's social constructions of gender identity at work. *Academy of Management Journal, 38*(3), 589–634.

Ely, R. J. (1995b). The role of dominant identity and experience in organizational work on diversity. In S. E. Jackson & M. N. Ruderman (Eds.), *Diversity in work teams: Research paradigms for a changing workplace* (pp. 161–186). Washington, DC: American Psychological Association.

Ferdman, F. M. (1995). Cultural identity and diversity in organizations: Bridging the gap between group differences and individual uniqueness. In M. M. Chemers, S. Oskamp, & M. A. Costanzo (Eds.), *Diversity in organizations: New perspectives for a changing workplace* (pp. 37–61). Thousand Oaks, CA: Sage.

Fernandez, J. P. (1991). *Managing a diverse work force.* Lexington, MA: Lexington Books.

Finkelstein, S., & Hambrick, D. C. (1990). Top management team tenure and organizational outcomes: The moderating role of managerial discretion. *Administrative Science Quarterly, 35*(3), 484–503.

Flynn, G. (1998, December). The harsh reality of diversity programs. *Workforce,* pp. 26–34.

Fondas, N. (1997). Feminization unveiled: Management qualities in contemporary writings. *Academy of Management Review, 22*(1), 257–282.

Fredrickson, J. W. (1984). The comprehensiveness of strategic decision processes: Extension, observations, future directions. *Academy of Management Journal, 27*(3), 445–466.

Fullerton, H. N., Jr. (1999). Labor force participation: 75 years of change, 1950–1998 and 1998–2025. *Monthly Labor Review, 122*(12), 3–12.

Gaertner, S. L., & Dovidio, J. F. (2000). *Reducing intergroup bias: The common ingroup identity model.* Philadelphia: Psychology Press.

Goffman, E. (1974). *Stigma: Notes on the management of spoiled identity.* New York: Aronson.

Gonsiorek, J. C., & Weinrich, J. D. (1991). The definition and scope of sexual orientation. In J. C. Gonsiorek & J. D. Weinrich (Eds.), *Homosexuality: Research implications for public policy* (pp. 1–12). Newbury Park, CA: Sage.

Hambrick, D. C., Cho, T. S., & Chen, M. J. (1996). The influence of top management team heterogeneity on firms' competitive moves. *Administrative Science Quarterly, 41*(4), 659–684.

Hambrick, D. C., & Mason, P. A. (1984). Upper echelons: The organization as a reflection of its top managers. *Academy of Management Review, 9*(2), 193–206.

Harrison, D. A., Price, K. H., & Bell, M. P. (1998). Beyond relational demography: Time and the effects of surface- and deep-level diversity on work group cohesion. *Academy of Management Journal, 41*(1), 96–107.

Heatherton. T. F., Kleck, R. E., Hebl, M. R., & Hull, J. G. (Eds.). (2000). *The social psychology of stigma.* New York: Guilford.

Hennig, M., & Jardim, A. (1976). *The managerial woman.* New York: Pocket Books.

Hogg, M. A., & Abrams, D. (1988). *Social identifications: A social psychology of intergroup relations and group processes.* London: Routledge.

Hogg, M. A., & Terry, D. J. (2000). Social identity and self-categorization processes in organizational contexts. *Academy of Management Review, 25*(1), 121–140.

Jackson, S. E., & Associates. (Eds.). (1992). *Diversity in the workplace: Human resources initiatives.* New York: Guilford.

Jackson, S. E., Brett, J. F., Sessa, V. I., Cooper, D. M., Julin, J. A., & Peyronnin, K. (1991). Some differences make a difference: Individual dissimilarity and group heterogeneity as correlates of recruitment, promotions, and turnover. *Journal of Applied Psychology, 76*(5), 675–689.

Jackson, S. E., May, K. A., & Whitney, K. (1995). Understanding the dynamics of diversity in decision-making teams. In R. A. Guzzo & E. Salas (Eds.), *Team effectiveness and decision making in organizations* (pp. 204–261). San Francisco: Jossey-Bass.

Jackson, S. E., & Ruderman, M. N. (1995). Introduction: Perspectives for understanding diverse work teams. In S. E. Jackson & M. N. Ruderman (Eds.), *Diversity in work teams: Research paradigms for a changing workplace* (pp. 1–13). Washington, DC: American Psychological Association.

Jackson, S. E., Stone, V. K., & Alvarez, E. B. (1992). Socialization amidst diversity: The impact of demographics on work team old-timers and newcomers. In L. L. Cummings & B. M. Staw (Eds.), *Research in organizational behavior* (Vol. 15, pp. 45–109). Greenwich, CT: JAI.

Jehn, K. A., Chadwick, C., & Thatcher, S. M. B. (1997). To agree or not to agree: The effects of value congruence, individual demographic dissimilarity, and conflict on workgroup outcomes. *International Journal of Conflict Management, 8*(4), 287–305.

Johnston, W. B., & Packer, A. E. (1987). *Workforce 2000: Work and workers for the 21st century.* Indianapolis, IN: Hudson Institute.

Kanter, R. M. (1977). *Men and women of the corporation.* New York: Basic Books.

Konrad, A. M. (in press). Defining the domain of workplace diversity scholarship. *Group and Organization Management.*

Konrad, A. M., & Gutek, B. A. (1987). Theory and research on group composition: Applications to the status of women and ethnic minorities. In S. Oskamp & S. Spacapan (Eds.), *Interpersonal processes: The Claremont symposium on applied social psychology* (pp. 85–121). Beverly Hills, CA: Sage.

Kossek, E. E., & Zonia, S. C. (1993). Assessing diversity climate: A field study of reactions to employer efforts to promote diversity. *Journal of Organizational Behavior, 14*(1), 61–81.

Larwood, L., Stromberg, A. H., & Gutek, B. A. (Eds.). (1985). *Women and work: An annual review* (Vol. 1). Beverly Hills, CA: Sage.

Lau, D. C., & Murnighan, J. K. (1998). Demographic diversity and fault lines: The compositional dynamics of organizational groups. *Academy of Management Review, 23*(2), 325–340.

Lawrence, B. S. (1997). The black box of organizational demography. *Organization Science, 8*(1), 1–22.

Linnehan, F., & Konrad, A. M. (1999). Diluting diversity: Implications for intergroup inequality in organizations. *Journal of Management Inquiry, 8*(4), 399–414.

Loden, M., & Rosener, J. B. (1991). *Work force America! Managing employee diversity as a vital resource.* Burr Ridge, IL: Irwin.

Lott, B., & Maluso, D. (Eds.). (1995). *The social psychology of interpersonal discrimination.* New York: Guilford.

Lyness, K. S., & Thompson, D. E. (2000). Climbing the corporate ladder: Do female and male executives follow the same route? *Journal of Applied Psychology, 85*(1), 86–101.

Maier, M. (1999). On the gendered substructure of organization: Dimensions and dilemmas of corporate masculinity. In G. N. Powell (Ed.), *Handbook of gender & work* (pp. 69–94). Thousand Oaks, CA: Sage.

Markus, H. R., & Cross, S. (1990). The interpersonal self. In L. A. Pervin (Ed.), *Handbook of personality: Theory and research* (pp. 576–608). New York: Guilford.

Martin, Y. M. (1985). Group sex composition in work organizations: A structural–normative model. In S. B. Bacharach & S. M. Mitchell (Eds.), *Research in the sociology of organizations* (Vol. 4, pp. 311–349). Greenwich, CT: JAI.

McCain, B. E., O'Reilly, C. A., & Pfeffer, J. (1983). The effects of departmental demography on turnover: The case of a university. *Academy of Management Journal, 26*(4), 626–641.

McGrath J. E., Berdahl, J. L., & Arrow, H. (1995). Traits, expectations, culture, and clout: The dynamics of diversity in work groups. In S. E. Jackson & M. N. Ruderman (Eds.), *Diversity in work teams: Research paradigms for a changing workplace* (pp. 247–253). Washington, DC: American Psychological Association.

McLeod, P. L., Lobel, S., & Cox, T. H. (1996). Ethnic diversity and creativity in small groups. *Small Group Research, 27*, 248–264.

Milliken, F. J., & Martins, L. L. (1996). Searching for common threads: Understanding the multiple effects of diversity in organizational groups. *Academy of Management Review, 21*(2), 402–433.

Mor Barak, M. E., Cherin, D. A., & Berkman, S. (1998). Organizational and personal dimensions in diversity climate: Ethnic and gender differences in employee perceptions. *Journal of Applied Behavioral Science, 34*(1), 82–104.

Morrison, A. M. (1992). *The new leaders: Guidelines on leadership diversity in America.* San Francisco: Jossey-Bass.

Mueller, C. W., Finley, A., Iverson, R. D., & Price, J. L. (1999). The effects of group racial composition on job satisfaction, organizational commitment, and career commitment: The case of teachers. *Work and Occupations, 26*(2), 187–219.

Mumby, D. K., & Putnam, L. L. (1992). The politics of emotion: A feminist reading of bounded rationality. *Academy of Management Review, 17,* 465–486.

Murray, A. I. (1989). Top management group heterogeneity and firm performance. *Strategic Management Journal, 10,* 125–141.

Nieva, V. F., & Gutek, B.A. (1981). *Women and work: A psychological perspective.* New York: Praeger.

Nkomo, S. M. (1992). The emperor has no clothes: Rewriting race in organizations. *Academy of Management Review, 17,* 487–513.

Nkomo, S. M. (1995). Identities and the complexity of diversity. In S. E. Jackson & M. N. Ruderman (Eds.), *Diversity in work teams: Research paradigms for a changing workplace* (pp. 17–46). Washington, DC: American Psychological Association.

Nkomo, S. M., & Cox, T. H., Jr. (1996). Diverse identities in organizations. In S. R. Clegg, C. Hardy, & W. R. Nord (Eds.), *Handbook of organization studies* (pp. 338–356). London: Sage.

Northcraft, G. B., Polzer, J. T., Neale, M. A., & Kramer, R. M. (1995). Diversity, social identity, and performance: Emergent social dynamics in cross-functional teams. In S. E. Jackson & M. N. Ruderman (Eds.), *Diversity in work teams: Research paradigms for a changing workplace* (pp. 69–96). Washington, DC: American Psychological Association.

Oakes, P. J., & Turner, J. C. (1986). Distinctiveness and the salience of social category memberships: Is there an automatic perceptual bias towards novelty? *European Journal of Social Psychology, 16*(4), 325–344.

O'Reilly, C. A., Caldwell, D. F., & Barnett, W. P. (1989). Work group demography, social integration, and turnover. *Administrative Science Quarterly, 34*(1), 21–37.

Pelled, L. H. (1996). Demographic diversity, conflict, and work group outcomes: An intervening process theory. *Organization Science, 7*(6), 615–631.

Pelled, L. H., Eisenhardt, K. M., & Xin, K. R. (1999). Exploring the black box: An analysis of work group diversity, conflict, and performance. *Administrative Science Quarterly, 44*(1), 1–28.

Pelled, L. H., Ledford, G. E., Jr., & Mohrman, S. A. (1999). Demographic dissimilarity and workplace inclusion. *Journal of Management Studies, 36,* 1013–1031.

Pettigrew, T. (1986). The intergroup contact hypothesis reconsidered. In M. Hewstone & R. Brown (Eds.), *Contact and conflict in intergroup encounters* (pp. 353–390). London: Basil Blackwell.

Pfeffer, J. (1983). Organizational demography. In L. L. Cummings & B. M. Staw (Eds.), *Research in organizational behavior* (Vol. 5, pp. 299–357). Greenwich, CT: JAI.

Powell, G. N. (1988). *Women and men in management.* Newbury Park, CA: Sage.

Powell, G. N. (1998). Reinforcing and extending today's organizations: The simultaneous pursuit of person–organization fit and diversity. *Organizational Dynamics, 27,* 50–61.

Priem, R. L., Lyon, D. W., & Dess, G. G. (1999). Inherent limitations of demographic proxies in top management team heterogeneity research. *Journal of Management, 25*(6), 935–953.

Ragins, B. R. (1997). Diversified mentoring relationships: A power perspective. *Academy of Management Review, 22*(2), 482–521.

Ragins, B. R., & Cornwell, J. M. (2001). Pink triangles: Antecedents and consequences of perceived workplace discrimination against gay and lesbian employees. *Journal of Applied Psychology, 86,* 1244–1261.

Ragins, B. R., Cornwell, J. M., & Miller, J. S. (in press). Heterosexism in the workplace: Do race and gender matter? *Group and Organization Management.*

Ragins, B. R., & Sundstrom, E. (1989). Gender and power in organizations: A longitudinal perspective. *Psychological Bulletin, 105*(5), 51–88 .

Richard, O. C. (2000). Racial diversity, business strategy, and firm performance: A resource-based view. *Academy of Management Journal, 43*(2), 164–177.

Riger, S., & Galligan, P. (1980). Women in management: An exploration of competing paradigms. *American Psychologist, 35*(10), 902–910.

Riordan, C. M., & Shore, L. M. (1997). Demographic diversity and employee attitudes: An empirical examination of relational demography within work units. *Journal of Applied Psychology, 82*(3), 342–358.

Robinson, G., & Dechant, K. (1997). Building a business case for diversity. *Academy of Management Executive, 11*(3), 21–30.

Schneider, S. K., & Northcraft, G. B. (1999). Three social dilemmas of workforce diversity in organizations: A social identity perspective. *Human Relations, 52*(11), 1445–1467.

Sessa, V. I., & Jackson, S. E. (1995). Diversity in decision-making teams: All differences are not created equal. In M. M. Chemers, S. Oskamp, & M. A. Costanzo

(Eds.), *Diversity in organizations: New perspectives for a changing workplace* (pp. 133–156). Thousand Oaks, CA: Sage.

Shaw, J. B., & Barrett-Power, E. (1998). The effects of diversity on small work group processes and performance. *Human Relations, 51*(10), 1307–1326.

Simon, B., Hastedt, C., & Aufderheide, B. (1997). When self-categorization makes sense: The role of meaningful social categorization in minority and majority members' self-perception. *Journal of Personality and Social Psychology, 73*(2), 310–320.

Simons, T., Pelled, L. H., & Smith, K. A. (1999). Making use of difference: Diversity, debate, and decision comprehensiveness in top management teams. *Academy of Management Journal, 42*(6), 662–673.

Smith, K. G., Smith, K. A., Olian, J. D., Sims, H. P., O'Bannon, D. P., & Scully, J. A. (1994). Top management team demography and process: The role of social integration and communication. *Administrative Science Quarterly, 39*(3), 412–438.

Society for Human Resource Management. (1997). *SHRM Survey of diversity programs.* Alexandria, VA: Society for Human Resource Management.

Stead, B. A. (Ed.). (1985). *Women in management* (2nd ed.). Englewood Cliffs, NJ: Prentice-Hall.

Tajfel, H. (1981). *Human groups and social categories: Studies in social psychology.* Cambridge, England: Cambridge University Press.

Tajfel, H., & Turner, J. C. (1986). The social identity theory of intergroup behavior. In S. Worchel & W. G. Austin (Eds.), *The psychology of intergroup relations,* (2nd ed., pp. 7–24). Chicago: Nelson-Hall.

Tharenou, P. (2001). Going up? Do traits and informal social processes predict advancing in management? *Academy of Management Journal, 44*(5), 1005–1017.

Thomas, D. A., & Ely, R. J. (1996). Making differences matter: A new paradigm for managing diversity. *Harvard Business Review, 74*(5), 79–91.

Thomas, R. R. (1990). From affirmative action to affirming diversity. *Harvard Business Review, 90*(2), 107–117.

Thomas, R. R. (1991). *Beyond race and gender: Unleashing the power of your total workforce by managing diversity.* New York: AMACOM.

Tolbert, P. S., Simons, T., Andrews, A. O., & Rhee, J. (1995). The effects of gender composition in academic departments on faculty turnover. *Industrial and Labor Relations Review, 48*(3), 562–579.

Triandis, H. C. (1995). The importance of contexts in studies of diversity. In S. E. Jackson & M. N. Ruderman (Eds.), *Diversity in work teams: Research paradigms for a changing workplace* (pp. 225–234). Washington, DC: American Psychological Association.

Triandis, H. C., Kurowski, L. L., & Gelfand, M. J. (1993). Workplace diversity. In H. C. Triandis, M. Dunnette, & L. Hough (Eds.), *Handbook of industrial and organizational Psychology* (4th ed., pp. 769–827). Palo Alto, CA: Consulting Psychologists Press.

Tsui, A. S., Egan, T. D., & O'Reilly, C. A. III. (1992). Being different: Relational demography and organizational attachment. *Administrative Science Quarterly, 37*(4), 549–579.

Tsui, A. S., & Gutek, B. A (1999). *Demographic differences in organizations*. New York: Lexington.

Tsui, A. S., & O'Reilly, C. A. III. (1989). Beyond simple demographic effects: The importance of relational demography in supervisor–subordinate dyads. *Academy of Management Journal, 32*(2), 402–423.

Turner, J. C. (1981). The experimental social psychology of intergroup behavior. In J. C. Turner & H. Giles (Eds.), *Intergroup behavior* (pp. 66–101). Chicago: University of Chicago Press.

Turner, J. C. (1987). *Rediscovering the social group: A self-categorization theory*. Oxford, England: Basil Blackwell.

U.S. Department of Census 2000. (n.d.). *Americans with disabilities: Table 4*. Retrieved October 15, 2001 from http://www.census.gov/hhes/www/disable/sipp/disab97t4.html

U.S. Department of Census 2000. (n.d.). *Black population in the U.S. March 2000 Table 1*. Retrieved on October 2, 2001 from http://www.census.gov/population/www/socdemo/race/ppl-142.html

Wagner, W. G., Pfeffer, J., & O'Reilly, C. A. (1984). Organizational demography and turnover in top-management groups. *Administrative Science Quarterly, 29*(1), 74–92.

Wallace, P. A. (Ed.). (1982). *Women in the workplace*. Boston: Auburn House.

Watson, W. E., Kumar, K., & Michaelsen, L. K. (1993). Cultural diversity's impact on interaction process and performance: Comparing homogeneous and diverse task groups. *Academy of Management Journal, 36*(3), 590–602.

Webber, S. S., & Donahue, L. M. (2001). Impact of highly and less job-related diversity on work group cohesion and performance: A meta-analysis. *Journal of Management, 27*(2), 141–162.

Webster, M., Jr., & Foschi, M. (Eds.). (1988). *Status generalization: New theory and research*. Stanford, CA: Stanford University Press.

Wharton, A. (1992). The social construction of gender and race in organizations: A social identity and group mobilization perspective. *Research in the Sociology of Organizations, 10*, 55–84.

Wiersema, M. F., & Bantel, K. A. (1992). Top management team demography and corporate strategic change. *Academy of Management Journal, 35*(1), 91–121.

Williams, K. Y., & O'Reilly, C. A., III. (1998). Demography and diversity in organizations: A review of 40 years of research. *Research in Organizational Behavior, 20*, 77–140.

Wright, P., Ferris, S. P., Hiller, J. S., & Kroll, M. (1995). Competitiveness through management of diversity: Effects on stock price valuation. *Academy of Management Journal, 38*(1), 272–287.

Yoder, J. D. (1991). Rethinking tokenism: Looking beyond numbers. *Gender and Society, 5*(2), 178–192.

# 5

# Organizational Justice: A Fair Assessment of the State of the Literature

Jason A. Colquitt
*University of Florida*

Jerald Greenberg
*The Ohio State University*

Social scientists long have noted that feelings of justice and injustice are experienced commonly in everyday life (Cohen, 1986). This is especially so on the job, where employees are sensitive to matters such as how much they are paid relative to others, how openly and consistently decisions are made, and how thoroughly and sensitively these decisions are explained to them (Greenberg, 1996). Such experiences reflect the domain of *organizational justice*—a term coined by Greenberg (1987) to refer to the extent to which people perceive organizational events as being fair. Specifically, organizational justice is widely regarded to take three major forms.

- *Distributive justice*: The perceived fairness of decision outcomes, such as pay. Distributive justice is promoted by following appropriate norms (e.g., equity, equality, or need) for allocating resources (Adams, 1965; Deutsch, 1975; Homans, 1961; Leventhal, 1976).
- *Procedural justice*: The perceived fairness of the procedures used to make decisions. Procedural justice is fostered by the use of certain

procedural rules, such as granting voice in the decision-making processes (i.e., *process control*), and making decisions in a manner that is consistent, accurate, correctable, and that suppresses bias (Leventhal, 1980; Leventhal, Karuza, & Fry, 1980; Thibaut & Walker, 1975).

- *Interactional justice*: The perceived fairness of how decisions are enacted by authority figures. Interactional justice has an interpersonal component that is fostered by dignified and respectful treatment, and an informational component that is fostered by adequate and honest explanations (Bies, 2001; Bies & Moag, 1986).

These types of justice have received considerable attention over the years, and have been the subject of detailed historical analyses (Byrne & Cropanzano, 2001; Cohen & Greenberg, 1982).

The organizational justice literature has grown dramatically during the 1990s. In fact, organizational justice was cited as the most popular topic of papers submitted to the Organizational Behavior Division of the Academy of Management for several years during the mid- to late 1990s (Cropanzano & Greenberg, 1997). A search of 20 psychology and management journals in the *Web of Science* database using the key terms "justice" or "fairness" further confirms this boom in popularity. From 1989 through 1992, there were only 15 publications using these key terms. From 1993 through 1996, there were 53; and from 1997 through 2000, the figure grew to 100. Clearly, the literature grew dramatically in the 1990s.

In part, this growth was fueled by the publication of a literature review by Greenberg (1990), that bookmarked the field's progress to that date. In that article, Greenberg delineated what already was established about organizational justice, what work was underway at the time, and what challenges he believed lay ahead. In this chapter, we examine the current state of the literature by updating the conceptual and empirical developments in organizational justice in the decade following Greenberg's (1990) review. In so doing, we follow Greenberg's lead by applying Reichers and Schneider's (1990) construct life cycle to the development of organizational justice. Our adaptation of their life cycle is summarized in Fig. 5.1.

FIG. 5.1    An adaptation of Reichers and Schneider's (1990) construct life cycle.

As Fig. 5.1 reveals, three stages are evident during the life of a construct or content area: evaluation, augmentation, and consolidation and accommodation. In the *evaluation stage* critical reviews of the literature question the conceptualization and operationalization of key constructs and point out equivocal empirical results. In the *augmentation stage* these weaknesses are addressed, as new conceptualizations appear and mediating and moderating variables are added. Finally, in the *consolidation and augmentation stage* controversies wane as definitions, antecedents, and consequences become well accepted. The end of this stage is signaled by the integration of the concept into mainstream literature and textbooks.

In his 1990 review, Greenberg argued that certain topics in the justice literature—distributive justice, for example—had reached the consolidation and accommodation stage. However, research on procedural justice was still in the evaluation or augmentation stage. Accordingly, he characterized the justice literature as being in its "intellectual adolescence" (Greenberg, 1993a, p. 135). We now ask: How far has the literature come in these intervening years? As we reveal, some questions now have been answered, consequently reaching the consolidation and accommodation stage. In contrast, other questions remain the subject of much debate. Our analysis of the development of the field of organizational justice will focus on four specific questions that have dominated the literature. These are as follows:

- How distinct are the various types of justice?
- How are justice judgments formed?
- What outcomes are associated with justice judgments?
- What are the boundary conditions for justice effects?

We detail the various stages through which each question has progressed, using Greenberg's (1990) review as our starting point. Finally, we conclude this chapter by offering observations about the field's current maturity and, acting as meddlesome caretakers, imposing our ideas about how to develop that maturity further.

## HOW DISTINCT ARE THE VARIOUS TYPES OF JUSTICE?

In studying justice in organizations, the question most commonly posed is, "How fair is X?" When X is defined as the outcome of an allocation decision, the subject of study is distributive justice. When X is defined as the procedures that led to that outcome, procedural justice is the phenomenon of interest. When X is defined as the enactment of a procedure by an authority figure, we are examining interactional justice. Although such distinctions are logical and convenient for social scientists, it is useful to determine whether this same trichotomy is acknowledged in common use (Greenberg, 1990). As such, the first question we examine concerns the distinctions among the various types of justice.

## Evaluation Stage

The evaluation stage is marked by several key criteria, most notably, the publication of critical reviews of the literature and the existence of equivocal empirical findings. Each of these criteria characterized the literature as the "how distinct" question entered the evaluation stage.

*Literature Reviews.* As the 1990s began, a variety of literature reviews were published, many of which discussed the distinctions among the various justice types. For example, Greenberg's (1990) review discussed support for the distributive–procedural distinction, including the results of open-ended content coding studies and the demonstration of different antecedents and consequences. However, Greenberg did not endorse the distinction between procedural and interactional justice proposed by Bies and Moag (1986). Instead, he conceived of interpersonal treatment and adequate explanations as "interpersonal aspects of procedural justice" (p. 411).

The combining of procedural and interactional justice is consistent with another review published that same year by Tyler and Bies (1990), which referred to interactional justice as the "interpersonal context of procedural justice" (p. 77). In so doing, they argued that the enactment of a procedure was not psychologically distinct from the formal qualities of the procedure itself. These sentiments echoed a prior review by Folger and Bies (1989), which had identified the interpersonal treatment and adequate explanations facets of interactional justice as "managerial responsibilities in procedural justice" (p. 82). Importantly, both of these reviews argued that the interactional form of justice included managers' consideration of subordinates' viewpoints, suppression of biases, and consistent application of criteria, in addition to the interpersonal treatment and adequate explanations facets introduced by Bies and Moag (1986). These additions, which overlap with Leventhal's (1980) criteria for procedural justice, further blurred the distinction between procedural and interactional justice.

*Equivocal Empirical Findings.* A second key characteristic of the evaluation stage is the existence of equivocal empirical findings. Equivocal results were found in efforts to distinguish the various types of justice empirically. For example, with respect to the distinction between distributive and procedural justice, some studies yielded weak to moderate correlations between these forms of justice (e.g., Daly & Geyer, 1994; Greenberg,

1994; White, Tansky, & Baik, 1995), whereas others reported correlations that were very high (e.g., Ball, Trevino, & Sims, 1993; Conlon & Ross, 1993; Gilliland, 1994). Similar inconsistencies were evident with respect to the procedural–interactional relationship: Some studies reported only modest relationships (e.g., White et al., 1995) whereas others found very high correlations (e.g., Kidwell & Bennett, 1994; Niehoff & Moorman, 1993). Still other studies made no effort to separate procedural and interactional justice at all (e.g., Brockner, Wiesenfeld, & Martin, 1995; Folger & Konovsky, 1989; Konovsky & Folger, 1991).

## Augmentation Stage

In the augmentation stage, we begin to find clarification of the conflicting results and conceptualizations evident in the evaluation stage. In the early-to-mid 1990s, this clarification began to occur for the distributive–procedural justice distinction.

*Confirmatory Factor-Analytic Studies.* One of the first sources of clarification was Moorman's (1991) confirmatory factor analysis of distributive and procedural justice in his study of organizational citizenship behavior. The best-fitting model was one in which the two justice types remained distinct. Sweeney and McFarlin (1993) also used confirmatory factor analysis to compare multiple models: one in which distributive and procedural justice were independent, and two that posited a causal connection between them. The models' fit statistics supported separation of distributive and procedural justice, and also showed that the addition of a causal connection did not enhance fit.

*Evidence of Outcome x Process Interactions.* A second source of clarification regarding the distributive–procedural distinction came by recognizing that these two forms of justice often interacted statistically in affecting outcomes. Brockner and Wiesenfeld (1996) reviewed studies using 45 independent samples published between 1983 and 1996 and noted that procedural justice was more strongly related to work attitudes when outcomes were low rather than high. Conversely, outcomes were more strongly related to work attitudes when procedures were unfair than when they were fair. Scientists have characterized this interaction in various ways, such as, "it is not only what you do, but how you do it" (Brockner & Wiesenfeld, 1996, p. 206) or "the means justify the ends" (Greenberg, 1987, p. 55). Regardless of how it is expressed, the robustness of the interaction demonstrates the importance of treating distributive and procedural justice as distinct concepts.

*New Conceptualizations.*     The distinction between procedural justice and interactional justice also received a great deal of attention throughout the 1990s. The augmentation stage is marked by the appearance of new conceptualizations of existing constructs. Greenberg (1993b) offered a new conceptualization of interactional justice by arguing that interactional justice should be broken down into two components: interpersonal justice, which captures the dignity and respect aspects of Bies and Moag's (1986) conceptualization, and informational justice, which captures the adequacy and honesty of explanations. It is noteworthy that Greenberg excluded such factors as consideration of others' viewpoints, suppression of biases, or consistent application of criteria—facets that were included in the conceptualizations by Folger and Bies (1989) and by Tyler and Bies (1990). This bit of reductionism began to clarify the construct boundaries of procedural and interactional justice.

*Distinguishing Justice Content From Justice Source.*     The procedural–interactional boundary was clarified further as researchers began distinguishing justice content (e.g., consistency vs. interpersonal treatment) from justice source (e.g., formal system vs. human agent). Although previous studies comparing procedural and interactional justice usually confounded these factors, recent studies have crossed them intentionally (Byrne & Cropanzano, 2000; Masterson, Bartol, & Moye, 2000; Tyler & Blader, 2000). For example, Byrne and Cropanzano (2000) used confirmatory factor analysis to separate four distinct justice dimensions: supervisor-originating procedural justice, supervisor-originating interactional justice, organization-originating procedural justice, and organization-originating interactional justice.

## Consolidation and Accommodation Stage

In the consolidation and accommodation stage we see a waning of controversies and a consensus regarding the definitions and correlates of key constructs. Such consensus currently is evident regarding the distributive–procedural justice distinction and the procedural–interactional justice distinction.

*Meta-Analytic Evidence of Consensus.*     One source of that consensus is provided by the first meta-analytic review of the justice literature (Colquitt, Conlon, Wesson, Porter, & Ng, 2001). Colquitt et al.'s review encompassed 183 articles with 242 independent samples, published between 1975 and 2001. Ninety-two of those samples included the correlation between distributive justice and procedural justice, which ranged from .34 to .57 depending on how procedural justice was captured (e.g., with respect to process control; Leventhal's [1980] criteria; or direct "how fair" measures). These results clearly show that distributive justice and procedural justice are unique, though highly intercorrelated.

The procedural–interactional distinction also has received clarification from meta-analytic findings. Notably, Colquitt et al. (2001) examined the validity of separating not just procedural and interactional justice, but also the interpersonal and informational aspects of Bies and Moag's (1986) construct. They found a correlation of .66 between interpersonal justice and informational justice (after correcting for unreliability). Because this correlation was not significantly different than the procedural-distributive correlation, the authors lent support to Greenberg's (1993b) four-dimensional conceptualization of organizational justice. The correlations between the two interactional facets and procedural justice also supported keeping those dimensions separate (.63 for procedural and interpersonal justice; .58 for procedural and informational justice). Colquitt's (2001) confirmatory factor analytic support for Greenberg's conceptualization provides further evidence for the four-dimensional view.

*Conceptual Reviews.* A second source of consolidation can be found in the theoretical review of the distributive–procedural distinction by Cropanzano and Ambrose (2001). These authors noted that, in an effort to separate the two constructs, justice scholars had perpetuated some artificial distinctions. For example, scholars generally examined distributive justice using some relative standard, whereas procedural justice was studied using more absolute rules or criteria. In fact, like distributive justice, procedural justice can be judged relative to social comparisons or individual expectations (Grienberger, Rutte, & Van Knippenberg, 1997). Another artificial distinction lies in the different sets of criteria used to foster the two types of justice. Equity, equality, and need—allocation norms used to promote distributive justice (Deutsch, 1975)—can be applied just as easily to procedural justice. For example, equal amounts of process control can be provided to all, or greater opportunities for correctability can be provided to those most in need of it. By separating true differences from artificial differences, Cropanzano and Ambrose provided consolidation and accommodation to the distributive–procedural distinction.

Bies (2001) provided another source of theoretical consolidation and accommodation in his review of the debate about whether to separate interactional justice from procedural justice. His conclusion, that "it makes theoretical and analytical sense to maintain the distinction between interactional justice and procedural justice" (p. 99) was identical to that reached by Bobocel and Holmvall (2001). Specifically, these theorists reached this conclusion by illustrating that procedural justice and interactional justice: (a) have different causal effects on outcomes, (b) have different antecedents, and (c) correlate with organizational outcomes to different degrees.

## Conclusion: How Distinct Are the Various Types of Justice?

The answer to the question "How distinct are the various types of justice?" has changed as the justice literature has developed (see Table 5.1). The equivocal results that characterized the evaluation stage called into question the existence of more than two types of justice. However, the new conceptualizations that appeared in the augmentation stage illustrated the independence of interactional justice, and even argued for its separation into interpersonal and informational facets. Furthermore, recent meta-analytic and narrative reviews have brought consolidation and accommodation to this critical question. This suggests that at least one key question in the justice literature has reached the final stage of Reichers and Schneider's (1990) life cycle.

# HOW ARE JUSTICE JUDGMENTS FORMED?

Once they clarified the types of justice that exist, scientists considered a more sophisticated question: How are justice judgments formed? Fig. 5.2 presents a model of this process around which we organize our discussion.

## Evaluation Stage

In the evaluation stage, the literature regarding the formation of justice judgments was based, in part, on a debate between *relational* and *instrumental* models of justice. These models had implications for the reasons that justice concerns were triggered, and the way that justice information was gathered once concerns had become salient. The evaluation stage also was marked by the development of referent cognitions theory (Folger, 1986a, 1986b, 1987), which offered a distinct but complementary view of the judgment process.

*Relational Versus Instrumental Models.* At the beginning of the last decade, questions about the motives underlying people's judgments of fairness were a central topic of critical reviews. For example, Greenberg (1990) provided an overview of the *self-interest model* and the *group value model* proposed by Lind and Tyler (1988). These models, which later were recast as the *instrumental model* and the *relational model* respectively (Tyler & Lind, 1992), proposed different triggers of the justice judgment process (see Fig. 5.2). The instrumental model argued that people attend to matters of justice in keeping with their long-term interest in control over economic outcomes (Lind &

# TABLE 5.1

## The Evolution of Key Questions in the Organizational Justice Literature

| Key Question | Stage of Development | | |
| --- | --- | --- | --- |
| | Evaluation | Augmentation | Consolidation and Accommodation |
| How distinct are the various types of justice? | • Reviews support DJ–PJ distinction, but blur PJ–IJ boundary | • Use of confirmatory factor analysis to support distinctions | • Colquitt et al. (2001) provided meta-analytic support for four-dimensional taxonomy |
| | • Inconsistent (and often high) correlations among justice types | • Process x Outcome interaction supports DJ–PJ separation | • Cropanzano and Ambrose (2001) reviewed artificial DJ–PJ differences |
| | | • Greenberg (1993b) presented reconceptualization of IJ | • Bies (2001) and Bobocel and Holmvall (2001) cemented PJ–IJ differences |
| | | • Justice source and content begin to be separated | |
| How are justice judgments formed? | • Tyler and Lind (1992) distinguished between instrumental and relational models of justice | • Lind et al. (1993) developed fairness heuristic theory, based on the relational model | • Not yet attained |
| | • Folger (1986a,1986b, 1987, 1993) introduce and update RCT | • Van den Bos, Lind, and colleagues conducted series of experiments testing fairness heuristic theory | |
| | | • Folger and Cropanzano (1998) developed fairness theory, based on RCT | |

*(continued on next page)*

TABLE 5.1 (*continued*)

| Key Question | Evaluation | Augmentation | Consolidation and Accommodation |
|---|---|---|---|
| What outcomes are associated with justice judgments? | • Reviews begin to distinguish distributive and procedural justice according to effects on system and person-referenced variables<br><br>• Reviews speculate on the relative effects of procedural and interactional justice | • Masterson et al. (2000) identified differences in mediators of justice effects<br><br>• Colquitt et al. (2001) conducted meta-analytic tests of two-factor and agent–system models<br><br>• New conceptualizations build on two-factor and agent–system models | • Not yet attained |
| What are the boundary conditions for justice effects? | • Reviews begin to make general extensions of justice effects (e.g., to dispute resolution, political, organizational, and interpersonal contexts)<br><br>• Empirical studies widen the bounds of justice applications to many specific contexts (e.g., performance evaluation, selection, compensation, organizational change) | • Researchers focus on explicit contextual moderators of justice effects (e.g., culture, uncertainty)<br><br>• Researchers focus on explicit individual moderators of justice effects (e.g., gender, personality) | • Not yet attained |

*Note.* DJ = distributive justice; PJ = procedural justice; IJ = interactional justice.

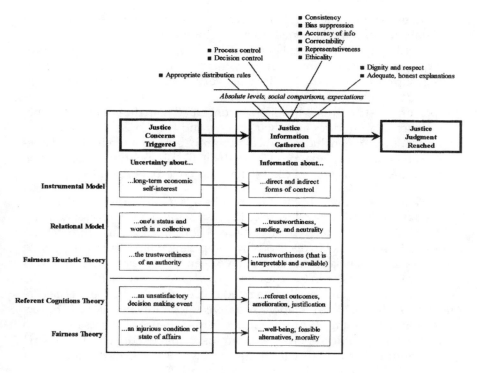

FIG. 5.2   A model of the justice judgment process.

Tyler, 1988; Thibaut & Walker, 1975). For example, process control is valued as a fair procedure insofar as it helps protect one's self-interest, making the future appear more predictable. The relational model, by contrast, argues that people attend to justice because fair procedures are "symbols of group values" (Tyler & Lind, 1992, p. 140), which signal that they are valued by others with whom they associate. Process control is valued in this case because it reinforces feelings of self-worth and acceptance by one's group.

These models also differ with respect to how individuals gather and organize information when forming justice judgments (see Fig. 5.2). From the instrumental perspective, the guiding question is, "Does this procedure enhance my control over desired outcomes?" In this regard, assessments of process control and decision control are critical pieces of information (Thibaut & Walker, 1975). However, they are not the *only* considerations. Leventhal's (1980) criteria, such as bias suppression, correctability, and representativeness, also make outcomes more controllable (or at least predictable). And, as Cropanzano and Ambrose (2001) noted, information relevant to the justice judgment process may be gathered in either absolute or relative terms (i.e., compared to some external standard or compared to one's own expectations).

According to the relational perspective (Tyler & Lind, 1992), three guiding questions organize information gathering: (a) What is my standing in this group? (b) Are the authorities trustworthy? and (c) Are the authorities neutral? Standing is based primarily on the dignity and respect criteria of interpersonal justice. Trustworthiness is concerned with the ethicality and benevolence of authorities and their actions, and therefore can depend on a number of criteria, including process control, representativeness, and adequate and honest explanations (Tyler, 1990). Finally, neutrality depends on bias suppression, as well as consistency and honesty (Tyler, 1990).

*Referent Cognitions Theory.*    Greenberg's (1990) review also discussed one other theory relevant to the justice judgment process: Folger's (1986a, 1986b, 1987) referent cognitions theory (RCT). This approach argues that people react to decisions by comparing what actually happened to their assessments of what might have been. These *referent cognitions,* as they are termed, come in three forms: *referent outcomes* (which compare the decision event to other easily imagined outcomes), the *likelihood of amelioration* (which considers whether a negative outcome eventually will be rectified), and *justification* (which compares the sequence of events that led to the outcome to other—perhaps, more justifiable—sequences). The first two cognitions concern distributive justice, whereas the third is concerned with procedural justice (Folger, 1986a, 1986b, 1987).

RCT assumes that a discrete event triggers the justice judgment process (see Fig. 5.2). Once the referent cognitions process begins, justice information is gathered and organized around the three RCT elements. Referent outcomes draw on distributive information. In contrast, the likelihood of amelioration draws on explanations (which could shed light on future outcomes) or on consistency and correctability (which could signal whether future outcomes will differ). Justification draws on any information conveying the fairness of the decision-making process, from process control to bias suppression to ethicality. Finally, we note that subsequent work has expanded the scope of the justification cognition. Folger (1993) argued that procedures have value beyond their "means to an end" function, because they signal whether certain moral obligations have been met. Thus, in assessing fairness, information on ethicality or dignity and respect could be considered, even if it has no bearing on any material outcomes.

## Augmentation Stage

As we described previously, the augmentation stage is marked by the introduction of new conceptualizations that clarify debates in the literature.

In the mid-1990s, new conceptualizations of the justice judgment process began to appear that were based on the approaches offered by the relational model (Tyler & Lind, 1992) and RCT (Folger, 1987). Subsequently, these developed into the formal conceptualizations known as fairness heuristic theory (see Lind, 2001a; Van den Bos, 2001a; Van den Bos, Lind, & Wilke, 2001) and fairness theory (see Folger & Cropanzano, 1998, 2001).

*Fairness Heuristic Theory.* Fairness heuristic theory originated as an extension of Tyler and Lind's (1992) relational model (Lind, Kulik, Ambrose, & de Vera Park, 1993). The relational model argues that fair treatment signals that authorities are legitimate—and therefore, that compliance with their directives will result in beneficial consequences (Tyler & Lind, 1992). Accordingly, fairness can be used as a *heuristic* that alleviates the need to fully explore all consequences of all responses to an authority figure's decisions (Lind et al., 1993).

Because it is useful and efficient, people are motivated to form this heuristic during the early stages of interaction with potentially untrustworthy authorities or other organizational parties (see Fig. 5.2). Importantly, this means that procedural issues play a larger role than distributive justice in forming justice judgments because procedural information typically is more readily available than distributive information. Van den Bos, Vermunt, and Wilke (1997) tested this notion in an experiment in which the order of presentation of procedural and distributive information was manipulated. They showed that individuals' justice judgments were driven more by the accuracy of the procedure when that information was presented first. However, when information on outcome favorability was presented first, that information proved to be the primary driver of justice judgments.

Subsequent research has shed further light on the development of fairness heuristics. In addition to the order and timing of information (Lind, Kray, & Thompson, 2001; Van den Bos, Vermunt, et al., 1997), the interpretability of information also is critical (Van den Bos, Lind, Vermunt, & Wilke, 1997; Van den Bos, Wilke, Lind, & Vermunt, 1998). Specifically, when distributive justice is difficult to judge (e.g., when social comparisons are impossible) procedural issues have a greater impact on fairness heuristics than distributive issues. Likewise, procedural issues also are more important when the trustworthiness of authorities is difficult to determine (Van den Bos, Wilke, & Lind, 1998).

*Fairness Theory.* The augmentation stage also has seen the introduction of a second reconceptualized theory relevant to the justice judgment process. Fairness theory (Folger & Cropanzano, 1998, 2001) builds on RCT by examining people's reactions to negative decisions. Like RCT, fairness theory is built on cognitive representations of what might have been. In

RCT, these are called referent cognitions, whereas in fairness theory they are referred to as *counterfactuals* (i.e., simulated events contrary to the facts). Three counterfactuals determine reactions to decisions: (a) the *would* counterfactual, which compares the current state of well-being with other potential states; (b) the *could* counterfactual, which assesses whether other feasible behaviors were available to the authority; and (c) the *should* counterfactual, which compares an authority figure's actions with prevailing moral standards.

Although the three counterfactuals can be constructed in any order, the logical trigger is some negative decision outcome—what Folger and Cropanzano (2001) called "an injurious condition or state of affairs" (p. 3; see Fig. 5.2). The impact of this negative outcome, procedure, or interpersonal interaction then is gauged by means of the would counterfactual, which takes into account relevant social comparisons, expectations, and referent standards. Attention then turns to issues of accountability. Could the authority have acted differently, or were the actions the result of some external influence? Should the authority have acted differently: Were his or her actions justified on moral or ethical grounds? All three counterfactuals are necessary for inferring injustice. As the authors noted, "If the chain is broken in any place, then a social injustice has not occurred … injury, conduct, and standards are the constituent elements from which blame is built" (Folger & Cropanzano, 2001, p. 5).

Despite its newness, predictions based on fairness theory have been supported by two recent studies. Gilliland, Groth, Baker, and Dew (2001) applied fairness theory to job applicants' reactions to rejection letters by creating explanations based on each of the counterfactuals. For example, an explanation based on the could counterfactual attributed the rejection to a hiring freeze, and an explanation based on the should counterfactual attributed the rejection to an ethically appropriate selection process. They found that the perceived fairness of the negative outcomes was enhanced when they were explained by the counterfactuals. Similar results were obtained by Colquitt and Chertkoff (2002), who manipulated whether or not participants in their laboratory study received desired outcomes (a requested partner on a group task). Explanations geared toward the should counterfactual had especially strong effects when the outcome was unexpectedly negative (thereby maximizing the would counterfactual).

## Consolidation and Accommodation Stage

As noted previously, the consolidation and accommodation stage is marked by a waning of controversies and a consensus regarding key questions and concepts. However, given that the differences between fairness heuristic theory and fairness theory have spurred debate among some proponents of the theories (Cropanzano, Byrne, Bobocel, & Rupp, 2001a, 2001b; Lind, 2001b), it appears that this stage has not yet been reached with respect to the justice judgment process. This manifests itself in terms of the theories' different claims regarding the cognitive loads placed on the people making justice judgments. Specifically, whereas fairness theory requires some controlled processing, fairness heuristic theory relies more on automatic processing (on this distinction, see Bargh & Ferguson, 2000). In this connection, several points are particularly critical to our discussion.

*Differences in Triggers of Justice Judgments.* The two theories differ with respect to the triggers of the justice judgment process. Fairness theory, for example, suggests that the process is triggered whenever an injurious condition or state of affairs arises. However, according to fairness heuristic theory, an injurious state might *not* trigger the justice judgment process because it would force individuals to revisit a heuristic they already have been using comfortably (Lind, 2001a; Van den Bos et al., 2001). The theory argues that individuals are motivated to avoid revisiting the heuristics formed during early stages of interaction.

However, this apparent difference can be reconciled by considering the *magnitude* of an injurious event. If an event is only slightly injurious, then the would counterfactual would not be fully activated and no search for blame and accountability occurs. In such a case, neither theory would predict a full iteration of the judgment process. On the other hand, if an event is highly injurious, then the would counterfactual is activated and the search for blame and accountability moves forward. In the case of fairness heuristic theory, Lind (2001a) argued that certain events are "phase shifting"—that is, they are able to end the use of the heuristic and prompt a fresh judgment. For example, events may be phase shifting because they signal a change in an organizational relationship or because they lie significantly outside one's expectations. Thus, assuming that the injurious event is of sufficient magnitude to trigger phase shifting, both theories would predict a full iteration of the justice judgment process.

*Differences in Central Concerns.* Other differences between the theories cannot be as easily reconciled. For example, whereas trust is the central concern of fairness heuristic theory, blame is the central concern of fairness theory. To illustrate this point, consider a case in which a trusted authority figure fails to provide the expected level of process control during a decision, when he or she could have (and should have) done so. The trust felt for the authority will likely deter a dysfunctional response by the employee, but it will not necessarily prevent the assessment of blame and accountability. Instead, employees are likely to conclude that although the authority figure is to blame, they owe that individual another chance. Thus, fairness theory does not put much importance on trust because it offers no mechanism to account for its effects on blame.

Analogously, fairness heuristic theory does not place much importance on blame. In fact, the theory argues that the injury (would), conduct (could), and standards (should) elements never would be processed fully by the person forming the judgment. Instead, whatever information was available first, or was most easily interpreted, would determine the selection of a fairness heuristic. Not only would blame not be an outcome of the process, but the information purportedly needed to assess it would not be completely considered. Thus, the two theories differ with respect to both the triggers of the justice judgment process and the manner in which the information on which those judgments are based is used.

If the consolidation and accommodation stage is to be reached, the importance of the blame and trustworthiness components of the theories must be reconciled. To do so requires a more comprehensive research design than typically is used in justice research. In addition to measuring the distributive, procedural, informational, and interpersonal inputs into the judgment process, researchers also must measure explicitly the motives, goals, and mechanisms underlying those judgments. If repeated investigations failed to yield significant main, moderating, or mediating effects of trust and blame, then revisions to the theories would have to be made. However, to fully assess the mechanics of the judgment process such research would have to rely on more detailed measurement methods than typically are used (e.g., interviews or verbal protocol analysis).

### Conclusion: How Are Justice Judgments Formed?

The answer to the question "How are justice judgments formed?" has changed as the literature has developed (see Table 5.1). The initial conceptualizations that were introduced in the evaluation stage provided preliminary views of the triggering and organizing steps of the judgment process. However, the new conceptualizations that appeared in the augmentation stage have proposed more complete and integrative processes. Two such theories—fairness theory and fairness heuristic theory—have important differences that must be reconciled if the consolidation and accommodation stage is to be reached.

## WHAT OUTCOMES ARE ASSOCIATED WITH JUSTICE JUDGMENTS?

Although our model in Fig. 5.2 ends with a justice judgment, practicing managers and applied researchers generally are more concerned with the next step—the effects of those judgments. Do decisions perceived to be fair promote beneficial reactions (e.g., commitment) and discourage counterproductive behavior (e.g., aggressive behavior and stealing)? In an attempt to answer this question, justice researchers have examined the practical impact of justice judgments.

## Evaluation Stage

Critical reviews published during the evaluation stage revealed patterns in the relationships between justice judgments and certain key outcomes. Initially, these patterns concerned the relative predictive power of distributive and procedural justice, but more current reviews considered the relative predictive power of procedural justice and interactional justice.

*The Two-Factor Model.* Three studies at the close of the 1980s examined distributive and procedural justice as predictors of key organizational outcomes, such as organizational commitment, pay satisfaction, trust in management, and leader evaluation (Alexander & Ruderman, 1987; Folger & Konovsky, 1989; Konovsky, Folger, & Cropanzano, 1987). These studies supported conclusions by Lind and Tyler (1988) that procedural justice was a stronger predictor than distributive justice of system-referenced evaluations (e.g., organizational commitment, trust in management), and that distributive justice was a stronger predictor than procedural justice of person-referenced outcomes (e.g., pay satisfaction). In reviewing this research, Greenberg (1990) concluded, "Whereas procedural justice perceptions tend to be associated with organizational system evaluations ... distributive justice perceptions tend to be associated with the outcomes received" (p. 407).

Two studies by McFarlin and Sweeney further support this pattern. McFarlin and Sweeney (1992) regressed pay satisfaction, job satisfaction, leader evaluation, and organizational commitment on procedural and distributive justice in a sample of bank employees. They found that distributive justice was the best predictor of satisfaction, but that procedural justice was the best predictor of leader evaluation and organizational commitment. In a follow-up study, Sweeney and McFarlin (1993) verified this pattern of effects using structural equation modeling. Specifically, they contrasted four structural equation models containing distributive and procedural justice, pay satisfaction, and organizational commitment. The best fitting model was the one in which procedural justice had a direct effect on commitment only and distributive justice had a direct effect on satisfaction only. This model, which Sweeney and McFarlin (1993) dubbed the "two-factor model," fit the data better than alternative models containing multiple effects for the justice variables.

*The Agent–System Model.*    Examinations of the two-factor model focused only on distributive and procedural justice, ignoring the predictive effects of interactional justice—a factor that some theorists considered the key determinant of reactions to authorities (Bies & Moag, 1986; Folger & Bies, 1989; Tyler & Bies, 1990). For example, Tyler and Bies (1990) suggested that "Evidence that procedures are being inappropriately implemented should be particularly important in undermining people's support for the authorities with whom they are dealing" (p. 93). The idea that interactional justice is a stronger predictor of agent-referenced outcomes whereas procedural justice is a stronger predictor of system-referenced outcomes has recently been termed the "agent–system model" (Colquitt et al., 2001).

The agent–system model received little testing at the beginning of the 1990s because the belief prevailed that interactional justice was a subset of procedural justice. As we noted earlier, many researchers combined the two dimensions into a single variable, precluding assessment of their relative effects (e.g., Brockner, Wiesenfeld, & Martin, 1995; Folger & Konovsky, 1989; Konovsky & Folger, 1991). Importantly, this practice had a critical side effect on many of the tests of the two-factor model. For example, Folger and Konovsky's findings that procedural justice predicted organizational commitment and trust in one's supervisor, but that distributive justice predicted pay satisfaction, must be interpreted in light of the fact that their procedural measure included criteria of an interactional nature (e.g., honesty, explanations). Similarly, given the nature of their measure, Brockner et al.'s (1995) significant correlation between a procedural–interactional composite and trust could be taken as support for either the two-factor model or the agent–system model.

## Augmentation Stage

As exemplified by the first two focal questions identified in this review, the augmentation stage clarifies some of the controversies in the literature by introducing new conceptualizations and adding moderating and mediating variables. At the end of the 1990s, although such clarification began to occur for the two-factor model and the agent–system model, other developments increased confusion associated with justice effects.

*Addition of Mediating Variables.*    Hagedoorn, Buunk, and Van de Vliert (1998) described the relationship between justice and outcome variables as a "black box" (p. 41), suggesting that the intervening mechanisms linking justice with various reactions are not well understood. One way of opening that "black box" is by measuring the mediators that link justice dimensions to certain outcomes. Masterson, Lewis, Goldman, and Taylor

(2000) provided a good example of such an approach in two field studies. Their first study demonstrated that interactional justice predicted an agent-referenced outcome (supervisor legitimacy), whereas procedural justice predicted two system-referenced outcomes (organizational commitment and turnover intentions).

In their second study, Masterson et al. (2000) added mediators for their predicted effects, and found that interactional justice predicted agent-referenced outcomes (e.g., supervisor-directed citizenship behaviors) through the intervening mechanism of leader–member exchange (LMX; Graen & Uhl-Bien, 1995). In contrast, procedural justice predicted system-referenced outcomes (e.g., organizational citizenship behavior, OCB) through the mechanism of perceived organizational support (Eisenberger, Huntington, Hutchinson, and Sowa, 1986). Cropanzano, Prehar, and Chen (2002) found similar results in their study of LMX as a mediator of procedural and interactional justice effects. Like Masterson et al. (2000), they found that although LMX mediated the effects of interactional justice on agent-referenced outcomes, it did not mediate the effects of procedural justice.

*New Conceptualizations.* Colquitt et al.'s (2001) meta-analytic review provided a powerful test of both the two-factor model and the agent–system model. It is important to note, however, that their review was based on Greenberg's (1993) four-dimensional conceptualization of justice, with interactional justice decomposed into its interpersonal and informational components. In assessing the two-factor and agent–system models, Colquitt et al. regressed 11 different outcome variables onto the four justice dimensions. Importantly, any study that used a procedural–interactional composite index was omitted from this analysis, allowing for a "confound-free" test of the two models.

The two-factor model received support for the most commonly examined attitudinal outcomes. Specifically, procedural justice was the strongest predictor of job satisfaction and organizational commitment, but distributive justice was the strongest predictor of outcome satisfaction. However, the model did not accurately capture behavioral effects. Although the two-factor model predicts that procedural justice would be the most significant antecedent of OCB, withdrawal, job performance, and counterproductive behavior, this prediction was not supported. Apparently, the two-factor model is more accurate for attitudes, which by definition have focal objects that can be classified as person versus system-referenced. However, because behavior generally lacks such a classifiable referent, it is not as readily predictable.

Mixed results were also found for the agent–system model. Using this model, one *would not* expect strong relationships between interpersonal or informational justice and system-referenced variables like job satisfaction and organizational commitment. However, one *would* expect strong relationships with agent-referenced variables like agent-referenced evaluation of authority and OCB. Colquitt et al.'s (2001) meta-analytic evidence supported each of these predictions. However, the agent–system model underestimated the effects of interpersonal and informational justice on behavioral outcomes. Specifically, systemic outcomes like withdrawal, organization-directed citizenship, and counterproductive behaviors were strongly predicted by interpersonal and informational justice, even though such effects are inconsistent with the agent–system model.

A new conceptualization of the two-factor model could potentially clarify these equivocal results. Ambrose and Hess (2001) presented a new version of the two-factor model that encompasses all four dimensions of organizational justice. Drawing on Greenberg's (1993b) taxonomy, they suggested that the informational–interpersonal distinction mimics the procedural–distributive distinction. Specifically, they claimed that both procedural and informational justice capture aspects of a long-standing decision-making system, particularly when informational justice provides important details about that system. Similarly, both distributive and interpersonal justice can capture aspects of a discrete decision event, particularly when interpersonal justice provides sincere and respectful treatment to ameliorate the effects of an unfavorable outcome. Accordingly, the Ambrose and Hess (2001) model predicts that procedural and informational justice will predict system- referenced outcomes, whereas distributive and interpersonal justice will predict person-referenced outcomes. This new conceptualization adequately captures Colquitt et al.'s (2001) results for system-referenced evaluations of authority, which were predicted strongly by procedural and informational justice but not by interpersonal and distributive justice. Much like the original two-factor model and the agent–system model, the Ambrose and Hess model fails to predict behavioral effects. Still, as more researchers employ a four-dimensional view of justice, this revised two-factor model could potentially become a more accurate gauge of the impact of various justice judgments.

Another new conceptualization is offered by Byrne and Cropanzano (2000) in their research distinguishing justice content from justice source. As we noted earlier, these investigators used confirmatory factor analysis to distinguish four distinct justice dimensions: supervisor-originating procedural justice, supervisor-originating interactional justice, organization-originating procedural justice, and organization-originating interactional justice. They also used structural equation modeling to determine the degree to which each type of justice is associated with specific supervisor and organization-referenced outcomes (e.g., citizenship, commitment, job performance). This conceptualization offers a new spin on both the two-factor and the agent–system model by suggesting that *source* (rather than *content*) may be the critical factor driving justice effects.

## Consolidation and Accommodation Stage

Two key characteristics of the consolidation and accommodation stage are the waning of controversies and the reaching of consensus regarding key questions and concepts. Certainly it is not controversial to state that justice judgments exhibit significant zero-order correlations with a variety of important organizational outcomes. Indeed, of the 82 justice-outcome correlations included in Colquitt et al.'s (2001) meta-analytic review, only 5 failed to reach statistical significance. However, important controversies remain when the question is which of the four dimensions of justice have the *strongest unique effects* on certain outcomes.

We believe that the question regarding outcomes associated with justice judgments has not yet reached the consolidation and accommodation stage. Rather, it lies at the same point as the question regarding justice judgment processes. Unfortunately, the two questions differ with respect to the level of theory building geared toward each. We believe it may be easier to reach consensus about the nature of the justice judgment process insofar as the relative merits of fairness theory and fairness heuristic theory can be assessed. These theories have provided the necessary frameworks for reconciling the remaining disagreements. However, no such framework exists that provides insights into the matter of justice effects. We see two possible ways to reconcile this controversy.

*Should There Be a Moratorium on Comparative Research?*   One way of eliminating controversies about the relative effects of different types of justice is to stop doing this type of research altogether. After all, fairness heuristic theory would suggest that there is little value in considering all four dimensions of justice given that only the information encountered first would be fully considered. Consider a case in which informational justice is a stronger predictor of supervisor-referenced evaluations than distributive justice. This would be consistent with both the two-factor model and the agent–system model. It also could be interpreted as showing stronger effects for supervisor-originating justice than for organization-originating justice. However, it may be that the information needed to gauge informational justice was simply available first (Van den Bos, Vermunt, et al., 1997) or that it was easier to judge (Van den Bos, Wilke, et al., 1998). In contrast, if distributive information were available first, or if it were easier to judge, then distributive justice might have had the stronger effect. In this case, any inferences supporting the two-factor model, the agent–system model, or the justice source model would be misleading.

Minimally, this suggests that the testing of the models cannot occur absent the context in which justice judgments are formed. At most, this suggests that a more effective way to connect justice judgments to various outcomes is by involving a "general justice" or "organizational justice" variable (Lind, 2001b). For example, a second-order structural equation model could be created with "organizational justice" as a latent variable, using distributive, procedural, interpersonal, and informational justice as latent indicators of it. Any difference in factor loadings across the four latent indicators would be a function of mechanisms such as availability of information or ease of interpretation, as proposed by fairness heuristic theory. The latent organizational justice variable could then be connected to the outcomes of interest. Researchers still would have an incentive to measure all four types of justice—not to compare their regression weights, but to maximize the construct and predictive validity of the organizational justice factor.

On the other hand, to design justice interventions effectively, we must understand the unique effects of justice dimensions on key outcomes (Greenberg & Lind, 2000). In practice, limited time and resources necessarily restrict the scope of such interventions. Should an organization devote its time and resources to improving the consistency and accuracy of formal procedures (thereby promoting procedural justice), or to publicizing and explaining the elements of procedures (thereby promoting informational justice)? Likewise, if supervisors are to be trained in justice principles (e.g., Skarlicki & Latham, 1996, 1997), would it be more effective to invest limited time in improving the way procedures are designed or the manner they are enacted? The answers to such questions can only be derived from comparative research.

*Building Better Theory.*    If we accept that making comparative inferences is important, then it is clear that better theory will be needed to support such inferences. Whetten (1989) suggested that a good theory explains when and how a relationship occurs. The issue of *when* concerns the boundary conditions, or moderators of the theory (an issue we discuss in the next section). The issue of *how* concerns the intervening mechanisms, or mediators of the theory. As we noted, however, very few studies have included mediators when linking justice judgments to outcome variables. Rather, the mechanisms tend to remain obscured in a "black box" (Hagedoorn et al., 1998, p. 41). In the absence of such mediators, it is difficult to explain, for example, why informational justice is strongly related to evaluation of authority, but weakly related to organizational commitment (Colquitt et al., 2001).

Some justice theories specify mediators of outcome linkages. For example, the relational model suggests that justice judgments influence outcomes through the mechanism of *legitimacy* (Tyler, 1990; Tyler & Lind, 1992). The belief that authorities are legitimate fosters voluntary compliance, stemming not from external rewards or punishments, but from internal beliefs and expectations. Illustrating this, Tyler (1990) assessed the legitimacy of the police and the court system using items such as "The basic rights of citizens are well protected in the courts" and "I feel that I should support the courts." He found that these perceptions were more strongly predicted by procedural justice than by distributive justice. This is consistent with Colquitt et al.'s (2001) finding that procedural justice effects were strongly predicted by three outcomes that are conceptually related to legitimacy—organizational commitment, system-referenced evaluation of authority, and trust.

Subsequent work by Tyler (1999; Tyler & Blader, 2000) offers a second potentially useful mediator of justice judgment effects—*identification,* the extent to which individuals define themselves in terms of their membership in a group or organization. Measuring identification with items such as "The organization in which I work says a lot about who I am as a person" and "When I talk about where I work, I usually say 'we' rather than 'they,'" Tyler and Blader (2000) found that procedural justice increases identification. Presumably, this is because individuals feel respected by the group, enhancing their pride in membership (Tyler, 1999; Tyler & Blader, 2000) when that group uses procedures perceived to be fair. Not surprisingly, Tyler and Blader (2000) also found identification to be an important antecedent of compliance, in-role behavior, and extra-role behavior. This is in keeping with the strong procedural justice effects Colquitt et al. (2001) found for job performance and OCB—two variables that seem to be driven by identification.

A third potential mediator is *blame,* which may mediate justice effects on counterproductive behaviors, such as theft (Greenberg, 1998), aggression (Greenberg & Alge, 1998), or organizational retaliation (Skarlicki & Folger, 1997). According to fairness theory, blame is placed whenever an authority could have and should have acted differently, and when one's well-being would have been better as a result (Folger & Cropanzano, 1998, 2001). Mikula (1993) argued similarly, claiming that blame results when an actor is intentionally responsible for some violation of an entitlement in the absence of a sufficient explanation. Thus, it appears that several types of injustice are relevant to blame. Low distributive justice provides the violation, low informational justice satisfies the absence of an explanation, and low procedural justice supplies the intent. With this in mind, it is not surprising that the "negative reactions" and withdrawal variables in Colquitt et al.'s (2001) review were driven by all four forms of justice.

## Conclusion: What Outcomes Are Associated With Justice Judgments?

The answer to the question "What outcomes are associated with justice judgments?" has changed as the literature has developed (see Table 5.1). Initial conceptualizations sought to predict the relative effects of different types of justice according to the referent of the dependent variable. New conceptualizations updated this practice while adding critical mediators to explain why certain effects occur. To reconcile the remaining controversies surrounding the effects of distributive, procedural, interpersonal, and informational justice, it would be useful to identify and explicitly measure additional intervening mechanisms.

## WHAT ARE THE BOUNDARY CONDITIONS FOR JUSTICE EFFECTS?

To this point, we have discussed the processes through which justice judgments are formed and the outcomes associated with those judgments. Now, we address the next logical question: What are the boundary conditions of justice effects? In other words, are there certain individual or contextual variables that qualify the nature of the justice judgment process or the strength of justice–outcome relationships? The existence of such boundary conditions has important implications not only for theory development, but also for enhancing justice in organizations (Greenberg & Lind, 2000).

### Evaluation Stage

Many of the critical reviews that marked the beginning of the decade were concerned with illustrating the wide applicability of organizational justice. In other words, rather than illustrating when justice *was not* important, the reviews focused on when it *was* important. Such efforts were understandable given that the justice literature was still in its infancy. Some reviews focused on laying out more general extensions of justice phenomena; others focused on specific contexts.

*General Extensions.* Lind and Tyler's (1988) landmark review described a variety of contexts in which justice principles apply. For example, justice principles long have been considered critical in legal and dispute-resolution contexts. This is evident in Thibaut and Walker's (1975) original conceptualization of procedural justice and in Tyler's (1990) work linking procedural justice to evaluations of judges, police officers, and court systems. Likewise, the importance of justice principles has also been established in the political arena, such as in investigations of people's reactions to political figures and systems (Lind & Tyler, 1988).

A key extension has come in recognizing that procedural justice accounts for behavior in organizations (Folger & Greenberg, 1985; Greenberg & Folger, 1983). These authors argued that justice principles might be even more important in organizations than in legal or political settings insofar as there is generally more variation in organizational procedures. Typically, organizational procedures are not constrained by institutional precedents, and the variety of decisions made by the procedures creates even more variation. Even within a single organization, for example, the procedures governing selection, training, performance evaluation, and compensation decisions may offer different levels of such key procedural variables as process control, consistency, and correctability.

Other reviews also discussed general extensions of justice principles and effects. For example, Tyler and Bies (1990) argued that justice effects are not bounded by the characteristics of formalized legal, political, or organizational procedures. Instead, they claimed, these effects extend to how decision makers conduct themselves interpersonally while implementing formal procedures. Moreover, Tyler and Lind (1992) suggested that justice principles are relevant in any context in which an authority figure seeks compliance from others.

*Specific Extensions.*    Aside from these more general extensions, other reviews focused on the specific organizational contexts in which justice effects have been observed. For example, Greenberg (1986a, 1986b, 1990) detailed the application of justice principles to performance evaluation contexts. Allowing employees to have a voice in the process and ensuring that justice judgments are based on accurate and consistent information improves the acceptance of the evaluation (regardless of its favorability). Analogously, Greenberg (1990) reviewed the applicability of justice to managerial dispute resolutions. In this context as well, fair procedures enhanced acceptance of dispute decisions.

Several other specific extensions widened the bounds of justice applications during the early to mid-1990s. For example, Gilliland (1993) applied justice principles to a selection context by detailing the criteria for a fair selection process. In an empirical test, he showed that the fairness of the selection process was related to intentions to recommend a job to others, as well as to efficacy and performance on the job (Gilliland, 1994). Similarly, Konovsky and Cropanzano (1991) showed that the perceived fairness of employee drug testing procedures was related to trust in management, organizational commitment, and job performance.

The boundaries of justice applications have also been extended to other areas of human resource management. Quinones (1995), for example, examined the perceived fairness of being assigned to remedial training rather than advanced training. He found that trainees' perceptions of fairness were correlated with their motivation to learn and job performance. Welbourne, Balkin, and Gomez-Mejia (1995) applied justice principles to compensation by examining the perceived fairness of a gainsharing system. They found that the system was more effective when employees believed that the formulas used to establish payouts were fair. Others have applied justice concepts to areas such as mentoring (Scandura, 1997), comparable worth (Greenberg & McCarty, 1990), and affirmative action (Parker, Baltes, & Christiansen, 1997).

Justice principles have also been applied in cases of wide-scale organizational change. For example, many have examined the perceived fairness of layoff decisions (e.g., Brockner et al., 1995; Brockner, Wiesenfeld, Reed, Grover, & Martin, 1993). In general, the more fairly layoffs are handled, the more committed layoff survivors are to their organization (Brockner & Greenberg, 1990), and the less likely layoff victims are to sue on the grounds of wrongful termination (Lind, Greenberg, Scott, & Welchans, 2000). Daly and Geyer (1994) examined organizational justice in the context of job relocations. They found that the perceived fairness of the relocation was correlated with intention to remain. Others have applied justice concepts to the implementation of corporate strategies (Kim & Mauborgne, 1993).

## Augmentation Stage

Many of the studies performed during the evaluation stage sought to widen the boundaries of justice applications—to show when and where justice is important. However, other work has focused on determining when and where justice *is not* important. Specifically, researchers have focused on explicit moderators of justice effects, including both contextual variables (e.g., culture, uncertainty) and individual variables (e.g., gender, personality). Here, we describe some of these key variables.

*Voluntariness of Association.* Tyler (1986) was one of the first to discuss moderators of justice effects in a review that asked, "When does procedural justice matter in organizational settings?" (p. 7). One moderator suggested by Tyler was voluntariness of association, with justice effects purported to be stronger when association was involuntary. Gordon and Fryxell (1989) later tested this proposition by assessing the relationship between justice judgments and satisfaction with union and management. They found that these relationships were stronger when union membership was mandatory rather than voluntary. It may be that the imposition of an association reinforces a lack of control, triggering control-based justice concerns.

*National Culture.* Another contextual variable that has been examined as a moderator of justice effects is national culture. Lind, Tyler, and Huo (1997) tested the relational model of justice in two studies using samples from the United States, Germany, Hong Kong, and Japan. Specifically, they examined the relationships between relational justice information (i.e., trustworthiness, standing, and neutrality) and procedural justice judgments. In the second study, standing was more strongly related to procedural justice in the United States than in Japan, suggesting that American and Japanese people have different expectations regarding standing. Brockner et al. (2001) also found that national culture moderated justice effects. Specifically, in four independent studies they found that people responded less favorably to low levels of voice in low-power distance countries (the United States and Germany) than in high-power distance countries (the People's Republic of China, Mexico, and Hong Kong). Taken together, these studies suggest that national culture is an important moderator of justice effects.

*Contextual Moderators Inspired by Fairness Heuristic Theory.* Additional moderators have been identified in research designed to test fairness heuristic theory. As shown in Fig. 5.2, this theory suggests that justice concerns are triggered by uncertainty about trustworthiness, and that justice information is gathered to serve as indirect evidence of trustworthiness. In support of fairness heuristic theory, Van den Bos, Wilke, et al. (1998) showed that the relationship between process control and reactions was stronger when participants lacked information on trustworthiness than when they had such information. In a recent extension, Van den Bos (2001b) showed that uncertainty also moderates the effects of justice. Specifically, when individuals were asked questions that aroused feelings of uncertainty, process control had a stronger effect on reactions than when no such questions were asked.

More recent work by Van den Bos and his colleagues has examined inclusion as a moderator of justice effects (Van Prooijen, Van den Bos, & Wilke, 2001). In a lab study, individuals who were included in a group reacted more strongly to variations in process control than those who were excluded. A lack of inclusion weakened the effects of justice-relevant information. A similar effect was observed by Holbrook and Kulik (2001) among bank customers applying for loans. The longer they did business with the bank, the more strongly they reacted to the level of process control granted during the loan process.

*Norms as Contextual Moderators.*    Norms also are likely to moderate justice effects. Leung and Tong (2001) recently proposed a "normative model of justice" that articulates the roles of norms in making and responding to justice judgments. Specifically, their model suggests that injustice creates feelings of resentment among those who were treated unfairly. This resentment occurs not only because of its effects on outcomes, status, or trustworthiness, but because it often violates important norms regarding the treatment of others. These norms may arise from codes of ethics, cultures, or moral obligations (Greenberg, in press) or from violated expectations of prevailing practices (Greenberg, Eskew, & Miles, 1991). Importantly, Leung and Tong (2001) noted that norms are dependent on context. In other words, they claim that differences in socialization and experiences can cause norms to differ across certain subgroups, which may alter people's expectations for justice and their responses to injustice.

*Gender Effects.*    Just as context can amplify certain justice effects, so too can various characteristics of individuals. Gender, for example, has been found to moderate the effects of an equity allocation norm; males tend to value equity whereas females tend to value equality (e.g., Brockner & Adsit, 1986; Major & Deaux, 1982). This effect is consistent with the finding that women have lower outcome expectations than men (McFarlin, Frone, Major, & Konar, 1989). More recent research has focused on gender as a moderator of procedural justice effects. Sweeney and McFarlin (1997) speculated that women are more sensitive to characteristics of formal procedures because of past discrimination and lack of access to informal advancement mechanisms. Not surprisingly, they found that procedural justice exerted stronger effects on intention to remain employed by an organization among females than among males.

*Traditional Personality Variables.*    Personality is another moderator of procedural justice effects. For example, Sweeney, McFarlin, and Cotton (1991) found that the relationship between process control and procedural justice was stronger for internal locus of control individuals. This is in keeping with earlier research showing that reactions to procedural violations were more extreme among people who highly endorsed the Protestant work ethic (Greenberg, 1979), a correlate of internal locus of control. Additional research has shown that people who are predisposed to delay gratification are highly sensitive to the nature of organizational procedures (Joy & Witt, 1992). After all, such individuals are inclined to take a long-term view on their organizations. In addition, Skarlicki, Folger, and Tesluk (1999) examined the moderating effects of affectivity and agreeableness. Specifically, individuals high in negative affectivity (NA) and low in agreeableness were more likely to react to unfair treatment by retaliating against the organization than those who scored in an opposite manner on these dimensions.

*Justice-Related Personality Variables.* In contrast to these studies, which investigated traditional personality variables, others have focused on aspects of personality specifically geared to justice concerns. Notably, equity sensitivity moderates individuals' reactions to departures from an equity allocation norm (e.g., Huseman, Hatfield, & Miles, 1987; King, Miles, & Day, 1993). Individuals showing an "entitled" pattern react weakly to overpayment inequity whereas individuals with a "benevolent" pattern react weakly to underpayment inequity. Between these extremes are "equity sensitives," who react to either type of inequity.

Another justice-based personality variable, known as sensitivity to befallen injustice (SBI), has been studied by Schmitt (1996). This construct assesses the intensity of anger following injustice, the intrusiveness of thoughts about unjust events, and people's inclination to punish the agent of the injustice. Schmitt (1996) treated people unfairly in the course of a laboratory experiment. He found that participants who scored most highly on SBI believed that the injustice was more extreme, leaving them angrier, more resentful, and more inclined to redress that injustice.

## Consolidation and Accommodation Stage

With respect to boundary conditions, we do not believe that the organizational justice literature has reached the consolidation and accommodation stage because consensus has not been reached regarding key questions and because controversies remain. Despite the broad scope of the justice literature, research on explicit moderators has been extremely limited. Such work is not only relatively uncommon, but also "scattershot" in nature when conducted. With the exception of culture and gender, most of the moderators have been examined in single investigations. Many of the moderators also are so narrow in scope that they are based on little or no specific literatures. As a result, our knowledge of justice moderation remains limited.

*A Framework for Justice Moderation.* To facilitate explanations of justice moderation, we propose the integrative framework shown in Fig. 5.3. This model expands Fig. 5.2 by including reactions to decision-making events. Existing research has focused on both linkages proposed in this model. Specifically, some studies have identified amplifiers or neutralizers of the relationship between such variables as equity and voice on justice judgments, whereas others have identified variables that strengthen or weaken the effects of justice judgments on subsequent attitudes (e.g., satis-

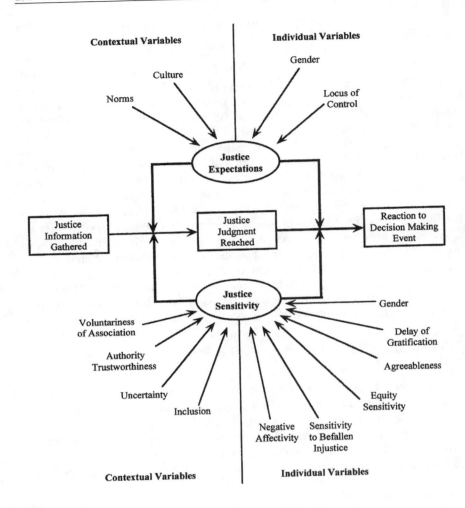

FIG. 5.3   A framework for examining justice moderation.

faction, anger) or behaviors (e.g., retaliation, withdrawal; for a review, see Greenberg, 2000).

As Fig. 5.3 illustrates, these moderators include both characteristics of the context (e.g., norms or uncertainty) and characteristics of the individual (e.g., gender or personality). The figure further classifies moderators into two types—justice expectation moderators and justice sensitivity moderators. *Justice expectation moderators* are variables affecting expectations of what justice means and the degree of justice expected. For example, an individual's native culture may influence his or her expectations regarding the qualities that characterize a "fair procedure." Indeed, it has been argued that culture's justice effects are moderated primarily by expectations (Kidder & Miller, 1991; Steiner, 2001). For example, people from cultures considered low with respect to Hofstede's (1980) power distance dimension (e.g., the United States and Germany) were found to express lower levels of organizational commitment in response to limited opportunities for voice than people from countries that are high in power distance (e.g., the People's Republic of China, Mexico, and Hong Kong; Brockner et al., 2001). Apparently, differing cultural expectations about the appropriateness of acknowledging status differences led to different reactions among people from those cultures when expectations with respect to this were violated.

*Justice sensitivity moderators* are variables that make concerns about justice more salient and reactions to justice more severe. The two most obvious examples of this kind of moderator are equity sensitivity and SBI, both of which were conceived to assess this type of effect. However, other individual variables also capture a sensitivity to justice issues, albeit more indirectly. For example, Skarlicki et al.'s (1999) results suggest that individuals scoring high in negative affectivity or low in agreeableness are especially sensitive to injustice, promoting stronger attitudinal and behavioral reactions. The same can be said for contextual variables like uncertainty and inclusion. This is illustrated by Van den Bos's (2001b) finding that uncertainty heightens concerns over predictability, increasing sensitivity to variations in process control.

In Fig. 5.3 we represent justice expectations and justice sensitivity as unmeasured, latent variables to acknowledge that these variables have not been measured explicitly in past research. Instead, more narrow variables have been used as indirect indicators of justice expectations and sensitivity. For example, Sweeney et al. (1991) speculated that people scoring high on internal locus of control expected higher levels of process control, but failed to measure such expectations directly. We also should caution that the indicators of justice expectations and sensitivity shown in Fig. 5.3 are not meant to be an exhaustive list. Rather, they reflect the variables that researchers have examined in at least one study during the past decade.

## Conclusion: What Are the Boundary Conditions for Justice Effects?

As in the case of the other questions we have examined, the answer to the question "What are the boundary conditions for justice effects?" has changed as the organizational justice literature has developed. Early reviews focused primarily on illustrating the contexts in which justice was relevant. Shortly thereafter, researchers began to examine individual and contextual moderators in an effort to determine when justice was and was not important. At present, the matter of boundary conditions has received less research attention than the three other questions we have identified. However, by offering a framework for understanding boundary conditions (see Fig. 5.3), we hope that future researchers will pay closer attention to them, further moving this area toward the consolidation and accommodation stage.

## HOW DOES THE FUTURE OF FAIRNESS FARE?

Three of the four focal issues that currently dominate the organizational justice literature have failed to reach Reichers and Schneider's (1990) final stage of construct development, consolidation, and accommodation (see Table 5.1). As a whole, therefore, the field may be characterized as falling between the augmentation stage and the consolidation and accommodation stage. However, to the extent that we can refine answers to the four focal questions we have been addressing, full maturity will have been attained. With this, our understanding of organizational justice will have advanced to the state in which it provides a useful reservoir of valid knowledge that can be drawn on as the basis for promoting fairness in organizations (Greenberg & Lind, 2000). For this to occur it will be necessary to more throughly integrate knowledge of organizational justice within the overarching discipline of organizational behavior. We believe that such linkages may be most fruitfully developed in three key areas: leadership, climate, and motivation.

### Justice and Leadership

Perhaps the most natural connection can be made between justice and leadership. After all, many of the practices advocated in the popular management literature offer recipes for effective leadership that bear a striking resemblance to the established practices for maintaining justice (e.g., Kouzes, Posner, & Peters, 1996). These include: give employees a voice, treat people in an unbiased and consistent fashion, be respectful of people, and explain decisions fully and sincerely. Likewise, many of the specific dimensions on which taxonomies of leader behavior are based parallel those from the justice literature. For example, Yukl's taxonomy of leader behaviors includes rewarding, consulting, supporting, and informing (Yukl & Van Fleet, 1992)—behaviors that echo distributive justice, process control, interpersonal justice, and informational justice, respectively. Similarly, Bass's (1985) transactional and transformational leadership behaviors include contingent rewards (reflecting distributive justice), intellectual stimulation (reflecting, in part, process control), and individual consideration (reflecting interpersonal justice). Finally, according to LMX theory (Graen & Uhl-Bien, 1995), high-quality leader–member relationships are founded on high levels of respect, trust, and mutual discretion—dimensions that correspond to high levels of interpersonal justice, informational justice, and process control.

Several leadership researchers have developed more explicit linkages between leadership and justice. For example, Vecchio, Griffeth, and Hom (1986) linked LMX to distributive justice perceptions, and Keller and Dansereau (1995) showed that the practice of empowering others promoted their perceptions of procedural justice. Justice scholars have also used evaluations by leaders as a dependent variable and have examined justice issues in the context of leader behavior. For example, Skarlicki and Latham (1996, 1997) trained leaders on various justice principles, which led to increased OCB among followers. Although such efforts are a good beginning, we believe that both literatures would benefit by more deeply integrating their theories and concepts.

This may be accomplished in several ways. For example, leadership theories have long been interested in predicting leader behaviors using characteristics of the leader, the situation, and followers (House & Aditya, 1997; Yukl & Van Fleet, 1992). In contrast, the justice literature has all but ignored what causes leaders to act fairly. Specifically, we know little about personality differences between fair and unfair leaders and how characteristics such as gender or age impact a leader's fairness. Likewise, we do not know the specific contexts that trigger fair or unfair treatment. Perhaps injustice is more common in complex, stressful, or novel contexts. Finally, we know little about the characteristics of followers that prompt leaders to employ fair treatment (for a notable exception, see Korsgaard, Roberson, & Rymph, 1998, who linked followers' assertiveness to leaders' use of interpersonal and informational justice). Perhaps diligent, hard-working subordinates engender fair treatment on the part of leaders. Examining such questions would bring more balance to a literature that has virtually ignored the *actor* who creates fairness, in favor of the *observer* who reacts to it.

Another potential source of theoretical integration can be drawn from contingency theories of leadership, which examine critical moderators that make some behaviors more appropriate under certain circumstances (House & Aditya, 1997; Yukl & Van Fleet, 1992). Following from this tradition, it is likely that various characteristics of the situation and of the followers might alter the appropriateness of high levels of process control or informational justice. For example, new employees may be too inexperienced for process control, and may remain on a "need to know basis" until they prove themselves. Also, situations in which team-based rewards are used may alter the appropriateness of an equity norm, possibly in favor of an equality norm. In this connection, the literature on "substitutes for leadership" (Kerr & Jermier, 1978) might be used to predict conditions under which the effects of perceived injustices are likely to be most damaging.

## Justice and Climate

Forehand and Gilmer (1964) defined organizational climate as a set of enduring characteristics that describe an organization, distinguish it from other organizations, and influence its members' attitudes and behaviors. Although the conceptualizations and methods used to study climate vary widely, most scholars assume that certain organizational attributes (e.g., size, structure, practices, procedures, routines, symbols, jargon, ceremonies) create shared perceptions of "the way things are around here" (Ostroff, Kinicki, & Tamkins, in press; Reichers & Schneider, 1990). The content of those shared perceptions also varies widely, with some scholars assessing one global form of climate, others assessing climate with multiple general dimensions (e.g., reward, risk, warmth, support), and still others referencing climate to very specific issues (e.g., safety, service, transfer of training).

This last form of climate represents the clearest bridge to the justice literature. If scholars can examine a "climate for safety" or a "climate for service," why not also consider a "climate for justice"? Naumann and Bennett (2000) did precisely this. Building on work by Mossholder, Bennett, and Martin (1998), Naumann and Bennett showed that bank employees converged on perceptions of procedural justice, particularly in branches in which work groups were highly cohesive and in which leaders were highly visible. This "procedural justice climate" explained variance in individuals' helping behavior, even after controlling for individuals' own justice perceptions. Colquitt, Noe, and Jackson (2002) extended this work in two ways. First, they identified group characteristics that lead to "strong climates," characterized by high levels of perceptual convergence. Second, they showed that justice climates in work groups had stronger effects on performance and absenteeism when climate strength was high rather than low.

The notion of justice climate fills a void in the justice literature by acknowledging the multilevel influences and effects of justice. Specifically, because formal procedures and practices exist at the group level, their effects should go beyond individual perceptions. As such, justice climate may be used to link justice to various team-, department-, and organization-level variables (e.g., retention, goal achievement, profitability). Justice climate also is important insofar as it acknowledges that justice perceptions are socially constructed, derived from a complex process of social comparison and normative influences. Although the social construction of justice perceptions has been acknowledged in the case of distributive justice, it has received little attention with respect to procedural justice (Cropanzano & Ambrose, 2001). However, by virtue of its focus on social information processing, future research on justice climate is destined to direct justice researchers to the processes underlying the social construction of procedural justice perceptions.

To strengthen the connection between justice and climate, it would be helpful to know the specific organizational characteristics that comprise the most important drivers of climate. Representing a step in this direction, Schminke, Ambrose, and Cropanzano (2000) examined the relationships between individual justice judgments and organizational size, centralization, and formalization—three attributes often linked to climate. They found that size hindered interpersonal justice whereas centralization hindered procedural justice. It also would be important to know what factors differentiate strong climates from weak climates. For example, it may be that procedural justice climates, which are based in part of long-standing formalized practices, are stronger than interpersonal justice climates, and therefore have greater impact. This represents a potentially fruitful direction for future research.

## Justice and Motivation

Another path for integrating organizational justice into mainstream OB may be taken through the literature on motivation. In several respects, the justice literature and the motivation literature already are closely tied. For example, equity theory routinely is described in the motivation chapter of OB textbooks, and a discussion of justice is featured prominently in Kanfer's (1991) motivation chapter in the *Handbook of Industrial and Organizational Psychology*. In other ways, however, the linkage is less well developed. Making this point, Colquitt and Chertkoff (2002) noted that few, if any, justice scholars have measured motivation explicitly.

Why is it that job satisfaction and organizational commitment are popular dependent variables in justice research, but motivation is virtually ignored? Is it that justice scholars do not believe that unjust treatment will result in a decrease in the intensity or persistence of task-related effort (apart from the predicted effects of underpayment inequity)? Or, is it that justice scholars simply view motivation as an intervening mechanism whose influence is so obvious that it can remain unmeasured? In our opinion, neither view holds much merit. To the contrary, we believe that by more closely considering motivation it would be possible to clarify the inconsistent effect of procedural justice on job performance that has been reported in the literature. For example, Colquitt et al. (2001) found that procedural justice had a meta-analytic correlation of .36 with performance, but that relationship varied widely across studies and across procedural justice conceptualizations. Given that motivation is often cited as a determinant of task performance (e.g., Porter & Lawler, 1968), it makes sense to pay closer attention to motivation as a variable in future studies of organizational justice.

Drawing on Kanfer's (1991) taxonomy, various motivational theories suggest different ways in which this may be done. For example, *need-motive-value* theories (e.g., Alderfer, 1972; Maslow, 1954) are founded on the notion that meeting one's needs triggers task effort. To the extent that maintaining fairness is a universal need, as Kanfer argued, it follows from the instrumental model of justice that people will be motivated to engage in behavior designed to satisfy it. Likewise, the idea that people are motivated to satisfy needs for affiliation and recognition is in keeping with relational models of justice.

*Cognitive choice* theories (e.g., Bandura, 1991; Carver & Scheier, 1981; Vroom, 1964) emphasize the cognitive reasoning required when deciding to initiate a given level of effort. As such, they are relevant to justice in two key ways. First, justice judgments affect (and are affected by) many of the same ingredients found in cognitive choice theories. For example, perceptions of distributive justice and procedural justice affect performance-outcome contingencies, thereby altering instrumentality (Vroom, 1964). Second, the status and self-worth signals that accompany fair treatment (Tyler & Lind, 1992) could affect effort-performance contingencies, thereby altering expectancy.

*Self-regulation* theories (e.g., social cognitive theory, Bandura, 1991; control theory, Carver & Scheier, 1981) emphasize the self-governed allocation of cognitive resources that control the persistence of effort. These regulatory processes may be used to explain the counterfactual and phase shifting mechanisms described by fairness theory (e.g., Folger & Cropanzano, 2001) and the development of heuristics described by fairness heuristic theory (Lind, 2001a). Efforts to juxtapose these underlying mechanisms promise to benefit both literatures.

Given these kinds of linkages, it should be possible to build a theory of motivation built primarily on justice needs, justice concerns, and justice judgment processes. Such a theory would clarify many of the inconsistencies that currently exist in the literature. For example, it could be used to ground predictions about which types of justice are most influential for various forms of outcomes. This would be responsive to our earlier plea to develop mediators that support comparative predictions. A justice-based theory of motivation also would integrate justice with other variables relevant to motivation, such as goals, job characteristics, and individual difference variables. This broader view of motivated behavior could then be used to combine justice interventions with other kinds of performance improvement strategies.

# CONCLUSION

Clearly, the field of organizational justice has grown out of its "intellectual adolescence" (Greenberg, 1993a, p. 135). Its "stumbling awkwardness" (p. 136) now has given way to a fairly linear progression of better theory, more refined conceptualizations, and research characterized by more rigorous methodology. This is not to say, however, that the field has reached the consolidation and accommodation stage, signaling full maturity. Witness the compelling nature of the issues that remain, as chronicled in our analyses of the state of the field's most rudimentary research questions. Given this state of affairs, we conclude that the field of organizational justice has blossomed into a "promising young adult"—and a very popular one, at that.

We acknowledge that this popularity may be both a blessing and a curse. Although the arrival of new theories and research directions promises to move the field forward, this may come at the expense of jeopardizing the field's current structure and coherence. However, by revisiting where the field has been and by offering suggestions as to where it should be going, we hope that other theorists will be inspired to preserve the field's integrity while improving its coherence. To the extent that future work can bring closure to the four key questions identified here, we will be well on our way to reaching that elusive final stage of maturity. Then, by building stronger connections to other areas of OB research, the concept of organizational justice will stand a good chance of being not only one of OB's most popular topics, but among its most important ones as well. When this occurs, the field of organizational justice promises to have a fruitful, mature life without ever having to face retirement. It is hoped that our remarks have paved the way for this to occur.

# REFERENCES

Adams, J. S. (1965). Inequity in social exchange. In L. Berkowitz (Ed.), *Advances in experimental social psychology* (Vol. 2, pp. 267–299). New York: Academic.

Alderfer, C. P. (1972). *Existence, relatedness, and growth*. New York: The Free Press.

Alexander, S., & Ruderman, M. (1987). The role of procedural and distributive justice in organizational behavior. *Social Justice Research, 1*, 177–198.

Ambrose, M. L., & Hess, R. L., Jr. (2001, September). *Individuals' responses to fairness: A consideration of management and marketing models*. Paper presented at the International Roundtable on Innovations in Organizational Justice Research, Vancouver, British Columbia, Canada.

Ball, G. A., Trevino, L. K., & Sims, H. P., Jr. (1993). Justice and organizational punishment: Attitudinal outcomes of disciplinary events. *Social Justice Research, 6*, 39–67.

Bandura, A. (1991). Social cognitive theory of self-regulation. *Organizational Behavior and Human Decision Processes, 50*, 248–287.

Bargh, J. A., & Ferguson, M. J. (2000). Beyond behaviorism: On the automaticity of higher mental processes. *Psychological Bulletin, 126,* 925–945.

Bass, B. M. (1985). *Leadership and performance beyond expectations.* New York: The Free Press.

Bies, R. J. (2001). Interactional (in)justice: The sacred and the profane. In J. Greenberg & R. Cropanzano (Eds.), *Advances in organizational justice* (pp. 89–118). Stanford, CA: Stanford University Press.

Bies, R. J., & Moag, J. F. (1986). Interactional justice: Communication criteria of fairness. In R. J. Lewicki, B. H. Sheppard, & M. H. Bazerman (Eds.), *Research on negotiations in organizations* (Vol. 1, pp. 43–55). Greenwich, CT: JAI.

Bobocel, D. R., & Holmvall, C. M. (2001). Are interactional justice and procedural justice different? Framing the debate. In S. Gilliland, D. Steiner, & D. Skarlicki (Eds.), *Theoretical and cultural perspectives on organizational justice* (pp. 85–110). Greenwich, CT: Information Age.

Brockner, J., Ackerman, G., Greenberg, J., Gelfand, M. J., Francesco, A. M., Chen, Z. X., Leung, K., Bierbauer, G., Gomez, C., Kirkman, B. L., & Shapiro, D. (2001). *Journal of Experimental Social Psychology, 37,* 300–315.

Brockner, J., & Adsit, L. (1986). The moderating impact of sex on the equity-satisfaction relationship: A field study. *Journal of Applied Psychology, 71,* 585–590.

Brockner, J., & Greenberg, J. (1990). The impact of layoffs on survivors: An organizational justice perspective. In J. Carroll (Ed.), *Advances in applied social psychology: Business settings* (pp. 45–75). Hillsdale, NJ: Lawrence Erlbaum Associates.

Brockner, J., & Wiesenfeld, B. M. (1986). An integrative framework for explaining reactions to decisions: Interactive effects of outcomes and procedures. *Psychological Bulletin, 120,* 189–208.

Brockner, J., Wiesenfeld, B. M., & Martin, C. L. (1995). Decision frame, procedural justice, and survivors' reactions to job layoffs. *Organizational Behavior and Human Decision Processes, 63,* 59–68.

Brockner, J., Wiesenfeld, B. M., Reed, T., Grover, S., & Martin, C. (1993). Interactive effect of job content and context on reactions of layoff survivors. *Journal of Personality and Social Psychology, 64,* 187–197.

Byrne, Z. S., & Cropanzano, R. (2000, April). *To which source do I attribute this fairness? Differential effects of multi-foci justice on organizational work behaviors.* Paper presented at the meeting of the Society for Industrial and Organizational Psychology, New Orleans, LA.

Byrne, Z. S., & Cropanzano, R. (2001). The history of organizational justice: The founders speak. In R. Cropanzano (Ed.), *Justice in the workplace: Vol. 2. From theory to practice* (pp. 3–26). Mahwah, NJ: Lawrence Erlbaum Associates.

Carver, C. S., & Scheier, M. F. (1981). *Attention and self-regulation: A control theory approach to human behavior.* New York: Springer-Verlag.

Cohen, R. L. (1986). *Justice: Views from the social sciences.* New York: Plenum.

Cohen, R. L., & Greenberg, J. (1982). The justice concept in social psychology. In J. Greenberg & R. L. Cohen (Eds.), *Equity and justice in social behavior* (pp. 1–41). New York: Academic.

Colquitt, J. A. (2001). On the dimensionality of organizational justice: A construct validation of a measure. *Journal of Applied Psychology, 86,* 386–400.

Colquitt, J. A., & Chertkoff, J. (2002). Explaining injustice: The interactive effect of explanation and outcome on fairness perceptions and task motivation. *Journal of Management.* 28, 591–610.

Colquitt, J. A., Conlon, D. E., Wesson, M. J., Porter, C. O. L. H., & Ng, K. Y. (2001). Justice at the millennium: A meta-analysis of 25 years of organizational justice research. *Journal of Applied Psychology, 86,* 425–445.

Colquitt, J. A., Noe, R. A., & Jackson, C. L. (2002). Justice in teams: Antecedents and consequences in procedural justice climate. *Personnel Psychology, 55,* 83–109.

Conlon, D. E., & Ross, W. H. (1993). The effects of partisan third parties on negotiator behavior and outcome perceptions. *Journal of Applied Psychology, 78,* 280–290.

Cropanzano, R., & Ambrose, M. L. (2001). Procedural and distributive justice are more similar than you think: A monistic perspective and a research agenda. In J. Greenberg & R. Cropanzano (Eds.), *Advances in organizational justice* (pp. 119–151). Stanford, CA: Stanford University Press.

Cropanzano, R., Byrne, Z. S., Bobocel, D. R., & Rupp, D. E. (2001a). Moral virtues, fairness heuristics, social entities, and other denizens of organizational justice. *Journal of Vocational Behavior, 58,* 164–209.

Cropanzano, R., Byrne, Z. S., Bobocel, D. R., & Rupp, D. E. (2001b). Self- enhancement biases, laboratory experiments, George Wilhelm Friedrich Hegel, and the increasingly crowded world of organizational justice. *Journal of Vocational Behavior, 58,* 260–272.

Cropanzano, R., & Greenberg, J. (1997). Progress in organizational justice: Tunneling through the maze. In C. L. Cooper & I. T. Roberson (Eds.), *International review of industrial and organizational psychology* (Vol. 12, pp. 317–372). Chichester, England: Wiley.

Cropanzano, R., Prehar, C. A., & Chen, P. Y. (2002). Using social exchange theory to distinguish procedural from interactional justice. *Group Organization Managment, 27,* 324–351.

Daly, J. P., & Geyer, P. D. (1994). The role of fairness in implementing large-scale change: Employee evaluations of process and outcome in seven facility relocations. *Journal of Organizational Behavior, 15,* 623–638.

Deutsch, M. (1975). Equity, equality, and need: What determines which value will be used as the basis for distributive justice? *Journal of Social Issues, 31,* 137–149.

Eisenberger, R., Huntington, R., Hutchinson, S., & Sowa, D. (1986). Perceived organizational support. *Journal of Applied Psychology, 71,* 500–507.

Folger, R. (1986a). A referent cognitions theory of relative deprivation. In J. M. Olson, C. P. Herman, & M. P. Zanna (Eds.), *Relative deprivation and social comparison: The Ontario symposium* (Vol. 4, pp. 33–55). Hillsdale, NJ: Lawrence Erlbaum Associates.

Folger, R. (1986b). Rethinking equity theory: A referent cognitions model. In H. W. Bierhoff, R. L. Cohen, & J. Greenberg (Eds.), *Justice in social relations* (pp. 145–162). New York: Plenum.

Folger, R. (1987). Reformulating the preconditions of resentment: A referent cognitions model. In J. C. Masters & W. P. Smith (Eds.), *Social comparison, justice,* and relative deprivation: Theoretical, empirical, and policy perspectives (pp. 183–215). Hillsdale, NJ: Lawrence Erlbaum Associates.

Folger, R. (1993). Reactions to mistreatment at work. In K. Murnighan (Ed.), Social psychology in organizations: Advances in theory and research (pp. 161–183). Englewood Cliffs, NJ: Prentice-Hall.

Folger, R., & Bies, R. J. (1989). Managerial responsibilities and procedural justice. Employee Responsibilities and Rights Journal, 2, 79–89.

Folger, R., & Cropanzano, R. (1998). Organizational justice and human resource management. Thousand Oaks, CA: Sage.

Folger, R., & Cropanzano, R. (2001). Fairness theory: Justice as accountability. In J. Greenberg & R. Cropanzano (Eds.), Advances in organizational justice (pp. 89–118). Stanford, CA: Stanford University Press.

Folger, R., & Greenberg, J. (1985). Procedural justice: An interpretive analysis of personnel systems. In K. Rowland & G. Ferris (Eds.), Research in personnel and human resources management (Vol. 3, pp. 141–183). Greenwich, CT: JAI.

Folger, R., & Konovsky, M. A. (1989). Effects of procedural and distributive justice on reactions to pay raise decisions. Academy of Management Journal, 32, 115–130.

Forehand, B., & Gilmer, B. V. (1964). Environmental variation in studies of organizational behavior. Psychological Bulletin, 62, 361–382.

Gilliland, S. W. (1993). The perceived fairness of selection systems: An organizational justice perspective. Academy of Management Review, 18, 694–734.

Gilliland, S. W. (1994). Effects of procedural and distributive justice on reactions to a selection system. Journal of Applied Psychology, 79, 691–701.

Gilliland, S. W., Groth, M., Baker, R. C., & Dew, A. F. (2001). Improving applicants' reactions to rejection letters: An application of fairness theory. Personnel Psychology, 54, 669–703.

Gordon, M. E., & Fryxell, G. E. (1989). Voluntariness of association as a moderator of the importance of procedural and distributive justice. Journal of Applied Social Psychology, 19, 993–1009.

Graen, G. B., & Uhl-Bien, M. (1995). Relationship-based approach to leadership: Development of leader–member exchange (LMX) theory of leadership over 25 years: Applying a multi-level multi-domain perspective. Leadership Quarterly, 6, 219–247.

Greenberg, J. (1979). Protestant ethic endorsement and the fairness of equity inputs. Journal of Research in Personality, 13, 81–90.

Greenberg, J. (1986a). The distributive justice of organizational performance evaluations. In H. W. Bierhoff, R. L. Cohen, & J. Greenberg (Eds.), Justice in social relations (pp. 337–351). New York: Plenum.

Greenberg, J. (1986b). Organizational performance appraisal procedures: What makes them fair? In R. J. Lewicki, B. H. Sheppard, & M. H. Bazerman (Eds.), Research on negotiation in organizations (Vol. 1, pp. 25–41). Greenwich, CT: JAI.

Greenberg, J. (1987). A taxonomy of organizational justice theories. Academy of Management Review, 12, 9–22.

Greenberg, J. (1990). Organizational justice: Yesterday, today, and tomorrow. Journal of Management, 16, 399–432.

Greenberg, J. (1993a). The intellectual adolescence of organizational justice: You've come a long way, maybe. *Social Justice Research, 6*, 135–148.

Greenberg, J. (1993b). The social side of fairness: Interpersonal and informational classes of organizational justice. In R. Cropanzano (Ed.), *Justice in the workplace: Approaching fairness in human resource management* (pp. 79–103). Hillsdale, NJ: Lawrence Erlbaum Associates.

Greenberg, J. (1994). Using socially fair treatment to promote acceptance of a work site smoking ban. *Journal of Applied Psychology, 79*, 288–297.

Greenberg, J. (1996). *The quest for justice on the job*. Thousand Oaks, CA: Sage.

Greenberg, J. (1998). The cognitive geometry of employee theft: Negotiating "the line" between taking and theft. In R. W. Griffin, A. O'Leary-Kelly, & J. Collins (Eds.), *Dysfunctional behavior in organizations: Vol. 2. Nonviolent behaviors in organizations* (pp. 147–193). Greenwich, CT: JAI.

Greenberg, J. (2000). Promote procedural justice to enhance acceptance of work outcomes. In E. A. Locke (Ed.), *A handbook of principles of organizational behavior* (pp. 191–195). Oxford, England: Blackwell.

Greenberg, J. (in press). Who stole what, and when? Individual and situational determinants of employee theft. *Organizational Behavior and Human Decision Processes*.

Greenberg, J., & Alge, B. (1998). Aggressive reactions to workplace injustice. In R. W. Griffin, A. O'Leary-Kelly, & J. Collins (Eds.), *Dysfunctional behavior in organizations: Vol. 1. Violent behavior in organizations* (pp. 119–145). Greenwich, CT: JAI.

Greenberg, J., Eskew, D., & Miles, J. A. (1991, August). *Adherence to participatory norms as a moderator of the fair process effect: When voice does not enhance procedural justice*. Paper presented at the meeting of the Academy of Management, Miami Beach, FL.

Greenberg, J., & Folger, R. (1983). Procedural justice, participation, and the fair process effect in groups and organizations. In P. Paulus (Ed.), *Basic group processes* (pp. 235–256). New York: Springer-Verlag.

Greenberg, J., & Lind, E. A. (2000). The pursuit of organizational justice: From conceptualization to implication to application. In C. L. Cooper & E. A. Locke (Eds.), *I/O psychology: What we know about theory and practice* (pp. 72–108). Oxford, England: Blackwell.

Greenberg, J., & McCarty, C. (1990). Comparable worth: A matter of justice. In G. R. Ferris & K. M. Rowland (Eds.), *Research in personnel and human resources management* (Vol. 8, pp. 265–301). Greenwich, CT: JAI.

Grienberger, I. V., Rutte, C. G., & Van Knippenberg, A. F. M. (1997). Influence of social comparisons of outcomes and procedures on fairness judgments. *Journal of Applied Psychology, 82*, 913–919.

Hagedoorn, M., Buunk, B. P., & Van de Vliert (1998). Opening the black box between justice and reactions to unfavorable outcomes in the workplace. *Social Justice Research, 11*, 41–57.

Holbrook, R. L., & Kulik, C. T. (2001). Customer perceptions of justice in service transactions: The effects of strong and weak ties. *Journal of Organizational Behavior, 22*, 743–757.

Homans, G. C. (1961). *Social behaviour: Its elementary forms*. London: Routledge & Kegan Paul.

House, R. J., & Aditya, R. N. (1997). The social scientific study of leadership: Quo vadis? *Journal of Management, 23*, 409–473.

Huseman, R. C., Hatfield, J. D., & Miles, E. W. (1987). A new perspective on equity theory: The equity sensitivity construct. *Academy of Management Review, 12*, 222–234.

Joy, V. L., & Witt, L. A. (1992). Delay of gratification as a moderator of the procedural justice-distributive justice relationship. *Group and Organization Management, 17*, 297–308.

Kanfer, R. (1991). Motivation theory and industrial and organizational psychology. In M. D. Dunnette & L. M. Hough (Eds.), *Handbook of industrial and organizational psychology* (Vol. 1, pp. 75–170). Palo Alto, CA: Consulting Psychologists Press.

Keller, T., & Dansereau, F. (1995). Leadership and empowerment: A social exchange perspective. *Human Relations, 48*, 127–146.

Kerr, S., & Jermier, J. M. (1978). Substitutes for leadership: Their meaning and measurement. *Organizational Behavior and Human Performance, 22*, 375–403.

Kidder, L. H., & Miller, S. (1991). What is "fair" in Japan? In H. Steensma & R. Vermunt (Eds.), *Social justice in human relations: Vol. 2. Societal and psychological consequences of justice and injustice* (pp. 139–154). New York: Plenum.

Kidwell, R. E., & Bennett, N. (1994). Employee reactions to electronic control systems: The role of procedural fairness. *Group and Organization Management, 19*, 203–218.

Kim, W. C., & Mauborgne, R. A. (1993). Procedural justice, attitudes, and subsidiary top management compliance with multinationals' corporate strategy decisions. *Academy of Management Journal, 36*, 502–526.

King, W. C., Jr., Miles, E. W., & Day, D. D. (1993). A test and refinement of the equity sensitivity construct. *Journal of Organizational Behavior, 14*, 301–317.

Konovsky, M. A., & Cropanzano, R. (1991). Perceived fairness of employee drug testing as a predictor of employee attitudes and job performance. *Journal of Applied Psychology, 76*, 698–707.

Konovsky, M. A., & Folger, R. (1991). The effects of procedures, social accounts, and benefits level on victims' layoff reactions. *Journal of Applied Social Psychology, 21*, 630–650.

Konovsky, M. A., Folger, R., & Cropanzano, R. (1987). Relative effects of procedural and distributive justice on employee attitudes. *Representative Research in Social Psychology, 17*, 15–24.

Korsgaard, M. A., Roberson, L., & Rymph, R. D. (1998). What motivates fairness? The role of subordinate assertive behavior on managers' interactional fairness. *Journal of Applied Psychology, 83*, 731–744.

Kouzes, J. M., Posner, B. Z., & Peters, T. (1996). *The leadership challenge*. San Francisco: Jossey-Bass.

Leung, K., & Tong, K. K. (2001, September). *Toward a normative model of justice*. Paper presented at the International Roundtable on Innovations in Organizational Justice Research, Vancouver, British Columbia, Canada.

Leventhal, G. S. (1976). The distribution of rewards and resources in groups and organizations. In L. Berkowitz & W. Walster (Eds.), *Advances in experimental social psychology* (Vol. 9, pp. 91–131). New York: Academic.

Leventhal, G. S. (1980). What should be done with equity theory? New approaches to the study of fairness in social relationships. In K. Gergen, M. Greenberg, & R. Willis (Eds.), *Social exchange: Advances in theory and research* (pp. 27–55). New York: Plenum.

Leventhal, G. S., Karuza, J., & Fry, W. R. (1980). Beyond fairness: A theory of allocation preferences. In G. Mikula (Ed.), *Justice and social interaction* (pp. 167–218). New York: Springer-Verlag.

Lind, E. A. (2001a). Fairness heuristic theory: Justice judgments as pivotal cognitions in organizational relations. In J. Greenberg & R. Cropanzano (Eds.), *Advances in organizational justice* (pp. 56–88). Stanford, CA: Stanford University Press.

Lind, E. A. (2001b). Thinking critically about justice judgments. *Journal of Vocational Behavior, 58*, 220–226.

Lind, E. A., Greenberg, J., Scott, K. S., & Welchans, D. (2000). The winding road from employee to complainant: Situational and psychological determinants of wrongful termination claims. *Administrative Science Quarterly, 45*, 557–590.

Lind, E. A., Kray, L., & Thompson, L. (2001). Primacy effects in justice judgments: Testing predictions for fairness heuristic theory. *Organizational Behavior and Human Decision Processes, 85*, 189–210.

Lind, E. A., Kulik, C., Ambrose, M., & de Vera Park, M. (1993). Individual and corporate dispute resolution: Using procedural fairness as a decision heuristic. *Administrative Science Quarterly, 38*, 224–251.

Lind, E. A., & Tyler, T. R. (1988). *The social psychology of procedural justice*. New York: Plenum.

Lind, E. A., Tyler, T. R., & Huo, Y. J. (1997). Procedural context and culture: Variation in antecedents of procedural justice judgments. *Journal of Personality and Social Psychology, 73*, 767–780.

Major, B., & Deaux, K. (1982). Individual differences in justice behavior. In J. Greenberg & R. L. Cohen (Eds.), *Equity and justice in social behavior* (pp. 43–76). New York: Academic.

Maslow, A. H. (1954). *Motivation and personality*. New York: Harper & Row.

Masterson, S. S., Bartol, K. M., & Moye, N. (2000, April). *Interactional and procedural justice: Type versus source of fairness*. Paper presented at the meeting of the Society for Industrial and Organizational Psychology, New Orleans, LA.

Masterson, S. S., Lewis, K., Goldman, B. M., & Taylor, M. S. (2000). Integrating justice and social exchange: The differing effects of fair procedures and treatment on work relationships. *Academy of Management Journal, 43*, 738–748.

McFarlin, D. B., Frone, M., Major, D. B., & Konar, E. (1989). Predicting career-entry pay expectations: The role of gender-based comparisons. *Journal of Business and Psychology, 3*, 331–340.

McFarlin, D. B., & Sweeney, P. D. (1992). Distributive and procedural justice as predictors of satisfaction with personal and organizational outcomes. *Academy of Management Journal, 35*, 626–637.

Mikula, G. (1993). Exploring the experience of injustice. *European Journal of Social Psychology, 4*, 223–244.

Moorman, R. H. (1991). Relationship between organizational justice and organizational citizenship behaviors: Do fairness perceptions influence employee citizenship? *Journal of Applied Psychology, 76*, 845–855.

Mossholder, K. W., Bennett, N., & Martin, C. L. (1998). A multilevel analysis of procedural justice context. *Journal of Organizational Behavior, 19*, 131–141.

Naumann, S. E., & Bennett, N. (2000). A case for procedural justice climate: Development and test of a multilevel model. *Academy of Management Journal, 43*, 881–889.

Niehoff, B. P., & Moorman, R. H. (1993). Justice as a mediator of the relationship between methods of monitoring and organizational citizenship behaviors. *Academy of Management Journal, 36*, 527–556.

Ostroff, C., Kinicki, A. J., & Tamkins, M. M. (in press). Organizational culture and climate. In W. C. Borman, D. R. Ilgen, & R. J. Klimoski (Eds.), *Comprehensive handbook of psychology: Vol. 12. Industrial and organizational psychology.* New York: Wiley.

Parker, C. P., Baltes, B. B., & Christiansen, N. D. (1997). Support for affirmative action, justice perceptions, and work attitudes: A study of gender and racial–ethnic group differences. *Journal of Applied Psychology, 82*, 376–389.

Porter, L. W., & Lawler, E. E., III. (1968). *Managerial attitudes and performance.* Homewood, IL: Irwin.

Quinones, M. A. (1995). Pretraining context effects: Training assignment as feedback. *Journal of Applied Psychology, 80*, 226–238.

Reichers, A. E., & Schneider, B. (1990). Climate and culture: Life cycles of constructs. In B. Schneider (Ed.), *Organizational climate and culture* (pp. 5–39). San Francisco: Jossey-Bass.

Scandura, T. A. (1997). Mentoring and organizational justice: An empirical investigation. *Journal of Vocational Behavior, 51*, 58–69.

Schminke, M., Ambrose, M. L., & Cropanzano, R. S. (2000). The effect of organizational structure on perceptions of procedural justice. *Journal of Applied Psychology, 85*, 294–304.

Schmitt, M. (1996). Individual differences in sensitivity to befallen injustice (SBI). *Personality and Individual Differences, 21*, 3–20.

Skarlicki, D. P., & Folger, R. (1997). Retaliation in the workplace: The roles of distributive, procedural, and interactional justice. *Journal of Applied Psychology, 82*, 434–443.

Skarlicki, D. P., Folger, R., & Tesluk, P. (1999). Personality as a moderator in the relationship between fairness and retaliation. *Academy of Management Journal, 42*, 100–108.

Skarlicki, D. P., & Latham, G. P. (1996). Increasing citizenship behavior within a labor union: A test of organizational justice theory. *Journal of Applied Psychology, 81*, 161–169.

Skarlicki, D. P., & Latham, G. P. (1997). Leadership training in organizational justice to increase citizenship behavior within a labor union: A replication. *Personnel Psychology, 50*, 617–633.

Steiner, D. D. (2001). Cultural influences on perceptions of distributive and procedural justice. In S. Gilliland, D. Steiner, & D. Skarlicki (Eds.), *Theoretical and cultural perspectives on organizational justice* (pp. 111–138). Greenwich, CT: Information Age.

Sweeney, P. D., & McFarlin, D. B. (1993). Workers' evaluations of the "ends" and "means": An examination of four models of distributive and procedural justice. *Organizational Behavior and Human Decision Processes, 55*, 23–40.

Sweeney, P. D., & McFarlin, D. B. (1997). Process and outcome: Gender differences in the assessment of justice. *Journal of Organizational Behavior, 18*, 83–98.

Sweeney, P. D., McFarlin, D. B., & Cotton, J. L. (1991). Locus of control as a moderator of the relationship between perceived influence and procedural justice. *Human Relations, 44*, 333–342.

Thibaut, J., & Walker, L. (1975). *Procedural justice: A psychological analysis.* Hillsdale, NJ: Lawrence Erlbaum Associates.

Tyler, T. R. (1986). When does procedural justice matter in organizational settings? In R. J. Lewicki, B. H. Sheppard, & M. H. Bazerman (Eds.), *Research on negotiations in organizations* (Vol. 1, pp. 7–23). Greenwich, CT: JAI.

Tyler, T. R. (1990). *Why people obey the law: Procedural justice, legitimacy, and compliance.* New Haven, CT: Yale University Press.

Tyler, T. R. (1999). Why people cooperate with organizations: An identity-based perspective. In B. M. Staw & R. Sutton (Eds.), *Research in organizational behavior* (Vol. 21, pp. 201–246). Greenwich, CT: JAI.

Tyler, T., & Bies, R. J. (1990). Beyond formal procedures: The interpersonal context of procedural justice. In J. Carroll (Ed.), *Applied social psychology and organizational settings* (pp. 77–98). Hillsdale, NJ: Lawrence Erlbaum Associates.

Tyler, T. R., & Blader, S. L. (2000). *Cooperation in groups: Procedural justice, social identity, and behavioral engagement.* Philadelphia : Psychology Press.

Tyler, T. R., & Lind, E. A. (1992). A relational model of authority in groups. In M. P. Zanna (Ed.), *Advances in experimental social psychology* (Vol. 25, pp. 115–191). San Diego, CA: Academic.

Van den Bos, K. (2001a). Fairness heuristic theory: Assessing the information to which people are reacting has a pivotal role in understanding organizational justice. In S. Gilliland, D. Steiner, & D. Skarlicki (Eds.), *Theoretical and cultural perspectives on organizational justice* (pp. 63–84). Greenwich, CT: Information Age.

Van den Bos, K. (2001b). Uncertainty management: The influence of uncertainty salience on reactions to perceived procedural fairness. *Journal of Personality and Social Psychology 80*, 931–941.

Van den Bos, K., Lind, E. A., Vermunt, R., & Wilke, H. A. M. (1997). How do I judge my outcome when I do not know the outcome of others? The psychology of the fair process effect. *Journal of Personality and Social Psychology, 72*, 1034–1046.

Van den Bos, K., Lind, E. A., & Wilke, H. A. M. (2001). The psychology of procedural and distributive justice viewed from the perspective of fairness heuristic theory. In R. Cropanzano (Ed.), *Justice in the workplace: Vol. 2. From theory to practice* (pp. 49–66). Mahwah, NJ: Lawrence Erlbaum Associates.

Van den Bos, K., Vermunt, R., & Wilke, H. A. M. (1997). Procedural and distributive justice: What is fair depends more on what comes first than on what comes next. *Journal of Personality and Social Psychology, 72*, 95–104.

Van den Bos, K., Wilke, H. A. M., & Lind, E. A. (1998). When do we need procedural fairness? The role of trust in authority. *Journal of Personality and Social Psychology, 75*, 1449–1458.

Van den Bos, K., Wilke, H. A. M., Lind, E. A., & Vermunt, R. (1998). Evaluating outcomes by means of the fair process effect: Evidence for different processes in fairness and satisfaction judgments. *Journal of Personality and Social Psychology, 74*, 1493–1503.

Van Prooijen, J. W., Van den Bos, K., & Wilke, H. A. M. (2001, September). *A group dynamics focus model of procedural justice.* Presented at the International Roundtable on Organizational Justice, Vancouver, British Columbia, Canada.

Vecchio, R. P., Griffeth, R. W., & Hom, P. W. (1986). The predictive utility of the vertical dyad linkage approach. *Journal of Social Psychology, 126*, 617–625.

Vroom, V. H. (1964). *Work and motivation.* New York: Wiley.

Welbourne, T. M., Balkin, D. B., & Gomez-Mejia, L. R. (1995). Gainsharing and mutual monitoring: A combined agency-organizational justice interpretation. *Academy of Management Journal, 38*, 881–899.

Whetten, D. A. (1989). What constitutes a theoretical contribution? *Academy of Management Review, 14*, 490–495.

White, M. M., Tansky, J. A., & Baik, K. (1995). Linking culture and perceptions of justice: A comparison of students in Virginia and South Korea. *Psychological Reports, 77*, 1103–1112.

Yukl, G., & Van Fleet, D. D. (1992). Theory and research on leadership in organizations. In M. D. Dunnette & L. M. Hough (Eds.), *Handbook of industrial and organizational psychology* (Vol. 3, pp. 147–197). Palo Alto, CA: Consulting Psychologists Press.

# 6

# Personal Reputation in Organizations

Gerald R. Ferris
*Florida State University*

Fred R. Blass
*Florida State University*

Ceasar Douglas
*Florida State University*

Robert W. Kolodinsky
*James Madison University*

Darren C. Treadway
*Florida State University*

For as long as we have been studying behavior in organizations, scholars have been interested in qualities, characteristics, and behaviors of individuals that contribute to their personal influence and effectiveness. Personal reputation is a construct that appears to incorporate such factors of individuals at work, and it seems worthy of serious scholarly attention by organizational scientists. Interestingly, and quite unfortunately, the notion of reputation has been virtually ignored as an individual-level focus of scientific inquiry and as a possible determinant of individual effectiveness in the management literature. However, we find that reputation has been studied for many years in other scientific disciplines and areas of scientific inquiry, but those literatures have remained reasonably parallel to one another, thus preventing integration and the building of a more extensive knowledge base.

In this chapter, we review the previous literature on reputation in organizations, and supplement this review with a systematic examination of reputation as it has been investigated in the accounting, sociology, economics, marketing, and organization theory and strategy fields. The current status of work on personal reputation is addressed in the next section, noting established findings and generally agreed on themes, concepts, and issues. Finally, we propose important directions for the future and address the potential richness in studying personal reputation in organizations.

## THE NATURE AND MEANING OF REPUTATION

Although the use of the term *personal reputation* is omnipresent in everyday work life today, we find that its status as a scientific construct has not emerged commensurate with its usage. The fact of the matter is that, with the exception of anecdotal use, we have developed little to date in the way of a collective and common understanding of the construct. Part of the reason for this state of affairs is that reputation has been studied in a number of different scientific disciplines, at different levels of analysis, and employing a variety of different definitions.

In this section of the chapter, we first review previous work to examine the various ways reputation has been defined, and then propose a working definition of the personal reputation construct that we believe representatively reflects the content domain and captures the essence of existing views. Then, we report on a review of the reputation literature that spans several disciplines and areas of inquiry. Whereas much of this review concerns itself with the reputations of organizations, groups, departments, and brands of products, we argue that the underlying foundational principles of reputation generalize, and thus can serve our interest in developing a more informed understanding of personal reputation in organizations.

### Domain and Definition of Reputation

Definitions of reputation include such descriptive statements as "estimation in which a person or thing is commonly held, whether favorable or not" (*Webster's New World College Dictionary*, 1997), and terms such as standing, prestige, and status. Recently, interest has been demonstrated in the reputations of organizations, which we would argue identify processes similar, in many respects, to how individuals develop and use reputations to exercise influence and maximize effectiveness.

*Considerations in Reputation Definition.* Organizational research-ers commonly cite reputation as an end worthy of pursuit or defense Peteraf & Shanley, 1997; Pfeffer & Salancik, 1978. In one of the few attempts to define organizational reputation, Barney (1991) described reputation as a substitute for a guarantee, contract, or control mechanism. Similarly, most studies on organizational reputation approach it from a re-source-based perspective. From this point of view, reputation is presented as an intangible asset that significantly contributes to organizational per-formance due to its inimitable nature (Barney, 1991; Fombrun & Shanley, 1990; Galang, Elsik, & Russ, 1999; Gioia, Shultz, & Corley, 2000; Teece, Pisano, & Shuen, 1997). The notion of a reputation being inimitable is cer-tainly applicable to personal reputation, because it makes sense that the value of a reputation is at least partly related to its degree of uniqueness.

Herbig, Milewicz, and Golden (1994) quantified the relationship between reputation and credibility by differentiating between the effects of transac-tions on the reputation and credibility of the signaling firm. They argued that a firm's reputation and subsequent credibility are the result of a continuous process of successful transactions that reinforce reputation and credibility. Suchman's (1995) discussion of legitimacy certainly has potential implica-tions for the reputation of organizations, and Galang et al. (1999) argued that legitimacy is a necessary condition for organization reputation. Suchman did make brief mention of what he called "personal legitimacy," and this concept appears to have quite strong parallels with the reputation of individuals.

In a study examining corporate human resource reputation, Jones (1996) suggested that an organization's human resource reputation refers to the ex-tent to which employees regard their organization as a "good" place to work. He argued that a human resource reputation exists as a distinct con-cept, and that it is largely the product of an innovative climate and job satis-faction. Similarly, Turban and Greening (1996) investigated the relationship between firms' corporate social performance and their reputation and at-tractiveness as employers. Their results indicated that independent ratings of corporate social performance are related to firms' reputations and attrac-tiveness as employers. Cable and Graham (2000) suggested that the type of industry in which a firm operates, the opportunities that a firm provides for employee development, and organizational culture affect the perceptions of an organization's reputation by job seekers. Indeed, Berkson, Harris, and Ferris (1999) suggested that recruitment interview processes can be vehicles to promote organizational reputation through persuasive communication of recruiters, focusing on attractive attributes of the organization.

*Sharpening the Focus on Personal Reputation.* Descriptions of repu-tation within various areas of research are reflective of their underlying as-sumptions, and more often implicit rather than explicit. For example, social scientists interested in networks tend to view reputation as a form of communication or exchange between members of those networks, and that this communiqué can serve as an implicit control on individual behavior (Granovetter, 1985). In these exchanges, norms for individual behavior are largely defined by an individual's role within a context of the network. As individuals interact with others, a network of roles and their attending behavioral expectations, known as role-sets, are established. These role-sets hold certain prescriptions and proscriptions regarding expected behavior of each role (Katz & Kahn, 1978; Merton, 1968; Tsui, 1984). As Tsui (1984) pointed out, a manager's reputation is determined by the degree to which he or she is effective at meeting the expectations of each of multiple constituents of that managerial role-set.

From a social network perspective, the network to which an individual belongs can be a factor in developing an individual's reputation as a good performer (Kilduff & Krackhardt, 1994). In what is probably the most comprehensive work on personal reputation to date, Bromley (1993) argued that reputation, as a form of influence, exerts itself in self-esteem, social identity, individual behavior, and social interactions. Furthermore, he suggested that individuals share with others their impressions of certain individuals, which become consolidated into collective impressions. These collective impressions then influence the attitudes, expectations, choices, and actions of the members within a given social network.

Similar to Bromley's (1993) approach, other researchers have presented reputation as an assessment of how others view an individual within an organization. From this perspective, reputation is the result of others' perceptual interpretations or determinations of an individual's job performance, suggesting that reputation is a substitute for firsthand knowledge of an individual (Baron & Markman, 2000; Doby & Caplan, 1995; Kydd, Ogilvie, & Slade, 1990). Some even have argued that an individual's reputation is partially attributable to the reputation of the organization (Staw & Epstein, 2000) or of a group or team (Simons, 1998), and some individuals seek to raise their own status and reputation through formal associations with prestigious organizations. Indeed, one would be hard pressed to argue that a new PhD (i.e., who presumably has not yet formed a well-known scholarly reputation) does not gain in reputational stature by accepting an offer for a faculty position at a prestigious university.

The varying descriptive approaches to reputation also have yielded inconsistent operationalizations. In one of the first studies to highlight the concept of individual reputation, Gladstone (1963) equated reputation with competence. Later, Jones and Shrauger (1970) operationalized reputation as the perceived value of external information on the individual. Baumeister (1982) used public feedback of a personality assessment as a proxy for reputation. Reputation also has been operationalized as performance history and performance comparisons with referent others (Gioia & Sims, 1983; Tsui, 1984).

Similar to the wide range of operationalizations and descriptions, definitions of reputation reflect the orientation of the researcher or the unit of analysis. For instance, those interested in organizations have defined reputation as "the collective judgments of an organization's overall character by groups of similarly interested and informed people that are based primarily on the past actions of the firm" (Hannon & Milkovich, 1996, p. 408). Fiol, O'Connor, and Aguinis (2001) defined the reputation of a group as "the set of beliefs others hold about how powerful the unit is" (p. 225), and Simons (1998) demonstrated the spillover effects of group reputation on individuals when suggesting that a team sergeant can enhance his own reputation if the team for which he has responsibility trains effectively.

At the individual level, reputation has been defined as "a nucleus of interconnected impressions shared and expressed by a high proportion of members of a defined social network" (Bromley, 1993, p. 42). Finally, at a product level, marketing literature has defined reputation as "the estimation of the consistency over time of an attribute of an entity" (Milewicz & Herbig, 1994, p. 41).

In addition to these stated considerations of reputation across different levels of analysis, reviewing the various treatments of reputation across those different levels presents an opportunity to offer a few noteworthy observations. First, reputation appears to be largely perceptual in nature. Specifically, reputation is defined by the perceptions of others with regard to a specific context (e.g., Bailey, 1971; Fombrun, 1996). Second, reputations are used by others to make decisions under conditions of incomplete information (e.g., Kreps & Wilson, 1982). Third, reputation has a value that is recognized by both the holder and the perceiver of the reputation (e.g., Bok, 1993; Riahi-Belkaoui & Pavlik, 1992). Fourth, reputations are a product of the agent, the situation, and the target. Fifth, reputations are influenced by deliberate or chance events, and as such are at times manageable, and at others unmanageable. Finally, reputations are the result of continuous processes.

*Toward a Working Definition of Personal Reputation.*   The similarities between the various descriptions of reputation at both the individual and organization levels imply that a general definition of personal reputation may be possible. Borrowing from previous research across fields and disciplines, the following definition of personal reputation is offered:

> Reputation is a perceptual identity reflective of the complex combination of salient personal characteristics and accomplishments, demonstrated behavior, and intended images presented over some period of time as observed directly and/or as reported from secondary sources.

There are several points we would like to emphasize about the different parts of this definition. First, we characterize reputation as "an" (i.e., singular) identity, implicitly suggesting that one can potentially have a number of different, even conflicting, reputations. Even when confining our interest and relevant domain of inquiry to the organizational setting, it is still quite possible that an individual could possess different work-related reputations perceptually identified and interpreted by different constituent target individuals or groups. This aspect of our definition addresses key parts of Tsui's (1984) work on role-sets, and thus it is conceivable one could reflect different reputations to different constituent persons or groups in different work contexts. Bromley (1993) suggested that an individual may have at least as many reputations as the number of distinct social groups within which they interact.

However, it is also possible that an individual could elicit a single and consistent reputational response from different individuals or groups across work contexts. For example, for all of the various reputational ways a CEO might be described by subordinates and close confidants, he or she is likely to be perceived reasonably consistently by other CEOs in various industries. Furthermore, whereas one can reflect multiple reputations, based on the different constituencies to which one attends, there probably needs to be some degree of general agreement, shared perspective, or consensus building regarding each within-constituency reputation perception (Becker, 1982).

Second, it is important to note that we see reputation as perceptual and highly subjective in nature, defined in the "eye of the beholder," more of a socially constructed reality than an objective one (e.g., Fine, 1996; Gamson, Croteau, Hoynes, & Sasson, 1992; Goffman, 1959; Gowler & Legge, 1989; Kapsis, 1983; Noorman, 1984; Rao, 1994), and, as some scholars have concluded, more of a political than an objective scientific construct (e.g., Ferris, Fedor, & King, 1994; Kanter & Brinkerhoff, 1981). Furthermore, such perceptual processes may operate and be formed at a distance, or involve some relationship between the parties (Bellah, 1986; Chong, 1992).

Third, this definition suggests that reputation is influenced by an individual's personal characteristics and accomplishments, which reflect certain observable qualities or attributes of an individual (e.g., gender, race or ethnicity, age), as well as human capital variables (e.g., education, institution granting degrees, experience), which can serve as signals of reputation (e.g., Ferris et al., 1994; Spence, 1974). Certainly, another important part of our definition of reputation has to do with other characteristics one possesses such as personality traits, social and political skill, and so forth, and the behavioral manifestations of such underlying traits and characteristics.

Fourth, we see a temporal dimension to reputation in that it is not something that occurs instantaneously, but rather emerges over some period of time, either through direct observation by others or through the communication of reputational information through secondary sources (e.g., Gotsi & Wilson, 2001; Hall, 1993; Herbig et al., 1994; Kennedy, 1977; Milewicz & Herbig, 1994).

Finally, we note that various aspects of one's behavior and decisions can come together in complex ways to create reputation. Particularly when a person's various reputations are viewed as positive, there appears to be a synergy that is created by the combination of these elements that suggests a unique reputational entity that can be greater than the simple sum of the individual parts. Indeed, we would argue further that well-developed reputations can possess such synergistic effects and uniqueness that are very difficult (if not impossible) to imitate or copy. As such, we view reputation as an intangible resource that can reflect value and potentially represent a source of personal sustained competitive advantage (e.g., Barney, 1991; Dollinger, Golden, & Saxton, 1997; Hall, 1992).

Consider the case of Jack Welch, former chairman and CEO of General Electric. The reputation he has enjoyed as a visionary and savvy business manager has brought him great wealth, consistent employment, and international acclaim. His unique and powerful business reputation not only benefits him as an individual, but any organization aligned with him. The foregoing was merely an effort to articulate and briefly explain the definition of personal reputation. In the next section, we carefully examine the behavioral sciences literature in several disciplines and areas of scientific inquiry to help build a more collective understanding of personal reputation.

## Research on Reputation in Different Fields, Disciplines, and Areas of Inquiry

The examination of research on personal reputation per se has been rather limited to date. However, when we expand the domain of inquiry to consider the way reputation has been studied in different fields, disciplines, and areas of scientific inquiry, we find a quite extensive literature from which we can begin to build a more informed understanding of personal reputation in organizations

*Accounting.* Generally, the discipline of accounting has referred to reputation as *goodwill* (Shenkar & Yuchtman-Yaar, 1997). Riahi-Belkaoui and Pavlik (1992) provided an interesting examination of corporate reputation from an accounting perspective, which essentially regards reputation as a valuable asset that can generate future returns to the organization. They argued that reputation-building efforts are conducted through the transmission of signals to the marketplace regarding the financial performance and effectiveness of the firm, but additionally include signals regarding the social performance of the organization that are also believed to reap returns (e.g., Keller, 1974; Matthews, 1984). Similarly, Fombrun and Shanley (1990) showed that financial statements are reflective of an organization's current state of affairs based on the organization's past activities, and as such, directly contribute to the firm's reputation.

*Sociology.* The notion that reputation is socially a constructed phenomenon is a recurrent theme in the sociological literature (Becker, 1982; Caldeira, 1983; Fine, 1996; Kapsis, 1983; Raub & Weesie, 1990; Simons, 1998). Another common perspective is that of informational asymmetries. From this viewpoint, uncertainty in a situation is directly and positively related to the value of reputation as a source of information (Chong, 1992; Kollock, 1994). Reputation has been presented as a viable resource contributing to the ability to influence others (Gamson, 1966), as a characteristic or attribute ascribed by others (Raub & Weesie, 1990), and as a result of a process of consensus building (Becker, 1982). Whitmeyer (2000) contended that reputation systems "are a ubiquitous feature of modern society, facilitating important economic activities such as employment and consumption and affecting social interaction" (p. 204).

*Economics.* Economists have been quite interested in reputation from several viewpoints. From the game-theory perspective, reputation is characterized as a primary criterion for decision making. In this context, reputation constitutes a summary of the behaviors a player has demonstrated in previous trials of a game. This categorized behavior represents a perceived likelihood of future behavior of the individual that is consistent with one's reputation, and is the basis for determining the nature of future interactions with that individual (Ching, Holsapple, & Whinston, 1992; Lahno, 1995; Rosenthal & Landau, 1979; Whitmeyer, 2000).

Characteristic of the game-theory perspective is Ching et al.'s (1992) description of reputation as a proxy for true ability within a given role that can be adjusted as actual performance confirms or disconfirms the original reputation. Additionally, they introduced the notion of a generic reputation that they presented as an aggregate of reputations across a range of roles, and suggested that this generic reputation is the measure of an individual's overall value as perceived by the organization. For example, an employee may have a reputation for being a hard worker, reliable, politically skilled, knowledgeable, and prompt, all helping to "add up" to having an overall reputation for being a valued organizational asset. What is unclear, however, is what happens when there are inconsistencies across the various "subreputations"; that is, we do not know whether they still come together in perhaps a weighted linear combination to form the overall or generic reputation, or if the overall reputation is disproportionately influenced by significant events in the subreputations.

Alt, Calvert, and Humes (1988) illustrated the relationship between reputation and hegemonic stability, specifically arguing that an actor with a reputation for toughness can serve to establish an equilibrium of cooperation among actors. Focusing on economic outcomes, Milgrom and Roberts (1992) suggested that reputation is important in situations where repeated transactions are likely and or desirable to either party.

What is actually being characterized here is how economic theory has dealt with conditions of imperfect information. Indeed, work in the economics literature for at least three decades has considered the nature of imperfect information, market signaling, and reputation in the operation of markets. For example, Kreps and Wilson (1982) investigated how reputational effects can exercise influence over others as these effects materialize in situations of uncertainty or imperfect information. Under such ambiguous conditions, reputation can fulfill a "signaling" function, which conveys potentially useful and uncertainty-reducing information to the marketplace about an entity. As Spence (1974) argued: "Market signals are activities or attributes of individuals in a market which, by design or accident, alter the beliefs of, or convey information to, other individuals in the market" (p. 1). Therefore, to the extent we have prior behavioral information about a person, such reputational information has predictive utility in reducing the uncertainty concerning how that person will behave in the future (i.e., under similar circumstances). Signaling theory also suggests that observable qualities of individuals such as skills, abilities, and so forth can serve as useful proxies for, or signals about, inherently unobservable underlying characteristics, like reputation (Ferris et al., 1994).

Another perspective taken by the economics field has been to examine the nature of reputation relative to trust. Indeed, this perspective is simply an elaboration on how reputation is a signal or source of information that allows one to predict future behavior. Similarly, trust is frequently viewed as a confidence, or increased probability, that one will behave a certain way in the future (e.g., Kramer & Tyler, 1996). Therefore, research in this field has linked these two constructs. Whitmeyer (2000) discussed the critical role positive reputation systems play in placing trust. This author defined *positive reputation* as "an attribute attached to actors (or perhaps objects) that signals that they are more likely to be desirable for some sort of interaction than those without the attribute" (p. 189). Furthermore, Whitmeyer argued that reputation is important "because it informs the formation of the subjective probability relevant to placing trust" (p. 190). Transmission of reputational information and placing trust can occur more informally in smaller social systems (or organizations). However, such processes often become more bureaucratic in larger social systems where more formalized reputation systems are needed (Klein, 1997).

Whereas the foregoing discussion reviewed research that examined how trust is allocated based on reputation, other research in this and other fields has considered the effects or outcomes of trust allocation based on reputation. Wernerfelt (1988) investigated principal–agent relationships and suggested that principals engage in less monitoring of agents who are considered to have better reputations. Although not directly investigated in this research, these results imply that reputation has informational, predictive, and trust-enhancing value, which leads us to treat individuals with greater reputations differently (and more favorably) than we do those with lesser reputations.

Greenberg (1990) made a similar argument concerning reputational effects by linking the process to Hollander's (1958) notion of "idiosyncrasy credit." Greenberg suggested that marginal latitude or "benefit of the doubt" was granted to those with particularly defined reputations. More specifically, Greenberg stated that: "A reputation for fairness may help give managers the benefit of the doubt in situations in which judgments of fairness may not be easily made—a process similar to the issuance of 'idiosyncrasy credit' (Hollander, 1964)" (p. 143).

Finally, Knoke (1983) demonstrated that greater latitude is allocated to organizations that have a high "influence reputation," defined simply as "an actor's reputation for influence" (p. 1068). Characterizing influence reputation in terms of both past and expected behaviors, Knoke suggested that: "The greater the reputed influence, the higher the organization's capacity to act autonomously within a network of organizations" (p. 1068). So, it seems to be the case that increased reputation carries with it greater behavioral latitude, discretion, and autonomy.

*Marketing.* In the marketing literature, reputation is generally presented as an aggregation of performances, actions, or images representing consumer knowledge about a brand (Aaker, 1991; Cobb-Walgren, Ruble, & Donthu, 1995; Feldwick, 1996; Keller, 1993). Prabhu and Stewart (2001) suggested that reputational beliefs are inferences drawn about the intentions and abilities of an entity. Bickerton (2000) essentially equated reputation to branding. This perspective suggests that reputation is a resource that can be used to guide processes that generate value (Macrae, 1999).

Other researchers have suggested that the company's core business processes represent a set of credentials tied together by the organization's brand (Knox & Maklan, 1998), and that the resulting reputation represents a powerful asset consisting of the sum of brand names, corporate logos, and customer loyalty (Aaker, 1991; Biel, 1992; Milewicz & Herbig, 1994). Bennett and Gabriel (2001) showed that positive corporate reputations increased buyer commitment by moderating the impact of trust on commitment in buyer–seller relations. Similar to Milgrom and Roberts (1992),

Herbig et al. (1994) suggested that a reputation is the result of a continuous process of credibility transactions.

Highlighting the associative aspects of reputation, Moorthy (1985) argued that brand names can serve as representations or repositories of a company's reputation, and as such serve as a transference vehicle from one product to another. Furthermore Weiss, Anderson, and MacInnis (1999) suggested that an organization monitors and actively manages its reputation through decisions regarding the composition of its workforce. This signaling perspective suggests that an inherent property of reputation is its ability to send signals on which others act (Aaker, 1991; Cabral, 2000; Cooke & Ryan, 2000; Gwinner & Eaton, 1999; Herbig & Milewicz, 1997; Kirmani & Rao, 2000; Prabhu & Stewart, 2001; Shapiro, 1982; Spence, 1974; Swait, Erdem, Louviere, & Dubelaar, 1993).

*Organization Theory and Strategy.*   Gotsi and Wilson (2001) presented organization reputation as a stakeholder's evaluation of the organization over some period of time. This evaluation is the target of organizational signaling as managers seek to influence stakeholders' assessments of the firm's salient characteristics (Fombrun, 1996; Fombrun & Shanley, 1990). Fombrun (1996) suggested that this approach to reputation management is so critical to organizational success that it must be coordinated and integrated with traditional corporate functions such as human relations, finance, and operations.

Petrick, Scherer, Brodzinski, Quinn, and Ainina (1999) stated that "reputation can be regarded as the outcome of a competitive process in which firms signal their key characteristics to stakeholders in order to maximize their socioeconomic and moral status" (p. 60). Additionally, they argued that reputation should receive constant leadership attention. Staw and Epstein (2000) demonstrated that organizational reputation was enhanced both within the organization and to external constituents when popular management techniques were implemented. Standifird (2001) showed that reputation plays a critical role in the emergence of Internet-based commerce. He argued that the high degree of uncertainty stemming from a separation of payment from delivery was mitigated through an ad hoc reputation system.

A resource-based view of the firm presents yet another perspective of organization reputation. This perspective highlights reputation as an intangible resource leading to sustained competitive advantage (Barney, 1991; Fombrun & Shanley, 1990; Galang et al., 1999; Gioia et al., 2000; Hall, 1992; Teece et al., 1997). A positive reputation is considered an important resource because it projects a degree of the firm's attractiveness, therefore enticing others to contract with it (Fombrun & Shanley, 1990; Weigelt & Camerer, 1988). Additionally, a reputation is developed through the accumulation of interactions over time. This implies reputation is more a reflection of deed than rhetoric (Caudron, 1997; Fombrun & Shanley, 1990; Hall, 1993), although rhetoric and managed meaning certainly have been found to play a role in reputation development and transmission (e.g., Fine, 1996; Gowler & Legge, 1989; Noorman, 1984; Rao, 1994).

Others have suggested that reputation is an assessment of an entity's desirability by constituents external to the firm (Kirmani & Rao, 2000; Rindova & Fombrun, 1998; Weigelt & Camerer, 1988), and that a firm's ability to manipulate its reputation is limited by the constituents' interpretation of the influence attempts (Standifird, 2001). Media coverage of organizations can be viewed as a forum from which organizations can influence their corporate reputations, as a barometer of public knowledge and opinion, and as a record or history of a firm's reputation as reflected in the media (Deephouse, 2000; Dutton & Dukerich, 1991; Elsbach, 1994; Elsbach & Sutton, 1992). This perspective of the relationship between media and organizations implicates the media as an active participant in the reputation formation process (Ferrier, 1997; Fine, 1996; Gamson et al., 1992; Hannon & Milkovich, 1996).

*Power.*    Pfeffer (1992) suggested that individuals seek reputations that portray them as powerful, and that once that reputation is gained it brings even more power. He went on to argue that this results in increased influence, which permits an individual to accomplish things with less effort, resulting in more getting done. In turn, this further enhances an individual's reputation.

Pfeffer's (1992) notion that reputation brings increased power also might make reference to the relevant concepts of idiosyncrasy credit and referent power (mentioned in an earlier section of this chapter). Hollander (1958) suggested that as individuals make useful and valued contributions to a group, they store up these idiosyncrasy credits, which provide them the unchallenged right to deviate from established behavioral norms. The accumulated credits create a sense of status (or reputation), whereby such individuals can cash in this idiosyncratic capital to buy increased discretion in being able to deviate from established rules and norms.

Indeed, Gioia and Sims (1983) demonstrated that managerial reputation contributed significantly to subordinate perceptions of legitimate, referent, and expert power. In a similar argument, Fiol et al. (2001) suggested that, over time, individuals develop consistent perceptions regarding the power of others. They argued that this power reputation leads to predictable behaviors within specific contexts. Furthermore, Matthews (1988) suggested that reputation is power, and that this power is based less on reality than on appearance.

French and Raven (1959) developed the notion of referent power to characterize the influence one person has over another based on attraction and identification. We would argue that individuals of higher reputation possess greater referent power due to other individuals' attraction to them and desire to identify with them. Furthermore, as information and resources contribute to social power bases, personal reputations of individuals should increase as they can more readily access such information and resources (Kilduff & Krackhardt, 1994; Tsui, 1984), which should enhance their perceived influence and power (Brass, 1984; Brass & Burkhardt, 1993).

*Recruitment Research.* Cable and Turban (2001) observed that researchers interested in personnel recruitment often confound the terms image, culture, reputation, and familiarity. Research has shown that recruits are attracted to organizations based on familiarity (Gatewood, Gowan, & Lautenshlager, 1993), organizational culture or image (Cable & Judge, 1996), or on the opinion others hold of the organization (Kilduff & Krackhardt, 1994). An emergent theme across this research is that an organization's reputation refers to the extent to which employees regard their organization as a "good" place to work (Jones, 1996). Echoing this theme, Rynes (1991) recommended that future recruitment research "determine the major components of organizational image and whether any of these can be cost-effectively modified or communicated to improve applicant attraction" (p. 436).

Maurer, Howe, and Lee (1992) observed that many parallels exist between marketing and organizational recruiting. They suggested that organizations view the labor market much as they would a consumer market (Breaugh, 1992; Matthews & Redman, 1994). Consistent with this argument, Martin and Franz (1994) suggested that human resource planners should adopt a marketing strategy when competing with other firms for the most qualified applicants. However, Turban, Forret, and Hendrickson (1998) suggested moving with caution regarding the modification of organizational image components because their results indicated that disconfirmation of expected attributes based on preconceived perceptions of reputation may result in a lower evaluation of an organization.

*Human Resources Reputation.* An organization that is perceived as socially responsible and one that offers competitive benefits is likely to be perceived by potential applicants as having a good reputation (Cable & Graham, 2000; Ferris et al.,1998; Turban & Greening, 1996). Indeed, Galang and Ferris (1997) noted that symbolic actions are stronger predictors of human resources department power than unionization, human resources performance, and top management attitudes. Koys (1997) argued that a primary method for human resource executives to influence corporate reputation is by "encouraging the fair treatment of employees either as an end in itself or as a way to attract and retain qualified people" (p. 98). Certainly, Greenberg's (1990) discussion of the role of fairness in reputation building is critical and quite relevant here to highlight Koys's findings.

Others have suggested that a good human resources reputation can decrease labor costs by reducing turnover (Jones, 1996; Stigler, 1962), and that human resources reputations are based on policies such as above-average pay, grievance systems, and attitude surveys (Guest, 1989). In a related study, Hannon and Milkovich (1996) investigated the relationship between human resources reputation and share prices of the firm. They found only partial support and stated that only the organization that was named "Best for Working Mothers" by *Working Mother* magazine, 1986 to 1989, showed a consistent pattern of share price increase relative to reputation-enhancing announcements.

*Psychology and Impression Management.* Focusing on the individual as the unit of analysis, research in psychology and impression management offers many insights into personal reputation. According to Bozeman and Kacmar (1997), people are motivated to manage their impressions because they have a goal of creating and maintaining a specific identity. Ultimately, this goal is achieved by exhibiting behaviors consistent with the desired identity (Baumeister & Jones, 1978; Tsui, 1984), and once formed, the reputation then serves to constrain future behavior to a degree consistent with the existing reputation (Baumeister, 1982). Reputations may provide the feedback to the individual that the goal has been obtained (Doby & Caplan, 1995; Kydd et al., 1990).

Jones and Shrauger (1970) argued that "reputation has a direct impact on interpersonal attraction and that the approval generated in others by an individual's expressed self-estimate varies as a function of his reputation" (p. 285). As individuals assess their identities, they do so in a multiplicity of comparative contexts, implying that individuals may have multiple reputations (Schlenker, 1980; Turner, 1991). Ashforth and Mael (1989) suggested that because of this role multiplicity, an individual's identity is actually an amalgam of loosely coupled identities.

Tedeschi and Norman (1985) posited that impression management behaviors can be categorized as tactics (i.e., short-term) or as strategies (i.e., long-term). Greenberg (1990) argued that "impression management strategies have the effect of reputation-building" (p. 138), and that repeated consistent behavior, whether real or perceived, may contribute to the formation of a reputation. Reputations not only may be developed and sustained by impression management behaviors, they also may be deliberately manipulated (Bromley, 1993). For instance, Kilduff and Krackhardt (1994) showed that perceptions of affiliation with prominent others boosted an individual's reputation as a good performer. Similar to the associative property of reputation illustrated in the marketing literature (Moorthy, 1985), Gladstone (1963) demonstrated that schoolchildren with a reputation for competence were perceived as possessing a higher degree of morality than those with a reputation for incompetence.

Consistent with the previously mentioned work of Turban et al. (1998), Rosen, Cochran, and Musser (1990) found that a mismatch between style and reputation probably elicits the greatest attention when individuals are gathering information regarding an entity. Subsequently, this mismatch itself becomes information, thus enabling an individual to quickly eliminate the least suitable alternative among multiple choices.

In other research focusing on the individual as the unit of analysis, reputation has been associated with achievement. From this perspective, achievement is presented as consistent high performance or responsible behavior, which then serves to establish trust with significant others, thereby resulting in a "good reputation" (Gowler & Legge, 1989). This connection of reputation and trust was discussed in an earlier section of this chapter based on the work of several authors (Klein, 1997; Wernerfelt, 1988; Whitmeyer, 2000).

Echoing the sociologist's perspective, Bailey (1971) argued that reputation is not a quality possessed by an individual, rather it is an accumulation of opinions that others have formed. Additionally, Gowler and Legge (1989) suggested that the notion of reputation presents a paradox in that "it is both a possession and not a possession" (p. 446). In a similar argument, Hepworth (1975) suggested that reputations consist of attributions made by others, and as such, their value is worthless unless others are prepared to subscribe to it. Ferris et al. (1994) presented managerial reputation as more of a sociopolitical construct than a rational one, arguing that managers achieve reputational effectiveness to the extent their behaviors are consistent with others' expectations. Hogan and Shelton (1998) suggested that at least one interpretation of personality is from an external perspective and that this "is equivalent to a person's reputation, it is defined in terms of traits, and used to predict a person's performance" (p. 132). In this sense, reputation may take on such descriptors as dominant, passive, considerate, and ruthless (Hogan, 1991).

*An Integrative Perspective.*    Shenkar and Yuchtman-Yaar (1997) presented an integrative perspective of reputation. They argued that what economists refer to as reputation, marketing scholars refer to as image, sociologists point to as prestige, and accounting and law researchers call goodwill, are all essentially referring to the same thing—an entity's general standing among counterparts. They suggested that "standing can be regarded as a social mechanism designed to reduce uncertainty faced by multiple constituencies who lack the ability to discern quality, performance, value, or other relevant attributes due to the nature of the observable phenomenon, lack of knowledge, or lack of access to information" (p. 1373).

This integrative attempt by Shenkar and Yuchtman-Yaar (1997) is at least a first step toward building a collective understanding of the reputation construct, which has been needed in the field. By examining the way reputation has been conceptualized and investigated in different fields, we can begin to extract some common themes and generally accepted findings that can provide the building blocks for a more informed understanding of personal reputation in the organizational sciences.

## CURRENT STATUS OF KNOWLEDGE ON REPUTATION

The foregoing review of the reputation literature has provided a much more extensive base of work from which to develop a more informed understanding of the personal reputation construct. In this section of the chapter, we focus on the discussion of themes that have emerged in prior research on which we see some general consensus, and therefore, on which we can begin to identify new directions for future work.

### Manipulation and Transmission of Reputation

Over 40 years ago, Goffman spoke of controlling others through a projected image. He related this image to that of a "theatrical performance." This dramaturgical perspective was argued to be the way in which the individuals in organizations present themselves to guide and control the perceptions that others form of them. It is clear from previous research that an individual's reputation has value and can be manipulated (e.g., Greenberg, 1990; Schlenker, 1980; Tedeschi & Norman, 1985). However, besides efforts to manage impressions about reputation, we also see that prior research has provided a basis for better understanding how reputations are transmitted.

We found that signaling theory expands on the notion of a theatrical performance and provides a useful perspective from which to consider reputations. Originally proposed by Spence (1973, 1974), signaling theory suggests that individuals coexist in markets of exchange. Within these markets, individuals signal others in the market in an attempt to convey information or alter their beliefs. Spence distinguished between potential and actual signals, arguing that potential signals represent observable, alterable characteristics, whereas actual signals are potential signals that influence others. From this perspective, reputation can be viewed as an actual signal in that it represents observable and alterable characteristics that influence others.

Focusing on the "alterable" aspect of a signal, Ferris and Judge (1991) suggested that reputation can be an intentional effort at signaling. They argued that individuals send various signals to others, and that these signals are more political than scientific, with intentions to influence perceptions and meaning. More recently, Ferris, Hochwarter, Buckley, Harrell-Cook, and Frink (1999) implied that reputations actually may be shaped or influenced by the individual to which the reputation is referent. They cited the influential role of reputation and its signaling capacity in an organizational setting by introducing Rosenbaum's (1989) tournament theory. According to tournament theory, those who experience advancement early in their careers are likely to experience greater success over the course of their careers due to the perceptions that others form of them. This clearly supports the idea of reputation as a signal to decision makers, whereby fast-track employees are identified and subsequently promoted based on their reputations of early success. In such cases, it is difficult, if not virtually impossible, to distinguish the use of the terms reputation and potential, which become conventional criteria for such decisions.

## Evolution of Personal Reputation

There appears to be rather widespread agreement that reputation is a temporal-dependent phenomenon that materializes over some period of time (e.g., Gotsi & Wilson, 2001; Hall, 1993; Herbig et al., 1994; Kennedy, 1977). Reputation, though arduously constructed and painstakingly maintained, is a fragile commodity. Reputations can take a lifetime to construct and yet a moment to destroy—consider the rapid fall from the national political spotlight suffered by Newt Gingrich, Bob Packwood, and Gary Condit. As previously mentioned, third parties and indirect ties are the legitimizing force behind reputations. Gulati (1995) suggested that networks or "reputational circuits" serve as enforcers in that bad behavior with any one member of the network will be reported to the other members, thus creating a deterrent against behavior inconsistent with expectations. Herbig et al. (1994) argued that credibility transactions that involve mixed or false signals are devastating to reputation and credibility. They showed that damage to reputation comes in the form of a loss of confidence in subsequent marketing signals, and this loss lingers for a substantial period of time. Additionally, their results showed that reputation is a fragile and valuable commodity, and that milking a reputation for short-term goals can be dangerous.

Previous research clearly suggests that reputations evolve through two distinct processes over time: development and maintenance (Bozeman & Kacmar, 1997; Bromley, 1993; Petrick et al., 1999; Weiss et al., 1999). The time frames surrounding each process are likely to differ widely as a function of both personal and contextual factors, so it is impossible to provide precise prescriptions regarding when an individual moves from one process to another. Furthermore, it is certainly possible, and even likely, that there is overlap of processes so that, for example, one is demonstrating behaviors indicative of the maintenance process while still involved in the development process.

As mentioned earlier, the study of legitimacy offers many interesting parallels to the study of reputation. One such parallel is the temporal aspect of legitimacy. Suchman (1995) depicted legitimacy as either episodic or continual in nature. Similarly, reputation can be presented as possessing both episodic and continuous aspects. This is important when considering the evolution of a reputation because it can at once be episodic as well as continual. In other words, the continual processes of developing and maintaining a reputation are punctuated by episodic events.

Reputations are formed within a specific context. As previously mentioned, context includes an actor's role set(s), social norms, and environment. Individual actions in the development of a reputation can range from passive conformity to others' expectations to active manipulation of the context. Actual behavior feeds back into perceptions of past behavior, and hence the reputation process is both cyclic and continuous in nature.

Maintaining a reputation requires that others' perceptions of actual behavior must remain consistent with expected behavior. Any inconsistency, positive or negative, will result in adjustments to the reputation, which in turn redefine the context. Unlike developing a reputation, however, the task of maintaining a reputation may be nearly routinized behavior.

To maintain a reputation, an individual must simply be aware of the reputation and act in accordance with the behaviors prescribed by it. Fombrun (1996) called this "practicing mundane management," and characterized it as those decisions that consistently produce expected behaviors. This does not imply that all maintenance behaviors are merely behaviors that conform to the reputation. Indeed, contexts are constantly changing, thus requiring a continuous calibration of the reputation. Similar to Suchman's (1995) strategies for maintaining legitimacy, it appears that maintaining a reputation involves anticipating and perceiving future changes in context, as well as protecting and defending the existing reputation.

Another form of maintaining a reputation is in its defense, which can involve accounts, apologies, excuses, justifications, and other forms of defensive impression management behaviors (Greenberg, 1990). In defending a reputation, the primary concern is the protection of the perceived reputation. Defense of a reputation may be called for following an unfortunate event or in response to a deliberate attempt to damage the reputation. Certainly, damaging a competitor's reputation by way of criticism, misinformation, distortion, or rumor can be an effective way to advance in an organization (Bromley, 1993). Furthermore, Fine (1996) demonstrated how historical accounts of prominent people (e.g., U.S. presidents) frequently involve the social construction of reputations, whereby interested parties provide interpretations of the "facts" of history in self-serving ways (i.e., casting a positive or a negative reputation) that use "reputational politics" to maximize the interests of particular constituencies.

We have to look no further than our own legal system to see defense of reputations in action. As Hepworth (1975) noted, because of the important role it played in everyday society as an "increasingly significant mainstay of conventional order," reputation began to attract "the protection of the courts" (p. 15). Indeed, reputational blackmail became a significant problem at that time, taking on the perspective of "moral murder" (Hepworth, 1975, p. 15). Logan (2001) reported that, from 1980 to 2000, courts awarded over $620 million to plaintiffs suing the media for damage to personal reputations. However, he pointed out that this figure is misleading and does not account for all those individuals unwilling to endure proceedings that put the plaintiff's reputation under close scrutiny. This implies that although some people will defend their reputations vigorously, others concede that the defense is more costly than developing a new reputation. Fombrun (1996) suggested that the best defense against potential reputational damage is through an active offense. He argued that aggressive maintenance behaviors, such as anticipating changes in future contexts, may prevent a reputational crisis from occurring.

## Indicators or Outcomes of Personal Reputation

The indicators of an effective personal reputation include the work-related outcomes we typically use as measures of success in organizations. Thus, performance evaluations, promotions, and salary are ways we can assess the nature and level of reputation an individual has attained. However, in addition to these, we also gauge reputational effectiveness through one's level of power attained (as we saw in the discussion of this topic in an earlier section of this chapter), and indications of external recognition (e.g., awards, honors, etc.).

As previously mentioned, Tsui (1984) suggested that the most reputationally effective manager is the one who is able to meet the expectations of all or most of the constituencies in the role set. This manager will most likely be rewarded more and advance faster in the organization than another manager who is unable to meet such expectations. This advancement record will, in turn, serve to enhance the overall reputation of effectiveness. Consistent with this reasoning, Dixit and Nalebuff (1991) stated that a "reputation becomes self-perpetuating as it becomes more valuable" (p. 148).

The very nature of the reputational effectiveness context is complex, dynamic, and deserving of careful examination. So, in this section, we discuss key issues that relate to reputation and indicators of effectiveness in an effort to more clearly portray these relationships.

*Performance Evaluation.*    One indicator of a favorable reputation is high performance, and because we have objective measurement of performance in few jobs, we typically operationalize job performance as the subjective ratings provided by immediate supervisors. As we have seen in recent years, supervisory ratings of employee performance can be subject to influence, bias, and distortion, and they can even depart from a strict focus on actual job performance behaviors, and instead be driven by other issues. Influence tactics have been found to affect performance ratings, even when there are no actual differences in job performance (e.g., Ferris & Judge, 1991; Higgins, Judge, & Ferris, 2002). Pfeffer (1981) suggested that we sometimes even evaluate individuals on the basis of beliefs, values, or effort.

Because goals can be considered a proxy for effort, and a surrogate measure of performance, we might envision workers being evaluated on the basis of self-set goals. Indeed, Dossett and Greenberg (1981) found that regardless of subsequent performance, supervisors gave the highest performance ratings to those individuals who set the highest goals. Because the goals themselves become disproportionately salient in the evaluation context, they dominate the focus of attention and the impression formation process, and they drive the determination of the performance rating, relegating subsequent performance to a secondary consideration at best. If subsequent performance is high, consistent with the self-set goal, it is simply used to support or validate the initial impression. If subsequent performance is lower than the self-set goal, and thus inconsistent with the initial impression, the lower performance level is likely attributed to nonpersonal causes and explained away.

As we have seen, personal reputations need to be built or developed, and they later need to be protected or defended. Because job performance plays a key role in affecting reputation, people might try to exercise influence over the way their own performance evaluation operates. March (1984) and Ferris et al. (1994) suggested that individuals may try to manage their reputations by getting others to evaluate them on the basis of process measures, such as effort, rather than outcomes, such as actual objective results. In some cases, intentional vagueness or even strategic ambiguity might be employed advantageously in such efforts to manipulate the performance criterion focus of evaluation (e.g., Eisenberg, 1984; Williams & Goss, 1975), and enhance and/or preserve reputation as a result.

*Promotions and Mobility.*    Another indicator of an effective reputation is the number of promotions one has received. Actually, rather than the mere examination of the number of promotions, we typically examine the number of promotions one has received within a specified period of time, and thus regard velocity of mobility as an indicator of reputation. Similar in nature to the performance evaluation process, promotion decisions can be influenced quite strongly by subjective assessments of qualities and characteristics that depart considerably from objective work behavior. Perhaps this is why promotions are widely considered to be among the most political decisions made in organizations (e.g., Ferris & Judge, 1991). Early impressions by decision makers also are very important in promotion decisions, and this is characterized in an interesting way through discussions of tournament mobility, and how people get positioned and can influence their ability to be successful in such competitions (e.g., Cooper, Graham, & Dyke, 1993; Rosenbaum, 1989).

An indicator of reputation similar in nature to promotions is mobility. Promotions necessarily address movement or mobility, but promotions may be confined to movement within a single organization over time. Use of the broader term *mobility* suggests the examination of movement through different positions, perhaps in a number of different organizations over a reasonably extended period of time (e.g., over a person's entire career). Here, the number of moves over a specified time period is not the focal issue. Instead, the nature of the positions obtained, the quality of the organizations at which one accepts positions, and so forth become the relevant indicators of reputation, and this is all examined relative to one's cohort as a gauge on how one is tracking. If one is receiving offers "ahead of schedule" (i.e., relative to what we would expect for people in the person's relevant cohort), and these are positions at relatively reputable or high status organizations, these can be indicators of an effective reputation.

*Compensation.* There is perhaps no more visible or salient indicator of individuals' reputations than the salary they are paid. There are several perspectives on the meaning of compensation to individuals, which include the actual monetary value and buying power of high salaries, as well as the symbolic and status-enhancing signal sent out about a person who is paid a high salary. Bartol and Martin (1990) showed that managers awarded higher pay raises to subordinates when the managers were dependent on the subordinates' expertise, implying a reputation of expertness is directly related to financial reward.

It is perhaps relevant to raise the question "Just what is it that we pay for when we assign salaries?" Because compensation level in organizations tends to be driven by the assessed worth of jobs (i.e., applying a point–factor method or some other method of job evaluation), one answer would justify salary as that it is paying for someone to effectively execute the duties of a job judged to be of a specific value. However, there is also considerable discretion remaining to compensate someone additionally for other things he or she brings to the job, like experience or education level, but it is also apparent that particularly in some jobs, we pay for reputation (Zajac & Westphal, 1995). In such cases, salaries can be quite high because reputational effectiveness increases one's negotiating power. We can readily observe the influence of reputation on salaries for movie stars, professional athletes, physicians, and college professors, to name a few.

This section has presented outcomes or indicators of reputation, but we need to explain a bit about how reputation relates to these outcomes. Performance evaluations, promotions, salary, and so forth are not simply or necessarily unidirectional outcomes of reputational effectiveness. Instead, we perceive a more complex, and in some cases, a reciprocal quality to the reputation–outcomes relationship. To build an effective reputation, one needs to establish a record of high performance. However, achieving an effective reputation also will contribute to high performance evaluations. Furthermore, personal reputation is an aggregate and temporally dependent construct, in that it takes time to build a reputation by demonstrating value-added behavior in a consistent and reasonably predictable manner (Ensminger, 2001). Additionally, reputation is likely generated more quickly and maintained more effectively by the extent to which the person achieves several different indicators or outcomes as discussed.

Of course, the various indicators of reputation discussed are not totally independent of one another, as some of the same individuals will be responsible for making decisions about performance ratings, promotability, and salary for a particular individual, so there are inevitably going to be cross-decision biases. However, it does seem to be the case that the greater the attainment of different reputation indicators or outcomes by an individual, the more confidence perceivers will have in their assessments of that person's reputation, and the less detractors will be able to persuade others of a negative reputation.

## Capital as Metaphor: Assessing the Value of Personal Reputation

Common across all research streams and levels of analysis is the notion that reputation has value. Yet, the exact nature or source of that value is rarely adequately addressed. In one of the few attempts to define reputational capital, Fombrun (1996) suggested that it is "the amount by which the company's market value exceeds the liquidation value of its assets" (p. 92). This is a useful definition from an organizational perspective, but it is also helpful when considering personal reputation. First, his definition suggests that reputation is something greater than the sum of its disaggregated parts, and second, it implies a market of exchange.

We assert that personal reputation has a value, and that the source of this value is the degree to which a reputation is useful in accurately predicting future behavior. By extension, we suggest that the inherent value of a reputation is in its ability to increase benefits relative to transaction costs. Tyler and Kramer (1996) suggested that the value of reputational effects stems from the degree of trust elicited in social interactions. From this social network perspective, indirect or third-party ties are a source of information that serve to enhance the trust one places in another. This triangulation effect on an individual's reputation, in turn, increases the reputation value among multiple constituents as well as increasing the reputational costs of noncooperative behavior (Gulati & Westphal, 1999).

Organizations, through their human resource systems, provide cues for the cultivation and maintenance of a positive reputation. The promotion system, when coupled with the performance evaluation system, provides a significant amount of information regarding the degree to which an organization values an individual. These systems provide signals to new or disenfranchised employees on how to develop or adjust behavior if they desire success in the organization. As noted by Kydd et al. (1990), people's assessment of their own reputations in an organization is the result of their interpretation of the organization's current opinion of their job performance.

Expanding on this notion, we suggest that an individual's reputation within the organization is reflective of the degree of trust the organization bestows on the individual regarding the expectations of future performance. Tyler and Kramer (1996) suggested that social institutions sanction those who violate trust, and that by making untrustworthy behavior costly, these social institutions assert both formal and informal control. In a similar argument, Ensminger (2001) argued that the longer a reputation has been in the making, the greater the costs are for disconfirming behavior. Consequently, as the value of a reputation increases, so do the opportunity costs for shirking, therefore making reputation self-reinforcing.

In 1969, Likert and Bowers called for human resource accounting methods that reflect a line of reasoning assuming that the human component of an organization can be capitalized, and that this capitalization can then be used to evaluate the financial implications of human resources in an organization (Geffin, 1980; Swann, 1978). This approach implies that the value of an individual's contribution to the organization is not an isolated incident of effective performance, or one that could be attributed to factors other than the individual himself or herself. Similarly, we suggest that an effective personal reputation relies on a number of things, not the least of which is an internal attribution by the perceiver that the accomplishments, performance, or other indicators of success are due to the qualities of the person, and not attributed externally to luck, the situation, or others (Hepworth, 1975; Raub & Weesie, 1990).

Feldman and Weitz (1992) noted that what many managers actually do in their jobs is for the most part unobservable. In these ill-defined situations, the image of success they project then becomes a proxy for actual success. The less objective the measures are in individual job performance, the greater the ambiguity in performance evaluations and promotions, and the greater the emphasis on personal reputations when making key personnel decisions. As Bok (1993) pointed out, "When things turn out badly, one never need apologize for having selected a leading figure in the field; it is the person who tries to save money by choosing a practitioner of uncertain quality who will have the explaining to do. There is likewise no need to spend precious time investigating the qualifications of leading figures in the field; their reputations speak for themselves" (p. 225). Reputations need only be classified as positive or negative based on the perceived utility of the reputation to the decision maker using it. Beyond that distinction, different types of reputation very well may be too numerous to categorize.

Implicit in our discussion of reputational capital is the idea that the value of an individual is not really associated with current ability or talent, rather it is based on future expectations of performance. Certainly, we need to look no further than the entertainment industry to make this point. A movie star or a sports star is not contracted based on what they have already accomplished or their current talent per se; rather they are contracted based on their expected performance and the degree to which this expected performance will generate revenue for the contracting organization. Similarly, Zajac and Westphal (1995) suggested that CEO compensation is often justified to stockholders based on future expectations of firm performance. However, the general belief in behavioral consistency would suggest that the best predictor of future behavior is past and present behavior in similar situations, and thus as the economic perspective has informed us, reputation reduces uncertainty for us because it provides predictability of future behavior based on one's past record.

## DIRECTIONS FOR FUTURE RESEARCH

The discussion in the previous section suggests that there are indeed some common themes and generally agreed on issues in the area of personal reputation in organizations. Additionally, there are many important issues that need to be investigated in future work. We discuss a number of these issues in this section.

### Theoretical Development and Measurement Challenges

One obvious need in this area is for the development of a theory of personal reputation that more precisely articulates antecedents, consequences, moderators, and mediators, and begins to address some critical issues and questions concerning this complex construct and how it is intertwined with other constructs and processes. Whereas we have accumulated considerable collective information about the reputation construct by examining research across different disciplines and fields of study, we still have much to learn about how personal reputations are constructed, the associated costs, their exchange value, and their potential constraining effects on human behavior. As we learn about how reputations are constructed, we may gain new insights into personal motivation and behavior in the workplace.

Of course, implicit in such discussions of future research is that there will be measurement instruments available to measure the relevant constructs. Reputation is a much less developed area than other organizational science constructs, and so as we see new theoretical development in this area, we also need to develop psychometrically sound instruments to measure personal reputation at work.

## Cross-Sectional and Longitudinal Research

Although initial research efforts might focus on investigation of aspects of personal reputation in organizations cross-sectionally, other future research in reputation will undoubtedly benefit from longitudinal studies as well. We need to explore the effects of different reputations as they affect job and career outcomes in short-, medium-, and long-range time frames. Also, in examination of longer term outcomes, we need to examine how people develop and maintain reputations through conscious and calculated strategies that are designed or become emergent over a long period of time, and how the choice of reputational tactics and strategies might change at different points in the evolution of one's reputation. Such longitudinal research on reputation might be productively approached through an examination of careers and how they progress over time. Gowler and Legge (1989) characterized careers and reputations as closely linked and naturally dependent constructs. Their social construction and meaning management notions might provide useful bases on which to ground such investigations.

## Personal Reputation and Social Influence

At least anecdotally, reputation and social influence (including power) appear to be virtually inextricably intertwined, as reputations typically are influential and can be used in influential ways (e.g., Caldeira, 1983; Goldthorpe & Hope, 1972; Pfeffer, 1992). However, future research needs to investigate this more systematically, perhaps taking into account some of the following points.

In communication research, the effectiveness of influence attempts is a function of the individual possessing appropriate resources, and the prestige or reputation of the influencer is one of the most important resources (Klapper, 1960). Thus, the integration of influence tactics and reputation is such that one's reputation can serve as a contextual backdrop for influence in a number of ways. This backdrop may serve as both an enabler and constrainer of the effectiveness of influence attempts. Further, both the reputation of the individual making the influence attempt and also that of the target(s) may affect the influence outcome.

Tedeschi and Melburg (1984) offered one of the most important conceptual works integrating both influence and reputational constructs. They suggested that individuals endeavor to build or defend their reputations in part by using various forms of impression management tactics, stating that:

> Each person earns a reputation for having certain traits, abilities, values, and experiences. Most people learn to care about the kind of reputation they develop, and they act in a manner calculated to protect and build particular reputational characteristics. Among the most important of these characteristics ... are attractiveness, prestige, esteem, status, and credibility (p. 43)

Just as people make financial investments to yield long-term monetary returns, "so do they invest time and effort in developing a reputation for possessing characteristics that will yield long-term effectiveness in influencing other people" (p. 42). They further suggested that the building of a reputation primarily involves strategic and assertive tactics, whereas one uses tactical and defensive tactics to defend one's reputation.

Indeed, some research to date has examined the nature of influence attempts as they play out and are interpreted against a reputational context. As Schlenker (1980) pointed out, "successful people can afford to be modest and thus acquire images of success and humility" (p. 193). Presumably, such behavior demonstrated against a positive and successful reputational context would be interpreted much more favorably than highly self-promoting behavior, which might raise questions in perceiver interpretation as a function of the reputational backdrop. However, this might not necessarily be the case, as seen in another study.

Rosen et al. (1990) investigated applicants' self-presentational style and work reputation on interviewer evaluations of the job candidates' job suitability. They reported that the boastful (i.e., self-presentational style)–superior (i.e., work reputation) job applicant was recommended highest over all others. Closer examination revealed that the modest–superior applicant was more highly recommended than the boastful–inferior and the modest–inferior combined. These results further indicate that we need to more carefully consider the relationship of influence attempts as they are demonstrated against a particular reputational context.

Dixit and Nalebuff (1991) argued that reputation affects the way we interpret certain behaviors. Furthermore, Klapper (1960) noted that prestige or reputation is a resource of influence, and as such, must be carefully considered when other forms of influence are added to one's situational behavioral repertoire. Reputation can serve to indirectly affect outcomes by causing the influencer to consider their own reputation as well as the reputation of the parties of influence prior to the choosing of influence behaviors. This is consistent with Tedeschi and Melburg's (1984) assertion that within the tactical/defensive quadrant, maintenance of one's reputation may influence one's choice of influence behaviors. From this perspective, we suggest that the influence tactics chosen must be consistent with the reputation or the reputation will be redefined, however incrementally.

Finally, the impression management implications of reputation and influence and power have been suggested by others as well. Pfeffer (1992) argued that people engage in efforts to build reputations that reflect power, which then result in those individuals wielding even more power (or at least being perceived as such). Reflecting on such processes, Matthews (1988), in characterizing Washington-type politics, contended that people become powerful by doing things that make them appear powerful, which has subsequent effects on their power broker reputations.

Therefore, a potentially fruitful area for future research is in studying the relationship between influence attempts and reputation. Further, reputation might play an important facilitating (i.e., moderating) function that could help to better explain some of the inconsistent findings between influence tactics and outcomes to date (Higgins et al., 2002). It would seem also quite useful to examine reputation within the context of leadership, which would fit in easily with the general agreement in the field that leadership involves influence, and that reputation can be seen in light of influence mechanisms. Particularly interesting might be the extent to which leaders may rely on the media to enhance their reputation through active efforts to play to such audiences (e.g., Deephouse, 2000; Fine, 1996).

## CONCLUSION

Personal reputation in organizations reflects a critically important but not well understood construct, which has the potential to leverage careers, ideas, and empires. An individual's reputation affects not only the choice of work behaviors, but the effectiveness of the enacted tactics and strategies. Upon enactment, these behaviors simultaneously craft and reinforce the very reputation from which the action and interpretation were derived. The ebb and flow of this reputational balance represents both the temporal and delicate nature of the context of social influence behavior in organizations. It is within this context that our personal reputation resides, and it is the inability to detach individual behavior from this reputational context that makes the further evaluation of reputation necessary to extend our understanding of behavior within organizations.

## REFERENCES

Aaker, D. A. (1991). *Brand equity: Capitalizing on the value of a brand name.* New York: The Free Press.

Alt, J. E., Calvert, R., & Humes, B. D. (1988). Reputation and hegemonic stability: A game theoretic analysis. *American Political Science Review, 82,* 445–466.

Ashforth, B. E., & Mael, F. (1989). Social identity theory and the organization. *Academy of Management Review, 14,* 20–39.

Bailey, F. G. (1971). Gifts and poison. In F. G. Bailey (Ed.), *Gifts and poison: The politics of reputation* (pp. 1–25). Oxford, England: Basil Blackwell.

Barney, J. (1991). Firm resources and sustained competitive advantage. *Journal of Management, 17,* 99–120.

Baron, R. A., & Markman, G. D. (2000). Beyond social capital: How social skills can enhance entrepreneurs' success. *Academy of Management Executive, 14,* 106–116.

Bartol, K. M., & Martin, D. C. (1990). When politics pays: Factors influencing managerial compensation decisions. *Personnel Psychology, 43,* 599–614.

Baumeister, R. F. (1982). Self-esteem, self-presentation, and future interaction: A dilemma of reputation. *Journal of Personality, 50,* 29–45.

Baumeister, R. F., & Jones, E. E. (1978). When self-presentation is constrained by the target's prior knowledge: Consistency and compensation. *Journal of Personality and Social Psychology, 36,* 608–618.

Becker, H. S. (1982). *Art worlds.* Berkeley: University of California Press.

Bellah, R. N. (1986). The meaning of reputation in American society. *California Law Review, 74,* 743–751.

Bennett, R., & Gabriel, H. (2001). Reputation, trust, and supplier commitment: The case of shipping company/seaport relations. *Journal of Business and Industrial Marketing, 16,* 424–438.

Berkson, H. M., Harris, M. M., & Ferris, G. R. (1999). Enhancing organizational reputation to attract applicants. In R. W. Eder & M. M. Harris (Eds.), *The employment interview handbook* (pp. 83–98). Thousand Oaks, CA: Sage.

Bickerton, D. (2000). Corporate reputation versus corporate branding: The realist debate. *Corporate Communications, 5,* 42–48.

Biel, A. L. (1992). How brand image drives brand equity. *Journal of Advertising Research, 6,* RC6–RC12.

Bok, D. C. (1993). *The cost of talent: How executives and professionals are paid and how it affects America.* New York: The Free Press.

Bozeman, D. P., & Kacmar, K. M. (1997). A cybernetic model of impression management processes in organizations. *Organizational Behavior and Human Decision Processes, 69,* 9–30.

Brass, D. J. (1984). Being in the right place: A structural analysis of individual influence in an organization. *Administrative Science Quarterly, 29,* 518–539.

Brass, D. J., & Burkhardt, M. E. (1993). Potential power and power use: An investigation of structure and behavior. *Academy of Management Journal, 36,* 441–470.

Breaugh, J. A. (1992). *Recruitment: Science and practice.* Boston: PWS-Kent.

Bromley, D. B. (1993). *Reputation, image and impression management.* New York: Wiley.

Cable, D. M., & Judge, T. A. (1996). Person organization fit, job choice decisions, and organizational entry. *Organizational Behavior and Human Decision Processes, 67,* 294–311.

Cable, D. M., & Graham, M. E. (2000). The determinants of job seekers' reputation perceptions. *Journal of Organizational Behavior, 21,* 929–947.

Cable, D. M., & Turban, D. B. (2001). Establishing the dimensions, sources, and value of job seekers' employer knowledge during recruitment. In G. R. Ferris (Ed.), *Research in personnel and human resources management* (Vol. 20, pp. 115–163). Oxford, England: JAI/Elsevier Science.

Cabral, L. M. B. (2000). Stretching firm and brand reputation. *RAND Journal of Economics, 31,* 658–673.

Caldeira, G. A. (1983). On the reputation of state supreme courts. *Political Behavior, 5,* 83–108.

Caudron, S. (1997, February). Forget image: It's your reputation that matters. *Industry Week,* 13–16.

Ching, C., Holsapple, C. W., & Whinston, A. B. (1992). Reputation, learning and coordination in distributed decision-making contexts. *Organization Science, 3,* 275–297.

Chong, D. (1992). Reputation and cooperative behavior. *Social Science Information, 31,* 683–709.

Cobb-Walgren, C. J., Ruble, C. A., & Donthu, N. (1995). Brand equity, brand preference, and purchase intent. *Journal of Advertising, 24,* 25–40.

Cooke, S., & Ryan, P. (2000). Brand alliances: From reputation endorsement to collaboration on core competencies. *Irish Marketing Review, 13,* 36–41.

Cooper, W. H., Graham, W. J., & Dyke, L. S. (1993). Tournament players. In G. R. Ferris (Ed.), *Research in personnel and human resources management* (Vol. 11, pp. 83–132). Greenwich, CT: JAI.

Deephouse, D. L. (2000). Media reputation as a strategic resource: An integration of mass communication and resource-based theories. *Journal of Management, 26,* 1091–1112.

Dixit, A. K., & Nalebuff, B. (1991). *Thinking strategically: The competitive edge in business, politics, and everyday life.* New York: Norton.

Doby, V. J., & Caplan, R. D. (1995). Organizational stress as threat to reputation: Effects on anxiety at work and at home. *Academy of Management Journal, 38,* 1105–1123.

Dollinger, M., Golden, P., & Saxton, T. (1997). The effect of reputation on the decision to joint venture. *Strategic Management Journal, 18,* 127–140.

Dossett, D. L., & Greenberg, C. I. (1981). Goal setting and performance evaluation: An attributional analysis. *Academy of Management Journal, 24,* 767–779.

Dutton, J., & Dukerich, J. (1991). Keeping an eye on the mirror: The role of image and identity in organizational adaptation. *Academy of Management Journal, 34,* 517–554.

Eisenberg, E. M. (1984). Ambiguity as strategy in organizational communication. *Communications Monographs, 51,* 227–242.

Elsbach, K. D. (1994). Managing organizational legitimacy in the California cattle industry: The construction and effectiveness of verbal accounts. *Administrative Science Quarterly, 39,* 57–88.

Elsbach, K. D., & Sutton, R. I. (1992). Acquiring organizational legitimacy through illegitimate actions: A marriage of institutional and impression management theories. *Academy of Management Journal, 35,* 699–738.

Ensminger, J. (2001). Reputations, trust, and the principal agent problem. In K. S. Cook (Ed.), *Trust in society* (pp. 185–201). New York: Sage.

Feldman, D. C., & Weitz, B. A. (1992). From invisible hand to gladhand: Understanding a careerist orientation to work. *Human Resource Management, 30,* 237–257.

Feldwick, P. (1996). What is brand equity anyway, and how do you measure it? *Journal of the Marketing Research Society, 38,* 85–104.

Ferrier, W. J. (1997). Tough talk and market leaders: The role of overt signaling and reputation building in sustaining industry dominance. *Corporate Reputation Review, 1,* 98–102.

Ferris, G. R., Arthur, M. M., Berkson, H. M., Kaplan, D. M., Harrell-Cook, G., & Frink, D. D. (1998). Toward a social context theory of the human resource management-organization effectiveness relationship. *Human Resource Management Review, 8,* 235–264.

Ferris, G. R., Fedor, D. B., & King, T. R. (1994). A political conceptualization of managerial behavior. *Human Resource Management Review, 4,* 1–34.

Ferris, G. R., Hochwarter, W. A., Buckley, M. R., Harrell-Cook, G., & Frink, D. D. (1999). Human resources management: Some new directions. *Journal of Management, 25,* 385–415.

Ferris, G. R., & Judge, T. A. (1991). Personnel/human resources management: A political influence perspective. *Journal of Management, 17,* 447–488.

Fine, G. A. (1996). Reputational entrepreneurs and the memory of incompetence: Melting supporters, partisan warriors, and images of President Harding. *American Journal of Sociology, 101,* 1159–1193.

Fiol, M. C., O'Connor, E. J., & Aguinis, H. (2001). All for one and one for all? The development and transfer of power across organizational levels. *Academy of Management Review, 26,* 224–242.

Fombrun, C. J. (1996). *Reputation: Realizing value from the corporate image.* Boston: Harvard Business School Press.

Fombrun, C. J., & Shanley, M. (1990). What's in a name? Reputation building and corporate strategy. *Academy of Management Journal, 33,* 233–258.

French, J. R. P., Jr., & Raven, B. (1959). The bases of social power. In D. Cartwright (Ed.), *Studies in social power* (pp. 150–168). Ann Arbor: Institute for Social Research, University of Michigan.

Galang, M. C., Elsik, W., & Russ, G. S. (1999). Legitimacy in human resources management. In G. R. Ferris (Ed.), *Research in personnel and human resources management* (Vol. 17, pp. 41–79). Stamford, CT: JAI.

Galang, M. C., & Ferris, G. R. (1997). Human resource department power and influence through symbolic action. *Human Relations, 50,* 1403–1426.

Gamson,W. (1966). Reputation and resources in community politics. *American Journal of Sociology, 72,* 121–131.

Gamson, W., Croteau, D., Hoynes, W., & Sasson, T. (1992). Media images and the social construction of reality. *Annual Review of Sociology, 18,* 373–393.

Gatewood, R. D., Gowan, M. A., & Lautenshlager, G. J. (1993). Corporate image, recruitment image, and initial job choice decisions. *Academy of Management Journal, 36,* 414–427.

Geffin, A. B. (1980). Human resource accounting and modern day theorists. *Psychologia Africana, 19,* 41–52.

Gioia, D. A., Schultz, M., & Corley, K. G. (2000). Organizational identity, image, and adaptive instability. *Academy of Management Review, 25,* 63–81.

Gioia, D. A., & Sims, H. P. (1983). Perceptions of managerial power as a consequence of managerial behavior and reputation. *Journal of Management, 9,* 7–26.

Gladstone, R. (1963). The moral reputation correlates of competence reputation. *Journal of Social Psychology, 59,* 283–288.

Goffman, E. (1959). *The presentation of self in everyday life.* Garden City, NY: Doubleday.

Goldthorpe, J. H., & Hope, K. (1972). Occupational grading and occupational prestige. In K. Hope (Ed.), *The analysis of social mobility* (pp. 19–79). Oxford, England: Clarendon.

Gotsi, M., & Wilson, A. M. (2001). Corporate reputation: Seeking a definition. *Corporate Communications: An International Journal, 6,* 24–30.

Gowler, D., & Legge, K. (1989). Rhetoric in bureaucratic careers: Managing the meaning of management success. In M. B. Arthur, D. T. Hall, & B. S. Lawrence (Eds.), *Handbook of career theory* (pp. 437–453). New York: Cambridge University Press.

Granovetter, M. (1985). Economic action and social structure: The problem of embeddedness. *American Journal of Sociology, 91,* 481–510.

Greenberg, J. (1990). Looking fair vs. being fair: Managing impressions of organizational justice. In B. M. Staw & L. L. Cummings (Eds.), *Research in organizational behavior* (Vol. 12, pp. 111–157). Greenwich, CT: JAI.

Guest, D. E. (1989). Human resource management: Its implications for industrial relations and trade unions. In J. Storey (Ed.), *New perspectives on human resource management* (pp. 41–55). London: Routledge & Kegan Paul.

Gulati, R. (1995). Social structure and alliance formation patterns: A longitudinal analysis. *Administrative Science Quarterly, 40,* 619–652.

Gulati, R., & Westphal, J. D. (1999). Cooperative or controlling? The effects of CEO–board relations and the content of interlocks on the formation of joint ventures. *Administrative Science Quarterly, 44,* 473–506.

Gwinner, K. P., & Eaton, J. (1999). Building brand image through event sponsorship: The role of image transfer. *Journal of Advertising, 28,* 47–57.

Hall, R. (1992). The strategic analysis of intangible resources. *Strategic Management Journal, 13,* 135–144.

Hall, R. (1993). A framework linking intangible resources and capabilities to sustainable competitive advantage. *Strategic Management Journal, 14,* 607–618.

Hannon, J. M., & Milkovich, G. T. (1996). The effect of human resource reputation signals on share prices: An event study. *Human Resource Management, 35,* 405–424.

Hepworth, M. (1975). *Blackmail: Publicity and secrecy in everyday life.* London: Routledge & Kegan Paul.

Herbig, P., & Milewicz, J. (1997). The relationship of reputation and credibility to brand success. *Pricing Strategy and Practice, 5,* 25–29.

Herbig, P., Milewicz, J., & Golden, J. (1994). A model of reputation building and destruction. *Journal of Business Research, 31,* 23–31.

Higgins, C. A., Judge, T. A., & Ferris, G. R. (2002). *Influence tactics and work outcomes: A meta-analysis.* Paper presented at the 17th annual conference of the Society for Industrial and Organizational Psychology, Toronto.

Hogan, R. T. (1991). Personality and personality measurement. In M. D. Dunnette & L. M. Hough (Eds.), *Handbook of industrial and organizational psychology* (2nd ed., Vol. 2, pp. 873–919). Palo Alto, CA: Consulting Psychologists Press.

Hogan, R. T., & Shelton, D. (1998). A socioanalytic perspective on job performance. *Human Performance, 11,* 129–144.

Hollander, E. (1958). Conformity, status, and idiosyncrasy credit. *Psychological Review, 65,* 117–127.

Jones, O. (1996). Human resources, scientists, and internal reputation: The role of climate and job satisfaction. *Human Relations, 49,* 269–294.

Jones, S. C., & Shrauger, J. S. (1970). Reputation and self-evaluation as determinants of attractiveness. *Sociometry, 33,* 276–286.

Kanter, R. M., & Brinkerhoff, D. (1981). Organizational performance: Recent developments in measurement. *Annual Review of Sociology, 7,* 321–349.

Kapsis, R. E. (1983). Reputation building and the film art world: The case of Alfred Hitchcock. *The Sociological Quarterly, 30,* 15–35.

Katz, D., & Kahn, R. L. (1978). *The social psychology of organizations* (2nd ed.). New York: Wiley.

Keller, K. L. (1993). Conceptualizing, measuring, and managing customer-based brand equity. *Journal of Marketing, 57,* 1–22.

Keller, W. (1974, February). Accounting for corporate social performance. *Management Accounting,* 39–41.

Kennedy, S. H. (1977). Nurturing corporate images: Total communication or ego trip? *European Journal of Marketing, 11,* 120–164.

Kilduff, M., & Krackhardt, D. (1994). Bringing the individual back in: A structural analysis of the internal market for reputation in organizations. *Academy of Management Journal, 37,* 87–108.

Kirmani, A., & Rao, A. (2000). No pain, no gain: A critical review of the literature on signaling unobservable product quality. *Journal of Marketing, 64,* 66–79.

Klapper, J. T. (1960). *The effects of mass communication.* Glencoe, IL: The Free Press.

Klein, D. B. (1997). Promise keeping in the great society: A model of credit information sharing. In D. B. Klein (Ed.), *Reputation: Studies in the voluntary elicitation of good conduct* (pp. 1–9). Ann Arbor: The University of Michigan Press.

Knoke, D. (1983). Organization sponsorship and influence reputation of social influence associations. *Social Forces, 61,* 1065–1087.

Knox, S., & Maklan, S. (1998). *Competing on value: Bridging the gap between brand and customer value.* London: Financial Times Pitman Publishing.

Kollock, P. (1994). The emergence of exchange structures: An experimental study of uncertainty, commitment, and trust. *American Journal of Sociology, 100,* 313–345.

Koys, D. J. (1997). Human resource management and *Fortune's* corporate reputation survey. *Employee Responsibilities and Rights Journal, 10,* 93–101.

Kramer, R. M., & Tyler, T. R. (Eds.). (1996). *Trust in organizations: Frontiers of theory and research.* Thousand Oaks, CA: Sage.

Kreps, D. M., & Wilson, R. (1982). Reputation and imperfect information. *Journal of Economic Behavior, 27,* 253–279.

Kydd, C. T., Ogilvie, J. R., & Slade, L. A. (1990). I don't care what they say, as long as they spell my name right: Publicity, retention, and turnover. *Group and Organization Studies, 15,* 53–74.

Lahno, B. (1995). Trust, reputation, and exit in exchange relationships. *Journal of Conflict Resolution, 39,* 495–510.

Likert, R., & Bowers, D. G. (1969). Organizational theory and human resource accounting. *American Psychologist, 24,* 585–592.

Logan, D. A. (2001). Libel law in the trenches: Reflections on current data on libel litigation. *Virginia Law Review, 87,* 503–529.

Macrae, C. (1999). Chartering brand identity—why this matters in emerging markets. *Journal of Business and Industrial Marketing, 14,* 162–164.

March, J. G. (1984, August). Notes on ambiguity and executive compensation. *Journal of Management Studies,* 53–64.

Martin, J. H., & Franz, E. B. (1994). Attracting applicants from a changing labor market: A strategic marketing framework. *Journal of Managerial Issues, 6,* 33–53.

Matthews, B. P., & Redman, T. (1994). Professionalizing marketing: The public face portrayed in recruitment advertisements. *Marketing Intelligence and Planning, 12,* 30–36.

Matthews, C. (1988). *Hardball: How politics is played told by one who knows the game.* New York: Harper Perennial.

Matthews, M. R. (1984, Fall). A suggested classification for social accounting. *Journal of Accounting and Public Policy,* 199–222.

Maurer, S. D., Howe, V., & Lee, T. W. (1992). Organizational recruiting as marketing management: An interdisciplinary study of engineering graduates. *Personnel Psychology, 45,* 807–833.

Merton, R. K. (1968). *Social theory and social structure* (Enl. ed.). New York: The Free Press.

Milewicz, J., & Herbig, P. (1994). Evaluating the brand extension decision using a model of reputation building. *Journal of Product and Brand Management, 3,* 39–47.

Milgrom, P., & Roberts, J. (1992). *Economics, organizations, and management.* Englewood Cliffs, NJ: Prentice-Hall.

Moorthy, K. A. (1985). Theoretical modeling in marketing. *Journal of Marketing Research, 22,* 262–282.

Noorman, R. (1984). *Service management: Strategy and leadership in service businesses.* Chichester, England: Wiley.

Peteraf, M., & Shanley, M. (1997). Getting to know you: A theory of strategic group identity. *Strategic Management Journal, 18,* 165–186.

Petrick, J. A., Scherer, R. F., Brodzinski, J. D., Quinn, J. F., & Ainina, M. F. (1999). Global leadership skills and reputational capital: Intangible resources for sustainable competitive advantage. *Academy of Management Executive, 13,* 58–69.

Pfeffer, J. (1981). Management as symbolic action: The creation and maintenance of organizational paradigms. In L. L. Cummings & B. M. Staw (Eds.), *Research in organizational behavior* (Vol. 3, pp. 1–52). Greenwich, CT: JAI.

Pfeffer, J. (1992). *Managing with power: Politics and influence in organizations.* Boston: Harvard Business School Press.

Pfeffer, J., & Salancik, G. R. (1978). *The external control of organizations: A resource dependence perspective.* New York: Harper & Row.

Prabhu, J., & Stewart, D. W. (2001). Signaling strategies in competitive interaction: Building reputations and hiding the truth. *Journal of Marketing Research, 38,* 62–72.

Rao, H. (1994). The social construction of reputation: Certification contests, legitimization, and the survival of organizations in the American automobile industry: 1895–1912. *Strategic Management Journal, 15,* 29–44.

Raub, W., & Weesie, J. (1990). Reputation and efficiency in social interactions: An example of network effects. *American Journal of Sociology, 96,* 626–654.

Riahi-Belkaoui, A., & Pavlik, E. L. (1992). *Accounting for corporate reputation.* Westport, CT: Quorum Books.

Rindova, V., & Fombrun, C. J. (1998). The eye of the beholder: The role of corporate reputation in defining organizational identity. In D. Whetten & P. Godfrey (Eds.), *Identity in organizations: Building theory through conversations* (pp. 62–66). Thousand Oaks, CA: Sage.

Rosen, S., Cochran, W., & Musser, L. M. (1990). Reactions to a match versus mismatch between an applicant's self-presentational style and work reputation. *Basic and Applied Social Psychology, 11,* 117–129.

Rosenbaum, J. E. (1989). Organization career systems and employee misperceptions. In M. B. Arthur, D. T. Hall, & B. S. Lawrence (Eds.), *Handbook of career theory* (pp. 329–353). New York: Cambridge University Press.

Rosenthal, R. W., & Landau, H. J. (1979). A game-theoretic analysis of bargaining with reputations. *Journal of Mathematical Psychology, 20,* 233–255.

Rynes, S. L. (1991). Recruitment, job choice, and post-hire consequences: A call for new research directions. In M. D. Dunnette & L. M. Hough (Eds.), *Handbook of in-*

*dustrial and organizational psychology* (2nd ed., Vol. 2, pp. 399–444). Palo Alto, CA: Consulting Psychologists Press.

Schlenker, B. R. (1980). *Impression management: The self-concept, social identity, and interpersonal relations.* Belmont, CA: Brooks/Cole.

Shapiro, C. (1982). Consumer information, product quality, and seller reputation. *Bell Journal of Economics, 13,* 20–35.

Shenkar, O., & Yuchtman-Yaar, E. (1997). Reputation, image, prestige, and goodwill: An interdisciplinary approach to organizational standing. *Human Relations, 50,* 1361–1381.

Simons, A. (1998). How ambiguity results in excellence: The role of hierarchy and reputation in U.S. Army Special Forces. *Human Organization, 57,* 117–123.

Spence, A. M. (1973). Job market signaling. *Quarterly Journal of Economics, 87,* 845–856.

Spence, A. M. (1974). *Market signaling: Informational transfer in hiring and related screening processes.* Cambridge, MA: Harvard University Press.

Standifird, S. S. (2001). Reputation and e-commerce: eBay auctions and the asymmetrical impact of positive and negative ratings. *Journal of Management, 27,* 279–295.

Staw, B. M., & Epstein, L. D. (2000). What bandwagons bring: Effects of popular management techniques on corporate performance, reputation, and CEO pay. *Administrative Science Quarterly, 45,* 523–566.

Stigler, G. J. (1962). Information in the labor market. *Journal of Political Economy, 69,* 49–73.

Suchman, M. C. (1995). Managing legitimacy: Strategic and institutional approaches. *Academy of Management Review, 20,* 571–610.

Swait, J., Erdem, T., Louviere, J., & Dubelaar, C. (1993). The equalization price: A measure of consumer-perceived brand equity. *International Journal of Research in Marketing, 10,* 23–45.

Swann, H. V. (1978). Human resource accounting: Some aspects which require psychologists' attention. *Journal of Occupational Psychology, 51,* 301–314.

Tedeschi, J. T., & Melburg, V. (1984). Impression management and influence in the organization. In S. B. Bacharach & E. J. Lawler (Eds.), *Research in the sociology of organizations* (Vol. 3, pp. 31–58). Greenwich, CT: JAI.

Tedeschi, J. T., & Norman, N. (1985). Social power, self-presentation, and the self. In B. R. Schlenker (Ed.), *The self and social life* (pp. 293–322). New York: McGraw-Hill.

Teece, D. J., Pisano, G., & Shuen, A. (1997). Dynamic capabilities and strategic management. *Strategic Management Journal, 18,* 509–533.

Tsui, A. S. (1984). A role set analysis of managerial reputation. *Organizational Behavior and Human Performance, 34,* 64–96.

Turban, D. B., Forret, M. L., & Hendrickson, C. L. (1998). Applicant attraction to firms: Influences of organization reputation, job and organizational attributes, and recruiter behaviors. *Journal of Vocational Behavior, 51,* 1–35.

Turban, D. B., & Greening, D. W. (1996). Corporate social performance and organizational attractiveness to prospective employees. *Academy of Management Journal, 40,* 658–672.

Turner, J. C. (1991). *Social influence.* Pacific Grove, CA: Brooks/Cole.

Tyler, T. R., & Kramer, R. M. (1996). Whither trust? In R. M. Kramer & T. R. Tyler (Eds.), *Trust in organizations: Frontiers of theory and research* (pp. 1–15). Thousand Oaks, CA: Sage.

*Webster's New World College Dictionary* (3rd ed.). (1997). New York: Macmillan.

Weigelt, K., & Camerer, C. (1988). Reputation and corporate strategy: A review of recent theory and applications. *Strategic Management Journal, 9,* 443–454.

Weiss, A. M., Anderson, E., & MacInnis, D. J. (1999). Reputation management as a motivation for sales structure decisions. *Journal of Marketing, 40,* 658–672.

Wernerfelt, B. (1988). Reputation, monitoring, and effort. *Information Economics and Policy, 3,* 207–218.

Whitmeyer, J. M. (2000). Effects of positive reputation systems. *Social Science Research, 29,* 188–207.

Williams, M. L., & Goss, B. (1975). Equivocation: Character insurance. *Human Communication Research, 1,* 265–270.

Zajac, E. J., & Westphal, J. D. (1995). Accounting for explanations of CEO compensation: Substance and symbolism. *Administrative Science Quarterly, 40,* 283–308.

# 7

# The Past, Present, and Future of Workplace Deviance Research

Rebecca J. Bennett
*University of Toledo*

Sandra L. Robinson
*University of British Columbia*

Payroll files at Acme Corporation are mysteriously deleted. Maria finds an obscene note taped to her chair when she returns from lunch. Marlene belittles the secretary in front of the department. Steven takes a 2-hour lunch break. Lawrence is running his own Web-based business on his computer at work. Intoxicated, Lee drives a forklift through a window. Janice cheats on her expense account. The aforementioned actions all have one thing in common: All fit the definition of employee deviance. All these behaviors are intentional acts initiated by organizational members that violate norms of the organization, and have the potential to harm the organization or its members.

Deviant actions such as these are pervasive in organizations. Every day, in every organization, harmful acts occur. Annually, 1.5 million American workers become the victim of violent behavior at work and another half a million become the victim of reported robberies (Warchol, 1998). Not surprisingly, the costs associated with dysfunctional workplace behavior are staggering. Annual cost estimates range from $4.2 billion for violence (Bensimon, 1997), to $200 billion for theft (Buss, 1993), to $5.3 billion for employees' recreational Web surfing (Bronikowski, 2000). Add in less direct costs such as increased insurance premiums and tarnished reputations (Allen & Lucero, 1996; Bensimon, 1997; Slora, Joy, & Terris, 1991) and it is apparent that workplace deviance poses one of the most serious problems facing organizations today.

Fortunately, workplace aggression has garnered considerable interest in the media (e.g., Bensimon, 1997) and in the organizational behavior literature (e.g., Bies, Tripp, & Kramer, 1997; Greenberg & Alge, 1998; O'Leary-Kelly, Griffin, & Glew 1996), where research has burgeoned. Nevertheless, given the complexity and scope of workplace deviance, much research remains to be done. The purpose of this chapter is to provide an overview of this research—what has been done, what is being done, and in particular, where the future of research on workplace deviance is going. We explore issues surrounding the definition and conceptualization of workplace deviance, research on its antecedents and consequences, as well as methodological challenges facing the future study of workplace deviance. This review is not intended to be comprehensive, but rather to highlight some interesting past and present trends that suggest what the future holds for those studying workplace deviance.

## CONCEPTUALIZATIONS OF WORKPLACE DEVIANCE

Reichers and Schneider (1990) suggested that the first stage of a construct's life cycle is the evaluation stage where critical reviews of the literature question the conceptualization and operationalization of key constructs. As such, a good starting point for a review of research on workplace deviance is a close look at how it has been conceptualized and how that conceptualization has matured over time. This section of our chapter reviews the progression of the conceptualization of workplace deviance from isolated and independent operational definitions to more inclusive definitions.

### Past

Early efforts to study deviant behaviors in the workplace were typically focused on particular types of behavior that happened to be deviant. Usually, the focus of these studies was not necessarily on deviant behavior per se, but they included variables that we would now consider to be a type of workplace deviance. Examples of such research include the studies on theft by Greenberg (1987, 1990, 1993), on responses to frustration by Spector and his colleagues (Chen & Spector, 1992; Spector, 1975, 1978), and on absenteeism (Rosse & Hulin, 1985).

These pioneering studies on undesirable organizational behaviors provided useful insights, to be sure. However, because they focused on just one type of deviant behavior, their value to understanding the broader phenomenon of workplace deviance was limited. Hence, although we may have clear evidence that procedural injustice impacts theft among employees (Greenberg, 1987, 1990, 1993), we cannot know from these studies what impact procedural injustice may have on other types of deviant behavior, such as work slowdowns or sabotage.

The arguments for developing and using broader conceptualizations of behavioral responses are convincing to us. Roznowski and Hulin (1992) proposed that looking at broader categorizations of behavior (e.g., withdrawal behaviors, rather than tardiness, absenteeism, or turnover) offers increased ability to generalize to unstudied but related behaviors. In addition, aggregating across several forms of deviant behavior ameliorates problems with skewed distributions that come as a result of studying individual behaviors with low variances (Hanisch & Hulin, 1991). The final argument for using broader measures of deviant behavior is that strong attitude–behavior correlations will occur only when there is correspondence between the levels of aggregation represented in the attitude and behavioral measures (Fishbein & Ajzen, 1975).

## Present

In line with the foregoing prescription, current researchers of deviant workplace behavior have, fortunately, shifted toward the use of broader conceptualizations of the construct. Initially, deviant behavior did not need to be defined beyond its operationalization within an individual study. However, as the concept of workplace deviance expanded to include a wide range of behaviors, the need for a broad definitional boundary around these behaviors was required. As such, we see more studies now that are using broader conceptualizations of workplace deviance than was the case 10 years ago.

Although researchers are now relying on broader definitions and conceptualizations of deviant workplace behavior, they have not reached any consensus. Indeed, as the study of workplace deviance emerged, so too did a multitude of constructs to capture this domain. Robinson and Greenberg (1998) identified no less than six distinct terms, with distinct definitions, to refer to essentially the same domain of behaviors: antisocial behavior (Giacalone & Greenberg, 1997), workplace deviance (Robinson & Bennett, 1995), workplace aggression (Baron & Neuman, 1996; Folger & Baron, 1996), retaliatory behavior (Skarlicki & Folger, 1997), organizational misbehavior (Vardi & Wiener, 1996), and organizationally motivated aggression (O'Leary-Kelly et al., 1996). Burroughs (1999) provided additional nomenclature used to describe either the same set of behaviors, or a specific subset of those behaviors: anticitizenship (Youngblood, Trevino, & Favia, 1992), negative citizenship behavior (Fisher & Locke, 1992), antirole behavior (McLean Parks & Kidder, 1994), counterproductive workplace behavior (Fox & Spector, 1999; Spector & Fox, in press), delinquency (Hogan & Hogan, 1989), harassment (Bjorkqvist, Osterman, & Hjelt-Back, 1994), incivility (Andersson & Pearson, 1999), maladaption (Perlow & Latham, 1993), noncompliant behavior (Puffer, 1987), revenge (Bies et al., 1997; Stuckless & Goranson, 1992), tyranny (Ashforth, 1994), and violence (Kinney, 1995; Kinney & Johnson, 1993; VandenBos & Bulatao, 1996).

These multiple constructs emerged because each researcher was throwing his or her net over the potential set of deviant behaviors from a somewhat different vantage point. Some researchers cast their net over behaviors that resulted from a particular cause. O'Leary-Kelly et al. (1996), for example, were interested in "organization-motivated" aggression and violence, only those actions instigated by factors in the organization itself. Similarly those with a revenge perspective (Bies & Tripp, 1996, 1998; Bies et al., 1997; Skarlicki & Folger, 1997; Skarlicki, Folger, & Tesluk, 1999; Stuckless & Goranson, 1992) approached this definitional challenge by focusing on only behaviors that are typically interpersonal retaliatory reactions for perceived mistreatment. Spector and his colleagues (Fox & Spector, 1999; Fox, Spector, & Miles, 2001; Spector, 1997; Spector & Fox, in press) zeroed in on behaviors that were emotional responses to frustration, and the industrial psychologists (Hogan & Hogan, 1989; Ones, Viswesvaran, & Schmidt, 1993) looked for behaviors symptomatic of dishonesty.

Others were more interested in the organizational or interpersonal consequences of the behaviors, and so sought to capture behaviors that are purposefully harmful to the organization (Baron & Neuman; 1996; Giacalone & Greenberg, 1997) or to individuals within the organization (Ashforth, 1994; O'Leary-Kelly, Paetzold, & Griffin, 2000; Perlow & Latham, 1993). Still others, such as Vardi and Weiner (1996), Andersson and Pearson (1999), Puffer (1987), Youngblood et al. (1992), and Robinson and Bennett (1995), were concerned with those behaviors that violated significant organizational norms. Despite these different starting points for conceptualizing workplace deviance, a closer examination of the end products of these definitions reveals tremendous consistencies and overlap. Indeed, regardless of label, orientation, or emphasis, the final set of behaviors under each conceptual umbrella shares many of the same features with the others. First, the majority of constructs captures behaviors that are perpetrated by organizational members and that are directed at either the organization or its members (e.g., Ashforth, 1994; Baron & Neuman, 1996; Bjorkqvist et al., 1994; Folger & Baron, 1996; Fox & Spector, 1999; O'Leary-Kelly et al., 1996; Robinson & Bennett, 1995; VandenBos & Bulatao, 1996) or, according to some definitions, prior organizational members or other stakeholders of the organization (e.g., Giacalone &

Greenberg, 1997; Perlow & Latham, 1993). Second, the behaviors captured by these constructs have the propensity to cause harm. All but one definition (Vardi & Wiener, 1996) posit that the concept is focused on organizationally related behavior that either *causes harm* or has the *potential to cause harm*. Third, these constructs focus on behavior that is intentional, as opposed to accidental (e.g., Andersson & Pearson, 1999; Bies & Tripp, 1998; McLean Parks & Kidder, 1994; Ones et al., 1993; Puffer, 1987; Robinson & Bennett, 1995; Vardi & Wiener, 1996) or, according to some definitions, intentionally harmful (e.g., Folger & Baron, 1996; Neuman & Baron, 1997; O'Leary-Kelly et al., 1996).

## Future Issues on the Conceptualization of Deviance

The study of workplace deviance in organizational behavior has gone from operationalizations of specific behaviors such as theft and absenteeism to competing definitions of broader constructs such as antisocial behavior, deviance, and misbehavior. Where will we go next with regard to conceptualizing workplace deviance?

*Definitional Directions.*   As this domain of study matures, we expect the emphasis on definitions and territorial behavior around these definitions to subside. Although one would have expected one or two definitions or conceptualizations to have emerged as dominant, this has not yet occurred. Although it may still happen, we anticipate that the opposite may occur, that individual researchers will adapt and use concepts and definitions of workplace deviance as the research question or project warrants. Indeed, it is our hope that multiple concepts can coexist. Although it is important to have solid definitions of one's construct before embarking on future research, we do not want to get mired in semantics and subtle distinctions between related constructs to the point of paralyzing publications. What matters most is not whose definition of workplace deviance is used in a given study, but only that the definition match the theory and the operationalizations in question. So long as we understand what we are trying to study and we use valid operationalizations of those constructs, the study of deviant behavior can successfully move forward.

*Expanding the Domain of Perpetrators.*   Although most conceptual definitions of workplace deviance characterize the perpetrators broadly as "organizational members," our empirical studies have not yet embraced this expanded perspective. Prior studies have focused on full-time, lower level paid employees of for-profit organizations. We believe that an expanded understanding of organizational member is necessary for the understanding of employee deviance to progress. In the following paragraphs, we review the typical perpetrators observed in prior research, followed by our thoughts on how expanding our notion of the deviant perpetrator will be beneficial.

It is interesting to note that the study of deviance, to date, has primarily focused on the behavior of employees, with a bias toward blue-collar and lower level workers. Early participants in studies of employee deviance were typically manufacturing plant workers (Greenberg, 1990), lower level workers in the health care field (Jones, 1981; Rosse, 1988); and retail clerks (Terris & Jones, 1982). Cross-sectional studies (e.g., Fox et al., 2001) often included upper level employees, of course, but unless controlled for in the analyses, the patterns of behavior of the disproportionately smaller numbers of higher level employees would have been drowned out by the behaviors of lower level employees. Hence, we wonder if patterns of behavior that heretofore have been found for lower level employees or for cross-sectional samples of employees will hold true for management-level employees as well.

We can think of a number of interesting questions raised by considering how the findings of studies looking at workplace deviance of the typical blue-collar worker might be applied to white-collar workers. For instance, we wonder if underpayment inequity is as strongly related to deviant behaviors for underpaid professional or executive-level employees. Are sales managers who have been treated in an unjust manner more inclined to engage in organizational deviance such as withholding effort or cheating on their expense accounts, or in interpersonal deviance, such as bullying their subordinates or spreading rumors? Does locus of control have as much influence on the physical aggression of stockbrokers as it does for direct care workers in a facility for mentally handicapped clients (Perlow & Latham, 1993)? Do the traits of personal honesty and thrill seeking explain the deviant behavior of executives who cheat on their expense accounts and who misrepresent their corporation's earnings to the same extent that they explain the behavior of convenience store clerks who steal from their employers (Terris & Jones, 1982)?

Just as the prior studies on workplace deviance have tended to be narrowly focused on blue-collar and lower level workers, so too have they been narrowly focused on full-time employees. This is an important lapse because we have no reason to believe that temporary or part-time employees (perhaps without benefits and job security) have the same opportunities, constraints, or motivations to engage in workplace deviance as do permanent, full-time employees. Moreover, part-time workers have been estimated to make up as much as 20% of the United States workforce and some industries rely heavily on contingent workers (Nardone, 1986). Given that so few studies have looked at part-time or contingent workers in the study of workplace deviance, we really know little about the deviance of a significant portion of the workforce.

We wonder if employees in part-time or temporary positions engage in different types or frequencies of deviant behaviors than full-time workers. Stamper and VanDyne (2001) investigated the effect of part-time employment on positive work behaviors that go above and beyond required tasks. Bennett and Robinson (1998), as part of an Academy of Management symposium on part-time workers, reanalyzed some of their earlier data, but found no effects for part-time status. We expect that moderators, such as whether the employee *chooses* to work part-time, will play an important role in this relationship as they have been shown to for the organizational citizenship behavior of part-time workers (Stamper & VanDyne, 2001).

Organizational members also refers to unpaid workers (i.e., volunteers or family members who "help out" in the family business for no compensation). Again, we do not know if deviant behavior of these types of workers is different than those of paid employees, given the absence of research on the former. Do volunteer members of charitable organizations (e.g., Habitat for Humanity workers) engage in the same or different forms and frequencies of deviant employee behavior than paid employees do? Do family members who volunteer on evenings, weekends, and vacations to help a fledgling business get off the ground engage in any workplace deviance or are they always exemplary employees? Our question is: Do unpaid organizational members have different reasons for interpersonal abuse, work slowdowns, and theft than those who get paid for the work they do?

We believe future research on workplace deviance should, and will, focus on broader samples of organizational members to include all levels of employees from a broad spectrum of occupations and industries. From pharmacists and attorneys to garbage collectors and restaurant busers, from universities and prisons to dry cleaners and construction crews, is deviance universal? Or does it take on different forms and frequencies given the environment?

It is also noteworthy that almost all conceptualizations of workplace deviance have been limited to the actions of individuals. Although this is a great starting point, we envision important future research to expand our models and studies to include the deviant actions of groups, whole organizations, or even industries. Of particular interest would be studies that examine antisocial pockets or groups within organizational contexts, or organizational (or even industry-level) cultures of dysfunctional or antisocial behavior. Once we move to consider groups and organizations, the interplay between these multiple levels opens up fascinating new directions. For example, how is the "good citizen" employee viewed and treated within a work group of deviant co-workers? How does the deviant or unethical behavior of an organization influence the potential for workplace deviance among groups or individuals within that organization? How do industry norms influence organizations' attitudes toward questionable behavior or the behavior of employees within that industry?

*Expanding the Domain of Behaviors.* Given that prior research has tended to focus on blue collar or lower level employees, it is not surprising that the types of behaviors that have been studied under the umbrella of workplace deviance tend to be oriented toward more plant floor behaviors such as theft, sabotage, and shirking, rather than actions more typical in the boardroom such as fraud, harassment, or embezzlement. Thus, as one important future direction, research in the area of workplace deviance needs to focus more attention on white collar deviant behaviors and behaviors that infect all levels of the organization, such as sexual harassment (O'Leary-Kelly et al., 2000), incivility (Andersson & Pearson, 1999), and abusive supervision (Hoobler & Tepper, 2001).

Another important way to expand the domain of behaviors under the umbrella of deviance is to consider deviant behaviors that have emerged from the advent of new technologies. Technological advancement has at once revolutionized the way we do work and, at the same time, multiplied the opportunities employees have to be unproductive at work. Computer misuse or "cyberloafing" in the workplace is something that employers are, or should be, increasingly concerned about (Lim, Loo, & Teo, 2001; Mastrangelo, Everton, & Jolton, 2001). Lim et al. (2001) defined cyberloafing as the act of employees using their company's Internet access during work hours to surf non-work-related Web sites and to send personal e-mail, both of which are unproductive uses of time at work. Additional high-technology deviance may include sabotaging computer programs, stealing proprietary information, executing viruses, and hacking into private computer space. Not surprisingly, organizations spend billions annually to offset cyberattacks, some of which may be done by their very own people (Mendoza, 2000). Yet the research into these forms of deviance lags far behind its prevalence in today's workplace.

Another future conceptual direction worth noting here is for the study of deviance to move toward more subtle social forms of deviance. Considerable attention has been given already to property deviance (e.g., theft, sabotage), production deviance (e.g., withdrawal, absenteeism), and serious social forms of deviance, such as aggression, harassment, and violence. Relatively little attention has been directed at the more commonplace, less serious forms of deviance. Examples of such behavior include political backstabbing, spreading rumors, verbal abuse, and incivility.

"Incivility is low intensity, deviant behavior that displays lack of regard for others, and that occurs in violation of norms for respect in social interactions" (Pearson, Andersson, & Porath, 1999, p. 7). Incivilities in organizations are often the first step in an upward spiral that leads to more direct and active forms of interpersonal deviance (Andersson & Pearson, 1999; Baron & Neuman, 1996). Consequently, we would like to see further work done to expand insight into incivility and its causes as well as to develop theory that weaves understanding of this form of deviance into the mainstream knowledge base of interpersonal deviance.

Another recent example of interest in more minor forms of interpersonal deviance is the studies on "abusive supervision" (Hoobler & Tepper, 2001), which has been defined as a sustained display of hostile verbal and nonverbal behaviors. Keashly and Jagatic (2000, in press) referred to a similar construct as emotional abuse. Northern European scholars have been interested in this concept for a few years; they refer to these behaviors as "mobbing" or "bullying" (Einarsen, 2000; Einarsen, Raknes, & Matthiesen, 1994; Rayner, 1997) and some report that the majority of this behavior is coming from managers (Rayner, 1997, 2000). Ashforth's (1994) definition of "petty tyranny" also refers to this brutal misuse of power by managers in organizations. Many factors have been speculated to affect tyrannical and abusive management styles: personality, beliefs, situational factors, and even cultural factors such as power distance (Ashforth, 1994; Einarsen, 2000). Clearly, these fruitful arenas of research, which heretofore have existed largely unto themselves, need to be blended into the domain of workplace deviance.

Finally, we are curious as to what forms deviance might take in an organization that is itself considered deviant. Do members of organizations engaged in illegal behavior (e.g., drug rings, chop shops, counterfeiters, prostitution rings, child pornography publishers) engage in similar types and forms of what we would call employee deviance? In other words, do those transporting illegal drugs steal merchandise? Do those publishing child pornography occasionally call in sick when they are not? Do prostitutes not work as hard as they could or spread rumors about their boss? Do counterfeiters threaten each other with interpersonal insults and physical assault? If not, what forms of *workplace* deviance do emerge in these businesses?

## ANTECEDENTS OF WORKPLACE DEVIANCE

Much of the research done to date, and likely to continue into the future, has been focused on causes or predictors of workplace deviance. Given the prevalence and costs associated with workplace deviance, fully understanding why it occurs is paramount. In this section, we visit some of the past and current trends around the study of antecedents and consider future trends of research in this area.

## Past and Present Research

A large number of empirical studies have examined potential antecedents of workplace deviance. Each study takes a somewhat different focus, examining a set of potential predictors that are aligned with a particular orientation. Taken together, we observe at least three trends in this research: those studies that treat deviance as a reaction to experiences, those that examine deviance as a reflection of one's personality, and those that explore deviance as adaptation to the social context.

*Deviance as Reactions to Experiences.*    Much of the past research that examines antecedents of workplace deviance has focused on how deviance, such as theft, vandalism, and aggression, reflects a reaction to perceived experiences of the employee in the organization. In particular, research has focused on deviance as a reaction to frustration, perceived injustices, lack of control, and threats to self.

Within organizational behavior, one of the "original" antecedents of employee deviance is frustration, studied now for more than 25 years. Spector and his colleagues (Chen & Spector, 1992; Fox & Spector, 1999; Fox et al., 2001; Spector, 1997; Storms & Spector, 1987) have built strong empirical support for the view that employee deviance is an emotional response to the experience of frustrating job stressors. Their studies offer support for the notion that acts of employee deviance are aggressive responses to thwarted goals.

Another, yet similar stream of research, has examined how deviance is predicted by experiences of perceived injustices in the workplace. Studies have shown that theft increases as a reaction to distributive and procedural injustice (Greenberg, 1990, 1993; Greenberg & Alge, 1998) as do sabotage (Ambrose, Seabright, & Schminke, 2001), aggression (Folger & Baron, 1996; O'Leary-Kelly et al., 1996; Skarlicki & Folger, 1997), and less serious interpersonal forms of interpersonal deviance (Burroughs, 2001).

One interesting future direction for these studies will be to distinguish the relative impact of different forms of injustice on interpersonal and organizational forms of deviance. A study by Aquino, Lewis, and Bradfield (1999), for example, provides some evidence supporting differential relationships in that they showed that although interactional justice was negatively related to both organizational and interpersonal deviance, distributive justice was negatively related only to interpersonal deviance. They argued that distributive justice was more strongly related to interpersonal deviance than organizational deviance because people are more likely to blame individuals than systems when making attributions for unfair outcomes. In contrast, they suggested that because interactional justice provokes the most intentional emotional response of all the types of injustice (Bies, 2001), it should result in a broader range of deviant behaviors. Further research should delve deeper into these arguments and into predicted differences between the different forms of injustice.

Ashforth (1989) defined powerlessness as a lack of autonomy and participation. The first stage of adjustment to experienced powerlessness proposed by Ashforth is reactance, where the individual attempts to (re)gain the control originally expected or desired. Deviant behavior, then, is argued to be a cathartic or corrective means to restoring an employee's sense of control over his or her environment. In fact the experience of powerlessness *has* been studied as a provocation for workplace deviance, such as sabotage (Ambrose et al., 2001; Bennett, 1998; DiBattista, 1991), violence (Lam, 1993; Perlow & Latham, 1993), and destructive behaviors (Allen & Greenberger, 1980). This line of reasoning is something to further investigate as we seek to understand deviant behavior in changing organizational environments. Does empowerment result in less organizational deviance as some preliminary studies indicate (Bennett, 1998)? Does the practice of "micromanagement" result in increased organizational and interpersonal deviance as humiliated professionals attempt to regain a perception of control and self-worth?

A final, related stream of research looks at how workplace experiences can create feelings of shame, which in turn elicit deviance in the form of aggression. Shame yields a painful scrutiny and negative evaluation of the entire self, with corresponding feelings of shrinking and becoming small (Gilligan, 1996; Kaufman, 1996; Morrison, 1996; Tangney, Wagner, Hill-Barlow, Marschall, & Gramzow, 1996). Shame has been found to be a strong precursor for violence in many settings (Gilligan, 1996; Tangney et al., 1996). Gilligan (1996) and Poulson (2001) provided convincing examples and arguments that much violence is a result of perceived insults against an individual's self-respect.

Exploration of deviance as reactions to organizational experiences will likely continue into the future. Of particular interest will be studies that seek to determine why individuals differ in their responses to perceived frustration, injustice, or insult; that is, why do some employees react with deviance whereas others forgive and forget? Why do some individuals react with aggression whereas others gravitate to other types of deviant responses? Some studies have begun to look at potential moderators of the experience–reaction relationship (Ambrose et al., 2001; Beugre, 1998; Skarlicki et al., 1999) and additional future efforts in this direction are needed to determine whether even more complex relationships are present.

Recent work by Aquino and his colleagues (Aquino & Bennett, 2002; Aquino, Galperin, & Bennett, 2001; Aquino, Tripp, & Bies, 2001) suggests that one's status has a strong effect on how one responds to the offenses one experiences. A study of revenge and reconciliation in the aftermath of a personal offense, Aquino, Tripp, & Bies (2001) found that the relationship between the attribution of blame for the offense and revenge directed toward the perpetrator was stronger for persons with low as compared to high hierarchical status. In support of an interaction between status and personality, Aquino and Bennett (2002) found that low status persons were more inclined to seek revenge against the offender when they are high in authoritarianism. It has been argued that lower status employees may be more inclined to perceive an offense as disrespect and to consequently feel shamed by that experience (Gilligan, 1996; Baumeister, Smart, & Boden, 1996). As was suggested earlier, shame can be a powerful motivator for aggression. So an important question is: When will aggression follow shame?

*Deviance as Reflections of One's Personality.*   The belief that deviant workplace behavior reflects one's personality has been widely held but not strongly supported by research. Although some past studies have identified some relationships between deviant acts and specific personality traits (see Trevino, 1986, for a review), these personality variables typically explain relatively little variance (Robinson & Greenberg, 1998). One exception may be dispositional aggressiveness, the extent to which people use implicit reasoning biases to justify aggressive behavior (James, 1998). Recent research has confirmed the existence of a direct relationship between dispositional aggressiveness and workplace deviance (Burroughs, Bing, & James, 1999; Burroughs, LeBreton, Bing, & James, 2000; Sablynski, Mitchell, James, & McIntyre, 2001).

Larry James and his colleagues have recently begun investigating the differing predictive power of implicit (unconscious) personality factors and explicit factors (those measured at a conscious level) on dysfunctional workplace behaviors. Their argument for using implicit measures such as the Conditional Reasoning Scale (James, 1998) is that because there are pressures to present oneself in a socially desirable manner, explicit measures of socially undesirable personality traits (e.g. aggression, Machiavellianism, negative affectivity, etc.) may be less accurate. This may explain the limited ability of explicit factors to predict much variance alone. Bing, Burroughs, Whanger, Green, and James (2002) proposed an interactive model where both implicit and explicit measures explain variance in workplace aggression. Continued investigation into these measures and the underlying constructs they measure will enlighten this aspect of deviance research.

Future research on the relationship between individual differences and workplace deviance is likely to take two directions. One direction will likely involve more research on the role of individual differences as moderators of the relationship between environment and workplace deviance. We contend that if personality plays a role, it is more likely as an indirect one, as a moderator of the relationship between situational influences and the deviant response to that situation. Some current research from a personality perspective suggests this may be the case. Negative affect has been found to moderate the relationship between deviant behavior and frustrating job stressors (Spector & O'Connell, 1994) and between deviance and perceived unfairness (Skarlicki et al., 1999). Moreover, those high in trait anger are more likely to respond to anger in provocative situations (Deffenbacher, 1992) and to engage in interpersonal deviance (Fox & Spector, 1999). Along similar lines, cognitive tendencies such as hostile attribution bias and belief in a negative reciprocity norm have been linked to dysfunctional reactions to perceived offenses (Eisenberger, Lynch, & Rohdieck, 1999; Greenberg & Alge, 1998).

Another direction for future research will be to explore personality effects from a broader perspective. Although prior studies have not found strong relationships between individual traits and deviance, more promise may be found in studies looking at larger personality trends, such as the Big Five. Indeed, very recent research suggests that the relationship between the Big Five personality factors and workplace deviance is significant (Cullen & Ones, 2001; Lee, Ashton, & Shin, 2001).

Lee et al. (2001) found that selected Big Five personality factors predicted distinct types of employee deviance. Specifically, they observed that organizational deviance was associated with low conscientiousness and that interpersonal deviance was associated with extraversion and low agreeableness. They also found the trait of honesty (which they propose—with good evidence—as the sixth factor of personality) to be significantly and negatively related to exploitation of others (i.e., interpersonal deviance) *and* to organizational deviance (Ashton, Lee, & Son, 2000; Lee et al., 2001). However, they found the relationship with (dis)honesty to be stronger for organizational deviance, which they suggested was due to the fact that organizational deviance is more heavily represented by dishonesty (e.g., time theft, falsifying records) than is that of interpersonal deviance, whose item content reflects malevolence in social interaction (e.g., making fun of others, assault) as well as deceit (Lee et al., 2001). Future research might investigate whether dispositional aggressiveness as measured by the conditional reasoning scale is a subfactor of this new factor of honesty.

*Deviance as Adaptation to the Social Context.*    A third trend in the study of antecedents of workplace deviance is that focusing on the role of social norms, cues, and constraints. Although, by definition, workplace deviance may involve the violation of significant organizational norms espoused by the dominant administrative coalition, it may be that local workgroup social pressures and norms espousing and supporting acts of deviance are essential for it to occur.

Robinson and O'Leary-Kelly (1998) found that a primary predictor of workplace antisocial behavior was the extent to which one's co-workers engaged in similar behavior. In terms of specific types of workplace deviance, social norms have been found to influence sabotage (Giacalone, Riordan, & Rosenfeld, 1997), workplace aggression (Greenberg & Alge, 1998), and theft (Greenberg, 1998).

O'Leary-Kelly and her colleagues (O'Leary-Kelly et al., 1996) suggested social learning theory as a theoretical explanation for aggression. Although social learning theorists acknowledge that some individuals are more prone to violence than others (Bandura, 1973; Berkowitz, 1993), their overarching premise is that aggression is learned as an adaptive response through cues in one's environment. The environment may provide these cues through modeling (Bandura, 1973) or through reinforcements or punishments present in their surroundings (Bandura, 1973; Harris, Wolf, & Baer, 1964).

## Future Directions on the Antecedents of Deviance

Future research on antecedents of workplace deviance is likely to follow down these three prior paths. In addition, we offer several very new directions that may be fruitful to explore in to fully comprehend why workplace deviance occurs.

*Contextual Variables.* Almost all of the predictors of workplace deviance to date have been limited to factors within the organization. This is not surprising given that this bias is inherent in almost all research in organizational behavior. Only recently has attention turned to the "contextualization" of organizational behavior (Dietz, Robinson, Folger, Baron, & Schultz, 2002); that is, examining factors outside the organization that may influence the behavior of organizational members. Nevertheless, we believe that a focus on external organizational factors may open up all kinds of new and interesting research on workplace deviance.

Some new research suggests that some forms of deviance are in fact influenced by factors beyond organizational walls. Recent research suggests that a significant predictor of workplace violence is the rate of violence in the community surrounding the organization (Dietz et al., 2002). Along similar lines, state-level community characteristics such as economic deprivation, family disruption, and population density have been found to significantly predict workplace homicide (Dietz & Nolan, 2001).

Another contextual factor that we expect might impact deviant behavior at work is national culture. Japan has long boasted of a low national crime rate (Australian Institute of Criminology, 2002). Criminologists attribute the low incidence of violent and nonviolent crime to a cultural and social heritage that values conformity and self-control (Taj, 1981). The obedience to authority found in Japan and other Asian cultures is largely due to a collectivist culture that promotes order through shared beliefs in interdependence, cooperation, and ethnocentrism. Individualistic cultures such as the United States value independence, egocentrism, and individual rights (Hofstede, 1980; Triandis, 1995). We would expect, therefore, that deviance in a collectivist culture would be less likely to occur than in an individualistic culture. When it does exist, we would expect it to take more passive forms. Hence, in the United States, if a supervisor offends you at work, the "Wild-West-every-man-for-himself" culture supports the notion of retaliation.

Another macrolevel variable that we believe affects deviant workplace behavior is the income (and status) distribution of the company in which the employee works. Medical sociologists have determined that the variance in distribution of wealth significantly affects the health and mortality of the country's citizens (Wilkinson, 1999). In the developed world, it is not the richest countries that have the best health, but the most egalitarian. We believe there may be a parallel pattern in organizations. If the salaries in the organization vary greatly such that the compensation for the CEO is many times that of the lowest paid employee, we would expect that the "health" of the organization would be poorer as well. Organizational health could be measured in a variety of ways; for instance, performance, absenteeism, turnover, or rates of other forms of organizational deviance and interpersonal deviance.

We strongly encourage future empirical studies to look at external factors as antecedents of workplace deviance of all kinds. Such future research may include national or community-level variables such as poverty, ethnic culture, and news coverage of deviant workplace behavior. It might also include individual-level external variables such as marital discord or other life stressors, lack of sleep, recreational drug use, or availability of social support as predictors of workplace deviance. Although these context variables may not all be directly controllable by the organization itself, knowledge of these influential factors may enable researchers to explain more variance in their models as well as help organizations to counteract their effects.

*Victim Variables.*    As our review suggests, the vast majority of research exploring antecedents of workplace aggression has been limited to variables about the individual perpetrator or the organizational context in which it occurs. Relatively little research has considered variables about the victims themselves that may facilitate the occurrence of workplace deviance. Perhaps this reluctance to look at victim predictors stems from a fear of encouraging a "blame the victim" mentality. Nevertheless, research outside of organizational behavior suggests that this approach may be warranted. We contend this will be a valuable and important future area of research on the causes of workplace deviance.

Theories of victimology (Felson & Steadman, 1983; Hepburn, 1973) from sociology and criminology have identified certain common personality and behavioral characteristics of victims. For example, studies of bullying in schools identify two types of victims: the "submissive victim," who is weak, anxious, and insecure; and the "provocative victim," who is both anxious and aggressive (Olweus, 1978, 1993). A few recent studies in organizational behavior have applied this victimization research to the workplace. Employees who are high in "victim traits" such as dependency, fear, and hostility (Aquino, Grover, et al., in press) or external locus of control (Rayner, 2000), have been found to report higher levels of victimization.

On the other hand, Hoobler and Teppers's (2001) longitudinal study paints a more complex relationship. They found support for a reciprocal causation model where poor performance, job dissatisfaction, and lack of affective commitment lead to abusive supervision, which in turn leads to additional poor performance and a downward spiral from there. The learned helplessness model from operant conditioning theory showed that those experiencing noncontingent punishment (part of the definition of tyrannical and abusive management) were unable to respond in a productive manner, even when the contingency changed. Hence, a poorly performing employee who fears the wrath of his or her boss will continue to perform poorly and will continue to be bullied. Research on how this dysfunctional cycle can be broken should be undertaken.

Without a doubt, future research efforts on understanding the causes of workplace deviance should also be focused on the role of the victim. Although it is important to avoid holding the victims responsible for workplace deviance, our understanding of how to prevent it may be enhanced by asking ourselves what is it about the victims themselves that might account for some of the variance in workplace deviance.

## CONSEQUENCES OF WORKPLACE DEVIANCE

The past and present focus on consequences of workplace deviance has tended to be limited to the costs of harm done to the organization. When the astronomical costs of deviance are calculated, they typically focus on losses in productivity and material resources, heightened security, and increased insurance premiums. In contrast, costs to the individual victims have only recently been considered, and consequences for witnesses, perpetrators, and secondary victims have been largely neglected.

*Victim Focus.*    Although numerous studies have calculated the costs associated with workplace deviance from a corporate perspective, the costs to individual victims is less clear. We know that employees perceive more stress as a result of concern about being a victim of violence at work (Johnson, 2000) and that victims suffer in terms of lost work time and effort (Pearson, 1998). However, very little research or theory in organizational behavior has been devoted to understanding what happens to the witnesses or victims of workplace deviance, or how it impacts them over time. One exception to this is the literature on abusive supervision, which has investigated some individual effects of experiencing hostile workplace behaviors.

Keashly and Jagatic's (in press) review of studies of emotional abuse shows that the effects of these seemingly minor behaviors on the victim are extensive, affecting all levels of functioning from personal (cognitive, psychological, physical) to interpersonal (aggressive behaviors, marital and family conflict) to professional (satisfaction, turnover, withdrawal) and organizational (productivity, commitment). In addition, the spiraling effect of interpersonal deviance has been shown to both (a) trigger a vicious circle where the abused employee becomes less productive and more withdrawn and hence is perceived worthy of greater abuse (Ashforth, 1994; Keashly & Jagatic, 2000), and also (b) create a ripple effect where the abusive behavior spreads to a wider and wider circle of "secondary victims" such as family and friends of the victim (Andersson & Pearson, 1999; Barling, 1996; Bennett, 1998; Glomb, 2001). These provocative findings should be extended and applied to other forms of deviant behavior.

*Functional Benefits.* To date, most of the research has assumed only negative consequences and costs associated with workplace deviance. Given the conceptual focus of the construct, this is not surprising. Moreover, it is relatively easy to observe the individual and organizational costs of deviant actions such as violence, theft, and shirking. However, in spite of these obvious negative outcomes, more and more researchers are challenging the conventional wisdom that workplace deviance yields only negative outcomes. In recent years, more researchers have focused on the potential functional aspects of workplace deviance.

A variety of perspectives have been used to explain how behaviors defined as deviant can also prove beneficial to individuals and organizations (Bies & Tripp, 1996, 1998; Coleman, 1985; Greenberg & Scott, 1996; Vardi & Wiener, 1996). Bies and Tripp (1997) proposed that behaviors commonly perceived of as "deviant" (e.g., revenge behaviors) can be conceived of as prosocial because they serve several beneficial purposes in the organization, such as correcting the perpetrator's behavior and restoring justice.

Vardi and Wiener (1996) proposed that the desirability (or lack thereof) of deviant behavior is inherently "a judgment matter" and the definition of whether deviance is "good" or "bad," therefore, depends on who is viewing the behavior. For instance, whistle blowing may be viewed as deviant by the organization, but society at large would find such behavior commendable. Dehler and Welsh (1998) further developed the argument for the functional nature of deviant behavior by asserting that the current definitions of workplace deviance are mere social constructions that support the status quo and sustain the control of the organizational elite. Critical theory is proposed as a better lens through which to view behavior that violates norms of the organization.

Morgan (1986, as cited by Dehler & Welsh, 1998, p. 185) dispelled the myth of organizational rationality by positing a number of unaddressed questions: Behavior is rational, efficient, and effective for whom? Whose goals are being pursued? What interests are being served? Who benefits? Rationality (or deviance, in this case) is a tool used to justify the agenda of the organizational elite. As Morgan (1986) stated, "rationality is always political" (p. 195). Critical theory allows deviant behavior to be "constructive" by allowing individuals to respond to the discrepancy they observe between their own cognitions of what will benefit the organization and the organization's officially sanctioned behaviors. Hence, constructive deviance refers to adaptive behaviors that employees engage in to bridge the gap between their personal expectations and the organization's standards of behavior. This allows organizational norms to develop that accommodate the turbulent environment in which organizations today exist. For instance, leaving early or taking care of personal business while at work may be tolerable in an organization employing many working parents who are involved in the lives of their children. The peace of mind that comes from knowing the children are home from school or being able to attend soccer games and piano recitals engenders commitment, positive morale, and greater productivity. Organizations that embrace such "deviance" will likely become trendsetters. Future research will need to be more open to considering the beneficial role of norm-violating behaviors for the individual, the group, and the organization.

Does constructive deviance take different forms? Galperin (2001) considered a variety of behaviors fitting the definition of constructive deviance and found support for a three-factor model of constructive deviance. Her first factor reflects innovative behaviors that enhanced performance. These behaviors (e.g., developed creative solutions to problems) did not seem to violate organizational norms and so would not be considered deviant (according to our definition). The second factor was labeled "challenging organizational deviance" and it reflected constructive acts of deviance (e.g., violated company procedures to solve a problem). These behaviors were distinguished from the third factor by their impersonal nature. The third factor reflected behaviors that challenged other individuals within the organization (e.g., "disobeyed your supervisor's instructions to perform more efficiently"). Despite the differences in these behaviors, they

share the goal of improving organizational functioning. Future researchers interested in broadening insight into the nature of constructive deviance and its role in organizational learning, adaptation, and long-term
viability will benefit from Galperin's carefully developed measure.

We posit that future research will persist in considering the long-term effects of employee deviance on victims and on organizations. The escalating
pattern of employee deviance and abusive supervision begs the question of
which came first and makes us wonder where else this pattern may occur.
Hence, longitudinal studies investigating reciprocal effects should be conducted for other forms of deviance as well. We would hope that future investigations into employee deviance will be broad-minded enough to consider the
functional effects of deviance for individuals, groups, and organizations.

## OTHER FUTURE DIRECTIONS FOR RESEARCH ON WORKPLACE DEVIANCE

We have, thus far, considered trends regarding the vast amount of research
on workplace deviance, which focuses primarily on its antecedents and consequences. However, we believe there are also a number of other interesting
future research trends in this domain that go beyond the scope of either predictors or outcomes. Discussed in the following are three such trends.

### Sense-Making and Perception

In many ways our conceptualization of workplace deviance has been relatively simplistic as we tend to ignore the fact that the concept of workplace
deviance is socially constructed (Giacalone & Greenberg, 1997; Robinson &
Bennett, 1995). We define workplace deviance as if there were some objective standard by which to determine what behavior is potentially harmful or
whether or not it violates organizational norms. Our belief is that there is a
moral standard widely accepted by society of which behaviors are right and
wrong. Yet the judgment of whether some behaviors are norm-violating or
not, or whether they are potentially harmful or not, can be very subjective.
The determination of what is and is not deviant workplace behavior sometimes depends on who is asked to make that assessment. Indeed, managers
across diverse organizations, or various employee groups and management
within the same organization, may in some circumstances view specific
workplace deviant behaviors quite differently.

Although the subjective and socially constructed nature of workplace
deviance may pose challenges to those of us seeking to study it in the future, different research possibilities may arise as a result. How do different
social entities view workplace deviance and what determines their differing perspectives? How do organizations and managers socially construct

and communicate their perspective of deviant behavior to the rest of the organization? Likewise, how do the perpetrators of potentially deviant behavior construct or justify that behavior so as to feel comfortable about what they do? If we are willing to move beyond our relatively simplistic assumptions that the construct of workplace deviance is objective, and can embrace the fact that it is instead, socially created, many interesting research possibilities open up and our understanding of workplace deviance will be richer.

## Dynamic Nature of Employee Deviance

To date, almost all the theoretical and empirical models of workplace deviance have taken a snapshot or static perspective on this set of behaviors. Although a number of noteworthy studies have employed longitudinal designs demonstrating the effects of predictors on workplace deviance at later points in time (Dietz et al., 2002; e.g., Greenberg, 1990; Jagatic & Keashly, 2001), the dynamics per se of workplace deviance have not been captured. But how does workplace deviance grow, change, and unfold over time within individuals, groups, or the organization itself? Do some forms of deviance lead into other forms of deviance over time? Is it that employees or groups begin with more minor forms of deviance and gradually escalate to more serious forms? How quickly do unchecked incidents of workplace deviance evolve into more frequent episodes by the perpetrators or spread to other employees? These are but a few potential questions yet to be answered regarding the dynamics of workplace deviance.

## Links to Other Organizational Behavior Constructs

The future study of workplace deviance might also benefit from examining the relationship between deviance and related constructs in organizational behavior. This may help to not only further our understanding of deviance, but also these other literatures. Two constructs that we believe may have interesting connections to workplace deviance are citizenship behavior and trust.

*Citizenship Behavior.*    There has, and continues to be, an intriguing divide between the two well-established literatures on employee citizenship behavior and workplace deviance; those that study one seem to avoid the other, and although these constructs and measures seem closely related, very little research has explored their relationship. In one sense, workplace deviance and citizenship behaviors are similar in that both reflect organizational members' behavior with reference to the norms of the social context. Whereas workplace deviance reflects doing what one *should not* do and not doing, or doing less of what one *should* do, citizenship behavior reflects going beyond the call of duty, surpassing what one should do or suppressing the desire to do what one should not do. Consequently, measures of these constructs are often intertwined, as measures of positive discretionary behaviors have often included deviant behaviors in their measures (negatively scored). However, little research has attempted to theoretically explicate or empirically compare these two constructs.

At least one recent study has looked at the co-occurrence and the underlying dimensionality of the larger group of discretionary behaviors, both positive and negative. Bennett and Stamper (2001) used multidimensional scaling and q-sort techniques to empirically demonstrate that two dimensions underlie all of these behaviors, whether the behavior is directed at the organization or at individuals within the organization and whether the behavior is positive or negative. Hence, what had previously been defined as "helping behaviors" fell into the prosocial, interpersonal quadrant. "Loyalty behaviors" fell into the prosocial, organizational quadrant. Negative behaviors also could be categorized by whether they were directed at the organization or at persons within the organization. Hence, individuals seem to perceive discretionary behaviors as falling along one continuum from positive to negative. Nonetheless, future research should investigate questions of causality for behaviors between and within dimensions. For instance, are behaviors at opposite ends of the positive–negative continuum caused by opposite phenomena (presence or lack of justice or control)? Are behaviors within quadrants substitutable? Do individuals engage in both positive and negative behaviors concurrently? If so, how do they justify their actions?

*Trust.* In recent years, the study of trust in organizations has been burgeoning (see Dirks & Ferrin, in press, for a review). To date, however, little research has explored the potentially strong relationship between trust and workplace deviance. It is highly likely that as workplace deviance increases within an organization, management's trust in employees declines. What is less obvious is how management's trust in employees will affect employees' subsequent deviant behavior. Organizations often seek to deter deviance in organizations by installing increased security and surveillance systems (Jones & Gautschi, 1988) yet some evidence suggests that these control systems and procedures may actually encourage, rather than deter, workplace deviance (e.g., Cialdini, 1996; Kruglanski, 1970). Recent research by Deutsch-Salamon and Robinson (2002) suggests that if management communicates to employees that they are not trusted, norms of responsibility do not develop and thus more deviance occurs. Along similar lines, Lawrence and Robinson (2001) suggested that the mere act of seeking to exert power over employees may encourage them to rebel, and Bennett (1998) implied that organizational cultures that minimize employee control engender destructive behaviors by employees trying to regain a sense of efficacy in their environment. Clearly this relationship between trust, power, and workplace deviance demands further exploration.

The reciprocating nature of variables such as trust, deviance, power, and control demonstrates how important it is to consider workplace deviance as a fluid, subjective phenomenon. The challenge is for future researchers to not settle for simplistic studies, but to create longitudinal research designs with feedback models that account for the interactive effects of these variables.

## METHODOLOGICAL CHALLENGES

In this last section, we address a number of methodological issues pertaining to the study of deviance in organizations. First, we address the issue of studying such a sensitive topic. Next we briefly discuss some interesting methodological approaches from other research domains that may be useful for future research on workplace deviance.

### Overcoming Sensitivity

Our concern is that too few people have studied workplace deviance for fear it is too challenging to observe and assess because it is relatively covert and sensitive. Although part of the challenge of studying workplace deviance is overcoming reluctance of deviant actors to admit to their deviant behavior, several methods have been successfully used to address this challenge. Bennett and Robinson (2000), for example, used anonymous mail-in surveys from the general population to elicit information on the degree of workplace deviance. Respondents were surprisingly forthcoming, indicating participation rates ranging from 25% to 84%. Moreover, Dalton and colleagues have developed several useful techniques for protecting confidentiality of respondents as well as increasing accuracy of response rates for sensitive behaviors. As discussed elsewhere (e.g., Robinson & Greenberg, 1998), such techniques include unmatched block, unmatched count, and randomized response technique (Dalton, Daily, & Wimbush, 1997; Dalton, Wimbush, & Daily, 1994).

Our main point here is that researchers should not be dissuaded from embarking on research in this area on the grounds that it is too sensitive, covert, or socially undesirable to adequately observe and measure. Although techniques thus far may be underestimating the degree of actual deviant behavior, they do reveal enough variance in deviance to make its empirical study possible.

## Methodological Techniques for Future Research

Researchers studying employee deviance to this point in time have largely relied on self-report measures of employee deviance. We believe that many research doors may be opened, however, by considering additional methods for examining workplace deviance. By employing new methodologies, we may be able to examine research questions that, to date, have not been considered. We now discuss some methods used in other research areas that should be considered by researchers of workplace deviance.

*Event Sampling Methodology.*  Numerous researchers, primarily in the area of workplace emotions, have begun to employ event sampling methodology (ESM). ESM involves having employees complete numerous short self-reports throughout a fixed time period, at either set time intervals or at times they are signaled to do so. The advantage of ESM is that it potentially captures psychological states or behavior in relatively "real" versus retrospective time, and the resulting data are useful for examining changes in psychological states or behavior over time. For some good reviews of this method, see Wheeler and Reis (1991), and for an excellent example of an application, see Diener, Smith, and Fujita (1995).

We believe this method may be particularly useful for future research on workplace deviance. Asking employees to report on their own or observed workplace deviance at random intervals during the day may help determine the actual frequency of deviant acts as this method would reduce biases associated with retrospective or global judgments. It might also be valuable for examining what real-time correlates occur with workplace deviance; that is, how is the employee feeling at the time before, during, or after acts of workplace deviance? Or what specific events tend to precede the act of workplace deviance? This method might also enable us to look at within-person behavioral changes as they pertain to workplace deviance. Respondents' concern about anonymity might be resolved by having them complete the ESM online using a confidential code number known only to themselves.

*Technology.*  As new technology makes new forms of deviance available, it also makes new methodologies for studying workplace deviance possible. For example, the use of Web surveys, and computer and video monitoring of employees may enhance our study of the frequency and correlates of deviant behaviors. In particular, over 75% of major corporations now monitor and record Web pages and e-mail used by their employees

(American Management Association, 2000). To our knowledge, this vast amount of data has not been used to study organizational behavior in general, or workplace deviance in particular. We believe, however, that content analysis of these data, combined with surveys or ESM, may yield some incredibly rich results.

Another potentially rich source of technology-inspired data on workplace deviance may come from in-house "cyberventing" Web pages. Cyberventing (Leonard, 1999) allows disgruntled employees the cathartic opportunity to blow off steam on a special Web page set up by the employer on the organization's intranet for that purpose. The hope is that the opportunity to vent anonymously will dispel frustrations that might otherwise build to a boiling point and result in employee deviance. Whether cyberventing provides a release and reduces deviance, or whether it only adds fuel to employees' fire, is a question that has yet to be empirically investigated.

*Others' Reports.*    Traditional fields of workplace behavior have tended to rely on self-report. However, the reports by others—peers, customers, and supervisors—have occasionally been used successfully to assess deviant workplace behavior (Burroughs, Woehr, Bing, & McIntyre, 2001; Skarlicki & Folger, 1997; Skarlicki et al., 1999). The advantage of this method over self-report is that it can reduce common method bias, it may elicit more honest or accurate assessments of behavior, and it might provide a different perspective on employee deviance. A recently developed peer-report measure of workplace deviance (Burroughs et al., 2001) found support for two dimensions of employee deviance as measured by peer ratings that are consistent with Bennett and Robinson's (2000) two-dimensional measure of self-reported deviant behavior.

*Critical Incident Method.*    This technique involves asking employees for examples of deviance and their reactions to those offenses. This can be preceded by other measures, such as psychological assessments, assessments of employees' perceptions of organizational and subgroup climates, opportunities for deviance in the organization, or expected consequences for these behaviors. Critical incidents allow researchers the richness of case studies while also allowing for content analysis, coding, and quantitative comparisons. Situational, demographic, and individual difference variables can be controlled for to determine what affects reactions to deviant behaviors experienced in organizations. An example of the critical incident method can be found in Pearson, Andersson, and Wegner (in press).

*Policy Capturing.*    Related to critical incident methodology is policy capturing, where one gives respondents a set of "critical incidents" that vary in terms of different dimensions. Respondents are then asked to rate and react to those incidents or scenarios. This method allows the researcher to use regression analysis to compute the relative importance that respondents put on each variable for making the judgments that they are asked to make. The end product is a statistical equation or "captured rating policy" that represents an expression of how one arrives at his or her judgment about incidents of deviance. This, and similar methods, have been recently used to successfully study deviant behaviors in the workplace (e.g., Rotundo & Sackett, 2001). A variety of techniques are coming into view that allow researchers the opportunity to test natural responses of participants. The use of these techniques undoubtedly will expand our knowledge of employee deviance.

## SUMMARY AND CONCLUSION

In this chapter we have provided an overview of research on workplace deviance—sampling what has been done, what is being done, and most importantly, where we believe the future of research on organizational deviance is going. Our goal has not been to provide an exhaustive review of this research domain, but rather to highlight what we believe are interesting past, current, and future trends in the study of workplace deviance. We hope our efforts encourage much needed future research on this fascinating topic.

We began this chapter with a consideration of the definition and conceptualization of workplace deviance. We discussed how the construct has evolved from one of narrow operationalizations of individual behaviors to numerous broader conceptualizations encompassing a wide range of behaviors committed by organizational members. Although no particular conceptual definition stands out as ideal, we encourage future researchers to focus on using a definition that best suits their research question and matches their operationalizations of workplace deviance. We also encourage researchers to expand their focus to include a wide range of organizational members and a wide range of potentially deviant behaviors, beyond those already explored.

In the next section, we addressed antecedents of workplace deviance. Given the apparent value of understanding this costly behavior, it is no surprise that most research on workplace deviance has focused on its antecedents. Taken together, we identified three common trends in the study of antecedents of workplace deviance: examining workplace deviance as reactions to experiences such as injustice, as reflections of one's personality, and as adaptations to the social environment. Some of our suggestions for future directions on the study of antecedents of workplace deviance include examining contextual variables outside the organization, such as societal-level violence or national culture, as well as more focus on the role that victims may play in instigating interpersonal workplace deviance.

Following our discussion of research on antecedents of workplace deviance, we turned our attention to the research on its consequences. Although statistics abound regarding the costs of deviance to organizations, we know relatively little about the potential costs to individuals. As such, we anticipate future research on the consequences of workplace deviance to emphasize the costs of deviance on individual victims and third-party witnesses. We also anticipate future studies to address not only the negative consequences of workplace deviance, but also their benefits and functions to individuals and organizations.

Along with identifying future research directions on antecedents and consequences of workplace deviance, we also sought to identify a number of other future research avenues in this domain. We focused on three potentially interesting routes. One route is to address the role of sensemaking and perceptions of both individuals and collectives in the construction and interpretation of workplace deviance. A second route is to explore the dynamic and changing nature of workplace deviance, in particular how it evolves throughout an organization. And finally, we believe our understanding of workplace deviance will be enhanced with more emphasis on connecting it to related constructs in organizational behavior, such as organizational citizenship behavior and trust.

We finalized our chapter with consideration of the methodological challenges facing future researchers of workplace deviance. First, we highlighted a number of ways in which researchers have successfully empirically assessed this relatively covert, low base rate, sensitive behavior. Next, we highlighted a number of novel methodologies from other domains that may be usefully applied to this domain, such as event sampling methodology, policy capturing, and critical incident methods. Our goal here was to suggest innovative ways to study workplace deviance and to provide encouragement to those who believe it may be too challenging to study.

The tale of employee deviance continues to unfold. We have seen the definition of the construct unfold, and we've watched the cast of characters continue to expand. As the manifold authorship of this story converges, we expect to explore the setting of where deviance is likely to exist, to gain insight into the story line of why and how employees engage in interpersonal and organizational deviance, and to watch the characters develop. Organizations and society will benefit from a greater understanding of this story and all should watch with interest as the story is written.

## ACKNOWLEDGMENTS

The authors wish to thank Bella Galperin, Susan Burroughs, and Karl Aquino for their helpful advice on the chapter.

# REFERENCES

Allen, R. E., & Lucero, M. A. (1996, August). *An empirical investigation of organization-ally-targeted insider aggression.* Paper presented at the meeting of the Academy of Management, Las Vegas, NV.

Allen, V., & Greenberger, D. B. (1980). Destruction and perceived control. In A. Baum & J. Singer (Eds.), *Advances in environmental psychology* (pp. 85–89). Hillsdale, NJ: Lawrence Erlbaum Associates.

Ambrose, M., Seabright, M., & Schminke, M. (2001). *Sabotage in the workplace: The role of organizational justice.* Unpublished manuscript, University of Central Florida, Orlando.

American Management Association. (2000). *Annual electronic monitoring and surveil-lance survey.* New York: Author.

Andersson, L. M., & Pearson, C. M. (1999). Tit for tat? The spiraling effect of incivil-ity in the workplace. *Academy of Management Review, 24,* 452–471.

Aquino, K., & Bennett, R. J. (2002). *Holding on or letting go: The interactive effects of authori-tarianism and organizational status variables on revenge, forgiveness and reconciliation in the aftermath of personal offense.* Unpublished manuscript, University of Delaware, Newark.

Aquino, K., Galperin, B. L., & Bennett, R. J. (2001, August). *Social status and aggressive-ness as moderators of the relationship between international justice and workplace deviance.* Paper presented at the meeting of the Academy of Management, Washington, DC.

Aquino, K., Grover, S. L., Goldman, B., & Folger, R. (in press). When push doesn't come to shove: Interpersonal forgiveness in workplace relationships. *Journal of Management Inquiry.*

Aquino, K., Lewis, M. U., & Bradfield, M. (1999). Justice constructs, negative affectivity, and employee deviance: A proposed model and empirical test. *Journal of Organizational Behaviour, 20,* 1073–1091.

Aquino, K., Tripp, T. M., & Bies, R. J. (2001). How employees respond to personal of-fense: The effects of blame attribution, victim status, and offender status on re-venge and reconciliation in the workplace. *Journal of Applied Psychology, 86,* 52–59.

Ashforth, B. (1989). The experience of powerlessness in organizations. *Organiza-tional Behavior and Human Decision Processes, 43,* 207–242.

Ashforth, B. (1994). Petty tyranny in organizations. *Human Relations, 47,* 755–777.

Ashton, M. C., Lee, K., & Son, C. (2000). Honesty as the sixth factor of personality: Correlations with Machiavellianism, primary psychopathy, and social adroit-ness. *European Journal of Personality, 14,* 359–368.

Australian Institute of Criminology. (2002). *International data on crime.* Harcourt Inc. Retrieved February 1, 2002, from http://www.google.com?search?hl=en&q+international+data+on+crime

Bandura, A. (1973). *Aggression: Social learning analysis.* Englewood Cliffs, NJ: Prentice-Hall.

Barling, J. (1996). The prediction, psychological experience and consequences of workplace violence. In G. VandenBos & E. Q. Bulatao (Eds.), *Violence on the job:*

*Identifying risks and developing solutions* (pp. 129–150). Washington, DC: American Psychological Association.

Baron, R., & Neuman, J. (1996). Workplace violence and workplace aggression: Evidence on their relative frequency and potential causes. *Aggressive Behaviour, 22,* 161–173.

Baumeister, R. F., Smart, L., & Boden, J. M. (1996). Retaliation of threatened egotism to violence and aggression. The dark side of high self-esteem. *Psychological Review 103,* 5–33.

Bennett, R. J. (1998). Perceived powerlessness as a cause of employee deviance. In R. Griffin, A. O'Leary-Kelly, & J. Collins (Eds.), *Dysfunctional behavior in organizations: Violent and deviant behavior 23(A)* (pp. 221–239). Stamford, CT : JAI.

Bennett, R. J., & Robinson, S. L. (1998, August). *Are part-timers more deviant than full-timers?* Paper presented at the meeting of the Academy of Management, San Diego, CA.

Bennett, R. J., & Robinson, S. L. (2000). The development of a measure of workplace deviance. *Journal of Applied Psychology, 85,* 349–360.

Bennett, R. J., & Stamper, C. L. (2001). Corporate citizenship and deviancy: A study of discretionary work behavior. In C. Galbraith & M. Ryan (Eds.), *International research in the business disciplines: Strategies and organizations in transition 3* (pp. 269–290). Amsterdam: Elsevier Science.

Bensimon, H. (1997). What to do about anger in the workplace. *Training and Development,* 28–32.

Berkowitz, L. (1993). *Aggression: Its causes, consequences and control.* New York: McGraw-Hill.

Beugre, C. D. (1998). Understanding organizational insider-perpetrated workplace aggression: An integrative model. *Research in the Sociology of Organizations, 15,* 163–196.

Bies, R. J. (2001). Interactional (in)justice: The sacred and the profane. In J. Greenberg & R. Cropanzano (Eds.), *Advances in organizational justice* (pp. 89–118). Stanford, CA: Stanford University Press.

Bies, R. J., & Tripp, T. M. (1996). Beyond distrust : "Getting even" and the need for revenge. In R. M. Kramer & T. R. Tyler (Eds.), *Trust in organizations* (pp. 246–260). Newbury Park, CA: Sage.

Bies, R. J., & Tripp, T. M. (1998). Revenge in organizations: The good, the bad, and the ugly. In R. W. Griffin, A. O'Leary-Kelly, & J. M. Collins (Eds.), *Dysfunctional behavior in organizations: Violent and deviant behavior* (pp. 221–239). Stamford, CT: JAI.

Bies, R.J., Tripp, T. M., & Kramer, R. M. (1997). At the breaking point: Cognitive and social dynamics of revenge in organizations. In R. A. Giacalone & J. Greenberg (Eds.), *Antisocial behavior in organizations* (pp. 18–36). Thousand Oaks, CA: Sage.

Bing, M. N., Burroughs, S. M., Whanger, J. C., Green, P. D., & James, L. R. (2002). *The integrative model of personality assessment for aggression: Implications for personnel selection and predicting deviant workplace behavior.* Unpublished manuscript, University of Tennessee, Knoxville.

Bjorkqvist, K., Osterman, K., & Hjelt-Back, M. (1994). Aggression among university employees. *Aggressive Behavior, 20*, 173–184.

Bronikowski, L. (2002). Esniff.com sniffs out cyberslacking. *ColoradoBiz, 27*(11), 46.

Burroughs, S. M. (1999). *Using a model contingent fairness to explain workplace deviance: The role of situational stimuli, dispositional aggressiveness, and organizational injustice.* Unpublished manuscript.

Burroughs, S. M. (2001). *The role of dispositional aggressiveness and organizational injustice on deviant workplace behavior.* Unpublished doctoral dissertation, University of Tennessee, Knoxville.

Burroughs, S. M., Bing, M. N., & James, L. R (1999, April). Reconsidering how to measure employee reliability: An empirical comparison of self-report and conditional reasoning methodologies. In S. Burroughs & L. Williams (Chairpersons), *New developments using conditional reasoning to measure human reliability.* Symposium presented at the meeting of the Society for Industrial and Organizational Psychology, Atlanta, GA.

Burroughs, S. M., LeBreton, J. M., Bing, M. N., & James, L. R. (2000, April). *Validity evidence for the conditional reasoning test of employee aggression.* Paper presented at the meeting of the Society for Industrial and Organizational Psychology, New Orleans, LA.

Burroughs, S. M., Woehr, D. J., Bing, M. N., & McIntyre, M. D. (2001, April). *Factor analytic and construct validity evidence for peer reports of organizational deviance.* Paper presented at the meeting of the Society for Organizational and Industrial Psychologists, San Diego, CA.

Buss, D. (1993, April). Ways to curtail employee theft. *Nation's Business*, 36–38.

Chen, P. Y., & Spector, P. E. (1992). Relationship of work stressors with aggression withdrawal, theft and substance use: An exploratory study. *Journal of Occupation and Organizational Psychology, 65*, 177–184.

Cialdini, R. B. (1996). Social influence and the triple tumor structure of organizational dishonesty. In D. M. Messick & A. E. Tenbrunsel (Eds.), *Codes of conduct: Behavioral research into business ethics* (pp. 44–56). New York: Russell Sage.

Coleman, J. W. (1985). *The criminal elite: The sociology of white collar crime.* New York: The Free Press.

Cullen, M. J., & Ones, D. S. (2001, April). *The role of conscientiousness and neuroticism in predicting police corruption.* Paper presented at the meeting of the Society for Industrial and Organizational Psychology, San Diego, CA.

Dalton, D. R., Daily, C. M., & Wimbush, J. C. (1997). Collecting "sensitive" data in business ethics research: A case for the unmatched block technique. *Journal of Business Ethics, 116*, 1049–1057.

Dalton, D. R., Wimbush, J. C., & Daily, C. M. (1994). Using the unmatched count technique (UCT) to estimate base-rates for sensitive behavior. *Personnel Psychology, 47*, 817–828.

Deffenbacher, J. L. (1992). Trait anger: Theory, findings, and implications. In C. D. Spielberger & J. N. Butcher (Eds.), *Advances in personality assessment* (Vol. 9, pp. 177–201). Hillsdale, NJ: Lawrence Erlbaum Associates.

Dehler, G. E., & Welsh, M. A. (1998). Problematizing deviance in contemporary organizations: A critical perspective. In R. W. Griffin, A. O'Leary-Kelly, & J. M. Collins (Eds.), *Dysfunctional behavior in organizations: Violent and deviant behavior, 23(A)* (pp. 241–269). Stamford, CT: JAI.

Deutsch-Salamon, S., & Robinson, S. L. (2002, August). *Does trust climate deter workplace deviance? An organizational level analysis.* Paper presented at the Academy of Management annual meeting, Denver, CO.

DiBattista, R. A. (1991). Creating new approaches to recognize and deter sabotage. *Public Personnel Management, 20,* 347–352.

Diener, E., Smith, H., & Fujita, F. (1995). The personality structure of affect. *Journal of Personality and Social Psychology, 69,* (1) 130–141.

Dietz, J., & Nolan, N. (2001). *Workplace homicides: A state-level study.* Paper presented at the 2001 Academy of Management Conference, Washington, DC.

Dietz, J., Robinson, S. L., Folger, R., Baron, R., & Schultz, M. (2002). *When colleagues become violent: Employee threats as a function of societal violence and organizational justice.* Unpublished manuscript.

Dirks, K. T., & Ferrin, D. L. (in press). Trust in leadership: Meta-analytic findings and implications for organizational research. *Journal of Applied Psychology.*

Einarsen, S. (2000). Harassment and bullying at work: A review of the Scandinavian approach. *Aggression and Violent Behavior: A Review Journal, 5,* (4) 379–401.

Einarsen, S., Raknes, S., & Matthiesen. P. (1994). Bullying and harassment at work and their relationships to work environment quality: An exploratory study. *European Work and Organizational Psychology, 4,* (4) 381–401.

Eisenberger, R., Lynch, P., & Rohdieck, S. (1999). *Biocultural influences on revenge.* Unpublished manuscript, University of Delaware, Newark.

Felson, R. B., & Steadman, H. J. (1983). Situational factors in disputes leading to criminal violence. *Criminology, 21,* 59–74.

Fishbein, M., & Ajzen, I. ( 1975 ). *Belief, attitude, intention and behavior.* Reading, MA: Addison-Wesley.

Fisher, C. D., & Locke, E. A. (1992). The new look in job satisfaction research and theory. In C. Cranny, P. Smith, & E. Stone (Eds.), *Job satisfaction: How people feel about their jobs and how it affects their performance* (pp. 165–194). New York: Lexington.

Folger, R., & Baron, R. A. (1996). Violence and hostility at work: A model of reactions to perceived injustice. In G. R. VandenBos & E. Q. Bulatao (Eds.), *Violence on the job: Identifying risks and developing solutions* (pp. 51–85). Washington, DC: American Psychological Association.

Fox, S., & Spector, P. E. (1999). A model of work frustration—aggression. *Journal of Organizational Behavior, 20,* 915–931.

Fox, S., Spector, P. E., & Miles, D. (2001). Counterproductive work behavior (CWB) in response to job stressors and organizational justice: Some mediator and moderator tests for autonomy and emotions. *Journal of Vocational Behavior, 59,* 1–19.

Galperin, B. L. (2001). *The development of a measure of workplace constructive deviance.* Unpublished manuscript, Concordia University, Montreal, Canada.

Giacalone, R. A., & Greenberg, J. (1997). *Antisocial behavior in organizations.* Thousand Oaks, CA: Sage.

Giacalone, R. A., Riordan, C. A., & Rosenfeld, P. (1997). In R. Giacalone & J. Greenberg (Eds.), *Antisocial behavior in organizations* (pp. 109–129). Thousand Oaks, CA: Sage.

Gilligan, J. (1996). *Violence: Reflections on a national epidemic.* New York: Vintage.

Glomb, T. M. (2001). *Workplace aggression: Antecedents, behavioral components and consequences.* Manuscript under review, University of Minnesota, Minneapolis.

Greenberg, J. (1987). Reactions to procedural injustice in payment distributions: Do the means justify the ends? *Journal of Applied Psychology, 72,* 55–61.

Greenberg, J. (1990). Employee theft as a reaction to underpayment inequity: The hidden cost of pay cuts. *Journal of Applied Psychology, 75,* (5) 561–568.

Greenberg, J. (1993). Stealing in the name of justice: Informational and interpersonal moderators of theft reactions to underpayment inequity. *Organizational Behavior and Human Decision Processes, 54,* 81–103.

Greenberg, J. (1998). The cognitive geometry of employee theft: Negotiating "the line" between taking and stealing. Dysfunctional behavior in organizations: Non-violent dysfunctional behavior. In R. W. Griffin, A. O'Leary-Kelly, & J. M. Collins, (Eds.), *Monographs in organizational behavior and industrial relations, 23(B)* (pp. 147–193). Stamford CT: JAI.

Greenberg, J., & Alge, B. (1998). Aggressive reactions to workplace injustice. In R. W. Griffin, A. O'Leary-Kelly, & J. Collins (Eds.), *Dysfunctional behavior in organizations: 1. Violent behavior in organizations* (pp. 119–145). Greenwich, CT: JAI.

Greenberg, J., & Scott, K. S. (1996). Why do workers bite the hands that feed them? Employee theft as a social exchange process. In B. M. Staw & L. L. Cummings (Eds.), *Research in organizational behavior, 18* (pp. 111–150). Greenwich, CT: JAI.

Hanisch, K. A., & Hulin, C. L. (1991). General attitudes and organizational withdrawal: An evaluation of a causal model. *Journal of Vocational Behaviour, 39,* 110–128.

Harris, F. R., Wolf, M. M., & Baer, D. M. (1964). Effects of social reinforcement of child behavior. *Young Children, 20,* 8–17.

Hepburn, J. R. (1973). Violent behavior in interpersonal relationships. *Sociological Quarterly, 14,* 419–429.

Hofstede, G. H. (1980). *Culture's consequences: International differences in work-related values.* Beverly Hills, CA: Sage.

Hogan, J., & Hogan, R. (1989). How to measure employee reliability. *Journal of Applied Psychology, 74,* 273–279.

Hoobler, J. M., & Tepper, B. J. (2001, August). *An examination of the causal relationships between abusive supervision and subordinates' attitudes, distress and performance.* Paper presented at the meeting of the Academy of Management, Washington, DC.

Jagatic, K., & Keashly, L. (2001). Negative interactions with faculty: Graduate student experiences. *Conflict Management in Higher Education Report, 1,* (3) 187–195.

James, L. R. (1998). Measurement of personality via conditional reasoning. *Organizational Research Methods, 1, (2) 131–163.*

Johnson, A. (2000). "Fear and loathing on the job," *MSNBC Online.* Retrieved 9/4/00 from http://www.msnbc.com/news/default.asp?sept=340

Jones, J. W. (1981). Attitudinal correlates of employee theft of drugs and hospital supplies among nursing personnel. *Nursing Research, 30*(6), 349–350.

Jones, T. M., & Gautschi, F. H. III. (1988). Will the ethics of business change? A survey of future executives. *Journal of Business Ethics, 7,* 231–248.

Kaufman, G. (1996). *The psychology of shame* (2nd ed.). New York: Springer.

Keashly, L., & Jagatic, K. (2000, August). *The nature, extent, and impact of emotional abuse in the workplace: Results of a statewide survey.* Paper presented at the meeting of the Academy of Management, Toronto, Ontario, Canada.

Keashly, L., & Jagatic, K. (in press). By any other name: American perspectives on workplace bullying. In S. Einarsen, H. Hoel, D. Zapf, & C. Cooper (Eds.), *Bullying and emotional abuse at work: International perspectives on research and practice.* London: Taylor Francis.

Kinney, J. A. (1995). *Violence at work.* Englewood Cliffs, NJ: Prentice-Hall.

Kinney, J. A., & Johnson, D. L. (1993). *Breaking point: The workplace violence epidemic and what to do about it.* Chicago: National Safe Workplace Institute.

Kruglanski, A. (1970). Attributing trustworthiness in supervisor-worker relations. *Journal of Experimental Social Psychology, 6,* 214–232.

Lam, T. (1993, May 11). Stifling military style lingers in the postal system. *Detroit Free Press,* pp. 1B–6B.

Lawrence, T., & Robinson, S. L. (2001). *Workplace deviance as resistance to power.* Unpublished manuscript.

Lee, K., Ashton, M. C., & Shin, K. (2001, August). *Personality correlates of workplace antisocial behavior.* Paper presented at the meeting of the Academy of Management, Washington, DC.

Leonard, B. (1999). Cyberventing. *HR Magazine, 44*(12), 34–39.

Lim, V. K. G., Loo, G. L., & Teo, T. S. H. (2001, August). *Perceived injustice, neutralization and cyberloafing at the workplace.* Paper presented at the meeting of the Academy of Management, Washington, DC.

Mastrangelo, P., Everton, W., & Jolton, J. (2001). *Computer misuse in the workplace.* Unpublished manuscript, University of Baltimore, Baltimore.

McLean Parks, J., & Kidder, D. L. (1994). "Till death us do part …" Changing work relationships in the 1990s. In C. L. Cooper & D. M. Rousseau (Eds.), *Trends in organizational behavior 1* (pp. 111–113). New York: Wiley.

Mendoza, M. (2000). Tech executives say government little help in fighting cybercrime. The Augusta Chronicle (online version). Retrieved 9/20/01 form http://www.augustachronicle.com/stories/040900/tee_124-1776.shtml

Morgan, G. (1986). *Images of organization.* Newbury Park, CA: Sage.

Morrison, A. (1996). *The culture of shame.* New York: Ballantine.

Nardone, T. J. (1986, February). Part-time workers: Who are they? *Monthly Labor Review,* 13–18.

Neuman, J. H., & Baron, R. A. (1997). Aggression in the workplace. In R. Giacalone & J. Greenberg (Eds.), *Antisocial behavior in organizations* (pp. 37–57). Thousand Oaks, CA: Sage.

O'Leary-Kelly, A., Griffin, R., & Glew, D. (1996). Organization-motivated aggression: A research framework. *Academy of Management Review, 21*, 225–253.

O'Leary-Kelly, A., Paetzold, R., & Griffin, R. (2000). Sexual harassment as aggressive behavior: An actor-based perspective. *Academy of Management Review, 25*, 372–388.

Olweus, D. (1978). *Aggression in the schools: Bullies and whipping boys.* Washington, DC: Hemisphere Wiley.

Olweus, D. (1993). *Bullying at school. What we know and what we can do.* Oxford, England: Basil Blackwell.

Ones, D. S., Viswesvaran, C., & Schmidt, F. L. (1993). Comprehensive meta-analysis of integrity test validities: Findings and implications for personnel selection and theories of job performance. *Journal of Applied Psychology, 78*(4), 679–703.

Pearson, C. (1998). Organizations as targets and triggers of violence: Framing rational explanations for dramatic organizational deviance. In S. Bacharach (Ed.), *Research in the sociology of organizations, 15* (pp. 197–223). Greenwich, CT: JAI.

Pearson, C. M., Andersson, L. M., & Porath, C. (1999, August). *Assessing and attacking workplace incivility.* Paper presented at the meeting of the Academy of Management, Chicago.

Pearson, C. M., Andersson, L. M., & Wegner, J. W. (in press). When workers flout convention: A study of workplace incivility. *Human Relations.*

Perlow, R., & Latham, L. L. (1993). The relationship of client abuse and locus of control and gender: A longitudinal study in mental retardation facilities. *Journal of Applied Personality, 78*(5), 831–834.

Poulson, C. (2001). *Shame: The root of violence.* Paper presented at the standing conference on organizational symbolism: Organization(s), institutions and violence, Dublin, Ireland.

Puffer, S. M. (1987). Prosocial behavior, non-compliant behavior, and work performance among commission salespeople. *Journal of Applied Psychology, 72*(4), 615–621.

Rayner, C. (1997). Incidence of workplace bullying. *Journal of Community and Applied Social Psychology, 7*(3), 199–208.

Rayner, C. (2000). *Bullying and harassment at work: Summary of findings.* Paper presented at the meeting of the Academy of Management, Toronto, Ontario, Canada.

Reichers, A. E., & Schneider, B. (1990). Climate and culture: Life cycles of constructs. In B. Schneider (Ed.), *Organizational climate and culture* (pp. 5–39). San Francisco: Jossey-Bass.

Robinson, S. L., & Bennett, R. J. (1995). A typology of deviant workplace behaviors: A multidimensional scaling study. *Academy of Management Journal, 38*, 555–572.

Robinson, S. L., & Greenberg, J. (1998). Employees behaving badly: Dimensions, determinants, and dilemmas in the study of workplace deviance. In C. L. Cooper & D. M. Rousseau (Eds.), *Trends in organizational behavior, 5* (pp. 1–30). New York: Wiley.

Robinson, S. L., & O'Leary-Kelly, A. M. (1998). Monkey see, monkey do: The influence of work groups on the antisocial behavior of employees. *Academy of Management Journal, 41,* 658–672.

Rosse, J. G. (1988). Relations among lateness, absence, and turnover: Is there a progression of withdrawal? *Human Relations, 41*(7), 517–531.

Rosse, J. G., & Hulin, C. L. (1985). Adaptation to work: An analysis of employee
health, withdrawal, and change. *Organizational Behavior and Human Decision Processes, 36,* 324–347.

Rotundo, M., & Sackett, P. R. (2001, April). *The relative importance of task, citizenship,
and counterproductive performance to global ratings of performance: A policy-capturing
approach.* Paper presented at the 16th annual conference of the Society for Industrial and Organizational Psychology, San Diego, CA.

Roznowski, M., & Hulin, C. (1992). The scientific merit of valid measures of general
constructs with special reference to job satisfaction and job withdrawal. In C. J.
Cranny, P. C. Smith, & E. F. Stone (Eds.), *Job satisfaction* (pp. 123–163). New York:
Lexington.

Sablynski, C. J., Mitchell, T. C., James, L. R., & Mcintyre, M. D. (2001, August). *Identifying aggressive individuals via conditional reasoning: An experimental study.* Paper
presented at the meeting of the Academy of Management, Washington, DC.

Skarlicki, D. P., & Folger, R. (1997). Retaliation in the workplace: The role of distributive, procedural, and interactional justice. *Journal of Applied Psychology, 82*(3),
434–443.

Skarlicki, D. P., Folger, R., & Tesluk, P. (1999). Personality as a moderator in the relationship between fairness and retaliation. *Academy of Management Journal, 42*(1),
100–108.

Slora, K. B., Joy, D. S., & Terris, W. (1991). Personnel selection to control employee violence. *Journal of Business and Psychology, 5*(3), 417–426.

Spector, P. E. (1975). Relationships of organizational frustration with reported behavioral reactions of employees. *Journal of Applied Psychology, 60,* 635–637.

Spector, P. E. (1978). Organizational frustration: A model and review of the literature. *Personnel Psychology, 31,* 815–829.

Spector, P. E. (1997). The role of frustration in antisocial behaviour at work. In R. A.
Giacalone & J. Greenburg (Eds.), *Antisocial behavior in organizations* (pp. 1–17).
Thousand Oaks, CA: Sage.

Spector, P. E., & Fox, S. (in press). An emotion centered model of voluntary work behaviors: Some parallels between counterproductive work behavior (CWB) and
organizational citizenship behavior. *Human Resources Management Review.*

Spector, P. E., & O'Connell, B. J. (1994). The contribution of personality traits, negative affectivity, locus of control and Type A to the subsequent reports of job stressors and job strains. *Journal of Occupational and Organizational Psychology, 67,* 1–11.

Stamper, C. L., & Van Dyne, L. (2001). Work status and organizational citizenship
behavior: A field study of restaurant employees. *Journal of Organizational Behavior, 22,* 517–536.

Storms, P. L., & Spector, P. E. (1987). Relationships of organizational frustration with reported behavioral reactions: The moderating effect of locus of control. *Journal of Occupational Psychology, 60*, 227–234.

Stuckless, N., & Goranson, R. (1992). The vengeance scale: Development of a measure of attitudes toward revenge. *Journal of Social Behavior and Personality, 7*(1), 25–42.

Taj, K. (1981, Spring). Crime control: Japanese society's "Internal Policeman" helps keep the public safe. *Trapedia International.* Retrieved February 10, 2002, from http://www.geocities.com/SoHo/Gallery/2710/crime.html

Tangney, J. P., Wagner, P. E., Hill-Barlow, D., Marschall, D. E., & Gramzow, R. (1996). Relation of shame and guilt to constructive versus destructive responses to anger across the lifespan. *Journal of Personality and Social Psychology, 70*, 797–809.

Terris, W., & Jones, J. (1982). Psychological factors related to employees' theft in the convenience store industry. *Psychological Reports, 51*, 1219–1238.

Trevino, L. K. (1986). Ethical decision making in organizations: A person–situation interactions model. *Academy of Management Review, 11*(3), 601–617.

Triandis, H. C. (1995). *Individualism and collectivism.* Boulder, CO: Westview.

Tripp, T. M., & Bies, R. J. (1997). What's good about revenge? The avenger's perspective. In R. J. Lewicki, R. J. Bies, & B. H. Sheppard (Eds.), *Research on negotiation in organizations* (Vol. 6, pp. 145–160). Greenwich, CT: JAI.

VandenBos, G. R., & Bulatao, E. Q. (Eds.). (1996). *Violence on the job: Identifying risks and developing solutions.* Washington, DC: American Psychological Association.

Vardi, Y., & Weiner, Y. (1996). Misbehavior in organizations: A motivational framework. *Organizational Science, 7*(2), 151–165.

Warchol, G. (1998). *Workplace violence, 1992–1996* (Bureau of Justice Statistics Special Report). Washington, DC: U.S. Department of Justice.

Wheeler, L., & Reis, H. (1991). Self-recording of everyday life events: Origins, types and uses. *Journal of Personality, 59*, 339–354.

Wilkinson, R. G. (1999). *Unhealthy societies: The afflictions of inequality.* London: Routledge.

Youngblood, S. A., Trevino, L. K., & Favia, M. (1992). Reaction to unjust dismissal and third-party dispute resolution: A justice framework. *Employee Rights and Responsibilities Journal, 4*, 283–307.

# 8

# Conflicting Stories: The State of the Science of Conflict

Kurt T. Dirks
*Washington University*

Judi McLean Parks
*Washington University*

It makes me nervous when someone says, "I agree with everything you say." Not even I agree with everything I say.

—Jeremy Rifkin (as quoted in van Biema, 1988, p. W13)

Conflict is, perhaps, one of, if not *the* most pervasive phenomena of organizational life. Although organizations are predicated on the achievement of a collective goal, they inherently foster conflict. The individual's attempt to define the collective goal and the means to achieve that goal bring personal agendas to pursue, as well as different personal values and work styles, all the while working under incentive systems that tend to generate competition, rather than cooperation. In other words, organizations provide the impetus for conflict, and in turn, they incubate that conflict.

It would be difficult to deny the importance of conflict, and hence of conflict research. Conflict has captured the attention of researchers from a variety of disciplines, including anthropology, economics, organizational behavior, political science, social psychology, and sociology. A recent search on only the electronic database, *PsychINFO,* produced over 30,000 references to conflict.

The goal of this chapter is to review some of the theory and research on the topic of organizational conflict, and to point out fruitful areas for future research. Our reviews are necessarily selective, and reflect what we believe to be the most important or potentially important paths for conflict researchers to follow. Our analysis begins by providing our working definition of conflict, to bound our discussion and to frame our subsequent investigation. This is followed by a discussion of "the way we were"—the historical perspective on conflict research and how it has evolved. Next, we turn our focus to current perspectives on conflict, to address the question of where the research is headed. Finally, we move to where we believe conflict research should go, including an enriched perspective of the relationship between culture and conflict, as well as a discussion of conflict and trust, suggesting future research questions and a model for conflict research as it moves forward.

## SETTING THE STAGE: A DEFINITION

### What Is Conflict?

There have been numerous attempts to define conflict. Early theorists tended to emphasize the competitive and destructive aspects of conflict (Deutsch, 1990). Yet, most perspectives on conflict can be reduced to a simple model of antecedents, processes, and outcomes (Wall & Callister, 1995; see Fig. 8.1). Pondy (1967) conceptualized conflict as a dynamic process between two or more individuals, incorporating five stages of conflict: (a) latent conflict, in which the conditions for conflict are present (although

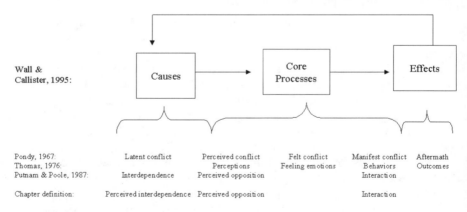

FIG. 8.1   The conflict process and a comparison of conflict definitions.

perhaps not in evidence); (b) perceived conflict, where one or more parties become aware of a conflict (the perception does not have to be accurate); (c) felt conflict, where conflict becomes personalized and the party may feel anxious or even hostile; (d) manifest conflict, where the conflict is enacted through behaviors (such as aggression); and (e) conflict aftermath, or the outcomes of the conflict episode. A few years later, Thomas's (1976) definition specified that conflict is a process that includes perceptions, emotions, behaviors, and outcomes, although he limited his definition to dyads, to avoid encompassing coalitions and political behaviors. Both of these definitions are quite broad, and by including antecedents (Pondy's latent conflict conditions), processes, emotions, behaviors, and outcomes, necessarily limited the focus of research, such that such behaviors and outcomes were frequently "assumed" rather than empirically explored in detail. Consequently, there was less focused effort on, for example, determining what actual factors contribute to latent conflict or what factors may induce the individual to perceive conflict and subsequently take action. In 1987, Putnam and Poole defined conflict as "the interaction of interdependent people who perceive opposition of goals, aims, and values, and who see the other party as potentially interfering with the realization of these goals" (p. 552). This definition narrowed and refined the previous conceptualizations, focusing the conflict definition on three key characteristics that had been part of the previous definitions, albeit perhaps with less clarity and focus (see Fig. 8.1). These defining characteristics were (a) interaction, (b) interdependence, and (c) incompatible goals.

In this chapter, our working definition of conflict is: the interaction of interdependent entities who perceive opposition in goals, aims, and values and who perceive the other entity or entities as potentially interfering with the realization of these goals. Thus we have retained the three key characteristics of interaction, interdependence, and incompatible goals. However, our definition has two important differences from that of Putnam and Poole (1987). First, we incorporate entities rather than restricting our definition of conflict to people. By doing so, we recognize the frequency not only of conflicting people, but of conflicting groups, teams, divisions, departments, and organizations in business. In that sense, we treat each of these entities as if they have the ability to act and engage in behaviors designed to further specific goals. One can argue whether or not groups, teams, organizations, and the like can engage in behaviors, and that our definition risks anthropomorphizing groups and organizations. However, regardless of whether organizations actually think and behave, perceivers *react* to organizations as if they do engage in goal-directed behavior, and may in fact *believe* they do. Our second difference is that our definition makes explicit that conflict can be defined in terms of *perceptions* that the other party can interfere with one's goals. Although perception may have been implied with Putnam and Poole's use of the word "sees," we have made it explicit. We believe this is important because it is perceptions that create the sense of conflict. If one perceives that there is a conflict—that the other party can interfere or reduce one's outcomes—then it is the perception that drives conflict behavior, not the reality that the other party may not be able to interfere or impact outcomes. In this sense, what is perceived becomes a self-fulfilling prophecy, by perhaps altering the first party's behavior in such a way that they other party now feels threatened and a conflict spiral can result. In this sense, then, our definition explicitly returns Pondy's (1967) awareness component to the definition of conflict.

## THE WAY WE WERE: A BRIEF HISTORY OF CONFLICT RESEARCH

As noted earlier, the literature on conflict is enormous, and has attracted the attention of scholars from a variety of disciplines. Yet, as Wall and Callister (1995) noted, most conflict, regardless of the level at which it occurs or the type of conflict, follows a generic format (see Fig. 8.1), with causes, underlying processes, and outcomes. Thus, our selective review of the conflict literature is categorized roughly into two of these three component parts, the antecedents or causes and the conflict process (although we acknowledge that our placement may be somewhat arbitrary, as some factors can clearly impact multiple aspects of this format). We now turn our attention to what we know about the causes of conflict.

### Causes of Conflict

The focus of conflict researchers, for the most part, has not been on determining the causes of conflict (Deutsch, 1990; Wall & Callister, 1995). However, the definition of conflict suggests several potential causes, and empirical and other evidence provides additional cues. Given our definition of conflict, three factors stand out as potential causes of conflict: the *interdependence* of the disputants, with actual or perceived *differences in goals, values, or aims,* who view the other party as potentially *interfering with the attainment* of those goals, values, or aims. These variables set the stage for conflict to emerge.

Pondy (1967) suggested that a primary cause of conflict in organizations arises because of competition over scarce resources as different interested parties or organizational units attempted to allocate and control the resources. How resources are allocated—the rules used for allocation—has been a focus of a significant body of research. When faced with allocation decisions, a number of different rules can be invoked (Deutsch, 1975; Griffith, 1989). Invoking these can resolve a conflict over scarce resources. The rules selected, especially if seen as unfair, however, can themselves become a source of conflict. Among these resource allocation rules are *equity rules*, which specify that allocations should be based on the strength of the parties' cases (i.e., commensurate with their contributions or benefits), *equality rules*, which specify that all parties receive the same allocation, *need rules*, which make allocations to each according to need or deprivation, and *rank rules*, which specify allocations based on status. Equity and equality rules have received the bulk of the empirical attention (e.g. Adams, 1965; Deutsch, 1975; Leventhal, 1976; Pruitt, 1981; Tornblom, Jonsson, & Foa, 1985), with fewer studies addressing the rank and need rules. This body of research suggests that preferences (and hence satisfaction with the results of the rule's application) for one rule or another are impacted by whether resources are being *allocated* or *recovered* (Mannix, Neale, & Northcraft, 1995; McLean Parks, Conlon, Ang, & Bontempo, 1999; Tornblom & Jonsson, 1985), the *attributes* of the resource to be allocated, such as the ease with which the resource can be divided (McLean Parks et al., 1996; Messick, 1993; Young, 1995), one's *culture* (Chen, 1995; McLean Parks et al., 1999), as well as one's "vested" *interests* (egoism, which we discuss shortly in more detail).

Thomas (1992) presented several "structural elements"—parameters of the situation that are static or slow to change—that may influence and regulate conflict episodes and their resolution, suggesting that some of these factors will foster collaboration between the disputants and reduce conflict levels. Several of these factors provide incentives for the formulation of integrative agreements (agreements that expand, rather than divide the pie) in a bargaining context. For example, integrative incentives will be higher when there are high stakes issues, especially when time is not a factor and the issues are clearly defined. Thus we might expect such situations to have less conflict. Similarly, commitment to an overarching goal will also reduce conflict between parties (Sherif, 1958), where we would expect potential disputants to join together to achieve the overarching goal. A positive relationship between the parties, especially when there is an absence of power differences and mutual trust, also provides integrative incentives and the potential for less conflict. Finally, a system that rewards collaboration and holds the expectation of future interactions (Pruitt & Rubin, 1986) will also magnify the integrative potential and decrease conflict.

## The Black Box of Conflict Process: Negotiations and Conflict Resolution Research

Once the conditions for conflict have activated felt conflict, the conflict *process* comes into place. Historically, early research regarding the conflict process examined the negotiation aspects of conflict from the perspectives of economic modeling (e.g., game theory), structural effects, personality and individual differences, and behavioral approaches (see Neale & Bazerman, 1985a). For the purposes of this chapter, we limit our discussion to the cognitive perspective, which we believe may be particularly fruitful. We impose this limitation not only because of space constraints, but also because some approaches, such as the individual difference perspective, may explain little variance (Thompson, 1998) and hence are more limited for our purposes (e.g., Bazerman et al., 2000; Neale & Bazerman, 1985a).

*The Cognitive Perspective on Negotiations.*     The cognitive perspective on bargaining and negotiations primarily has explored why disputants define the conflict situation as they do, and how the cognitive biases that form the foundation of these assessments impact the process and outcomes of a conflict situation. This line of research (see review by Neale & Bazerman, 1985a) views negotiations as a judgment process in which judgments and disputant choices are impacted by cognitive biases, five of which are briefly reviewed here: (a) the anchoring effect, (b) the fixed pie bias, (c) the framing effect, (d) the overconfidence effect, and (e) egocentric biases.

The first of these biases is the *anchoring effect*, where disputants anchor on a reference point (which may be relevant or irrelevant) and adjust up or down from that value in creating their expectations or setting aspiration levels (e.g., Northcraft & Neale, 1987; Thompson, 1995). Thus anchors that reduce the perceived bargaining range may result in more contentious and protracted conflicts as well as higher impasse rates. In addition, higher opening offers form higher anchors for the negotiation, which tends to result in higher individual outcomes (Raiffa, 1982). In fact, initial offers can be correlated as high as .85 with the final outcomes of a negotiation (Galinsky & Mussweiler, 2000), suggesting the potential importance of the initial offer in a negotiation. Yet these high anchors can create unrealistically high opening offers or high aspirations. When combined with the overconfidence bias (see later), these high aspirations can lead to more stalemates and impasses.

The second cognitive bias is the *fixed pie bias*, where disputants assume that their interests are directly opposed to those of their counterparts. In other words, they assume that the size of the bargaining pie is fixed—what one wins, the other necessarily loses. Consequently the disputants may miss opportunities to make beneficial trade-offs (Bazerman, 1983; Bazerman, Magliozzi, & Neale, 1985; Thompson & Hastie, 1990), reducing potential value that could be gained from the negotiation. The pervasiveness of the fixed pie bias is striking. Thompson (1998) estimated that between 67% and 80% of negotiators fall prey to the fixed pie bias and throw value away, despite experience levels and even knowledge of the fixed pie bias. Believing themselves in a win–lose situation, fixed pie negotiators are likely to be more contentious and intransigent, fearing that any concession is tantamount to a loss of value to one's own position.

The third cognitive bias is the *framing effect*, where losses—cognitively perceived as more painful than equivalent gains are pleasurable—result in the disputants being risk seeking in the domain of losses and risk averse in the domain of gains. Hence, disputants who view a situation in terms of what they have to *lose* will be more likely to go to impasse (Bazerman & Neale, 1983) and are less successful and less concessionary (e.g., Bazerman et al., 1985; Bottom & Studt, 1993) than their counterparts who are positively framed.

The *overconfidence effect* results in disputants who are overconfident and optimistic about their potential outcomes. When disputants believe that their offer is more likely to be accepted, their reservation point is likely to become more extreme and they will be less willing to compromise (Bazerman, 1998). Believing that the negotiated outcome is more likely to favor themselves (Bazerman, Moore, & Gillespie, 1999; Lim 1997), disputant overconfidence can result in less concessionary behavior and lower performance (Neale & Bazerman, 1985b). Farber and Bazerman (1986) found that both disputants involved in a third-party dispute resolution process believed that the neutral third party would be more likely to decide in their favor (a logical impossibility), suggesting a higher potential for unreasonable demands and expectations by the disputants. Overconfidence is so pervasive that it even invades the judgments of experts in their fields of expertise (Russo & Schoemaker, 1989).

More recent research has explored the *egocentric bias* whereby disputants—despite the fact that they may believe themselves to be "objective"—tend to overweight views that favor their own position, resulting in a motivational bias (Babcock & Lowenstein, 1997; Diekmann, Samuels, Ross, & Bazerman, 1997). We have all been in the situation where we have tried to determine a fair rule for splitting a restaurant check. At dinner during professional meetings, the faculty member who ordered the most expensive meal may suggest splitting the check equally among all diners. The dean, who ate only a salad and soup, is likely to ask for separate checks. The graduate student may feel that his or her meal should be "absorbed" by the relatively more well off faculty member and dean. Both the faculty member and the graduate student may believe that the dean, as ranking member of the party, should pick up the check. Each of these allocation rules has some justification in "fairness"—equality, equity, need, and rank rules all have their proponents under some circumstances. Yet our tendency to be egocentric biases our judgment such that we believe what is fair is the rule that implicitly favors our position. The faculty prefers an equality rule (because he or she would like to diffuse the cost of an expensive meal), the dean prefers an equity rule (because he or she did not eat very much), and the poverty-stricken graduate student prefers a need rule. The lower status faculty member and graduate student may also subscribe to a rank rule. Thus, when disputants try to agree on a fair solution, their perceptions of what is fair are likely to be egocentrically biased. The egocentric bias is especially strong when faced with ambiguous information (e.g., Babcock & Olson, 1992), which can be more easily interpreted subjectively than less ambiguous information. Yet, even when disputants are aware of the potential for an egocentric bias or know the opposing view, they still have a tendency to act egocentrically (Babcock, Loewenstein, Issacharoff, & Camerer, 1995). The more one's view is egocentric, the more difficult the dispute will be to resolve (e.g., Camerer & Lowenstein, 1993; Thompson & Lowenstein, 1992). Egocentric biases even appear in assessments of our own behaviors when compared to others.

## Summary

The research on negotiations and conflict resolution has provided insight into what goes on "inside the black box" of the *process* in a conflict situation, as well as in determining some of the antecedents of conflict. We believe that the research on cognitive biases has been particularly important in the conflict and negotiation domain. Cognitive biases may help us understand how disputants view the situation that creates or activates a conflict situation. In addition, cognitive biases may impact one's willingness to make concessions or to go to impasse, making the disputant more or less cooperative or more or less competitive in their tactics and strategies. We now shift our attention from the historical research on conflict and negotiation and conflict resolution to the current state of the research—the way we are.

## THE WAY WE ARE: CONFLICT RESEARCH

Although conflict research interest has, perhaps, waned in terms of exploring the structural causes of conflict, the research on negotiations, including the cognitive perspective just reviewed, is continuing to expand our knowledge base. In this section, we explore current research trends. We first turn our attention to the recent surge of interest in the impact of culture. Then we examine research exploring the types of conflict, which attempts to unravel the anomalies of the past in terms of when conflict is beneficial and when it is detrimental.

## Culture and Conflict

One's culture—the "software of the mind" (Hofstede, 1996)—will affect conflict and the conflict resolution process in a variety of ways. Culture, which determines what we value and disvalue, will impact preferences for given outcomes. Culture also creates "right" ways of doing things, so will also impact the nature of the process through which conflicts are resolved. In other words, culture is likely to affect both the content and the process of conflict.

Wall and Callister (1995) noted that parties from different cultures value conflict itself quite differently, with some cultures comfortable with conflict, even to the point of believing it to be beneficial (e.g., many Western, individualistic cultures such as the United States and Canada). In contrast, other cultures regard conflict itself as pejorative and to be avoided at all costs (e.g., many Eastern, collectivist cultures, such as Japan and Korea). As a consequence, conflict—at least manifest conflict—may be more apparent in individualistic cultures than in collectivist cultures.

Crossing cultures, where disputants represent different cultures and hold different cultural values, is also quite likely to engender conflict. As noted by Tinsley, Curhan, and Kwak (1999), resolving disputes across cultures bears some similarity to dancing when one person dances a waltz and another a tango. Cultural differences impact the assumptions and expectations that each party brings to the table, and may result in a particularly difficult conflict resolution process. Although we know that people negotiating from *within* a culture frequently leave unclaimed value, those negotiating *across* cultures are likely to leave even more unclaimed value (Brett, 2000). For example, Brett and Okumura (1998) found that Japanese and American intercultural negotiation dyads reached lower joint outcomes than intra-cultural dyads (American–American and Japanese–Japanese), at least in part because those involved in intercultural negotiations more frequently failed to understand the priorities of the other culture.

The cross-cultural negotiation research domain predominantly has suggested that cultural differences in negotiations can be conceptualized along four basic dimensions: individualism–collectivism, power distance, communication context, and conception of time (Bazerman et al., 2000), as well as risk preferences (uncertainty avoidance). Individualism–collectivism is a cultural dimension that captures the degree to which members of a culture place emphasis on valuing the individual or the collective. For an individualist, a key goal in the negotiation process may be to maximize one's own gain, and one identifies as an independent individual. In contrast, collectivist cultures are more likely to find their identity in the interdependent social collective and to emphasize the welfare of the group in setting negotiation goals. Consistent with American individualism, Brett and Okumura (1998) found that American disputants focused on their own self-interest, more so than the more collectivist Japanese disputants. Lewicki and Robinson (1998) found, consistent with the goals of individualism, that Americans are more accepting of competitive bargaining tactics than other, less individualistic nationalities. Yet, collectivist cultures tend to exhibit a stronger in-group favoritism bias, such that when group identity boundaries are salient, collectivists become more competitive than individualists (Espinoza & Garcia, 1985), especially when they believe their identity group to be in the minority.

Power distance—a cultural dimension that captures the extent to which members of a culture are comfortable with power differences—also impacts the negotiations in the intercultural dyads. At a very basic level, we would expect to see fewer conflicts in high power distance cultures, where the norms for low-status members is to avoid challenging high-status members (Brett, 2000). In high power distance cultures, within rank conflicts are more likely to be deferred to a superior to resolve (Leung, 1987). In low power distance cultures, disputants are more likely to challenge others, regardless of their status. From a power distance perspective, Americans primarily viewed their power in terms of their ability to leave the bargaining table, whereas the Japanese viewed their source of power in the negotiation as residing in their role assignments (Brett & Okumura, 1998).

Differences in risk perceptions also vary by culture. Although there may not be differences in actual risk *judgments* by nationality, those from different countries, and hence different cultures, do weigh the *elements* of risk differently (Bontempo, Bottom, & Weber, 1997). In general, Bontempo et al. (1997) found that cultures varied in the relative emphasis that was given in risk assessments to the fear of failure and to the desire to succeed (losses vs. gains), such that the impact of the gain frame in promoting risk aversion was mitigated in Eastern cultures. In addition, whereas the *probability* of loss had a greater impact on risk perceptions in Western cultures, it was the *magnitude* of the potential loss that impacted risk for Eastern cultures (Bontempo et al., 1997). Thus the differences in cultural risk preferences and assessments may be important in conflict resolution, as these differences may enable disputants to capitalize on their *differences* (e.g., by writing contingent contracts, essentially "betting" that their own risk assessment is correct) rather than following the more conventional wisdom of relying on commonalities to facilitate conflict resolution (e.g., Bontempo et al., 1997).

Different cultures also have distinctly different styles of communicating (Hall, 1973). In high-context cultures, meaning relies heavily on "reading between the lines," or understanding what is said through the context of the situation. In contrast, in low-context cultures, meaning is explicitly delineated—what you say is what you mean. Even with the 20–20 vision of hindsight, one wonders what role communication style may have played in the September 11, 2001 terrorist attack on the World Trade Center in New York City. In the 3 years before the terrorist attack, the United States and Taliban leaders met to discuss bringing the terrorist Osama bin Laden to justice. According to former CIA station chief Milton Bearden (Ottaway & Stephens, 2001), "We never heard what they were trying to say.... We had no common language. Ours was, 'Give up bin Laden.' They were saying, 'Do something to help us give him up.'" (p. A01). When the Taliban publicly stated that they no longer knew where bin Laden was, the low-context United States interpreted it as an effort to evade responsibility for turning him over. However, a more high-context interpretation of the statements suggests that the Taliban more than once set up bin Laden for capture by the United States. Bearden noted (Ottaway & Stephens, 2001), "Every time the Afghans said, 'He's lost again,' they are saying something. They are saying, 'He's no longer under our protection'... They thought they were signaling us subtly, and we don't do signals" (p. A01). High-context cultures communicate using signals, yet low-context cultures apparently don't "do" signals, potentially with disastrous results.

By exploring the impact of cultural differences on conflict, this research is beginning to expand our knowledge of its impact both on the process of negotiation and conflict resolution and on the parties' preferences for given outcomes, as well as setting up the conditions for conflict in the first place. We now turn our attention to the second area of current research that we address, the different types of conflict.

## The Nature of the Conflict: Current Research Provides an Answer to "When and Under What Circumstances?"

In the conflict domain, for many years, researchers attempted to determine how conflict could be reduced, eliminated, and resolved in organizations. The implicit assumption was that conflict was detrimental to the organization and that it would be beneficial to reduce or eliminate conflict. More recently, researchers have asked perhaps the better question: When and under what circumstances is conflict detrimental and when and under what circumstances does it benefit the organization? Although historically and frequently naively assumed to be pejorative, conflict is neither good nor bad, but rather, it can be both good *and* bad. Coser (1957) saw conflict as providing the impetus for change and innovation, and avoiding stagnation in organizations. Thus perhaps the practical question becomes that posed by Deutsch (1973, 1983) and others, where we do not attempt to prevent conflict, but rather attempt to manage it in a way that will ameliorate or eliminate its destructive effects while capitalizing on and enhancing its constructive effects.

Until recently, the research results on conflict and its beneficial and detrimental effects have been mixed. These conflicting findings have been at least partially resolved by more recent research, which has demonstrated that conflict is a multidimensional construct (e.g., Jehn, 1992; Pinkley, 1990). Consequently, prior mixed research results may have been a consequence of one type of conflict having a negative impact, whereas another type of conflict had a positive impact. In other words, more recent thinking and empirical research suggests conflict can be a benefit or a detriment. Which it is depends largely on the type of conflict and how it is managed.

Researchers have identified several different types of conflict, albeit with some lack of precision in the delineation of definitions. Unfortunately this situation has resulted in a proliferation of terminology, despite significant conceptual overlap. In particular, the concepts of interpersonal, relational, affective, and emotional conflict appear to be somewhat indistinguishable, as are the concepts of task, debate, substantive, and cognitive conflict.

Simons, Pelled, and Smith (1999) defined task debate as a discussion of task-related differences concerning different approaches to the task at hand; Jehn and Mannix (2001) defined task conflict as an awareness of differences in viewpoints and opinions pertaining to a group task, including conflict about ideas and differences of opinion; Amason (1996) defined cognitive conflict as task-oriented debates focused on perceptual diversity; and Lovelace, Shapiro, and Weingart (2001) measured task disagreement as disagreement concerning issues related to new product development. Admittedly, Simons et al. (1999) differentiated their construct from that of Jehn and her colleagues as more behavioral in focus than perceptual. Yet other researchers have also used a behavioral focus (e.g., Amason, 1996), and in some scales, the behavioral and attitudinal are mixed. Hence we have collapsed them and we subsume these and related constructs under the umbrella of *substantive conflict*.

Affective/emotional conflict is defined as emotional and aimed at personal disputes (Amason, 1996), and measured as personality clashes, degree of anger, degree of friction, and general amount of emotional conflict (Barsade, Ward, Turner, & Sonnenfeld, 2000), or interpersonal clashes characterized by anger, frustration, or other negative feelings (Pelled, Eisenhardt, & Xin, 1999). Relationship conflict is defined as interpersonal tension (Jehn, 1995) and frustration and uneasiness (Walton & Dutton, 1969). Given the conceptual overlap, we subsume affective/emotional and relationship conflict under the rubric of *affective conflict*. Lastly, researchers also discuss process conflict (Jehn, 1997), which appears to be different from either affective or substantive conflict. The three types of conflict are briefly defined in the following.

- *Substantive conflict:* the discussion or awareness of differences in viewpoints and opinions pertaining to a group task, including conflict about ideas, differences in opinion, and differences in preferences or approaches to a task.
- *Affective conflict:* an awareness of personality clashes or interpersonal tension or conflict, characterized by anger, frustration, and uneasiness.
- *Process conflict:* an awareness of controversies about aspects of how task accomplishment will proceed, specifically concerning issues of duty, responsibilities and accountability, and resource delegation (Jehn, 1997; Jehn, Northcraft, & Neale, 1999).

Several authors have suggested a variety of factors, which impact the constructive or destructive effects of conflict on a variety of organizational outcomes, as well as factors that impact conflict levels (see Table 8.1). Key among these is the type of conflict, whether substantive, process, or affective. The predominant predictor of substantive conflict in the studies reviewed was various forms of diversity, which generally can be classified as either *social* (e.g., age, gender, ethnicity, values) or *informational* (e.g., functional area, education, tenure with firm; Jehn, Chadwick, & Thatcher, 1997; Jehn et al., 1999). Although many, if not most of the studies reviewed here were cross-sectional, at least intuitively, the various factors can be classified as antecedents or outcomes (recognizing, of course, that the relationships are quite likely to be reciprocal), and within the "outcome" category, as *task* or *relationally* focused.

*Substantive Conflict.* Substantive conflict, involving different opinions, preferences, or approaches to a task, can be a key defense against group-think (Janus, 1972), where a group's need for consensus and agreement can interfere with the analysis of a problem, resulting in faulty decisions. Among the possible antecedents of substantive conflict, research has generally supported the relationship between different types of diversity and substantive conflict, such as educational (Jehn et al., 1997), value differences (Jehn, 1994; Jehn et al., 1997; Jehn et al., 1999), functional diversity (Lovelace et al., 2001; Pelled et al., 1999), and racial and age diversity (Pelled et al., 1999). The primary relationship identified between diversity and conflict is positive, such that, in general, the more diverse a group, the greater the level of conflict, especially substantive and affective conflict. Top management teams with high levels of trait-based positive affect (a generalized tendency to be enthusiastic, energetic, mentally alert, and determined; Watson, Clark, & Tellegen, 1988) experience lower levels of substantive and affective conflict regardless of their affective diversity. However, substantive and affective conflict are higher in teams with low levels of trait-based positive affect that were affectively diverse (Barsade et al., 2000). In other words, dispositionally "unhappy" teams may find affective variation disconcerting and uncomfortable, resulting in greater substantive and affective conflict. The enthusiastic "Tigger" will be seen by "Eeyores"[1] of the group as downright irritating!

Substantive conflict tends to exhibit a positive relationship with task-related outcomes, such as decision outcomes (Amason, 1996), decision comprehensiveness (Simons et al., 1999), constructive communications (Lovelace et al., 2001), task progress and efficiency (Tjosvold & De Dreu, 1997; Wong, Tjosvold, & Lee, 1992), and performance (Jehn, 1994; Shah & Jehn, 1993), par-

---

[1]Based on A. A. Milne's characters in *Winnie the Pooh*, Tigger is enthusiastic, optimistic, full of energy, and frequently has "bouncy" days. In contrast, Eeyore is slow and ponderous, and generally sad.

## TABLE 8.1
### Selected Empirical Relationships With Conflict Type

| | Substantive Conflict | Process Conflict | Affective Conflict |
|---|---|---|---|
| Amason, 1996 | +Decision outcomes | | |
| Barsade et al., 2000 | +Affectively diverse "unhappy" teams<br>–"Happy" teams<br>– Affectively homogeneous teams | | +Affectively diverse "unhappy" teams<br>–"Happy" teams<br>–Affectively homogeneous teams |
| Bourgeois, 1985 | +Firm financial performance | | |
| Duffy, Shaw, & Stark, 2000 | | | +Satisfaction high task interdependence and low self-esteem attenuate—relationship between conflict and peer evaluations<br>High task interdependence and low self-esteem magnify<br>+Relationship between conflict and absenteeism |
| Earley & Moskowski, 2000 | | | –Performance<br>–Satisfaction<br>–Efficacy of communication<br>–Planning efficacy<br>–Diversity<br>Partial mediation of diversity–performance link |

| Study | | | |
|---|---|---|---|
| Eisenhardt & Bourgeois, 1988<br>Jehn, 1994<br>Jehn, 1995 | + Successful companies<br>+Vvalue diversity<br>–Satisfaction<br>+Performance<br>–Satisfaction<br>–Liking of group members<br>–Intent to remain in group<br>–Performance for routine tasks<br>+Performance for nonroutine tasks | | –Value diversity<br>Satisfaction<br>–Performance<br>–Satisfaction<br>–Liking of group members<br>–Intent to remain in group |
| Jehn, 1997 | | –Performance<br>–Productivity<br>+Intent to leave the group<br>+Perceived unfairness<br>+Role ambiguity | –Performance<br>–Satisfaction |
| Jehn et al., 1997 | +Education diversity<br>–Value congruence | | +Demographic diversity<br>–Value congruence |
| Jehn et al., 1999 | +Value diversity<br>–Commitment<br>–Satisfaction<br>–Intent to remain<br>–Actual performance | +Value diversity<br>–Commitment<br>–Satisfaction<br>–Intent to remain<br>–Actual performance | +Value diversity<br>–Commitment<br>–Satisfaction<br>–Intent to remain<br>–Perceived performance<br>–Actual performance |
| Jehn & Mannix, 2001 | –Trust (static)<br>–Respect (static)<br>–Liking (static)<br>–Cohesiveness (static)<br>–Performance (static) | –Trust (static)<br>–Respect (static)<br>–Cohesiveness (static)<br>–Performance (static) | –Trust (static)<br>–Respect (static)<br>–Cohesiveness (static) |

(continued on next page)

**TABLE 8.1** (*continued*)

| | Substantive Conflict | Process Conflict | Affective Conflict |
|---|---|---|---|
| Lovelace et al., 2001 | +Functional diversity<br>–Innovativeness<br>–Leadership<br>–Free to express doubts<br>+Contentious communications | | |
| Pelled et al., 1999 | +Racial diversity<br>+Age diversity<br>+Functional background diversity | | +Gender diversity<br>+Age diversity<br>+Company tenure diversity<br>+Functional background diversity |
| Shah & Jehn, 1993 | +Performance | –Performance | |
| Simons et al., 1999 | + Decision comprehensiveness<br>+ Interaction with TMT[a] diversity enhances performance | | –Performance |
| Tjosvold & De Dreu, 1997 | + Task progress<br>+Efficiency<br>+Work relationships<br>+Expectations of future collaboration | | |
| Wong, Tjosvold, & Lee, 1992 | +Task progress<br>+Efficiency<br>+Work relationships<br>–Expectations of future collaboration | | |

[a]top management team
[b]Task conflict (debate) magnifies the impact of TMT diversity on firm level performance.

ticularly on nonroutine tasks (Jehn, 1995). However, in some situations, task performance is negatively related to substantive conflict (e.g., Jehn et al., 1999). In her 1995 study, Jehn examined task routineness, finding a negative relationship between substantive conflict and performance when the task was routine. Although not specifically examining task characteristics, Jehn et al. (1999) found a negative relationship in task groups in the household moving industry. Although groups examined ranged from mail sorters to strategic planners, the relative ratios of each in the sample were not given. Arguably, given the industry, the preponderance of the groups in the sample may have been engaged in relatively routine tasks, accounting for the negative relationship between substantive conflict and performance.

In routine tasks, conflict may detract attention from the routine task at hand and result in process loss within the group and poorer performance. In a study of product development teams, Lovelace et al. (2001) examined two very different types of performance measures: constraint adherence (targeted expenditures, etc.) and innovation. They did not find a significant relationship between substantive conflict and constraint adherence. However, they did find that substantive conflict inhibited the expression of doubts and had a negative impact on innovation. With few exceptions, research has explored high versus low levels of substantive conflict and its effects, yet intuitively, one would expect that the relationship is curvilinear—too much substantive conflict may easily paralyze groups and lead to lower performance. Hence it may be the case that moderate levels of substantive conflict are optimal. In one of the few, if not the only study testing this concave relationship, Jehn (1995) found that too much or too little substantive conflict can be detrimental, but moderately high levels of substantive conflict are beneficial, supporting the u-shaped hypothesis.

The impact of substantive conflict on more relational outcomes is generally negative. Specifically, researchers have found that substantive conflict negatively impacts relational outcomes such as trust, respect, cohesiveness (Jehn & Mannix, 2001), liking (Jehn, 1995; Jehn & Mannix, 2001), perceptions of leadership (Lovelace et al., 2001), satisfaction (Jehn, 1994), and intent to stay (Jehn et al., 1999). In other cases, substantive conflict appears to positively impact relational outcomes, including the expectations of future collaborations (closely related to intent to stay) and work relationships (Tjosvold & De Dreu, 1997; Wong et al., 1992). However, it should be noted that the studies by Tjosvold and his colleagues involved Dutch and Chinese samples, where cultural factors may have had an impact on the findings (Tjosvold & De Dreu, 1997; Wong et al., 1992). Alternatively, the construct of constructive controversy—the conflict measure used in the Dutch and Chinese samples—explicitly involves a more positive and respectful tone in terms of its wording, whereas substantive conflict can often lack those factors (Dirks, Shah, & Chervany, 2001), which may also account for the difference in findings.

*Process Conflict.*    Jehn et al. (1999) found a positive relationship between value diversity and process conflict, such that the more diverse a group's values were from each other, the more they were likely to experience conflict over the allocation of responsibilities and resources to complete the task. Unlike substantive conflict, the relationship between process conflict and task outcomes tends to be negative. The greater the disagreement over delegation of responsibility and accountability and procedures for resource allocation, the lower the performance. Specifically, actual (Jehn, 1997; Jehn et al., 1997; Jehn & Mannix, 2001; Shah & Jehn, 1993) and perceived (Jehn et al., 1999) performance and productivity (Jehn, 1997) are all lower when there are higher levels of process conflict. Similarly, process conflict also appears to fracture relational outcomes, increasing the propensity to leave (Jehn, 1997; Jehn et al., 1999), role ambiguity, and perceived unfairness (Jehn, 1997), while decreasing cohesiveness (Jehn & Mannix, 2001), satisfaction, commitment (Jehn et al., 1999), trust, and respect (Jehn & Mannix, 2001). In summary, process conflict appears to be detrimental to both task and relationally focused outcomes.

*Affective Conflict.*    In general, demographic diversity increases levels of affective conflict (Jehn et al., 1997) along gender, age, company tenure, and functional background lines (Pelled et al., 1999). The impact of differences in values, however, is mixed (Jehn, 1994; Jehn et al., 1997; Jehn et al., 1999). Affective conflict, which involves personality clashes, may inhibit the free and open exchange of information, and is likely to result in more contentious behaviors. Not surprisingly, affective conflict generally has a detrimental effect on relational outcomes such as satisfaction (Earley & Moskowski, 2000; Jehn, 1994, 1995, 1997; Jehn et al., 1999), intent to remain (Jehn, 1995; Jehn et al., 1999), commitment (Jehn et al., 1999), cohesiveness, respect, and trust (Jehn & Mannix, 2001). Similarly, the impact of affective conflict is generally detrimental on task-focused outcomes such as perceived (Jehn et al., 1999) and actual performance (Earley & Moskowski, 2000; Jehn, 1994, 1997; Jehn et al., 1999; Shah & Jehn, 1993), as well as the efficacy of communicative and planning activities (Earley & Moskowski, 2000). Like process conflict, affective conflict appears to increase in the face of diversity and appears to have a predominantly detrimental impact on task and relational outcomes.

## Summary and Future Directions

By differentiating among types of conflict, the more recent conflict research has been able to unravel some of the anomalous and contradictory findings of the past. With few exceptions, the research reviewed here suggests that whether or not conflict is detrimental or beneficial depends on the type of conflict, as well as the task at hand. By and large, process and affective conflict are detrimental both on task and relationally focused outcomes. Substantive conflict can be beneficial for task related outcomes, but whether or not it is depends on the type of task and the type of outcome that is the focus of the research, and perhaps on the actual level of substantive conflict (a curvilinear relationship). Substantive conflict tends to have a detrimental impact on relational outcomes such as trust, liking, respect, and group cohesiveness. For routine tasks, conflict is simply detrimental. For nonroutine tasks, substantive conflict appears to be beneficial for task-focused outcomes, with the exception of innovation, and perceived freedom to express doubt.

It is plausible, and even likely, that the different forms of conflict interact with one another in their effect on task and relational outcomes. The interactive effects of conflict type (substantive, process, and affective) may produce quite different effects (see Fig. 8.2). Low affective and process conflict provide a supportive environment with responsibilities clearly understood and delineated, encouraging cohesiveness and positive interactions among the parties. When faced with high substantive conflict, the positive personal relationships derived from relational outcomes provide a platform for the exchange of information and viewpoints, and a more open-minded approach to the issues. These relational outcomes provide a supportive and "safe" environment in which one can disagree. A more complete evaluation of alter-

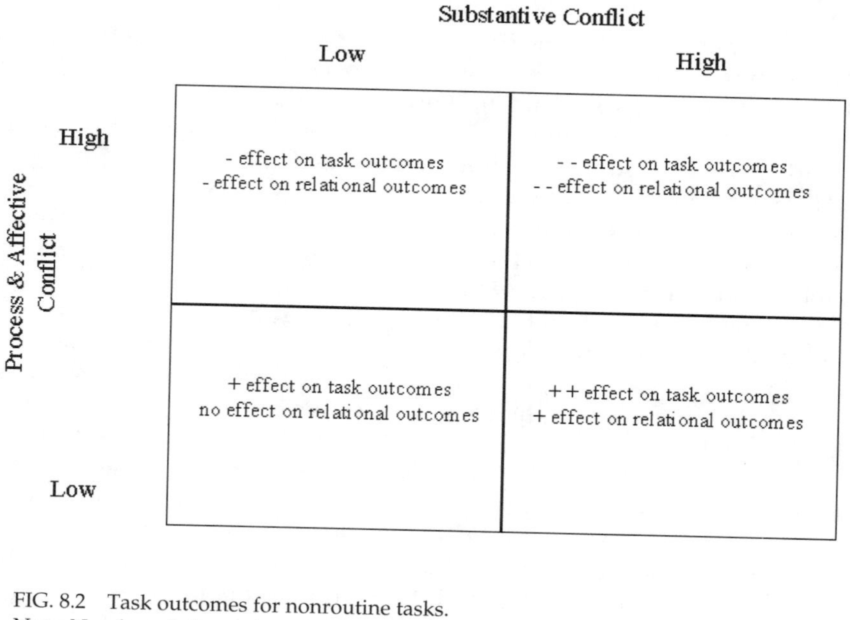

Substantive Conflict

|  | Low | High |
|---|---|---|
| **High**<br><br>Process & Affective Conflict | - effect on task outcomes<br>- effect on relational outcomes | - - effect on task outcomes<br>- - effect on relational outcomes |
| **Low** | + effect on task outcomes<br>no effect on relational outcomes | + + effect on task outcomes<br>+ effect on relational outcomes |

FIG. 8.2   Task outcomes for nonroutine tasks.
Note: Number of plus and minus signs indicates relative strength of the effect.

natives is likely to emerge through constructive discussion, resulting in the potential for innovative and novel solutions. Under these circumstances, we might expect to see the most positive results in terms of the task outcomes such as decision quality and performance. Through airing differences concerning how to go about the task (substantive conflict) and constructive discussion, relational outcomes are also likely to be enhanced, as each party feels respected and believes they have "had their say." However, if substantive conflict is low, the parties may not be energized to share information, falling into a "common knowledge" trap, whereby members assume that information they possess is common knowledge and hence do not share it, depriving the group of a resource available that might enhance performance (Gigone & Hastie, 1993, 1997). It is precisely this situation, where there is no apparent disagreement, in which the situation is ripe for groupthink. "If everyone is thinking alike, then someone isn't thinking" (attributed to General George S. Patton, Jr.).

When there is high affective and process conflict, the parties clash personally while lacking agreement over the specification of responsibilities and accountability. Such high levels of affective and process conflict will divert the parties' energies from the task at hand, and may potentially intensify grudges and feuds, increasing political behaviors and resulting in damaged relationships. When process conflict is high, negative task outcomes may result in finger pointing, and the parties may invoke "plausible deniability." Nothing will be learned from the negative outcomes and the finger pointing will result in damaged relational outcomes. Under these circumstances, information sharing and constructive discussions are unlikely to take place, resulting in substandard decisions and a spiral of substandard performance. If substantive conflict is low, groups may "bungle through," with no attempt to critically examine the effectiveness of their task process. Decisions once made may find little buy-in and implementation may become problematic, resulting in less effective decisions and lower performance. The lack of commitment to group decisions may leave the parties alienated and cynical. The combination of high affective and process conflict and high substantive conflict over a nonroutine task may be particularly deadly. In this situation, high affective and process conflict results in personal clashes among the parties (affective conflict) who are unwilling or unable to specify responsibilities and accountability (process conflict). Information will be hoarded, ideas will be suppressed, and the high levels of conflict on all fronts will result in fractious and contentious discussions. As a result, the group is unlikely to resolve their differences and performance is likely to suffer. Once again, negative outcomes will result in finger pointing and the "blame game," creating negative relationships among the parties.

The current research on conflict, although providing additional insight by differentiating different types of conflict in predicting conflict outcomes, is not well integrated with the literature reviewed earlier addressing the process of conflict; in particular, the research on cognitive biases in negotiations and the cross-cultural research. For example, are anchors, framing, overconfidence, and egoism more or less problematic when dealing with substantive conflict or with affective conflict? Is an egoistic bias more damaging to individualists or collectivists? And how do cultural differences impact preferences, which may, in turn, create a perceived conflict?

## MISSING LINKS: DIRECTIONS FOR FUTURE RESEARCH

Given our review of the conflict literature thus far, the research suggests that factors such as informational diversity, social diversity, and values diversity can engender conflict. Based on the research to date, that conflict is generally recognized as taking one of the three forms: substantive, process, and affective. Yet, there is much that we do not know about conflict, which may provide fruitful avenues for future research. In particular, we identified two areas where we believe future research is likely to yield important results: (a) a richer perspective of the impact of cultural differences, and (b) the decisive role of trust in shaping the conflict process. We now turn our attention to each of these areas.

## A RICHER UNDERSTANDING OF THE IMPACT OF CULTURE

We believe that the research on culture and conflict has much more to contribute. The first way that our examination of culture and conflict can be enriched is by a broader conceptualization of the dimensions through which culture exerts its influence. To date, the majority of the cross-cultural negotiations research has focused on individualism–collectivism, power distance, communication context, time (Bazerman, et al., 2000), and risk preferences. These dimensions are based primarily on the seminal cross-cultural study by Hofstede (1980), leaving other empirically supported cross-cultural dimensions wanting. The second way conflict research can be enriched by culture is by exploring multiple dimensions simultaneously and by examining not just the intensity of a culture, but also its crystallization.

### A Richer Conceptualization of Cultural Differences

Although the current body of research has resulted in an intriguing set of findings, we believe that a broader dimensionalization of cultural differences may be beneficial in understanding how cross-cultural disputants differ in preferences, expectations, and assumptions. In particular, recent research by Trompenaars and Hampden-Turner (1998) has explored a dimension that we believe particularly important in explaining culture's effects on negotiations, that of universalism–particularism. Universalistic cultures depend on rules for defining what is right or wrong, appropriate or inappropriate. Hence universalistic cultures tend to rely on courts to enforce these rules (Trompenaars & Hampden-Turner, 1998). To the extreme universalist, what is important is that a rule (normative or legal) was broken, and if broken, one must pay the price. In contrast, the particularist includes more of the context in the interpretation of right or wrong. For example, did the party *mean* to break the rule? Did they realize that there was a rule? Did they understand the consequences? Was there any damage as a result? Hence, for the extreme particularist, what is important in determining whether a wrong has been done is the understanding and reasons and motivation of the actor. Based on these two perspectives, one might believe that the extreme universalist will find the particularist untrustworthy—because he or she makes exceptions. In contrast, the extreme particularist will find the universalist untrustworthy—because he or she won't even help a friend (Trompenaars & Hampden-Turner, 1998). Clearly, this cultural difference is likely to affect conflict, where, as we later suggest, the issue of trust may be paramount. For the cultural aspects of conflict to continue to be fruitful, we must go beyond the few dimensions that have received virtually all of the research attention and examine other cultural dimensions.

In addition, we believe it is important to examine the profile of a culture on multiple dimensions, rather than simply one or two dimensions at a time. The values expressed by different cultural dimensions may be more or less important to different cultures. Different cultural dimensions may, at times, conflict in terms of the preferences they imply. For example, egalitarian cultures are uncomfortable with status differences. Collectivist cultures avoid making one person the focus of attention. Hence, a culture that is both hierarchical and collectivist may clash "internally," making it important to understand when and under what circumstances hierarchical attitudes and behaviors will dominate and when and under what circumstances collectivist attitudes and behaviors will dominate. However, exploring only a single cultural dimension at a time would not make such issues and potential contradictions obvious. Hence, simply comparing the position of two cultures on the dimensions, rather than the profile of dimensions, may produce a rather impoverished view. By taking the more complex view, we may better understand the implications of culture in conflict, and how different cultural dimensions may interact with one another.

# Crystallization as Well as Intensity

The second way in which our examination of culture and conflict can be enriched is by not only exploring the positioning of a given culture on the cultural dimensions, but also by looking at the level of consensus around that cultural position. At the societal level, cultures can be described in terms of their intensity and their crystallization. To date, most of the research has examined the intensity of culture, or how extreme a given culture is on one of the cultural dimensions. For example, in terms of power distance, Saudi Arabia is a very hierarchical culture and Sweden is very egalitarian, whereas Canada is between the two (Hofstede, 1980). Thus, Saudi Arabia and Sweden, as two extremes (extremely hierarchical and extremely egalitarian, respectively), are more intense, whereas Canada is less intense. Yet, the positioning of a given culture on the power distance continuum represents a *distribution*, around which there may be significant variation within the culture.

Drawing from the literature on norms (e.g., Jackson, 1966) and an extension of that literature into organizational culture (Chatman, 1989), we can characterize national culture as more or less crystallized. In the context of group norms, Jackson (1966) defined a crystallized norm as one in which there is agreement across individuals in terms of what is appropriate or inappropriate. It is a norm in which there is little room for deviation—analogous to our statistical definition of the standard deviation. Like norms, cultures also may be more or less crystallized. The greater the agreement or consistency in the culture on each cultural dimension, the more the culture is crystallized. Although we might obtain the same "score" in terms of cultural intensity on a given dimension such as individualism or collectivism, the degree of variation around that score means that the character of the culture and what we predict may be quite different. In cultures where there is more variation, attitudes and behaviors derived from the cultural dimension may be less consistent, and there may be identifiable subcultures that may conflict with one another, and in which people who are "different" may be more able to fit in, as they have a variety of subcultures from which to "select." It may also be the case that in more diffuse cultures, behaving outside the norm is more acceptable and might even be encouraged. In contrast, in highly crystallized cultures, we would expect to find more consistent attitudes and behaviors, and perhaps less acceptance of differences. In this case, substantive conflict could easily evolve into affective conflict. Depending on the crystallization of the culture, we might expect to find very different results when comparing the benefits or detriments of diversity and the benefits and detriments of conflict.

The combined view of intensity and crystallization also may yield interesting predictions. When two intense but different cultures collide that are highly crystallized, we would expect greater conflict. In fact, juxtaposing these two aspects of culture (intensity and crystallization) reveals potentially very different results (see Fig. 8.3). For example, in cultures that are neither intense nor crystallized, we would expect that the impact of culture would reduce our ability to observe culturally instantiated attitudes and behaviors, perhaps explaining some of the mixed or nonsignificant results in some cross-cultural research. In addition, two such cultures that come in contact and conflict may have rather low levels of conflict, and may be more able to control affective conflict and benefit from substantive conflict. In contrast, two cultures that are both intense and crystallized form the basis of a "strong context," a context that is culturally driven. As Mischel (1977) noted, strong contexts can drive behaviors, and in this instance, drive the behaviors in a way that will make them more consistent with the cultural differences between the parties. Consequently, we might expect to find strong evidence of culturally instantiated behaviors and attitudes, which could manifest themselves quite predictably in terms of the preferences of the parties for culturally related outcomes and conflict resolution processes. In addition, when cultures that are both intense and crystallized are "opposites" (e.g., individualists vs. collectivists), they will be more likely to "clash" and it may be more difficult to capitalize on the potential benefits of substantive conflict. Conflicts characterized by two opposite intense and crystallized cultures may easily result in conflict spirals and intractability. When the two cultures are opposite and intense and

Crystallization

|  | Low | High |
|---|---|---|
| High | Culture has moderate predictive ability<br><br>Moderate levels of culture "clash" | Culture has very high predictive ability<br><br>Extremely high levels of culture "clash" |
| Low | Culture has low predictive ability<br><br>Low levels of culture "clash" | Culture has moderately high predictive ability<br><br>Moderately high levels of culture "clash" |

Intensity

FIG. 8.3  Cultural intensity and crystallization.

crystallized on *multiple cultural dimensions*—in other words, their *profiles* are incongruent—this effect is likely to be magnified.

We now turn our attention to the second area that we believe provides a foundation for future conflict research, an integration of the literature on conflict and on trust. We first review past and present research on trust, defining trust as we use it, and finally provide a model integrating trust and conflict.

## THE DECISIVE ROLE OF TRUST IN SHAPING THE CONFLICT PROCESS

Because conflict does not occur in a vacuum, and because it is inherently a problem associated with *relationships* between individuals or collectives, it is quite likely that expectations and interpretations play a role. How do I expect you to treat me? How do I expect you to react? Can I work with you? Can I predict your reactions? What do I think motivates you? Do you want to do what is best, or what is best for you? What happens when you violate my expectations? Such questions get at what we believe is an essential part of the conflict process and how it unfolds: trust. The issue of trust—a concept dealing with all of these factors—is a fundamental part of the conflict process, a fundamental that has been relatively ignored in conflict research. Trust allows potential disputants to give each other the benefit of the doubt in an emerging dispute, determining whether or not conflict actually erupts. Trust (or distrust) in the other party impacts one's interpretation of events and behaviors. Trust may make disputants less contentious, possibly avoiding conflict spirals.

In this section, we explore how trust shapes the conflict process by determining how different forms of conflict are related to each other, and the extent to which they impact task and relational outcomes. Although research has explored how trust is a direct determinant (De Dreu, Giebels, & Van de Vliert, 1998) or a direct outcome (Jehn & Mannix, 2001) of the conflict process, we suggest a more complex role for trust that, like a richer view of culture, helps address the question explored earlier in this chapter: When and under what circumstances can conflict be detrimental or beneficial?

### What Is Trust?

Like the literature on conflict, the research on trust is studied in several disciplines (see reviews by Dirks & Ferrin, 2002; Kramer, 1999; Ross & Lacroix, 1996). Perhaps as a result, trust has been conceptualized in several different ways in past research. Prior research had studied trust as a personality trait, as a behavior, and as a psychological state (belief, behavioral intention). These three specifications are quite different and in many contexts only loosely related to each other. For instance, trusting behavior may occur for many reasons that are unrelated to trust as a belief (Mayer, Davis, & Schoorman, 1995; Rousseau, Sitkin, Burt, & Camerer, 1998). And, data suggest that on average, trust as a personality construct—trust of others in general—is correlated with trust as a psychological state—trust in a specific partner—at very low levels ($r = .16$; Dirks & Ferrin, 2002). Most contemporary empirical research in organizational behavior studies trust as a psychological state.

Although most definitions of trust seem to have a common conceptual core (Rousseau et al., 1998), the construct of trust involves specifying two independent facets: the referent of the trust and the type of trust. Hence, followers are asked to assess a particular referent—perhaps a peer or a manager—on a particular dimension or type of trust. Early empirical research treated trust as a unidimensional belief or expectation in the other party. More recently, organizational scholars have begun to explore whether trust is comprised of multiple dimensions. McAllister (1995), for instance, distinguished between *cognitive* trust, which reflects issues of the reliability, integrity, or fairness of another party, and *affective* trust, which reflects a special relationship with the other party involving care and concern about that party's welfare. There is presently no consensus on what the exact structure of the construct should be, as there has been a proliferation of different specifications[2] (e.g., Cummings & Bromiley, 1996; Lewicki & Bunker, 1996; McAllister, 1995). There appears to be, however, an emerging consensus that recognizing different types will gain precision in understanding the antecedents and consequences of trust.

In addition to specifying the content of trust (Trust on what dimension?), trust must have a referent (Trust in whom?). Past research has involved leaders (e.g., supervisor, senior management), peers (e.g., co-worker, teammate, negotiation partner), subordinates, and other entities (e.g., organizations, institutions). Thoughtfully specifying the referent is important because trust in different referents may be caused by different factors and result in different outcomes in a given situation. For instance, in a review of the literature on trust in leadership, Dirks and Ferrin (2002) found that trust in supervisors and trust in senior management were differentially related to outcomes and antecedents such that trust in supervisors was highly related to job-focused variables (e.g., job performance, job satisfaction) and trust in senior management related to organizational variables (e.g., organizational commitment).

In this chapter, we use an adaptation of Rousseau et al.'s (1998) "cross-disciplinary" definition of trust that captures the core elements of most definitions: "a psychological state comprising positive expectations

---

[2]Mayer, Davis, and Schoorman (1995) added an additional suggestion that trust perceptions be referred to as "trustworthiness" and the behavioral intent of willingness to risk to be referred to as "trust."

about the behavior or intentions of another party, when one is vulnerable to that party" (p. 395). Where appropriate, we discuss the different referents of trust and the type of trust in question.

## What Do We Know About How Trust Operates?

Early work, particularly in economics, predominantly regarded trust in probabilistic terms—more or less a Bayesian updating model. If, on an initial encounter, one party is cooperative and facilitative, then it is possible to update expectations to reflect that given instance. At the next encounter, if the same behavior is observed, the intuitive Bayesian updating can once again take place. However, from a behavioral perspective, this view of trust is less than satisfactory, particularly with the recognition that trust includes affective elements and that it may operate in multiple and complex ways. Recent research is providing insight into the multiple and complex ways in which trust operates.

Trust may influence the conflict process in two distinct ways (Dirks & Ferrin, 2001). First, trust facilitates the willingness to take a risk in a relationship. Trust in this context is *prospective* in nature; that is, it involves the estimation of future behavior. Second, trust impacts how another party, and his or her actions, is perceived. In this case, trust is *retrospective* in nature because it deals with interpretation of existing actions, frequently based on the interpretation and recall of previous actions. (We use these terms throughout to distinguish between the effects.)

The prospective effect is summarized by Mayer et al. (1995), who suggested that trust results in behaviors that involve "risk taking in a relationship." "Risk taking" may be manifested in different forms in particular contexts: cooperative behavior in a prisoner's dilemma or social dilemma, sharing sensitive information with a negotiation partner, bringing up a controversial idea in a group discussion, or investing resources or sharing knowledge with a joint venture partner. Two sets of theories are frequently used to describe how and why trust facilitates this set of behaviors. The first logic focuses on cognitive processes, rational choice, and the conscious calculation of risks (Kramer, 1999). Specifically, the logic focuses on how perceptions of another party and his or her character impact one's willingness to put oneself at risk to that party (e.g., Mayer et al., 1995; Pruitt & Kimmel, 1977). For example, if one believes the other party is not trustworthy, one may be unwilling to engage in cooperative behavior for fear of being exploited (e.g., see Dirks, 1999). The second logic focuses on relational issues and draws on social exchange theory (e.g., Blau, 1964). Under this set of principles, individuals are willing to reciprocate care and concern that the other party may express in the relationship. For instance, individuals who feel that the other party demonstrates care and consideration will reciprocate this sentiment in the form of desired behaviors.

The retrospective effect builds on psychological research indicating that preexisting beliefs and evaluations guide what information one perceives and how one subsequently interprets and evaluates the information. Trust is a fundamental belief that is likely to be a key facet of how we understand other parties in professional and personal relationships (Holmes, 2001; Kramer, 1999). For example, Robinson (1996) found that employees with low trust tended to experience breach of contract as intentional and negative, whereas individuals with high trust tended to interpret the breach as unintentional or as a misunderstanding. Likewise, Schurr and Ozanne (1985) found support for trust as a moderator of the relationship between bargaining stance of the other party (tough vs. soft) and several outcomes (integrative behavior, distributive behavior, and agreements reached) in a bargaining situation. For example, under high trust a tough bargaining stance led to integrative behavior and high levels of agreement; under low trust a tough bargaining stance resulted in more distributive behavior and low levels of agreement. The authors suggested that this was the case because prior levels of trust frame the perceptions of the party's behavior (e.g., toughness) and the motives underlying it.

These two perspectives provide a theoretical basis for understanding the effect of trust on the conflict process. The previous section reviewed the "typical" relationships between conflict and task and relational outcomes. We suggest that the nature of the relationship changes dramatically contingent on the level of trust between parties. Retrospective trust, based on current interpretations of events or of past events applied to the present, provides a foundation for trust to ameliorate the detrimental effects of conflict suppressing the potentially negative interpretations of criticisms and differences of opinion. Prospective trust will enable risk taking, allowing parties to reciprocate positive behaviors without fear of being exploited. This reciprocation will provide additional "oil" to grease the machinery of the relationship.

## AN INTEGRATED MODEL

### The Impact of Trust on Relationships Between Different Forms of Conflict

Trust impacts the conflict process via the retrospective effect by impacting the extent to which substantive conflict is translated into affective conflict. Simons and Peterson (2000), for example, found that trust moderated the relationship between substantive conflict and affective conflict. They proposed that under low levels of trust, substantive conflict would be interpreted negatively and subsequently result in affective conflict, but that under high levels of trust, a neutral (or even positive) interpretation of the intent behind the conflict behaviors would occur, thus preventing the transference. In other words, substantive conflict behaviors that are well intentioned may be interpreted very differently in low trust relationships than in high trust relationships, effectively resulting in a "sinister attribution error" or paranoid cognitions (Kramer, 1996). Under low trust well-intentioned behaviors may be taken as a sign of devaluation of the relationship, a situation that quickly spins into affective conflict. The moderating effects are illustrated in Fig. 8.4.

The effects may be exaggerated when diversity exists. Diversity increases conflict (a direct, positive effect; see Fig. 8.4). Simultaneously, it may sometimes reduce trust levels (e.g., Pelled & Xin, 2000). Observed similarity is often used as a proxy for similar goals and values, promoting "swift trust" (Kramer, Brewer, & Hanna 1996). Diversity, or dissimilarity, consequently may result in swift distrust. This dual detrimental effect is compounded when trust tends to affect the extent to which substantive conflict translates into other forms of conflict.

These effects may create a confound in the ability to cleanly separate the unique effects of different types of conflict, because one type of conflict may affect another.

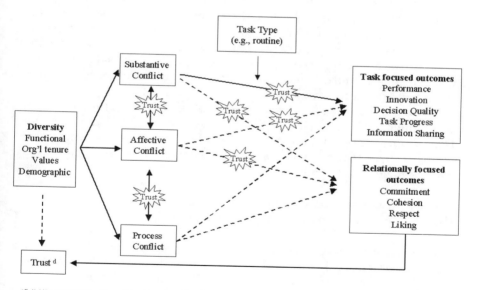

[a]Solid lines indicate positive relationships, dotted lines indicate negative relationships
[b]We use the symbol ⚡Trust⚡ to indicate that trust moderates the relationship
[c]As shown in Table 2, the different forms of conflict may interact to impact outcomes
[d]As suggested by our arguments, trust plays multiple roles in the process. For simplicity of the diagram, some relationships are omitted.

FIG. 8.4   Simplified model of relationships between conflict, trust, and outcomes[a,b,c].

## The Impact of Trust on Relationships
## Between Conflict and Task-Focused Outcomes

As previously noted, substantive conflict appears to have a generally positive impact on task-focused outcomes and affective and process conflict
appears to have a generally negative impact. The effect of substantive conflict on outcomes such as performance, innovation, and decision quality
rests on the assumption that different opinions, ideas, and talents will be
offered and subsequently used. The prospective role of trust is necessary if
individuals are willing to take the risk of offering their unique opinions
and ideas. In other words, unless individuals feel that the environment is
"safe" or trusting, they are unlikely to offer unique or controversial ideas
that may subject them to negative evaluations by co-workers (Edmondson, 1999). Or, the individual may fail to trust the competence of the partner to use the idea that has been offered. Once the idea has been offered, the
retrospective role of trust may complement this effect by impacting
whether the other party is willing to accept the idea. For instance, failing to
trust the integrity of the individual contributing the idea may make one
question why the idea is being offered, calling into question the underlying motivation for offering the idea in the first place. Or, failing to trust the
capability may make one question the value of the idea. In summary, the
beneficial relationship between substantive conflict and task outcomes is
likely to be significantly greater with increasing levels of trust between the
two parties. Substantive conflict provides the "raw materials" for better
task outcomes, but trust among the parties is required for those resources
to be converted into actual outcomes.

In contrast, under low levels of trust, any possible positive effects of
substantive conflict on task outcomes are likely to be neutralized. The neutralization of the positive effects of substantive conflict allows the negative
effects of affective conflict on trust to dominate (see Fig. 8.4)—and perhaps
even be magnified by low levels of trust.

## Trust's Impact on Relationships Between
## Conflict and Relationally Focused Outcomes

The impact of affective and process conflict on outcomes may occur due to
a perceived lack of valuation and respect for the other party involved in the
conflict. The retrospective impact of trust is likely to play an important role
in determining the magnitude of the effect. In low-trust relationships, affective conflict is likely to be interpreted negatively and will be seen as a
sign of the continued poor relationship. In a high-trust relationship, the effect is likely to be muted in most cases. For instance, affective conflict in a
high-trust relationship (although uncomfortable) may be discounted as an

anomaly and may be attributed to external forces. Supporting this idea, Holmes and Rempel (1989) found that parties in close interpersonal relationships with high trust tend to assess the flow of events in their relationships over a more extended period of time than individuals in low-trust relationships. Hence, individuals in high-trust relationships use a longer time metric and tend to discount any single negative incident more readily than those individuals with low trust. This explanation is consistent with the patterns of conflict found by Jehn and Mannix (2001). Over time, conflict levels may ebb and flow, but in high-performance groups, conflict has a curvilinear form across time, ebbing, perhaps, as trust kicks in.

The effects described are often observed in labor–management negotiations. The phenomenon is not surprising, given that a recent survey by the AFL-CIO (2001) found that almost two thirds of their members report having little or no trust for management. These patterns may also be observed in conflict between Israel and Palestine: The parties simply do not trust one another; hence even neutral actions are interpreted with sinister motivations, resulting in a conflict spiral.

## Cyclical Effects

Lastly, we propose that trust may facilitate positive or negative cycles of conflict in the model shown in Fig. 8.4 via the prospective and retrospective effects of trust. In high-trust relationships, we believe that the parties are likely to take a risk with each other (prospective effect) because they believe they will not be exploited. The risky action is interpreted positively and the other party responds in kind. Observing the in-kind reaction (retrospective effect), the trust levels are enhanced. These factors may lead to a reduction in affective conflict between the parties, and hence better relational and task outcomes. And the process cycles again. With a positive experience between them, the parties begin their next encounter with a better relationship, and even if things go wrong, are more likely to interpret them either in a neutral manner, or by attributing the "cause" of the negative experience to external forces (bad economy, bad luck) rather than to the motivations or traits of the other party.

In contrast, a low-trust relationship is likely to experience a cycle involving withholding information and a negative interpretation of such actions. Withholding information will make the parties less willing to accept responsibility, increasing process conflict while the negative attributions concerning the other party's motivations will result in an increase in affective conflict. With both process and affective conflict escalating, the result will be a detrimental impact on both relational and task outcomes. Scholars have noted how such cycles of conflict can play out in settings ranging from the Cold War to various forms of prisoners' dilemmas (e.g., Axelrod, 1984;

Lindskold, 1978). The proposed solution to these dilemmas typically tends to involve the development of trust by gradual acts of cooperation.

## Summary and Future Directions
## for Research on Conflict and Trust

Recent advances in the respective literatures of trust and conflict provide new insights into the interrelationships between the constructs. In summarizing and extending current research, we advance several propositions. First, trust appears to affect the relationships between different types of conflict by providing a lens for the interpretation of events in a conflict episode. If trust is high, conflict behaviors will be interpreted as neutral and underlying motivations as unintended. If trust is low, conflict behaviors will be interpreted negatively, and as intended to harm, exploit, or take advantage. Second, we propose that trust impacts the extent to which conflict relates to task and relationally focused outcomes because it allows one party to be willing to take a risk (e.g., share an idea), and it impacts whether the other party is willing to reciprocate in kind. Third, the attributions and willingness to risk engender a cycle whereby the level of trust and conflict reinforce each other to spiral up or down. As of yet, there appears to be very little empirical research examining these factors as they operate in organizational settings. Interestingly, despite being frequently referenced conceptually, our search of the literature also turned up very few empirical studies that examined the role of trust (as psychological state) between negotiators (for a prior review, see Ross & LaCroix, 1996). We believe that a program of research on trust investigating the impact of trust on the conflict process could enrich our understanding of conflict and how to control its detrimental effects while capitalizing on its beneficial effects.

Although there are a number of other issues for future research, we note two issues particularly deserving given their scientific and practical significance. One issue involves identifying methods of repairing broken trust. This topic may be particularly helpful for preventing a downward spiral of trust and conflict. Researchers examining the topic have previously focused on initiating a gradual de-escalation of negative or destructive conflict and by gradual acts of cooperation (e.g., Lindskold, 1978). Clearly, however, this strategy is more easily proposed than it is implemented, given the perceived risk in doing so when one does not trust a partner. Scholars or practitioners might identify and test practical methods of applying this strategy to conflicts that occur in groups and organizations. The use of the strategy also presupposes that all types of trust may be rebuilt the same way. We suspect that trying to rebuild trust in integrity may be different than rebuilding trust in competence or trust involving care and concern. For example, although one may be able to demonstrate renewed care and concern or renewed competence through behavior, one may not be able to demonstrate renewed integrity (an oxymoron?) or attempting to do so may require such a long period of time as to be impractical. Researchers might therefore investigate the different strategies needed for repairing different types of trust. It might also explore factors that serve as substitutes or neutralizers of the negative effects of broken trust such as structural factors like sanctions (e.g., Yamagishi, 1986) or more personal factors such as apology and forgiveness (e.g., Ohbuchi, Kameda, & Agarie, 1989) for cases where other methods fail.

A second issue that may have theoretical and practical implications for conflict research involves the building and repairing of trust in cross-cultural relationships and negotiations. Despite recognition of the growing frequency and significance of cross-culture relationships in business and political contexts, there has been little research in organizational behavior on this issue. Building on the earlier discussion, different cultures often have different values and different styles of communicating. Clearly, these differences provide additional opportunities for trust to be broken, or at least lowered (see research on relational demography; Pelled & Xin, 2000). For example, messages sent by individuals from high-context cultures may be interpreted as being intentionally evasive by individuals from low-context cultures that may simultaneously damage trust and create difficulty in resolving a conflict. The problem of building and repairing trust is obviously magnified when lack of commonalities create misunderstandings. To address this issue, research might, for instance, explore how cross-cultural relationships initiate and leverage the positive cycle of trust and conflict by focusing on commonalities on other dimensions such as gender, other values, or goals.

## CONCLUSION

In this chapter we have attempted to summarize selected research on conflict in organizations. Recent advances exploring different types of conflict have provided important advances in knowledge in conflict and its management. In particular, this work has helped move past the assumption that conflict is good or bad to a more sophisticated understanding about what types of conflict may be beneficial or detrimental and under what circumstances, circumstances that we believe may be impacted by culture and trust.

Although advances have been made, the topic of conflict is still alive and well. As has been often noted, today's workplace is an increasingly diverse context. This fact clearly provides the fodder for both greater substantive conflict and affective conflict. The ability to tap into the former while managing the latter represents a crucial task for managers and an important research agenda for scholars. Ironically, this challenge comes in the face of low trust within organizations (AFL-CIO, 2001) and a societal decline in trust over the past several decades (Putnam, 2000).

Our chapter discusses at least three issues that we believe provide interesting opportunities for researchers. First, we suggest looking beyond the main effects and at the *interactions* between the different types of conflict. This perspective suggests that effects of conflict on outcomes are likely to be complex and interdependent. Second, we should expand our conceptualization of cultural differences to go beyond the often-researched construct of individualism–collectivism to include other cultural dimensions and their impact, such as universalism–particularism. We should also address the circumstances under which culture will have its greatest impact in determining preferences and behaviors and in creating the conditions for conflict. Third, we suggest that trust plays a decisive role in the conflict process and may help understand the situations in which the effects of different forms of conflict on outcomes are accentuated or muted. Although trust has long been associated with conflict, we found very little empirical research that actually studied the association. By continuing to peel apart the different levels and types of conflict, as well as the factors that influence their effects, researchers may help resolve the "conflicting stories" found in existing literature.

Finally, space limitations forced us to ignore one potential area of research that we believe is underexplored and potentially important. We would like to suggest that researchers focus more attention on conflicts that occur between an organization and various external and perhaps amorphous constituencies, such as the public. As part of the context of culture, we believe that more research needs to be done in this domain. At this level, organizations may provide the stage from which conflicts are heard and enacted, frequently involving the court of public opinion. For example, as noted by Lambrecht (2001):

> In the waning years of the 1990s, Monsanto mutated in the minds of many from a typical American company.... to a corporate demon. Indeed, "Monsatan" was coined as a suitable *nom de guerre* for a company with the temerity to cross the boundaries of species to set the global table and upset the food business ... Monsanto—"Mutanto," another choice label ... was a lightning rod. (p. 23)

This produced a situation in which the mere name, "Monsanto," could create conflict. Clearly, as the Monsanto example suggests, such conflicts have the potential to become flashpoints and may be particularly intractable. Issues of trust (in large organizations) and culture (of the United States vs. the European countries that reacted so negatively to Monsanto's foray into the realm of genetically modified crops) are likely to play out at this level of analysis as well. The relative paucity of such research appears to us to be unfortunate, and by turning attention to these issues, we may see a resurgence in interest in important research questions concerning whistle blowing (Near & Miceli, 1986) and principled organizational dissent (Graham, 1986), areas that have not received a great deal of research attention.

What advice do we have for managers? In answering that question, we are reminded of Don Francis, the CDC researcher in the movie about the search for the cause of AIDS, *And the Band Played On.* Francis would start each research meeting by asking, "What do we know?" and "What do we think we know?" In terms of conflict, to the extent that there is a body of research, there are some things we "know." And, based on the integration offered here, there are some things we "think we know." We know that substantive conflict appears to be beneficial when the task itself is complex and nonroutine. Hence the manager needs to manage the work to reduce substantive conflict when tasks are routine, and to make sure that substantive conflict does not escalate to a point where it becomes dysfunctional in complex and nonroutine tasks. We know that process and affective conflict are almost always detrimental, so steps should be taken to resolve such conflicts when they arise. We think we know that different types of conflict interact, that high levels of affective and process conflict may be particularly detrimental when combined with high levels of substantive conflict. We think we know that culture will impact the potentially beneficial and detrimental effects of conflict. We also think we know that trust and its formation play a key role in turning process and affective conflict into a neutral or perhaps even a positive. Similarly, we think we know that trust can go a long way to ameliorate the pejorative effects of any type of conflict—and in that role trust is an asset that managers must cultivate.

## ACKNOWLEDGMENTS

We would like to acknowledge Emily DiFilippo for her assistance in the review of the literature.

## REFERENCES

Adams, J. S. (1965). Inequity in social exchange. In L. Berkowitz (Ed.), *Advances in social psychology, 2* (pp. 267–299). New York: Academic.

AFL-CIO (2001). *Workers' rights in America: What employers think about their jobs and employers.* Washington, DC: Peter D. Hart Associates.

Amason, A. C. (1996). Distinguishing the effects of functional and dysfunctional conflict on strategic decision making: Resolving a paradox for top management teams. *Academy of Management Journal, 39,* 123–148.

Axelrod, R. (1984). *The evolution of cooperation*. New York: Basic Books.

Babcock, L., & Lowenstein, G. (1997). Explaining bargaining impasse: The role of self-serving biases. *Journal of Economic Perspectives, 11*, 109–126.

Babcock, L., Lowenstein, G., Issacharoff, S., & Camerer, C. (1995). Biased judgments of fairness in bargaining. *The American Economic Review, 85*, 1337–1343.

Babcock, L., & Olson, C. (1992). The causes of impasses in labor disputes. *Industrial Relations, 31*, 348–360.

Barsade, S., Ward, A., Turner, J., & Sonnenfeld, J. (2000). To your heart's content: A model of affective diversity in top management teams. *Administrative Science Quarterly, 45*, 802–836.

Bazerman, M. (1983). Negotiator judgment: A critical look at the rationality assumption. *American Behavioral Scientist, 27*, 618–634.

Bazerman, M. (1998). *Judgment in managerial decision making* (4th ed.). New York: Wiley.

Bazerman, M., Curhan, J., Moore, D., & Valley, K. (2000). Negotiation. *Annual Review of Psychology, 51*, 279–314.

Bazerman, M., Magliozzi, T., & Neale, M. (1985). The acquisition of integrative response in a competitive market. *Organizational Behavior and Human Decision Processes, 34*, 294–313.

Bazerman, M., Moore, D., & Gillespie, J. (1999). The human mind as a barrier to wiser environmental agreements. *American Behavioral Scientist, 42*, 1254–1276.

Bazerman, M., & Neale, M. (1983). Heuristics in negotiations: limitations to effective dispute resolution. In M. Bazerman & R. Lewicki (Eds.), *Negotiating in organizations* (pp. 51–67). Beverly Hills, CA: Sage.

Blau, P. (1964). *Exchange and power in social life*. New York: Wiley.

Bontempo, R., Bottom, W., & Weber, E. (1997). Cross-cultural differences in risk perception: A model-based approach. *Risk Analysis, 17*, 479–488.

Bottom, W., & Studt, A. (1993). Framing effects and the distributive aspect of integrative bargaining. *Organizational Behavior and Human Decision Processes, 56*, 459–474.

Bourgeois, L. J. (1985). Strategic goals, environmental uncertainty, and economic performance in volatile environments. *Academy of Management Journal, 28*, 548–573.

Brett, J. (2000). *Negotiating globally: How to negotiate deals, resolve disputes, and make decisions across cultural boundaries*. San Francisco, CA: Jossey-Bass.

Brett, J., & Okumura, T. (1998). Inter- and intra-cultural negotiations: U.S. and Japanese negotiators. *Academy of Management Journal, 41*, 495–510.

Camerer, C. F., & Lowenstein, G. (1993). Information, fairness, and efficiency in bargaining. In B. A. Mellers & J. Baron (Eds.), *Psychological perspectives on justice: Theory and applications* (pp. 155–179). New York: Cambridge University Press.

Chatman, J. (1989). Organizational research: A model of person–organization fit. *Academy of Management Review, 14*, 333–349.

Chen, C. (1995). New trends in reward allocation preferences: A Sino–U.S. comparison. *Academy of Management Journal, 38*, 408–428.

Coser, L. A. (1957). Social conflict and the theory of social change. *British Journal of Sociology, 8*, 197–207.

Cummings, L. L., & Bromiley, P. (1996). The Organizational Trust Inventory (OTI): Development and validation. In R. M. Kramer & T. R. Tyler (Eds.), *Trust in organizations* (pp. 302–330). Thousand Oaks, CA: Sage.

De Dreu, C., Giebels, E., & Van de Vliert, E. (1998). Social motives and trust in integrative negotiation: The disruptive effects of punitive capability. *Journal of Applied Psychology, 83,* 408–423.

Deutsch, M. (1973). *The resolution of conflict.* New Haven, CT: Yale University Press.

Deutsch, M. (1975). Equity, equality and need: What determines which value will be used as the basis for distributive justice? *Journal of Social Issues, 31,* 137–149.

Deutsch, M. (1983). Conflict resolution: Theory and practice. *Political Psychology, 4,* 431–453.

Deutsch, M. (1990). Sixty years of conflict. *The International Journal of Conflict Management, 1,* 237–263.

Diekmann, K., Samuels, S., Ross, L., & Bazerman, M. (1997). Self-interest and fairness in problems of resource allocation: Allocators versus recipients. *Journal of Personality and Social Psychology, 72,* 1061–1074.

Dirks, K. T. (1999). The effects of interpersonal trust on work group performance. *Journal of Applied Psychology, 84,* 445–455.

Dirks, K. T., & Ferrin, D. (2001). The role of trust in organizational settings. *Organization Science, 12,* 450–467.

Dirks, K. T., & Ferrin, D. L. (2002). Trust in leadership: Meta-analytic findings and implications for research and practice. *Journal of Applied Psychology, 87,* 611–628.

Dirks, K. T., Shah, P. P., & Chervany, N. (2001). The impact of friendship networks on team performance: A story of equifinality. In D. Nagao (Ed.), *Academy of Management meeting best papers proceedings,* ( OB, E1–E5). Briarcliff Manor, NY: Academy of Management.

Duffy, M., Shaw, J., & Stark, E. (2000). Performance and satisfaction in conflicted interdependent groups: When and how does self-esteem make a difference? *Academy of Management Journal, 43,* 772–782.

Earley, E. C., & Moskowski, E. (2000). Creating hybrid team cultures: An empirical test of transnational team functioning. *Academy of Management Journal, 43,* 26–39.

Edmondson, A. (1999). Psychological safety and learning behavior in work teams. *Administrative Science Quarterly, 44,* 350–383.

Eisenhardt, K. M., & Bourgeois, L. J. (1988). Politics of strategic decision making in high velocity environments: Toward a midrange theory. *Academy of Management Journal, 31,* 737–770.

Espinoza, J., & Garcia, R. (1985). Social group salience and interethnic cooperation. *Journal of Experimental Social Psychology, 21,* 380–392.

Farber, H., & Bazerman, M. (1986). The general bias of arbitrator behavior: An empirical analysis of conventional and final offer arbitration. *Econometrica, 54,* 1503–1528.

Galinsky, A., & Mussweiler, T. (2000). *Promoting good outcomes: Effects of regulatory focus on negotiation outcomes.* Manuscript in preparation.

Gigone, D., & Hastie, R. (1993). The common knowledge effect: Information sharing and group judgment. *Journal of Personality and Social Psychology, 65,* 959–974.

Gigone, D., & Hastie, R. (1997). The impact of information on small group choice. *Journal of Personality and Social Psychology, 72,* 132–140.

Graham, J. (1986). Principled organizational dissent: A theoretical essay. In B. M. Staw & L. L. Cummings (Eds.), *Research in organizational behavior* (Vol. 8, pp. 1–52). Greenwich, CT: JAI.

Griffith, W. I. (1985). The allocation of negative outcomes. In E. Lawler (Ed.), *Advances in group processes, 6,* 107–137.

Hall, E. (1973). *The silent language.* New York: Anchor.

Hofstede, G. (1980). *Cultures consequences: International differences in work related values.* Thousand Oaks, CA: Sage.

Hofstede, G. (1996). *Cultures and organizations.* New York: McGraw-Hill.

Holmes, J. G. (2001). The exchange process in close relationships: Microbehavior and macromotives. In M. J. Lerner & S. C. Lerner (Eds.), *The justice motive and social behavior* (pp. 261–284). New York: Plenum.

Holmes, J. G., & Rempel, J. K. (1989). Trust in close relationships. In C. Hendrick (Ed.), *Close relationships* (pp. 187–220). Thousand Oaks, CA: Sage.

Jackson, J. (1966). A conceptual and measurement model for norms and roles. *Pacific Sociological Review, 9,* 35–47.

Janus, I. (1972). *Victims of groupthink.* Boston: Houghton-Mifflin.

Jehn, K. (1992). *The impact of intragroup conflict on effectiveness: A multimethod examination of the benefits and detriments of conflict (group effectiveness).* Unpublished doctoral dissertation, Northwestern University, Chicago.

Jehn, K. (1994). Enhancing effectiveness: An investigation of advantages and disadvantages of value-based intragroup conflict. *International Journal of Conflict Management, 5,* 223–238.

Jehn, K. (1995). A multimethod examination of the benefits and detriments of intragroup conflict. *Administrative Science Quarterly, 40,* 256–282.

Jehn, K. (1997). A quantitative analysis of conflict types and dimensions in organizational groups. *Administrative Science Quarterly, 42,* 530–557.

Jehn, K., Chadwick, C., & Thatcher, M. (1997). To agree or not to agree: The effects of value congruence, individual demographic dissimilarity, and conflict on workgroup outcomes. *International Journal of Conflict Management, 8,* 287–305.

Jehn, K., & Mannix, E. (2001). The dynamic nature of conflict: A longitudinal study of intragroup conflict and performance. *Academy of Management Journal, 44,* 238–251.

Jehn, K., Northcraft, G., & Neale, M. (1999). Why differences make a difference: A field study of diversity, conflict and performance in workgroups. *Administrative Science Quarterly, 43,* 741–763.

Kramer, R. (1996). Divergent realities and convergent disappointments in the hierarchic relation: Trust and the intuitive auditor at work. In R. M. Kramer & T. R. Tyler (Eds.), *Trust in organizations: Frontiers of theory and research* (pp. 216–245). Thousand Oaks, CA: Sage.

Kramer, R. (1999). Trust and distrust in organizations: Emerging perspectives, enduring questions. *Annual Review of Psychology, 50,* 569–598.

Kramer, R., Brewer, M., & Hanna, B. (1996). Collective trust and collective action: The decision to trust as a social decision. In R. M. Kramer & T. R. Tyler (Eds.), *Trust in organizations: Frontiers of theory and research* (pp. 357–389). Thousand Oaks, CA: Sage.

Lambrecht, B. (2001). *Dinner at the New Gené Café: How genetic engineering is changing what we eat, how we live, and the global politics of food.* New York: Thomas Dunne.

Leung, K. (1987). Some determinants of reactions to procedural models for conflict resolution: A cross-national study. *Journal of Personality and Social Psychology, 53,* 898–905.

Leventhal, G. (1976). *Fairness in social relationships.* Morristown, NJ: General Learning Press.

Lewicki, R., & Bunker, B. (1996). Developing and maintaining trust in work relationships. In R. Kramer & T. Tyler (Eds.), *Trust in organizations: Frontiers of theory and research* (pp. 114–139). Thousand Oaks, CA: Sage.

Lewicki, R., & Robinson, R. (1998). Ethical and unethical bargaining tactics: An empirical study. *Journal of Business Ethics, 19,* 665–682.

Lim, R. (1997). Overconfidence in negotiation revisited. *International Journal of Conflict Resolution, 8,* 52–79.

Lindskold, S. (1978). Trust development, the GRIT proposal, and the effects of conciliatory acts on conflict and cooperation. *Psychological Bulletin, 85,* 772–793.

Lovelace, K., Shapiro, D., & Weingart, L. (2001). Maximizing cross-functional new product teams' innovativeness and constraint adherence: A conflict communications perspective. *Academy of Management Journal, 44,* 779–793.

Mannix, E., Neale, M., & Northcraft, G. (1995). Equity, equality or need? The effects of organizational culture on the allocation of benefits and burdens. *Organizational Behavior and Human Decision Processes, 63,* 276–286.

Mayer, R. C., Davis, J. H., & Schoorman, F. D. (1995). An integrative model of organizational trust. *Academy of Management Review, 20,* 709–734.

McAllister, D. J. (1995). Affect- and cognition-based trust as foundations for interpersonal cooperation in organizations. *Academy of Management Journal, 38,* 24–59.

McLean Parks, J., Boles, T., Conlon, D., DeSouza, E., Gatewood, W., Gibson, K., Halpern, J., Locke, D., Straub, P., Wilson, G., & Murnighan, J. (1996). The fair distribution of adventitious outcomes. *Organizational Behavior and Human Decision Processes, 67,* 181–200.

McLean Parks, J., Conlon, D., Ang, S., & Bontempo, R. (1999). The manager giveth, the manager taketh away: Variation in distribution/recovery rules due to resource type and cultural orientation. *Journal of Management, 25,* 723–757.

Messick, D. (1993). Equality as a decision heuristic. In B. Mellers & J. Baron (Eds.), *Psychological perspectives on justice* (pp. 111–131). Cambridge, England: Cambridge University Press.

Milne, A. A. (2001). *The complete tales of Winnie the Pooh* (75th anniversary ed.). New York: Dutton.

Mischel, W. (1977). The interaction of person and situation. In D. Magnusson & N. S. Endler (Eds.), *Personality at the crossroads: Current issues in interactional psychology* (pp. 333–352). Hillsdale, NJ: Lawrence Erlbaum Associates.

Neale, M. A., & Bazerman, M. H. (1985a). Perspectives for understanding negotiation: Viewing negotiation as a judgmental process. *Journal of Conflict Resolution, 29*, 33–35.

Neale, M. A., & Bazerman, M. H. (1985b). When will externally set aspiration levels improve negotiator performance? A look at integrative behavior in competitive markets. *Journal of Occupational Behavior, 6*, 19–32.

Near, J., & Miceli, N. (1986). Organizational dissidence: The case of whistle-blowing. *Journal of Business Ethics, 4*, 1–16.

Northcraft, G., & Neale, M. (1987). Expert, amateurs and real estate: An anchoring and adjustment perspective on property pricing decisions. *Organizational Behavior and Human Decision Processes, 39*, 228–241.

Ohbuchi, K., Kameda, M., & Agarie, N. (1989). Apology as an aggression control: Its role in mediating appraisal of and response to harm. *Journal of Personality and Social Psychology, 56*, 219–227.

Ottaway, D., & Stephens, J. (2001, October 29). Diplomats meet with Taliban on bin Laden: Some contend U.S. missed its chance. *The Washington Post*, p. A01.

Pelled, L., Eisenhardt, K., & Xin, K. (1999). Exploring the black box: An analysis of work group diversity, conflict, and performance. *Administrative Science Quarterly, 44*, 1–28.

Pelled, L., & Xin, K. (2000). Relational demography and relationship quality in two cultures. *Organization Studies, 21*, 1077–1094.

Pinkley, R. (1990). Dimensions of conflict frame: Disputant interpretations of conflict. *Journal of Applied Psychology, 75*, 117–126.

Pondy, L. R. (1967). Organizational conflict: Concepts and models. *Administrative Science Quarterly, 12*, 296–320.

Pruitt, D. (1981). *Negotiation behavior*. New York: Academic.

Pruitt, D., & Kimmel, M. (1977). Twenty years of experimental gaming: Critique, synthesis, and suggestions for the future. *Annual Review of Psychology, 28*, 363–392.

Pruitt, D., & Rubin, J. (1986). *Social conflict: Escalation, stalemate, and settlement*. New York: Random House.

Putnam, L., & Poole, M. (1987). Conflict and negotiation. In F. Jablin, L. Putnam, K. Roberts, & L. Porter (Eds.), *Handbook of organizational communication: An interdisciplinary perspective* (pp. 459–499). Thousand Oaks, CA: Sage.

Putnam, R. (2000). *Bowling alone: The collapse and revival of the American community*. New York: Simon & Schuster.

Raiffa, H. (1982). *The art and science of negotiation*. Cambridge, MA: Belknap.

Robinson, S. (1996). Trust and the breach of the psychological contract. *Administrative Science Quarterly, 41*, 574–599.

Ross, W., & LaCroix, J. (1996). Multiple meanings of trust in negotiation theory and research: A literature review and integrative model. *International Journal of Conflict Management, 7*, 314–360.

Rousseau, D. M., Sitkin, S. B., Burt, R. S., & Camerer, C. (1998). Not so different after all: A cross-discipline view of trust. *Academy of Management Review, 23*, 393–404.

Russo, J. E., & Schoemaker, P. (1989). *Decision traps: Ten barriers to brilliant decision making and how to overcome them.* New York: Doubleday.

Schurr, P., & Ozanne, J. (1985). Influences on exchange processes: Buyers' preconceptions of a seller's trustworthiness and bargaining toughness. *Journal of Consumer Research, 11,* 939–953.

Shah, P., & Jehn, K. (1993). Do friends perform better than acquaintances? The interaction of friendship, conflict and task. *Group Decision and Negotiation, 2,* 149–165.

Sherif, M. (1958). Superordinate goals in the reduction of intergroup conflict. *The American Journal of Sociology, 63,* 349–356.

Simons, T., Pelled, L., & Smith, K. (1999). Making use of difference: Diversity, debate and decision comprehensiveness in top management teams. *Academy of Management Journal, 42,* 662–673.

Simons, T., & Peterson, R. (2000). Task conflict and relationship conflict in top management teams: The pivotal role of intra-group trust. *Journal of Applied Psychology, 85,* 102–111.

Thomas, K. (1976). Conflict and conflict management. In M. Dunnette (Ed.), *Handbook of industrial and organizational psychology* (pp. 889–935). Chicago: Rand McNally.

Thomas, K. (1992). Conflict and negotiation processes in organizations. In M. Dunnette & L. Hough (Eds.), *Handbook of industrial and organizational psychology* (pp. 651–717). Palo Alto, CA: Consulting Psychologists Press.

Thompson, L. (1995). The impact of minimum goals and aspirations on judgments of success in negotiations. *Group Decisions and Negotiations, 4,* 513–524.

Thompson, L. (1998). *The mind and heart of the negotiator.* Upper Saddle River, NJ: Prentice-Hall.

Thompson, L., & Hastie, R. (1990). Lose–lose agreements in interdependent decision making. *Psychological Bulletin, 120,* 396–409.

Thompson, T., & Lowenstein, G. (1992). Egocentric interpretations of fairness and interpersonal conflict. *Organizational Behavior and Human Decision Process, 51,* 176–197.

Tinsley, C., Curhan, J., & Kwak, R. (1999). Adopting a dual lens approach for overcoming the dilemma of difference in international business negotiation. *International Negotiation, 4,* 1–18.

Tjosvold, D., & De Dreu, C. (1997). Managing conflict in Dutch organizations: A test of the relevance of Deutsch's cooperation theory. *Journal of Applied Social Psychology, 27,* 2213–2227.

Tornblum, K., & Jonsson, D. (1985). Subrules of the equality and contribution principles: Their perceived fairness in distribution and retribution. *Social Psychology Quarterly, 48,* 249–261.

Tornblum, K., Jonsson, D., & Foa, U. (1985). Nationality, resource class, and preferences among three allocation rules: Sweden vs. USA. *International Journal of Intercultural Relations, 9,* 51–77.

Trompenaars, F., & Hampden-Turner, C. (1998). *Riding the waves of culture: Understanding diversity in global business.* New York: McGraw-Hill.

van Biema, D. (1988, January 17). Biotech gadfly buzzes Italy. *The Washington Post Magazine,* p. W13.

Wall, J., & Callister, R. (1995). Conflict and its management. *Journal of Management, 21*, 515–558.

Walton, R., & Dutton, J. (1969). The management of interdepartmental conflict: A model and review. *Administrative Science Quarterly, 14*, 73–84.

Watson, D., Clark, L. A., & Tellegen, A. (1988). Development and validation of brief measures of positive and negative affect: The PANAS scales. *Journal of Personality and Social Psychology, 54*, 1063–1070.

Wong, C., Tjosvold, D., & Lee, F. (1992). Managing conflict in a diverse work force: A Chinese perspective in North America. *Small Group Research, 23*, 302–321.

Yamagishi, T. (1986). The provision of a sanctioning system as a public good. *Journal of Personality and Social Psychology, 51*, 110–116.

Young, H. P. (1995). Dividing the indivisible. *American Behavioral Scientist, 38*, 904–920.

# III

## Cross-Level Themes

# 9

## Construct Validation in Organizational Behavior Research

Jeffrey R. Edwards
*University of North Carolina*

A theory comprises two sets of relationships, one that links constructs that constitute the substance of the theory, and another that maps constructs onto phenomena that can be directly observed and measured (Bagozzi & Phillips, 1982; Costner, 1969). In organizational behavior (OB) research, theory development emphasizes relationships among constructs but devotes relatively little attention to relationships between constructs and measures (Schwab, 1980). These latter relationships are crucial to theory development, because they provide the means by which constructs become accessible to empirical research and theories are rendered testable. Moreover, because the relationships between constructs and measures are integral to a theory, theory testing is incomplete unless these relationships are scrutinized. Thus, the relationships between constructs and measures constitute an auxiliary theory that itself is subject to empirical testing and falsification (Costner, 1969; Cronbach & Meehl, 1955; Schwab, 1980).

Relationships between constructs and measures are the essence of construct validity. At its most fundamental level, construct validity concerns the degree to which a measure captures its intended theoretical construct (Cronbach & Meehl, 1955). Although the notion of construct validity is straightforward, procedures used to assess construct validity are complex and have evolved considerably during the past several decades. These procedures present a potentially bewildering array of choices for OB researchers confronted with crucial task of establishing the correspondence between theoretical constructs and their measures.

This chapter provides a chronological treatment of approaches to construct validation. The chapter begins by defining constructs and measures, the basic elements of construct validation. Construct validity is then defined and distinguished from other forms of validity. Next, approaches to construct validation are discussed, focusing on formulations of the relationship between constructs and measures and statistical procedures to assess reliability and convergent and discriminant validity. These approaches are organized chronologically in terms of classical approaches prevalent from the 1950s through the 1970s, modern approaches of the 1980s and 1990s, and emerging approaches that capture recent developments and future trends. The chapter concludes with recommendations for assessing and enhancing the construct validity of measures used in OB research.

## DEFINITIONS

This section offers definitions of the terms *construct, measure,* and *construct validity.* Definitions of these terms have evolved over the years, as evidenced by successive publications of the American Psychological Association standards for educational and psychological testing (American Psychological Association, 1966, 1985, 1999) and treatises on construct validity by Campbell (1960, 1996), Cronbach (1971, 1989; Cronbach & Meehl, 1955), and Messick (1975, 1981, 1995). However, the nuances that mark this evolution are anchored in core ideas that have remained stable. This stability is reflected in the definitions adopted here, which provide a consistent backdrop against which to track the development of construct validation procedures.

### Construct

A *construct* is a conceptual term used to describe a phenomenon of theoretical interest (Cronbach & Meehl, 1955; Edwards & Bagozzi, 2000; Messick, 1981). Constructs are terms researchers invent to describe, organize, and assign meaning to phenomena relevant to a domain of research (Cronbach & Meehl, 1955; Messick, 1981; Nunnally, 1978; Schwab, 1980). Although constructs are literally constructed, or put together, by researchers (Nunnally, 1978; Schwab, 1980), the phenomena constructs describe are real and exist independently of the researcher (Arvey, 1992; Cook & Campbell, 1979; Loevinger, 1957; MacCorquodale & Meehl, 1948; Messick, 1981). For example, attitudes such as job satisfaction and organizational commitment are real subjective experiences of people in organizations, and characteristics of social relationships such as trust and conflict are real to people engaged in those relationships. Although constructs refer to real phenomena, these phenomena cannot be observed directly or objectively. Rather, researchers view these phenomena through the distorted epistemological lenses that constructs provide and rely on flawed measures that yield imperfect empirical traces (Cook & Campbell, 1979; Loevinger, 1957; Messick, 1981). This definition represents a critical realist perspective on the meaning of constructs (Bhaskar, 1978; Cook & Campbell, 1979). It is realist because it asserts that constructs refer to actual psychological and social phenomena that exist separately from our attempts to study them, and it is critical because it recognizes that these phenomena cannot be assessed with complete accuracy, due to imperfections in our sensory and methodological apparatus (Cook & Campbell, 1979; Delanty, 1997; Loevinger, 1957; Messick, 1981; Zuriff, 1998).

## Measure

A *measure* is an observed score gathered through self-report, interview, observation, or some other means (DeVellis, 1991; Edwards & Bagozzi, 2000; Lord & Novick, 1968; Messick, 1995). Put simply, a measure is a quantified record, such as an item response, that serves as an empirical representation of a construct. A measure does not define a construct, as in strict operationalism (Campbell, 1960; Cronbach & Meehl, 1955), but rather is one of various possible indicators of the construct, all of which are considered fallible (Messick, 1995). As defined here, a measure is not an instrument used to gather data, such as a questionnaire, interview script, or observation protocol, nor is it the process by which data are generated and gathered (Alreck & Settle, 1995; Rea & Parker, 1992; Sudman, Bradburn, & Schwarz, 1996). Rather, a measure is an observed record or trace that serves as imperfect empirical evidence of a construct.

## Construct Validity

*Construct validity* refers to the correspondence between a construct and a measure taken as evidence of the construct (Cronbach & Meehl, 1955; Nunnally, 1978; Schwab, 1980). Construct validity does not refer to the inherent properties of a measure or instrument. Instead, it concerns the degree to which a measure represents a particular construct and allows credible inferences regarding the nature of the construct (Cronbach, 1971; Cronbach & Meehl, 1955). Thus, a particular measure may demonstrate different degrees of construct validity depending on the construct for which the measure is taken as evidence. Moreover, construct validity is not an all-or-nothing phenomenon, such that a measure that demonstrates certain properties is deemed construct valid. Rather, construct validity is a matter of degree based on the cumulative evidence bearing on the correspondence between a construct and measure (Cronbach & Meehl, 1955). Finally, construct validation is not a task that is accomplished and then set aside. To the contrary, construct validation is an ongoing process, such that each application of an instrument provides further evidence regarding the construct validity of the instrument and the measures it generates (Cronbach, 1989; Nunnally, 1978).

Construct validity may be separated into trait validity and nomological validity (Campbell, 1960). Trait validity focuses on the relationship between the construct and measure isolated from the broader theory in which the construct is embedded. Evidence for trait validity is provided by convergence of measures intended to represent the same construct and divergence among measures designed to represent different constructs. Convergence of measures sharing the same method (e.g., all self-report) indicates reliability, whereas convergence of measures using different methods represents convergent validity (Campbell, 1960; Campbell & Fiske, 1959). Divergence among measures using the same or different methods demonstrates discriminant validity (Campbell, 1960; Campbell & Fiske, 1959). Reliability and convergent validity provide evidence for a construct acting as a common cause of the measures, and discriminant validity provides evidence against the intrusion of other unintended constructs (Messick, 1995). Nomological validity is based on evidence that measures of a construct exhibit relationships with measures of other constructs in accordance with relevant theory (Carmines & Zeller, 1979; Cronbach & Meehl, 1955). Thus, nomological validity entails the evaluation of a measure within a broader theory that describes the causes, effects, and correlates of the construct and how they relate to one another (Campbell, 1960; Cronbach & Meehl, 1955).

Construct validity may be distinguished from content validity and criterion-oriented validity (Nunnally, 1978). Content validity is the degree to which a measure represents a particular domain of content. Content validity is achieved by defining the content domain of interest, selecting or developing items that represent the domain, and assembling the items into a test, survey, or other instrument. Content validity is not assessed using empirical or statistical procedures, but instead relies on "appeals to reason" (Nunnally, 1978, p. 93) that the procedures used to develop an instrument ensure that important content has been adequately sampled and represented.[1] Criterion-oriented validity refers to the relationship between the measure of interest and some criterion measure deemed important, such as job perfor-

---

[1] The assessment of item content after an instrument has been developed has been described as face validity (Nunnally, 1978) or content adequacy (Schriesheim, Cogliser, Scandura, Lankau, & Powers, 1999), and statistical procedures for its assessment have been developed (Schriesheim et al., 1999).

mance. Criterion-oriented validity places less emphasis on the conceptual interpretation of a measure than on its ability to predict a criterion.

Construct validity may be distinguished from other forms of validity that are vital to the research process. Cook and Campbell (1979) organized these forms of validity into three broad categories. Statistical conclusion validity is whether a study can establish the presence and magnitude of the relationship between two variables. Internal validity concerns whether the relationship between a presumed cause and effect is free from alternative explanations that implicate other causes or methodological artifacts. Finally, external validity is whether the findings from a study can be generalized to other samples, settings, and time frames. Because these forms of validity do not bear directly on the relationships between constructs and measures, they are not discussed further in this chapter (for thorough treatments, see Cook & Campbell, 1979; Cook, Campbell, & Peracchio, 1990).

## CONSTRUCT VALIDATION APPROACHES

The past several decades have brought significant developments in procedures used to assess construct validity. These developments are signified by increasingly sophisticated views of the relationship between constructs and measures and advances in statistical procedures for assessing reliability and convergent and discriminant validity. Methods for studying nomological validity have advanced as well, but these advancements have tracked general developments in analyzing relationships among constructs, as marked by the evolution from analysis of variance to multiple regression, path analysis, and structural equation modeling (Cohen, 1968; Jöreskog, 1974; Werts & Linn, 1970; Williams & James, 1994). These developments implicate the whole of applied statistics, and reviewing them is well beyond the scope of this chapter. Rather, the following discussion tracks the evolution of three core elements of construct validation: (a) the specification of the relationship between constructs and measures; (b) reliability; and (c) convergent and discriminant validity. These three elements provide a focused treatment of construct validation approaches and encompass many important analytical developments that deal specifically with mapping constructs onto measures. Moreover, these aspects of construct validation should be addressed prior to investigating nomological validity, because if a measure does not display construct validity when examined in isolation, it is unwise to embed the measure within a broader theoretical framework. Thus, the elements of construct validation examined in this chapter are natural precursors to the essential task of nomological validation (Cronbach & Meehl, 1955).

For expository purposes, the construct validation approaches discussed here are separated chronologically into classical, modern, and emerging approaches to construct validation. The boundary between classical and modern approaches roughly coincides with the advent of confirmatory factor analysis (CFA), and the boundary between modern and emerging approaches is marked by developments that increase the complexity of the relationship between constructs and measures and relax traditional assumptions that underlie analytical procedures used for construct validation. As will become evident, the classification of construct validation approaches into these three time frames reflects their usage in the OB literature more than their development in the statistical literature. For instance, although CFA is the hallmark of modern approaches to construct validation, its development predates its general use in the OB literature by over a decade (Jöreskog, 1969). Likewise, some approaches that are just beginning to emerge in the OB literature, such as generalizability theory (DeShon, 2002), can be traced back more than three decades (Cronbach, Gleser, Nanda, & Rajaratnam, 1972). These time lags are natural for the development and use of methodological procedures in general, and it is hoped that this chapter will help accelerate the diffusion of recently developed construct validation procedures in OB research.

## Classical Approaches

Classical approaches to construct validation are rooted in seminal work on measurement and psychometric theory of the 1950s and 1960s (e.g., Campbell, 1960; Campbell & Fiske, 1959; Cronbach & Meehl, 1955; Lord & Novick, 1968; Nunnally, 1967). This work laid the foundation for conceptualizing and analyzing relationships between constructs and measures and established the language of construct validation. These approaches are discussed below.

*Relationship Between Constructs and Measures.* The fundamental equation of classical measurement theory (Gulliksen, 1950; Lord & Novick, 1968) is as follows:

$$X_i = T + e_i \tag{1}$$

where $X_i$ is the ith measure of $T$, $T$ is an unobserved true score, and $e_i$ is measurement error, which encompasses all sources of variance in $X_i$ other than $T$. It is assumed that $e_i$ is a random variable with zero mean and is uncorrelated with $T$ and with the true scores and errors of other measures (Lord & Novick, 1968). Figure 9.1 portrays the relationships between a single true score and three measures, along with their associated

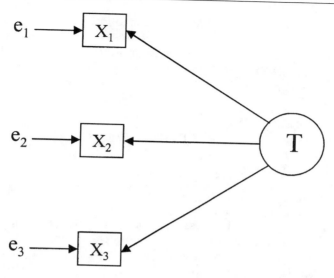

FIG. 9.1 Relationship between true score and measures according to classical measurement theory.

error terms. (In this and subsequent figures, variables that signify constructs are represented by circles, and variables that represent measures are indicated by squares.) As will be seen, Fig. 9.1 provides a useful point of departure for comparing classical measurement theory to modern and emerging approaches to construct validation.

The interpretation of Equation 1 in terms of the relationship between a construct and measure hinges on the meaning of the true score $T$. In classical measurement theory (Lord & Novick, 1968; Nunnally, 1978), a true score is typically defined as the hypothetical average of an infinite number of scores for a particular subject. As the number of scores constituting the average approaches infinity, the proportion of error variance in the average approaches zero. Therefore, a true score may be interpreted as a subject's score on $X_i$ that is free from random measurement error. This score might not accurately represent the value of the construct, because any systematic errors in $X_i$, such as mean bias or floor and ceiling effects, become part of the hypothetical average that defines the true score (Cronbach et al., 1972). Thus, a true score may be interpreted as the value of a construct for a subject if: (a) the measure $X_i$ is unbiased, such that repeated measures of $X_i$ converge on the correct value of the construct; and (b) measurement errors are uncorrelated with the construct, such that errors do not tend to be positive or negative depending on the level of the construct (Lord & Novick,

1968). These assumptions are adopted in the following discussion, thereby framing $T$ as the value of the construct of interest.

Equation 1 allows several useful derivations that provide the basis for understanding the correspondence between constructs and measures. We begin with the variance of $X_i$, which may be written as:

$$
\begin{aligned}
V(X_i) &= V(T+e) \\
&= V(T)+V(e_i)+2C(T,e_i) \\
&= V(T)+V(e_i)
\end{aligned}
\tag{2}
$$

where V(.) and C(.) refer to the variance and covariance, respectively, of a given term for multiple subjects. Equation 2 follows from standard rules of covariance algebra and the assumption that $T$ and $e_i$ are uncorrelated. From Equation 2, it can be seen that the variance of a measure is the sum of the variance of the true score and the variance of measurement error. Because a true score signifies an error-free measure of a construct, $V(T)$ indicates the amount of variance in $X$ that is attributable to the construct. Naturally, it is desirable for $V(T)$ to be large relative to $V(e_i)$.

Next, consider the covariance of $X_i$ with $T$, which captures the magnitude of the relationship between a measure and its associated construct:

$$
\begin{aligned}
C(X_i,T) &= C[(T+e_i),T] \\
&= C(T,T)+C(T,e_i) \\
&= V(T).
\end{aligned}
\tag{3}
$$

Equation 3 indicates that the covariance between a measure and its true score, and hence the construct of interest, is represented by the variance of the true score.

Finally, the covariance between two measures, designated here as $X_i = T_p + e_i$ and $X_j = T_q + e_j$, may be written as:

$$
\begin{aligned}
C(X_i,X_j) &= C[(T_p+e_i),(T_q+e_j)] \\
&= C(T_p,T_q)+C(T_p,e_j)+C(T_q,e_i)+C(e_i,e_j) \\
&= C(T_p,T_q).
\end{aligned}
\tag{4}
$$

Equation 4 shows that the covariance between the true scores $T_p$ and $T_q$ equals the covariance between their respective measures $X_i$ and $X_j$. Thus, the covariance between the constructs underlying two measures is indicated by the covariance between the measures themselves.

If $X_i$ and $X_j$ in Equation 4 refer to the same construct, they are termed *congeneric*, meaning their true scores are perfectly correlated but need not have the same value. If $X_i$ and $X_j$ have the same true scores, such that $T_p = T_q = T$, they are termed *tau equivalent*. Under tau equivalence, $C(T_p, T_q) = C(T, T) = V(T)$, which indicates that the covariances between all pairs of tau equivalent measures have the same value and equal the variance of their common true score. These properties also hold for measures that are *essentially tau equivalent*, which have true scores that differ by no more than a constant (Novick & Lewis, 1967). Finally, if $X_i$ and $X_j$ have the same true scores as well as the same error variances, such that $V(e_i) = V(e_j) = V(e)$, they are termed *parallel*. Because parallel measures have equal true score variances and equal error variances, the measures themselves also have equal variances, which in turn implies that the covariances and correlations among pairs of parallel measures are equal. These principles and the associated derivations form the basis of classical measurement theory and provide the foundation for subsequent developments.

*Reliability.*   Reliability refers to the proportion of true score variance in a measure. The reliability of $X$ may be expressed algebraically as follows:

$$\rho_{x_i} = V(T) / V(X_i). \tag{5}$$

For a single item, $\rho_{x_i}$ cannot be estimated, given that $V(X_i)$ is known but $V(T)$ is unknown. This dilemma spawned various approaches to the estimation of reliability. One approach is based on the notion of parallel measures of $T$. By definition, the correlation between parallel measures equals their covariance divided by the product of their standard deviations. As noted previously, the covariance between parallel measures equals $V(T)$, and the variances of parallel measures have a common value $V(X_i)$, which in turn implies that the product of their standard deviations is also $V(X_i)$. Hence, the correlation between parallel measures equals $V(T) / V(X_i)$ and represents the reliability of either measure. This reasoning underlies the alternative forms method of reliability estimation (Carmines & Zeller, 1979; Nunnally, 1978). Although simple in concept, this approach carries the practical problem of developing measures that meet the rather stringent conditions of parallel measurement.

One way to address the problem of developing parallel measures is to administer the same measure twice, based on the premise that a measure is parallel with itself. This approach underlies the test–retest method of reliability estimation, which uses the correlation between a measure collected on two occasions as an estimate of the reliability of the measure. The test–retest approach has several drawbacks, such as the inability to distinguish low reliability from actual change in the true score, practice and consistency effects that may inflate test–retest correlations, and the possibility that biases and other artifacts embedded in measurement errors are correlated over time, thereby violating a key assumption of classical measurement theory (Bohrnstedt, 1983; Nunnally, 1978).

An alternative to the test–retest approach is the split-half approach, in which a set of items is administered on a single occasion and scores on the items are divided into two subsets. Given that the subsets are drawn from the same set, they are considered alternative forms, which means that their correlation represents the reliability of either subset. Because the subsets contain fewer items than the full set, the correlation between the subsets of items underestimates the reliability of a measure created by summing the full set. This underestimation can be corrected by applying the Spearman-Brown prophecy formula (Nunnally, 1978):

$$\rho_X = \frac{2r_{X_1 X_2}}{1 + r_{X_1 X_2}}$$

(6)

where $X_1$ and $X_2$ are sums of items from the two split halves and $r_{X_1 X_2}$ is the correlation between these sums. Despite its advantages, the split-half approach carries a fundamental ambiguity, in that a set of items can be split in numerous ways, each of which may yield a different reliability estimate.

The ambiguity of the split-half approach is resolved by Cronbach's alpha (Cronbach, 1951), which equals the average of all possible split-half reliability estimates for a set of items. Alpha may be interpreted as the proportion of true score variance in a sum of essentially tau equivalent items. The intuition behind alpha can be grasped by considering the following sum of $k$ tau equivalent items:

$$\sum_{i=1}^{k} X_i = \sum_{i=1}^{k} (T + e_i).$$

(7)

The true score $T$ is not indexed because it is assumed to be the same for all $X_i$. The variance of the item sum may be written as:

$$V\left(\sum_{i=1}^{k} X_i\right) = V\left[\sum_{i=1}^{k} (T + e_i)\right]$$
$$= V\left[(T + e_1) + (T + e_2) + \ldots (T + e_k)\right]$$
$$= V(kT + e_1 + e_2 + \ldots + e_k)$$
$$= k^2 V(T) + \sum_{i=1}^{k} V(e_i).$$

(8)

The amount of true score variance in the sum is represented by $k^2 V(T)$. Therefore, the proportion of true score variance is $k^2 V(T) / V\left(\sum_{i=1}^{k} X_i\right)$.

$V\left(\sum_{i=1}^{k} X_i\right)$ can be computed by taking the variance of the item sum, and $V(T)$ can be obtained by recalling that, for essentially tau equivalent items, $V(T)$ equals the covariance between any two items. Because all interitem covariances are equal for essentially tau equivalent items, any one of the covariances will serve as an estimate of $V(T)$. In practice, interitem covariances usually vary, in which case it is sensible to use the average interitem covariance to represent $V(T)$ (McDonald, 1999). This approach leads to the following equation for alpha (Cronbach, 1951):

$$\alpha = \frac{k^2 \overline{C}(X_i, X_j)}{V\left(\sum_{i=1}^{k} X_i\right)}.$$

(9)

An algebraically equivalent expression can be computed from the variances of the items and their sum (Cronbach, 1951; Nunnally, 1978):

$$\alpha = \frac{k}{k-1} \frac{V\left(\sum_{i=1}^{k} X_i\right) - \sum_{i=1}^{k} V(X_i)}{V\left(\sum_{i=1}^{k} X_i\right)}.$$

(10)

The assumption of essential tau equivalence is crucial to alpha. To the extent this assumption is violated, alpha underestimates the reliability of the item sum (Heise & Bohrnstedt, 1970). Hence, alpha should be considered a lower bound estimate of reliability and equals reliability when the items constituting the sum are essentially tau equivalent.

*Convergent and Discriminant Validity.* Classical approaches to construct validation have generally relied on two methods for assessing convergent and discriminant validity. One method involves submitting measures to principal components analysis or common factor analysis and determining whether measures of the same construct cluster together and measures of different constructs separate from one another. The principal components model may be written as follows (Harman, 1976; Kim & Mueller, 1978):

$$C_j = b_{j1} X_1 + b_{j2} X_2 + \ldots + b_{jk} X_k$$

$$= \sum_{i=1}^{k} b_{ji} X_i \tag{11}$$

where $C_j$ represents the jth principal component and $b_{ji}$ is a coefficient linking the ith measure to the jth component. Equation 11 shows that a principal component is treated as a weighted linear combination of measures, and measurement error is disregarded. In contrast, the common factor model is as follows (Harman, 1976; Kim & Mueller, 1978):

$$X_i = b_{i1} F_1 + b_{i2} F_2 + \ldots + b_{im} F_m + d_i U_i$$

$$= \sum_{j=i}^{m} b_{ij} F_j + d_i U_i \tag{12}$$

where $F_j$ represents the jth common factor, $b_{ij}$ is a coefficient linking the ith measure to the jth factor, $U_i$ is the uniqueness of $X_i$, or the part of $X_i$ that is not explained by the common factors, and $d_i$ is a coefficient linking $U_i$ to $X_i$. $U_i$ combines random measurement error and measure specificity, which refers to stable sources of variance in a particular $X_i$ that are not shared with other $X_i$. Because the common factor model incorporates measurement error and treats measures as outcomes of factors, it is more consistent with classical measurement theory, as captured by Equation 1. Nonetheless, principal components analysis and common factor analysis typically yield similar conclusions regarding the convergence and divergence of measures (Velicer & Jackson, 1990), although they tend to yield different estimates of population parameters that quantify the relationships between constructs and measures (Mulaik, 1990; Snook & Gorsuch, 1989; Widaman, 1993).

A more systematic approach to assessing convergent and discriminant validity is based on the multitrait–multimethod (MTMM) matrix (Campbell & Fiske, 1959). A MTMM matrix arranges correlations among measures of several traits, or constructs, using different methods such that criteria for assessing convergent and discriminant validity can be readily applied. Table 9.1 shows a hypothetical MTMM matrix for three traits labeled A, B, and C, and three methods designated 1, 2, and 3. The solid triangles contain heterotrait-monomethod values, which are correlations among measures of different traits using the same method. The dashed triangles contain heterotrait-heteromethod values, which are correlations among measures of different traits using different methods. In boldface are monotrait-heteromethod values, which represent correlations between measures

**Table 9.1**

**Multitrait-Multimethod Matrix With Three Traits and Three Methods**

| | Constructs | Method 1 | | | Method 2 | | | Method 3 | | |
|---|---|---|---|---|---|---|---|---|---|---|
| | | A | B | C | A | B | C | A | B | C |
| Method 1 | Construct A | $(\alpha_{A1})$ | | | | | | | | |
| | Construct B | $r_{A1B1}$ | $(\alpha_{B1})$ | | | | | | | |
| | Construct C | $r_{A1C1}$ | $r_{B1C1}$ | $(\alpha_{C1})$ | | | | | | |
| Method 2 | Construct A | $r_{A1A2}$ | $r_{B1A2}$ | $r_{C1A2}$ | $(\alpha_{A2})$ | | | | | |
| | Construct B | $r_{A1B2}$ | $r_{B1B2}$ | $r_{C1B2}$ | $r_{A2B2}$ | $(\alpha_{B2})$ | | | | |
| | Construct C | $r_{A1C2}$ | $r_{B1C2}$ | $r_{C1C2}$ | $r_{A2C2}$ | $r_{B2C2}$ | $(\alpha_{C2})$ | | | |
| Method 3 | Construct A | $r_{A1A3}$ | $r_{B1A3}$ | $r_{C1A3}$ | $r_{A2A3}$ | $r_{B2A3}$ | $r_{C2A3}$ | $(\alpha_{A3})$ | | |
| | Construct B | $r_{A1B3}$ | $r_{B1B3}$ | $r_{C1B3}$ | $r_{A2B3}$ | $r_{B2B3}$ | $r_{C2B3}$ | $r_{A3B3}$ | $(\alpha_{B3})$ | |
| | Construct C | $r_{A1C3}$ | $r_{B1C3}$ | $r_{C1C3}$ | $r_{A2C3}$ | $r_{B2C3}$ | $r_{C2C3}$ | $r_{A3C3}$ | $r_{B3C3}$ | $(\alpha_{C3})$ |

of the same trait using different methods. These values constitute the validity diagonal within the heteromethod blocks formed by the correlations between all measures obtained from a given pair of methods. Finally, the parentheses contain monotrait-monomethod values, which signify the reliabilities of the measures.

Campbell and Fiske (1959) proposed the following criteria for assessing convergent and discriminant validity using the MTMM matrix. Convergent validity is evidenced when the monotrait-heteromethod values are significantly different from zero and large enough to warrant further examination of validity. This criterion demonstrates that measures of the same construct using different methods are related. Discriminant validity rests on three criteria. First, monotrait-heteromethod values should be larger than values in the same row and column in the heterotrait-heteromethod triangles. For instance, $r_{A1A2}$ in Table 9.1 should be larger than $r_{A1B2}$, $r_{A1C2}$, $r_{B1A2}$, and $r_{C1A2}$. This criterion establishes that measures of the same construct using different methods correlate more highly than measures of different constructs using different methods. Second, the monotrait-heteromethod values for each measure should be larger than values in the heterotrait-monomethod triangles that entail that measure. To illustrate using the measure of construct A using method 1, $r_{A1A2}$ and $r_{A1A3}$ should be larger than $r_{A1B1}$ and $r_{A1C1}$.

This criterion shows that a measure correlates more highly with measures of the same construct using different methods than with measures of different constructs that happen to use the same method. Third, the pattern of correlations among the traits in each heterotrait triangle should be the same regardless of the method employed. For instance, if the relative magnitudes of the correlations among constructs A, B, and C measured with method 1 are $r_{A1B1} > r_{A1C1} > r_{B1C1}$, then the same ordering should be obtained for methods 2 and 3. This criterion may also be applied to individual measures. For example, if construct A measured with method 1 correlates more strongly with construct B than with construct C when both are measured with method 1 (i.e., $r_{A1B1} > r_{A1C1}$), then it should also correlate more strongly with construct B than with construct C when the two are measured with methods 2 and 3 (i.e., $r_{A1B2} > r_{A1C2}$ and $r_{A1B3} > r_{A1C3}$ should both hold). In addition to these criteria for convergent and discriminant validity, Campbell and Fiske (1959) pointed out that differences between corresponding values in the monomethod and heteromethod triangles provide evidence for method variance. Returning to Table 9.1, if $r_{A1B1}$ is larger than $r_{A1B2}$, then the correlation between measures of constructs A and B using method 1 is presumably inflated by their reliance on the same method. Differences between correlations in a MTMM matrix can be tested using procedures for comparing dependent correlations (Steiger, 1980), and differences in patterns of correlations can be tested using Kendall's coefficient of concordance, which yields a chi-square statistic representing the difference between two rankings (Bagozzi, Yi, & Phillips, 1991; McNemar, 1962).

The Campbell and Fiske (1959) procedure for assessing convergent and discriminant validity has many important strengths, perhaps the foremost of which is the distinction between traits and methods as two systematic sources of variance in a measure. However, the procedure has several shortcomings. First, it does not quantify the degree to which convergent and discriminant validity have been demonstrated (Bagozzi et al., 1991; Schmitt & Stults, 1986). Instead, the procedure yields a count of the number of confirming and disconfirming comparisons involving the correlations of the MTMM matrix. Second, the procedure does not separate method variance from random measurement error (Schmitt & Stults, 1986). This shortcoming might be addressed by conducting MTMM analyses using disattenuated correlations (Althauser & Heberlein, 1970; Jackson, 1969), but doing so prevents the use of conventional statistical tests for comparing correlations. Third, and perhaps most important, the Campbell and Fiske (1959) criteria yield unambiguous conclusions regarding convergent and discriminant validity only under highly restrictive assumptions regarding the magnitudes of trait and method effects and the correlations between method factors (Althauser, 1974; Althauser & Heberlein, 1970; Schmitt & Stults, 1986). Many of these shortcomings were recognized by Campbell and Fiske (1959), but their resolution awaited the application of CFA to MTMM matrices, which is a hallmark of modern approaches to construct validation.

## Modern Approaches

Modern construct validation approaches were spawned by the advent of CFA, which brought many important developments to the construct validation process. These developments are discussed in general sources on CFA (Bollen, 1989; Jöreskog, 1971, 1974; Long, 1983) and follow logically from the application of CFA to reliability and construct validity (Bagozzi et al., 1991; Schmitt & Stults, 1986). These developments and their relevance to construct validation are discussed below.

*Relationships Between Constructs and Measures.* In CFA, the relationship between a construct and measure may be expressed as:

$$X_i = \lambda_i \xi + \delta_i. \tag{13}$$

Although Equation 13 is similar to Equation 1 based on classical measurement theory, several differences should be noted. First, $\xi$ does not signify the hypothetical average of $X_i$, but instead represents a latent variable or factor that corresponds to a theoretical construct (Bollen, 1989; Jöreskog & Sörbom, 1996). Second, unlike Equation 1, Equation 13 includes the coefficient $\lambda_i$ on $\xi$, which allows the relationships between $\xi$ and the $X_i$ to vary. Third, whereas the $e_i$ in Equation 1 represents random measurement error, the $\delta_i$ in Equation 13 signify the uniquenesses of the $X_i$, which are composed of random measurement error and measurement specificity (i.e., stable aspects of each $X_i$ that are not explained by the common factor $\xi$). It is assumed that the $\delta_i$ have zero means and are uncorrelated with one another and with $\xi$, analogous to the assumptions underlying classical measurement theory (Bollen, 1989; Jöreskog & Sörbom, 1996). Figure 9.2 displays the relationship between a construct and three measures, and comparing Fig. 9.1 to Fig. 9.2 further reinforces the basic distinctions between classical and modern approaches to specifying relationships between constructs and measures.

Drawing from the assumptions underlying Equation 13, several useful expressions can be derived, similar to those developed under classical measurement theory. First, the variance of $X_i$ can be written as:

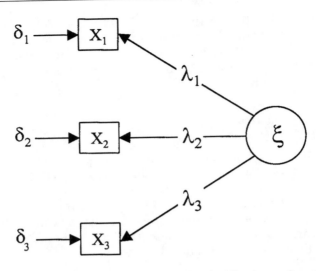

FIG. 9.2   Relationship between construct and measures following confirmatory factor analysis.

$$V(X_i) = V(\lambda_i \xi + \delta_i)$$
$$= \lambda_i^2 V(\xi) + V(\delta_i) + 2\lambda_i C(\xi, \delta_i)$$
$$= \lambda_i^2 V(\xi) + V(\delta_i)$$
$$= \lambda_i^2 \phi + \theta_{\delta_{ii}} \tag{14}$$

where $\phi$ represents the variance of $\xi$ and $\theta_{\delta_{ii}}$ is the variance of $\delta_i$, respectively (Bollen, 1989; Jöreskog & Sörbom, 1996). According to Equation 14, the amount variance in $X_i$ attributable to the construct $\xi$ is represented by $\lambda_i^2 \phi$. Next, the covariance between $X_i$ and $\xi$ is:

$$C(X_i, \xi) = C\big[(\lambda_i \xi + \delta_i), \xi\big]$$
$$= \lambda_i C(\xi, \xi) + \lambda_i C(\xi, \delta_i)$$
$$= \lambda_i V(\xi)$$
$$= \lambda_i \phi. \tag{15}$$

Finally, the covariance between two measures $X_i = \lambda_i \xi_p + \delta_i$ and $X_j = \lambda_j \xi_q + \delta_j$ is:

$$C(X_i, X_j) = C\left[(\lambda_i \xi_p + \delta_i), (\lambda_j \xi_q + \delta_j)\right]$$
$$= \lambda_i \lambda_j C(\xi_p, \xi_q) + \lambda_i C(\xi_p, \delta_j) + \lambda_j C(\xi_q, \delta_i) + C(\delta_i, \delta_j)$$
$$= \lambda_i \lambda_j C(\xi_p, \xi_q)$$
$$= \lambda_i \lambda_j \phi_{pq}.$$

$$(16)$$

where $\phi_{pq}$ is the covariance between $\xi_p$ and $\xi_q$. If $X_i$ and $X_j$ refer to the same construct, such that $\xi_p = \xi_q = \xi$, then Equation 16 simplifies to:

$$C(X_i, X_j) = \lambda_i \lambda_j \phi .$$

$$(17)$$

Equations 14, 16, and 17 may be used to calculate the covariance matrix among the measures as reproduced by the CFA model, which provides the basis for evaluating the fit of the model to the data (Jöreskog & Sörbom, 1996).

The foregoing equations depict the $X_i$ as congeneric, given that: (a) each $X_i$ can have a different true score, since the composite term $\lambda_i \xi$ can vary across measures; and (b) the variances of the measurement errors can differ, as depicted by the $\theta_{\delta_{ii}}$. If the $X_i$ were tau equivalent, the $\lambda_i$ would be equal, and if the $X_i$ were parallel, the $\theta_{\delta_{ii}}$ would also be equal. These assumptions can be readily examined with CFA by imposing equality constraints on the relevant parameters and testing the decrease in model fit using the chi-square difference test (Jöreskog & Sörbom, 1996).

*Reliability.* Because Equation 11 relaxes the assumption of tau equivalence, it leads to a less restrictive formula for the reliability of an item sum. This formula can be derived by extending Equation 13 to represent the sum of $k$ congeneric items:

$$\sum_{i=1}^{k} X_i = \sum_{i=1}^{k} (\lambda_i \xi + \delta_i).$$

$$(18)$$

The variance of the item sum is:

$$
\begin{aligned}
\left( V \sum_{i=1}^{k} X_i \right) &= V\left[ \sum_{i=1}^{k} (\lambda_i \xi + \delta_i) \right] \\
&= V\left[ (\lambda_1 \xi + \delta_1) + (\lambda_2 \xi + \delta_2) + \ldots + (\lambda_k \xi + \delta_k) \right] \\
&= V\left[ \left( \sum_{i=1}^{k} \lambda_i \right) \xi + \sum_{i=1}^{k} \delta_i \right] \\
&= \left( \sum_{i=1}^{k} \lambda_i \right)^2 V(\xi) + \sum_{i=1}^{k} V(\delta_i) \\
&= \left( \sum_{i=1}^{k} \lambda_i \right)^2 \phi + \sum_{i=1}^{k} \theta_{\delta_{ii}}.
\end{aligned}
\tag{19}
$$

In Equation 19, the first term on the right represents the amount of true score variance in the item sum. Thus, the proportion of true score variance in the item sum may be written as:

$$
\omega = \frac{\left( \sum_{i=1}^{k} \lambda_i \right)^2 \phi}{V \sum_{i=1}^{k} X_i}.
\tag{20}
$$

Coefficient omega ($\omega$) represents the proportion of true score variance in a sum of $k$ congeneric items (McDonald, 1970). If the items are tau equivalent, omega reduces to alpha. Otherwise, omega gives a higher estimate of reliability than that given by alpha, depending on the degree to which the $\lambda_i$ differ from one another. An alternative expression for $\omega$ is obtained by substituting Equation 19 for the denominator of Equation 20 (Jöreskog, 1971; McDonald, 1970):

$$
\omega = \frac{\left( \sum_{i=1}^{k} \lambda_i \right)^2 \phi}{\left( \sum_{i=1}^{k} \lambda_i \right)^2 \phi + \sum_{i=1}^{k} \theta_{\delta_{ii}}}.
\tag{21}
$$

This substitution rests on the assumption that the $\delta_i$ are mutually independent. If this assumption does not hold, then Equation 21 will yield a biased estimate of reliability (Raykov, 2001). This bias is avoided by Equation

20, which incorporates the correct expression for the variance of the item sum regardless whether the $\delta_i$ are independent.

CFA also yields estimates of the reliabilities of the individual $X_i$. As shown by Equation 14, the variance of $X_i$ equals $\lambda_i^2 \phi + \theta_{\delta_{ii}}$, which in turn implies that the proportion of true score variance in $X_i$ is $\lambda_i^2 \phi / V(X_i)$. The quantities needed to calculate this ratio can be obtained from a CFA, provided multiple $X_i$ are available to achieve model identification (Bollen, 1989). Note that this approach limits true score variance to variance attributable to the common factor $\xi$, thereby treating measurement specificity and random measurement error in the same manner.

*Convergent and Discriminant Validity.* Shortcomings of the Campbell and Fiske (1959) procedure for analyzing MTMM matrices prompted the development of alternative approaches. Of these, CFA has emerged as the most widely used approach (Schmitt & Stults, 1986). This approach treats each measure as a function of a trait factor, a method factor, and measurement error, as indicated by the following equation (Jöreskog, 1971; Werts & Linn, 1970):

$$X_i = \lambda_{iTp} \xi_{Tp} + \lambda_{iMq} \xi_{Mq} + \delta_i \qquad (22)$$

where $\xi_{Tp}$ is trait $p$, $\xi_{Mq}$ is method $q$, and $\lambda_{iTp}$ and $\lambda_{iMq}$ are coefficients relating $X_i$ to $\xi_{Tp}$ and $\xi_{Mq}$, respectively. Thus, $X_i$ has two systematic sources of variance, one due to the substantive trait or construct of interest, and another generated by the method of data collection. These sources of variance, along with variance due to the error term $\delta_i$, can be seen by taking the variance of Equation 22:

$$
\begin{aligned}
V(X_i) &= V\left(\lambda_{iTp} \xi_{Tp} + \lambda_{iMq} \xi_{Mq} + \delta_i\right) \\
&= \lambda_{iTp}^2 V\left(\xi_{Tp}\right) + \lambda_{iMq}^2 V\left(\xi_{Mq}\right) + 2\lambda_{iTp} \lambda_{iMq} C\left(\xi_{Tp}, \xi_{Mq}\right) + V(\delta_i) \\
&= \lambda_{iTp}^2 \phi_{Tp} + \lambda_{iMq}^2 \phi_{Mq} + 2\lambda_{iTp} \lambda_{iMq} \phi_{TpMq} + \theta_{\delta_{ii}}.
\end{aligned}
\qquad (23)
$$

Models that include correlations between traits and methods are particularly prone to estimation problems, such as nonconvergence and improper solutions (Schmitt & Stults, 1986; Widaman, 1985). Therefore, traits are usually specified as independent of methods (Brannick & Spector, 1990; Marsh & Bailey, 1991; Schmitt & Stults, 1986), whereby Equation 23 simplifies to:

$$V(X_i) = \lambda_{iTp}^2 \phi_{Tp} + \lambda_{iMq}^2 \phi_{Mq} + \theta_{\delta_{ii}}. \qquad (24)$$

In Equation 24, the amount of trait variance in $X_i$ is represented by $\lambda^2_{iTp} \phi_{Tp}$, and the amount of method variance is captured by $\lambda^2_{iMq} \phi_{Mq}$. If the trait and method factors are standardized, such that their variances equal unity, then the amount of trait variance and method variance in $X_i$ equals its squared loadings on these two factors ($\lambda^2_{iTp}$ and $\lambda^2_{iMq}$, respectively). Dividing these quantities by $V(X_i)$ gives the proportion of trait and method variance in $X_i$.

Equation 22 also provides the basis for decomposing the correlations in a MTMM matrix into trait and method components (Althauser, 1974; Althauser & Heberlein, 1970; Alwin, 1974; Kalleberg & Kluegel, 1975; Schmitt, 1978; Werts & Linn, 1970). This decomposition yields important insights regarding the interpretation of these correlations and their implications for the criteria developed by Campbell and Fiske (1959). The process begins by introducing a second measure, $X_j$, which is expressed as follows:

$$X_j = \lambda_{jTr} \xi_{Tr} + \lambda_{jMs} \xi_{Ms} + \delta_j. \tag{25}$$

Analogous to $X_i$, $X_j$ is a function of a trait factor $\xi_{Tr}$, a method factor $\xi_{Ms}$, and measurement error $\delta_j$. Assuming measurement errors are random and trait factors are independent of method factors, the covariance between $X_i$ and $X_j$ may be written as:

$$C(X_i, X_j) = \lambda_{iTp} \lambda_{jTr} \phi_{TpTr} + \lambda_{iMq} \lambda_{jMs} \phi_{MqMs}. \tag{26}$$

By using different subscripts on trait factors and method factors, Equation 26 applies to measures that represent different traits and methods, corresponding to the heterotrait-heteromethod values in a MTMM matrix. If $X_i$ and $X_j$ share the same method, Equation 26 becomes:

$$C(X_i, X_j) = \lambda_{iTp} \lambda_{jTr} \phi_{TpTr} + \lambda_{iMq} \lambda_{jMq} \phi_{Mq} \tag{27}$$

where the subscript $q$ indicates the shared method. Thus, Equation 27 refers to the heterotrait-monomethod values in a MTMM matrix. Conversely, if $X_i$ and $X_j$ represent the same trait, Equation 26 simplifies to:

$$C(X_i, X_j) = \lambda_{iTp} \lambda_{jTp} \phi_{Tp} + \lambda_{iMq} \lambda_{jMs} \phi_{MqMs} \tag{28}$$

where the subscript $p$ identifies the shared trait. Equation 28 corresponds to the monotrait-heteromethod values, or validity diagonals, of a MTMM matrix.

To illustrate how Equations 26, 27, and 28 can be used to decompose correlations in a MTMM matrix, consider the model in Fig. 9.3, which has

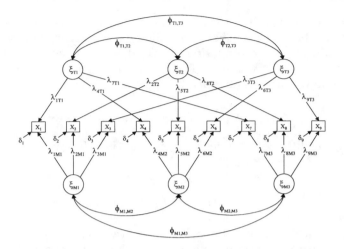

FIG. 9.3   Confirmatory factor analysis model for a MTMM matrix with three traits and three methods.

three trait factors and three method factors. For simplicity and without loss of generality, we assume all factors and measures are standardized. Recall that convergent validity is inferred from correlations between measures of the same trait using different methods. Applying Equation 28 to the correlation between $X_1$ and $X_4$ yields:

$$r_{X_1 X_4} = \lambda_{1T1} \lambda_{4T1} + \lambda_{1M1} \lambda_{4M2} \phi_{M1 M2}. \qquad (29)$$

As Equation 29 shows, the correlation between $X_1$ and $X_4$ has two components, one driven by the loadings of $X_1$ and $X_4$ on their common trait, and another that represents their loadings on their respective methods and the correlation between the methods. These two components correspond to the two pathways that connect $X_1$ and $X_4$ in Fig. 9.3 (these pathways may be derived formally using the tracing rule; Blalock, 1969). It is the former component, not the latter, that signifies the convergent validity of $X_1$ and $X_4$, because convergent validity frames the correlation between two measures in terms of their shared trait (Alwin, 1974; Marsh & Grayson, 1995). Assuming $X_1$ and $X_4$ contain some degree of method variance, such that $\lambda_{1M1}$ and $\lambda_{4M2}$ are nonzero, the correlation between $X_1$ and $X_4$ gives unambiguous evidence for convergent validity only if the correlation between the method factors is zero (Schmitt & Stults, 1986), which is unlikely in practice.

Similar procedures may be applied to comparisons among correlations taken as evidence for discriminant validity. For instance, the first criterion for discriminant validity stipulates that monotrait-heteromethod correlations should be larger than heterotrait-heteromethod correlations. This criterion is illustrated by comparing the correlation between $X_1$ and $X_4$ to the correlation between $X_1$ and $X_5$. The former correlation is shown in Equation 29, and the latter is obtained by applying Equation 26, which yields:

$$r_{X_1X_5} = \lambda_{IT1}\lambda_{5T2}\phi_{T1T2} + \lambda_{IM1}\lambda_{5M2}\phi_{M1M2}. \tag{30}$$

Thus, the difference between $r_{X1X4}$ and $r_{X1X5}$ is as follows:

$$r_{X_1X_4} - r_{X_1X_5} = \lambda_{IT1}\lambda_{4T1} + \lambda_{IM1}\lambda_{4M2}\phi_{M1M2} - \lambda_{IT1}\lambda_{5T2}\phi_{T1T2} + \lambda_{IM1}\lambda_{5M2}\phi_{M1M2}$$
$$= \lambda_{IT1}\left(\lambda_{4T1} - \lambda_{5T2}\phi_{T1T2}\right) + \lambda_{IM1}\phi_{M1M2}\left(\lambda_{4M2} - \lambda_{5M2}\right). \tag{31}$$

As Equation 31 shows, the difference between $r_{X1X4}$ and $r_{X1X5}$ is a function of terms representing the loadings and correlations of the trait and method factors underlying $X_1$, $X_4$, and $X_5$. Of these terms, $\phi_{T1T2}$ is the most relevant to discriminant validity, because this term can be used to assess whether the correlation between the two traits underlying the measures is less than unity, thereby indicating that the traits are distinct (Marsh & Grayson, 1995; Werts & Linn, 1970). Equation 31 provides this information only under restrictive conditions. For example, if all trait and method loadings have the same value $\lambda$ (Althauser & Heberlein, 1970), Equation 31 simplifies to:

$$r_{X_1X_4} - r_{X_1X_5} = \lambda^2\left(1 - \phi_{T1T2}\right). \tag{32}$$

For a particular loading $\lambda$, Equation 32 is a function of the term $(1 - \phi_{T1T2})$ and therefore captures discriminant validity (Althauser, 1974). Equation 32 also results when loadings on the trait factors are equal and either $X_1$ has no method variance or the method factors are uncorrelated. Because Equation 32 is based on conditions that are highly restrictive, it is rarely useful for assessing discriminant validity (Althauser, 1974; Althauser & Heberlein, 1970). A more direct approach is to assess whether $\phi_{T1T2}$ is statistically and meaningfully less than unity (Bagozzi et al., 1991; Kenny, 1976; Schmitt, 1978; Werts & Linn, 1970). The procedure used to obtain Equation 31 can be also used to express the second and third criteria for discriminant validity in equation form (Althauser, 1974; Kalleberg & Kluegel, 1975; Schmitt, 1978). In both cases, the resulting expressions are functions that yield a direct test of discriminant validity only under highly restrictive conditions.

The CFA approach to analyzing MTMM matrices also provides tests of overall model fit, thereby indicating whether the specified trait and method factor structure is consistent with the data. The specified model can also be compared to alternative models that impose various restrictions (Althauser, Heberlein, & Scott, 1971; Schmitt, 1978; Widaman, 1985). Widaman (1985) proposed a framework that separately specifies trait and method factors as follows: (a) no factors, such that measures assigned to each trait or method are uncorrelated; (b) factors with correlations fixed to unity, which translates into a single general trait factor or method factor; (c) factors with correlations fixed to zero, such that the trait or method factors are orthogonal; and (d) unconstrained factor correlations, such that correlations among trait factors and among method factors are freely estimated. Applying these specifications to trait factors and method factors yields 16 models with different representations of trait variance, method variance, and convergent and discriminant validity.[2] For instance, fixing trait correlations to unity creates a model in which trait factors exhibit no discriminant validity. Comparing the chi-square from this model to one from a model in which trait correlations are freely estimated yields an omnibus test of discriminant validity. In addition, the difference in chi-squares between models with and without trait factors provides an omnibus test of convergent validity. Analogously, the chi-square difference between models with and without method factors yields an omnibus test of method variance.

Although the CFA approach to analyzing MTMM matrices is appealing in several respects, it also suffers from a number of problems. First, the residual terms in the CFA model confound measurement specificity with random measurement error (Bagozzi et al., 1991; Marsh & Hocevar, 1988). This confounding occurs because the model represents reliability not as the internal consistency of the items that constitute each measure, but instead as the variance in each measure explained by its trait and method factors. As a result, low loadings might reflect small trait or method effects, attenuation due to measurement error, or some combination thereof (Marsh & Hocevar, 1988). Second, although the CFA model corrects the correlations among trait and method factors for measurement error, it does not remove the effects of measurement error from the correlations among the measures that constitute the MTMM matrix, because these measures are used as single indicators (Marsh & Hocevar, 1988). Third, the interpretation of trait and method factors is often ambiguous. For example, a set of correlated method factors might reflect a general trait factor not captured by the separate trait factors in the model (Marsh, 1989). The converse holds as well, such that a set of correlated trait factors might represent a general method effect. Fourth,

---

[2]As noted by Widaman (1985), some of the models derived from the framework cannot be meaningfully compared. For instance, a model with a single trait factor and no method factors is indistinguishable from a model with a single method factor and no trait factors.

the CFA model treats trait and method effects as additive, whereas trait and method factors might combine multiplicatively (Campbell & O'Connell, 1967, 1982).

Perhaps the most serious problem with the CFA model is that, in most cases, the model suffers from nonconvergence and improper solutions, such as negative error variances, factor correlations that exceed unity, and excessively large standard errors (Brannick & Spector, 1990; Marsh & Bailey, 1991; Wothke, 1987). This problem is particularly prevalent for models that include correlations between trait and method factors (Marsh, 1989), but it is also common for models in which trait factors are uncorrelated with method factors (Brannick & Spector, 1990; Marsh & Bailey, 1991; Wothke, 1987). This problem can be traced to identification issues inherent in the CFA model (Grayson & Marsh, 1994; Kenny & Kashy, 1992; Millsap, 1992; Wothke, 1987). Theoretically, the model is identified if it contains at least three trait factors and three method factors (Alwin, 1974; Werts & Linn, 1970). However, if the parameters in the model follow certain patterns, the model is empirically under-identified, meaning that a unique set of estimates cannot be obtained even though the model is theoretically identified. For example, if the correlations among the trait factors and among the method factors are unity and the trait and method factors are independent, the CFA model is equivalent to an exploratory factor model with two orthogonal factors. This model is not identified unless one of the loadings is fixed to establish the orientation of the factors (Wothke, 1987). Likewise, the model is not identified if, for each trait and method factor, the loadings are equal for all measures assigned to that factor (Kenny & Kashy, 1992). This pattern is a special case of a factor loading matrix that is not of full column rank, which is sufficient to establish that the model is not identified (Grayson & Marsh, 1994). Even if the loadings do not exactly conform to a pattern that produces deficient column rank, as would be expected when loadings are freely estimated using real data, estimation problems are likely if the loadings roughly approximate such a pattern (Kenny & Kashy, 1992). One way to address these estimation problems is to impose constraints on the trait and method factor loadings. For instance, Millsap (1992) identified conditions for rotational uniqueness for the CFA model that translate into equality constraints on selected trait and method loadings. Although rotational uniqueness does not solve the general identification problem (Bollen & Jöreskog, 1985), it can avoid improper solutions common in CFA models (Millsap, 1992). Estimation problems with the CFA model can also be addressed by adopting different models for analyzing MTMM data, as discussed in the following section.

## Emerging Approaches

Emerging approaches to construct validation are characterized by advances in CFA that relax traditional assumptions regarding the form of the relationship between constructs and measures and address shortcomings that became evident in initial applications of CFA to estimating reliability and convergent and discriminant validity. These advancements and their relevance to construct validation are summarized below.

*Relationships Between Constructs and Measures.* Most applications of CFA specify the relationship between constructs and measures according to Equation 13. However, alternative specifications that elaborate or reframe this relationship have gained increased attention. One alternative introduces an intercept into the equation relating constructs to measures, as follows:

$$X_i = \tau_i + \lambda_i + \xi + \delta_i \qquad (33)$$

Intercepts are useful when the means of $\xi$ and the $X_i$ are of interest, as in studies that compare the means of constructs between samples, such as experimental groups, or within a sample over time. To estimate models with means and intercepts, the input covariance matrix of the $X_i$ is supplemented by a vector of means, and parameters representing intercepts and means are freed, subject to restrictions required to achieve model identification (Bollen, 1989; Jöreskog & Sörbom, 1996).

Another alternative to Equation 13 reverses the direction of the relationship between the construct and measure, as depicted by the following equation:

$$\eta = \lambda_i X_i + \zeta \qquad (34)$$

where $\eta$ is the construct, $\gamma_i$ is a coefficient linking the measure to the construct, and $\zeta$ is that part of $\eta$ not captured by $X_i$ (Bollen & Lennox, 1991; Edwards & Bagozzi, 2000; MacCallum & Browne, 1993). Figure 9.4 depicts the relationship between a construct and three measures according to Equation 34. The $X_i$ in Equation 34 are termed *formative* measures because they form or induce the construct (Fornell & Bookstein, 1982). In contrast, the $X_i$ in Equation 13 are *reflective* measures, meaning they reflect or manifest the construct. In OB research, measures have been treated as formative when they describe different facets or aspects of a broad concept, as when measures of facet satisfaction are combined to represent overall job satisfaction (Law, Wong, & Mobley, 1998). Although simple in principle, formative

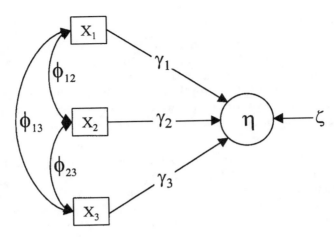

FIG. 9.4   Relationship between construct and measures following a formative measurement model.

measures introduce complex issues of model identification and interpretation (Edwards, 2001; MacCallum & Browne, 1993). Moreover, treating measures as formative implicitly ascribes causal potency to scores, which is difficult to defend from a philosophical perspective (Edwards & Bagozzi, 2000). In most cases, formative measures of a general construct are better treated as reflective measures of specific constructs that cause the general construct (Blalock, 1971; Edwards & Bagozzi, 2000).

A third alternative to Equation 13 incorporates indirect relationships between constructs and measures (Edwards & Bagozzi, 2000). This alternative is exemplified by second-order factor models in which measures are assigned to several specific constructs that in turn serve as indicators of a general construct (Rindskopf & Rose, 1988). Figure 9.5 illustrates a second-order factor model with one second-order factor, three first-order factors, and three measures of each first-order factor. A second-order factor model is represented by the following two equations:

$$\eta_j = \gamma_j \xi + \zeta_j \tag{35}$$

$$y_i = \lambda_{ij}\eta_j + \varepsilon_i \tag{36}$$

where $\xi$ is a general construct, the $\eta_j$ are specific constructs, and the $y_i$ are measures of the $\eta_j$. The indirect relationships between $\xi$ and the $y_i$ may be seen by substituting Equation 35 into Equation 36, which yields:

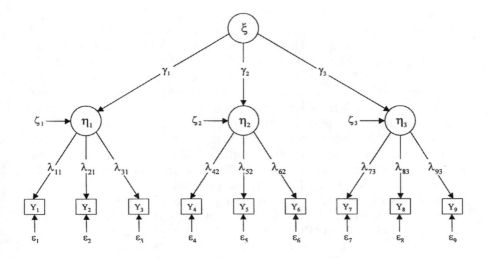

FIG. 9.5   Second-order confirmatory factor model with three first-order factors and one second-order factor.

$$y_i = \lambda_{ij}(\gamma_j\xi + \zeta_j) + \varepsilon_i$$

$$y_i = \lambda_{ij}\gamma_j\xi + \lambda_{ij}\zeta_j + \varepsilon_i \ . \qquad (37)$$

Equation 37 shows that the relationships between $\xi$ and the $y_i$ are represented by the products $\lambda_{ij}\gamma_j$. Equation 37 also shows that, when viewed as indicators of $\xi$, the $y_i$ have two sources of error: (a) $\lambda_{ij}\zeta_j$, which captures aspects of the $\eta_j$ not explained by $\xi$; and (b) $\varepsilon_i$, which represents measurement error in the usual sense. The basic model illustrated here can be extended to include multiple second-order factors. In addition, indirect relationships can be specified for formative measures that induce specific constructs that in turn combine to form a general construct (Edwards & Bagozzi, 2000). However, it is often more reasonable to treat such measures as reflective indicators of specific constructs that form a general construct, in which case the relationships between the measures and general construct are spurious rather than indirect (Edwards, 2001; Edwards & Bagozzi, 2000).

Equation 13 may also be expanded to include sources of systematic variance other than $\xi$. A prominent example of this approach is provided by Equation 22, which includes trait and method factors as systematic sources of variance in $X_i$. This example may be viewed as a special case of the family of models encompassed by generalizability theory (Cronbach et al., 1972). Generalizability theory treats measures as samples from a universe of admissible observations. The universe is defined in terms of facets that describe conditions believed to influence scores. Examples of such facets include items, persons, traits, methods, raters, and time. Building on this premise, generalizability theory specifies a measure as a function of an overall universe score (i.e., the mean score across facets), facet scores representing the deviation of each measure from the universe score, interactions among facets, and a residual. Generalizability theory provides a framework for decomposing the variance of a measure into variance attributable to the main and interactive effects of facets and the residual. These variance components can be used to calculate generalizability coefficients that represent the dependability of measures for different conditions of measurement, of which coefficient alpha is a special case. Although generalizability theory was developed over three decades ago, it has yet to gain widespread usage, due in part to the technical nature of its initial presentation (Cronbach et al., 1972). Fortunately, introductory treatments have become available (DeShon, 2002; Marcoulides, 2000; Shavelson & Webb, 1991), and linkages between generalizability theory and methods more familiar to OB researchers, such as CFA, are being explored (DeShon, 1998; Marcoulides, 1996).

Finally, Equation 13 may be respecified to capture nonlinear relationships between constructs and measures. Although nonlinear relationships are rarely considered within the context of construct validation in OB research, the required statistical foundations have been in place for decades. For instance, McDonald (1963, 1967a; Etezadi-Amoli & McDonald, 1983) developed nonlinear factor analytic models in which measurement equations analogous to Equation 13 are supplemented by factors raised to various powers, such as squares, cubics, and so forth. McDonald (1967b) adapted this approach to accommodate interactions, such that the measurement equations contain products of two or more factors. Nonlinear models also form the basis of item response theory (IRT) (Drasgow & Hulin, 1990; Embretson & Reise, 2000; Lord, 1952; Lord & Novick, 1968), which focuses on relationships between constructs and categorical measures. For dichotomous measures, IRT specifies the relationship as a logistic or normal ogive function bounded by the two scores the dichotomous measure can take. This function may be conceived as the probability of a positive (e.g., correct) response for a particular level of the underlying construct. IRT models are also available for polychotomous measures that have multiple nominal or ordinal response options (Drasgow & Hulin, 1990; Thissen & Steinberg, 1984; Zickar, 2002). Although IRT models were developed to accommodate violations of multivariate normality caused by items with a small number of discrete response options, these models can also be applied to continuous measures to uncover nonlinearities in the relationship between the measure and its underlying construct. For instance, IRT functions associated with each level of an agree–disagree scale can be compared to determine whether the shape and spacing of the functions is consistent with a linear or nonlinear relationship between the construct and measure (Drasgow & Hulin, 1990; Zickar, 2002). Although such applications of IRT remain infrequent (Drasgow & Hulin, 1990), they hold promise for scrutinizing the linearity assumptions underlying most models relating constructs to measures.

*Reliability.* Classic and modern approaches to reliability estimation focus on the proportion of true score variance in an item sum, as represented by alpha and omega. However, the relevance of this quantity is questionable when items are used as reflective measures of latent variables in structural equation models. Because these models do not incorporate item sums, the proportion of true score variance contained in these sums is less relevant than the proportion of true score variances captured by the individual items themselves. Nonetheless, it is worthwhile to consider the proportion of true score variance captured by the items collectively. This quantity can be estimated using principles of multivariate regression analysis, which provides multivariate $R^2$ values for the proportion of variance explained in a set of dependent variables by one or more independent variables (Cohen, 1982; Dwyer, 1983). Applying this approach to the relationship between a construct and a set of measures yields the following equation:

$$R_m^2 = \frac{\left|\hat{\Sigma}\right| - \left|\hat{\Theta}_\delta\right|}{\left|\hat{\Sigma}\right|}$$

(38)

where $R_m^2$ represents the multivariate $R^2$, $\left|\hat{\Sigma}\right|$ is the determinant of reproduced covariance matrix of the $X_i$, and $\left|\hat{\Theta}_\delta\right|$ is the determinant of the covariance matrix of the $\delta_i$ (which usually contains the variances of the $\delta_i$ along the diagonal and zeros elsewhere). The determinant of a covariance matrix may be interpreted as the generalized variance of the variables that constitute the matrix (Cohen, 1982). Thus, the numerator of Equation 38 is the generalized total variance of the $X_i$ as implied by the model minus the generalized unexplained variance of the $X_i$. The difference between these quantities is therefore the generalized variance of the $X_i$ explained by $\xi$. Equation 38 divides the generalized explained variance by the generalized total variance, such that $R_m^2$ represents a multivariate analog to $R^2$. $R_m^2$ is a special case of the coefficient of determination, which captures the total effect of the exogenous variables on the endogenous variables in a structural equation model (Bollen, 1989; Jöreskog & Sörbom, 1996). The reasoning underlying Equation 38 may also be applied to estimate the proportion of variance in a set of first-order factors explained by a second-order factor, corresponding to $\eta_j$ and $\xi$ in Equation 35 (Edwards, 2001).

When measures are formative rather than reflective, as in Equation 34, the latent variable $\eta$ is not a construct that is free from measurement error, but instead is a weighted composite that incorporates all the variance of the $X_i$, including variance that represents measurement error. If reliability estimates of the $X_i$ are available, it is possible to identify the proportion of variance in $\eta$ that represents measurement error in the $X_i$, using principles of covariance algebra such as those used to derive omega. Nonetheless, this measurement error is carried into $\eta$ and therefore can bias parameter estimates for models in which $\eta$ is embedded. One solution to this problem is to treat each $X_i$ as a reflective indicator of a $\xi_i$ and fix the variances of the $\delta_i$ to nonzero values that represent the amount of error variance in the $X_i$ (Edwards, 2001; Edwards & Bagozzi, 2000). The $\xi_i$ are then treated as causes of $\eta$ and do not bring measurement error into the composite they form. For such models, it is informative to estimate the proportion of variance in the $\xi_i$ as a set captured by the formative construct $\eta$. This quantity is represented by the adequacy coefficient, here labeled $R_a^2$ (Edwards, 2001). $R_a^2$ is used in canonical correlation analysis to represent the relationship between a set of variables and their associated canonical variate (Thompson, 1984) and is algebraically equivalent to the percentage of variance captured by a principal component (Kim & Mueller, 1978). For the relationship between $\eta$ and a set of $\xi_i$, $R_a^2$ can be calculated by summing the squared correlations between $\eta$ and each $\xi_i$ and dividing by the number of $\xi_i$. The information necessary to calculate $R_a^2$ is available from the covariance matrix of $\eta$ and $\xi_i$ reported by programs such as LISREL (Jöreskog & Sörbom, 1996).

*Convergent and Discriminant Validity.*    As noted previously, analyzing MTMM matrices using the standard CFA model with correlated traits and correlated methods (hereafter termed the CTCM model) suffers from problems of nonconvergence and improper solutions. To overcome these problems, alternatives to the CTCM model have been proposed. One alternative is the correlated uniqueness (CU) model (Kenny, 1976; Marsh, 1989; Marsh & Hocevar, 1988), which replaces method factors with correlations among the residual terms for measures collected using the same method. Figure 9.6 portrays the CU model for measures representing three traits and three methods. When three methods are involved, the CU model is mathematically equivalent to a CFA model with correlated trait factors and uncorrelated method factors (i.e., a CTUM model; Marsh & Bailey, 1991). With more than three factors, the CU model can be compared to the CTUM model to test whether the measures are congeneric with respect to the method factors, meaning that each method factor adequately explains the

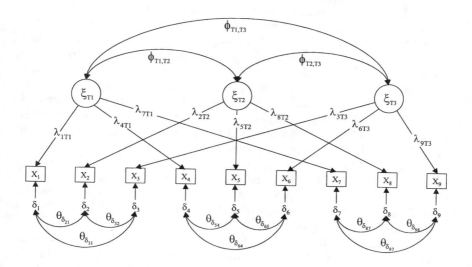

FIG. 9.6   Correlated uniqueness model for a MTMM matrix with three traits and three methods.

covariation among measures collected using that method after the effects of the trait factors have been removed (Kenny & Kashy, 1992; Marsh & Bailey, 1991). Compared to the CTCM model, the CU model is more likely to converge and yield proper solutions (Marsh & Bailey, 1991). However, because it does not contain method factors, the CU model does not provide a direct estimate of the amount of method variance in each measure. Nonetheless, it can be shown that the average correlation among the uniqueness for a particular method yields an estimate of the amount of variance attributable to that method (Conway, 1998a; Scullen, 1999). A more serious limitation is the assumption that methods are uncorrelated. If methods are positively correlated, the CU model tends to overestimate trait variances and covariances, thereby artificially inflating convergent validity and reducing discriminant validity (Byrne & Goffin, 1993; Kenny & Kashy, 1992).

Another alternative to the CTCM model is the composite direct product (CDP) model (Browne, 1984; Swain, 1975). The CDP model traces its origins to observations made by Campbell and O'Connell (1967), who noted that MTMM matrices often display a pattern in which sharing a common method inflates heterotrait correlations to a greater extent when trait correlations are high rather than low. Based on this observation, Campbell and O'Connell (1967) suggested that trait and method factors might operate multiplicatively rather than additively. The CDP model incorporates multiplicative effects by specifying the true score of each measure as the product of its corresponding trait and method scores (Browne, 1989). Assuming trait and method factors are independent and normally distributed with zero means, this specification produces a covariance structure in which the covariance between any pair of true scores equals the covariance between their traits times the covariance between their methods (Bohrnstedt & Goldberger, 1969; Browne, 1984, 1989). This covariance structure can be written in matrix form as the right direct product between the trait and method covariance matrices (Browne, 1984; Swain, 1975), from which the CDP model acquired its name. Applications of the CDP model show that it is often less prone to estimation problems than the CTCM model (Goffin & Jackson, 1992). Results from the CDP model can be mapped onto the Campbell and Fiske (1959) criteria (Browne, 1984; Cudeck, 1988), although convergent and discriminant validity can be assessed more precisely using estimates of specific model parameters (Reichardt & Coleman, 1995).

The strengths of the CDP model are offset by several shortcomings. First, although the CDP model suffers from fewer estimation problems than the CTCM model, it is nonetheless prone to improper solutions (Becker & Cote, 1994; Conway, 1996). Second, the CDP model does not provide separate estimates of the trait and method variance in each measure. Rather, these two sources of variance are combined into a single commonality estimate (Conway, 1996; Goffin & Jackson, 1992; Kenny, 1995). As a result, the model does not indicate how well each measure represents its intended underlying construct (Bagozzi & Yi, 1990). Third, the model does not provide a test of the assumption that true scores are a function of the product of trait and method factors. Some researchers have suggested that if the CDP model fits the data, method effects are likely to be multiplicative (Bagozzi & Yi, 1990; Bagozzi et al., 1991). However, model fit does not constitute a test of the multiplicative structure on which the CDP model is built, and data fit by the CDP model can often be fit by additive models such as the CTCM or CU models (Coenders & Saris, 2000; Corten et al., 2002; Kumar & Dillon, 1992). In effect, estimating the CDP model is analogous to testing interactions using product terms without controlling for their constituent main effects, which does not provide proper tests of interactions and can produce misleading results (Cohen, 1978; Evans, 1991). A final issue is that the CDP model is not required to capture the observations of Campbell and O'Connell (1967) that method effects are stronger when trait correlations are higher (Kumar & Dillon, 1992; Marsh & Grayson, 1995). This pattern can be produced when higher trait correlations are accompanied by stronger method effects, as indicated by larger method loadings in the CTCM model or higher correlations among uniquenesses in the CU model. The CDP model represents a special case of this pattern, given that the CDP model can be parameterized as a restricted version of the CU model with nonlinear constraints on the covariances among the uniquenesses (Coenders & Saris, 2000; Corten et al., 2002).

Other models have been developed in which the number of factors is one less than the combined number of traits and methods. By excluding one factor and its associated parameters, these models provide one approach to address the identification problems common in the CTCM model. Eid (2000) proposed a model that is equivalent to the CTCM model with one method factor removed. The excluded method factor serves as a standard of comparison to evaluate the effects of the included method factors on observed scores. For example, if a MTMM design uses self-reports, interviews, and observations as methods and excludes a self-report method factor, the interview and observation factors explain how the covariances among measures collected with these methods differ from the covariances among measures collected using self-reports. Although this model is identified in many cases where the CTCM model is not (Eid, 2000), it confounds trait and method variance for measures corresponding to the excluded method factor and generally yields different fit depending on which method factor is excluded. Kenny and Kashy (1992) presented a model in which method factor loadings are fixed to represent contrasts among the methods, such that the effects of each method factor sum to zero. The effect sizes of the method contrasts are represented by the variances of the method factors, which are freely estimated. Like the model proposed by Eid (2000), the Kenny and Kashy (1992) model does not provide estimates of method variance for each measure. Moreover, Kenny and Kashy (1992) reported that the model inappropriately lowered discriminant validity and inflated convergent validity to a greater extent than the CU model. Finally, Wothke (1987, 1995, 1996) developed a covariance components analysis (CCA) model that includes a general factor, $t-1$ contrast factors to represent traits, and $m-1$ contrast factors to represent methods ($t$ and $m$ signify the number of traits and methods, respectively). The variances of the trait and method factors indicate the magnitudes of their associated contrasts, consistent with the interpretation of the method contrast factors in the Kenny and Kashy (1992) approach. However, the CCA model does not provide estimates of trait or method variance for each measure, and its interpretation of its results in terms of convergent and discriminant validity is not straightforward (Kumar & Dillon, 1992; Wothke, 1996).

Each of the foregoing models uses a single indicator to represent each trait measured with each method. Other models have been developed that use multiple indicators for each trait–method combination. These models are feasible when the measures that constitute a MTMM matrix are created by summing multiple items, as is often the case (Marsh, 1993). Of these models, perhaps the most straightforward model assigns individual items directly to their associated trait and method factors (Tomás, Hontangas, & Oliver, 2000). Models specified in this manner are less prone to nonconvergence and improper solutions than models that treat each trait–method unit as a single indicator (Tomás et al., 2000). However, this model does not separate specificity from random measurement error, which remain confounded in the residual of each measure. This limitation can be overcome by adding a factor specific to each trait–method combination, yielding a first-order factor model in which each item is assigned to a trait factor, a method factor, and a specificity factor (Kumar & Dillon, 1990). One drawback of this approach is that it separates trait, method, and specific variance for individual items rather than the trait–method combinations that comprise the items, which are usually the focus of MTMM studies. This drawback is avoided by second-order CFA models in which items are assigned to first-order factors representing trait–method units, which in turn are assigned to second-order trait and method factors (Marsh, 1993; Marsh & Hocevar, 1988). In such models, the residual for each first-order factor captures specific variance from which the effects of measurement error have been removed, and loadings of the first-order factors on the second-order factors can be used to obtain estimates of trait and method variance for each trait–method unit. In addition, methods for comparing alternative CTCM models (Widaman, 1985) can be applied to the second-order factor structure imposed on the correlations among the first-order factors, which are corrected for measurement error at the level of the trait–method unit (Marsh, 1993; Marsh & Hocevar, 1988). Hybrid models have also been proposed in which traits are specified as second-order factors and methods and trait–method units are treated as first-order factors (Anderson, 1985, 1987). Research is needed to evaluate the relative strengths of these alternative models.

Finally, models have been developed that include measures that serve as direct indicators of method factors. These measures are intended to give explicit substantive meaning to method factors, as opposed to relying on broad distinctions between methods to infer what method factors might represent. Models with direct measures of method factors have been used to examine the effects of negative affectivity on work attitudes (Williams & Anderson, 1994; Williams, Gavin, & Williams, 1996) and the effects of general impressions and interpersonal affect on performance ratings (Conway, 1998b). This approach might be applied to MTMM analyses by including measures that represent substantive dimensions believed to differentiate the methods of measurement used in a particular study. Doing so would enable researchers to treat method variance from a theoretical standpoint, such that method factors are not merely a nuisance to be avoided, but instead represent substantive processes worthy of study in their own right (Cronbach, 1995; Schmitt, 1994).

## GUIDELINES FOR CONSTRUCT VALIDATION IN OB RESEARCH

The foregoing discussion has traced the evolution of classical, modern, and emerging approaches to construct validation. Much of the material reviewed has drawn not from the OB literature *per se*, but instead from the methodological literature in which construct validation approaches have been developed. Within the OB literature, it is perhaps fair to say that much empirical research draws from construct validation procedures that represent the classical era. This tendency is evidenced by the widespread use of alpha to estimate reliability, the associated reliance on classical measurement theory to frame the relationship between a construct and its measures, and the application of principal components analysis and common factor analysis to assess the convergence and divergence of measures. The use of CFA, which is the hallmark of the modern era, has grown substantially during the past decade, but few studies have estimated reliability with omega, and MTMM studies using CFA to evaluate convergent and discriminant validity are rare. Applications of emerging approaches to construct validation are beginning to appear, primarily through the use of second-order factor analysis, the framing of measures as formative rather than reflective, and scattered applications of the CU and CDP models to analyze MTMM data. This state of affairs does not justify an indictment of the OB literature, but instead reflects the natural time lag required for methodological developments to disseminate through any applied science.

Lessons learned from tracing the development of the classical, modern, and emerging approaches suggest several recommendations for construct validation in OB research. First, OB researchers should carefully scrutinize the models they implicitly or explicitly use to relate constructs to measures. In most instances, the model underlying classical measurement theory will prove too restrictive. The standard CFA model will be appropriate in many cases, provided measures may be viewed as alternative indicators of a single underlying construct. If measures describe qualitatively different manifestations of the same general concept, then the measures might be assigned to first-order factors that serve as reflective indicators of a second-order factor. Alternately, if measures describe distinct dimensions that combine to define a broader concept, then the measures might be assigned to first-order factors that are cast as formative indicators of a general construct. Typically, models of this type should be preferred to models that treat the measures themselves as formative indicators, due to philosophical problems with the assumption that measures, as numeric quantities, are capable of causing constructs of interest in OB research (Edwards & Bagozzi, 2000).

Second, the widespread reliance on alpha to assess reliability should be reconsidered. As noted earlier, alpha rests on the assumption of tau equivalence, which is unlikely to be met in practice. Omega relaxes this assumption and reduces to alpha when measures are tau equivalent. Therefore, it would seem advantageous to adopt omega for estimating the internal consistency reliability of summed scales. However, both alpha and omega lose their relevance when summed scales are replaced by latent variables with multiple indicators in structural equation models, as is becoming increasingly common in OB research. Such models shift the focus of reliability from sums of measures to the individual measures themselves. In addition, the variance explained in a set of measures by their underlying construct can be quantified using $R_m^2$, which gives a single index of the proportion of true score (i.e., construct) variance in a set of measures. Reframing reliability in this manner aligns the meaning of reliability with the treatment of measures as indicators of latent constructs rather than elements of summed scales.

Third, the assessment of convergent and discriminant validity should no longer rely on the Campbell and Fiske (1959) criteria. Research has convincingly shown that these criteria do not distinguish the various factors that give rise to MTMM correlations and therefore yield ambiguous conclusions regarding convergent and discriminant validity. These ambiguities can be avoided by analyzing MTMM data using CFA models. However, the CTCM model, which is the most widely used CFA model for analyzing MTMM data, is prone to nonconvergence and improper solutions attributable to inherent identification problems. Of the alternatives to the CTCM model, the CU model has received the greatest attention and is perhaps the simplest to estimate and interpret. However, the CU model incorporates the rather stringent assumption that methods are independent. The CDP and CCA models have attractive statistical features, but these models do not permit a straightforward decomposition of the variance of a measure into trait, method, and error components. Moreover, these models specify trait and method factors in ways that fundamentally differ from the CTCM model, and the substantive meaning of these different specifications have not been fully addressed. Second-order CFA models treat each trait–method combination as a latent variable with multiple indicators, and limited evidence suggests that these models are less susceptible to problems that plague the CTCM model. However, identification problems that arise from the structure of the item loadings in the CTCM may apply to the first-order factor loadings in the second-order factor model. Despite this possibility, available evidence warrants cautious optimism regarding the application of the second-order CFA model to MTMM analyses.

Finally, including measures that serve as indicators of method factors provides the dual advantage of reducing identification problems and clarifying the processes believed to underlie method effects. Establishing that method variance exists should be considered an initial step that is followed by research that assigns meaning to method factors and explains how and why they operate.

A final recommendation concerns guidelines for developing measures that exhibit strong construct validity. Guidelines such as these are discussed elsewhere (e.g., Converse & Presser, 1986; DeVellis, 1991; Spector, 1992; Stone-Romero, 1994), and a thorough treatment is beyond the scope of this chapter. Stated succinctly, researchers should begin with a clear definition of the construct of interest and assemble or develop items that provide alternative descriptions of the construct. Researchers should resist the temptation to use items that describe different facets of a concept, because such items often exhibit poor internal consistency and produce scales and factors that cannot be unambiguously interpreted. If different facets of a general concept are of interest, then it is advisable to use items that provide alternative descriptions of each facet and treat the facets as dimensions of a multidimensional construct (Edwards, 2001). The item pool may be screened by judges who rate the degree to which each item describes its intended construct (Schriesheim, Cogliser, Scandura, Lankau, & Powers, 1999), and the resulting ratings may be used to select, revise, or discard items before using them to collect data. Item ratings may also be used to specify CFA models that form the basis for assessing reliability and convergent and discriminant validity, using procedures discussed in this chapter. Finally, the items should be analyzed within broader models that include causes, correlates, and effects of the construct of interest, thereby generating evidence relevant to nomological validity. By following these guidelines, OB researchers can enhance the validity of measures taken as evidence of constructs that constitute the substance of OB theories and thereby promote theory testing and knowledge accumulation in the field.

## ACKNOWLEDGMENTS

The author thanks Richard P. DeShon, Fritz Drasgow, and Larry J. Williams for their helpful comments on an earlier version of this chapter.

## REFERENCES

Alreck, P. L., & Settle, R. B. (1995). *The survey research handbook: Guidelines and strategies for conducting a survey*. Chicago: Irwin.

Althauser, R. P. (1974). Inferring validity from the multitrait–multimethod matrix: Another assessment. In H. L. Costner (Ed.), *Sociological methodology* (pp. 106–127). San Francisco: Jossey-Bass.

Althauser, R. P., & Heberlein, T. A. (1970). Validity and the multitrait–multimethod matrix. In E. F. Borgatta & G. W. Bohrnstedt (Eds.), *Sociological methodology* (pp. 151–169). San Francisco: Jossey-Bass.

Althauser, R. P., Heberlein, T. A., & Scott, R. A. (1971). A causal assessment of validity: The augmented multitrait–mulitmethod matrix. In H. M. Blalock, Jr. (Ed.), *Causal models in the social sciences* (pp. 374–399). Chicago: Aldine.

Alwin, D. F. (1974). Approaches to the interpretation of relationships in the multitrait–multimethod matrix. In H. L. Costner (Ed.), *Sociological methodology* (pp. 79–105). San Francisco: Jossey-Bass.

American Psychological Association. (1966). *Standards for educational and psychological tests and manuals*. Washington, DC: American Psychological Association.

American Psychological Association. (1985). *Standards for educational and psychological testing*. Washington, DC: American Psychological Association.

American Psychological Association. (1999). *Standards for educational and psychological testing*. Washington, DC: American Psychological Association.

Anderson, J. C. (1985). A measurement model to assess measure-specific factors in multiple informant research. *Journal of Marketing Research, 22,* 86–92.

Anderson, J. C. (1987). An approach for confirmatory measurement and structural equation modeling of organizational properties. *Management Science, 33,* 525–541.

Arvey, R. D. (1992). Constructs and construct validation: Definitions and issues. *Human Performance, 5,* 59–70.

Bagozzi, R. P., & Phillips, L. W. (1982). Representing and testing organizational theories: A holistic construal. *Administrative Science Quarterly, 27,* 459–489.

Bagozzi, R. P., & Yi, Y. (1990). Assessing method variance in multitrait–multimethod matrices: The case of self-reported affect and perceptions at work. *Journal of Applied Psychology, 75,* 547–560.

Bagozzi, R. P., Yi, Y., & Phillips, L. W. (1991). Assessing construct validity in organizational research. *Administrative Science Quarterly, 36,* 421–458.

Becker, T. E., & Cote, J. A. (1994). Additive and multiplicative method effects in applied psychological research: An empirical assessment of three models. *Journal of Management, 20,* 625–641.

Bhaskar, R. (1978). On the possibility of social scientific knowledge and the limits of naturalism. *Journal for the Theory of Social Behaviour, 8,* 1–28.

Blalock, H. M. (1969). Multiple indicators and the causal approach to measurement error. *American Journal of Sociology, 75,* 264–272.

Blalock, H. M. (1971). Causal models involving unobserved variables in stimulus-response situations. In H. M. Blalock (Ed.), *Causal models in the social sciences* (pp. 335–1347). Chicago: Aldine.

Bohrnstedt, G. W. (1983). Measurement. In P. H. Rossi, J. D. Wright, & A. B. Anderson (Eds.), *Handbook of survey research* (pp. 69–121). New York: Academic Press.

Bohrnstedt, G. W., & Goldberger, A. S. (1969). On the exact covariance of products of random variables. *American Statistical Association Journal, 64,* 1439–1442.

Bollen, K. A. (1989). *Structural equations with latent variables.* New York: Wiley.

Bollen, K. A., & Jöreskog, K. G. (1985). Uniqueness does not imply identification: A note on confirmatory factor analysis. *Sociological Methods and Research, 14,* 155–163.

Bollen, K., & Lennox, R. (1991). Conventional wisdom on measurement: A structural equation perspective. *Psychological Bulletin, 110,* 305–314.

Brannick, M. T., & Spector, P. E. (1990). Estimation problems in the block-diagonal model of the multitrait–multimethod matrix. *Applied Psychological Measurement, 14,* 325–339.

Browne, M. W. (1984). The decomposition of multitrait–multimethod matrices. *British Journal of Mathematical and Statistical Psychology, 37,* 1–21.

Browne, M. W. (1989). Relationships between an additive model and a multiplicative model for multitrait–multimethod matrices. In R. Coppi & S. Bolasco (Eds.), *Multiway data analysis* (pp. 507–520). Amsterdam: Elsevier.

Byrne, B. M., & Goffin, R. D. (1993). Modeling MTMM data from additive and multiplicative covariance structures: An audit of construct validity concordance. *Multivariate Behavioral Research, 28,* 67–96.

Campbell, D. T. (1960). Recommendations for APA test standards regarding construct, trait, or discriminant validity. *American Psychologist, 15,* 546–553.

Campbell, D. T. (1996). Unresolved issues in measurement validity: An autobiographical overview. *Psychological Assessment, 8,* 363–368.

Campbell, D. T., & Fiske, D. W. (1959). Convergent and discriminant validation by the multitrait–multimethod matrix. *Psychological Bulletin, 56,* 81–105.

Campbell, D. T., & O'Connell, E. J. (1967). Method factors in multitrait–multimethod matrices: Multiplicative rather than additive? *Multivariate Behavioral Research, 2,* 409–426.

Campbell, D. T., & O'Connell, E. J. (1982). Methods as diluting trait relationships rather than adding irrelevant systematic variance. In D. Brinberg & L. H. Kidder (Eds.), *Forms of validity in research. New directions for methodology of social and behavioral science* (No. 12, pp. 93–111). San Francisco: Jossey-Bass.

Carmines, E. G., & Zeller, R. A. (1979). *Reliability and validity assessment.* Newbury Park, CA: Sage.

Coenders, G., & Saris, W. E. (2000). Testing nested additive, multiplicative, and general multitrait–multimethod models. *Structural Equation Modeling, 7,* 219–250.

Cohen, J. (1968). Multiple regression as a general data-analytic system. *Psychological Bulletin, 70,* 426–443.

Cohen, J. (1978). Partialed products *are* interactions: Partialed powers *are* curve components. *Psychological Bulletin, 85,* 858–866.

Cohen, J. (1982). Set correlation as a general multivariate data-analytic method. *Multivariate Behavioral Research, 17,* 301–341.

Converse, J. M., & Presser, S. (1986). *Survey questions: Handcrafting the standardized questionnaire.* Beverly Hills, CA: Sage.

Conway, J. M. (1996). Analysis and design of multitrait-multirater performance appraisal studies. *Journal of Management, 22,* 139–162.

Conway, J. M. (1998a). Estimation and uses of the proportion of method variance in multitrait–multimethod data. *Organizational Research Methods, 1*, 209–222.

Conway, J. M. (1998b). Understanding method variance in multitrait–multirater performance appraisal matrices: Examples using general impressions and interpersonal affect as measured method factors. *Human Performance, 11*, 29–55.

Cook, T. D., & Campbell, D. T. (1979). *Quasi-experimentation: Design and analysis issues for field settings*. Boston: Houghton Mifflin.

Cook, T. D., Campbell, D. T., & Peracchio, L. (1990). Quasi experimentation. In M. D. Dunnette & L. M. Hough (Eds.), *Handbook of industrial and organizational psychology* (2nd ed., Vol. 1, pp. 491–576). Palo Alto, CA: Consulting Psychologists Press.

Corten, I. W., Saris, W. E., Coenders, G., van der Veld, W., Aalberts, C. E., & Kornelis, C. (2002). Fit of different models for multitrait–multimethod experiments. *Structural Equation Modeling, 9*, 213–232.

Costner, H. L. (1969). Theory, deduction, and the rules of correspondence. *American Journal of Sociology, 75*, 245–263.

Cronbach, L. J. (1951). Coefficient alpha and the internal structure of tests. *Psychometrika, 16*, 297–334.

Cronbach, L. J. (1971). Test validation. In R. L. Thorndike (Ed.), *Educational measurement* (2nd ed., pp. 443–507). Washington, DC: American Council on Education.

Cronbach, L. J. (1989). Construct validation after thirty years. In R. L. Linn (Ed.), *Intelligence* (pp. 147–171). Chicago: University of Illinois Press.

Cronbach, L. J. (1995). Giving method variance its due. In P. E. Shrout & S. T. Fiske (Eds.), *Personality research, methods, and theory: A festschrift honoring Donald W. Fiske* (pp. 145–157). Hillsdale, NJ: Lawrence Erlbaum Associates.

Cronbach, L. J., Gleser, G., Nanda, H., & Rajaratnam, N. (1972). *The dependability of behavioral measurements: Theory of generalizability for scores and profiles*. New York: Wiley.

Cronbach, L. J., & Meehl, P. C. (1955). Construct validity in psychological tests. *Psychological Bulletin, 52*, 281–302.

Cudeck, R. (1988). Multiplicative models and MTMM matrices. *Journal of Educational Statistics, 13*, 131–147.

Delanty, G. (1997). *Social science: Beyond constructivism and realism*. Minneapolis: University of Minnesota Press.

DeShon, R. (1998). A cautionary note on measurement error corrections in structural equation modeling. *Psychological Methods, 3*, 412–423.

DeShon, R. (2002). Generalizability theory. In F. Drasgow & N. Schmitt (Eds.), *Measuring and analyzing behavior in organizations* (pp. 189–220). San Francisco: Jossey-Bass.

DeVellis, R. F. (1991). *Scale development: Theories and applications*. Newbury Park, CA: Sage.

Drasgow, F., & Hulin, C. L. (1990). Item response theory. In M. D. Dunnette & L. M. Hough (Eds.), *Handbook of industrial and organizational psychology* (2nd ed., Vol. 1, pp. 577–636). Palo Alto, CA: Consulting Psychologists Press.

Dwyer, J. H. (1983). *Statistical models for the social and behavioral sciences*. New York: Oxford University Press.

Edwards, J. R. (2001). Multidimensional constructs in organizational behavior research: An integrative analytical framework. *Organizational Research Methods, 4,* 144–192.

Edwards, J. R., & Bagozzi, R. P. (2000). On the nature and direction of the relationship between constructs and measures. *Psychological Methods, 5,* 155–174.

Eid, M. (2000). A multitrait–multimethod model with minimal assumptions. *Psychometrika, 65,* 241–261.

Embretson, S. E., & Reise, S. P. (2000). *Item response theory for psychologists.* Mahwah, NJ: Lawrence Erlbaum Associates.

Etezadi-Amoli, J., & McDonald, R. P. (1983). A second generation nonlinear factor analysis. *Psychometrika, 48,* 315–342.

Evans, M. G. (1991). The problem of analyzing multiplicative composites: Interactions revisited. *American Psychologist, 46,* 6–15.

Fornell, C., & Bookstein, F. L. (1982). Two structural equation models: LISREL and PLS applied to consumer exit-voice theory. *Journal of Marketing Research, 19,* 440–452.

Goffin, R. D., & Jackson, D. N. (1992). Analysis of multitrait–multirater performance appraisal data: Composite direct product method versus confirmatory factor analysis. *Multivariate Behavioral Research, 27,* 363–386.

Grayson, D. A., & Marsh, H. W. (1994). Identification with deficient rank loading matrices in confirmatory factor analysis: Multitrait–multimethod models. *Psychometrika, 59,* 121–134.

Gulliksen, H. (1950). *Theory of mental tests.* Hillsdale, NJ: Lawrence Erlbaum Associates.

Harman, H. H. (1976). *Modern factor analysis* (3rd ed.). Chicago: University of Chicago Press.

Heise, D. R., & Bohrnstedt, G. W. (1970). Validity, invalidity, and reliability. In E. F. Borgatta & G. W. Bohrnstedt (Eds.), *Sociological methodology* (pp. 104–129). San Francisco: Jossey-Bass.

Jackson, D. N. (1969). Multimethod factor analysis in the evaluation of convergent and discriminant validity. *Psychological Bulletin, 72,* 30–49.

Jöreskog, K. G. (1969). A general approach to confirmatory maximum likelihood factor analysis. *Psychometrika, 34,* 183–202.

Jöreskog, K. G. (1971). Statistical analysis of sets of congeneric tests. *Psychometrika, 36,* 109–133.

Jöreskog, K. G. (1974). Analyzing psychological data by structural analysis of covariance matrices. In D. H. Krantz, R. C. Atkinson, R. D. Luce, & P. Suppes (Eds.), *Contemporary developments in mathematical psychology* (Vol. 2, pp. 1–56). San Francisco: Freeman.

Jöreskog, K. G., & Sörbom, D. (1996). *LISREL 8: User's reference guide.* Chicago: Scientific Software International.

Kalleberg, A. L., & Kluegel, J. B. (1975). Analysis of the multitrait–method matrix: Some limitations and an alternative. *Journal of Applied Psychology, 60,* 1–9.

Kenny, D. A. (1976). An empirical application of confirmatory factor analysis to the multitrait–multimethod matrix. *Journal of Experimental Social Psychology, 12,* 247–252.

Kenny, D. A. (1995). The multitrait–multimethod matrix: Design, analysis, and conceptual issues. In P. E. Shrout & S. T. Fiske (Eds.), *Personality research, methods, and theory: A festschrift honoring Donald W. Fiske* (pp. 111–124). Hillsdale, NJ: Lawrence Erlbaum Associates.

Kenny, D. A., & Kashy, D. A. (1992). Analysis of the multitrait–multimethod matrix by confirmatory factor analysis. *Psychological Bulletin, 112,* 165–172.

Kim, J. O., & Mueller, C. W. (1978). *Factor analysis.* Beverly Hills, CA: Sage.

Kumar, A., & Dillon, W. R. (1990). On the use of confirmatory measurement models in the analysis of multiple-informant reports. *Journal of Marketing Research, 27,* 102–111.

Kumar, A., & Dillon, W. R. (1992). An integrative look at the use of additive and multiplicative covariance structure models in the analysis of MTMM data. *Journal of Marketing Research, 29,* 51–64.

Law, K. S., Wong, C. S., & Mobley, W. H. (1998). Toward a taxonomy of multidimensional constructs. *Academy of Management Review, 23,* 741–755.

Loevinger, J. (1957). Objective tests as instruments of psychological theory. *Psychological Reports, 3,* 635–694.

Long, J. S. (1983). *Confirmatory factor analysis.* Beverly Hills, CA: Sage.

Lord, F. M. (1952). A theory of test scores. *Psychometric Monograph, 7.*

Lord, F. M., & Novick, M. R. (1968). *Statistical theories of mental test scores.* Reading, MA: Addison-Wesley.

MacCallum, R., & Browne, M. W. (1993). The use of causal indicators in covariance structure models: Some practical issues. *Psychological Bulletin, 114,* 533–541.

MacCorquodale, K., & Meehl, P. E. (1948). On a distinction between hypothetical constructs and intervening variables. *Psychological Review, 55,* 95–107.

Marcoulides, G. A. (1996). Estimating variance components in generalizability theory: The covariance structure analysis approach. *Structural Equation Modeling, 3,* 290–299.

Marcoulides, G. A. (2000). Generalizability theory. In H. E. A. Tinsley & S. D. Brown (Eds.), *Handbook of applied multivariate statistics and mathematical modeling* (pp. 527–551). San Diego, CA: Academic Press.

Marsh, H. W. (1989). Confirmatory factor analyses of multitrait–multimethod data: Many problems and a few solutions. *Applied Psychological Measurement, 13,* 335–361.

Marsh, H. W. (1993). Multitrait–multimethod analyses: Inferring each trait–method combination with multiple indicators. *Applied Measurement in Education, 6,* 49–81.

Marsh, H. W., & Bailey, M. (1991). Confirmatory factor analyses of multitrait–multimethod data: A comparison of alternative models. *Applied Psychological Measurement, 15,* 47–70.

Marsh, H. W., & Grayson, D. (1995). Latent variable models of multitrait–multimethod data. In R. H. Hoyle (Ed.), *Structural equation modeling: Concepts, issues, and applications* (pp. 177–198). Thousand Oaks, CA: Sage.

Marsh, H. W., & Hocevar, D. (1988). A new, more powerful approach to multitrait–multimethod analyses: Application of second-order confirmatory factor analysis. *Journal of Applied Psychology, 73,* 107–117.

McDonald, R. P. (1963). A general approach to nonlinear factor analysis. *Psychometrika, 27,* 397–415.

McDonald, R. P. (1967a). Nonlinear factor analysis. *Psychometric Monographs,* 15(167).

McDonald, R. P. (1967b). Factor interaction in nonlinear factor analysis. *British Journal of Mathematical and Statistical Psychology, 20,* 205–215.

McDonald, R. P. (1970). The theoretical foundations of principal factor analysis, canonical factor analysis, and alpha factor analysis. *British Journal of Mathematical and Statistical Psychology, 23,* 1–21.

McDonald, R. P. (1999). *Test theory: A unified treatment.* Mahwah, NJ: Lawrence Erlbaum Associates.

McNemar, Q. (1962). *Psychological statistics* (3rd ed.). New York: Wiley.

Messick, S. (1975). The standard problem: Meaning and values in measurement and evaluation. *American Psychologist, 30,* 955–966.

Messick, S. (1981). Constructs and their vicissitudes in educational and psychological measurement. *Psychological Bulletin, 89,* 575–588.

Messick, S. (1995). Validity of psychological assessment. *American Psychologist, 50,* 741–749.

Millsap, R. E. (1992). Sufficient conditions for rotational uniqueness in the additive MTMM model. *British Journal of Mathematical and Statistical Psychology, 45,* 125–138.

Mulaik, S. A. (1990). Blurring the distinctions between component analysis and common factor analysis. *Multivariate Behavioral Research, 25,* 53–59.

Novick, M. R., & Lewis, C. (1967). Coefficient alpha and the reliability of composite measures. *Psychometrika, 32,* 1–13.

Nunnally, J. C. (1967). *Psychometric theory.* New York: McGraw-Hill.

Nunnally, J. C. (1978). *Psychometric theory* (2nd ed.). New York: McGraw-Hill.

Raykov, T. (2001). Bias of coefficient alpha for fixed congeneric measures with correlated errors. *Applied Psychological Measurement, 25,* 69–76.

Rea, L. M., & Parker, R. A. (1992). *Designing and conducting survey research.* Newbury Park, CA: Sage.

Reichardt, C. S., & Coleman, S. C. (1995). The criteria for convergent and discriminant validity in a multitrait–multimethod matrix. *Multivariate Behavioral Research, 30,* 513–538.

Rindskopf, D., & Rose, T. (1998). Some theory and application of confirmatory second-order factor analysis. *Multivariate Behavioral Research, 23,* 51–67.

Schmitt, N. (1978). Path analysis of multitrait–multimethod matrices. *Applied Psychological Measurement, 2,* 157–173.

Schmitt, N. (1994). Method bias: The importance of theory and measurement. *Journal of Organizational Behavior, 15,* 393–398.

Schmitt, N., & Stults, D. M. (1986). Methodology review: Analysis of multitrait–multimethod matrices. *Applied Psychological Measurement, 10,* 1–22.

Schriesheim, C. A., Cogliser, C. C., Scandura, T. A., Lankau, M. J., & Powers, K. J. (1999). An empirical comparison of approaches for quantitatively assessing the content adequacy of paper-and-pencil measurement instruments. *Organizational Research Methods, 2,* 140–156.

Schwab, D. P. (1980). Construct validity in organizational behavior. In L. L. Cummings & B. M. Staw (Eds.), *Research in organizational behavior* (Vol. 2, pp. 3–43). Greenwich, CT: JAI.

Scullen, S. E. (1999). Using confirmatory factor analysis of correlated uniquenesses to estimate method variance in multitrait–multimethod matrices. *Organizational Research Methods, 2,* 275–292.

Shavelson, R. J., & Webb, N. M. (1991). *Generalizability theory: A primer.* Newbury Park, CA: Sage.

Snook, S. C., & Gorsuch, R. L. (1989). Component analysis versus common factor analysis: A Monte Carlo study. *Psychological Bulletin, 106,* 148–154.

Spector, P. E. (1992). *Summated rating scale construction.* Newbury Park, CA: Sage.

Steiger, J. H. (1980). Tests for comparing elements of a correlation matrix. *Psychological Bulletin, 87,* 245–251.

Stone-Romero, E. (1994). Construct validity issues in organizational behavior research. In J. Greenberg (Eds.), *Organizational behavior: The state of the science* (pp. 155–179). Hillsdale, NJ: Lawrence Erlbaum Associates.

Sudman, S., Bradburn, N. M., & Schwarz, N. (1996). *Thinking about answers: The application of cognitive processes to survey methodology.* San Francisco: Jossey-Bass.

Swain, A. J. (1975). *Analysis of parametric structures for variance matrices.* Unpublished doctoral dissertation, University of Adelaide, Adelaide, Australia.

Thissen, D., & Steinberg, L. (1984). A response model for multiple choice items. *Psychometrika, 47,* 501–519.

Thompson, B. (1984). *Canonical correlation analysis: Uses and interpretation.* Newbury Park, CA: Sage.

Tomás, J. M., Hontangas, P. M., & Oliver, A. (2000). Linear confirmatory factor models to evaluate multitrait–multimethod matrices: The effects of number of indicators and correlation among methods. *Multivariate Behavioral Research, 35,* 469–499.

Velicer, W. F., & Jackson, D. N. (1990). Component analysis versus common factor analysis: Some issues in selecting an appropriate procedure. *Multivariate Behavioral Research, 25,* 1–28.

Werts, C. E., & Linn, R. L. (1970). Path analysis: Psychological examples. *Psychological Bulletin, 74,* 193–212.

Widaman, K. F. (1985). Hierarchically nested covariance structure models for multitrait–multimethod data. *Applied Psychological Measurement, 9,* 1–26.

Widaman, K. F. (1993). Common factor analysis versus principal component analysis: Differential bias in representing model parameters? *Multivariate Behavioral Research, 28,* 263–311.

Williams, L. J., & Anderson, S. E. (1994). An alternative approach to method effects by using latent-variable models: Applications in organizational behavior research. *Journal of Applied Psychology, 79,* 323–332.

Williams, L. J., Gavin, M. B., & Williams, M. L. (1996). Measurement and nonmeasurement processes with negative affectivity and employee attitudes. *Journal of Applied Psychology, 81,* 88–101.

Williams, L. J., & James, L. R. (1994). Causal models in organizational behavior research: From path analysis to LISREL and beyond. In J. Greenberg (Ed.), *Organizational behavior: The state of the science* (pp. 181–205). Hillsdale, NJ: Lawrence Erlbaum Associates.

Wothke, W. (1987). *Multivariate linear models of the multitrait–multimethod matrix.* Paper presented at the meeting of the American Educational Research Association, Washington, DC. (ERIC No. ED 283 850, TM 870 369)

Wothke, W. (1995). Covariance components analysis of the multitrait–multimethod matrix. In P. E. Shrout & S. T. Fiske (Eds.), *Personality research, methods, and theory: A festschrift honoring Donald W. Fiske* (pp. 125–144). Hillsdale, NJ: Lawrence Erlbaum Associates.

Wothke, W. (1996). Models for multitrait–multimethod matrix analysis. In G. A. Marcoulides & R. E. Schumacker (Eds.), *Advances in structural equation modeling* (pp. 7–56). Hillsdale, NJ: Lawrence Erlbaum Associates.

Zickar, M. J. (2002). Modeling data with polytomous item response theory. In F. Drasgow & N. Schmitt (Eds.), *Measuring and analyzing behavior in organizations* (pp. 123–155). San Francisco: Jossey-Bass.

Zuriff, G. (1998). Against metaphysical social constructionism in psychology. *Behavior and Philosophy, 26,* 5–28.

# 10

# The Search for Universals in Cross-Cultural Organizational Behavior

Herman Aguinis
*University of Colorado at Denver*

Christine A. Henle
*University of North Carolina at Charlotte*

Globalization is one of the central themes of the 21st century. Goods, information, and people move across countries and continents at unprecedented speed. For instance, the volume of trade between the United States and other countries has increased exponentially over the past few years. In 2000, U.S. exports equaled $1,068,741 million whereas imports totaled $1,437,606 million (Bureau of the Census, Foreign Trade Division, 2001). Regarding the exchange of information, hundreds of millions of individuals can now communicate instantly across continents using the Internet. In addition to the international transfer of goods and information, immigration movements in Europe (e.g., from the former Soviet bloc and Northern Africa to Western European countries), the Americas (e.g., from South and Central America to the United States), and Asia (e.g., from mainland China to Hong Kong) show that people are also moving across national boundaries. Finally, the formation of economic blocs has made it even easier to transfer goods, information, and people within these blocs. Examples of these economic blocs include North American Free Trade Area (NAFTA), Southern Cone Common

Market (MERCOSUR), European Union (EU), Association of Southeast Asian Nations (ASEAN), Economic Community of West African States (ECOWAS), Andean Pact, and Central American Common Market. In short, globalization is no longer an abstract concept and it affects the daily lives of millions of people around the world. The field of organizational behavior (OB) must adapt to this new reality and place greater emphasis on cross-cultural issues or it risks becoming a parochial dinosaur with the level of curiosity of a "mid-twentieth-century fossil" (Boyacigiller & Adler, 1991, p. 263). The fact that this chapter is included in the second edition of *Organizational Behavior: The State of the Science* is a good indication that cross-cultural OB is becoming a mainstream topic.

Interest in examining the influence of culture on OB primarily developed in North America and Western Europe after World War II as the business environment slowly started to become more globalized (Bhagat & McQuaid, 1982). The crux of this research centered on testing Western-based theories in cross-cultural settings and, thus, had an individualistic bias due to the perspective of researchers in these countries. As Triandis (1994) pointed out, 90% of this research was being conducted by less than 15% of the world's population.

The 1960s witnessed an increased volume of research in cross-cultural OB with Haire, Ghiselli, and Porter's (1966) first large cross-national study of managers, and the first round of Hofstede's survey on values in a multinational organization around 1968, which culminated in his now-seminal work (i.e., Hofstede, 1980, 2001). Also of importance in the United States were the changes in immigration policy, which increased diversity in many areas of the country. The following decade was characterized by further research and culminated with the first reviews of the cross-cultural OB literature (e.g., Barrett & Bass, 1976; Roberts, 1970). Interest in the effects of culture on OB continued throughout the next couple of decades and even developed into partnerships among researchers from various countries. Erez (1994) offered several reasons for this growth of cross-cultural OB research, including increased diversity in the workplace, foreign acquisition and mergers, locating organizational divisions in different parts of the world, the necessity to understand diverse customer needs, technology enabling worldwide communication, and the unification of countries (e.g., Germany) as well as continents (e.g., Europe).

Looking back at the past 20 years of research on cross-cultural OB, there is unequivocal evidence that cultural differences in societies and groups affect OB. For instance, Adler and Bartholomew (1992) reviewed articles in the fields of OB and human resources management that included the concept of culture and reported that over 93% of studies found that culture was related to the substantive variables under investigation. More recently, House,

Wright, and Aditya (1997) concluded that there is massive evidence that cultural differences in societies and in organizations account for significant amounts of variance in individuals' expectations and assumptions about their environments, attitudes toward others, modes of social interaction, expressions of emotions and global behavior patterns, and reactions to others. This conclusion is strongly supported by the following reviews of the cross-cultural OB and psychology literatures spanning over 20 years, for example, Arvey, Bhagat, and Salas (1991), Aycan and Kanungo (2001), Bhagat, Kedia, Crawford, and Kaplan (1990), Bhagat and McQuaid (1982), Bond and Smith (1996a), Drenth and Groenendijk (1984), Erez (1994), Hui and Luk (1997), Kagitçibaşi and Berry (1989), Ronen and Kumar (1987), Segall (1986), Tannenbaum (1980), and Triandis (1994).

From a developmental perspective of the field of cross-cultural OB, the massive empirical evidence accumulated thus far indicates that the "cultural pervasiveness hypothesis" (House et al., 1997, p. 613) should no longer be questioned and is part of the past. At present, the relevant question is no longer whether culture influences OB. There is overwhelming empirical evidence demonstrating this fact. A more challenging question is whether, in spite of the observed culture-based differences, there is knowledge generated by the field of OB that is universal and culture free. We view this question as the central challenge of the present and future of cross-cultural OB.

The goal of this chapter is to discuss universals in eight major topics in the field of OB. Addressing universals necessarily demands that we adopt a developmental view of cross-cultural OB. First, we adopt a past orientation by locating universals previously identified in the literature. Second, we adopt a present orientation by proposing universals not previously identified as such. Third, we adopt a future orientation because the universals we propose will, it is hoped, be put to future empirical tests. Thus, the identification of universals addresses the past, present, and future of cross-cultural OB.

Addressing cross-cultural universals is a challenging task because culturally diverse groups can be both similar and dissimilar at the same time. This ambivalent situation is at the heart of the universalist–particularist debate. In spite of differences in behaviors, there seem to be deeper level functions and generalizations that remain constant across cultures (Kagitçibasi & Berry, 1989; Smith, 1997). So, we address the universalist–particularist debate by framing our review of each OB topic by identifying universals that have been found, or we hypothesize to be, culturally invariant.

A few clarifications are in order. First, we began our review by content-analyzing the most updated editions of 10 OB textbooks and identifying content areas covered in all or most textbooks. This review resulted in 17 areas, which are listed in the left column of Table 10.1. Second, we examined

## TABLE 10.1

### Coverage of Cross-Cultural Organizational Behavior and Psychology Literature Reviews in Book Chapter and Refereed Journals (1980–Present)

| Topic | Arvey, Bhagat, & Salas (1991) | Aycan & Kanungo (2001) | Bhagat, Kedia, Crawford, & Kaplan (1990) | Bhagat & McQuaid (1982) | Bond & Smith (1996a) | Drenth & Groenendijk (1984) |
|---|---|---|---|---|---|---|
| Attitudes and values | ✓ | | ✓ | ✓ | ✓ | ✓ |
| Communication | ✓ | | | | | |
| Conflict and negotiation | ✓ | | ✓ | | | |
| Decision making | | | | | ✓ | |
| Environment, strategy, and technology | | | | | ✓ | |
| Group behavior and teamwork | | | ✓ | | ✓ | |
| Interpersonal behavior | | | | | | |
| Job design | | | | | ✓ | |
| Leadership | ✓ | | | | ✓ | |
| Organizational change and development | | ✓ | | | ✓ | |
| Organizational culture | | | | | | |
| Organizational structure and design | ✓ | | ✓ | ✓ | ✓ | ✓ |
| Perception, attribution, and learning | ✓ | | ✓ | | ✓ | ✓ |
| Personality | ✓ | | | | ✓ | |
| Power and politics | ✓ | | | | ✓ | |
| Stress management | ✓ | | ✓ | | ✓ | |
| Work motivation | ✓ | | ✓ | ✓ | ✓ | |

*Article*

| Topic | Erez (1994) | Hui & Luk (1997) | Kağitçibaşi & Berry (1989) | Article Ronen & Kumar (1987) | Segall (1986) | Tannenbaum (1980) | Triandis (1994) |
|---|---|---|---|---|---|---|---|
| Attitudes and values | | ✓ | ✓ | | ✓ | ✓ | ✓ |
| Communication | | | | | | | ✓ |
| Conflict and negotiation | | ✓ | | | | | ✓ |
| Decision making | ✓ | ✓ | | ✓ | | ✓ | ✓ |
| Environment, strategy, and teamwork | | | | | | | |
| Group behavior and teamwork | | ✓ | | | | ✓ | ✓ |
| Interpersonal behavior | | | | | | ✓ | ✓ |
| Job design | | | | | | | ✓ |
| Leadership | ✓ | ✓ | | | | ✓ | ✓ |
| Organizational change, and development | | ✓ | | ✓ | | | |
| Organizational culture | | | | | | ✓ | ✓ |
| Organizational structure, and design | | | | | | | |
| Perception, attribution, and learning | | | ✓ | ✓ | ✓ | | |
| Personality | | | ✓ | | | | |
| Power and politics | | | | | | | |
| Stress management | | | | | | | |
| Work motivation | | | | ✓ | ✓ | ✓ | ✓ |

reviews of the cross-cultural OB literatures published as journal articles and book chapters over the past 20 years and tabulated whether each review covered each of the 17 OB areas identified in our content analysis. Results of this analysis, also shown in Table 10.1, serve as a useful resource for researchers interested in updated reviews on specific topics. In addition, this table shows that some topics (e.g., work motivation) have received more extensive coverage than others (e.g., organizational change and development). Third, due to space constraints, we could only include a discussion of a subset of topics. Our selection was guided conceptually by a choice to discuss a combination of diverse topics spanning the national, organizational, group, dyad, and individual levels of analysis. In addition, our selection was based on areas for which sufficient primary-level studies exist to warrant a review. Based on this selection, our discussion follows a macro-to-micro sequence and includes the following topics: (a) national values, (b) organization development and change, (c) organizational culture, (d) work teams, (e) conflict and negotiation, (f) leadership, (g) work motivation, and (h) decision making. Before we begin the discussion of each of these areas, however, we define the construct of culture.

## CULTURE: DEFINITION AND OPERATIONALIZATION

A common criticism of cross-cultural research is the lack of a shared conceptual definition of culture. This lack of consensus leads to operationalizations of culture that vary widely across studies (House et al., 1997). In fact, in the 1950s researchers had listed over 160 definitions of culture (Kroeber & Kluckhohn, 1952) and Ajiferuke and Boddewyn (1970) noted that "Culture is one of those terms that defy a single all-purpose definition, and there are almost as many meanings of 'culture' as people using the term" (p. 154). Even worse than a lack of agreement over the definition and operationalization of culture, many researchers do not even define culture or simply use national affiliation to represent culture (Bond & Smith, 1996a). Researchers must take into account many different dimensions of culture (Child, 1981; Lytle, Brett, Barsness, Tinsley, & Janssens, 1995; Ronen, 1997). Recently, much cross-cultural research has focused on the dimension of individualism–collectivism, if any dimension is delineated at all. Unfortunately, if this dimension is used, often it is not measured directly (Hui & Luk, 1997); rather, it is inferred from country membership. This method is no longer acceptable due to the availability of measures of individualism–collectivism (e.g., Hui, 1988; Hui & Yee, 1994) and the numerous other dimensions of culture that have been proposed (see Lytle et al., 1995, for a review). In summary, culture needs to be defined a priori and its dimensions clearly specified or it will not be possible to link cultural differences to the dependent variables of interest.

In spite of a historical variation in its definition, culture is increasingly and pervasively defined as a set of psychological commonalities shared by a group that limits the behavioral choices of its members. Represented in this definition is what House et al. (1997) referred to as "shared psychological properties," Poortinga (1992) referred to as "shared constraints," Lytle et al. (1995) referred to as "frame that prescribes behavior," and Ronen (1997) referred to as "common ways of viewing events and objects." First, we should note that culture is determined by common experiences, geography, language, and history. These are antecedents of culture, and not culture per se. Antecedents of culture should not be confused with the construct of culture. Second, culture sets the stage for behavior, but does not include behavior. Behaviors are consequences of culture and should not be confused with the construct. Third, culture is a stable system in equilibrium (Ronen, 1997). However, as geography, history, religion, and other shared experiences change, so does culture. Fourth, culture is a latent construct that can be examined only through a host of less than perfect indicators (Lytle et al., 1995). Lytle et al. reviewed several types of indicators including definitions of self and others (e.g., ascription–achievement, pragmatism–idealism), motivational orientation (e.g., high need for power–low need for power, intrinsic orientation–extrinsic orientation), and relations between societal members (e.g., individualism–collectivism, particularism– universalism), among others. We can assess the extent to which individuals are members of the same cultural group by gathering information on a subset of these indicators. Fifth, culture is a multidimensional construct. Defining a cultural group in a unidimensional manner (i.e., using one indicator of culture such as individualism–collectivism only) leads to underspecifying the construct of culture and is no longer acceptable (Earley & Erez, 1997). Sixth, culture is a multilayered construct and not a dichotomy but a matter of degree. An individual is a member of a cultural group to the extent that he or she has shared experiences (e.g., geography, history) with the other members. However, given that individuals have shared experiences with members of several groups (e.g., based on religion, ethnicity, gender, socioeconomic status, etc.; De Cieri & Dowling, 1995), they share, to different degrees, the cultural characteristics in each of several groups. Thus, we are all multicultural to the extent that we belong in various cultural groups.

Next, we review the aforementioned eight OB topics in search for universals following a downward sequence regarding levels of analysis. Specifically, we use the following macro-to-micro sequence: national (national values), organizational (organizational change and development, organizational culture), group and dyad (work teams, conflict and negotiation, leadership), and individual (work motivation, decision making).

# NATIONAL LEVEL OF ANALYSIS

## National Values

The topic of values is arguably one of the most frequently studied subjects in cross-cultural research. In fact, Table 10.1 shows that virtually every review of the cross-cultural OB and psychology literatures in the past 20 years has addressed this topic. Values can be defined as "a broad tendency to prefer certain states of affairs over others" (Hofstede, 2001, p. 5). Similarly, values have been defined as "desirable, transsituational goals, varying in importance, that serve as guiding principles in people's lives" (Schwartz & Sagie, 2000, p. 467). Put simply, values represent what is important (Bond & Smith, 1996a). As noted earlier in this chapter, cross-cultural researchers usually use values as indicators of the latent construct of culture. Thus, values have been studied in connection to each of the other topics addressed in this chapter. And, in spite of recent skepticism regarding the usefulness of the value construct for cross-cultural psychology (Bond, 1997), there is no sign that the interest in values in OB is waning.

Although cultural groups may or may not endorse specific values, a relevant universal–particular question is whether specific values created in one cultural context make sense in other cultural contexts. Stated differently, are values typically studied by cross-cultural researchers universally understood? Do we have sufficient accumulated knowledge to identify a universal taxonomy of values?

Hofstede's (1980) book describes the first systematic attempt at studying work-related values that are universally understood on a large international scale. National values were operationalized as the average scores for a given value in each of the 40 countries participating in the study (Hofstede & Bond, 1988, reported data on an additional 10 countries and three geographic regions). Hofstede (1980) derived, via a combination of exploratory factor analysis and theoretical considerations, the following four values: power distance, uncertainty avoidance, individualism–collectivism, and masculinity–femininity. It is important to note that these values were derived at the country level using ecological factor analysis (e.g., the mean values derived from each country were subjected to the factor analysis, and not the scores provided by the over 116,000 individuals who participated). This is a crucial distinction because results refer to national (however defined) values, as opposed to what the values of average citizens are in each country (see Bond, 1988, and Schwartz, 1992, for analyses at the individual level).

Power distance refers to the degree of inequality between a supervisor and his or her subordinate; it was derived from questions addressing perceptions of (a) a supervisor's style of decision making, (b) co-workers' fear to disagree with superiors, and (c) the type of decision making that subordinates prefer in their supervisor. Uncertainty avoidance refers to the degree of tolerance for uncertainty and it was derived from questions addressing (a) rule orientation, (b) employment stability, and (c) stress. Individualism refers to the type of relationship between the individual and the collectivity that prevails in a given society and was derived from questions addressing work goals (e.g., have a job that leaves sufficient time for my personal or family life, have considerable freedom to adapt my own approach to the job). Masculinity–femininity refers to the degree of endorsement of "masculine" (i.e., advancement and earnings as more important) as opposed to "feminine" (i.e., interpersonal aspects, rendering service, and the physical environment as more important) goals.

Hofstede (1980) demonstrated that each of the four country-level values showed significant relationships with a diverse set of country-level variables. For instance, countries with higher power distance scores are more likely to be situated in a more tropical latitude, countries with higher uncertainty avoidance scores are more likely to show higher national anxiety levels, countries with higher individualism scores are likely to have higher gross national product per capita, and countries with higher masculinity scores are likely to have a lower percentage of women in professional and technical jobs.

Hofstede's (1980) seminal work has led to hundreds of follow-up studies and is arguably the most influential single investigation of cross-national differences in values (see Hofstede, 2001, for a review of follow-up studies, and Smith, in press, for an in-depth analysis and critique). Possibly, the appeal of Hofstede's value-based country classification among social scientists is that "soft" constructs were related to "hard" country-level indexes of economic performance. In addition, Hofstede's labels have a psychological flavor intrinsically appealing to Western researchers trained in individual-centered disciplines (e.g., OB, psychology). From a practical standpoint of research logistics, values are easy to measure by asking study participants to provide their endorsement of lists of terms used to justify actions in various societies. For example, values measured using the Chinese Value Survey (CVS) took about 5 minutes to complete (Chinese Culture Connection, 1987, p. 148).

The universality of Hofstede's (1980) four-value taxonomy was challenged by the Chinese Culture Connection (1987). The goal of the Chinese Culture Connection's study was to create an indigenous CVS to ascertain whether values originated from within the Chinese culture (i.e., "Eastern" instrument) would correlate with values found in Hofstede's study (i.e., "Western" instrument). The survey was distributed in 22 countries, 20 of which had participated in Hofstede's study. This allowed for an empirical comparison of values derived from two separate instruments in a sample of

20 countries. Results of an ecological factor analysis yielded a value taxonomy including the following four dimensions: (a) integration (i.e., tolerance of others, harmony with others, noncompetitiveness), (b) Confucian work dynamism (i.e., ordering relationships, thrift, persistence, having a sense of shame), (c) human-heartedness (i.e., kindness, patience, courtesy), and (d) moral discipline (i.e., moderation, having few desires, keeping oneself disinterested and pure). Integration, human heartedness, and moral discipline were related to Hofstede's values (e.g., integration was correlated with individualism, human heartedness was correlated with masculinity). However, the value "Confucian work dynamism" was not related to any of Hofstede's dimensions. Confucian work dynamism refers to Confucian work ethics and is reflected by the endorsement of such items as persistence, thrift, and having a sense of shame. Results from the Chinese Culture Connection demonstrated that although Hofstede's four values seem to be universally understood, Confucian work dynamism is a value indigenous to non-Western regions (e.g., China) that is not captured in Hofstede's four-value taxonomy.

Smith, Dugan, and Trompenaars (1996) also challenged Hofstede's (1980) four-value taxonomy by distributing a value survey to 8,841 managers and employees in 43 countries. Items emphasized measures of universalism–particularism, achievement–ascription, and individualism–collectivism. Results of multidimensional scaling analysis yielded a three-dimension solution of values related to individualism–collectivism (Hofstede, 1980), power distance (Hofstede, 1980), integration (Chinese Culture Connection, 1987), and Confucian work dynamism (Chinese Culture Connection, 1987). Results showed that power distance and individualism–collectivism are not distinct factors and can be conceptualized as representing varying orientations toward continuity of group membership (loyal involvement/utilitarian involvement) and varying orientations toward the obligations of social relationship (conservatism/egalitarian commitment). Also, Hofstede's dimensions of uncertainly avoidance and masculinity–femininity did not emerge from the analysis. Smith et al. provided possible explanations for the lack of emergence of these dimensions including the fact that their measures were not designed to measure these dimensions directly. Overall, Smith et al. (1996) concluded that their results suggest "considerable replicability in the results emerging from value surveys sampling relatively large numbers of nations" (p. 259). Also, they concluded that the individualism–collectivism dimension is present in virtually every multination study. Therefore, Smith et al. asserted that "it is probably safe to infer that this dimension is the most important yield of cross-cultural psychology to date" (p. 237).

Schwartz and colleagues (Schwartz, 1992, 1994a, 1994b; Schwartz & Bilsky, 1987, 1990) developed a theory of individual-level values that can also be applicable at the national level of analysis when scores are aggregated across individuals (e.g., Schwartz & Sagie, 2000). In contrast with Hofstede's inductive approach, Schwartz's central goal was to identify a theory-based structure of values that would generalize across cultures. Schwartz's systematic research efforts have led to a taxonomy of 10 motivationally distinct types of values that includes self-direction, stimulation, achievement, hedonism, power, security, conformity, tradition, benevolence, and universalism (see Schwartz & Sagie, 2000, for a recent summary and description). These 10 value types are grouped along two orthogonal and bipolar dimensions. The first dimension opposes openness to change (self-direction and stimulation) to conservation (conformity, tradition, and security). The second dimension opposes self-transcendence (universalism and benevolence) to self-enhancement (achievement and power). The universality of this two-dimensional structure has been confirmed by results obtained in dozens of countries (Schwartz, 1992, 1994a; Schwartz & Sagiv, 1995). Although the relative importance given to the two dimensions varies from country to country, there seems to be a near universal structure of motivational oppositions and compatibilities that organizes the espoused values.

More recently, the GLOBE project developed measures to assess Hofstede's (1980) four values as well as humane orientation, performance orientation, and long- versus short-term orientation (House et al., 1997). Although results are not yet published, humane orientation is likely to yield results similar to human heartedness and performance orientation, and long- versus short-term orientation are likely to be related to Confucian work dynamism. Therefore, it seems unlikely that the GLOBE project will result in value dimensions not studied previously.

To summarize, what do we know about the universality of country-level values? First, Hofstede's (1980) four-value classification represents the first attempt at deriving a universal taxonomy of values at the nation level of analysis. Second, there is substantial evidence to suggest that the individualism-collectivism dimension is universally understood and relevant in numerous, if not all, cultural contexts. Third, there is substantial evidence that Schwartz's (1992, 1994a) theory-based value taxonomy, often applied at the individual level of analysis, can be applied in a near universal way at the national level of analysis. Fourth, we have abundant information regarding how various countries and cultural groups differ along several values (e.g., individualism–collectivism, power distance, Confucian work dynamism, openness to change–conservation; e.g., Bond, 1988; Chinese Culture Connection, 1987; Hofstede, 1980; Schwartz & Sagiv, 1995; Smith et al., 1996; Trompenaars, 1993). Fifth, some of the efforts regarding the development of value taxonomies have originated by researchers in only one cultural context and, consequently, did not include values indigenous to other contexts (e.g., Hofstede, 1980, 2001, were originated by Western researchers and the Chinese Culture Connection, 1987, was based on a set of values specifically relevant to China). These efforts are likely to lead to value taxonomies that may include universal values, but are likely to not include relevant local values. In conclusion, although specific values have been shown to be universally applicable (e.g., Hofstede's individualism–collectivism), Schwartz's value taxonomy seems to be the only comprehensive taxonomy of universal values applicable in many regions of the world. Looking to the future, we hope that researchers will continue to attempt to identify critical values indigenous to underinvestigated geographic regions (e.g., Africa, Latin America, and the Arab countries).

Next, we continue our review in a macro-to-micro sequence by moving down to the organization level of analysis and discussing organizational development and change followed by organizational culture.

## ORGANIZATION LEVEL OF ANALYSIS

### Organization Development and Change

Organization development (OD) was created virtually concurrently in the United States and the United Kingdom in the 1940s as a social science response to societal problems including minority affairs (e.g., Collier, 1945; Lewin, 1946), repatriation of war veterans (e.g., Bion, 1948), and postwar needs of industry to increase productivity (Faucheux, Amado, & Laurent, 1982). In its broadest meaning, OD is a long-term planned effort that utilizes the theories and knowledge of the behavioral sciences to produce changes in organizations (Aguinis, 1993). A more focused definition is the following: "Organizational Development is concerned with the deliberate, reasoned, introduction, establishment, reinforcement, and spread of change for the purpose of improving an organization's effectiveness and health" (Huse, 1980, p. 23).

Some common OD interventions include survey feedback (i.e., information is collected and fed back to participants), sensitivity training or T-groups (i.e., small-group interactions that allow group members to learn about themselves), total quality management (i.e., organization wide intervention aimed at managing and improving service and product quality), job enrichment (i.e., job redesign aimed at giving employees greater control over their jobs), job enlargement (i.e., job redesign aimed at giving employees greater task variety on their jobs), team building (i.e., small-group interactions to allow group members to improve group dynamics), grid training (i.e., organization wide intervention aimed at improving concern for production and people), quality of work life programs (i.e., organizationwide intervention aimed at increasing employee involvement in decision making), and management by objectives (i.e., goal setting aimed at improving individual and organizational performance).

Is there evidence regarding the universality of some of these popular OD intervention techniques? Are there any underlying principles or functions that make certain OD interventions effective globally?

Unfortunately, there is substantial empirical evidence indicating that many OD techniques that originated in the United States and other Western countries are not likely to be effective outside of these cultural contexts. For example, management by objectives programs allowing frank and open discussion between supervisor and subordinate generally have not been successful in France due to management's inclination to exert control through the implementation of objectives (Trepo, 1973). Similarly, Mirvis and Berg (1977) compiled a large number of cases describing the failure of OD interventions outside of the United States. One such case includes the investigation of why a group development program had been terminated in a company in Switzerland (Bennis, 1977). Bennis concluded that the reason for the termination was that the hierarchical and authority-oriented values of the company's Swiss Army-trained president collided with the goals of the program. More recently, Hui and Luk (1997) conducted a selective review of OD interventions in Africa, Arab countries, Japan, Latin America, the Philippines, Scandinavia, Singapore, Turkey, and the former Soviet Union republics. Hui and Luk concluded that "OD programs are not always successful … Perhaps we have to seriously rethink the basic premises and utility of OD programs as they are applied in another culture" (p. 394).

A universal principle underlying why OD interventions fail seems to be a mismatch between local cultural values and the values underlying OD interventions (Jaeger, 1986). OD's values are consistent with McGregor's (1960) Theory Y and include, among others, (a) moving away from blocking the expression of feeling and moving toward making possible both appropriate expression and effective use of feelings, (b) moving away from the use of status for maintaining power and personal prestige and moving toward the use of status for organizationally relevant purposes, (c) moving away from avoiding risk taking and moving toward willingness to risk, and (d) moving away from emphasizing competition and moving toward emphasizing collaboration (Tannenbaum & Davis, 1969). Jaeger (1986) posited that the greater the congruence between the contextual (i.e., organizational and societal) and OD values, the greater the chance that an OD intervention will be accepted and succeed. So, for example, an OD intervention is not likely to succeed in an environment where individuals do not express their feelings, use status to maintain power, avoid risk, and emphasize competition at the expense of cooperation. Although it is not expected that all values will be congruent (after all, OD interventions attempt to help individuals move toward these values), extreme incongruence is a recipe for failure.

Jaeger (1986) compared the values underlying OD interventions (as described by Tannenbaum & Davis, 1969) with the values studied by Hofstede (1980) and concluded that OD interventions espouse low power distance, low uncertainty avoidance, low masculinity, and medium individualism. Thus, OD interventions are most likely to be successful in countries espousing these values and unsuccessful in countries where these values are not prevalent. Jaeger noted that Denmark, Norway, and Sweden have the most congruent cultural profile. On the other hand, numerous developing countries (e.g., Argentina, Brazil, Chile, Colombia, Pakistan, Peru, the Philippines, Yugoslavia) espouse values that are quite different from those adopted by OD (Bourgeois & Boltvinik, 1981; Jaeger, 1986). Developing countries are those in greatest need of organizational improvement, but this culture incongruence may not allow traditional OD techniques to be successful. Thus, Jaeger recommended that an analysis of process/culture fit be undertaken before implementing an OD intervention. Many OD failures could have been avoided had such an analysis been undertaken prior to the intervention. For instance, DiBella (1993) described how goal-setting assumptions do not apply well in the Philippines, and participants of a funding program, aimed at helping them develop their own business, set glamorous and unattainable goals so as to get more funds but were not concerned about whether these goals would be met.

Interventions congruent with the local cultural context are likely to be popular and effective. For example, the most common OD technique in Singapore is survey feedback (Putti, 1989). A major difference between North American and many Asian countries is that, due to the fear of losing face or making someone else lose face, employees in Asia are less likely to favor open and frank discussions (Aguinis & Roth, 2001). Survey feedback is typically conducted in an anonymous manner, and Hui and Luk (1997) noted that anonymity is the likely reason for its popularity.

Based on the process/culture fit analysis, it is then desirable to adapt or "indigenize" OD techniques to local cultural contexts (Aycan & Kanungo, 2001). For example, Aguinis (1990) described a large-scale change effort that took place in Argentina in the late 1980s, after a decade of brutal and repressive dictatorship, to increase the level of participation of students in university governance structures. Aguinis adapted typical OD interventions such as T-groups to the local cultural context of extreme fear and distrust. Another example includes the implementation of the nurturant-task leadership model in India (Aycan & Kanungo, 2001). In this OD intervention, there is an emphasis on performance and task accomplishment that allows for the expression of collectivistic values including group harmony and cooperation (Sinha, 1980).

In summary, the past has taught us that there seems to be no universally effective OD intervention. Instead, a universal underlying principle is that a process/culture fit analysis needs to be undertaken before an OD intervention is implemented. First, the overall values of OD (cf. Tannenbaum & Davis, 1969) and then the specific assumptions underlying the proposed OD technique need to be scrutinized vis-à-vis the local culture. If the gap between OD values and the organizational and societal culture is too large, then the chances that the OD intervention will be accepted and successful are reduced substantially. As noted by Faucheux et al. (1982), "planned organizational change can only be a gimmick when it does not fully integrate the contextual dimension that provides life, meaning, and raison d'être to organizations" (p. 366). Looking to the future, researchers need to attempt to understand what is a "tolerable" and "acceptable" gap for an OD intervention to succeed in a culturally incongruent context.

## Organizational Culture

Organizational culture refers to a pattern of shared basic assumptions about the environment, human nature, social relationships, and reality that employees have learned as they addressed and resolved problems of external adaptation and internal integration (Schein, 1984). Assumptions are abstract and hard for organizational members to identify because they are taken for granted and out of consciousness. Nevertheless, these assumptions are passed on to new employees as the correct method for dealing with problems. Shared and enduring assumptions reduce ambiguity, encourage desired behavior, and promote a common understanding and response to environmental challenges and opportunities (Schein, 1996). Further, organizational culture helps explain why organizations differ and how organizations and their employees interact.

Schein (1985) noted that, in addition to assumptions, organizational culture has two other levels of manifestation: values and artifacts. Values represent a more concrete level of organizational culture as compared to assumptions, and they guide behavior in organizations by delineating standards by which employees can judge the appropriateness of their actions. Artifacts refer to visible aspects of culture such as technology, arts, attire, architecture, stories, rituals, symbols, and ceremonies.

Although some authors have acknowledged that national culture affects organizational culture (e.g., Hofstede, Neuijen, Ohayv, & Sanders, 1990; Konrad & Susanj, 1999), studies examining the relationship between the two are rare (Adler & Jelinek, 1986; Aycan, Kanungo, & Sinha, 1999; Hofstede et al., 1990; Triandis, 1994). This is unfortunate because successful implementation of human resource practices (Schneider, 1988) and employee job satisfaction (Lincoln, Hanada, & Olson, 1981) rely on the congruence between organizational and national culture. Next, based on the small body of available research investigating organizational and societal culture, we propose potential universals for each of the three levels of manifestation of organizational culture (i.e., assumptions, values, and artifacts).

*Assumptions.*    Underlying assumptions affect how employees perceive and respond to the organizational environment. Schein (1985) asserted that assumptions regarding work tasks and employees are important aspects of organizational culture. Task assumptions refer to the nature of work tasks and how they can be accomplished most effectively, whereas employee assumptions refer to employee nature and behavior. The model of culture fit first proposed by Kanungo and Jaeger (1990) included these assumptions. According to this model, task (i.e., task goal, task orientation, and competitive orientation) and employee (i.e., futuristic orientation, locus of control, malleability, proactivity vs. reactivity, obligation toward others, responsibility seeking, and participation) assumptions are influenced by external environment characteristics such as industry, market, ownership, and resource availability, as well as cultural dimensions such as paternalism, power distance, and uncertainty avoidance. Both task and employee assumptions, which represent organizational culture, in turn influence individual and group behavior. Initial support for the model was found in Canadian and Indian samples (Aycan et al., 1999; Mathur, Aycan, & Kanungo, 1996); however, we recommend further research on the applicability of these assumptions in other cultures. There is evidence that societal culture affects organizational culture, but it is unclear if different cultures define organizational culture using the same underlying assumptions.

*Values.*    Many researchers argue that organizational culture can be represented by values (e.g., Howard, 1998) instead of assumptions. Quinn and McGrath (1985) proposed a typology of organizational culture based on the following two values: internal versus external orientation and flexibility versus control orientation. This typology results in four types of organizational culture. First, group culture has an internal and flexible orientation characterized by group cohesiveness, participation, cooperation, individual growth, open communication, and organizational commitment. Second, developmental culture represents an external and flexible orientation marked by searches for new information in the external environment, innovation, creativity, openness to change, risk taking, and tolerance for ambiguity. Third, a hierarchical culture represents a combination of internal and control orientations, and it focuses on rationality, respect for authority, clearly defined rules and procedures, stability, formality, and security. Finally, a rational culture refers to the combination of external and control orientations, which results in rational planning, goal setting, and an achievement orientation. A few studies have used this typology in the

United States (e.g., Howard, 1998), United Kingdom (e.g., West & Anderson, 1992), and Europe (e.g., Konrad & Susanj, 1999; van Muijen & Koopman, 1994). However, much empirical research is needed to determine the universality of these organizational culture values.

Xenikou and Furnham (1996) also sought to identify common values representing organizational culture. These researchers factor analyzed four commonly used U.S. measures of organizational culture that assess behavioral norms and values (i.e., Organizational Culture Inventory by Cooke & Lafferty, 1989; Culture Gap Survey by Kilman & Saxton, 1983; Organizational Beliefs Questionnaire by Sashkin, 1984; and Corporate Culture Survey by Glaser, 1983). Using two British organizations, this study found five dimensions of organizational culture across the measures: openness to change in a cooperative culture (emphasis on change, innovation, and achievement in a cooperative and supportive environment), task-oriented organizational growth (emphasis on continuous improvement and organizational development), human factor in a bureaucratic culture (emphasis on conventionality, formalization, and central planning), negativism and resistance to new ideas (emphasis on power, competition, and confrontation), and positive social relations in the workplace (emphasis on human relations, development of friendships, and socializing).

Although the values proposed by Quinn and McGrath (1985) and Xenikou and Furnham (1996) are similar and overlap considerably, they were both derived from a Western perspective. According to Adler and Jelinek (1986), research on organizational culture has been limited to the United States and has failed to be integrated into cross-cultural OB research because of its U.S.-based approach. Future research should not only investigate the universality of these values underlying organizational culture, but also explore other values that may be specific to cultures other than the United States.

*Artifacts.*    The final level of organizational culture is artifacts (i.e., the visible aspects of culture). Hofstede et al. (1990) asserted that organizational culture is best measured by organizational practices (i.e., a type of artifact) instead of more abstract assumptions and values. In their study of 10 companies in Denmark and the Netherlands, Hofstede et al. found six practices that could be used to measure organizational culture. The practices were process versus results oriented (e.g., "People put in maximal effort"), employee versus job oriented (e.g., "Important decisions are made by individuals"), parochial versus professional (e.g., "Job competence is the only criterion in hiring people"), open versus closed system (e.g., "Organization and people are closed and secretive"), loose versus tight control (e.g., "Everybody is cost-conscious"), and normative versus pragmatic (e.g., "Results are more important than procedures"). Again, we must qualify that these practices were found in northwest European organizations and that further investigation is necessary to determine if they can be applied to other cultures.

In summary, one broad universal we can conclude is the presence of a relationship between societal and organizational culture; however, we need to explore the nature and magnitude of this relationship across cultures. Looking to the future, we have proposed potential universals at the three levels of organizational culture. However, these proposals are preliminary and empirical evidence is far too limited to declare their generalizability with confidence. Further research is imperative in this area before strong conclusions can be drawn about universal and culture-specific aspects of organizational culture.

Next, we continue our macro-to-micro journey and move down from the organization to the group and dyad levels of analysis and review the topics of work teams, conflict and negotiation, and leadership.

## GROUP AND DYAD LEVELS OF ANALYSIS

### Work Teams

Teams are an important aspect of organizational functioning. In recent years, there has been a trend toward alternative work arrangements with organizing work in teams being a common choice. Many organizations are organizing around teams in hopes of deriving increased productivity, enhanced creativity and problem solving, and greater satisfaction with the work environment. Unfortunately, there is a paucity of research comparing team-related phenomena across cultures (Kirkman & Shapiro, 1997) to determine the generalizability of the touted benefits of teams. Indeed, most previous research has focused on multicultural teams or teams compiled of individuals from different cultures (e.g., Ilgen, LePine, & Hollenbeck, 1997; Prieto & Arias, 1997) instead of teams operating within a specific culture.

A team can be defined as two or more individuals who interact and are to some degree dependent on each other in the pursuit of common goals, solving problems, or completing tasks (Hackman, 1987; Sundstrom, De Meuse, & Futrell, 1990). This dependence is a result of members possessing unique skills, duties, and roles within the team. In addition, not only do these individuals perceive themselves as a team, but outsiders who are familiar with them do as well. Even though some researchers have noted a distinction between groups and teams, we use the terms interchangeably.

Although groups are a naturally occurring phenomenon (Mann, 1980), preferences for working in them and the nature of behavior within them seems to vary substantially across cultures. For instance, it is well accepted that workers from individualistic cultures find working alone substantially more motivating than working as part of a team, whereas collectivistic societies tend to prefer group situations. In fact, Kirkman and Shapiro (1997) proposed that employees from individualistic cultures will actively resist work organized in teams, whereas employees from collectivistic cultures will openly embrace teams because they value the well-being of groups of which they are a part.

Another marked difference in group behavior between individualistic and collectivistic cultures is in the area of social loafing. Social loafing refers to individuals not working as hard in groups as they would individually and it is a common occurrence in Western cultures but it does not exist or is even reversed in others. In countries such as China (Earley, 1989), Israel (Earley, 1993), Japan (Matsui, Kakuyama, & Onglatco, 1987), and Taiwan (Gabrenya, Wang, & Latané, 1985), performance actually increases when individuals work as part of a group as compared to when they work alone. Thus, work organized in teams may hinder employee performance in individualistic cultures like the United States, whereas it may facilitate performance in collectivistic cultures like Japan.

Although preference for working in teams is particular to the type of culture, we can identify a potential universal regarding teams even in this area. That is, whereas individualists prefer working alone and collectivists favor working in teams, both demonstrate lower performance levels when working with out-group members (Earley, 1993). Once again, the magnitude of this effect depends on the culture of employees, with those in collectivistic cultures posing greater opposition to working with out-group members than employees from individualistic cultures.

As Mann (1980) pointed out in his review of the small-group research literature, in all cultures groups pressure individual members to conform to group norms. For teams to be successful, a certain amount of conformity and cooperation is imperative. Without cooperation, teams would be hard pressed to achieve their goals and tasks. Mann's review found that conformity to group pressure existed in every country studied using the Asch (1956) method. The original study by Asch indicated that about 33% of participants conformed to group pressure and replications found similar levels of conformance in countries such as Brazil (34%), Fiji (36%), Hong Kong (32%), Japan (25%), Lebanon (31%), and slightly higher rates in Rhodesia (51%; Chandra, 1973; Frager, 1970; Whittaker & Meade, 1967). However, a meta-analysis of studies replicating Asch's conformity study indicated that collectivists had higher levels of conformity than individualists (Bond & Smith, 1996b). Thus, although all groups require some degree of compliance with group norms, those in collectivistic cultures are likely to exhibit the most compliance. Finally, not only is it universal for teams to exert pressure on their members to conform to group norms, teams typically reject those members that refuse to conform at least to some degree (Mann, 1980).

In summary, team research has focused on performance in multinational teams, whereas team behavior has not been investigated extensively in different cultures. Research that has been conducted in cross-cultural settings indicates that there are differences among cultures in preference for working in teams as well as productivity levels due to the presence, lack of, or reversal of social loafing. However, research also provides evidence that teams universally exert pressure on their members to conform to group norms and that those individuals who do not conform, at least to some extent, are ostracized from the team. In the future, knowledge about the effects of culture on work teams will benefit greatly from empirical research examining between-culture differences in team organization and dynamics.

## Conflict and Negotiation

Conflict between parties, typically holding opposing interests, is an all-too-frequent event in organizational life. In fact, managers in the United States report spending approximately 20% of their time resolving conflicts (Cropanzano, Aguinis, Schminke, & Denham, 1999; Thomas & Schmidt, 1976). Because of the pervasiveness of conflict, individuals use a variety of negotiation approaches in an attempt to end the conflict (Cropanzano et al., 1999). These negotiation approaches derive from the extent to which one has the dual concern with one's own outcomes and with the other party's outcomes (Leung, 1997). Having low concerns for both is likely to lead to an avoidance or inaction approach, whereas having high concerns for both is likely to lead to a problem-solving approach. If concern for one's outcomes is high and for other's outcomes is low, a contending or competition approach is likely, and if concern for one's outcomes is low and for other's outcomes is high, yielding is likely. Lastly, if concern for one's outcomes is moderate and for other's outcomes is high, compromise is likely (van de Vliert, 1990).

Janosik (1987) noted the following four paradigms to studying the relationship between culture and negotiation: (a) culture as learned behavior (i.e., assumes that people sharing a geographic region are socialized into similar patterns and therefore display similar negotiation behaviors), (b) culture as shared values (i.e., assumes that people with a common culture share values that directly affect their negotiation behaviors), (c) culture as dialectic (i.e., assumes that people sharing a common culture share values that are in constant tension that directly affect their negotiation behaviors), and (d) culture in context (i.e., assumes that people sharing a common culture share values and a host of other factors that affect their negotiation behaviors). Reviews by Wilson, Cai, Campbell, Donohue, and Drake (1995) and Leung (1997) make it clear that the vast majority of empirical studies regarding culture and negotiation have adopted the culture as shared values perspective, in which a cultural dimension (e.g., individualism–collectivism) is predicted to have a main effect on preferences for or actual negotiation behaviors.

Wilson et al.'s (1995) review of studies of individualism–collectivism revealed that, in general, negotiators from more collectivistic societies tend to report a preference for nonconfrontational (e.g., avoiding, accommodating) behaviors as compared to negotiators from more individualistic societies. In addition to these procedural preferences, there are several studies concluding that there are cross-national differences in discourse and nonverbal features of negotiation interaction. For example, Graham (1985) compared Japanese, Brazilian, and U.S. negotiators and found that Japanese interactions contained more conversational gaps, whereas Brazilian interactions contain more direct eye contact and touch; in addition, Brazilians used the word "no" 10 times more frequently than did Japanese and U.S. managers. Numerous similar illustrations exist regarding cross-national differences in the number of conversational gaps and overlaps (Graham, Evenko, & Rajan, 1992), vocal backchannels (Fant, 1989), and the use of self- versus other-oriented markers (Fant, 1989).

In sharp contrast with the findings described here, Wilson et al.'s (1995) review also revealed that no such clear differences were found in intracultural negotiations for the direct effect of cultural dimensions such as individualism–collectivism on (a) actual negotiator behaviors, and (b) negotiation outcomes (e.g., nature of the settlement, profits for buyers and sellers; note, however, that there is evidence that intercultural negotiations show lower levels of joint gains as compared to intracultural negotiations, Brett & Okumura, 1998). For example, Adler, Graham, and Gehrke (1987) found that Mexican dyads (i.e., assumed to be collectivistic) did not differ from Canadian and U.S. dyads (i.e., assumed to be individualistic) regarding the use of cooperative tactics and the size of profits derived from settlements. As a second illustration, Cai (1993, cited in Wilson et al., 1995) did not find that culture had a main effect on the actual use of face management tactics (i.e., a tactic designed to protect one's identity, Aguinis & Roth, 2001) in samples of students from Taiwan and the United States.

Taken together, results gathered over the past decades suggest that although culture affects *reported* preferences for negotiation behaviors and actual conversational and communication styles, there is no clear evidence of a direct effect of cultural differences on *actual* negotiation behaviors and outcomes. Rather than a main effect, culture may play the role of a mediator (Leung, 1997) or a moderator (Wilson et al., 1995) variable. For instance, a negotiator's culture-based preference may be overridden by the desire to reciprocate (Adler et al., 1987) or accommodate (Gallois, Franklyn-Stokes, Giles, & Coupland, 1988) the other party's negotiation behaviors. Thus, it appears that culture is just one of several antecedents of negotiation behaviors including number and linkage between issues, time constraints, and the personalities and roles of the negotiators involved. Accordingly, Janosik's (1987) culture-in-context paradigm seems to be the most promising conceptual framework for understanding the role of culture as an antecedent to conflict management. It seems that "any attempt to understand negotiation behavior as a genre of human action which attends only to the culturally defined values of the negotiator will, ultimately, be inadequate" (Janosik, 1987, p. 537).

In summary, returning to the question of universals, it seems that negotiators do have culture-specific preferences for various behaviors, hold different perceptions regarding which behaviors may be appropriate or preferred, and perceive the same conflict situation differently (Gelfand et al., 2001; Wilson & Waltman, 1988). However, behaviors in actual situations are not explained clearly by cultural differences and negotiators from different cultures arrive at similar outcomes. Thus, an apparent universal in the cross-cultural literature on conflict and negotiation is that negotiators, regardless of their cultural background, reach similar outcomes. Culture is just one of several variables that ultimately affect these outcomes and more complex conceptual models are needed to explain the remarkable finding that, in spite of conversational and communication differences, negotiation outcomes seem to remain cross-culturally invariant. Future research is needed to examine the precise effect of culture (e.g., mediator, moderator), and the strength of this effect.

## Leadership

There is no consensual definition of leadership in the OB literature. A recent meeting of the GLOBE project including 84 scholars representing 56 countries yielded the following definition of organizational leadership: "… the ability of an individual to influence, motivate, and enable others to contribute toward the effectiveness and success of the organizations of which they are members" (House et al., 1997, p. 548).

The universal–particular question is whether there are specific leadership functions that are universal and culture free. There is empirical support for two such functions: (a) transactional–transformational leadership, and (b) task–relationship orientation leadership.

*Transactional–Transformational Leadership.*    There is abundant evidence suggesting that the transactional–transformational paradigm transcends cultural boundaries (Bass, 1997; Bass & Avolio, 1993; Bass, Burger, Doktor, & Barrett, 1979). Bass and colleagues have concluded that subordinates' ideal regarding a leader is transformational and not transactional. Transformational leaders display attributes including charisma, intellectual stimulation of followers, and individualized attention and consideration toward followers. On the other hand, transactional leaders establish relationships with followers based on contingent rewards.

The transformational–transactional paradigm is a good example of a basic universal underlying function that is enacted by a variety of behavioral manifestations across cultures. For example, House et al. (1997) illustrated that the charisma dimension of transformational leadership was enacted in a highly aggressive manner in the cases of John F. Kennedy, Martin Luther King, Jr., and Theodore Roosevelt in the United States and Winston Churchill in the United Kingdom. Alternatively, charismatic leadership was enacted in a more quiet and nonaggressive manner in the cases of Mahatma Gandhi and Mother Teresa in India and Nelson Mandela in South Africa. Similarly, Smith (1997) concluded that "charisma may be best thought of as a quality that is global but imputed to leaders on the basis of behaviors that are culture-specific" (p. 628).

*Task–Relationship Orientation Leadership.* The task versus relationship orientation of situational leadership theory (Hersey & Blanchard, 1988) is a second function that crosses cultural borders. Misumi's (1985) work in Japan identified the two fundamental leadership functions of performance (P) and maintenance (M). The P function refers to task requirements and the M function refers to the maintenance of good relationships between the leader and the followers and among the followers. Misumi emphasized that these leader functions surface through behaviors that are culture-specific. Stated differently, although the P and M functions are universal, the behavioral manifestations of these functions vary across cultures. For example, an M-related behavior in the United States may consist of a leader inviting subordinates out for after-work drinks at a local bar, whereas an M-related behavior in Brazil may include a leader helping a subordinate secure a job for his or her spouse.

Several Western researchers have identified the same two functions, albeit labeled differently. For instance, Fiedler (1978) described a dimension related to the concern for establishing good relations with subordinates and a second dimension related to the concern with attaining successful task performance, and Bass (1990) described the "consideration" and "initiating structure" dimensions. Moreover, researchers in other non-Western regions of the world have also identified the same functions. For instance, Sinha (1995) described the task versus nurturing leadership functions, and asserted that leaders must perform both functions to be effective, and Ah Chong and Thomas (1997) confirmed Misumi's (1985) P and M dimensions in samples of Pakeha and Pacific Islanders in New Zealand.

In summary, we conclude that the transactional–transformational and task–relationship paradigms are universal underlying leadership functions. These functions are expressed in a large number of diverse and culture-specific behaviors, as described in reviews of the cross-cultural leadership literature (e.g., Bass, 1990; House et al., 1997).

Next, we discuss the following two areas at the individual level of analysis: work motivation and decision making.

## INDIVIDUAL LEVEL OF ANALYSIS

### Work Motivation

Work motivation is an important determinant of job performance and often a top priority of managers (i.e., managers spend much energy motivating employees to do good work). It has been defined as a set of processes that initiate, direct, and maintain effort toward desired work behaviors (e.g., Campbell & Pritchard, 1976; Pinder, 1998). OB research in the United States has focused much attention on this topic, but the transfer of American theories to other cultures has been neglected (e.g., Ambrose & Kulik, 1999) or has met with limited success (e.g., Silverthorne, 1996).

An explanation for the lack of empirical support of work motivation theories outside the United States can be found in Erez's (1997) culture-based model of work motivation. Building from the previously proposed model of cultural self-representation (Erez & Earley, 1993), Erez (1997) suggested that motivational practices be evaluated using the individualism–collectivism and power distance cultural dimensions. As previously described in the section on national values, the individualism–collectivism dimension refers to the inclination for working individually or in teams, whereas the power distance dimension refers to the degree that a power hierarchy and inequality are acceptable. When motivating practices, such as employee participation, are evaluated as contributing to employees' self-worth (i.e., they are congruent with employees' cultural values), employees are motivated to perform well, whereas negative evaluations lead to poor performance. For example, in low power distance cultures, where there are few power differentials and a willingness to challenge others' ideas, employee participation programs are likely to succeed because they are congruent with employees' cultural values.

Although Erez's (1997) cross-cultural model of work motivation explains why many motivating practices that succeed in the United States often fail overseas and vice versa, we believe there are some universal motivators. First, McClelland's need for achievement has been touted as universal (see Bhagat & McQuaid, 1982, for a more detailed review). Research demonstrates that many countries place high importance on the need for achievement such as Japan, Northern Ireland (Yamauchi, Lynn, & Rendell, 1994), Australia, Canada, Singapore, the United States (Popp, Davis, & Herbert, 1986), China, Lebanon, and Aborigine Australia (Holt & Keats, 1992). However, the magnitude of achievement motivation varies from country to country and the manifestations differ as well. That is, achievement may be behaviorally manifested as economic, task, personal, group, or family success. For example, achievement motivation is more socially oriented (e.g., need to belong, need to cooperate) in collectivistic cultures like East Asia instead of focused on the work itself or individual achievement like in the United States (Yu, 1995; Yu & Yang, 1994). In summary, employees worldwide develop a need for achievement, but the emphasis placed on that need and its behavioral manifestation vary somewhat among cultures.

There are other employee needs that may serve as universal motivators besides achievement (see Ambrose & Kulik, 1999, for a more extensive review). For instance, Harpaz (1990) randomly surveyed over 8,000 employees in seven countries (i.e., Belgium, Great Britain, Israel, Japan, the Netherlands, the United States, and West Germany) to determine important motivating factors at work. Although the motivators varied somewhat among the countries, interesting work and pay were consistently the two most important. However, the method of distributing pay to motivate employees may depend on cultural values (see Leung, 1997, for a more detailed discussion). Employees can be rewarded according to their performance (principle of equity), equally (principle of equality), or based on their needs (principle of need). Research supports using the equity principle in individualistic cultures and using the equality principle in collectivistic cultures (James, 1993). Individualistic cultures value competition, achievement, and personal goals, and therefore, desire to have pay plans that recognize individual contributions. Conversely, collectivistic cultures emphasize cooperation, interdependence, and group goals, and thus, prefer plans that support group harmony. However, a caveat should be noted. Collectivistic cultures differentiate between in-group and out-group members by applying the equality principle to in-group members and the equity principle to out-group members (Leung & Bond, 1984).

Two final motivators that may be universally applicable are the need for growth and the need to control one's environment. The need for growth was valued by employees in China, Russia, the United States (Silverthorne, 1992), Bulgaria, Hungary, the Netherlands (Roe, Zinovieva, Dienes, & Ten Horn, 2000), Australia, Canada, and Singapore (Popp et al.,

1986), whereas the need to control one's environment was deemed important by employees in foreign subsidiaries of an organization in Belgium, Colombia, Germany, Italy, Japan, Mexico, Spain, and Venezuela (Alpander & Carter, 1991). Thus, there is some support for additional universal motivators, at least among industrialized nations.

In summary, there appear to be some universal motivators such as achievement, interesting work, pay, growth, and environmental control, even though the magnitude of their importance and even their manifestations may vary among countries. Work motivation drives job performance and, thus, is an important issue for organizations worldwide. Therefore, cross-cultural research in this area needs to assist managers in identifying employee motivators that can be used regardless of the culture in which organizations are operating as well as acknowledging culture-specific aspects of work motivation.

## Decision Making

Effective decision making is crucial in today's competitive and global business environment. Managers are faced daily with a multitude of decisions demanding their attention. Choices made regarding these decisions can determine success of organizations and even individual careers. Indeed, it is not surprising that decision making has been labeled one of the most important duties of executives and managers alike (Mintzberg, 1988).

Decision making is the process of selecting a response for handling problems or opportunities (Huber, 1980). There are five basic steps in the decision-making process. First, a problem or opportunity must be recognized and clearly defined. Next, potential courses of action need to be generated and evaluated as to their feasibility. Third and fourth, a course of action is selected and implemented. Lastly, the outcome of the action is assessed and necessary adjustments are made. Although there are many areas of decision-making research, cross-cultural research tends to focus on who makes decisions, and specifically, on employee participation in decision making. Thus, we propose universals regarding the level of employee participation encouraged in decision making.

Managers can make decisions individually, consult others such as superiors or subordinates and then make decisions, ask employees to jointly make decisions with them, or defer decision-making power solely to employees. Although the level of participation may vary among cultures, as we discuss momentarily, participative decision making has increased worldwide (Córdova, 1982). Participatory decision making or industrial democracy (as it is referred to in Europe) can take many forms, such as voluntary implementation by organizations, collective bargaining (e.g., Great Britain, United States), mandated by national law (e.g., Norway, Peru), work councils (e.g., Germany, Austria, the Netherlands), producers' cooperatives (e.g., Spain), or representation on company boards (e.g., Luxembourg, Sweden, Denmark; see Strauss, 1982, for a detailed review).

Whether voluntarily adopted or required by legislation, Haire et al. (1966) noted that managers in 14 countries favored participative involvement by employees, but they believe that their employees are not capable of engaging in participative decision making. This finding was later replicated in other countries such as Cyprus, Greece, and Turkey (Banai & Katsounotos, 1993; Cummings & Schmidt, 1972; Kozan, 1993). In summary, managers believe that employee participation in decision making is worthwhile, but only when they perceive that employees have the necessary skills to successfully engage in participation (Heller & Wilpert, 1981). As the Industrial Democracy in Europe (1981) discovered in its research, participative decision making is only implemented when there are cultural norms promoting positive attitudes toward participation and actual involvement in it. Thus, the level of participation granted in decision making depends in part on culture.

Whereas some degree of employee participation in decision making is universally accepted in organizations, power distance has been proposed as a determinant of the amount of participation deemed appropriate by managers (e.g., Triandis, 1994; Wilpert, 1984). Specifically, it has been hypothesized that cultures characterized by high power distance as well as individualism are more likely to favor decisions made by individual managers or employees, whereas those cultures exemplified by low power distance and collectivism are more likely to favor participatory decision making (e.g., Erez, 1994; Triandis, 1994).

Evidence on the predictive power of power distance in participatory decision making is conflicting. On the other hand, findings regarding the effects of individualism–collectivism may be more explanatory. For example, Erez and Earley (1987) compared the effectiveness of assigned goals, representative goal setting, and participative goal setting in the United States and Israel. Results showed that the Israeli participants had lower performance than their U.S. counterparts when the goals were assigned. However, there was no performance difference for the representative and participative goal setting conditions in the U.S. sample. This study illustrates a situation involving a more collectivistic and lower power distance culture responding more negatively to nonparticipation in decision making than a more individualistic and higher power distance culture, which supports the foregoing hypothesis. However, Smith, Peterson, Akande, Callan, and Cho (1994) examined 16 countries and found that decisions were typically participatory in collectivistic high power distance countries, whereas decisions were usually made by individuals in individualistic low power distance countries. This finding is surprising because it has been proposed that employees in collectivistic high power distance cultures should readily accept decisions handed down by their supervisors, and even resist participation in decision making because of their unquestioning attitudes toward their supervisors. Support for this assertion was provided by Graf, Hemmasi, Lust, and Liang (1990), who found that Chinese managers approved of the nonparticipatory approach of their superiors and the lack of assertiveness by subordinates in decision making.

As previously noted, the individualism–collectivism dimension may provide a better explanation for why managers prefer different levels of participation in decision making. For instance, Peterson, Smith, Bond, and Misumi (1990) found employees in Japan, a collectivistic society, preferred managing events (i.e., making decisions) in conjunction with their co-workers, whereas employees in more individualistic cultures including the United Kingdom and United States preferred making decisions individually or deferring to their supervisors, respectively, instead of consulting with others. Similarly, studies by Radford, Mann, Ohta, and Nakane (1991, 1993) found Japanese employees tended to work with others when making decisions, whereas Australian employees, who are typically more individualistic, preferred to make decisions themselves.

In summary, decision making is a universal aspect of organizational life. Organizations that can make and implement decisions effectively will be those that prosper in today's global marketplace. There is a worldwide trend toward employee participation in decision making although the level of participation varies depending on the culture in which organizations are operating. Participative decision making may be most effective in collectivistic cultures because of their group orientation, which is likely to foster positive attitudes toward and value employee involvement in organizational decision making.

## CONCLUDING COMMENTS

The early stages of cross-cultural OB were marked by a great deal of enthusiasm and optimism. However, some researchers are at present skeptical. For instance, some believe that not much progress has been made, that theoretical models are lacking or underdeveloped (Aycan & Kanungo, 2001; Bond, 1997; Ilgen et al., 1997), and even that culture may not be a potent explanatory variable for OB. However, our chapter shows that cross-cultural OB has made impressive advances in the past few decades in identifying universals in several areas, including national values, organizational change and development, organizational culture, work teams, conflict and negotiation, leadership, work motivation, and decision making. For instance, there is substantial evidence to support the universal applicability of individualism–collectivism as a national value, the universal need to match contextual (i.e., organizational and societal) values with OD values to prevent change intervention failures, the universal similarity often found in negotiation outcomes in spite of the differences in negotiation process preferences, the universal applicability of the transformational– transactional leadership paradigm, and the universal presence of motivators including need for achievement and interesting work, to name a few.

Looking toward the future of cross-cultural OB, our chapter also includes a discussion of universals as well as directions for investigation that we hope will be subjected to empirical testing. For instance, we hope that future work will identify national values indigenous to underinvestigated regions such as Africa and Latin America, will assess what is an acceptable gap between contextual and OD values for an OD intervention to be effective, will ascertain whether similar task and employee assumptions (i.e., basic components of organizational culture) affect individual and group behavior universally, will examine team dynamics cross-culturally (and not just multinational teams within cultures), and will attempt to understand the surprisingly high level of similarity in negotiation outcomes in spite of cross-cultural differences in negotiation processes, to name a few.

The identification of universals, paired with the massive evidence in support of the culture pervasiveness hypothesis, explains how different cultural groups can be similar and dissimilar at the same time. The existence of behaviors that differ across cultures is not necessarily incompatible with underlying functions that are culture free. In spite of these common underlying functions (e.g., charismatic leadership), their behavioral manifestations can differ markedly from culture to culture (e.g., a quiet and nonaggressive manner in the case of Mahatma Gandhi and a highly aggressive manner in the case of Theodore Roosevelt). We have identified universals in eight OB areas spanning the national, organizational, group, dyad, and individual levels of analysis. We hope that future work will continue this trend and move beyond this admittedly selected subset of topics.

Many authors have noted that cross-cultural OB research is dominated by the United States (e.g., Adler, Doktor, & Redding, 1986). We echo this concern and believe that it is imperative that we move the field of OB beyond the U.S. borders. Related to this criticism is the complaint that the samples used in published studies are biased in that they overrepresent the United States and the West (Bond & Smith, 1996a). We feel that one of the causes for this state of affairs is the problem that the vast majority of U.S. researchers cannot read research results published in non-English outlets. One way to overcome this problem is to work with collaborators who know other languages. This is an important issue to address in the future and we hope that future reviews of the cross-cultural OB literature will include knowledge generated in countries other than the United

States and Western Europe and published in non-English journals. In addition, related to the need to collaborate with researchers who speak other languages is the need to include collaborators who are transcultural (Graen, Hui, Wakabayashi, & Wang, 1997). The United States has a privileged position in this regard due to the large number of immigrants. We should take advantage of this wonderful opportunity and include members of cultural minorities in our research teams.

In closing, we have a very optimistic view of the field of cross-cultural OB. A review of past research has allowed us to identify some universals and propose others that require future empirical test. The knowledge accumulated thus far is generating important theoretical propositions (e.g., Earley & Erez, 1997), as well as guidance for organizational practice and interventions (e.g., Hui & Luk, 1997).

## ACKNOWLEDGMENTS

We thank Michael H. Bond (Chinese University of Hong Kong, People's Republic of China), Kwok Leung (City University of Hong Kong, People's Republic of China), Edwin A. Locke (University of Maryland, United States), Charles A. Pierce (Montana State University, United States), Peter B. Smith (University of Sussex, United Kingdom), and David C. Thomas (Simon Fraser University, Canada) for constructive comments on previous drafts.

The research reported herein was supported, in part, by grants awarded to Herman Aguinis from the Institute for International Business and the Business School at the University of Colorado at Denver. Portions of the research reported herein were conducted while Herman Aguinis was on sabbatical leave from the University of Colorado at Denver and holding visiting appointments at China Agricultural University-The International College of Beijing (People's Republic of China), City University of Hong Kong (People's Republic of China), Nanyang Technological University (Singapore), University of Science Malaysia (Malaysia), and Universidad de Santiago de Compostela (Spain).

## REFERENCES

Adler, N. J., & Bartholomew, S. (1992). Academic and professional communities of discourse: Generating knowledge on transnational human resource management. *Journal of International Business Studies, 23*, 551–570.

Adler, N. J., Doktor, R., & Redding, S. G. (1986). From the Atlantic to the Pacific: Cross-cultural management reviewed. *Journal of Management, 12*, 295–318.

Adler, N. J., Graham, J. L., & Gehrke, T. S. (1987). Business negotiations in Canada, Mexico, and the United States. *Journal of Business Research, 15*, 411–429.

Adler, N. J., & Jelinek, M. (1986). Is "organization culture" culture bound? *Human Resource Management, 25*, 73–90.

Aguinis, H. (1990). Universities and youth. In M. Aguinis (Ed.), *Memoirs of a sowing: Utopia and practice of PRONDEC* (National Program for Culture Democratization) (pp. 239–245). Buenos Aires, Argentina: Planeta-Sudamericana.

Aguinis, H. (1993). Action research and scientific method: Presumed discrepancies and actual similarities. *Journal of Applied Behavioral Science, 29*, 416–431.

Aguinis, H., & Roth, H. A. (2001). *Teaching in China: Culture-based challenges*. Manuscript submitted for publication.

Ah Chong, L. M., & Thomas. D. C. (1997). Leadership perceptions in cross-cultural context: Pakeha and Pacific Islanders in New Zealand. *Leadership Quarterly, 8*, 275–293.

Ajiferuke, M., & Boddewyn, J. (1970). "Culture" and other explanatory variables in comparative management studies. *Academy of Management Journal, 13*, 153–163.

Alpander, G. G., & Carter, K. D. (1991). Strategic multinational intra-company differences in employee motivation. *Journal of Managerial Psychology, 6*, 25–32.

Ambrose, M. L., & Kulik, C. T. (1999). Old friends, new faces: Motivation research in the 1990s. *Journal of Management, 25*, 231–292.

Arvey, R. D., Bhagat, R. S., & Salas, E. (1991). Cross-cultural and cross-national issues in personnel and human resources management. In G. R. Ferris & K. M. Rowland (Eds.), *Research in personnel and human resources management* (Vol. 9, pp. 367–407). Greenwich, CT: JAI.

Asch, S. E. (1956). Studies of independence and conformity. A minority of one against a unanimous majority. *Psychological Monographs, 70* (No. 9, Whole No. 416).

Aycan, Z., & Kanungo, R. N. (2001). Cross-cultural industrial and organizational psychology: A critical appraisal of the field and future directions. In N. Anderson, D. S. Ones, H. K. Sinangil, & C. Viswesvaran (Eds.), *Handbook of industrial, work & organizational psychology* (Vol. 1, pp. 385–408). London: Sage.

Aycan, Z., Kanungo, R. N., & Sinha, J. B. P. (1999). Organizational culture and human resource practices: The model of culture fit. *Journal of Cross-Cultural Psychology, 30*, 501–526.

Banai, M., & Katsounotos, P. (1993). Participative management in Cyprus. *International Studies of Management and Organization, 23*, 19–34.

Barrett, G. V., & Bass, B. M. (1976). Cross-cultural issues in industrial and organizational psychology. In M. D. Dunnette (Ed.), *Handbook of industrial and organizational psychology* (pp. 1639–1686). Chicago: Rand McNally.

Bass, B. M. (1990). *Bass and Stogdill's handbook of leadership: Theory, research and managerial applications* (3rd ed.). New York: The Free Press.

Bass, B. M. (1997). Does the transactional–transformational paradigm transcend organizational and national boundaries? *American Psychologist, 52*, 130–139.

Bass, B. M., & Avolio, B. J. (1993). Transformational leadership: A response to critiques. In M. M. Chemers & R. Ayman (Eds.), *Leadership theory and research: Perspectives and directions* (pp. 49–80). Orlando, FL: Academic.

Bass, B. M., Burger, P. C., Doktor, R., & Barrett, G. V. (1979). *Assessment of managers: An international comparison*. New York: The Free Press.

Bennis, W. (1977). Bureaucracy and social change: An anatomy of a training failure. In P. H. Mirvis & D. N. Berg (Eds.), *Failures in organization development and change: Cases and essay for learning* (pp. 191–215). New York: Wiley.

Bhagat, R. S., Kedia, B. L., Crawford, S. E., & Kaplan, M. R. (1990). Cross-cultural issues in organizational psychology: Emergent trends and directions for research in the 1990s. In C. L. Cooper & I. T. Robertson (Eds.), *International review of industrial and organizational psychology* (Vol. 5, pp. 59–99). Chichester, England: Wiley.

Bhagat, R. S., & McQuaid, S. J. (1982). Role of subjective culture in organizations: A review and directions for future research. *Journal of Applied Psychology, 67*, 653–685.

Bion, W. R. (1948). Psychiatry at a time of crisis. *British Journal of Medical Psychology, 21*, 81–89.

Bond, M. H. (1988). Finding universal dimensions of individual variation in multi-cultural studies of values: The Rokeach and Chinese value surveys. *Journal of Personality and Social Psychology, 55*, 1009–1015.

Bond, M. H. (1997). Adding value to the cross-cultural study of organizational behavior. In P. C. Earley & M. Erez (Eds.), *New perspectives on international industrial/organizational psychology* (pp. 256–275). San Francisco: New Lexington.

Bond, M. H., & Smith, P. B. (1996a). Cross-cultural social and organizational psychology. *Annual Review of Psychology, 47*, 205–235.

Bond, R., & Smith, P. B. (1996b). Culture and conformity: A meta-analysis of studies using Asch's (1952b, 1956) line judgment task. *Psychological Bulletin, 119*, 111–137.

Bourgeois, L. J., & Boltvinik, M. (1981). OD in cross-cultural settings: Latin America. *California Management Review, 23*, 75–81.

Boyacigiller, N. A., & Adler, N. J. (1991). The parochial dinosaur: Organizational science in a global context. *Academy of Management Review, 16*, 262–290.

Brett, J. M., & Okumura, T. (1998). Inter- and intra-cultural negotiations: U.S. and Japanese negotiators. *Academy of Management Journal, 41*, 495–510.

Bureau of the Census, Foreign Trade Division. (2001, March). *Report FT900* (CB-01-84). Washington, DC.

Cai, D. (1993, November). *Determinants of facework in negotiation: An intercultural perspective.* Paper presented at the meeting of the Speech Communication Association, Miami, FL.

Campbell, J. P., & Pritchard, R. D. (1976). Motivation theory in industrial and organizational psychology. In M. D. Dunnette (Ed.), *Handbook of industrial and organizational psychology* (pp. 63–130). Chicago: Rand McNally.

Chandra, S. (1973). The effects of group pressure in perception: A cross-cultural conformity study. *International Journal of Psychology, 8*, 37–39.

Child, J. (1981). Culture, contingency and capitalism in the cross-national study of organizations. *Research in Organizational Behavior, 3*, 303–356.

Chinese Culture Connection. (1987). Chinese values and the search for culture-free dimensions of culture. *Journal of Cross-Cultural Psychology, 18*, 143–164.

Collier, J. (1945). United States Indian Administration as a laboratory of ethnic relations. *Social Research, 12*, 275–286.

Cooke, R. A., & Lafferty, J. C. (1989). *Organizational culture inventory*. Plymouth, MI: Human Synergistics.

Córdova, E. (1982). Workers' participation in decisions within enterprises: Recent trends and problems. *International Labour Review, 121*, 125–140.

Cropanzano, R., Aguinis, H., Schminke, M., & Denham, D. L. (1999). Disputant reactions to managerial conflict resolution tactics: A comparison among Argentina, the Dominican Republic, Mexico, and the United States. *Group and Organization Management, 24*, 124–154.

Cummings, L. L., & Schmidt, S. M. (1972). Managerial attitudes of Greeks: The roles of culture and industrialization. *Administrative Science Quarterly, 17*, 265–272.

De Cieri, H., & Dowling, P. J. (1995). Cross-cultural issues in organizational behavior. In C. L. Cooper & D. M. Rousseau (Eds.), *Trends in organizational behavior* (pp. 127–145). New York: Wiley.

DiBella, A. J. (1993). The role of assumptions in implementing management practices across cultural boundaries. *Journal of Applied Behavioral Science, 29*, 305–319.

Drenth, P. J. D., & Groenendijk, B. (1984). Work and organizational psychology in cross-cultural perspective. In P. J. D. Drenth, H. Thierry, P. J. Willems, & C. J. de Wolff (Eds.), *Handbook of work and organizational psychology* (Vol. 2, pp. 1197–1229). New York: Wiley.

Earley, P. C. (1989). Social loafing and collectivism: A comparison of the United States and the People's Republic of China. *Administrative Science Quarterly, 34*, 565–581.

Earley, P. C. (1993). East meets West meets Mideast: Further explorations of collectivistic and individualistic work groups. *Academy of Management Journal, 36*, 319–348.

Earley, P. C., & Erez, M. (1997). Reassessing what we know: Critical commentaries and new directions. In P. C. Earley & M. Erez (Eds.), *New perspectives on international industrial/organizational psychology* (pp. 732–737). San Francisco: New Lexington.

Erez, M. (1994). Toward a model of cross-cultural industrial and organizational psychology. In H. C. Triandis, M. D. Dunnette, & L. M. Hough (Eds.), *Handbook of industrial and organizational psychology* (Vol. 4, pp. 559–607). Palo Alto, CA: Consulting Psychologists Press.

Erez, M. (1997). A culture-based model of work motivation. In P. C. Earley & M. Erez (Eds.), *New perspectives on international industrial/organizational psychology* (pp. 193–242). San Francisco: New Lexington.

Erez, M., & Earley, P. C. (1987). Comparative analysis of goal-setting strategies across cultures. *Journal of Applied Psychology, 72*, 658–665.

Erez, M., & Earley, P. C. (1993). *Culture, self-identity, and work*. New York: Oxford University Press.

Fant, L. (1989). Cultural mismatch in conversation: Spanish and Scandinavian communicative behavior in negotiation settings. *Hermes: Journal of Linguistics, 3*, 247–265.

Faucheux, C., Amado, G., & Laurent, A. (1982). Organizational development and change. *Annual Review of Psychology, 33*, 343–370.

Fiedler, F. E. (1978). Contingency model and the leadership process. In L. Berkowitz (Ed.), *Advances in experimental social psychology* (Vol. 11, pp. 60–112). New York: Academic.

Frager, R. (1970). Conformity and anti-conformity in Japan. *Journal of Personality and Social Psychology, 15*, 203–210.

Gabrenya, W. K., Wang, Y., & Latané, B. (1985). Social loafing on an optimizing task. *Journal of Cross-Cultural Psychology, 16*, 223–242.

Gallois, C., Franklyn-Stokes, A., Giles, H., & Coupland, N. (1988). Communication accommodation in intercultural encounters. In Y. Y. Kim & G. B. Gudykunst (Eds.), *Theories of intercultural communication* (pp. 157–185). Newbury Park, CA: Sage.

Gelfand, M. J., Nishii, L. H., Holcombe, K. M., Dyer, N., Ohbuchi, K., & Fukuno, M. (2001). Cultural influences on cognitive representations of conflict: Interpretations of conflict episodes in the United States and Japan. *Journal of Applied Psychology, 86*, 1059–1074.

Glaser, R. (1983). *The corporate culture survey.* Bryn Mawr, PA: Organizational Design and Development.

Graen, G. B., Hui, C., Wakabayashi, M., & Wang, Z. (1997). Cross-cultural research alliances in organizational research: Cross-cultural partnership-making in action. In P. C. Earley & M. Erez (Eds.), *New perspectives on international industrial/organizational psychology* (pp. 160–189). San Francisco: New Lexington.

Graf, L. A., Hemmasi, M., Lust, J. A., & Liang, Y. (1990). Perceptions of desirable organizational reforms in Chinese state enterprises. *International Studies of Management and Organization, 20*, 47–56.

Graham, J. L. (1985). The influence of culture on the process of business negotiations: An exploratory story. *Journal of International Business Studies, 16*, 79–94.

Graham, J. L., Evenko, L. I., & Rajan, M. N. (1992). An empirical comparison of Soviet and American business negotiations. *Journal of International Business Studies, 23*, 387–415.

Hackman, J. R. (1987). The design of work teams. In J. W. Lorsch (Ed.), *Handbook of organizational behavior* (pp. 315–342). Englewood Cliffs, NJ: Prentice-Hall.

Haire, M., Ghiselli, E. E., & Porter, L. W. (1966). *Managerial thinking: An international study.* New York: Wiley.

Harpaz, I. (1990). The importance of work goals: An international perspective. *Journal of International Business Studies, 21*, 75–93.

Heller, F. A., & Wilpert, B. (1981). *Competence and power in managerial decision making.* New York: Wiley.

Hersey, P., & Blanchard, K. H. (1988). *Management of organizational behavior.* Englewood Cliffs, NJ: Prentice-Hall.

Hofstede, G. (1980). *Culture's consequences: International differences in work-related values.* Thousand Oaks, CA: Sage.

Hofstede, G. (2001). *Culture's consequences: Comparing values, behaviors, institutions, and organizations across nations* (2nd ed.). Thousand Oaks, CA: Sage.

Hofstede, G., & Bond, M. H. (1988). The Confucian connection: From cultural roots to economic growth. *Organizational Dynamics, 16*, 4–21.

Hofstede, G., Neuijen, B., Ohayv, D. D., & Sanders, G. (1990). Measuring organizational culture: A qualitative and quantitative study across twenty cases. *Administrative Science Quarterly, 35*, 286–316.

Holt, J., & Keats, D. M. (1992). Work cognitions in multicultural interaction. *Journal of Cross-Cultural Psychology, 23*, 421–443.

House, R. J., Wright, N. S., & Aditya, R. N. (1997). Cross-cultural research on organizational leadership: A critical analysis and a proposed theory. In P. C. Earley & M. Erez (Eds.), *New perspectives on international industrial/organizational psychology* (pp. 535–625). San Francisco: New Lexington.

Howard, L. W. (1998). Validating the competing values model as a representation of organizational cultures. *The International Journal of Organizational Analysis, 6*, 231–250.

Huber, G. P. (1980). *Managerial decision making.* Glenview, IL: Scott, Foresman.

Hui, C. H. (1988). Measurement of individualism–collectivism. *Journal of Research in Personality, 22*, 17–36.

Hui, C. H., & Luk, C. L. (1997). Industrial/organizational psychology. In J. W. Berry, M. H. Segall, & C. Kagitçibasi (Eds.), *Handbook of cross-cultural psychology* (Vol. 3, pp. 371–411). Boston: Allyn & Bacon.

Hui, C. H., & Yee, C. (1994). The shortened individualism–collectivism scale: Its relationship to demographic and work-related variables. *Journal of Research in Personality, 28*, 409–424.

Huse, E. F. (1980). *Organization development and change* (2nd ed.). St. Paul, MN: West.

IDE (Industrial Democracy in Europe—International Research Group). (1981). *Industrial democracy in Europe.* London: Oxford University Press.

Ilgen, D. R., LePine, J. A., & Hollenbeck, J. R. (1997). Effective decision making in multinational teams. In P. C. Earley & M. Erez (Eds.), *New perspectives on international industrial/organizational psychology* (pp. 377–409). San Francisco: New Lexington.

Jaeger, A. M. (1986). Organization development and national culture: Where's the fit? *Academy of Management Review, 11*, 178–190.

James, K. (1993). The social context of organizational justice: Cultural, intergroup, and structural effects on justice behaviors and perceptions. In R. Cropanzano (Ed.), *Justice in the workplace: Approaching fairness in human resource management* (pp. 21–50). Hillsdale, NJ: Lawrence Erlbaum Associates.

Janosik, R. J. (1987). Rethinking the culture–negotiation link. *Negotiation Journal, 3*, 385–395.

Kagitçibasi, C., & Berry, J. W. (1989). Cross-cultural psychology: Current research and trends. *Annual Review of Psychology, 40*, 493–531.

Kanungo, R. N., & Jaeger, A. M. (1990). Introduction: The need for indigenous management in developing countries. In A. M. Jaeger & R. N. Kanungo (Eds.), *Management in developing countries* (pp. 1–23). London: Routledge.

Kilman, R. H., & Saxton, M. J. (1983). *The Kilman-Saxton culture-gap survey.* Pittsburgh, PA: Organizational Design Consultants.

Kirkman, B. L., & Shapiro, D. L. (1997). The impact of cultural values on employee resistance to teams: Toward a model of globalized self-managing work team effectiveness. *Academy of Management Review, 22*, 730–757.

Konrad, E., & Susanj, Z. (1999). Crossnational study of cultures in European manufacturing organizations. *Studia Psychologica, 41*, 23–31.

Kozan, M. K. (1993). Cultural and industrialization level influences on leadership attitudes for Turkish managers. *International Studies of Management and Organization, 23*, 7–17.

Kroeber, A. L., & Kluckhohn, C. (1952). *Culture: A critical review of concepts and definitions*. (Papers of the Peabody Museum of American Archaeology and Ethnology, Vol. 47, No. 1). Cambridge, MA: Harvard University Press.

Leung, K. (1997). Negotiation and reward allocations across cultures. In P. C. Earley & M. Erez (Eds.), *New perspectives on international industrial/organizational psychology* (pp. 640–675). San Francisco: New Lexington.

Leung, K., & Bond, M. H. (1984). The impact of cultural collectivism on reward allocation. *Journal of Personality and Social Psychology, 47*, 793–804.

Lewin, K. (1946). Action research and minority problems. *Journal of Social Issues, 2*, 34–46.

Lincoln, J. R., Hanada, M., & Olson, J. (1981). Cultural orientations and individual reactions to organizations: A study of employees of Japanese-owned firms. *Administrative Science Quarterly, 26*, 93–115.

Lytle, A. L., Brett, J. M., Barsness, Z. I., Tinsley, C. H., & Janssens, M. (1995). A paradigm for confirmatory cross-cultural research in organizational behavior. *Research in Organizational Behavior, 17*, 167–214.

Mann, L. (1980). Cross-cultural studies of small groups. In H. C. Triandis & R. W. Brislin (Eds.), *Handbook of cross-cultural psychology* (Vol. 5, pp. 155–209). Boston: Allyn & Bacon.

Mathur, P., Aycan, Z., & Kanungo, R. N. (1996). Work cultures in Indian organisations: A comparison between public and private sector. *Psychology and Developing Societies, 8*, 199–222.

Matsui, T., Kakuyama, T., & Onglatco, M. L. (1987). Effects of goals and feedback on performance in groups. *Journal of Applied Psychology, 72*, 407–415.

McGregor, D. (1960). *The human side of enterprise*. New York: McGraw-Hill.

Mintzberg, H. J. (1988). *Mintzberg on management: Inside our strange world of organizations*. New York: The Free Press.

Mirvis, P. H., & Berg, D. N. (Eds.). (1977). *Failures in organization development and change: Cases and essay for learning*. New York: Wiley.

Misumi, J. (1985). *The behavioral science of leadership: An interdisciplinary Japanese research program*. Ann Arbor: University of Michigan Press.

Peterson, M. F., Smith, P. B., Bond, M. H., & Misumi, J. (1990). Personal reliance on alternative event-management processes in four countries. *Group and Organization Studies, 15*, 75–91.

Pinder, G. C. (1998). *Work motivation in organizational behavior*. London: Prentice-Hall.

Poortinga, Y. (1992). Towards a conceptualization of culture for psychology. In S. Iwawaki, Y. Kashima, & K. Leung (Eds.), *Innovations in cross-cultural psychology* (pp. 3–17). Amsterdam: Swets & Zeitlinger.

Popp, G. E., Davis, H. J., & Herbert, T. T. (1986). An international study of intrinsic motivation composition. *Management International Review, 26*, 28–35.

Prieto, J. M., & Arias, R. M. (1997). Those things yonder are no giants, but decision makers in international teams. In P. C. Earley & M. Erez (Eds.), *New perspectives on international industrial/organizational psychology* (pp. 410–445). San Francisco: New Lexington.

Putti, J. M. (1989). Organization development scene in Asia: The case of Singapore. *Group and Organization Studies, 14,* 262–270.

Quinn, R. E., & McGrath, M. R. (1985). The transformation of organizational cultures: A competing values perspective. In P. J. Frost, L. F. Moore, M. L. Louis, C. C. Lundberg, & J. Martin (Eds.), *Organizational culture* (pp. 315–334). Beverly Hills, CA: Sage.

Radford, M. H., Mann, L., Ohta, Y., & Nakane, Y. (1991). Differences between Australia and Japan in reported use of decision processes. *International Journal of Psychology, 26,* 35–52.

Radford, M. H., Mann, L., Ohta, Y., & Nakane, Y. (1993). Differences between Australian and Japanese students in decisional self-esteem, decisional stress and coping styles. *Journal of Cross-Cultural Psychology, 24,* 284–297.

Roberts, K. H. (1970). On looking at an elephant: An evaluation of cross-cultural research related to organizations. *Psychological Bulletin, 74,* 327–350.

Roe, R. A., Zinovieva, I. L., Dienes, E., & Ten Horn, L. A. (2000). A comparison of work motivation in Bulgaria, Hungary, and the Netherlands: Test of a model. *Applied Psychology: An International Review, 49,* 658–687.

Ronen, S. (1997). Personal reflections and projections: International industrial/organizational psychology at a crossroads. In P. C. Earley & M. Erez (Eds.), *New perspectives on international industrial/organizational psychology* (pp. 715–731). San Francisco: New Lexington.

Ronen, S., & Kumar, R. (1987). Comparative management: A developmental perspective. In B. M. Bass & P. J. D. Drenth (Eds.), *Advances in organizational psychology: An international review* (pp. 252–265). Thousand Oaks, CA: Sage.

Sashkin, M. (1984). *Pillars of excellence: Organizational beliefs questionnaire.* Bryn Mawr, PA: Organizational Design and Development.

Schein, E. H. (1984). Coming to a new awareness of organizational culture. *Sloan Management Review, 1,* 3–16.

Schein, E. H. (1985). *Organizational culture and leadership.* San Francisco: Jossey-Bass.

Schein, E. H. (1996). Culture: The missing concept in organization studies. *Administrative Science Quarterly, 41,* 229–240.

Schneider, S. C. (1988). National vs. corporate culture: Implications for human resource management. *Human Resource Management, 27,* 231–246.

Schwartz, S. H. (1992). Universals in the content and structure of values: Theoretical advances and empirical tests in 20 countries. In M. P. Zanna (Ed.), *Advances in experimental social psychology* (Vol. 25, pp. 1–65). New York: Academic.

Schwartz, S. H. (1994a). Are there universal aspects in the content and structure of values? *Journal of Social Issues, 50,* 19–45.

Schwartz, S. H. (1994b). Beyond individualism and collectivism: New cultural dimensions of values. In U. Kim, H. C. Triandis, C. Kagitçibasi, S. C. Choi, & G. Yoon (Eds.), *Individualism and collectivism: Theory, method, and applications* (pp. 85–119). Thousand Oaks, CA: Sage.

Schwartz, S. H., & Bilsky, W. (1987). Toward a universal psychological structure of human values. *Journal of Personality and Social Psychology, 53*, 550–562.

Schwartz, S. H., & Bilsky, W. (1990). Toward a theory of the universal content and structure of human values: Extensions and cross-cultural replications. *Journal of Personality and Social Psychology, 58*, 878–891.

Schwartz, S. H., & Sagie, G. (2000). Value consensus and importance: A cross-national study. *Journal of Cross Cultural Psychology, 31*, 465–497.

Schwartz, S. H., & Sagiv, G. (1995). Identifying culture specifics in the content and structure of values. *Journal of Cross Cultural Psychology, 26*, 92–116.

Segall, M. H. (1986). Culture and behavior: Psychology in global perspective. *Annual Review of Psychology, 37*, 523–564.

Silverthorne, C. P. (1992). Work motivation in the United States, Russia, and the Republic of China (Taiwan): A comparison. *Journal of Applied Social Psychology, 22*, 1631–1639.

Silverthorne, C. (1996). Motivation and management styles in the public and private sectors in Taiwan and a comparison with the United States. *Journal of Applied Social Psychology, 26*, 1827–1837.

Sinha, J. B. P. (1980). *The nurturant task leader.* New Delhi, India: Concept.

Sinha, J. B. P. (1995). *The cultural context of leadership and power.* Thousand Oaks, CA: Sage.

Smith, P. B. (1997). Cross-cultural leadership: A path to the goal? In P. C. Earley & M. Erez (Eds.), *New perspectives on international industrial/organizational psychology* (pp. 626–639). San Francisco: New Lexington.

Smith, P. B. (2002). Culture's consequences: Something old and something new. *Human Relations, 55*, 119–135.

Smith, P. B., Dugan, S., & Trompenaars, F. (1996). National culture and the values of organizational employees: A 45 nation study. *Journal of Cross-Cultural Psychology, 27*, 231–264.

Smith, P. B., Peterson, M. F., Akande, D., Callan, V., & Cho, N. G. (1994). Organizational event management in 14 countries: A comparison with Hofstede's dimensions. In A. M. Bouvy, F. J. R. van de Vijver, P. Boski, & P. Schmitz (Eds.), *Journeys into cross-cultural psychology* (pp. 364–373). Amsterdam: Swets & Zeitlinger.

Strauss, G. (1982). Workers' participation in management: An international perspective. In B. Shaw & L. L. Cummings (Eds.), *Research in organizational behavior* (Vol. 4, pp. 173–265). Greenwich, CT: JAI.

Sundstrom, E., De Meuse, K. P., & Futrell, D. (1990). Work teams: Applications and effectiveness. *American Psychologist, 45*, 120–133.

Tannenbaum, A. S. (1980). Organizational psychology. In H. C. Triandis & R. W. Brislin (Eds.), *Handbook of cross-cultural psychology* (Vol. 5, pp. 281–334). Boston: Allyn & Bacon.

Tannenbaum, R., & Davis, S. A. (1969). Values, man and organizations. *Industrial Management Review, 10*, 67–83.

Thomas, K. W., & Schmidt, W. H. (1976). A survey of managerial interests with respect to conflict. *Academy of Management Journal, 19*, 315–318.

Trepo, G. (1973, Autumn). Management style à la française. *European Business, 41,* 86–90.

Triandis, H. C. (1994). Cross-cultural industrial and organizational psychology. In H. C. Triandis, M. D. Dunnette, & L. M. Hough (Eds.), *Handbook of industrial and organizational psychology* (Vol. 4, pp. 103–172). Palo Alto, CA: Consulting Psychologists Press.

Trompenaars, F. (1993). *Riding the waves of culture.* London: Brealey.

van de Vliert, E. (1990). Positive effects of conflict: A field assessment. *International Journal of Conflict Management, 1,* 69–80.

van Muijen, J. J., & Koopman, P. L. (1994). The influence of national culture on organizational culture: A comparative study between 10 countries. *European Work and Organizational Psychology, 4,* 367–380.

West, M. A., & Anderson, N. (1992). Innovation, cultural values, and the management of change in British hospitals. *Work & Stress, 6,* 293–310.

Whittaker, J. O., & Meade, R. D. (1967). Social pressure in the modification and distortion of judgment: A cross-cultural study. *International Journal of Psychology, 2,* 109–113.

Wilpert, B. (1984). Participation in organizations: Evidence from international comparative research. *International Social Science Journal, 36,* 355–366.

Wilson, D. F., & Waltman, M. S. (1988). Assessing the Putnam-Wilson Organizational Communication Conflict Instrument (OCCI). *Management Communication Quarterly, 1,* 367–388.

Wilson, S. R., Cai, D. A., Campbell, D. M., Donohue, W. A., & Drake, L. E. (1995). Cultural and communication processes in international business negotiations. In A. M. Nicotera (Ed.), *Conflict and organizations: Communicative processes* (pp. 201–237). Albany: State University of New York Press.

Xenikou, A., & Furnham, A. (1996). A correlational and factor analytic study of four questionnaire measures of organizational culture. *Human Relations, 49,* 349–371.

Yamauchi, H., Lynn, R., & Rendell, I. (1994). Gender differences in work motivations and attitudes in Japan and Northern Ireland. *Psychologia, 37,* 195–198.

Yu, A. B. (1995). Ultimate Chinese concern, self, and achievement motivation. In M. H. Bond (Ed.), *The handbook of Chinese psychology* (pp. 227–246). Hong Kong: Oxford University Press.

Yu, A. B., & Yang, K. S. (1994). The nature of achievement motivation in collectivist societies. In U. Kim, H. C. Triandis, C. Kagitçibasi, S. C. Choi, & G. Yoon (Eds.), *Individualism and collectivism: Theory, method and applications* (pp. 239–250). Newbury Park, CA: Sage.

# IV

## Commentary

# 11

## Good Definitions: The Epistemological Foundation of Scientific Progress

Edwin A. Locke
*University of Maryland*

Bad terminology is the enemy of good thinking.

—Warren Buffet (2001, p. 10)

Definitions are the guardians of rationality, the first line of defense against the chaos of mental disintegration.

—Ayn Rand (1975, p. 77)

The truth or falsehood of all of man's conclusions, inferences, thought and knowledge rests on the truth or falsehood of his definitions.

—Ayn Rand (1990, p. 49)

I begin this chapter with a discussion of definitions, which is the main theme of my comments, because I believe that a major factor retarding progress in our field—and almost every intellectual field today—has been the use of sloppy, careless, or subjective definitions. Every chapter in this book suffers, to a lesser or greater degree, from this problem. I am not denying that considerable progress has been made in the areas covered by these chapters—an issue I discuss later. Rather, I argue that poor defini-

**415**

tions (and in some cases, a complete lack of definitions) undermine progress. This is because instead of fulfilling their proper function—the promotion of cognitive clarity—they sow cognitive confusion.

## THE EPISTEMOLOGICAL ROLE OF DEFINITIONS

What is a definition? According to Ayn Rand (1990), "A definition is a statement that identifies the nature of the units subsumed under a concept" (p. 40), thereby making it the final stage of concept formation (Locke, in press). A concept is a mental integration of perceptual concretes (or of higher level concepts traceable to concretes). A word (except in the case of proper nouns) is a symbol that stands for a concept. A valid definition of a word (i.e., concept) accomplishes two things: (a) it ties the concept to reality, and (b) it distinguishes the concept from other concepts.

Consider, for example, the definition of man as "a rational animal" (meaning that he possesses the power of reason). Animal is the genus in this definition; it is the wider category within which man belongs. As such, the definition connects our knowledge of men with our knowledge of other types of animals. Rationality is the differentia; it distinguishes man from all other species of animals. Observe also that the definition identifies only the most fundamental differentiator. Reason is the faculty that makes possible the myriad other differences between man and the lower animals (e.g., art, humor, tool making, language, writing, etc.).

A definition is not identical to a concept. The concept of man includes all the characteristics of man ever discovered and all the characteristics yet to be discovered (Rand, 1990). A definition is only a shorthand identification designed to ensure cognitive clarity. Definitions may change when new knowledge is discovered, but new definitions do not necessarily contradict previous ones. For example, historically, the concept "red" would have had to be defined ostensively (by pointing), "Red is this—for example, the color of this blood." Once electromagnetic radiation was discovered, it could be defined, for example, as "the form in which one experiences electromagnetic radiation of wavelengths between approximately 630 and 750 nanometers." This does not contradict the earlier definition; it merely makes it more scientifically exact.

Valid definitions and concepts are not arbitrary social constructions, as the postmodernists claim. They are based, first and foremost, on observing reality and then conceptualizing one's observations. Consider, for example, Rand's (1990) discussion of the concept of justice:

> … what fact of reality gave rise to the concept of "justice"? The fact that man must draw conclusions about the things, people and events around him, i.e., must judge and evaluate them. Is his judgment automatically right? No.

> What causes his judgment to be wrong? The lack of sufficient evidence, or his evasion of the evidence, or his inclusion of considerations other than the facts of the case. How, then, is he to arrive at the right judgment? By basing it exclusively on the factual evidence and by considering all the relevant evidence available.... Now, do I need a concept to designate the act of judging a man's character and/or actions exclusively on the basis of all the factual evidence available, and of evaluating it by means of an objective moral criterion? Yes. That concept is "justice." (p. 51)

A very useful policy to follow when considering how to formulate definition is to start with the question: What facts of reality give rise to this concept? Dictionaries can be very useful presumably because others already have done the conceptual work, although some dictionaries are much better than others. Looking at reality can eliminate a lot of confusion. Consider, for example, the long-standing controversy over the concept of intelligence. What facts of reality gave rise to this concept? The fact that some people are better able to grasp abstractions (concepts) than others. This observation implies certain types of measures to those who want to measure intelligence, for example, vocabulary or reading comprehension.

The definition also clearly rules out the use of this term for processes that do not entail grasping concepts, such as so-called "emotional intelligence" (Goleman, 1997), which is really little more than skill at identifying one's emotions through introspection or empathy with respect to other people's emotions. I think this is an invalid concept. The word intelligence was tacked on originally to give the work publicity value, but the processes mentioned have little to do with the ability to grasp concepts.

Professors have the unfortunate habit, when formulating definitions, of looking not at reality (and not at dictionaries), but solely at the (inevitably conflicting) definitions formulated by other professors. This often leads to total chaos. I recall one professor who complained that he had found over 100 definitions of the concept about which he was writing a book. This so paralyzed him that he declined to define the concept at all in his book. Such a procedure is not very conducive to scientific progress. It is hard to write a coherent book if one does not know the identity of that which one is writing about.

A valid definition of a concept is a prerequisite to valid measurement. One cannot attempt to measure something unless one knows what it is one is trying to measure. One symptom of this problem—and I have noticed it throughout my academic career—is reading articles in which the name of the concept bears almost no, or only a peripheral, relationship to the questionnaire items used to measure it. Furthermore, the process cannot be reversed by claiming, "the meaning of the concept is that which I am measuring." It begs the question of what it is that you are trying to measure.

# ASSESSMENTS OF KEY ORGANIZATIONAL BEHAVIOR CONCEPTS IN THIS BOOK: SOME DEFINING MOMENTS

Having described the nature of definitions in our scientific endeavor, the stage is now set to assess critically the definitions of concepts presented in this book. I now do this, taking each chapter in turn, ordering my remarks alphabetically by topic.

## Affect

Barsade, Brief, and Spataro argue that there has been an affective revolution in the field of organizational behavior. They claim that there is a new research paradigm, by which they seem to mean that a lot more people are studying emotion in organizations with "richer theory, stronger measures, more sophisticated methods, and ... a broader understanding of affective constructs." The authors are quite right in saying that more people now are studying emotions in the workplace than earlier and that a variety of emotions are being investigated in addition to the traditional one, job satisfaction. They also document the increased interest in dispositional causes of emotions, although they fail to mention the important work done by Judge and colleagues on *core evaluations* (e.g., Judge, Locke, Durham, & Kluger, 1998).

However, I cannot agree that a broader understanding of affect has been achieved. Symptomatic of the problem is that the term *emotion*, the subject of the chapter, is never even defined! Not that this should be surprising. A recent volume devoted entirely to the subject of emotions in the workplace has no reference to a definition of emotion in the index (Lord, Klimoski, & Kanfer, 2002). One reason that people are reluctant or unable to define the concept may be that many see it as a psychological primary—that is, as a basic given that cannot be analyzed further and that has no identifiable psychological (as opposed to physiological or biological) causes. This is a grave mistake. I discussed the nature of emotions over 25 years ago (Locke, 1976), but as this analysis has been pretty much ignored, I explain the issue again.

The form in which one experiences an emotional response is typically: object → emotion. For example, pay raise → satisfaction; boss humiliates → depression, anger. But it does not follow from this that no psychological processes are involved. To understand this, one has to use retrospective introspection—one has to look inward and back and ask: What processes are involved here? Let me illustrate by using a simple case. Assume you are hiking in a remote wilderness area, unarmed, and are suddenly confronted on the trail by a snarling grizzly bear. The experience is: bear → fear. However, there are actually four processes involved and some of them are subconscious.

1. *Perception.* The object has to be perceived. If the hiker is too blind or deaf to see or hear the bear, there will be no emotional response. This experience is conscious.

2. *Conceptual evaluation.* The subconscious automatically classifies the perceived object based on one's stored knowledge (e.g., this is a grizzly bear; they are potentially dangerous and have been known to kill people, etc.). Other knowledge that automatically comes into play would include location (How close am I to the bear?), escape possibilities (Is there is tree nearby?), and weapons (Do I have a gun? Do I know how to use it?). The importance of these assessments can be validated by a thought experiment. For example, how would it change the response if you recognized the bear as a trained pet? What if you knew you could climb a safe tree well before the bear could attack? How about if you were armed and confident of your shooting ability?

3. *Value appraisal.* Value appraisal is a form of subconscious, psychological measurement or evaluation; the standards of measurement are one's value standards. Let us assume that the value here is one's life. If the bear is perceived as a threat to one's life, the emotional response is fear. If one did not value one's life or health, there would be no fear. Every emotion has a unique and universal type of value appraisal (e.g., satisfaction is the response to having attained a value; guilt is the response to believing one has violated a moral principle; anger results when one sees another person act in a morally inappropriate manner; sadness results from the perceived loss of a value, etc.).

4. *Emotional experience.* The last stage is the emotional experience itself, which also involves physiological reactions and sometimes various symptoms (e.g., faintness, nausea). So my definition is: an emotion is the form in which one experiences automatic, subconscious value appraisals. Emotions, as part of the experience, contain built-in action tendencies or impulses (e.g., the action tendency in fear is to flee; in love, to approach and protect; in anger, to right the wrong; in hate, to harm the perpetrator, etc.). These tendencies do not compel action but the urge to action undoubtedly has survival value (e.g., fleeing a dangerous predator).

I define moods as enduring emotional states. Emotions can endure because the situation endures, or because one's subconscious continues to make appraisals without shutting off, or because one is consciously brooding over the issue causing continual re-appraisals, or because one's brain is somewhat miswired due to various chemical imbalances.

What one experiences consciously, as noted, is Stages 1 and 4. But Stages 2 and 3, despite being subconscious and automatic, are essential to understanding emotional responses. This model is not a research issue as such. The validation is through introspection—introspection that people can perform for themselves. It is very easy to do thought experiments to show that changing any of the inputs (Stages 1–3) changes the output (the emotion). (For a discussion of this topic, see Lazarus, 1991; and for a discussion of the relationship of reason and emotion, see Peikoff, 1991.)

I agree strongly with Barsade, Brief, and Spataro with respect to several key points. First, I agree with their claim that we need to conduct more studies of specific emotions in the workplace (aside from job satisfaction, that is), and that as a precondition of this we need to better understand the unique value appraisals behind each emotion. Second, I also agree with the authors' suggestion that we should study positive as well as negative emotions in organizations. In this connection, a recently published handbook of positive psychology (Snyder & Lopez, 2002) may be of interest. Third, I found interesting the authors' discussion of research on the issue of how people attempt to consciously manage their own emotions and those of others. Here again, more progress will be made if researchers understand the causal determinants of emotions.

Now let us consider the more complex issue of dispositional factors. I am not going to discuss possible hormonal imbalances, an issue more apropos to the field of medicine. Psychologically, Judge, Locke, and Durham (1997) argued that people make fundamental appraisals or core evaluations of themselves (e.g., as good or bad, efficacious or inefficacious) often at a young age, that form the background for emotional responses and that subsequently color them. However, Barsade, Brief, and Spataro prefer to look at dispositions pertaining to broadly focused emotional states (positive and negative affectivity, PA and NA). But the question is: What do these measures actually represent, especially when correlated with other measures? For example, a high PA person (i.e., I am a happy person) tends to have high job satisfaction (I am happy on my job). Are general emotional states actually the cause of specific emotional states? Or do specific experiences add up to cause the general states? Or, as seems likely, are both, in part, caused by core evaluations (Judge et al., 1998)? Clearly, this issue needs more work.

## Conflict

The chapter by Dirks and Parks was well organized and well written and I applaud their attempt to gain conceptual clarity. I take issue, however, with their definition of conflict: "the interaction of interdependent entities who perceive opposition in goals, aims, and values and who perceive the other entity or entities as potentially interfering with the realization of these goals." First, conflict does not require interdependence (e.g., a police officer and a criminal are not interdependent). Second, Why do they use the term entities—a much broader term that includes inanimate objects, which do not have conflicts, and animals—when they mean people? The term *parties* would include groups and teams by implication. Third, the dictionary definition is simpler, that is, "a state of disharmony between incompatible or antithetical persons, ideas or interests" (*American Heritage Dictionary*, 1992, p. 396).

The authors clearly and succinctly summarize factors that foster conflict resolution, the cognitive factors (e.g., anchoring, framing, etc.) that undermine successful negotiations, and cultural factors that affect the ability to resolve conflicts. However, I do not agree that communication could have saved the September 11 situation. The conflict here is about two fundamentally antagonistic value systems: theocracy, dictatorship, poverty, and the afterlife versus reason, freedom, capitalism, and love of this world, and the first wants to destroy the second.

The most interesting part of the chapter is on the types of conflict. Here, the authors attempt to bring order out of chaos by grouping the types into overarching categories. However, I still am not clear on the distinction between *substantive conflict*, which includes "preferences or approaches to a task," and *process conflict*, which pertains to "how task accomplishment will proceed." Both seem to involve substantive conflict. It might be better to use the term *substantive* for both and then, if necessary, to divide substantive conflict into subtypes (although I am unsure what these would be). Careful definitions are called for here.

The authors make two useful suggestions for future research on conflict that involve examining the role of culture and the role of trust. On the first point, they make an excellent suggestion: to look not just at mean levels on cultural dimensions but also the level of consensus (variation) around the mean. Trust is important, too (and not just in the conflict arena), but trust in what? Three types (two of which the authors acknowledge; see Salam, 2000) may be relevant here: trust in moral integrity, trust in competence, and trust in goodwill (e.g., you are not out to stab me in the back). Current terminology (e.g., cognitive and affective trust) is more confusing than clarifying. And the definition of trust (i.e., reliance on others) should not contain nonessential words, such as "vulnerability."

I would like to add one more topic for future research. I think that in the substantive conflict realm perceived amount of conflict is too coarse a measure. We need to go to a deeper level. What is relevant are questions such as: (a) Who in the team possesses the relevant elements of task knowledge? (b) Will members of the team recognize who knows what and make their decisions accordingly? (c) Will team members stimulate one another to gain new insights and to discover new knowledge? To answer such questions we need to look not just at the amount of conflict, but at its actual content. Of course, content would have to be separated from style or personality. The harmful effects of personality clashes may involve not only distracting people from focusing on the content, but also leading people to reject certain content ideas regardless of whether or not they are sound, simply because they dislike the other party.

## Construct Validity

Edwards provides a very detailed discussion of this concept with a heavy emphasis on the mathematical side. My focus is on whether construct validity is a valid concept. I have to confess here that the term has bothered me during the whole of my academic career.

To begin, consider the term *construct* itself. The dictionary treats construct as a rough synonym for concept. However, the term construct has much more of a "postmodern" implication—that one simply "constructs" something more or less arbitrarily. Postmodernism is the doctrine that no objective knowledge is possible. Thus concepts are not objective—they are "socially constructed" in accordance with the person's culture or social group. As such, they have no objective status—they are, in short, subjective. (As noted earlier, I consider concepts to be objective if formed by the correct method; see Rand, 1990.) Edwards defines a construct as a "conceptual term," but this is defining it in terms of a supposed synonym.

To Edwards's credit, he argues that the "phenomena constructs describe are real and exist independently of the observer." But then he undermines this by asserting that "these phenomena cannot be observed directly or objectively." If he is talking about psychological concepts (concepts pertaining to consciousness), then this is simply not true. All the phenomena relevant to forming psychological concepts are directly observable by introspection. If people could not introspect, that is, to selectively focus on their internal mental states, then there would be no way for people to know *conceptually* of the existence of psychological phenomena and thus no way for them to form or to understand psychological concepts at all—any more than they could grasp the concept of table without looking at the outside world.

What the idea of construct validity does is to substitute measurements and relationships between measures for introspection and definitions based on such introspection. The claim is that construct validity pertains to the correspondence between a construct and the measure(s) taken of it. But, in reality, it does not mean that at all. Consider Edwards's definition of *trait validity*—one form of construct validity—as convergence of measures (using different methods). But what does such a test prove? For example, if the different methods do not converge, are one or both in error? There is no way to tell. And if they do converge, how do we know if either of them is actually relevant to the concept? Again, we have no way of knowing. (If one of the two measures is known to be valid, the case is slightly better. If they are highly correlated, that is evidence they are measuring the same concept. However, if they are not highly correlated, there is no way to tell what the nonvalid measure is measuring.)

What about the second aspect of construct validity: *nomological validity?* This refers to the relationship between a measure and a network of theoretically related measures. Let's say the expected pattern of relationships does not materialize. Which is at fault, the theory or the measure? Again, there is no way to tell. Suppose the proposed relationships, as is typical, "sort of" come out (e.g., the correlations are inconsistent and moderate in size)? Is the theory sort of invalid or is the measure sort of invalid? Or both? We can't know from the data alone. No amount of statistical legerdemain can overcome this problem.

The questions I posed here are unanswerable because the construct validity approach skips three crucial steps. First, the concept has to be defined objectively so its exact meaning is specified at the outset. Second, the measures chosen must have a logical or commensurable relationship with the definition. The reader will note that I have just described what most would consider to be content validity. However, the focus in content validity is on sampling—items that cover the domain—but what I mean is more basic: Do the items relate logically to the concept? A better name for this would be *logical validity*—a term I introduced in 1976, although I have reformulated my definition here. My view is that logical validity always has to be primary. If you do not know what you are trying to measure, then the relationship of the chosen measure to other measures cannot be interpreted.

There is a third step involved in validation that I will call *measurement validity*. What I mean by this, in the case of psychological concepts is: Can the respondents introspect well enough to be able to provide accurate answers to the logically valid questions? All questionnaire studies assume that people can do this, but the truth is that some people do it much better than others, and we usually cannot identify these in advance. We probably could find out by careful direct questioning, but this is done rarely, if ever. Another aspect of this issue is determining whether the respondents can actually understand the questions, given their context of knowledge. Questions may have to be formulated differently for different groups, which poses the problem of logical equivalence. Usually, we simply assume we are getting valid answers to our questions. This may not be a disastrous assumption, but certainly we are getting some error in our measurements.

Only when we have a measure that is validated based on the preceding three steps are we able to interpret correlations with other measures *unequivocally*. If all the measures in question are valid, but not correlated, then they are not measuring the same phenomenon. If a causal relationship between variables is hypothesized in theory but is not supported empirically, then the theory is incorrect. However, I would not call these procedures establishing construct validity. Rather they entail the development of alternative measures or theory building.

In summary, I consider the term construct validity to be an invalid concept, and I think it should be dropped from our vocabulary. I think the concept of construct validity actually has had a pernicious influence on the field, because it has taken attention away from the most important parts of the validation process (clear definitions, logically related questions) and allowed people to think that they can be rescued from conceptual carelessness through statistical procedures. Concepts that are carefully defined and measured by questions logically related to the definition do not have to go through any construct validation process. Consider, by way of example, concepts like self-efficacy and goal. These are very powerful concepts that reliably explain action, yet they never went through any such process.

## Cross-Cultural Universals

Aguinis and Henle pose a very interesting question: Are there universal OB principles—that is, principles that cross cultures? To address this question one needs an objective definition of culture, but we are presented with a baffling array of definitions. The definition officially embraced by the authors is, "a set of psychological commonalities shared by a group that limits the behavioral choices of its members." I do not think this is a good definition. First, "psychological commonalities" is both too narrow and misleading. For example, "people become sad after suffering a loss" would be a psychological commonality, but is this an issue of culture or human nature? Second, the focus on "limits" is too negative (and belongs in a definition of a norm), as well as too narrow (e.g., it does not include cultural achievements or products). As the chapter progresses, a bewildering variety of other definitions are offered—among them, a pattern of shared basic assumptions, artifacts, (organizational) practices, learned behavior, shared values, and dialectic. All this variety simply makes for chaos.

Consider two alternative definitions: (a) "a nation's culture is the sum of the intellectual achievements of individual men, which their fellow citizens have accepted in whole or in part, and which have influenced the nation's way of life" (Rand, 1982, pp. 205–206); and (b) "The totality of socially transmitted behavior patterns, arts, beliefs, institutions, and all other products of human work and thought" (*American Heritage Dictionary*, 1992, p. 454). These are reasonably compatible definitions, although the first is more succinct and the second is more detailed. They can be adapted readily to an organizational context.

Now, consider the issue of common value dimensions (factors) across cultures. The discussion of this issue was not entirely clear. To test for common factors, employees from every country have to answer the same questionnaire, translated appropriately. To actually get common factors two criteria need to be met: (a) there has to be variance within cultures in the item responses, and (b) there must be more common variance among logically similar items than among logically dissimilar items. If common factors do not emerge (poor translations aside—a possible source of error that needs to be ruled out explicitly), it must be because either or both criteria are not satisfied (e.g., items that were meant to be logically similar may not be). There is, however, one additional possibility: The concept(s) from one culture may not have any directly comparable equivalent in another culture. This would make it impossible to make any meaningful translation at all. All these would be interesting issues to study, and I think they would have to be studied before any definitive answer could be given to the question of universal value dimensions.

A second issue that Aguinis and Henle discuss concerns the universality of the effectiveness of OB—which they limit mainly to OD—techniques across culture. But there are several distinct aspects of this issue that would have been useful for the authors to discuss: (a) Technique A does not work in culture B because people in Culture B refuse to use it (or because people refused to use it at first but were willing to try it eventually); (b) Technique A does not work in Culture B because people in Culture B tried it and it failed (perhaps because of poor implementation?); (c) Technique A works in Culture B only if the form in which it is implemented is modified to fit culture B (e.g., MBO with and without participation in goal setting); (d) Technique A works in many cultures, but better in some than in others; (e) Technique A works in some parts of Culture B but not others (e.g., some types of organizations).

Of course, we do not have a research base that is nearly big enough to reach any of these conclusions unequivocally (and certainly not on the basis of a very small number of studies), but these questions imply a more sophisticated approach to the cross-cultural issue than trying to reach blanket conclusions about what works across cultures and what does not. I totally agree with the authors that culture matters, but the issue is to show how it matters. In this connection, for example, the authors do a good job of showing how teamwork affects motivation in collectivistic versus individualistic cultures.

On the issue of culture and negotiation, there may be a difference of opinion between Dirks and Parks, who claim in their chapter that culture affects the process of conflict resolution, and Aguinis and Henle, who claim that culture has no direct effect on actual negotiation behaviors. Possibly the two sets of authors are focusing on different literatures.

Aguinis and Henle argue that there is cross-cultural agreement on the definition of and preferences for transformational versus transactional leadership, and on the distinction between performance-focused and relationship-focused supervision. On this topic, Chah and Locke (1996) found that the factor structure of leadership scales and the relationships between these factors and rated leader effectiveness were virtually identical in the United States and Korea. This may be because the tasks that leaders have to perform are similar across capitalistic countries, regardless of cultural difference.

Aguinis's and Henle's discussion of work motivation across cultures is quite interesting, especially their observation that need for achievement may manifest itself differently in different cultures and that individualism–collectivism affects preferences for different reward systems.

In summary, the generality of OB procedures across cultures is a very interesting and important topic. One issue that should be studied is the relative importance of the fact that people in all cultures share the same biological and psychological needs (qua human being) and, under capitalism, the same organizational imperatives, versus the fact that all cultures differ in certain respects in their value systems.

## Deviance

Bennett and Robinson's chapter is on organizational deviance, and I was glad to find that they provided a (correct) definition: "acts ... that violate the norms of the organization." In this case, however, I believe that chapter was mistitled. The term *deviance* as such (despite its negative connotations) is morally neutral in its denotation; deviance can be good or bad, beneficial or harmful depending on the nature of the norms and the nature of the deviance. The chapter, however, is concerned almost exclusively with the harmful effects of deviance; so a better title would have been something like Harmful (or Dysfunctional) Employee Actions. The authors complain that they do not want to get "mired in semantics." But words are symbols that stand for concepts that are the form in which a human consciousness grasps reality. Thus, precision is essential.

Let me explain further. Harmful actions of the type the authors discuss, if taken repeatedly by executives and managers, may not be deviant. They may be the norm! Thus the problem becomes not deviation from the norms, but the norms themselves. Similarly, employee responses to dysfunctional manager norms can also become normative, as the authors themselves note.

The authors do an excellent job of documenting the many types of harmful employee actions. However, it would have been very useful if they had attempted to classify these various types of actions into meaningful categories rather than just listing them.

It also might have been beneficial to discuss managers and subordinates under separate headings. The reason is that what the top executives and managers do, as suggested before, is often an instigating cause of what subordinates do. For example, the authors mention abusive (e.g., insulting) supervision, incivility (lack of consideration?), and injustice as examples. The subordinate section could then indicate the various ways people react to such mistreatment.

The claim that "frustrating job stressors" cause harmful behaviors is a bit simplistic. Lots of people are frustrated on the job and feel stress but that alone does not necessarily cause them to take actions that harm the organization. The same goes for "powerlessness." By powerlessness the authors seem to mean lack of autonomy, but this would not inevitably lead to harmful behavior; for example, it might simply lead to boredom.

I agree with the authors that personal traits are important here, both with respect to how managers act and how subordinates respond. For example, an honest subordinate would not respond to incivility by stealing but might instead respond by quitting. And a moral manager would not knowingly treat subordinates unjustly. As to hostility, which may be what the authors mean by aggressiveness, this would be harmful in any context as it would destroy morale.

Physical violence in the workplace is becoming increasingly problematic, but an explanation mainly in terms of role modeling simply will not do. People see violence all the time, especially on TV and in the movies, but only a minuscule number of people act it out. Mental illness plays a role (e.g., Raine & Sanmartin, 2001), in addition to a lack of moral scruples. The culture may reinforce this through the influence of postmodernism, which asserts that there are no objective moral principles, that moral statements are just subjective biases. Sooner or later the message gets through and infects, to varying degrees, the whole culture.

Bennett and Robinson are quite right to bring up the national culture issue, but they are mistaken in arguing that collectivism characteristically promotes peace and individualism encourages violence. Politically, it is quite the opposite. Collectivism is the doctrine that the group is the unit of value, and thus it promotes self-sacrifice. At the state level this promotes totalitarianism, in that man is compelled to live for the state (race, party, religion, etc.), which can dispose of him as it sees fit. The mass slaughter of the Nazis (Peikoff, 1982) and the Communists was the violent result. At the organization level, collectivism may promote superficial harmony because resentment caused by crushing individual desire is suppressed, but this does not promote organizational well-being.

Individualism is the doctrine that the individual, not the group, is the unit of value and implies a morality of rational self-interest and respect for the rights and dignity of each individual. This would encourage individu-

als to stand up for themselves when wronged but would not imply violence unless combined with postmodern amorality so that rational
self-interest deteriorated into mindless irrationalism. There is no doubt,
however, that American culture is heading in this direction today.

It is unfortunate that the authors advocate the use of postmodern concepts to better understand workplace deviance. As postmodernism ends
in total skepticism, such an analysis will not enlighten anyone. It is not that
hard to show that certain types of actions (e.g., dishonesty, sabotage) are
objectively harmful to an organization.

Finally, I agree strongly with Bennett and Robinson that we should
study what they call reciprocal causation models, which document how an
action initiated by a manager or subordinate provokes a response by the
other, which provokes a further response, thereby creating an escalating
cycle of harmful actions. By understanding such cycles, we could develop
ways to stop downward spirals.

## Diversity

From the point of view of providing a challenge to philosophical analysis,
the topic of diversity is perhaps the most interesting topic in this book.
Ragins and Gonzalez do an excellent job of reviewing this literature. But
let's look further. The authors never define the term, so let us begin with a
dictionary definition: "1a. The fact or quality of being diverse; difference.
b. A point or respect in which things differ. 2. Variety or multiformity"
(*American Heritage Dictionary*, 1992, p. 543). By this definition, obviously,
all organizations are diverse because no two people are the same. But this
is not what diversity advocates mean by the term. They mean racial, and
sometimes gender, diversity.

Here is where it gets interesting. Advocates of diversity have wanted
to encourage organizations to achieve racial and gender diversity. So,
they began by looking at the data. However, as Ragins and Gonzalez
note, the studies did not yield consistent results regarding the effect of racial or gender diversity on outcomes such as performance, satisfaction,
conflict, or turnover. Some of the studies even showed adverse effects. It
also was soon realized that, as the dictionary definition would imply,
there were other types of diversity that should be studied (e.g., age, education, job or industry experience, functional specialty, etc.). But these
studies did not yield consistent results either. And, I submit, they could
not. Diversity of *ideas* (depending on the ideas in question) may be important in organizations, but there is no one-to-one correspondence between
ideas and demographics. (Diversity in functional specialty may be important in some cases because of the different skills involved and the
need for coordination across areas.)

But rather than questioning the appropriateness of this type of research, Ragins and Gonzalez take the discussion in two new directions. First, they conclude that diversity is a "slippery construct," and then ask, "Who defines diversity and where does diversity reside? Is diversity objective or subjective? ... there is diversity even in the way diversity is defined." They suggest that "the definition of a construct emerges with the study of its properties, effects, and outcomes." Of course, it will not (see my earlier discussion of construct validity). They quote another researcher, with evident agreement, to the effect that "race and gender are not objective categories, but are social constructions grounded in perception." This, of course, is a contradiction; if race and gender are directly perceivable and the senses give us direct knowledge of reality, then the concepts are obviously objective. People really do differ by gender and race.

Calling diversity "slippery" will not help clarify it, nor will research in the absence of a definition be very enlightening. It will only lead to "slippery" research. The meaning of the term is quite clear: It means difference. So the relevant issue is: What kind of differences between people should we study and why?

This brings us to Ragins' and Gonzalez's second point. They advocate, in effect, forgetting about the outcome issue, and focusing instead on a different agenda: how people of different groups (racial, gender, and differences of many other types) view themselves and each other and how they come to be stigmatized, especially as a function of various, differential power relationship in organizations.

However, they do not mention that the most basic cause of such stigmatization is: collectivism—the premise, often held in the racial sphere by both Blacks and Whites, that one's group (e.g., racial) identity is the most important, determining fact about people. This is a fundamental error—an error because ideas are not caused by one's genes. By ideas I mean one's basic values, moral character, and knowledge. Race and gender are objective facts, but they are not the most important facts when it comes to an organization evaluating people.

The antipode of and antidote to collectivism is individualism, "the view that, in social issues, the individual is the unit of value" (Peikoff, 1991, p. 361). Only individuals exist and individuals have the volitional power to choose their own ideas and form their own character (Binswanger, 1991).

Racism, as a form of collectivism, can be viewed as a form of epistemological passivity in that directly perceivable characteristics are given primacy, because this requires a lot less mental work than evaluating on character, which requires observation of the person over a period of time and logical inference.

Rather than glorifying collectives and searching for victims under every bedpost, wouldn't it be more beneficial to organizations to take research in an entirely different direction? A useful direction would be to study how organizations might develop their own cultures to stress individualism. For example, what are the most important things that an organization needs to know about potential or actual employees? Three things, I believe, are most critical:

- The employee's moral character (e.g., honesty, integrity).
- The employee's willingness to exert effort to get the job done (e.g., motivation).
- The employee's ability, skills, and knowledge (i.e., competence).

One might add to this, in some contexts, the employee's willingness and ability to work as part of a team. If an organization stressed that these characteristics were all they cared about in hiring, promoting, and rewarding and acted accordingly (i.e., objectively), then a culture of individualism could emerge.

The diversity advocate could make two relevant points in response to this recommendation: (a) Even if individualism were the official doctrine of an organization, not everyone in it would necessarily agree with it. This is true, and it would be up to the leadership to reinforce their espoused philosophy in training and in hiring and reward decisions; for example, by insisting on scrupulously objective processes. (b) More difficult is the problem of subconscious bias—bias of which the person is not consciously aware, despite having good conscious premises. This is a valid point; some people clearly do have subconscious premises that contradict their conscious values.

But then wouldn't the following two problems be ideal candidates for research: (a) How can leaders and managers learn to be objective when making decisions about organizational members? (b) How can people be made aware of their subconscious biases and how can they be trained to overcome them? In short, how can people be helped to view other people as individuals and not simply as members of a racial, gender, or other collective? Wouldn't this have a far more salutary effect on organizations than glorifying collectivism by making group membership the most important topic of study?

I have thought for a long time that our current obsession with what racial or gender or other groups people belong to is actually a *cause* of racism and sexism, simply because it makes those collective memberships more important than who the people really are—that is, what they have made of themselves as individuals. I hasten to add that I am not advocating that people pretend that race and gender do not exist; they are real—but the issue is: What should be most important from the viewpoint of the organization?

## Justice

Justice is one of the most interesting of all OB topics, because it is one of the few that is specifically concerned with morality. Colquitt and Greenberg have done an outstanding job summarizing and integrating what we know about justice in the workplace. There is no doubt that it is a very important issue for employees and that whether they are treated justly or unjustly matters a great deal.

Notably, they never define the term *justice*. They define distributive and procedural justice but only in terms of the synonym "fairness." So what is the meaning of this concept? "'Justice' is the virtue of judging man's character and conduct objectively and of acting accordingly, granting to each man that which he deserves" (Peikoff, 1991, p. 276). Observe right away that there are two aspects to justice; one pertains to the realm of cognition and the other to the realm of action.

In the realm of cognition, as noted in the earlier quote from Ayn Rand, justice means looking at all the relevant evidence about the individual in question—in relation to the context in which one is doing the judging (e.g., fitness for promotion)—and integrating that evidence into a meaningful whole. It means consistently using reason, not emotion or bias, when processing the information. This includes taking the trouble to seek out all the facts about the person that are relevant in the context, as opposed to, say, looking only at the facts that support one's bias (e.g., gender or race) or only considering actions that one has observed recently to avoid mental effort.

It is clear that this aspect of justice is most similar to what has been called procedural justice in the literature. However, the term *procedure* derives from early work that was focused on justice in relation to the law. There are *procedural* safeguards that protect the rights of the accused (e.g., a fair and speedy trial, the right to hire a lawyer, the right to question the accusers, etc.). The word procedure, however, is too narrow. The cognitive aspect of justice pertains not just to procedure but how the person who judges actually thinks. It is interesting, in another definitional anomaly, that, as used, the term *procedural* actually includes, by implication, certain thought processes (e.g., freedom from bias). The thinking aspect is the more fundamental, however, because a procedure, however good, cannot be just if it is based on incomplete, wrong, or tainted information. A better term here, I believe, would be, *cognitive and procedural justice*. The core idea is that these precede (or should precede) the taking of action that allocates rewards and are the basis for such action. This would imply the need to measure, explicitly, issues like: Did the manager actually gather and examine all the relevant data (in the given context) on the employee? Did the manager integrate the data objectively—that is, separate the relevant (e.g., performance, character) from the irrelevant (e.g., demographics) facts? Here is a true injustice anecdote: Company $X$ refused to hire Ms. $Y$, who was very well qualified for the job, because, said the hiring manager, "You dress better than the wives of our top executives."

The action component of justice (which could be called *action justice*) entails acting on one's knowledge so that the employees get what they deserve. Observe that another virtue comes into play here—namely, integrity, loyalty to one's rational convictions in action. (Peikoff, 1991, argued that, in reality, all the virtues are interconnected.) Concluding that a person deserves a certain reward and then voluntarily withholding it is a breach of both integrity and justice. Clearly the action component of justice is most similar in meaning to what has been called distributive justice. The focus on the latter has typically been on pay or pay raises, but the issue is actually wider in that many actions aside from granting raises are justice-related. Some examples are giving recognition, granting promotions, assignments to new projects, giving punishments, layoffs, and so on.

Justice reflects "the trader principle.... *A man deserves from others that and only that which he earns*" (Peikoff, 1991, p. 287). (Observe that the principle of justice rules out need-based rewards as they are not based on anything the person did to earn them. The lack of something is not a badge of merit.)

In summary, justice in the organization requires two things: (a) the cause—a rational thinking process to gather and to integrate the relevant facts, and (b) the effect—actions based on the conclusions drawn from that process. In both cases, one must hold the full context. For example, a manager cannot spend his or her whole career gathering facts about his or her subordinates and never have time to get his or her other work done. And rewards cannot always be granted, if, for example, the company is in severe financial trouble.

Now let us consider so-called "interactional justice." This was asserted to involve "interpersonal treatment," but this is a very vague term. Logically it would imply that you treat everyone differently in face-to-face encounters, based on merit, but this is not what its proponents mean. They mean "dignified, respectful treatment," which implies that everyone is treated the same. It also was asserted, at least initially, that interactional justice was a category of procedural justice pertaining to how managers enact decisions. But this focus on action would imply that it was a component of the action part of justice (i.e., distributive justice). But this is not what is meant either.

Today, interactional justice is accepted as a concept separate from the other two forms of justice. But, what, then, does it mean? Here are its components, as listed by Bies (2001), who is one of the champions of the concept:

- The absence of deception, for example, lies.
- Keeping promises.
- Keeping secrets.
- Not invading privacy.
- Showing respect and consideration (e.g., refraining from public humiliations).
- Avoiding prejudice (e.g., racism).

- Avoiding the use of threats (e.g., "Do what I say, or you will be fired").
- Not causing undue stress.

Given all of these, what are we to make of the concept of interactional justice? In reality, we have total chaos. No single term could encompass all of these categories. For example, the absence of deception is actually a different virtue—that of honesty. The keeping of promises and secrets is yet another virtue, that of integrity. Not invading privacy is an issue of tact. Consideration, which has its roots in the old Michigan and Ohio State studies of supervision (see Bass, 1990), is stylistic and implies an attitude of benevolent good will toward employees. Avoiding prejudice pertains to the cognitive aspect of justice (i.e., rationality), and thus is already part of that concept. And the public humiliation and stress elements are aspects of consideration. In short, aside from the prejudice part that pertains to the cognitive aspect of justice, none of these other categories has anything directly to do with justice, nor can all these elements be described by means of a single concept.

How did such a mess occur? Due to an empirical research error caused by an epistemological error. Researchers typically asked employees to describe incidents that involved unfair treatment. And, in reply, the reported everything but the kitchen sink. This is not surprising. (My friend Tom Becker from the University of Delaware has been doing studies of integrity and, when asked for examples, subjects give examples of numerous other virtues in addition to integrity.) Most people do not hold very clear definitions of concepts, especially abstract, moral concepts, so they undoubtedly replied to the question about justice with examples of just about everything a boss ever did to make them unhappy. Their implicit definition of justice was probably something like this: "bad stuff that my bosses did to me to make me mad or upset." To get pertinent examples, the researchers should have defined the concept very carefully for the subjects and asked them to give only examples that fit that definition! Examples that did not fit the definition should have been discarded.

Under the pernicious influence of postmodernism, which views all concepts and definitions as arbitrary, the researchers might reply, "We are just looking at how people perceive justice in their own terms." But this will simply not do. There is no justification for accepting or promoting conceptual carelessness. It will lead only to incomprehensibility. If interactional justice can mean anything to anybody, then it has no objective meaning at all and coherent discussion of the concept is impossible. In my view the concept of interactional justice should be discarded and the correct terms should be used for the examples listed previously, if there is a practical interest in those examples.

Let me add that the finding of correlations of various sizes between the various justice scales does not prove anything about their content or the suitability of the labels. First, people may answer items with different content the same because they do not distinguish the concepts in their own minds, even though they are objectively different. Second, they may also answer different items similarly, because certain traits often go together (e.g., people who are biased thinkers give "biased" rewards; dishonest people typically lack integrity).What is relevant is the content of the scales themselves and the need to use the proper names for the actual concepts involved (logical validity).

What about a more recent add-on to the justice list: informational justice? Getting accurate feedback involves honesty, integrity, and knowledge on the part of the manager providing it. None of this pertains directly to justice. Justice could be involved in some cases, for example, the manager gives invalid feedback during a performance appraisal session because he or she did not bother to gather or evaluate the relevant information when preparing for the meeting. But this would be an aspect of the cognitive aspect of justice. I recommend the term informational justice also be discarded. Things should be called by their objectively proper names. Broadening the concept of justice to include everything in sight will render the concept meaningless.

This brings up a further research idea. Why confine studies of managers' moral behavior just to justice? Why not also honesty and integrity? By combining scales, one could develop a "morality" index by which subordinates could describe managers and leaders—which might or might not be practically useful. (I have drafted such a possible index, based on three virtues, in the Appendix.)

Finally, it is widely recognized that trust is an important concept in organizations, but there is rarely any mention of where it comes from. Moral trust comes from an appraisal of the manager's or leader's moral character. For example, to be trusted a manager should be honest. (What could be called practical trust comes from an appraisal of the manager's or leader's competence; Salam, 2000.)

## Reputation

The topic of this chapter by Ferris, Blass, Douglas, Kolodinsky, and Treadway is an important one. It could be argued that a person's or an organization's reputation is his or her or its most prized social asset. As the authors astutely point out, reputations have value. Given these points, it is unfortunate that the authors spend so many pages discussing poor definitions (e.g., reputation as a substitute for a guarantee, reputations as a substitute for firsthand knowledge, reputation as competence, etc.). All these definitions focus on nonessentials.

The authors end their discussion with this definition: "a perceptual identity reflective of the complex combination of salient personal characteristics and accomplishments, demonstrated behavior, and intended images presented over some period of time as observed directly and/or as reported from secondary sources." Now consider how much clearer and more essentialized the dictionary definition is: "1. The general estimation in which a person is held by the public. 2. The state or situation of being held in high esteem" (*American Heritage Dictionary*, 1992, p. 1533). The authors are quite right in implying that reputation is contextual. A reputation is usually for something specific (e.g., a reputation for fairness) and is granted by specific sets of people (e.g., subordinates, customers).

The authors title their chapter "Personal Reputation in Organizations," but the content of the chapter suggests that a more accurate title would have been: "Personal Reputation in *and of* Organizations," as there are numerous references to the latter topic. Furthermore, there also is mention of a possible causal relationship between the two in that being a member of an organization with a good reputation can enhance one's personal reputation. One could add the other side of this coin: An individual with a good reputation can enhance an organization's reputation, as in the case of a new CEO.

It does not follow, however, from the fact that reputation is a social phenomenon that reputation, as the postmodernists would claim, "is more of a socially constructed reality than an objective one." Unless people are flagrantly irrational, reputation is based on real characteristics and real actions of people. There are objective reasons why Jack Welch of General Electric has a better business reputation than Kenneth Lay of Enron. Ferris et al. argue that reputation enhances trust but the opposite is also true: Trust enhances reputation. For example, when people find they can trust certain businesspersons as a result of their actions, this enhances their reputations—which would have been objectively merited.

I think the chapter's theme would have come across more clearly had it been organized around several key questions. These include the following:

- How do individuals earn, maintain, and protect their reputations (including a discussion of earned reputation vs. hyped reputations)?
- How do organizations earn, maintain, and protect (and hype) their reputations?
- What are the practical consequences of individual and organizational reputations?
- How do individuals and organizations use their reputations as strategic assets?
- How can we discover if a reputation is deserved?

This latter question raises an important issue that would never occur to a postmodernist, and one that is not covered in the chapter. Many disastrous decisions are made because decision makers act blindly on the basis of reputation without looking at how it was attained. Academia is not immune from this error. As a case in point, it is well known that when applying to an academic job, the matter of where the candidate received his or her PhD is far more important to many recruiters than the quality of his or her work as presented in a professional colloquium.

The issue of how to judge a reputation objectively is an important one. I think the first requirement is independent thinking. Reputations may or may not be deserved; going along with the crowd when judging others without knowing how the crowd arrived at its estimate is a dangerous luxury. The best decision makers (e.g., Warren Buffett) are usually those who look beyond the glitz in search of the substance.

Ferris et al. make a number of good observations in their chapter—especially the point that reputation building is a dynamic process and that it can take a long time to create, and yet be destroyed quite rapidly. The exodus of clients from the Arthur Andersen accounting firm in the wake of its alleged role in the Enron scandal illustrates this point only too well. The authors argue that forming a reputation is a consequence of meeting the expectations of others. I think this is true, in part, but the formulation is too narrow. Reputations are often made by people for whom there are no prior expectations (e.g., writers and entrepreneurs, simply because no one knows who they are until after they have made their creative contribution). Even in the case of a manager, an employee may have no advance expectation. They may take a cautious, wait-and-see approach, or they even may approach their judgments with a cynical attitude. Managers' reputations are created by the actions they take.

Ferris et al. discuss at some length what they call "indicators" of reputation, such as salary or position. But of what are these indicators? Allegedly, in the case of salary, they are indicators of competence. Of course, the connection between competence and salary is far from perfect. And salary would not necessarily be an indicator of moral character. Other indicators (e.g., keeping promises, telling the truth) would be needed for that.

I strongly agree with Ferris et al. that the topic of reputation is worthy of a great deal more study, both from the viewpoint of the individual and the organization. They point out many fruitful areas for further work. To their list, I would like to add an additional research question of my own: Are people who consciously set out to build a public reputation as trustworthy as those who try to do what they believe is right and let the resulting reputation take care of itself? In other words, to what extent do active efforts to manipulate one's reputation backfire by unintentionally cultivating an image of oneself as being inappropriately self-promotional (suggesting that one has something to hide)? This strikes me as a particularly important question deserving of future research attention—and one with considerable practical value as well.

## Self-Fulfilling Prophecies

Eden and his colleagues have engaged in many years of impressive programmatic research to identify how managers' or leaders' expectations affect subordinates' performance. Especially impressive has been their attempt to identify the sequence of causal mechanisms by which the Pygmalion effect operates to influence performance. Specifically, leader's expectations → leader's actions (especially support) → subordinate's self-efficacy → increased motivation and effort → performance. The Pygmalion effect does not operate consciously; leaders deny that their expectations lead them to treat different people differently. Although much of the research was conducted in Israeli military settings, they have also used nonmilitary samples and settings. They also have expanded the initial studies, which used only female subjects, thereby enhancing the generalizability of the earliest reported effects.

That said, however, three particular issues still remain in Eden's work. First, all the studies have used deception to manipulate leaders' expectations. Although this may be acceptable in experimental studies conducted for theory-building purposes, it becomes problematic when the theory is applied practically (White & Locke, 2000). How do you justify lying to managers about their subordinates? Eden's answer is that "little lies create one big truth," implying that the lies have a good result. He argues that "deception is not deceit." If not, I would like to know what it is. In a bizarre twist of logic, Eden even asks if Pygmalion works, then isn't it unethical *not* to deceive managers? This argument is convincing only if you accept the philosophy of pragmatism (do what works for the moment), which I do not. If you can lie just because you get a good result at the time, this opens a huge Pandora's box, and I do not think any organization should want to open it. Eden later switches the focus of his argument to argue that it is all right to expect people to do better than their best previous performance. This, of course, is true, but this idea does not involve any deception, as almost anyone can learn to improve on what he or she has done before. The point is that it is not necessary for managers to be deceived regarding any group of employees. It should be quite sufficient to convince them that everyone can improve and to give them training in how to build the self-efficacy of all employees (White & Locke, 2000). This would take Pygmalion out of the realm of the subconscious and make efficacy building a conscious process, but that should be for the better because that puts the process more in the manager's direct control.

A second problem is that Pygmalion training programs for managers have, by and large, not worked. Based on the information provided by Eden, I agree that the central cause of these failures is the fact that in most of the studies the managers were dealing with employees with whom they had already worked rather than people they had never met (as in the case of the Israeli armed forces studies). Once managers have worked with someone, they get feedback about how that person performs, so trying to get them to ignore this information and to develop expectations divorced from this may be a hopeless task. It may be that training should be focused instead on teaching self-efficacy building techniques as proposed by Bandura (1997).

The third issue pertains to the concept of means efficacy. There is a definitional problem here. Self-efficacy is a psychological experience; it refers to task-specific confidence. However, the means (i.e., the technology) one uses to perform a task does not have efficacy because it does not have psychological experiences. Thus, the term *means efficacy* is not a valid concept. The proper term to use, in my opinion, would be *instrumentality*. This could be rated objectively (e.g., how much better— by some defined standard—is this machine than the old one?) or subjectively (e.g., "To what degree do you think this machine will help you to perform better?").

Now, let's consider the experiments on means efficacy. Note first that if the individual is actually using the new machine, after being trained, and gets feedback about performance, the self-efficacy rating should automatically take into account the machine's benefits and one's mastery of it. This is because self-efficacy is both task-specific and situation-specific—in other words, it enables people to assess how well they can perform a particular task in a particular setting. Unfortunately, no such measurements were taken in the experiments Eden reports. For example, in the Eden and Granat-Flomin study, computer self-efficacy was measured at the outset but time to account *performance* efficacy, after having used the new computer program and gotten feedback, was not measured, even though time to account was the dependent variable.

Second, the experimental group in this study was told, in effect, to expect "drastic improvements in average net file-processing time," whereas the control group was not told this. This, I submit is a none-too-subtle goal manipulation, and it may have been responsible for the treatment effect. To check on this, subjects could have been asked, after the manipulation, "How much would you think time to account should improve as a result of this new computer system?" Means efficacy ratings improved most in the experimental group, probably because they actually performed better. I cannot comment on the anti-aircraft gunnery experiment, because it was reported in far less detail.

I do not mean to imply from the foregoing that managers should not be concerned with giving their subordinates the best possible equipment and training. Certainly, this can lead to improved performance. But I believe that this occurs for reasons more closely tied to instrumentality than to the processes proposed by Eden.

## Stress

There can be no doubt that stress is an important element of modern life, especially working life, so a chapter on the state of the science is certainly needed. However, not very much of the chapter by Quick, Cooper, Nelson, Quick, and Gavin is about the state of the science. Most of it is about the prevalence of stress today, stress measures, changes in the modern workplace that cause stress, and recommendations for future research.

It is unfortunate that nowhere in the chapter do Quick et al. define the phenomenon that they are talking about. Nor do they define the term *strain* or explain its relationship to stress. So let me begin with my own definition of stress: the psychosomatic form in which one experiences threat. I think this is a bit more succinct than the dictionary definition that calls it a mentally or emotionally upsetting condition, which would not distinguish it from, say, unhappiness. Stress is not the same as job dissatisfaction. Satisfaction and its obverse are matters of getting or not getting what you want. The core emotions in stress are anxiety and fear.

As to theory, the employee demand versus abilities (D–A fit) model is on the right track if one views demands as job requirements and abilities as personal resources. Being asked to do more than one possibly can do would be experienced as threatening. However, I would not agree that stress is a result of "excessive involvement" in one's work unless that involvement is motivated by fear rather than love of the work.

The critical point to be made here is that demands, as such, are not threats to an employee who is able to meet them. Thus, stress is neither "out there" nor "in here," but in the relationship between the person and the situation. Nor is it the case that the threat is experienced and then diffused when people see that they have the resources to cope (although this may occur on complex issues, where problem solving is required). More typically, threat is not experienced in the first place because people make judgments automatically and subconsciously whenever a potential threat arises. Consider an example. A copilot is flying with a pilot in a small plane and the pilot suddenly dies of a heart attack. Scenario 1: The copilot is a student pilot on his first flight. His response would be immediate panic, because he does not know how to fly and his life is in danger. Scenario 2: The copilot is an experienced pilot. He might be upset at the pilot's demise, but there would be no panic because he knows that he knows how to fly and his life is not at risk.

The critical variable here, which Copper et al. do not mention, is self-efficacy, or task-specific confidence. Bandura (1997) showed that self-efficacy is the converse of anxiety. When people know they can carry out a course of action (e.g., give a public talk), they do not feel threatened. The demands–control (not to be confused with the demands–abilities) model is misleading because decision latitude is not the same as self-efficacy. One can have autonomy and still not know what to do (Bandura, 1997). Therefore, preventive stress management at the individual level should emphasize skill building on the part of employees and managers. From Quick et al.'s excellent description of the various potential threats in today's global economy, training—including training in job skills, how to manage one's career, and finding a new job—would seem to be needed more than ever.

The balance between work and family life that Quick et al. identify as a major source of stress is a serious issue, especially for ambitious people. By pursuing one value intensely, one threatens the other. Anyone who can figure this out should be able to make a great living as a therapist, trainer, or counselor!

To me, the most interesting part of Quick et al.'s chapter was the section on new, stress-reducing innovations in the workplace—especially the organizational health center, and the appointment of a chief psychological officer. The achievements of the U.S. Air Force in reducing stress-related problems by means of a health center headed by a chief psychological officer were truly impressive, especially considering that they were dealing with base closures and downsizing. This may be a model that other organizations could adopt, especially because it appears cost effective.

I also was impressed by Quick et al.'s emphasis on the need for self-reliance—so much the opposite of today's whiny insistence that we are not responsible for anything we do and that it is up to the government to save us from all the problems that life brings. They base this emphasis on self-reliance on Frese and Fay's (2001) excellent work on personal initiative that stresses the need to constantly update and enhance one's skills (i.e., one's self-efficacy) in a fast-changing world.

In concluding, allow me to comment about *eustress*—a term that has bothered me for at least 25 years. In my opinion, positive stress, if stress is defined as the form in which one experiences threat, is a contradiction in terms. One can experience the tension of unfulfilled purpose or the thrill of a challenging new project or arousal, but these do not involve actual stress unless one feels threatened. If one feels threatened, the emotion is not positive. If one does not feel threatened, the experience is not one of stress.

## CONCLUSION

Although I have been critical in my remarks, I have tried to be critical in a constructive way. I did not expect, when I agreed to write this overview chapter, that my theme would be the need for clear, valid definitions. The theme came to me as I read the chapters. The proximate cause of most of the definitional problems, other than giving no definition at all, is overreliance on others for one's definitions, especially the felt need to formulate definitions based on consensus. This implicit premise of this procedure is that other people have done all the thinking necessary so that all one has to do is to take the average of all the other definitions. To the degree that this is ever valid, it is best to start with a dictionary. I did not find one definition in any of the chapters that was as good as the dictionary definition. Often this was because the authors made the definitions too long-winded, convoluted, and full of nonessentials. Imagine an OB scholar defining man as: "the upright-walking, hairless biped with an opposable thumb and an advanced cognitive apparatus enabling the symbolic processing of information leading to complex, adaptive forms of individual and social behavior, including language behavior, that is beyond the capabilities of various other species who lack the same brain size and structure." What does this say, in terms of essentials, that "man is the rational animal" does not? And which is more succinct?

The deeper cause of definition problems is the failure to grasp the nature and role of definitions. Definitions are not "just words" and they are not arbitrary "social constructions." The human form of grasping reality is by means of concepts (Rand, 1990). Definitions are symbols that stand for concepts. They need to be clear and objective because reality is what it is—reality has identity. I think our science, and all science, will progress far more rapidly if we take pains to clearly identify the nature of that which we are talking about. This all goes to show that no science can be better than the epistemology on which it rests.

Let me end by giving one positive example of a clearly defined concept in OB, one to which I already have alluded briefly: self-efficacy. This has been defined from the beginning as task-specific confidence (Bandura, 1997). It has been logically differentiated from self-esteem (general self-worth or efficacy), instrumentality (expectancy of reward), locus of control (general ability to control outcomes), and effort–performance expectancy (which is one aspect of self-efficacy). There has never been any doubt as to what it meant for anyone who read Bandura's work carefully. Self-efficacy is easy to measure, given its clear definition, and the concept has proven to be extraordinarily useful as a motivational concept in numerous domains of human functioning. (A similar case could be made for the term goal.) I believe that scientific progress in all OB areas will be enhanced if we start our work with clear definitions.

## ACKNOWLEDGMENTS

I am indebted to Jerald Greenberg and Cathy Durham for their helpful comments on an earlier version of this chapter.

# Appendix
## Proposed Manager Morality Scale

*Note:* These items have *never* been tested. Although the components are conceptually distinguishable, they may be highly correlated and might readily be combined to form a single score. The scales should be highly correlated with trust in the manager, as they are the causes of the moral aspect of trust. (Practical trust would depend on the manager's perceived competence; Salam, 2000.) Obviously these items could be adapted to refer to peers, subordinates, top leaders, or others. (For a detailed discussion of moral virtue from a rational, nonreligious, perspective, see Peikoff, 1991.)

*Honesty (The refusal to fake reality)*

1.  My manager lies all the time.
2.  My manager never tries to evade relevant facts.
3.  My manager characteristically tells the truth.
4.  If my manager does not like some fact, he or she will deny it or make up some other fact(s) to suit his or her bias.
5.  My manager is honest: He or she never tries to fake reality.

*Integrity (Loyalty to rational convictions in action)*

6.  If my manager makes a promise, he or she keeps it unless the circumstances are totally beyond his or her control.
7.  My manager preaches one thing but typically does another.
8.  My manager breaks promises routinely.
9.  If my manager believes that something is the right thing to do, he or she always acts accordingly.
10. My manager has integrity: He or she acts in accordance with his or her rational convictions.

*Justice (Judging people's conduct or character objectively and acting accordingly, granting to each person that which he or she deserves)*

11. When preparing for a decision about a reward or punishment, my manager is very scrupulous about first gathering all the relevant facts.
12. When my manager prepares for a decision that will affect his or her subordinates, he or she lets feelings and biases override his or her rational judgment of the facts.
13. When my manager gives out raises or recognition, he or she gives them strictly in accordance with merit.

**14.** Those who work under my manager typically do *not* get what they deserve.

**15.** My manager is a fair person; he or she looks at all the facts and gives people what they earn.

## REFERENCES

American Heritage Dictionary. (1992). *The American heritage dictionary of the English language* (3rd ed.). New York: Houghton Mifflin.

Bandura A. (1997). *Self-efficacy: The exercise of control.* New York: Freeman.

Bass, B. M. (1990). *Bass and Stogdill's handbook of leadership: Theory, research, and managerial applications.* New York: The Free Press.

Bies, R. (2001). Interactional (in)justice: The sacred and the profane. In J. Greenberg & R. Cropanzano (Eds.), *Advances in organization justice* (pp. 89–118). Stanford, CA: Stanford University Press.

Binswanger, H. (1991). Volition as cognitive self-regulation. *Organizational Behavior & Human Decision Processes, 50,* 154–178.

Buffett, W. (2001). Chairman's letter. In *Berkshire Hathaway, Inc.: Annual report.* Omaha, NE: Berkshire Hathaway.

Chah, D. O. K., & Locke, E. A. (1996). Correlates of leadership effectiveness in the U.S. and Korea. In A. Rahim, R. Golembiewski, & C. Lundberg (Eds.), *Current topics in management* (Vol. 1, pp. 201–223). Greenwich, CT: JAI.

Frese, M., & Fay, D. (2001). Personal initiative: An active performance concept for work in the 21st century. In B. Staw & R. Sutton (Eds.), *Research in organizational behavior* (Vol. 23, pp. 133–187). Greenwich, CT: JAI.

Goleman, D. (1997). *Emotional intelligence.* New York: Bantam.

Judge, T., Locke, E. A., & Durham C. (1997). The dispositional causes of job satisfaction: A core evaluations approach. In L. Cummings & B. Staw (Eds.), *Research in organizational behavior* (Vol. 19, pp. 151–188). Greenwich, CT: JAI.

Judge, T., Locke, E. A., Durham, C., & Kluger, A. (1998). Dispositional effects on job and life satisfaction: The role of core evaluations. *Journal of Applied Psychology, 83,* 17–34.

Lazarus, R. (1991). *Emotions and adaptation.* New York: Oxford University Press.

Locke, E. A. (1976). The nature of causes of job satisfaction. In M. D. Dunnette & L. Hough (Eds.), *Handbook of industrial and organizational psychology* (pp. 1297–1349). Chicago: Rand McNally.

Locke, E. A. (in press). The epistemological side of teaching management: Teaching through principles. *Academy of Management Learning and Education.*

Lord, R., Klimoski, R., & Kanfer, R. (2002). *Emotions in the workplace.* San Francisco: Jossey-Bass.

Peikoff, L. (1982). *The ominous parallels: The end of freedom in America.* New York: Stein & Day.

Peikoff, L. (1991). *Objectivism: The philosophy of Ayn Rand.* New York: Dutton.

Raine, A., & Sanmartin, J. (2001). *Violence and psychopathy.* New York: Plenum.

Rand, A. (1975). *The romantic manifesto.* New York: Signet.

Rand, A. (1982). *Philosophy: Who needs it?* New York: Signet.

Rand, A. (1990). *Introduction to objectivist epistemology* (2nd ed.). New York: NAL Books.

Salam, S. (2000). Foster trust through competence, honesty and integrity. In E. A. Locke (Ed.), *Handbook of principles of organizational behavior* (pp. 274–288). New York: Basil Blackwell.

Snyder, C., & Lopez, S. (2002). *Handbook of positive psychology.* New York: Oxford University Press.

White, S., & Locke, E. A. (2000). Problems with the Pygmalion effect and some suggested solutions. *Leadership Quarterly, 11,* 389–415.

# Author Index

# Subject Index